Cultures of Politics
Politics of Cultures

Cultures of Politics Politics of Cultures

Re-visioning Latin American Social Movements

edited by
Sonia E. Alvarez
UNIVERSITY OF CALIFORNIA AT SANTA CRUZ

Evelina Dagnino
STATE UNIVERSITY OF CAMPINAS, SÃO PAULO

Arturo Escobar
UNIVERSITY OF MASSACHUSETTS

Westview Press
A Member of the Perseus Books Group

Published in 1998 in the United States of America by Westview Press, 5500 Central Avenue, Boulder, Colorado 80301-2877, and in the United Kingdom by Westview Press, 12 Hid's Copse Road, Cumnor Hill, Oxford OX2 9JJ

Library of Congress Cataloging-in-Publication Data
Cultures of politics/politics of cultures : re-visioning Latin American
social movements / edited by Sonia E. Alvarez, Evelina Dagnino,
Arturo Escobar.
p. cm.
Includes bibliographical references and index.
ISBN 0-8133-3071-8 (hardcover). — ISBN 0-8133-3072-6 (paperback)
1. Social movements—Latin America. 2. Civil society—Latin
America. 3. Political participation—Latin America. 4. Political
culture—Latin America. 5. Minorities—Latin America—Political
activity. I. Alvarez, Sonia E., 1956– . II. Dagnino, Evelina.
III. Escobar, Arturo, 1952– .
HN110.5.A8C845 1998
303.48'4'098—dc21 97-43513
CIP

The paper used in this publication meets the requirements of the American National Standard for Permanence of Paper for Printed Library Materials Z39.48-1984.

10 9 8 7 6 5 4 3

Contents

PART FOUR
THEORETICAL AND METHODOLOGICAL REFLECTIONS ON THE CULTURAL AND THE POLITICAL IN LATIN AMERICAN SOCIAL MOVEMENTS

Preface and Acknowledgments

This volume was originally inspired by the editors' shared discomfort with the narrow disciplinary boundaries within which analyses of contemporary Latin American social movements are too often confined. Dissatisfied with the compartmentalized and segmented approaches prevailing in our own disciplines of anthropology and political science, we wanted to draw attention to how social movements operate at the *interface* of culture and politics. On the one hand, by exposing the perhaps less visible, less measurable, yet vital ways in which movements continue to contest culturally specific notions of politics and the political, we hoped to retheorize the *cultural dimensions of politics* and thereby contest the often-made claim that the "political" significance of social movements has receded with the return of formal, electoral democracy to much of Latin America. On the other hand, in underscoring how the "cultural" struggles of social movements over meanings and representations are deeply entangled with their struggles for rights and economic and political-institutional power, we wished to further theoretical reflection on the *political dimensions of the cultural.* By examining simultaneously the cultural in the political and the political in the cultural, we hoped to rekindle the dialogue between these two arenas and the various disciplines devoted to their study and thereby re-vision contemporary social movement practices.

The ensuing chapters are the outgrowth of multiple theoretical, disciplinary, political, personal, and transcontinental encounters—entailing countless conversations, debates, conference sessions, seminars, and working meetings involving North American, European, and Latin American anthropologists, sociologists, literary critics, geologists, political scientists, and intellectual activists scattered across a vast array of locations in the Americas and around the globe. A product of genuinely transnational and transdisciplinary dialogue and collaboration, this book project spanned nearly four years and entailed a number of phases and processes.

Beginning in early 1994, the editors undertook extensive common readings in cultural and political theory, cultural studies, feminist theory, and other recent critical theoretical literatures in search of analytical guideposts around which to organize this collection. During 1994–1995, we came together in Atlanta, Rio de Janeiro, Campinas, Serra Negra, Florianópolis, and Washington, D.C., for several working sessions in which we refined the theoretical goals of the anthology, identified key contributors and themes, and reviewed chapter abstracts and preliminary drafts. We also wrote a preliminary introduction that attempted to map out the analytical terrain of the volume and circulated it to all contributors in August 1995.

Because we wanted to ensure the internal coherence and organicity of the volume, we engaged in ongoing dialogue with our contributors from the earliest stages of the project through its conclusion. To maximize debate and exchange among our contributing authors, the editors organized sessions at both the 1994 and 1995 international congresses of the Latin American Studies Association. We took a further, very important step toward that end by organizing a three-day working conference—funded by the Rockefeller Foundation and the State University of Campinas's Graduate Program in Social Sciences—at Campinas in March 1996. At that conference, all contributors presented a second draft of their chapters (circulated in advance to all conference participants) and received critical feedback from assigned discussants, editors, other contributors, and Brazilian colleagues and students present. We also invited four scholars whose work has been central to the study of social movements and cultural politics—Alberto Melucci, Elizabeth Jelin, Mary Louise Pratt, and Paulo Krischke—to provide summary reflections on the draft chapters and conference proceedings. Their essays assessing the book's theoretical and methodological contributions and signaling future research directions are assembled in Part Four of this volume.

After the conference, the editors and a few contributors stayed on in Campinas to revise and refine the arguments advanced in our draft introduction in light of conference debates and to provide detailed editorial feedback to each contributor. Chapter authors were encouraged to address the conceptual and theoretical issues raised by other contributors in their final revisions. After receiving these revisions in July and August 1996, the editors redrafted the introduction to reflect the final chapter arguments.

We of course incurred many debts of gratitude over the course of the numerous phases of this project. We are especially grateful to all our contributors for their hard work, perseverance, and assiduous enthusiasm and support for this collaborative undertaking. We also thank our Brazilian colleagues—Ana Maria Doimo, Antonio Augusto Arantes, Bela Feldman-Bianco, Caio Navarro Toledo, Claudia Lima Costa, Renato Ortiz, Suely Kofes, and Teresa Caldeira—who served as session coordinators and discussants at the 1996 Campinas conference and whose critical insights greatly enriched this collection. Ana Claudia Chaves Teixeira adeptly coordinated the often complex logistical arrangements for our international conference, juggling complicated travel schedules and catering to the every need of our contributors and other conference participants with extraordinary efficiency and invariable good humor. Suely Borges Costa, Janaina Damasceno, Luis Celso Machado, and the administrative staff of the Institute of Philosophy and Human Sciences also provided invaluable support in organizing the Campinas conference. We also thank the Graduate Program in Social Sciences at Campinas and the Rockefeller Foundation's Humanities Fellowships Program (through a 1995–1998 grant to the Culture and Politics Area of the interdisciplinary Ph.D. Program in Social Sciences, coordinated by Evelina Dagnino during 1995–1996) for their financial support of the conference.

Anne Blair ably translated the chapters authored by Sérgio Baierle and coauthored by Maria Celia Paoli and Vera Telles, and Brian Wampler was responsible for translating Olivia Gomes da Cunha's contribution (both translators were assisted by Sonia E. Alvarez). Arturo Escobar translated the chapter he coauthored with Carlos Rosero and Libia Grueso. Henrietta Brown, Cheryl Van Der Veer, and other staff at the University of California at Santa Cruz Document Publishing and Editing Center provided inestimable assistance with the preparation of the electronic manuscript. We also wish to thank Mr. Eduardo Costantini for generously granting us permission to use the Abaporu as the cover to this volume.

We are beholden to the many friends and colleagues who supported us at various places and phases of this book project. We want to acknowledge former Westview editor Barbara Ellington for her enthusiastic encouragement of this book in its earliest stages. Sonia thanks colleagues and staff at the Rio de Janeiro office of Ford Foundation—particularly Janice Rocha, Bradford Smith, and Sarah Hawker Costa—for supporting her efforts to remain active as a scholar and researcher while serving as program officer during 1993–1996. We all wish to express our deep appreciation to Armando (Fu) Marchesi, Magda Corredor, and Claudia Lima Costa for their intellectual and emotional *"parceria"* during the glamorous and not-so-glamorous moments of this book's preparation. Finally, we wish to thank one another—for the many lively, inspirational, trilingual, "bi/transdisciplinary" conversations (both "virtual" and "real"), for our several high culinary–cum–high theory extravaganzas (especially our oyster-eating sessions in Sambaqui and churrascos in Santinho), and for the camaraderie and friendship that grew ever stronger as this project progressed, infusing collegiality and scholarly collaboration with new meanings.

Sonia E. Alvarez
Santa Cruz, California

Evelina Dagnino
Campinas, São Paulo

Arturo Escobar
Amherst, Massachusetts

Cultures of Politics
Politics of Cultures

Chapter One

Introduction: The Cultural and the Political in Latin American Social Movements

SONIA E. ALVAREZ, EVELINA DAGNINO, AND ARTURO ESCOBAR

As we approach the millennium's end, what future is in store for Latin American societies? Unprecedented levels of violence, poverty, discrimination, and exclusion would seem to indicate that the "performance" and indeed the very design of Latin America's "new" democracies are far from satisfactory. And it is precisely over possible alternative blueprints for democracy that much of the political struggle is being waged in Latin America today. Social movements, we will claim, play a critical role in that struggle. Fundamentally in dispute are the parameters of democracy—to be sure, the very boundaries of what is to be properly defined as the political arena: its participants, its institutions, its processes, its agenda, and its scope.

Programs of economic and social adjustment, inspired by neoliberalism, have entered this dispute as formidable and pervasive contenders. In response to the allegedly "inevitable" logic imposed by the processes of economic globalization, neoliberal policies have introduced a new kind of relationship between the state and civil society and advanced a distinctive definition of the political domain and its participants—based on a minimalist conception of both the state and democracy.

As civil society is charged with taking on the social responsibilities now eschewed by neoliberalism's shrinking state, its capacity as a crucial political domain for the exercise of democratic citizenship is increasingly being downplayed. Citizens, in this view, should pull themselves up by their own private bootstraps, and citizenship is increasingly equated with individual integration into the market.

An alternative conception of citizenship—one advanced by several of the movements discussed in this volume—would view democratic struggles as encompassing a redefinition not only of the political system but also of economic, social, and cultural practices that might engender a democratic ordering for society as a whole. Such a conception calls our attention to a wide array of possible public spheres wherein citizenship might be exercised and societal interests not only represented but also fundamentally re/shaped. The scope of democratizing struggles would be extended to encompass not just the political system but also the future of "development" and the eradication of social inequalities such as those of race and gender, deeply shaped by cultural and social practices. This enlarged conception further acknowledges that the process of building democracy is not homogeneous but rather internally discontinuous and uneven: Different spheres and dimensions have distinct rhythms of change, leading some analysts to argue that this process is inherently "disjunctive" (Holston and Caldeira, forthcoming; see also Jelin and Hershberg 1996).

Social movements not only have sometimes succeeded in translating their agendas into public policies and in expanding the boundaries of institutional politics but also, significantly, have struggled to resignify the very meanings of received notions of citizenship, political representation and participation, and, as a consequence, democracy itself. Both the processes of translating movement agendas into policy and of redefining the meaning of "development" or "citizen," for example, entail the enactment of "cultural politics"—a concept developed in the field of cultural studies, which, we will argue, can help shed new light on social movements' cultural and political stakes in the contemporary struggle over the fate of democracy in Latin America.

Reconceptualizing the Cultural in Latin American Social Movements Research

From Culture to Cultural Politics

This book is intended primarily as an investigation into the relationship between culture and politics. We argue that this relationship can be productively explored by delving into the nature of the cultural politics enacted—with more or less clarity and to a greater or lesser extent—by *all* social movements and by examining the potential of this cultural politics for fostering social change.

Conventional social science has not systematically explored the connections between culture and politics. We alluded to this fact in our earlier work (Escobar and Alvarez 1992; Dagnino 1994). It is important to discuss the changing conceptions of culture and politics in anthropology, literature, and other disciplines as a backdrop to understanding how the concept of cultural politics arose from the intense interdisciplinary dialogue and blurring of boundaries that has taken place in the last decade, fostered by various poststructuralist currents. In our previous anthology, we pointed out that the conventional understanding of culture in various fields as static—embedded in a set of canonical texts, beliefs, and artifacts—has contributed greatly to rendering invisible everyday cultural practices as a terrain for, and source of, political practices. Theorists of popular culture such as de Certeau (1984), Fiske (1989), and Willis (1990) moved beyond this static understanding to highlight how culture involves a collective and incessant process of producing meanings that shapes social experience and configures social relations. Studies of popular culture thus pushed research in the humanities further away from the "high culture" emphasis originating in literature and the arts and closer to an anthropological understanding of culture. This closeness had already been propitiated by Raymond Williams's characterization of culture as "the signifying system through which necessarily (though among other means) a social order is communicated, reproduced, experienced and explored" (1981, 13). As Glenn Jordan and Chris Weedon note, "Culture in this sense, is not a sphere, but a dimension of all institutions—economic, social and political. Culture is a set of *material* practices which constitute meanings, values and subjectivities" (1995, 8).

In a recent influential volume, Williams's definition is elaborated upon to conclude that "in cultural studies . . . culture is understood *both* as a way of life—encompassing ideas, attitudes, languages, practices, institutions, and structures of power—and a whole range of cultural practices: artistic forms, texts, canons, architecture, mass-produced commodities, and so forth" (Nelson, Treichler, and Grossberg 1992, 5). This characterization of culture points to grounded practices and representations as central to culture yet, in practice, its main emphasis continues to be on textual and artistic forms. This accounts, we believe, for a number of critiques waged at cultural studies such as the seemingly problematic reliance on "quick and dirty" ethnographies, the salience of textual analyses, and the importance ascribed to the culture industries and to paradigms of reception and consumption of cultural products. Whatever the validity of these criticisms—as we shall explain below—it is fair to say that cultural studies has not given sufficient importance to social movements as a vital aspect of cultural production.[1]

The notion of culture is also actively debated in anthropology. Classical anthropology adhered to a realist epistemology and a relatively fixed understanding of culture as embodied in institutions, practices, rituals, symbols, and the like. Culture was seen as belonging to a group and bounded in time and space. This paradigm of organic culture suffered significant blows with the development of structural, political economy–oriented, and interpretive anthropology. Building on hermeneutics and semiotics, interpretive anthropology moved toward a nonpositivist, partial understanding of culture, partly driven by the metaphor of "cultures as texts." In the mid-1980s, a further displacement of culture sought to take account of the fact that "no one can write about others any longer as if they were discrete objects or texts," and took to developing "new conceptions of culture as interactive and historical" (Clifford and Marcus 1986, 25). Since then, the growing awareness of the globalization of cultural and economic production has pushed anthropologists to question spatial notions of culture, dichotomies between homogeneous "us" and discrete "others," and any illusion of clear boundaries between groups, self or other (see Fox 1991; Gupta and Ferguson 1992).[2]

One of the most useful aspects of the poststructuralist understanding of culture in anthropology is its insistence on the analysis of production and signification, of meanings and practices, as simultaneous and inextricably bound aspects of social reality. In this vein, Kay Warren (in this volume) argues that material conditions are too often viewed as "more autonomous, real, and basic than anything else. 'But what about exploitation?' is the critics' common reply, through which they seek to convey a materialist urgency that trumps cultural issues, no matter how worthy." Warren goes on to suggest that social movements' "material demands are in practice politically advanced selective constructions, conveyed in fields of social relations that also define their significance" and advocates an alternative conceptualization that "would confront the cultural issues (and political interests) infused in the construction of materialist politics as well as the materialist concerns (and political interests) infused in cultural framings of politics." While anthropologists have generally attempted to intertwine the analyses of "the symbolic and the material," advances in the theory of discourse and representation have provided tools for more nuanced accounts of the mutual constitution, indeed inseparability, of meanings and practices (see Comaroff and Comaroff 1991 for an excellent example of this approach).

This development has useful lessons for cultural studies; in fact it jibes well with what is perceived to be a central issue in the field, namely, what the metaphors of culture and textuality both help to explain and fail to address. The issue is expressed eloquently in Stuart Hall's retrospective account of the impact of the "linguistic turn" in cultural studies. For Hall, the discovery of discursivity and textuality brought forth the realization of "the crucial importance of language . . . to any study of culture" (1992, 283). It was thus that cultural studies practitioners found themselves always "driven back to culture." Yet despite the importance of the metaphor of the discursive, for Hall

> there is always something decentered about the medium of culture, about language, textuality, and signification, which always escapes and evades the attempt to link it, directly and immediately, with other structures. . . . [We must assume that] culture will always work through its textualities—and at the same time that textuality is never enough. . . . Unless and until one respects the necessary displacement of culture, and yet is always irritated by its failure to reconcile itself with other questions that matter, with other questions that cannot and can never be fully recovered by critical textuality in its elaborations, cultural studies as a project, an intervention, remains incomplete. (1992, 284)[3]

Hall's dictum that culture and textuality "are never enough," in our view, refers to the difficulty of pinning down, through culture and textuality, "other questions that matter," such as the structures, formations, and resistances that are inevitably permeated by culture, the "something nasty down below" to which Hall wants to return cultural studies from "the clean air of meaning and textuality" (1992, 278). Hall thus reintroduces politics into the midst of cultural studies, not only because his formulation provides a means to hold theoretical and political questions in tension but because it calls upon theorists—particularly those too prone to remain at the level of the text and the politics of representation—to engage with "the something nasty down below" as a question of both theory and politics.

In other words, the tension between the textual and that which underlies it, between representation and its grounding, between meanings and practices, between narratives and social actors, between discourse and power can never be resolved in the terrain of theory. But the "never enough" goes both ways. If there is always "something else" beyond culture, something that it not quite captured by the textual/discursive, there is also something else beyond the so-called material, something that is always cultural and textual. We shall see the importance of this reversal for the cases of social movements of very poor and marginalized people, for whom the first goal of the struggle is often to demonstrate that they are people with rights, so as to recover their dignity and status as citizens and even as human beings. In other words, this tension is only provisionally resolved in practice. We argue that social movements are a crucial arena for understanding how this perhaps precarious yet vital entanglement of the cultural and the political occurs in practice. Moreover, we believe that the conceptualization and investigation of the cultural politics of social movements is a promising theoretical detour that heeds Hall's call.

From Cultural Politics to Political Culture

Despite its commitment to a broader understanding of culture, much of cultural studies, particularly in the United States, continues to be heavily oriented toward the textual. This has to do with disciplinary, historical, and institutional factors (Yúdice, in this volume). This bias finds its way into the use of the concept of cultural politics. In its current usage—despite the interest of cultural studies scholars in examining the relations between cultural practices and power and their commitment to social transformation—"cultural politics" often refers to disembodied struggles over meanings and representations, the political stakes of which for concrete social actors are sometimes difficult to discern.

We concur with the definition of cultural politics advanced by Jordan and Weedon in their recent book by the same title:

> The legitimation of social relations of inequality, and the struggle to transform them, are central concerns of CULTURAL POLITICS. Cultural politics fundamentally determine the meanings of social practices and, moreover, which groups and individuals have the power to define these meanings. Cultural politics are also concerned with subjectivity and identity, since culture plays a central role in constituting our sense of ourselves. . . . The forms of subjectivity that we inhabit play a crucial part in deter-

> mining whether we accept or contest existing power relations. Moreover, for marginalized and oppressed groups, the construction of new and resistant identities is a key dimension of a wider political struggle to transform society. (1995, 5–6)

However, by focusing their analysis on the "dominant . . . conception of culture," which reduces it to "music, literature, painting and sculpture, theater and film," now broadened to include the cultural industries, "popular culture" and the "mass media," Jordan and Weedon appear to share in the assumption that the politics of representation—as gleaned mostly from textual forms and analysis—has a direct and clear link with the exercise of power and, correspondingly, with resistance to it. Not always, however, are these links made explicit in ways that illuminate the actual or potential stakes and political strategies of particular social actors. We argue that these links are evident in the practices, the *concrete actions,* of Latin American social movements, and we thereby wish to extend the concept of cultural politics in analyzing their political interventions.

It is important to emphasize the fact that in Latin America today all social movements enact a cultural politics. It would be tempting to restrict the concept of cultural politics to those movements that are more clearly cultural. In the 1980s, this restriction resulted in a division between "new" and "old" social movements. New social movements were those for which identity was important, those that engaged in "new forms of doing politics," and those that contributed to new forms of sociability. Indigenous, ethnic, ecological, women's, gay, and human rights movements were the candidates of choice. Conversely, urban, peasant, labor, and neighborhood movements, among others, were seen as more conventionally struggling for needs and resources. The following chapters clearly show that the urban popular movements of squatters, women, marginal people, and others also set into motion cultural forces. In their continuous struggles against the dominant projects of nation building, development, and repression, popular actors mobilize collectively on the grounds of very different sets of meanings and stakes. For all social movements, then, collective identities and strategies are inevitably bound up with culture.

Our contributors explore the ways in which manifold cultural politics come into play when collective actors mobilize. Cultural politics are perhaps most evident in movements that make culture-based claims—as in the case of the Colombian black movement discussed by Libia Grueso, Carlos Rosero, and Arturo Escobar or the Pan-Mayan movement analyzed by Kay Warren—or in those that deploy culture as a means to mobilize or engage participants, as illustrated in the case of the African-Brazilian movements discussed by Olivia Cunha or of Mexico's COCEI (the Coalition of Workers, Peasants, and Students of the Isthmus) considered by Jeffrey Rubin.

However, we want to stress that cultural politics are also enacted when movements intervene in policy debates, attempt to resignify dominant cultural interpretations of politics, or challenge prevailing political practices. George Yúdice,

David Slater, and Gustavo Lins Ribeiro, for example, each draw our attention to the "artful guerrilla media war" launched by the Zapatistas in combating neoliberalism and promoting democratization in Mexico. Sonia Alvarez emphasizes that the policy battles waged by those Latin American feminists who in recent years have entered the state or the international development establishment must also be understood as struggles to resignify prevailing notions of citizenship, development, and democracy. Jean Franco makes a similar point in underscoring that feminism should be described "as a position (not exclusive to women) that destabilizes both fundamentalism and the new oppressive structures that are emerging with late capitalism," and that feminism's confrontation with such structures "involves more urgently than ever the struggle for interpretative power." Sérgio Baierle's analysis of urban popular movements in Porto Alegre, Brazil, conceptualizes these as "strategic spaces wherein different conceptions of citizenship and democracy are debated," and Maria Célia Paoli and Vera Telles likewise stress the manifold ways in which popular movements and trade unions simultaneously engage in struggles over rights and significations.

As Evelina Dagnino argues, the concept of cultural politics is important for assessing the scope of the struggles of social movements for the democratization of society and for highlighting the less visible and often neglected implications of these struggles. She maintains that cultural contestations are not mere "by-products" of political struggle but are instead constitutive of the efforts of social movements to redefine the meaning and the limits of the political system itself. Jean Franco notes that "discussions over the use of words often seem like nit-picking; language seems to be irrelevant to 'real' struggles. Yet the power to interpret, and the active appropriation and invention of language, are crucial tools for emergent movements seeking visibility and recognition for the views and actions that filter out from their dominant discourses." Indeed, as David Slater suggests in his contribution, "social struggles can be seen as 'wars of interpretation.'"

Our working definition of cultural politics is enactive and relational. We interpret cultural politics as the process enacted when sets of social actors shaped by, and embodying, different cultural meanings and practices come into conflict with each other. This definition of cultural politics assumes that meanings and practices—particularly those theorized as marginal, oppositional, minority, residual, emergent, alternative, dissident, and the like, all of them conceived in relation to a given dominant cultural order—can be the source of processes that must be accepted as political. That this is rarely seen as such is more a reflection of entrenched definitions of the political, harbored in dominant political cultures, than an indication of the social force, political efficacy, or epistemological relevance of cultural politics. Culture is political because meanings are constitutive of processes that, implicitly or explicitly, seek to redefine social power. That is, when movements deploy alternative conceptions of woman, nature, race, economy, democracy, or citizenship that unsettle dominant cultural meanings, they enact a cultural politics.

We speak of cultural politics formations in this sense: They are the result of discursive articulations originating in existing cultural practices—never pure, always hybrid, but nevertheless showing significant contrasts in relation to dominant cultures—and in the context of particular historical conditions. Of course, cultural politics exist in social movements of the right and even within state formations as well; neoconservatives, for instance, purport to "resacralize political culture" through "the defense or re-creation of a traditionalist and authoritarian lifeworld" (Cohen and Arato 1992, 24). Jean Franco's chapter similarly shows how, during preparations for the Fourth World Conference of Women, conservative and fundamentalist movements joined the Vatican in seeking to undermine feminism "by staging an apparently trivial sideshow—namely, an attack on the use of the word 'gender.'" And Verónica Schild's contribution calls attention to neoliberalism's efforts to restructure culture as well as the economy in Chile.

But perhaps the most important angle from which to analyze the cultural politics of social movements is in relation to its effects on political culture(s). Every society is marked by a dominant political culture. For the purposes of this volume, we define political culture as the particular social construction in every society of what counts as "political" (see also Slater 1994a; Lechner 1987a). In this way, political culture is the domain of practices and institutions, carved out of the totality of social reality, that historically comes to be considered as properly political (in the same way that other domains are seen as properly "economic," "cultural," and "social"). The dominant political culture of the West has been characterized as "rationalist, universalist, and individualist" (Mouffe 1993, 2).[4] As we shall see, the dominant forms of political culture in Latin America differ somewhat, perhaps significantly in some cases, from this definition.

The cultural politics of social movements often attempt to challenge or unsettle dominant political cultures. To the extent that the objectives of contemporary social movements sometimes reach beyond perceived material and institutional gains; to the extent that social movements shake the boundaries of cultural and political representation and social practice, calling into question even what may or may not be seen as political; to the extent, finally, that the cultural politics of social movements enact cultural contestations or presupposes cultural differences—then we must accept that what is at stake for social movements, in a profound way, is a transformation of the dominant political culture in which they have to move and constitute themselves as social actors with political pretensions. If social movements purport to modify social power, and if political culture also involves institutionalized fields for the negotiation of power, then social movements of necessity wrestle with the question of political culture. In many cases, social movements do not demand inclusion into but rather seek to reconfigure the dominant political culture. Baierle's analysis of popular movements—which finds echo in the chapters by Dagnino and Paoli and Telles—suggests that these movements can sometimes play a foundational role, "aimed at transforming the very political order in which they operate," and stresses that the "new citizens" emerging from the participatory forums and popular councils in Porto Alegre and other Brazilian cities radically question the mode in which power is to be exercised rather than merely attempting to "conquer" it.

The cultural politics of social movements can also be seen as fostering alternative modernities. As Fernando Calderón put it, some movements pose the question of how to be both modern and different—"como entrar en la modernidad sin dejar de ser indios" (1988, 225). They may mobilize constructions of individuals, rights, economies, and social conditions that cannot be strictly defined within standard paradigms of Western modernity (see Slater 1994a; and Warren et al., in this volume; Dagnino 1994a, 1994b).[5]

Latin American political cultures are greatly influenced by and yet differ from those that have prevailed in Europe and North America. This influence is clearly expressed in the recurrent references to principles such as rationalism, universalism, and individualism. However, in Latin America, these principles historically combined in contradictory ways with other principles aimed at ensuring social and political exclusion and even control over the definition of what counts as political in extremely inequitable and hierarchical societies. Such a contradictory hybridization has fueled analyses of the peculiar adoption of liberalism as "ideas out of place" *(idéias fora do lugar)* (Schwarz 1988) and, with respect to more recent times, analyses of "facade" democracies (Whitehead 1993).

This "out of place" liberalism suited nineteenth-century Latin American elites both as a response to international pressures and as a means of maintaining exclusionary political power, insofar as it was built upon and coexisted with an oligarchic conception of politics, transferred from the social and political practices of latifundio (Sales 1994), where personal, social, and political power overlapped, constituting one and the same reality. This lack of differentiation between the public and the private—where not only the public is privately appropriated but also political relations are perceived as extensions of private relations—normalizes favoritism, personalism, clientelism, and paternalism as regular political practices. In addition, assisted by myths such as "racial democracy," these practices obscured inequality and exclusion. As a consequence, subaltern, excluded groups came to regard politics as the "private business" of the elites (as Baierle puts it, as "o espaço privado dos doutores"), resulting in an immense distance between civil and political society—even in moments when dominant mechanisms of exclusion were apparently to be redefined, as, for instance, with the republican advent (Carvalho 1991).

When in the first few decades of the twentieth century urbanization and industrialization made the political incorporation of the masses unavoidable, it is not surprising that this same tradition inspired the new predominant politico-cultural arrangement, populism. Having to share their political space with formerly excluded participants, Latin American elites established mechanisms for a subordinated form of political inclusion, in which their own personalized relations with political leaders ensured control and tutelage over a heteronomous popular participation. More than the alleged "irrationality of the masses," what was behind the emergence of populist leadership—identified by the excluded as their "father" and savior—was still the dominant logic of personalism.

Associated with these new mechanisms of political representation and the economic reforms necessitated by modernization—with respect to which economic liberalism had revealed its limits (Flisfich, Lechner, and Moulian 1986)—a redefinition of the role of the state became a crucial element in Latin American political cultures. Conceived as the promoter of changes from above and thus as the primary agent of social transformation, the ideal of a strong and interventionist state, whose functions were seen as including the "organization"—and, in some cases, the very "creation"—of society, came to be shared by populist, nationalist, and developmentalist political cultures, in both their conservative and leftist versions. The dimension assumed by this centrality of the state in most political projects inspired analysts to refer to a "cult to the State" or to "*estadolatria*" (Coutinho 1980; Weffort 1984). The definition of what counts as "political" now had a new and concrete reference, aggravating the difficulties for the emergence of new politically autonomous subjects and thereby adding to the exclusion populism purported to address through the concession of political and social rights.

Under international pressures to "keep democracy and capitalism alive in Latin America," military regimes emerged throughout much of the region in the 1960s and 1970s in reaction to attempts to radicalize populist alliances or explore democratic socialist alternatives. Exacerbated authoritarianism transformed political exclusion into political elimination through state repression and systemic violence. Bureaucratic and technocratic decisionmaking procedures provided an additional rationale for further contracting the definition of politics and its participants.

Basically organized around the administration of exclusion, dominant political cultures in Latin America—with perhaps a few short-lived exceptions—cannot be seen as examples of hegemonic orderings of society. In fact, all have been committed, in different forms and degrees, to the deeply rooted social authoritarianism pervading the exclusionary organization of Latin American societies and cultures.

It is significant that social movements emerging from civil society in Latin America over the course of the last two decades—both in countries under authoritarian rule and in formally democratic nations—developed plural versions of a cultural politics that go well beyond the (re)establishment of formal liberal democracy. Thus, emergent redefinitions of concepts such as democracy and citizenship point in directions that confront authoritarian culture through a resignifying of notions as rights, public and private spaces, forms of sociability, ethics, equality and difference, and so on. These multiple processes of resignification clearly reveal alternative definitions to what counts as political.

Reconceptualizing the Political in Latin American Social Movements Research

In exploring the political in social movements, we must view politics as more than just a set of specific activities (voting, campaigning, lobbying) that occur in clearly delimited institutional spaces such as parliaments and parties; it must also be seen to encompass power struggles enacted in a wide range of spaces culturally defined as private, social, economic, cultural, and so on. Power, in turn, should not be understood as "blocs of institutional structures, with pre-established, fixed tasks (to dominate, to manipulate), or as mechanisms for imposing order from the top downwards, but rather as a social relation diffused through all spaces." (García Canclini 1988, 474). A decentered view of power and politics, however, should not divert our attention from how social movements interact with political society and the state and "must not lead us to ignore how power sediments itself and concentrates itself in social institutions and agents" (475).

Thus, our contributors pay due attention to movements' relationships to the sedimented powers of parties, institutions, and the state while suggesting that examining that relationship is "never enough" to apprehend the political impact or significance of social movements.[6] As David Slater (in this volume) cogently argues, the claim that contemporary social movements have challenged or redrawn the frontiers of the political "can mean, for example, that movements can subvert the traditional givens of the political system—state power, political parties, formal institutions—by contesting the legitimacy and apparently normal and natural functioning of their effects within society. But, also, the role of some social movements has been to reveal the concealed meanings of the political encased in the social."

Just as the chapters that follow seek to move beyond static understandings of culture and the (textual) politics of representation, they similarly transgress the narrow, reductionistic conceptions of politics, political culture, citizenship, and democracy that prevail in both mainstream political science and in some versions of resource mobilization and political-process approaches to social movements.[7] Instead of assessing or measuring movement "success" principally or exclusively on the basis of whether and how movement demands are processed within the politics of (institutional) representation, our authors also endeavor to shed new light on how the discourses and practices of social movements might destabilize and thereby—at least partially—transform the dominant discourses and exclusionary practices of "actually existing [Latin American] democracy" (Fraser 1993).

Having experienced something of a renaissance in the fields of political science and sociology in recent years (Inglehart 1988), the concept of political culture has sought to shed the "westernization" biases of yesteryear (Almond and Verba 1963, 1980). It nonetheless remains largely restricted to those attitudes and beliefs about that narrow arena (the bounded political system) that the dominant culture historically came to define as properly political and to those beliefs that either buttress or undermine the established rules of a given "political game": "Political culture involves a number of different psychological orientations, including deeper elements of value and belief about how political authority should be structured and how the self should relate to it, and more temporary and mutable attitudes, sentiments, and evaluations concerning the political system" (Diamond and Linz 1989, 10). Thus, for many political scientists such as Larry Diamond and

Juan Linz, "values and behavioral dispositions (particularly at the elite level) of compromise, flexibility, tolerance, conciliation, moderation, and restraint" contribute significantly to the "maintenance of democracy" (12–13).

Such conceptions of political culture take the political as a given and fail to grapple with a key aspect of movement struggles explored by several of the chapters assembled here. As Slater (1994a) notes, too often politics is referred to in a way that already presumes a meaning that is consensual and foundational. And we concur with Norbert Lechner's assessment that "the analysis of political issues necessarily raises the question of why a given issue is political. Thus, we can assume that political culture conditions and expresses precisely this determination" (1987a, 8). The cultural politics enacted by social movements, in challenging and resignifying what counts as political and who—besides the "democratic elite"—gets to define the rules of the political game, can be crucial, we maintain, to fostering alternative political cultures and, potentially, to extending and deepening democracy in Latin America (see also Avritzer 1994; Lechner 1987a, 1987b; Dagnino 1994). Rubin (in this volume) maintains, for example, that it was the "fostering of a new and hybrid political culture that enabled COCEI to secure its power even as neoliberal economic restructuring and the demobilization of popular movements dominated policymaking elsewhere in Mexico and Latin America."

Moreover, although the elite cultural dispositions noted by Diamond and Linz no doubt would help strengthen elite-based representative democracy, they tell us little about how broader cultural patterns and practices that foster societal authoritarianism and egregious inequality obstruct the exercise of meaningful democratic citizenship for non-elite citizens (Sales 1994; Telles 1994; Oliveira 1994; Hanchard 1994). The rigid social hierarchies of class, race, and gender that typify Latin American social relations prevent the vast majority of de jure citizens from even imagining, let alone publicly claiming, the prerogative to have rights. As we have argued elsewhere, popular movements, along with feminist, Afro–Latin American, lesbian and gay, and environmental movements, have been instrumental in constructing a new conception of democratic citizenship, one that claims rights in society and not just from the state, and that challenges the rigid social hierarchies that dictate fixed social places for its (non)citizens on the basis of class, race, and gender:

> Social authoritarianism engenders forms of sociability and an authoritarian culture of exclusion that underlies social practices as a whole and reproduces inequality in social relations on all levels. In this sense, its elimination constitutes a fundamental challenge for the effective democratization of society. A consideration of this dimension necessarily implies a redefinition of that which is normally viewed as the terrain of politics and of the power relations to be transformed. And, fundamentally, this requires an expansion and deepening of the conception of democracy, so as to include all social and cultural practices, a conception of democracy which transcends the formal institutional level and extends into all social relations permeated by social authoritarianism and not just by political exclusion in the strict sense. (Dagnino 1994a, 104–105)

Teresa Caldeira's analysis (forthcoming) of how and why the defense of common criminals' human rights continues to be viewed as "something bad and reproachable" by the majority of citizens in democratic Brazil poignantly illustrates why—in light of enduring sociocultural authoritarianism—"social analysis should look beyond the political system" in theorizing democratic transitions and explore how "the limits of democratization are deeply embedded in popular conceptions of the body, punishment, and individual rights." The pervasiveness of cultural notions of the "unbounded body and individual," Caldeira argues, seriously inhibits the consolidation of basic individual and civil rights in Brazil: "This notion is repeatedly reiterated not only as a means of exercise of power in interpersonal relations, but also as an instrument to challenge in an explicit way the principles of universal citizenship and individual rights." The cultural politics of human rights movements, then, must work to resignify and transform dominant cultural conceptions of rights and the body.

Despite the renewed attention afforded to political culture in some recent political analyses, however, the cultural continues to play second fiddle to the classical electoral, party, and policy harmonies that inspire liberal (neo)institutionalist analysis. Most mainstream theorists conclude that social movements and civic associations play, at best, a secondary role in democratization, and they have therefore focused scholarly attention on political institutionalization, which is viewed as "the single most important and urgent factor in the consolidation of democracy" (Diamond 1994, 15).

Consequently, discussions of Latin American democratization today focus almost exclusively on the stability of formal representative political institutions and processes, for example, "the perils of presidentialism" (Linz 1990; Linz and Valenzuela 1994), the formation and consolidation of viable parties and party systems (Mainwaring and Scully 1995), and the "requisites of governability" (Huntington 1991; Mainwaring, O'Donnell, and Valenzuela 1992; Martins 1989). Prevailing analyses of democracy, in short, center on what political scientists have dubbed the "institutional engineering" required to consolidate representative democracy in the South of the Americas.

A recent trend in the study of Latin American social movements would appear to endorse this exclusive focus on the formally institutional (see Foweraker 1995). Although the early literature on the movements of the 1970s and early 1980s praised their putative eschewal of institutional politics, their defense of absolute autonomy, and their emphasis on direct democracy, many recent analyses maintain that these postures gave rise to an "ethos of indiscriminate rejection of the institutional" (Doimo 1993; Silva 1994; Coelho 1992; Hellman 1994) that made it difficult for movements to effectively articulate their claims in formal political arenas. Other theorists have highlighted the movements' parochial, fragmentary qualities and emphasized their inability to transcend the local and engage in the realpolitik necessitated by the return of electoral democracy (Cardoso 1994, 1988; Silva 1994; Coelho 1992).

Though social movements' relationships to parties and the state and the fragile, elitist, particularistic, and often corrupt institutions of Latin America's civilian regimes certainly warrant scholarly attention, such analyses too often disregard the possibility that nongovernmental or extra-institutional public arenas—principally inspired or constructed by social movements—might be equally essential to the consolidation of meaningful democratic citizenship for subaltern social groups and classes. By calling attention to the cultural politics of social movements and to other less measurable and sometimes less visible or submerged dimensions of contemporary collective action (Melucci 1988), our authors offer alternative understandings of how movements have contributed to cultural and political change since economic neoliberalism and (limited, and largely protoliberal) representative democracy became the twin pillars of domination in Latin America.

The contributors draw on a variety of theoretical debates that may help us transcend some of the shortfalls inherent in dominant understandings of the political and shed a different light on its imbrications with the cultural in the practices of Latin American social movements. Among these are the recent feminist, cultural studies, and the postmarxist and poststructuralist debates about citizenship and democracy, as well as correlate concepts such as social movement networks or "webs," civil society, and public spaces or sphere(s).

Culture and Politics in Social Movement Networks or Webs

One particularly fruitful way to explore how social movements' political interventions extend into and beyond political society and the state is to analyze the configuration of social movement networks or webs (Melucci 1988; Doimo 1993; Landim 1993a; Fernandes 1994; Scherer-Warren 1993; Putnam 1993; Alvarez, 1997). On the one hand, several of the following chapters call attention to the cultural practices and interpersonal networks of daily life that sustain social movements across mobilizational ebbs and flows and that infuse new cultural meanings into political practices and collective action. These frameworks of meaning may include different modes of consciousness and practices of nature, neighborhood life, and identity.

Rubin, for example, eloquently describes how radical popular movements in Juchitán, Mexico, drew strength from family, community, and ethnic ties. He stresses how seemingly apolitical "physical and social locations" such as market stalls, local bars, and family courtyards "contributed to the reelaboration of local cultural beliefs and practices" and became "important places for discussion and mobilization [in Juchitán] . . . their gender and class characteristics [providing] fertile ground for rethinking politics and getting people out into the streets." The centrality attributed to the submerged networks of daily life (Melucci 1988) in shaping movements' cultural politics finds echo in Libia Grueso, Carlos Rosero, and Arturo Escobar's discussion of Afro-Colombian struggles over nature and identity, Sérgio Baierle's treatment of Brazilian urban movements, and Olivia Gomes da Cunha's chapter on Brazilian black movements in this volume.

On the other hand, several chapters stress that social movements must be understood not only to rely and draw upon networks of everyday life but also to construct or configure new interpersonal, interorganizational, and politico-cultural linkages with other movements as well as with a multiplicity of cultural and institutional actors and spaces. These linkages expand movements' cultural and political reach far beyond local communities and family courtyards and, some of our authors contend, help counter movements' alleged parochial, fragmentary, and ephemeral propensities.

When evaluating the impact of social movements on larger processes of politico-cultural change, we must understand the reach of social movements as extending beyond their conspicuous constitutive parts and visible manifestations of protest. As Ana Maria Doimo suggests in her incisive study of the "popular movement" in Brazil:

> In general, when we study phenomena relative to explicitly political participation, such as parties, elections, parliament, etc., we know where to look for data and instruments to "measure" them. This is not the case with the movement field in question. . . . such a field rests upon interpersonal relationships which link individuals to other individuals, involving connections that go beyond specific groups and transversely cut across particular social institutions, such as the Catholic Church, Protestantism—national and international—the scientific academy, non-governmental organizations (NGOs), leftist organizations, trade unions and political parties. (Doimo 1993, 44)

Alvarez contends that the political demands, discourses, and practices as well as the mobilizational and policy strategies of many of today's movements are spread widely, and sometimes invisibly, through the social fabric, as their political-communicative networks stretch into parliaments, the academy, the Church, the media, and so on. Schild argues: "Vast networks of professionals and activists who are feminists, or who are at least sensitive to women's issues, are at work today in Chile and other Latin American countries. These networks are not only responsible for sustaining the work of grassroots organizations and . . . NGOs but are also engaged in the production of knowledge, including categories that become part of the moral repertoires used by the state." Moreover, as contributions by Yúdice, Slater, Lins Ribeiro, and Alvarez demonstrate, many Latin American movement networks are increasingly regional and transnational in scope (see also Lipschutz 1992; Keck and Sikkink 1992; Fernandes 1994).

The term "social movement webs" (in contrast to the more common "networks") conveys the intricacy and precariousness of the manifold imbrications of and ties established among movement organizations, individual participants, and other actors in civil and political society and the state. The "web" metaphor also enables us to more vividly imagine the multilayered entanglements of movement actors with the natural-environmental, political-institutional, and cultural-discursive terrains in which they are embedded.

In other words, movement webs encompass more than movement organizations and their active members; they include occasional participants in movement events and actions, and sympathizers and collaborators in NGOs, political parties, universities, other cultural and conventionally political institutions, the Church, and even the state who (at least partially) support a given movement's goals and help deploy its discourses and demands in and against dominant political cultures and institutions (Landim 1993a and 1993b). When we examine the impact of movements, then, we must gauge the extent to which their demands, discourses, and practices circulate in weblike, capillary fashion (e.g., are deployed, adopted, appropriated, co-opted, or reconstructed, as the case may be) in larger institutional and cultural arenas. Warren, for example, criticizes the prevalent notion that "the measure of success of a social movement is its ability to achieve mass mobilizations and public protests," arguing that in assessing the impact of a movement such as the Pan-Mayan—based on education, language, cultural reaffirmation, and collective rights—we must consider that there may not be any "demonstrations to count because this is not a mass movement that generates protest. But there will be new generations of students, leaders, teachers, development workers, and community elders who have been touched in one way or another by the Pan-Mayan movement and its cultural production."

We must also consider how movement dynamics and discourses are shaped by the important social, cultural, and political institutions that traverse movement networks or webs and how movements, in turn, shape the dynamics and discourses of those institutions. Schild, for example, notes that "government agencies and nonprofit, party-based initiatives working on behalf of women rely heavily on the efforts of women positioned in [feminist-inspired] networks" in contemporary Chile. And Alvarez analyzes the relatively rapid, if selective, absorption, appropriation, and resignification of Latin American feminist discourses and demands by dominant cultural institutions, parallel organizations of civil and political society, the state, and the development establishment.

Social Movements and the Revitalization of Civil Society

Like the notion of political culture, the concept of civil society has also witnessed a significant revival, indeed a veritable conceptual boom, in the social sciences over the past decade (Cohen and Arato 1992, 15; Walzer 1992; Avritzer 1994; Keane 1988). Andrew Arato attributes "the notable reemergence of this concept" to the fact that:

> It expressed the new dualist, radical, reformist, or revolutionary strategies of transformation of dictatorship, observed first in eastern Europe and later in Latin America, for which it provided a new theoretical understanding. These strategies were based on the autonomous organization of society and the reconstruction of social ties outside the

> authoritarian state and the conceptualization of a public sphere independent and separate from every form of official, state, or party-controlled communication. (1995, 19)

Indeed, as Alfred Stepan put it, "civil society became the political celebrity" of many recent Latin American transitions from authoritarian rule (Stepan 1988, 5) and was uniformly viewed as a significant (if secondary) player in the democratization literature. In his contribution to this anthology, Yúdice further claims that, under neoliberalism's shrinking state, civil society has "flourished." In other recent work, civil society has gone "international" (Ghils 1992), "transnational" (Lins Ribeiro 1994 and in this volume), "global" (Lipschutz 1992; Leis 1995; Walzer 1995), even "planetary" (Fernandes 1994 and 1995).

And though efforts to delimit the concept vary wildly—ranging from all-encompassing (in some versions, residual) definitions that signal everything that is *not* the state or the market to conceptions that restrict the notion to forms of organized or purposive associational life aimed at the expression of societal interests—most include social movements among its central and most vital components. Moreover, conservative and progressive analysts and activists alike tend overwhelmingly to sing the praises of civil society's democratizing potential on a local, national, regional, and global scale.

Our contributors generally endorse this positive view, to the extent that civil society has often constituted the only available or most important domain for organizing cultural and political contestation. However, they also draw attention to three important, but seldom explored, caveats. First, they highlight that civil society itself is not one homogeneous happy family or "global village" but is also a terrain of struggle mined by sometimes undemocratic power relations and the enduring problems of racism, hetero/sexism, environmental destruction, and other forms of exclusion (Slater, Alvarez, Lins Ribeiro, Schild). In particular, the growing predominance of NGOs within Latin American movements and their complex relationship to local grassroots movements and constituencies, on the one hand, and to bilateral, multilateral, and private agencies, foundations, and transnational NGOs based in North America, on the other, are also signaled as especially gnarly political and theoretical issues for the region's movements today (see also MacDonald 1992; Ramos 1995; Muçoucah 1995; Rielly 1994; Walzer 1992; Lebon 1993). Lins Ribeiro points out that "NGOs can indeed be an effective fragmented, decentered, political subject in a postmodern world, but the cost of flexibility, pragmatism, and fragmentation may well be reformism—their capability to promote radical change may weaken." Alvarez analyzes questions of representativeness, legitimacy, and accountability that often plague feminist NGOs and, along with Schild, calls attention to ways in which NGOs sometimes appear to act as "neo-" or "para-" rather than "non"-governmental organizations. And Yúdice asks: "[might not] the effervescence of NGOs [be] cut two ways: helping to buttress a public sector evacuated by the state and at the same time making it possible for the state to steer clear of what was once seen as its responsibility?"

Second, several of the ensuing chapters caution us against uncritically applauding the virtues of civil society in its local, national, regional, or global manifestations. Slater notes that "not infrequently civil society has been essentialized in a positive frame, as the terrain of the good and the enlightened," yet his chapter, along with chapters by Schild, Yúdice, Lins Ribeiro, and Alvarez, stresses that civil society is a terrain mined by unequal relations of power wherein some actors can gain greater access to power, as well as differential access to material, cultural, and political resources, than others. Because democratizing cultural and social relations—whether at the micro level of the household, the neighborhood, and the community association or the macro level of relations between women and men, blacks and whites, rich and poor—is an express goal of Latin American social movements, civil society must be understood as both their "terrain" and one of their privileged "targets" (see Cohen and Arato 1992, esp. chap. 10). In this sense, there is an evident link between the importance of democratizing struggles within civil society and the cultural politics of social movements.

Third, several chapters examine how the boundary between civil society and the state often becomes blurred in the practices of contemporary Latin American social movements. Schild emphasizes the frequent "transmigration" of Chilean feminist activists from NGOs to the state and back again and further calls attention to the fact that the state itself structures relationships *within* civil society, arguing that "this structuring relies on important cultural resources from civil society itself." And Slater contends that there are links between the state and civil society that make illusory the idea of a confrontation or even a delimitation between the two as fully fledged autonomous entities (Slater, in this volume).

Chapters by Rubin and Miguel Díaz-Barriga illustrate how the hybrid practices of social movements also often defy dichotomous representations of public life and private or domestic life. Rubin argues that COCEI's cultural politics were often enacted in the "blurred zones in between." And the *colonas* participating in Mexico City's urban movements, Díaz-Barriga maintains, similarly operate within "cultural borderlands." He further says that "both challenged and reinforced the cultural and political meanings of women's subordination as well as inhabited a social space wrought with ambiguity, irony, and conflict."

Social Movements and the Trans/formation of Public Politics

Different conceptions of the public—such as public spheres, public spaces, and subaltern counterpublics—have been recently proposed as hopeful approaches to exploring the nexus of culture and politics in contemporary social movements (Habermas 1987 and 1989; Fraser 1989 and 1993; Cohen and Arato 1992; Robbins 1993; Costa 1994) and are reworked and deployed in various ways in the chapters that follow.

George Yúdice argues that scholars in the Americas must "deal with [the] challenge to (re)construct civil society, and in particular the contending public spheres in which cultural practices are channeled and evaluated" (1994, 2). Jean Franco (quoted in Yúdice 1994) further suggests that we must examine "public spaces" rather than conventionally defined public spheres so as to identify zones of action that present possibilities of participation to the subordinated groups who use and move through these spaces. It is in the re/appropriation of public spaces such as shopping malls, one of Franco's examples, that it becomes possible for marginal groups to satisfy needs unforeseen in the conventional uses of such spaces (Yúdice 1994, 6–7). Rubin's analysis of family courtyards and local markets as important locations for the production of meanings about culture, politics, and participation; Díaz-Barriga's notion of "cultural borderlands" created by women active in Mexican popular struggles; Colombian black activists' use of river and forest environments; and the Zapatistas' creative uses of cyberspace are illustrative of the re/construction and appropriation of such public spaces by social movements.

To apprehend the politico-cultural impact of social movements and assess their contributions to undermining social authoritarianism and elite-based democratization, then, it is not enough to examine movement interactions with official public environments (such as parliaments and other national and transnational policy arenas). We must shift our gaze to also encompass other public spaces—constructed or appropriated by social movements—in which cultural politics are enacted and subaltern identities, demands, and needs are shaped.

Nancy Fraser persuasively argues that Habermas' account of the liberal public sphere is "informed by an underlying evaluative assumption, namely, that the institutional confinement of public life to a single, overarching public sphere is a positive and desirable state of affairs, whereas the proliferation of a multiplicity of publics represents a departure from, rather than an advance toward, democracy" (1993, 13). This critique is particularly relevant in the case of Latin America where—even in formally democratic political contexts—information about, access to, and influence in the governmental arenas in which collectively binding policy decisions are made have been restricted to a very small, privileged fraction of the population and effectively denied to subaltern groups and classes. Because the subaltern historically have been relegated to the status of de facto noncitizens in Latin America—several of our authors maintain—the multiplication of public arenas in which sociocultural, gender-based, racial, and economic, and not just political, exclusion might be contested and resignified, then, must also be seen as integral to the expansion and deepening of democratization.

The proliferation of alternative social movement "publics"—configured, several of our contributors suggest, out of intra- and intermovement political-communicative networks or webs—is thus positive for democracy not only because it serves to "check the power of the state" or because it "give[s] expression" to structurally preordained "popular interests," as Diamond and Linz would have it (1989, 35), but also because it is in these alternative public spaces that those very interests can be continually re/constructed. Fraser conceptualizes these alternative spaces as "subaltern counterpublics" in order to signal that they are "parallel discursive arenas where members of subordinated social groups invent and circulate counterdiscourses, so as to formulate oppositional interpretations of their identities, interests and needs" (Fraser 1993, 14). Social movements' contribution to Latin American democracy, then, can also be found in the proliferation of multiple public spheres, and not just in their success in processing demands within official publics.

As Baierle maintains, beyond the struggle for the realization of interests, such spaces make possible the processing of conflicts surrounding the construction of identities and the definition of spaces in which those conflicts can be expressed. Thus defined, "politics incorporates, in its paramount moment, the social construction of interest, which is never given a priori." For Paoli and Telles, the social struggles of the 1980s have left an important legacy for the 1990s: they created informal, discontinuous, and plural public spaces in which diverse demands can circulate and in which the recognition of others as the bearers of rights may occur. Paoli and Telles contend that popular and labor movements alike have helped constitute public arenas in which conflicts gain visibility, collective subjects constitute themselves as valid interlocutors, and rights structure a public language that delimits the criteria through which collective demands for justice and equity can be problematized and evaluated. Like Baierle and Dagnino, they further maintain that these new public arenas of representation, negotiation, and interlocution represent a "democratic field in construction" that signals at least the possibility of rethinking and expanding the parameters of actually existing Brazilian democracy.

As noted above, movement-based or movement-inspired publics are themselves riddled by unequal power relations. Indeed, rather than portraying social movements as "intrinsically politically virtuous," as Paoli and Telles put it, several of our chapters explore crucial questions regarding representation, accountability, and internal democracy *within* these alternative publics constructed or inspired by social movements. Nonetheless, we maintain that, however contradictory, the sustained public presence and proliferation of social movement webs and alternative publics has been a positive development for existing democracy in Latin America. In this sense, we concur with Fraser's assessment that:

> subaltern counterpublics are [not] always necessarily virtuous; some of them, alas, are explicitly antidemocratic and antiegalitarian; and even those with democratic and egalitarian intentions are not always above practicing their own modes of informal exclusion and marginalization. Still, insofar as these counterpublics emerge in response to exclusion within dominant publics, they help expand discursive space. In principle, assumptions that were previously exempt from contestation will now have to be publicly argued out. In general, the proliferation of subaltern counterpublics means a widening of discursive contestation, a good thing in stratified societies. (1993, 15)

Though the putatively democratizing role of movement publics is surely rendered more problematic by issues of representativeness and accountability explored in several of our chapters, the increased imbrication of alternative and official publics may nevertheless widen political and policy contestation *within* institutions of political society and the state. Indeed, as Dagnino's survey of movement activists in Campinas, São Paulo, demonstrates, participants in social movements have hardly "turned their backs" on parties and governmental institutions. Instead, her study reveals that whereas the overwhelming majority of Brazilian citizens mistrust politicians and view parties as mechanisms for the advancement of particularistic interests, over 70 percent of those active in social movements belong to or strongly identify with a political party and believe that representative institutions are crucial arenas for promoting social change.

Still, our chapters suggest that Colombian black activists, feminists at the UN, Pan-Mayan movement leaders, and Zapatistas alike are not merely struggling for access, incorporation, participation, or inclusion into the "nation" or the "political system" on terms predefined by dominant political cultures. Rather, as Dagnino stresses, what is also at stake for today's social movements is the right to participate in the very definition of the political system, the right to define that in which they wish to be included.

Globalization, Neoliberalism, and the Cultural Politics of Social Movements

In closing, it is necessary to consider the myriad ways in which globalization and the neoliberal economic project in vogue throughout Latin America have affected the cultural politics of social movements in recent years. On the one hand, globalization and its correlate concept, transnationalism (see the chapter by Lins Ribeiro on this distinction), appear to have opened up new possibilities for social movements—for example, facilitating efforts to promote a politics of nonterritorial democratization of global issues, as Slater contends. Lins Ribeiro finds that new communications technologies such as the Internet have made possible new forms of political "activism at a distance." And Yúdice notes that although "most leftist views of globalization are pessimistic, the turn to civil society in the context of neoliberal policies, and the uses of the new technologies on which globalization relies, have opened up new forms of progressive struggle in which the cultural is a crucial arena of struggle." In Colombia, ethnic struggles also find in the globalization of the environment—particularly the importance of biodiversity conservation—a potentially favorable conjuncture.

On the other hand, several contributors suggest that globalization and neoliberalism have not only intensified economic inequality—such that ever larger numbers of Americans on both sides of the equator live in absolute poverty, with those in the South deprived of even the minimal and always precarious safety net provided by the *Estados de mal-estar social* of yesteryear—but have also significantly redefined the politico-cultural terrain in which social movements must today undertake their struggles. Indeed, the overpowering neoliberal policies that have swept the continent in recent years appear in some cases to have weakened popular movements and unsettled existing languages of protest, placing movements at the mercy of other articulating agents, from conservative parties and narcotraffic to fundamentalist churches and transnational consumerism. Violence has taken on novel dimensions as a shaper of the social and the cultural in many regions; *clases emergentes,* linked to illicit businesses and transnational market-driven enterprises alike, have gained social and political ascendancy; and certain forms of racism and sexism have been accentuated in connection with changing divisions of labor that place the burden of adjustment on women, the nonwhite, and the poor.

It is becoming increasingly clear that one important politico-cultural dimension of economic neoliberalism is what could be called "social adjustment," the appearance in many countries of social programs targeted to those groups most clearly excluded or victimized by structural adjustment policies (SAPs). Whether it is FOSIS (Fondo de Solidaridad e Inversion Social) in Chile, Comunidade Solidaria in Brazil, Red de Solidaridad in Colombia, or PRONASOL (Programa Nacional de Solidaridad) in Mexico, these programs constitute—under the rubric of "solidarity," curiously enough—strategies of social adjustment that must necessarily accompany economic adjustment (see Cornelius, Craig, and Fox 1994; Graham 1994; Rielly 1994). We may properly speak, indeed, of "apparatuses and practices of social adjustment" (APSAs) at play here. With different degrees of reach, sophistication, state support, or even cynicism, the various APSAs not only make manifest once again the proclivity of Latin America's dominant classes to experiment and improvise with the popular classes—as we suggest above in our discussion of twentieth-century dominant political culture—but they purport to transform the social and cultural basis of mobilization. This is perhaps most clearly the case in Chile, where the process of refounding the state and society on neoliberal terms is most advanced—and, indeed, Chile's FOSIS is being hailed as a model for other Latin American countries to follow (see Schild, in this volume).

As we noted at the outset of this chapter, neoliberalism is a powerful and ubiquitous contender in the contemporary dispute over the meaning of citizenship and the design of democracy. Programs such as FOSIS operate by creating new client categories among the poor and by introducing new individualizing and atomizing discourses such as those of "personal development," "capacity building for self-management," "self-help," "active citizenship," and the like. These discourses pretend more than the self-management of poverty. In seemingly Foucaultian fashion (see Yúdice, Slater, and Schild's treatments of Foucault's concept of "governmentality" in this respect), they appear to introduce new forms of self-subjectification, identity formation, and discipline. It is thus that participants in these programs come to see themselves increasingly in the individualizing and economizing terms of the market. APSAs thus might depoliticize the basis for mobilization. This effect is sometimes facilitated by professionalized NGOs, which, as we have noted, in many cases act as mediators between the state and the popular movements.

We must be wary, however, when confronted with these developments, of thinking once again that "the world is going to hell in a handbasket." Nothing, to begin with, ensures that the Chilean model will be exported successfully to other countries—or will continue to be successful in Chile—and there is no guarantee that the effect of demobilization will be permanent. Surely, forms of resistance to APSAs will become increasingly clear. As Schild argues, we cannot foretell "what form the identity of today's 'marketized' citizen may take, or in what contexts such an identity may be deployed by different social groups," but goes on to insist, nonetheless, "that the terms in which citizenship may be adopted, contested, and struggled over are predetermined" by neoliberalism's cultural-economic offensive. Paoli and Telles, by contrast, stress that neoliberalism is not a coherent, homogeneous, or totalizing project; that the prevailing logic of structural adjustment is far from inevitable; and it is precisely at the interstices generated by these contradictions that social movements sometimes articulate their politics. Yet the fact remains that neoliberalism and globalization do transform significantly the conditions under which collective action may take place.

To what extent do neoliberal reformulations of citizenship and democracy and the now reigning and restricted conception of social policy embodied in the new APSAs entail cultural reconversions of importance? To what extent will popular groups and other social movements be able to negotiate or partially utilize the new social and political spaces carved out by APSAs or by neoliberalism's professed celebration of "civil society"?

Finally, we must raise a question regarding the possibility that the new conditions dictated by neoliberal globalization might transform the meaning itself of "social movement." Is what counts as a social movement being reconfigured? Are social movements ebbing in the seemingly demobilizing context of SAPs and APSAs? Should we not look critically at the participation of many previously progressive social movement organizations and NGOs in the apparatuses of social adjustment? Some of our chapters propose preliminary answers to these pressing questions.

Indeed, investigating the relationship between neoliberal renditions of citizenship, social adjustment, and the cultural politics of social movements is an especially urgent task. The stakes are high, no doubt, and for us—scholars, intellectuals, and intellectual activists—they are enmeshed with our perception of the world and the current state of our knowledge traditions. What we attempt to develop, in this anthology, is a collective inquiry that might allow us to gauge simultaneously one and the other, stakes and frameworks.

Notes

1. A recent, important exception is Darnovsky, Epstein, and Flacks 1995. This anthology focuses primarily on contemporary social movements in the United States and principally engages debates concerning "identity politics" and radical democracy.

2. But while some call for the abandonment of "culture," most critical anthropologists continue to believe that both fieldwork and the study of cultures remain important and perhaps exemplary, analytical, methodological, and political practices for examining the world at present, even if both fieldwork and culture—in their reflexive, poststructuralist modes—are now understood in significantly different ways than even a decade ago. To the extent that culture continues to be a space for the exercise of power, and given the persistent force of cultural differences despite globalization, cultural theorizing and fieldwork continue to be forceful intellectual and political projects.

3. The "decentering" and displacement associated with culture and the discursive Hall talks about originates in the fact that meaning can never be totally fixed, that any interpretation of reality can always be contested. So we have a permanent tension between a "material reality" that seems solid and stable and the ever changing semiosis that gives meanings to it and that, in the long run, is what makes the material real for concrete people. This tension, well known to hermeneutic philosophers and anthropologists, has witnessed a series of reworkings since the breakdown of the base/superstructure division. Foucaultian poststructuralism introduced first the division of discursive and nondiscursive formations, statements and visibilities, with discourse organizing and incorporating the nondiscursive (institutions, economies, historical conditions, and so on). Laclau and Mouffe (1985) attempted to radicalize the Foucaultian insight by dissolving the distinction, claiming the fundamental discursive nature of all social reality. For them, there is no materiality that is not mediated by discourse and no discourse unrelated to materiality. The differentiation of the material and the discursive can only be made, if at all, for analytical purposes.

4. Western political culture is of course not a monolithic entity. But whether it refers to elite or participatory democracy, rights-oriented liberalism or communitarianism, welfarist or neoconservative conceptions, one is dealing with contested conceptions within the established boundaries of political culture in the history of the modern West (Cohen and Arato 1992).

5. This is why we do not agree with the widely held opinion that restricts the scope of social movements to deepening the democratic imaginary of the West. To reject the ideas of unitary subject and single political space, as Mouffe (1993) wants us to do in endorsing antiessentialism, may require casting off more of the features of modernity than she, and most European and European-American political theorists, seem prepared to grant. Similarly, while we agree with the fact that social movements are a "key feature of a vital, modern, civil society," we disagree with the assertion that they should not be seen as "prefiguring a form of citizen participation that will or even ought to substitute for the institutional arrangements of representative democracy" (Cohen and Arato 1992, 19). In Latin America, which is characterized by hybrid cultures and a precarious differentiation between state, economy, and civil society, and where the conventionally political has rarely fulfilled the role it has been entrusted with, the normativity and structuration that European and North American political theorists want to uphold are tenuous and problematic at best. We find more compelling, for instance, the hypothesis of the existence of subaltern domains of politics, parallel to the dominant domain and articulated by different practices and idioms of protest (Guha 1988).

6. For an exhaustive overview of the existing literature focusing on movements' relationships to parties and the state in Latin America, see Foweraker 1995.

7. Recent reappraisals of resource mobilization (RM) theory have prompted scholars to explore simultaneously the institutional, structural, *and* cultural-symbolic sides of social

movements. RM theorists increasingly recognize that cultural processes—such as Tarrow's "collective action frames" (1992), Friedman and McAdam's "identity incentives" (1992), Taylor and Whittier's "politicization of symbolic presentations of everyday life" (1992), and the "transformation of hegemonic meanings and group loyalties" (Mueller 1992, 10)—are intimately intertwined with the unfolding of political opportunities and social movement strategies. Carol McClurg Mueller aptly summarizes this new research direction by highlighting how, while the economistic rational actor of resource mobilization theory minimized the role of ideas, beliefs, and cultural configurations, the new social movement actor constructs the meanings that designate from the outset the relevant types of grievances, resources, and opportunities (1992, 21–22). See also Johnston and Klandermans 1995; McAdam, McCarthy, and Zald 1996.

References

Almond, Gabriel, and Sidney Verba. 1963. *The Civic Culture.* Boston: Little, Brown.

Almond, Gabriel, and Sidney Verba, eds. 1980. *The Civic Culture Revisited.* Boston: Little, Brown.

Alvarez, Sonia E. 1997. "Reweaving the Fabric of Collective Action: Social Movements and Challenges to 'Actually Existing Democracy' in Brazil." In *Between Resistance and Revolution: Cultural Politics and Social Protest,* ed. R. Fox and O. Starn, 83–117. New Brunswick, N.J.: Rutgers University Press.

Arato, Andrew. 1995. "Ascensão, Declínio e Reconstrução do Conceito de Sociedade Civil: Orientações para Novas Pesquisas." *Revista Brasileira de Ciências Sociais* 10 (27):18–27.

Avritzer, Leonardo, ed. 1994. *Sociedade Civil e Democratização.* Belo Horizonte: Del Rey.

Caldeira, Teresa. Forthcoming. *City of Walls: Crime, Segregation, and Citizenship in São Paulo, Brazil.* Berkeley: University of California Press.

Calderón, Fernando. 1995. *Movimientos Sociales y Política.* Mexico City: Siglo XXI.

Calderón, Fernando, ed. 1988. *Imagenes Desconocidas: La Modernidad en la Encrucijada Postmoderna.* Buenos Aires: CLACSO.

Cardoso, Ruth Corrêa Leite. 1988. "Isso É Política? Dilemas da Participação entre o Moderno e o Pós-Moderno." *Novos Estudos do CEBRAP* 20:74–80.

______. 1994. "A Trajetória dos Movimentos Sociais." In *Anos 90: Política e Sociedade no Brasil,* ed. E. Dagnino. São Paulo: Brasiliense.

Carvalho, José Murilo de. 1991. *Os Bestializados.* São Paulo: Cia das Letras.

Clifford, James, and George Marcus, eds. 1986. *Writing Culture: The Poetics and Politics of Ethnography.* Berkeley: University of California Press.

Coelho, Simone C. T. 1992. "O Estado e os Movimentos Pró-Moradia: A Construção de uma Relação Democrática." Master's thesis, Universidade de São Paulo.

Cohen, Jean L., and Andrew Arato. 1992. *Civil Society and Political Theory.* Cambridge: MIT Press.

Comaroff, Jean, and John Comaroff. 1991. *Of Revelation and Revolution.* Chicago: University of Chicago Press.

Cornelius, Wayne A., Ann L. Craig, and Jonathan Fox, eds. 1994. *Transforming State-Society Relations: The National Solidarity Strategy.* San Diego: Center for U.S.-Mexican Studies, University of California at San Diego.

Costa, Sérgio. 1994. "Esfera Pública, Redescoberta da Sociedade Civil e Movimentos Sociais no Brasil: Uma Abordagem Tentativa." *Novos Estudos do CEBRAP* 38:38–52.

Coutinho, Carlos Nelson. 1980. *A Democracia como Valor Universal.* São Paulo: Ciências Humanas.

Dagnino, Evelina. 1994a. "Os movimentos sociais e a emergência de uma nova noção de cidadania." In *Anos 90: Política e Sociedade no Brasil,* ed. E. Dagnino. São Paulo: Brasiliense.

______. 1994b. "On Becoming a Citizen: The Story of D. Marlene." In *Migration and Identity,* ed. R. Benmayor and A. Skotnes. Oxford: Oxford University Press.

Dagnino, Evelina, ed. 1994. *Anos 90: Política e Sociedade no Brasil.* São Paulo: Brasiliense.

Darnovsky, Marcy, Barbara Epstein, and Richard Flacks, eds. 1995. *Cultural Politics and Social Movements.* Philadelphia: Temple University Press.

de Certeau, Michel. 1984. *The Practice of Everyday Life.* Berkeley: University of California Press.

Diamond, Larry. 1994. "Rethinking Civil Society: Toward Democratic Consolidation." *Journal of Democracy* 5 (3):4–17.

Diamond, Larry, and Juan J. Linz. 1989. "Introduction: Politics, Society, and Democracy in Latin America." In *Democracy in Developing Countries: Latin America,* ed. L. Diamond, J. Linz, and S. Lipset. Boulder: Lynne Rienner.

Doimo, Ana Maria. 1993. "O 'Movimento Popular' no Brasil Pos–70: Formacão de um Campo Ético-Político." Ph.D. dissertation, Universidade de São Paulo.

Escobar, Arturo, and Sonia E. Alvarez, eds. 1992. *The Making of Social Movements in Latin America: Identity, Strategy, and Democracy.* Boulder: Westview Press.

Fernandes, Rubem César. 1994. *Privado, porém Público: O Terceiro Setor na América Latina.* Rio de Janeiro: Relume-Dumará.

______. 1995. "Elos de uma Cidadania Planetaria." *Revista Brasileira de Ciências Sociais* 10 (28):15–34.

Fiske, John. 1989. *Understanding Popular Culture.* Boston: Unwin Hyman.

Flisfich, Angel, Norbert Lechner, and Tomas Moulian. 1986. *Problemas de la Democracia y la Política Democrática en América Latina.* Santiago: FLACSO/CLAEH.

Foweraker, Joe. 1995. *Theorizing Social Movements.* Boulder: Pluto Press.

Fox, Richard, ed. 1991. *Recapturing Anthropology: Working in the Present.* Santa Fe, N.Mex.: School of American Research.

Fraser, Nancy. 1989. "What's Critical about Critical Theory? The Case of Habermas and Gender." In *Unruly Practices: Power, Discourse, and Gender in Contemporary Social Theory,* ed. N. Fraser. Minneapolis: University of Minnesota Press.

______. 1993. "Rethinking the Public Sphere: A Contribution to the Critique of Actually Existing Democracy." In *The Phantom Public Sphere,* ed. B. Robbins. Minneapolis: University of Minnesota Press.

Friedman, Debra, and Doug McAdam. 1992. "Collective Identity and Activism: Networks, Choices, and the Life of a Social Movement." In *Frontiers of Social Movement Theory,* ed. A. Morris and C. Mueller. New Haven: Yale University Press.

García Canclini, Nestor. 1988. "Culture and Power: The State of Research." *Media, Culture and Society* 10:467–497.

Ghils, Paul. 1992. "International Civil Society: International Non-Governmental Organizations in the International System." *International Social Science Journal* 133:417–429.

Graham, Carol. 1994. "Mexico's Solidarity Program in Comparative Context: Demand-Based Poverty Alleviation Programs in Latin America, Africa, and Eastern Europe." In *Transforming State-Society Relations in Mexico: The National Solidarity Strategy,* ed. W. Cornelius, A. Craig, and J. Fox. San Diego: Center for U.S.-Mexican Studies, University of California at San Diego.

Guha, Ranajit. 1988. "The Prose of Counterinsurgency." In *Selected Subaltern Studies,* ed. R. Guha and G. Spivak. Delhi: Oxford University Press.

Gupta, Akhil, and James Ferguson. 1992. "Beyond Culture: Space, Identity, and the Politics of Difference." *Cultural Anthropology* 7 (1):6–23.

Habermas, Jürgen. 1987. *The Theory of Communicative Action.* Vol. 2, *Lifeworld and System: A Critique of Functionalist Reason,* trans. T. McCarthy. Boston: Beacon Press.

______. 1989. *The Structural Transformation of the Public Sphere: An Inquiry into the Category of Bourgeois Society,* trans. T. Burger with F. Lawrence. Cambridge: MIT Press.

Hall, Stuart. 1992. "Cultural Studies and Its Theoretical Legacies." In *Cultural Studies,* ed. L. Grossberg, C. Nelson, and P. Treichler. London: Routledge.

Hanchard, Michael George. 1994. *Orpheus and Power: The Movimento Negro of Rio de Janeiro and São Paulo, Brazil, 1945–1988.* Princeton: Princeton University Press.

Hellman, Judith Alder. 1994. "Mexican Popular Movements, Clientelism, and the Process of Democratization." *Latin American Perspectives* 21 (2):124–142.

Holston, James, and Teresa Caldeira. Forthcoming. "Democracy, Law, and Violence: Disjunctions in Brazilian Citizenship." In *Fault Lines of Democratic Governance in the Americas,* ed. F. Aguero and J. Stark. Miami and Boulder: North-South Center and Lynne Rienner.

Huntington, Samuel P. 1991. *The Third Wave: Democratization in the Late Twentieth Century.* Norman: University of Oklahoma Press.

Inglehart, Ronald. 1988. "The Renaissance of Political Culture." *American Political Science Review* 82: 1203–1230.

Jelin, Elizabeth, and Eric Hershberg, eds. 1996. *Constructing Democracy: Human Rights, Citizenship, and Society in Latin America.* Boulder: Westview Press.

Johnston, Hank, and Bert Klandermans, eds. 1995. *Social Movements and Culture.* Minneapolis: University of Minnesota Press.

Jordan, Glenn, and Chris Weedon. 1995. *Cultural Politics: Class, Gender, Race and the Postmodern World.* Oxford: Blackwell.

Keane, John. 1988. *Democracy and Civil Society: On the Predicaments of European Socialism, the Prospects for Democracy, and the Problem of Controlling Social and Political Power.* London: Verso.

Keck, Margaret, and Kathryn Sikkink. 1992. "International Issue Networks in the Environment and Human Rights." Paper presented at the Seventeenth International Congress of the Latin American Studies Association, September, Los Angeles.

Laclau, Ernesto, and Chantal Mouffe. 1985. *Hegemony and Socialist Strategy: Towards a Radical Democratic Politics.* London: Verso.

Landim, Leilah. 1993a. "A Invenção das ONGs: Do Servico Invisivel à Profisão sem Nome." Ph.D. dissertation, Programa de Pos-Graduação em Antropologia Social, Universidade Federal do Rio de Janeiro/Museu Nacional.

______. 1993b. *Para Alem do Mercado e do Estado? Filantropia e Cidadania no Brasil.* Rio de Janeiro: ISER–Textos de Pesquisa.

Lebon, Nathalie. 1993. "The Brazilian Feminist Movement in the Post-Constitutional Era: Assessing the Impact of the Rise of Feminist Non-Governmental Organizations." *Florida Journal of Anthropology* 18: 17–26.

Lechner, Norbert. 1987a. "Presentación." In *Cultura Política y Democratización,* ed. N. Lechner. Santiago: CLACSO, FLACSO, ICI.

______. 1987b. "La Democratización en el Contexto de una Cultura Posmoderna." In *Cultura Política y Democratización,* ed. N. Lechner. Santiago: CLACSO, FLACSO, ICI.

Lechner, Norbert, ed. 1987c. *Cultura Política y Democratización.* Santiago: CLACSO, FLACSO, ICI.

Leis, Hector Ricardo. 1995. "Globalização e Democracia." *Revista Brasileira de Ciências Sociais* 10 (28):55–70.

Linz, Juan. 1990. "The Perils of Presidentialism." *Journal of Democracy* 1 (1):51–70.

Linz, Juan, and Arturo Valenzuela, eds. 1994. *The Failure of Presidential Democracy: The Case of Latin America.* Baltimore: Johns Hopkins University Press.

Lipschutz, Ronnie D. 1992. "Reconstructing World Politics: The Emergence of Global Civil Society." *Millennium: Journal of International Studies* 21 (3):389–420.

MacDonald, Laura. 1992. "Turning to the NGOs: Competing Conceptions of Civil Society in Latin America." Paper presented at the Seventeenth International Congress of the Latin American Studies Association, September, Los Angeles.

Mainwaring, Scott. 1992. "Transitions to Democracy and Democratic Consolidation: Theoretical and Comparative Issues." In *Issues in Democratic Consolidation: The New South American Democracies in Comparative Perspective,* ed. S. Mainwaring, G. O'Donnell, and J. Valenzuela. Notre Dame, Ind.: University of Notre Dame Press.

Mainwaring, Scott, Guillermo O'Donnell, and J. Samuel Valenzuela, eds. 1992. *Issues in Democratic Consolidation: The New South American Democracies in Comparative Perspective.* Notre Dame, Ind.: University of Notre Dame Press.

Mainwaring, Scott, and Timothy Scully, eds. 1995. *Building Democratic Institutions: Party Systems in Latin America.* Stanford: Stanford University Press.

Martins, Luciano. 1989. "Ação Política e Governabilidade na Transição Brasileira." In *Dilemas da Consolidação Democrática,* ed. J. Alvaro Moises and J. Guilhon Alburquerque. São Paulo: Paz e Terra.

McAdam, Doug, John D. McCarthy, and Mayer M. Zald, eds. 1996. *Comparative Perspectives on Social Movements: Political Opportunities, Mobilizing Structures, and Cultural Framings.* Cambridge: Cambridge University Press.

Melucci, Alberto. 1988. "Social Movements and the Democratization of Everyday Life." In *Civil Society and the State: New European Perspectives,* ed. J. Keane. London: Verso.

Mouffe, Chantal. 1993. *The Return of the Political.* London: Verso.

Muçoucah, Paulo Sérgio. 1995. "As ONGs: dos Bastidores ao Centro do Palco." *Revista Brasileira de Ciências Sociais* 10 (28):35–37.

Mueller, Carol McClurg. 1992. "Building Social Movement Theory." In *Frontiers of Social Movement Theory,* ed. A. Morris and C. Mueller. New Haven: Yale University Press.

Nelson, Cary, Paula A. Treichler, and Lawrence Grossberg. 1992. "Cultural Studies: An Introduction." In *Cultural Studies,* ed. L. Grossberg, C. Nelson, and P. Treichler. London: Routledge.

O'Donnell, Guillermo, and Philippe C. Schmitter. 1986. *Transitions from Authoritarian Rule: Tentative Conclusions about Uncertain Democracies.* Baltimore: Johns Hopkins University Press.

Oliveira, Francisco de. 1994. "Da Dadiva aos Direitos: A Dialética da Cidadania." *Revista Brasileira de Ciências Sociais* 9 (25):42–44.

Putnam, Robert D. 1993. *Making Democracy Work: Civic Traditions in Modern Italy*. Princeton: Princeton University Press.

Ramos, Alcida Rita. 1995. "O Indio Hiper-Real." *Revista Brasileira de Ciências Sociais* 10 (28):5–14.

Rielly, Charles, ed. 1994. *Nuevas Políticas Urbanas, las ONGs y los Gobiernos Municipales en la Democratización Latinoamericana*. Arlington, Va.: Inter-American Foundation.

Robbins, Bruce. 1993. "Introduction: The Public as Phantom." In *The Phantom Public Sphere,* ed. B. Robbins. Minneapolis: University of Minnesota Press.

Sales, Teresa. 1994. "Raízes da Desigualdade Social na Cultura Política Brasileira." *Revista Brasileira de Ciências Sociais* 9 (25):26–37.

Scherer-Warren, Ilse. 1993. *Redes de Movimentos Sociais*. São Paulo: Loyola.

Schumaher, Maria Aparecida and Elisabeth Vargas. 1993. "Lugar no Governo: Alibi ou Conquista?" *Revista Estudos Feministas* 1 (2):348–365.

Schwarz, Roberto. 1988. *Ao Vencedor as Batatas*. São Paulo: Duas Cidades.

Silva, Catia Aida Pereira da. 1994. "Os Conselhos Tutelares da Criança e o Adolescente de São Paulo e os Segmentos Pró-Cidadania: Conflitos, Negociações e Impasses na Construção de Espaços Públicos." Master's thesis, Universidade de São Paulo.

Slater, David. 1994a. "Exploring Other Zones of the Postmodern: Problems of Ethnocentrism and Difference Across the North-South Divide." In *Racism, Modernity, and Identity,* ed. A. Rattansi and S. Westwood. Cambridge, England: Polity Press.

______. 1994b. "Power and Social Movements in the Other Occident: Latin America in an International Context." *Latin American Perspectives* 21 (2):11–37.

Stepan, Alfred. 1988. *Rethinking Military Politics: Brazil and the Southern Cone*. Princeton: Princeton University Press.

Tarrow, Sidney. 1992. "Mentalities, Political Cultures, and Collective Action Frames." In *Frontiers of Social Movement Theory,* ed. A. Morris and C. Mueller. New Haven: Yale University Press.

Taylor, Verta, and Nancy E. Whittier. 1992. "Collective Identity in Social Movement Communities: Lesbian Feminist Mobilization." In *Frontiers of Social Movement Theory,* ed. A. Morris and C. Mueller. New Haven: Yale University Press.

Telles, Vera da Silva. 1994. "Cultura da Dadiva, Avesso da Cidadania." *Revista Brasileira de Ciências Sociais* 9 (25):48–51.

Walzer, Michael. 1992. "The Civil Society Argument." In *Dimensions of Radical Democracy: Pluralism, Citizenship, Community,* ed. C. Mouffe. London: Verso.

Walzer, Michael, ed. 1995. *Toward a Global Civil Society*. Oxford: Berghahn Books.

Weffort, Francisco. 1984. *Por que Democracia?* São Paulo: Brasiliense.

Whitehead, Lawrence. 1993. "The Alternatives to 'Liberal Democracy': A Latin American Perspective." In *Prospects for Democracy,* ed. D. Held. Cambridge, England: Polity Press.

Williams, Raymond. 1981. *Culture*. Glasgow: Fontana.

Willis, Paul. 1990. *Common Culture*. London: Verso.

Yúdice, George. 1994. "Cultural Studies and Civil Society." Paper presented at the Eighteenth International Congress of the Latin American Studies Association, March, Atlanta.

Part One

The Cultural Politics of Citizenship, Democracy, and the State

Chapter Two

Culture, Citizenship, and Democracy: Changing Discourses and Practices of the Latin American Left

EVELINA DAGNINO

My primary objective in this chapter will be to identify changes in the approaches made by the Latin American Left to the relationship between culture and politics, as a result of the broader process of renovation within the Left that began to take place at the end of the 1970s. In addition, I will discuss the new directions emerging from concrete political contexts, namely the process of democratization and particularly the crucial role played by social movements in that process.

First, I will briefly address the previously dominant theoretical tendencies in the traditional Marxist approach to the relationship between culture and politics. Second, I will discuss the emergence of an alternative theoretical framework, built upon the influence of Antonio Gramsci, which decisively contributed to disrupting the previous ways of thinking about that relationship. Third, I will analyze new conceptions of democracy and citizenship emerging from the struggles of social movements, which have decisively contributed to new approaches to the relationship between culture and politics. Ultimately, these new approaches came to express a confluence between new theoretical influences and new political directions emerging from concrete contexts. Finally, I will explore the results of my own research on social movements' conceptions about democracy and citizenship

I would like to thank Raul Burgos for his generous bibliographical help and valuable insights for the discussion of the Latin American Left; Sonia Alvarez for a most stimulating and rewarding intellectual *parceria* from which emerged several of the ideas discussed here; and the Conselho Nacional de Desenvolvimento Científico e Tecnológico, CNPq, for its research support.

in order to substantiate these new directions. I will also suggest that emphasis on cultural change as an element of social movements' strategy is not confined to civil society as a privileged site for politics but extends to the state and political institutionality.

* * *

New ways of thinking about the relationship between culture and politics have emerged in connection with the broader process of theoretical-political renovation which from the beginning of the 1970s has affected the conceptions of the Left in Latin America. If this has been a global process, the specificities of our own concrete historical experience and theoretical tradition certainly justify reference to its particularity.

The main focuses of this process are already well known (Castañeda 1994; McCaughan 1995; Garcia 1986; Burgos 1994). The linearity of laws ruling historical development and economic determinism; the conception of the working class as the privileged subject of history; the role of the vanguard and its relationship with the masses; the notion of revolution; and the role of the state and civil society have been the most important questions subjected to debate and revision. In addition, a new vision of democracy came to integrate this redefined theoretical framework and to play an increasingly crucial role in political practice and theory (Coutinho 1980; Weffort 1984; Garcia 1986; Lechner 1986).

The relationship between culture and politics has not been in itself a privileged or central question in the debate in the Left. Doomed to subordination and negativity, imprisoned in an eternal secondary role, and confined to quick final chapters where its importance is rhetorically reiterated, the cultural problematic has certainly not played a visible, fundamental role in the dynamics of that debate. However, although in a less spectacular manner than themes such as democracy and the historical subject, it is possible to affirm and to identify a substantial transformation in the ways of thinking about this relationship, as an integral part of the Left's renovation.

If culture and its relationships to politics have not been a visible center of this renovation, under what conditions has the transformation of their theoretical status taken place? I would like to introduce the idea that such a problematic has been always underlying the Left's renovative critique about these questions, whether as a not always explicit premise or as a not always intended consequence of the reasonings advanced. In this sense, the general theoretical-political process of renovation in the Left has not only contributed decisively to breaking the straitjacket that traditional Marxism had imposed on the analysis of culture and its role in social transformation but also brought with it significant conceptual changes in the specific field of cultural analysis.

A fundamental input into this process of theoretical renovation has come from the social movements themselves and their actual struggles. With this I am not simply acknowledging that such a transformation obviously cannot be understood as endogenous to the field of theory. It constitutes a response to the concrete dynamics of society, Latin American and global, and to the challenges and impasses of the political practice of the Left. More than that, I want to emphasize the proactive role of social movements in raising new questions and in generating new directions for theoretical-political analysis. The redefinition of the notion of citizenship, as discussed below, exemplifies this affirmative role of social movements.

As a result of this renovation, the cultural problematic is seen today under a new light by a significant part of the Left. Before examining this issue, I will address the traditional Marxist approaches to the relationships between culture and politics.

From the Kingdom of Ideology and the State to the Apogee of Hegemony and Civil Society

The conceptual framework predominant in the analysis of the relationships between culture and politics until the inflection brought about by renovation was subordinated to basic premises derived from classical Marxism and was reinforced by the Althusserianism that had consolidated its influence in Latin America in the 1970s. The Marxist concept of ideology reigned supreme as the privileged theoretical instrument for analyzing the relations between culture and politics. The separation between infrastructure and superstructure, the determination of the superstructure by the economic infrastructure, and the conception of the realm of ideas as a reflex or an inverted image of reality form the constitutive principles of ideology (Williams 1977). Culture, especially popular culture, was the domain of alienation, false consciousness, and mystification; in sum, the kingdom of ideology.

The primacy of the concept of ideology in the end established a trap for cultural studies from which few analysts on the Latin American Left escaped. Its primary impact was to impregnate the cultural realm with negativity. First, it fostered a negativity derived from economic determinism that denied culture any possibility of its own dynamic, establishing culture as a separate sphere, a mere epiphenomenal expression of an economic "essence." Second, culture was entrapped in negativity in the sense that ideas, and culture itself, were seen predominantly as obstacles to social transformation. The masses should be taught the irrelevance of culture and the primacy of "true knowledge" and "class consciousness" through the enlightened actions of their true bearers: the intellectuals, the vanguard, the party. José Nun refers to this strategy, embedded in the Marxist theory of ideology, as a "radical therapy" for the working class: "With respect to them [the workers] Marxism cannot do less than propose a radical therapy: its discourse must displace the false discourse that the dominant ideas have instilled in the heads of these workers; and must displace it as a whole. . . . true ideas must penetrate the consciousnesses in order to dissolve the distortions that affect them." (1989, 17)

In addition, class reductionism erected in analytical categories the well-known dichotomies that opposed, as two monolithic blocs external to each other, dominant and dominated cultures, bourgeois ideology and working-class culture, examples of what Canclini (1988) calls deductivist approaches in cultural analysis. Dependency theory, formulated by Latin Americans in an effort to adjust Marxist class analysis to the complexity of the new developments in international political economy, maintained this dichotomous approach.[1]

If the relations between culture and politics were approached predominantly through the lens of ideology theory, politics itself was equated and identified with another ruling concept: the state. Under the heavy influence of Marxist structuralism, the state was conceived as a condensation of power relations and the specific locus of domination in society. As the privileged focus of attention in the analysis of politics and political transformation, the state was considered to be the only decisive arena of power relations and, therefore, the only relevant site and target of political struggle, in what came to be known as a "statist" view of politics. Latin American political culture came to reinforce such a view, since a conception of a strong and interventionist state, seen as historically linked to the building of the nation and as the primary agent of social transformation, has been central to all versions of populist, nationalist, and developmentalist projects, whether conservative or leftist. Examining the relation between culture and politics in these terms predominantly implied, then, an analysis of the use of culture as an instrument of domination. The strategies of the dominant classes seemed to exhaust cultural spaces, leaving no room for any other significant effect than their passive acceptance. The impact of the Frankfurt school only contributed to this direction in its analysis of the mass media, as did the pervasive reproductionist theories in education (Canclini 1988). The concept of state ideological apparatuses[2] reached its climax to the extent that, in consummating the marriage between the concepts of state and ideology, it in effect accounted for the dynamics of society.

An important consequence of this theoretical framework was the strengthening in the field of social sciences of a subordinated, marginal conception of the theme of culture itself. With the exception of scholars of anthropology, a field in which culture has always been a constitutive, fundamental theme but which seldom dealt appropriately with the connections between culture and power relations, sociologists and political scientists in the Latin American academic Left considered culture a secondary subject.[3]

From a strictly theoretical perspective, a significant number of authors and influences have ensured that the relationships between culture and politics could be reexamined along a multiplicity of new directions. It is not my purpose to assess all these influences here, but one can safely affirm that the contribution of Antonio Gramsci and the influence he exerted in Latin America represented a fundamental rupture in the ways of approaching these relationships within the Left. Such an influence was not always direct or explicit, but it is possible to identify a number of groupings and individuals who were clearly inspired by Gramsci; for a large number of leftist intellectuals, Gramsci's ideas came to integrate a new diversified theoretical-political set of references in development. In this sense, as I will argue below, the work of Gramsci served as a vehicle, a catalyst, and a pretext for a renovating discussion within the Left that included several other influences and that helped to consolidate an alternative set of conceptions to traditional Marxism.

The role played by the work of Gramsci as a whole in the broader process of renovation in the Left certainly defines his contribution to the specific field of the relations between culture and politics. In other words, the overall impact of his work contributed from the outset to changing significantly the theoretical-political status of these relations. The basis for the renovating impact of Gramscian thought lies in his powerful critique of economic reductionism. This critique asserts a deep imbrication among culture, politics, and the economy and establishes an equivalence between material forces and cultural elements within an integrated view of society as a whole. From this premise, Gramsci's work unfolds into a complex and wide-ranging reflection, the relevance of which for our discussion can be expressed in a number of points.

The first and most obvious of these points is the conception of hegemony, a process of articulation of different interests around the gradual and always renewed implementation of a project for the transformation of society. The dimension of culture is crucial for the hegemonic process for two fundamental reasons. First, hegemony requires in a very strong sense what Gramsci termed an *intellectual and moral reform*. Second and more importantly (although not always recognized or properly emphasized), it is in the terrain of culture that *active consent*, the specific mode of operation of hegemony, which defines the very concept of hegemony and distinguishes it from domination, is produced (or is not produced).[4] It is through the concept of hegemony that Gramsci formulates a new way of thinking about the relationship between culture and politics in which the former becomes radically constitutive of the latter.

The second point refers to the Gramscian conception of social transformation, in which revolution is no longer conceived as an insurrectional act of taking over state power but as a process in which intellectual and moral reform is an integral part rather than a possible consequence. As revolution is envisaged as the process of building of a new hegemony, which implies a new world conception, the role of ideas and culture assumes a positive character. Two crucial formulations underlie this conception of social transformation. The first refers to the very notion of power, understood by Gramsci not as an institution, a "thing" to be seized, but as a relationship among social forces that must be transformed.[5] The second is a strong emphasis on the character of social transformation as historical construction rather than as a fatalist and predetermined process. As a consequence, the issue of agency or the constitution of subjects is privileged over the dynamics of "objective" social structures, and the role ascribed to "subjective" elements such as will, passion, and faith received in Gramsci a consideration that was unprecedented in Marxist theory.

A third point is the emphasis placed by Gramsci on civil society as terrain of political struggle, which is conceived as a "war of position" rather than a "war of maneuver" or frontal attack on the state. This emphasis is one of the elements of Gramscian thought that came to play a decisive role in the new directions available to the Left in Latin America, implying not only a revision of the role up to then attributed to the state but also an enlargement of the political terrain and the plurality of power relations. This expansion of the political establishes new parameters for reflecting on the relations between culture and politics.

The influence played by these ideas reached its peak in Latin America in the period from the mid-1970s into the 1980s. Because it developed differently in different countries, Gramsci's impact has been assessed by a number of analysts.[6] Interesting evidence of Gramsci's forceful diffusion is found in an intelligence report presented to the Seventeenth Conference of American Armed Forces (Conferência dos Exércitos Americanos) in Mar del Plata in 1987, which conferred on him the status of "ideologue of the new strategy of the International Communist Movement." The report added: "For Gramsci, the method was not the 'revolutionary taking of power' but the cultural subversion of society as the immediate step in order to reach power in a progressive, peaceful and permanent way."[7]

Several reasons explain the wide dissemination of Gramsci's ideas. First, they opened up for a Left in crisis the possibility of exploring new theoretical and political directions without having to face a traumatic rupture. As José Aricó, one of the earlier Argentinean enthusiasts of Gramsci put it, "For us, Gramsci represented that solid backing from which we could enter into a multiplicity of theoretical directions without having to abdicate our socialist ideas or the critical capacity of Marxism" (Aricó 1988a, 39). In the words of a Brazilian, Gramsci made it possible for the Left "to be tranquilly heterodox," thus "softening the renovation of a Left that was willing to abandon 'Marxism-Leninism'" (Nogueira 1988, 135, 137).[8]

Second, the work of Gramsci offered the Latin American Left an appropriate framework with which to examine the historical specificity of their own societies, especially the particular kinds of relations established between state and society. Thus, "the search for the national reality" discovered in Gramsci a fertile supporting ground (Córdova 1987, 99; Aricó 1988a, 41; Portantiero 1977; Coutinho 1980, 56–60; Coutinho and Nogueira 1988, 106). Categories formulated by Gramsci in the analysis of Italian history such as "national-popular," "passive revolution," and "transformism" became sources of extensive study dedicated to analyzing experiences like populism and the role of the state in configuring Latin American societies, to which traditional Marxism had not been seen to contribute properly.

But it was toward the understanding of the new political processes that were then taking shape and the political challenges they posed that the routes opened up by Gramsci's influence were increasingly explored. Thus, the problematic of democracy and the whole set of new correlated questions it implied constituted the milieu in which the Gramscian boom manifested itself. This particular environment seems to have nurtured a strong emphasis on the progressive or "revolutionary" possibility of hegemony as a project for the transformation of society.[9] Such an emphasis contrasts with other readings of the concept; European theorists, for instance, consistently explored its application to an analysis of the maintenance of the status quo and dominant power relations.[10]

After the defeat of the armed struggle strategy, the Left's resistance to authoritarian regimes focused on a return to democratic rule. Democracy served as the unifying concept through which previous theoretical tenets and forms of struggle were to be redefined (Barros 1986). Emblematic of this rupture is the generalized acknowledgment that the idea of democracy had replaced that of revolution in the political and intellectual debate (Lechner 1988; Weffort 1984; Coutinho 1980; Barros 1986; Garcia 1986). The relationship with the masses, the organizational forms, the characterization of political subjects, the role of the state, and the conception of politics itself were issues of debate and revision. The strengthening of civil society was seen as paramount to the building of democracy, a view reinforced by the fact that the theoretical critique of the authoritarian state had led, as pointed out by Lechner, to a critique of statist conceptions of politics (Lechner 1988, 21).

It is not difficult to visualize how Gramscian concepts of hegemony, civil society, organic intellectuals, collective will, and intellectual and moral reform provided suitable means to both intellectual construction and political action in the new scenario. The remarkable incorporation of these words into the general political vocabulary of the 1980s indicates a broad recognition of their pertinence, even if not necessarily of their precise conceptual meaning.

The overarching notion of hegemony provided a general framework under which it was possible to revise old questions and, more importantly, to examine new ones and integrate them into a coherent setting. The debate during the seminar entitled "Hegemony and Political Alternatives in Latin America," held in Morelia, Mexico, in February 1980, taken by some as an emblem of the diffusion of Gramsci's influence in Latin America (Aricó 1988b, 31), revolved

> around the Gramscian concept of hegemony, its validity as a theoretical and political instrument to reconsider, from the perspective of the present, the limitations of the Marxist theory of politics and of the State; the reelaborations through which such a theory could reconquer its critical potential and its capacity of producing strategies of transformation on the concrete ground of Latin American reality and, finally, the relationship of *continuity* or *rupture* that could be established between the conceptions of Gramsci and the Leninist tradition." (Aricó 1985, 12)

The understanding of these concepts was, and is, far from homogeneous or univocal. It is a commonplace to acknowledge the multiplicity of readings inspired by the fragmentary, unsystematic, unfinished, and often preliminary entries of the *Prison Notebooks*. The uses of Gramsci, not by chance the title of one of the first thorough Gramscian studies produced in Latin America,[11] were many. However, I argue, the predominant reading of Gramsci within the Latin American Left stressed the confluence of three different tendencies: a renovative critique of traditional Marxism, an emphasis on the building of democracy with its correlated strengthening of civil society, and, in the interstices of these two, a new approach to the relationship between culture and politics.[12]

In this sense, the use made of the Gramscian concepts allowed and advanced such a confluence. In a 1985 debate in Brazil focusing on the Left and democracy, Francisco Weffort and Carlos Nelson Coutinho, the two most prominent proponents of democracy in the Brazilian intellectual Left and both renowned Gramscians, fielded questions about the inherent democratic nature of hegemony in a way that clearly acknowledged that selective posture toward Gramsci's work. After stressing the much-neglected Gramscian distinction between hegemony and domination, Weffort maintained: "In my view, if the notion of hegemony may have an anti-democratic meaning, we must look for a democratic meaning to it. . . . What I am proposing is that we invent, if there is not one, a notion of hegemony which is democratic." Coutinho maintained the need to articulate the idea of hegemony to that of pluralism in order to strengthen the contractual element already present in pluralism (Garcia 1986, 86, 98). Moreover, conceived under this articulation, hegemony as the construction from below of a collective will would express the search for "a unity within the diversity" of autonomous collective political subjects (Coutinho 1980, 31).[13]

For a significant part of the Left, the struggle against the authoritarian states unfolded into a struggle against all forms of authoritarianism and reinforced the refusal of orthodox and rigid conceptual categories for political analysis.[14] In addition, the increasing differentiation and complexity of Latin American societies no longer seem to fit the traditional categories and ways of doing politics. Errors from concrete past experience compounded the theoretical crisis and pushed it toward unexplored interpretations and heterodox combinations. An emphasis on pluralism, diversity, and flexibility inspired not only the particular appropriation of Gramsci's thought but also its blending with several other Marxist and non-Marxist authors. From Foucault to Cornelius Castoriadis and Agnes Heller, from Claude Leffort to Jürgen Habermas, Norberto Bobbio, Tocqueville, and Hannah Arendt, the renovation of the Left opened itself to an antiauthoritarian eclecticism that makes it difficult to single out particular influences.[15] Still, as pointed out above, for a representative part of the Left, Gramsci served as a solid launching pad from which it became easier to integrate several other influences deemed appropriate to address the new times. The need to account for and provide progressive directions to the new reality constituted the main force underlying not only the renovative impulse of the Left but also the particular reading of Gramsci conducted as part of such an impulse.[16]

The role to be played by civil society in the building of hegemony was paramount to its acceptance by the Left as an appropriate framework for the struggle for democracy. The need for theoretical analysis and political understanding of the set of social forces that emerged during the struggle against the authoritarian states was crucial for the Left. The characterization of civil society as an arena of politics and a target of hegemonic efforts, as well as a privileged terrain of intellectual and moral reform and a construction of the collective will, provided the analytical tools and political directions necessary to deal with an emergent element that did not fit old models. Well familiar with the "frontal attack," the Left had to learn how to conduct a "war of position" and operate in the multiplicity of trenches which such a conflict implies.

According to Weffort, "the discovery that in politics there was something other than the State" began as a personal experience for the Left, when victims of repression and political persecution found protection not in the political parties or in the judicial system but in the Catholic Church and with friends and families. The first signs of civil society were displayed as a defense against "State terror," as a reaction against the paralysis of fear, even for those who were not involved in politics (Weffort 1984, 93). The resistance against authoritarian states gradually took shape through the increasing organization of civil society. This original feature fostered a view that radically opposed civil society and the state.

Jorge Castañeda, in his appraisal of the Left, considered this disjunctive view contradictory to the most advanced European tendencies, such as Foucault's thought. He also attributed to Gramsci "the resurrection of the old duality State/civil society," with its risks of misunderstanding and confusion (1994, 171). In fact, this dichotomy had a precise concrete meaning in a situation where there was a clear antagonism between repressive authoritarian states and the sources in civil society from which resistance could emerge. In this sense, what this dichotomy expressed, more than a radical theoretical separation between state and civil society, was the distinction between two antagonistic political positions. In addition, if civil society was ever thought of as a homogeneous and unitary actor, the unfolding of the struggle for democracy soon dissolved that tactical illusion.

In theoretical terms, the emphasis of the theory of hegemony on civil society as an arena of politics implies not a dichotomy but precisely a continuity between state and civil society.[17] In societies where there is "a proper relation between State and civil society," the state is "only an outer ditch, behind which there stood a powerful system of fortresses and earthworks" (Gramsci 1971, 238). Hence, it is exactly because of this continuity that the effort toward the building of a new hegemony in those societies cannot privilege the state as its only target and neglect civil society as a proper arena for political struggle. In the same sense, to assert civil society as an arena for and target of the political struggle for hegemony necessarily involves acknowledging its heterogeneous and contradictory nature and refusing its mythification as a virtuous pole against an evil state.

If hegemony provided a new way to conceive the relation between state and civil society, it also contributed to understanding the changing dynamics of the latter. The emergence of social movements, expressing a plurality of interests and the increasing heterogeneity and complexity of Latin American societies, had aggravated a fundamental theoretical-political challenge for the Left: the question of the characterization of political subjects.

There is widespread recognition that the theory of hegemony implies a rupture with the notion that "preconstituted" political subjects are deduced from positions within the economic production process through class reductionism (Barros 1986; Aricó 1985, 1988b; Nun 1989; Coutinho 1980; Riz and Ipola 1985; Laclau and Mouffe 1985). The hegemonic construction requires "the attainment of a 'cultural-social' unity through which a multiplicity of dispersed wills, with heterogeneous aims, are welded together with a single aim, on the basis of an equal and common conception of the world" (Gramsci 1971, 349). As a process of articulation of the different interests necessary to build a "collective will" and achieve active consent, hegemony is itself a process of constitution of subjects. Such a process takes place on a ground that is not strictly defined by economic structural forces but by a broader process of moral and intellectual reform.[18] Thus, the capacity to transcend particular, corporative interests, to compromise and negotiate, are crucial hegemonic features insofar they make possible this articulation of different interests (Gramsci 1971, 161, 182). The "single aim" and the "equal and common conception of the world" are not points of departure ensured by predefined subjects and contents but a processual construction, an articulation always submitted to reelaboration and renewal, conceived as the basis for collective political action toward social transformation. Moreover, this conception of hegemony as articulation opens the door for a consideration of the autonomy of different subjects and the process of building their own collective identities. The collective elaboration of the basis for such an articulation embodies the core of and the greatest challenge to hegemonic construction.

This predominant view of hegemony as the terrain of constitution of political subjects, anchored in Gramsci's critique of economic reductionism and his emphasis on the primacy of politics understood as an ethical-cultural process, constituted an integrative basis from which it was possible to address the emerging social movements as well as the multiplicity of concerns and interests these movements brought to the political scene. For their bearers, such a view expresses a number of motivations: among them are an urge to break from class reductionism without falling into liberal pluralism and a need to account for difference without forsaking the historical concern of the Left with equality. In addition, addressing these new actors was intimately connected with the prospect of advancing the socialization of politics throughout civil society as the basis for a radically democratic socialization of power. In this sense, their reading of hegemony has been influenced by those theoretical elements considered appropriate to such motivations.[19]

As this interpretation of Gramscian hegemony had its validity and relevance established within the process of the renovation of the Latin American Left, it facilitated a new understanding of the relationships between culture and politics that extended well beyond the limits of the particular field of cultural analysis. The non-subalternity of cultural relations and the constitutive imbrication between culture and politics, established as principles by the theory of hegemony, had led those looking for new approaches to establish Gramsci as a necessary reference in the field of cultural studies. But because these two principles are intrinsic and central to the very core of the hegemony argument, as I have tried to show, the influence of hegemony in other fields carried with it a decisive contribution to the generalization of such principles as part of the renovation process in the Left.

As a consequence of this process, previous emphases on the approach toward culture have been largely abandoned or minimized. Major categories such as the separated infrastructure and superstructure and the relationship of determination between them, and ideology as an inverted reflex of reality, were replaced by a view that stressed the wholeness of social processes and that reinforced a conception of culture as inherently constitutive of them instead of as a separate, subordinate instance.[20] Gramsci's concept of a "historical bloc,"[21] through which he maintained the organic indissolubility between "material forces" and "ideologies" and their equivalence, was a crucial instrument in the theoretical turn that redefined the negative, subordinate status of culture. The idea of culture as materiality, which Louis Althusser had taken from Gramsci to ground his own state apparatuses of ideology, was recovered in order to assert not just the necessary embedding of culture into practices and institutions but its integration of a social material process.

Within this new framework, the relationship between culture and politics loses its externality; whereas previous approaches looked for the "politicization" of culture, which usually meant inserting elements of class consciousness into popular culture, culture, as emphasized by Horacio Tarcus and Blas de Santos (1990), is seen as internally constitutive of politics:

> Cultural politics is not an optional subject, that subject eternally pending in the Left programs, but a subject which does not resist to be simply added to them. Its mere presence questions and forces the reformulation of the whole way in which politics is conceived and practiced. For the lack of a cultural politics on the Left is not the lack of politics for an isolated compartment of the social, for a limited and detachable area, but a symptom, nothing more, nothing less, of a *lack of politics* at all.[22]

If the conception of culture as the attribution of meanings embedded in all social practices has been established in the field of anthropology, what the theory of hegemony brought to light was the fact that this attribution of meanings takes place in a context characterized by conflict and power relations. In this sense, the struggle over meanings and who has the power to attribute them is not only a political struggle in itself but is also inherent and constitutive of all politics (see this volume's Introduction).

The new theoretical status conferred on cultural relations and its role in the definition of politics and social transformation unfolded into a number of consequences for the field of cultural analysis. First, there was a significant change in the approach to popular culture itself. The negativity implicit in traditional Marxist analysis was replaced by a positive regard that emphasized creative autonomy, a capacity for symbolic reelaboration, and negotiation as features of the cultural practices of subaltern sectors. In a not unusual pattern in intellectual history where antithetical positions temporarily polarize the debate, this positivity at times appeared as a sheer celebration of "the voice of the people" and as the essentialist incarnation of the truth, paralleling the *basismo* that succeeded and reacted against populist and authoritarian forms of popular organization. At other times, "hegemonic" and "subaltern" cultures became just new denominations for previous deductivist monolithic dichotomies.

But a substantial direction in cultural analysis carried through the lessons of Gramsci's realistic and attentive assessment of the culture of the Italian masses as a conception of the world, characterized by heterogeneity, ambiguity, contradictions, and fragmentation as well as by specific forms of knowledge expressed in the notions of folklore, "common sense," and "good sense." Such a direction has affirmed the plural, discontinuous, and complex character of the process of constitution of social subjects "against all forms of reductionist simplifications" (Riz and Ipola 1985, 61).

The notions of common sense and good sense underlie the critique of the reduction of multiple rationalities to the Marxist conception of class consciousness and of its privileged bearer, the vanguard, in what Nun called "the other reductionism." Subjacent to "a vertical and authoritarian approach to politics," this "other reductionism," in addition, rejects a war of position, which precisely "requires the abandonment of any fixed idea of major staffs *[estados mayores]* or armies or pre-constituted discourses and their replacement for differentiated patrols *[destacamientos]* and significations, which emerge and mutate in the multiple spaces where antagonisms take place"[23] (Nun 1989, 50–51).

This theoretical turn also allowed the Left to legitimately consider the dimensions ignored by traditional Marxist analyses, the political relevance of which had become unquestioned in the changing Latin American scene of the 1980s. On the one hand, the increasing heterogeneity and complexity of Latin American societies, impelled by a modernization increasingly defined by their global connections, engendered a vast plurality of new cultural themes. On the other, the gradual erosion of the authoritarian states and the transition to democracy made possible the social groups' capacity for initiative and invention in civil society to reveal the multiple dynamics of the relations between culture and politics. Thus, an unprecedented attention to subjects such as daily life, subjectivity, youth culture, and consumption, began to take shape within the Left (Canclini 1987; Nun 1989; Lechner 1988).[24] As stated by Fernando Calderón, in concluding his article on the pertinence of Gramsci's thought to the Bolivian context, "so long as we do not interpret what moves people in their doings and dreamings, what they dream about and what they do every day, that is, understand and accept fully the multiple and various sociocultural manifestations, it is impossible to establish moral and intellectual direction of society as a goal" (1987, 18).

This new posture toward the relationship between culture and politics has been, as mentioned above, intimately connected with the emergence of a hegemonic building of democracy as the project of the Left. For that significant part of the Left that became engaged in this project, it posed as a central challenge the elaboration of what Lechner (1988) called "a collective reference," able to express a democratic collective will. The state, the vanguard, the party, previous authoritarian intended incarnations of such a collective reference, have been put under suspicion or rejected altogether. The market, as the universal reference proposed by neoliberalism in its depoliticizing version of the collective, has been just as obviously repudiated.

In addition, in Latin America, the building of a democratic collective reference from the Left's perspective can hardly rely on a redemption of historical elements from the past. Not by chance, the elaboration of a "new grammar" for politics is a recurrent metaphor used by analysts to express the foundational character attributed to the democratic challenge (Ipola and Portantiero 1984; Lechner 1988; Telles 1994b). The search for a new language, a new set of subjects, rules, and procedures, new ways of doing politics, very often summarized under the call for a new political culture, sometimes for a new culture *tout court,* outlines the scope of the transformations embedded in such a democratic project.

The plurality inherent to democracy; the multiplicity of subjects and spaces to be involved in its construction; and the replacement, expressed by hegemony, of a "logic of war" for a "logic of politics" that imposes the mutual recognition of different subjects (Lechner 1988, 27–28) constitute the main features perceived as framing that challenge. All these features point toward the need for a politico-cultural understanding of differences, without which their hegemonic collective articulation cannot even be envisioned.

In this sense, the new perception of the political meaning of culture, of its constitutive imbrication with politics, has been to a significant extent a consequence of changes in the general perception of the meaning of politics itself: where, how, by whom, and over what politics shall be done. As these interrogations are posed, the new answers provided by both theory and practice have entailed a new understanding of the relationship between culture and politics. Because the terrain of culture is recognized as political and as a locus of the constitution of different political subjects, when cultural changes are seen as the targets of political struggle and cultural struggle as an instrument for political change, a new definition of the relationship between culture and politics is underway.

For that part of the Latin American Left open to reviewing its own conceptions, these changes responded to a global tendency but have been strongly determined by the specific characteristics and demands of processes of democratic building in the particular settings of each country. Thus, the new approaches to the relationship between culture and politics and the new visions of politics in which they are embedded express a confluence between the theoretical influences discussed so far and the political directions emerging from concrete political contexts of democratization.[25] In order to illustrate this argument I will discuss the role of social movements in the process of democratization in Brazil and the political directions emerging from their concrete struggles.

Democracy and Citizenship: The Cultural Politics of Social Movements

As in most Latin American societies, political struggle in Brazil today is being waged around alternative designs for democracy. As stated in the Introduction to this volume, "Fundamentally in dispute are the parameters of democracy—to be sure, the very boundaries of what is to be properly defined as the political arena: its participants, its institutions, its processes, its agenda, and its scope." Social movements have been deeply involved in this struggle since the very beginning of the resistance to the authoritarian regime in the early 1970s.

Although the positive role of social movements in the transition to democracy has been largely acknowledged by analysts, since the return to civilian rule in 1985 their actual or potential contribution to the expansion and deepening of democracy has been questioned. In discussing this questioning,[26] conveyed by both mainstream theorists of "democratic consolidation" and some social movements analysts, I suggested that it has been based on a predominant focus on the institutional dimension of the democratic process: Social movements are presented either as irrelevant to and even destabilizing for democratic institutionalization or as incapable of adjusting to the new formal representative political arenas. What these objections may fail to acknowledge is precisely the existence of dispute among alternative conceptions of democracy and the political arena. As an emphasis on institutional "engineering" and consolidation has monopolized most of the intellectual efforts of analysts of the process of democratization in Latin America (and a great deal of the energies of its political technocrats), other crucial dimensions of the process, valued by those historically excluded from traditional representative democracy, are often disregarded.

The basic question I would like to address in this section is how social movements in Brazil have been contributing to resignifying the relations between culture and politics in their democratizing struggles. There are clear points of confluence between the main process of renovation on the Left and the political directions indicated by the struggles of social movements. In fact, such a confluence results from the intermingling of influences that takes place within a common ethical-political field.

The notion of a social movement's ethical-political field has been developed in order to account for the production and circulation of "a common field of references and differences for collective action and political contestation" (Baierle 1992, 19). In recent analyses of social movements' collective actions, such a notion has been connected to the emergence of "webs," or networks of social movements, to indicate the collective construction that results from this articulation of social movements of various kinds with other sectors and organizations, such as political parties, leftist organizations, the Catholic Church, scientific groups, nongovernmental organizations (NGOs), trade unions, and so on (Alvarez 1993; Alvarez and Dagnino 1995; Doimo 1995; Teixeira 1995; Scherer-Warren 1993).

Through the interchange of discourses and practices, "an active process of elaboration which reflects the dynamics of multiple emergent concrete practices of struggle and their internal conflicts" takes place in these webs, configuring a distinctive ethical-political field.[27]

I will argue first that social movements have advanced a conception of democracy that transcends the limits both of political institutions as traditionally conceived and of "actually existing democracy." The distinctive feature of this conception, which points toward the extension and deepening of democracy, is the fact that it has as a basic reference not the democratization of the *political regime* but of society as a whole, including therefore the cultural practices embodied in social relations of exclusion and inequality. Second, I will argue that the operationalization of this conception of democracy is being carried out through a redefinition of the notion of citizenship and of its core referent, the notion of rights. Finally, I will suggest that this societal emphasis does not imply, as some of the early literature on social movements argued, a refusal of political institutionality and the state but rather a radical claim for their transformation.

As social movements do not constitute homogeneous social actors or political subjects but indeed are characterized by heterogeneity and diversity, the conceptions discussed here are not to be taken as representative of the whole multiplicity of social movements existing today in Brazil. If it is true that a certain tendency to mystify their collective actions as incarnations of political virtue and bearers of all the new hopes for social transformation on the Left must be critically assessed, this should not be done at the expense of denying or obscuring the molecular changes that result from social movements' practice.

The adoption of an alternative perspective in examining the cultural politics of social movements and assessing the scope of their struggles for the democratization of society seeks to highlight the less visible and often neglected implications of these struggles. Emphasizing cultural implications implies the recognition of the capacity of social movements to produce new visions of a democratic society insofar as they identify the existing social ordering as limiting and exclusionary with respect to their values and interests. Fragmentary, plural, and contradictory as they may be, these cultural contestations are not to be seen as by-products of political struggle but as constitutive of the efforts by social movements to redefine the meaning and the limits of the political itself.

For the excluded sectors of Brazilian society, the perception of the political relevance of cultural meanings embedded in social practices is part of their daily life. As an exemplary case that can be easily generalized for Latin America as a whole, Brazilian society is one in which economic inequality and extreme levels of poverty have been only the most visible aspects of the unequal and hierarchical organization of social relations as a whole, what can be called *social authoritarianism*. Class, race, and gender differences constitute the main bases for a social classification that has historically pervaded Brazilian culture, establishing different categories of people hierarchically disposed in their respective "places" in society.

Underneath the apparent cordiality of Brazilian society, the notion of *social places* constitutes a strict code, very visible and ubiquitous, in the streets and in the homes, in the state and in society, which reproduces inequality in social relations at all levels, underlying social practices and structuring an authoritarian culture.[28]

The perception of the need for cultural changes as a fundamental element in the process of democratization has been obviously crucial to women, homosexuals, blacks, and other groups. A great part of their political struggle, in fact, is directed toward confronting this authoritarian culture. Yet, if the recognition of their struggles as cultural politics is more acceptable, there is still resistance to acknowledging their meaning in reconfiguring society as a whole and to redefining the political they imply.

What is seldom recognized, however, is the fact that urban popular movements reached this same understanding of the intermingling of culture and politics as soon as they realized that what they had to struggle for was not only their social rights, housing, health, education, and so on but their very right to have rights. As part of the authoritarian, hierarchical social ordering of Brazilian society, to be poor means not only to endure economic and material deprivation but also to be submitted to cultural rules that convey a complete lack of recognition of poor people as subjects, as bearers of rights. In what Telles (1993) called the incivility embedded in that tradition, poverty is a sign of inferiority, a way of being in which individuals lose their ability to exercise their rights. This cultural deprivation imposed by the absolute absence of rights, which ultimately expresses itself as a suppression of human dignity, then becomes constitutive of material deprivation and political exclusion.[29]

In this sense, the struggle for rights, for the right to have rights, exposed what had to be a political struggle against a pervasive culture of social authoritarianism, thus setting the stage for the urban popular movements to establish a connection between culture and politics as constitutive of their collective action. This connection has been a fundamental element in establishing a common ground for articulation with other social movements that are more obviously cultural, such as ethnic, women's, gay rights, ecological, and human rights movements, in the search for more egalitarian relations at all levels, helping to demarcate a distinctive, enlarged view of democracy.

A fundamental instrument used by social movements in the struggle for democratization in recent times has been the appropriation of the notion of citizenship, which operationalizes their enlarged view of democracy. The origins of the present redefined notion of a new citizenship can be partially found in the concrete experience of social movements in the late 1970s and 1980s. For urban popular movements, the perception of social needs, *carências,* as rights represented a crucial step and a turning point in their struggle.[30] For other social movements such as the ecological movement and those led by women, blacks, homosexuals, and others, the struggle for the right to equality and to difference found clear support in the redefined notion of citizenship. A significant part of this common experience was the elaboration of new identities as subjects, as bearers of rights, as equal citizens.

This turning point represented a rupture with the predominant strategies of political organization of the popular sectors characterized by favoritism, clientelism, and tutelage. Such strategies, still alive, of course, find support in and reinforce the dominant authoritarian culture insofar as they do not confront its systems of classification and exclusion and its basic hierarchies, thus legitimating the maxim, as put by Teresa Sales: "In Brazil either you give orders or you plead" *("No Brasil ou bem se manda ou bem se pede"),* expressing an oligarchic conception of politics that still obstructs the political organization of the excluded and that enlarges the political autonomy of the elites (see this volume's Introduction, p. 18).

A broader emphasis on the extension and deepening of democracy came to reinforce the concrete experience of social movements as a struggle for equal rights. Such an emphasis, as already discussed, was connected not only to the new political and theoretical status that the question of democracy had acquired throughout the world but also to the crisis of the authoritarian regime in Brazil and the new directions taken by the Brazilian, and Latin American, Left.

In recent years the use of the term "citizenship" has spread increasingly throughout Brazilian society. As the redefined notion continued to underlie popular struggles and the political practices of parties such as the PT (Partido dos Trabalhadores) and NGOs such as those associated with the Brazilian Association of Nongovernmental Organizations (ABONG), citizenship is squarely behind solidarity campaigns aimed at the mobilization of the middle classes, such as the Ação da Cidadania contra a Fome, headed by Herbert de Souza-Betinho, or associations of progressive entrepreneurs such as CIVES (Associação Brasileira de Empresarios pela Cidadania). The term "citizenship" also began to be reappropriated by neoliberal sectors and even by conservative traditional politicians, with obviously very different meanings and intentions.[31]

Neoliberal versions of citizenship, created in connection with the implementation of policies of economic and social adjustment now prevailing throughout Latin America, have been particularly energetic in their attempts to redefine "the political domain and its participants—based on a minimalist conception of both the state and democracy" (see this volume's Introduction). On the one hand, neoliberalism works with a view of citizenship as an alluring individual integration to the market. On the other, it systematically operates for the elimination of consolidated rights, transforming their bearers/citizens into the new villains of the nation, privileged enemies of political reforms intended to shrink state responsibilities. Moreover, social expenditures are directed toward the reversion of that major step in the organization of social movements that made possible the very emergence of the new citizenship, the definition of needs as rights: Transformed into public charity for the needy, the *carentes,* governmental social expenditures are decided without any real participation by civil society (Oliveira 1996).

The symbolic dispute around the meaning of citizenship attests to its political relevance and to the importance attributed by the different contenders to the redefinitions deployed by social movements. Such a dispute also requires an effort to clarify the notion referred to here as the "new citizenship."

A first crucial and distinctive element in this notion comes from the very conception of democracy it intends to operationalize: The new citizenship seeks to implement a strategy of democratic construction, of social transformation, that asserts *a constitutive link between culture and politics.* Incorporating characteristics of contemporary societies such as the role of subjectivities, the emergence of social subjects of a new kind and of rights of a new kind, and the broadening of the political space, this strategy acknowledges and emphasizes the intrinsic character of cultural transformation with respect to the building of democracy. In this sense, the new citizenship includes cultural constructions such as those underlying social authoritarianism as fundamental political targets of democratization. It is therefore my argument here that the redefinition of the notion of citizenship, as formulated by social movements, expresses not only a *political strategy* but also a *cultural politics.*

To assert the notion of citizenship as a political strategy (Wiener 1992) means to emphasize its character as a historical construct that expresses concrete interests and practices not previously defined by a given universal essence. In this sense, its contents and meanings are not previously defined and limited but constitute a response to the dynamics of real conflicts and the political struggle lived by a particular society at a given historical moment. Such a historical perspective poses a need to distinguish the new citizenship of the 1990s from the liberal tradition that coined this term at the end of the eighteenth century. Emerging as the state's response to claims from excluded social sectors, the liberal version of citizenship ended up essentializing the concept, in spite of the fact that it today performs functions entirely different from those that characterized its origin.

In a very preliminary way, it is possible to indicate some points that clarify this distinction. There is a similarity in the vocabulary that expresses common references, the most obvious being the very question of *democracy* and the notion of *rights,* central elements in both conceptions. But beyond this similarity, it is necessary to identify to what extent the political differences that emerge from different historical contexts are also expressed as conceptual differences.

1. The first point refers to the very notion of *rights.* The new citizenship assumes a redefinition of the idea of rights, and the point of departure is the conception of *a right to have rights.* This conception is not limited to legal provisions, access to previously defined rights, or the effective implementation of abstract, formal rights. It includes the invention and creation of *new* rights, which emerge from specific struggles and their concrete practices. In this sense, the very determination of the meaning of "right" and the assertion of some value or ideal as a "right" are themselves objects of political struggle. The right to autonomy over one's own body, the right to environmental protection, the right to housing, are examples (intentionally very different) of this creation of new rights. In addition, this redefinition comes to include not only the right to equality but also the right to difference, which specifies, deepens, and broadens the right to equality.[32]

2. The second point, which implies the right to have rights, is that the new citizenship, contrary to older conceptions, is not linked to the strategy of the domi-

nant classes and the state for the gradual political incorporation of excluded sectors for the purpose of greater social integration or as a legal and political condition necessary for the installation of capitalism.[33] The new citizenship requires the constitution of active social subjects (political agents), defining what they consider to be their rights and struggling for their recognition; it is even *thought of* as consisting of this process. In this sense, it is a strategy of the noncitizens, of the excluded, to secure a citizenship "from below."

3. The third point is the idea that the new citizenship transcends a central reference in the liberal concept, the claim to access, inclusion, membership, and belonging to an already given political system. What is at stake, in fact, is *the right to participate in the very definition of that system, to define what we want to be members of,* that is to say, the invention of a new society. The recognition of the right to citizenship, as defined by those who today in Brazil are excluded from it, points toward radical transformations in our society and in its structure of power relations. Recent political practices inspired by the new citizenship, such as those emerging in the cities governed by the Partido dos Trabalhadores/Frentes Populares, where popular sectors and their organizations have provided space for the democratic control of the state through the effective participation of citizens in power, help to visualize future possibilities.

The Participatory Budget Council (Conselho do Orçamento Participativo) of Porto Alegre, which began in 1989, is probably the most successful of these alternative democratic experiments (see Baierle, in this volume). But Porto Alegre is only one example among many. There is in Brazil today a proliferation of microexperiments that cannot be ignored since they reveal important possibilities of change as a result of the building of citizenship (Alvarez and Dagnino 1995). In addition, these experiences point to the efforts of social movements themselves to adjust to democratic institutionality. This has implied a qualitative change in their practices that challenges some well-known interpretations of the character of their political participation, such as the predominance of corporate interests that would force social movements to compete among themselves for state resources, or to develop a clientelistic relationship with the state or whoever could meet their demands, or even to move *against* the State.

It is not contradictory to emphasize these experiences of popular intervention in the state after having emphasized the importance of civil society and cultural transformation as crucial spaces of political struggle for the building of citizenship. These experiences show changes not only in the modes of decisionmaking within the state but also in the forms of relationship between state and society. In addition, there is no doubt that they express and contribute to reinforcing the existence of citizens-subjects and of a culture of rights that includes the right to be a coparticipant in city government. Moreover, this kind of experience contributes to the creation of public spaces, where private and common interests, specificities, and differences can be exposed, discussed, and negotiated (see Telles and Paoli, in this volume).

There are obviously real difficulties for the popular sectors in playing this new role. Most of the difficulties refer to inequalities in terms of information, uses of language, and technical knowledge. Nevertheless, they are not serving as an excuse to eliminate the new role for popular sectors but are being challenged in concrete practices.

4. The emphasis on the process of the constitution of subjects, on "becoming a citizen," on the diffusion of a "culture of rights," poses again the question of a democratic culture mentioned above and points to an additional, crucial distinction: the *broadening of the scope* of the new citizenship, the meaning of which is far from limited to the formal and legal acquisition of a set of rights and therefore to the political-judicial system. The new citizenship is a *project for a new sociability:* not only an incorporation into the political system in a strict sense, but a more egalitarian format for social relations at all levels, including new rules for living together in society (for the negotiation of conflicts, a new sense of a public order and public responsibility, a new social contract, and so on). A more egalitarian format for social relations at all levels implies the "recognition of the other as a subject bearer of valid interests and of legitimate rights" (Telles 1994b, 46; see also Telles and Paoli, in this volume). It also implies the constitution of a public dimension of society where rights can be consolidated as public parameters for the interlocution, debate, and negotiation of conflicts, making possible the reconfiguration of an ethical dimension of social life. Such a project unsettles not only social authoritarianism as the basic mode of social ordering in Brazil but also more recent neoliberal discourses that establish private interest as the measure for everything, denying alterity and hence obstructing the possibilities for an ethical dimension of social life.[34]

5. This broadened conception of citizenship implies, in contrast to the liberal view, that citizenship is no longer confined within the limits of the relationship with the state or between the state and the individual but must be established within civil society itself. The process of building citizenship as the affirmation and recognition of rights is, especially in Brazilian society, a process of transformation of practices rooted in society as a whole. Such a political strategy implies moral and intellectual reform: a process of social learning, of constructing new kinds of social relations, implying, obviously, the establishment of citizens as active social subjects. But also, for society as a whole, this strategy requires learning to live on different terms with these emergent citizens, who refuse to remain in the places that were socially and culturally defined for them. This is one point in which the radicality of citizenship as cultural politics seems quite clear.

Some of the results from a survey on democratic culture and citizenship in which I participated in Campinas, São Paulo, in 1993, may help to substantiate the analytical arguments developed above addressing the conceptions of citizenship and democracy deployed by social movements. The research was intended to investigate to what extent perceptions that emphasize the democratization of social relations as a whole, especially a refusal of social and cultural practices responsible for social authoritarianism, would be present in different sectors of organized civil society. One additional motivation underlying this research was that the emphasis on the need for cultural changes today in Brazil, where the worsening of economic inequalities, hunger, and extreme poverty has transformed social authoritarianism into social apartheid, violence, and genocide, has been often considered inappropriate. However, when the economic crisis determines what tends to be a certain "economic reductionism" in the analysis of the question of democracy, emphasizing the cultural dimension of citizenship seemed even more important.[35] Thus, I particularly wanted to investigate how the connection between social authoritarianism as a historical model of social ordering in Brazil and the present situation of deprivation lived by the majority of the population, which seemed clear at the theoretical level, was perceived by political leaders of civil society.

Fifty-one members of organized sectors of civil society were interviewed: both urban popular movements and social movements of a wider character (such as women's, black, and ecological movements), workers' and middle-class trade unions, entrepreneurs' associations, and elected members of the São Paulo City Council *(vereadores)*. The survey included a question asking the interviewees to select, from a list, which quality was most important for a country to be considered democratic. The alternatives were:

- There are several political parties.
- All have food and housing.
- Whites, blacks, men, women, rich, and poor are all treated equally.
- People can participate in unions and associations.
- People can criticize and protest.

My expectation was that social and economic equality would be overwhelmingly chosen, given the critical economic situation at that time and the economic claims that characterize the political activities of the associations surveyed. However, 58 percent of the sample selected equal treatment for whites, blacks, men, women, rich, and poor as most important (see Table 2.1). What these results indicate is that the existence of social authoritarianism and the hierarchization of social relations is perceived, more than economic inequality or the absence of freedom of expression and party and union organization, as a serious obstacle to the building of democracy.

The distribution of this preference among the various sectors interviewed is also very significant; it seems to be most important to social movements, to whose experience the emergence of the notion of a new citizenship is clearly associated. Even urban popular movements, certainly the sector most penalized by economic inequality within the sample, stressed an egalitarian code for social relations as the most important dimension of democracy. Entrepreneurs and members of the middle-class unions, sectors certainly less affected by the cultural practices of so-

TABLE 2.1 Dimensions of Democracy: Responses to the Question: "In your opinion, what is the most important thing for a country to be considered democratic?"

	Entrepreneurs	*Middle-Class Unions*	*Workers' Unions*	*Urban Movements*	*Wider Social Movements*	*City Council Members*	*General Sample*
Mentioned as Most Important:							
Political parties	12.5	12.5	–	–	–	14.3	5.8
Food and housing	12.5	25.0	10.0	11.1	20.0	14.3	15.4
Equal treatment	50.0	50.0	60.0	66.7	70.0	42.9	57.7
Particip. in unions and associations	12.5	–	10.0	22.2	–	14.3	9.6
Freedom of expression	12.5	12.5	10.0	–	10.0	14.3	9.6
Mentioned as Second Most Important:							
Political parties	12.5	12.5	–	11.1	–	14.3	7.7
Food and housing	25.0	37.5	10.0	22.2	40.0	28.6	26.9
Equal treatment	25.0	12.5	10.0	11.1	20.0	14.3	15.4
Particip. in unions and associations	12.5	12.5	30.0	11.1	20.0	14.3	17.3
Freedom of expression	25.0	37.5	60.0	22.2	10.0	14.3	28.8
Total	100.0	100.0	100.0	100.0	100.0	100.0	100.0

SOURCE: Research Cultura Democrática e Cidadania.

cial authoritarianism, nevertheless clearly identified its consequences for the democratization of society. Elected members of the City Council, where more conservative parties form the majority, seem to be the least sensitive to the egalitarian dimension of democracy. Significantly, social movements of both kinds as well as workers' unions clearly stated their position about the diminished importance of political parties to democracy by ignoring this category altogether.

This data seems to indicate that the classical dimensions of liberal democracy—freedom of expression and organization and the existence of political parties—are perceived as already ensured and that the emphasis should now be placed on the need to deepen and extend democracy. The deeply rooted existence of social authoritarianism as the dominant cultural mode of social relations at various levels of society and, secondarily, economic inequality (which received 15 percent of the first-place votes) constitute the two, clearly connected, central questions around which the struggle of social movements for citizenship is organized today in Brazil.

Open-ended questions enabled us to collect qualitative data that confirmed the perception of members of subaltern organizations of the contradiction between existing authoritarian cultural practices that permeate social relations at all levels and the building of citizenship and a democratic society. Asked whether or not they were treated as citizens, members of social movements of both kinds and of workers' trade unions revealed very different perceptions in relation to the two other sectors interviewed. While middle-classes interviewees and entrepreneurs stressed activities such as "paying taxes," "having a profession," "voting," or even "having money" as evidence of their citizenship (63 and 75 percent of these sectors, respectively, considered themselves treated as citizens), members of social movements and trade unions stressed that their nonexistence as citizens was related to the ways they were treated socially: A great majority of them mentioned disrespect, discrimination, and prejudice as part of their daily experience in the city; referred to their status as "second-class citizens"; and complained of mistreatment because of their race or because they were not dressed well. The state was repeatedly mentioned as being responsible for this treatment, mainly through references to police abuse and to the absence of basic services to the poor. Although 90 percent of the interviewees from these sectors affirm that they are not treated as citizens, they do consider themselves as such (wider social movements, 80 percent; urban popular movements, 90 percent; workers' trade unions, 60 percent), primarily because they "struggle for their rights."

Another set of questions in the study referred to the nature of politics (who engages in politics, who *should* engage in politics, and so on). The data showed that members of social movements and trade unions have an extended conception of the political arena; they indicated their belief that civil society and its organizations, including the social movements and trade unions themselves, are crucial terrains and agents of democratization, but that they had yet to be acknowledged as such by the official public sphere.[36]

The emphasis on civil society and on the cultural practices that underlie social relations as arenas of the struggle of social movements for democratization shall not be understood as a limiting choice that would exclude, again, the state and political institutionality as secondary arenas. The concrete experience of social movements in the transition to democracy in Brazil is full of examples that show this dichotomy to be false (Alvarez and Dagnino 1995).

This research showed that members of social movements, in contrast to much of the Brazilian population, have a very positive view of political institutions. Whereas both members of urban movements and of black, women's, and ecological movements clearly value political parties (89 and 80 percent, respectively), national surveys showed that 52 percent of the general population considered that "political parties only divide people"; only 35 percent saw them as "indispensable to democracy"; 61 percent believed that "parties only defend interests of politicians"; and 50 percent believed that "political parties make political participation more difficult."[37] In addition, members of both urban popular movements and wider social movements identify themselves or are affiliated with political parties (89 and 70 percent, respectively); consider voting an important instrument of participation in society; and would vote even if it were not mandatory (78 and 80 percent, respectively).

This positive view of traditional institutional mechanisms, however, is not a complacent one. This approach to institutional channels of political participation in representative democracy is far from implying the abandonment of the critical perspective that underlies the very emergence of social movements. It coexists with a clear demand for the improvement of the democratic content of such mechanisms, both through transformations in the political culture that would redefine their present significance and through the creation of new mechanisms that may expand and deepen the limits of actually existing democracy. Thus, when none of the members of social movements and trade unions mentioned the existence of parties as significant indicators of democracy (while members of entrepreneurial and middle-class associations did),they seem to be saying not only that the existence of political parties is not a sufficient or relevant indicator of democracy but that parties, such as those currently in existence in Brazil, do not constitute guarantees of democracy. In addition, for these sectors, dissatisfaction with political parties is not passive. Thus, the elimination of clientelistic and personal relations as criteria in electoral choices, the strengthening of relations between elected representatives and voters, and the adoption of mechanisms of control over elected representatives in order to ensure their accountability were pointed out both as motivating concrete practices executed by members of social movements and as examples of their demands for formal, functioning democratic institutions.

These statements suggest that social movements, in emphasizing the transformation of authoritarian social relations and cultural practices throughout civil society as fundamental in building democracy, are not selecting exclusive targets or turning their backs on political institutions. On the contrary, they perceive that their cultural politics can extend into formal representative political arenas.

In theoretical terms, the perspective explored here is certainly not intended to reproduce the compartmentalization and hierarchization of the multiple dimensions of democracy and its forms of struggle. In fact, it was exactly against the "schizophrenia" of political analysis of democratization—which segregates the institutional from the noninstitutional, the state from civil society, the political from the cultural—that I decided to work toward a theoretical framework that was able to take into account this complex multiplicity without obscuring what appeared to me as concrete and crucial aspects of the collective action of social movements.

In enacting an enlarged view of democracy and operationalizing this view in terms of a struggle for citizenship, social movements also convey an alternative vision of what counts as political in Latin American societies (see Slater, in this volume). The very existence of social movements has unsettled dominant notions of political subjects and spaces, as the theoretical redefinitions carried out by the Left's renovation showed. As they enter the dispute among the different blueprints for democracy, social movements, along with other political actors sharing the same perspective, offer new parameters for that dispute and react against reductionist conceptions of both democracy and politics itself. In politicizing what is not conceived of as political, in presenting as public and collective what is conceived of as private and individual, they challenge the political arena to enlarge its own boundaries and broaden its agenda. It is my contention that the cultural effects of such efforts upon this dispute and upon the social imaginary must be recognized as political, beyond the assessment of other successes or failures that may result from them.

Notes

1. For an example, see Dagnino 1972.

2. Through institutions such as the Church, family, trade unions, and educational, legal, political, and communications systems, the ideological state apparatuses function "massively and predominantly *by ideology*" to ensure "the reproduction of the relations of production, i.e. of capitalist relations of production" through the "subjection to the ruling ideology" (Althusser 1971, 133, 145, 154).

3. In this connection, it would be interesting to investigate the number of women intellectuals engaged in cultural subjects.

4. The silence about this fundamental component of the concept of hegemony is notable in Laclau and Mouffe 1985.

5. This formulation is from Portantiero 1977. Juan Carlos Portantiero was one of the first Latin American Gramscians and a member of Pasado y Presente, a unique and influential politico-cultural grouping of Gramscians that originated in Argentina in 1963 and was exiled to Mexico in 1976. For an extended account of Pasado y Presente, see Burgos 1996.

6. Gramsci's works arrived first in Latin America in Argentina between 1958 and 1962, then in Brazil between 1966 and 1968, and finally in Mexico in 1970 (although an out of print early translation had been available in Mexico since the late 1950s). For an account of Gramsci's "geography" on the continent, see Aricó 1988a, 1988b; Nogueira 1988; Coutinho and Nogueira 1988; Córdova 1987; Burgos, 1996.

7. Quoted by Clovis Rossi, *Folha de São Paulo,* September 25, 1988.

8. Ruptures with the Communist Party to which they belonged was part of the trajectory of the most significant Gramscian intellectuals in both Argentina (1963) and Brazil (1973).

9. See Burgos 1994 for a discussion of the influence of Gramscian hegemony on both Brazil's Partido dos Trabalhadores (PT) and El Salvador's Frente Farabundo Martí de Liberación Nacional (FMLN).

10. This last tendency seems to have been more developed in advanced capitalist societies. In some cases, the revolutionary potential of hegemony, so crucial to Gramsci's own thought, was simply ignored, and the concept was reduced to designating a "given" of any kind of exercise of dominant power in nonauthoritarian modern capitalist societies, its distinction with respect to domination and its specificity as a particular mode of exercising power therefore disregarded. An additional connected difference in these readings of Gramsci is the importance attributed in Latin America to the concept of hegemony crisis, often used to describe the lack of hegemony in our societies and seldom applied to advanced capitalist countries.

11. See Portantiero 1977.

12. For an example of the non-interchangeability of these three tendencies, see Vasconi 1990.

13. This last assertion expresses a concern not only with the association between hegemony and democracy but also with the affirmation of an indissoluble link between democracy and socialism. According to Coutinho, the search for unity within the diversity, concealed and mystified by liberalism, is not only an immediate tactical objective in the struggle against authoritarian regimes but, insofar as it implies the elevation of democracy to a higher level, it is also a strategic objective in the building of a socialist society based on political democracy (Coutinho 1980, 40–41). The debate around the critique of the Left's "instrumental" conception of democracy and the establishment of an intrinsic link between democracy and socialism constituted a significant part of the renovation process within the Left. See Coutinho 1980, Weffort 1984, Barros 1986, Garcia 1986, Chauí 1981, Toledo 1994.

14. See, for instance, Riz and Ipola 1985. The authors advocate a "flexible" posture toward theory, which denies it "the exorbitant right to fix 'forever' the exact meaning and the rules for using conceptual tools" but, on the contrary, confers on theory "the reasonable right to keep open the discussion about the various meanings and the multiple possibilities of a productive use of those tools." In addition, this same posture is reaffirmed with respect to Gramsci's thought (1985, 45). [Texto original: "flexible en la medida en que niega a los esquemas teóricos el exorbitante derecho de fijar 'para siempre' el sentido exacto y las reglas de empleo de las herramientas conceptuales y les otorga, en cambio, el razonable derecho de mantener abierta la discusión acerca de los varios sentidos y las multiples posibilidades de un uso fecundo de esas herramientas."]

15. A good example of this intermingling and the difficulty in isolating particular influences is a criticism by Tomás Vasconi referring to an alleged replacement of the "logic of

contradiction" by the "logic of conflict" in the renovative critique of the Left: "We must emphasize that although the authors invoke the ideas of Gramsci, the concepts that truly found these formulations are inspired by Foucault" (1990, 27).

16. For an explicit example of this self-titled "pragmatic" approach to Gramscian categories, see Riz and Ipola 1985, 45.

17. See Gramsci 1971, 257–264. The continuity between state and civil society is also addressed by the Gramscian concept of *integral state*.

18. See Gramsci 1971, 133 for Gramsci's view on the links between economic, intellectual, and moral reforms.

19. According to Riz and Ipola, the conditions in which Gramsci's thought can establish a new mode of analysis of Latin American social realities from a Marxist perspective cannot be "sacralized": "That is, if one does not close up a thinking, on the contrary, one works with it and from it (and, sometimes, *against it*) in order to account for concrete social realities" (1985, 61; my emphasis). Such a consciously selective reading, however, is not always made explicit. Thus, Gramsci's isolated assertion with respect to hegemonic capacity being restricted to "fundamental classes," which could be seen as problematic to the plurality of political subjects and the critique of economic reductionism, has not been properly addressed by the authors we examined. [Cita original: "La difusión más reciente del 'gramscismo' en América Latina y la profusión de distintas lecturas de Gramsci nacidas a la luz de las urgencias políticas del momento, abre la posibilidad de instalar en el centro de las reflexiones teórico-políticas sobre el presente un nuevo modo de análisis de las realidades latinoamericanas desde el marxismo. Pero esa posibilidad existe a condición de no operar una sacralización del pensamiento de Gramsci. Es decir, si no se clausura un pensamiento y, por el contrario, se trabaja con él y desde él (y a veces, contra ese pensamiento) para dar cuenta de realidades sociales concretas, único camino abierto a la constitución de una 'dirección intelectual y moral'(un pensamiento capaz de explicar y transformar esas realidades)]."

20. See Riz and Ipola 1985 for what is seen as a rupture between Gramsci and this "logic of separation." See also Mires 1984.

21. Gramsci 1971, 377. In this connection, see also p. 165: "Furthermore, another proposition of the philosophy of praxis is also forgotten: that 'popular beliefs' and similar ideas are themselves material forces."

22. Tarcus and Santos 1990. [Texto original: "La política cultural no es una materia optativa, la materia eternamente pendiente de los programas de la izquierda, sino una materia tal que no resiste, simplemente, ser adicionada en ellos. Su sola presencia pone en cuestion y obliga a reformular la totalidad de como se concibe y se practica la política. Pues la ausencia de una política para la cultura en la izquierda, no es la ausencia de política para un compartimiento estanco de lo social, para un area delimitada y recortable, sino que es síntoma, ni más ni menos, de *falta de política* a secas."]

23. [Texto original: "(Es que la complejidad misma de las 'sociedades de Occidente' sobre las que reflexionaba Gramsci) impone descartar cualcuer idea fija de estados mayores o ejércitos o discursos preconstituidos para sustituirla por la de destacamentos y significaciones diferenciados que van emergiendo y mutando en los múltiples espacios en que se dan los antagonismos."]

24. Lechner (1986, 33) points out how the experience of authoritarianism itself has contributed to developing a new sensitivity among intellectuals on the Left with respect to issues related to subjectivity and to the cultural practices that orient ordinary life.

25. That this particular kind of confluence between the Left and social movements' practices is not the only one possible is shown by Jeffrey Rubin's chapter in this volume.

26. See Alvarez and Dagnino 1995.

27. "As the 'discursive matrix' analyzed by Sader (1988) in the origins of the social movements in the 1970s, an ethical-political field refers to distinctive "ways of approaching reality which imply different attributions of meaning," deriving from the "elaboration of experiences previously silenced or interpreted differently" (Sader 1988, 19). The openness to include the new, for which there were not previous categories, can then be seen as a defining characteristic of an ethical-political field. This suggests, on the one hand, its internal plurality and nonhomogenous nature, and on the other hand, its oppositional character with respect to existing political fields, especially the dominant one" (Alvarez and Dagnino 1995, 14).

28. Referring to the historical rooting of authoritarianism will not obscure its constant renovation and reelaboration, with the emergence of new forms of exclusion and violence through which this deeply rooted mode of social ordering becomes adapted to the transformations engendered by the modernization, and postmodernization, of Brazilian society. Thus, if recent legislation proscribed the generalized existence of "service elevators" reserved for "noncitizens" (employees, domestic maids, but very often just plainly black people), the closing of streets to public transit in middle- and upper-class neighborhoods for alleged security reasons is already a pervasive habit in large cities.

29. Urban popular movements' perceptions of the intermingling of these different dimensions of exclusion and deprivation and how they affect each other first became evident to me through the experience of the Assembléia do Povo, an early (1979) *favelado* movement in Campinas, São Paulo. At the beginning of their struggle for the "right to the use of the land," their first public initiative was to ask the media to publicize the results of their own survey of the *favelas,* in order to show the city that they were not idle people, marginals, or prostitutes, as *favelados* were considered to be, but decent working citizens. See Dagnino 1995.

30. See Miguel Díaz-Barriga, in this volume, for the meaning attributed by Mexican *colonas* to *"necesidad."*

31. See Verónica Schild, in this volume, for how this appropriation is taking place in Chile with respect to the women's movement.

32. For a discussion of citizenship and the connections between the right to difference and the right to equality, see Dagnino 1994.

33. For other conceptions of citizenship deployed by dominant classes in recent Brazilian history, see the notions of *cidadania regulada* ("regulated citizenship") (Santos 1979), *cidadania concedida* ("citizenship by concession") (Sales 1994), and also Carvalho 1991.

34. For Vera Telles (1994a), the absence of these public and ethical dimensions, which leaves the moral codes of private life as the only available spaces for the formulation and solution of daily individual and collective dramas, is certainly behind the criminality, vigilante justice, police violence, and various kinds of prejudices that plague our [Brazilian] uncivil society.

35. Ironically, this "economic reductionism" is sustained not only by the traditional Left but also by neoliberals trying to solve social inequality by reducing poverty to supportable levels.

36. There were additional questions about whether or not the interviewees perceived themselves and their organizations as political actors, and about who engages in politics in Brazil today and who should engage in politics.

37. This information is drawn from CESOP (Centro de Estudos de Opinião Pública, Universidade Estadual de Campinas, São Paulo): DAT/BR90, Mar–00219, 1990.

References

Althusser, Louis. 1971. "Ideology and Ideological State Apparatuses." In *Lenin and Philosophy*. New York: Monthly Review Press.

Alvarez, Sonia E. 1993. "'Deepening Democracy': Popular Movement Networks, Constitutional Reform, and Radical Urban Regimes in Contemporary Brazil." In *Mobilizing the Community: Local Politics in the Era of the Global City*, ed. R. Fischer and J. Kling. Newbury Park, Calif.: Sage Publications.

Alvarez, Sonia E. and Evelina Dagnino. 1995. "Para Além da 'Democracia Realmente Existente': Movimentos Sociais, a Nova Cidadania e a Configuração de Espaços Públicos Alternativos." Paper presented at the Nineteenth Annual Meeting of the Associaçao Nacional de Pos-Graduaçao e Pesquisa em Ciências Sociais (ANPOCS), Caxambu, Minas Gerais, Brazil.

Aricó, José. 1985. "Prólogo." In *Hegemonia y Alternativas Políticas en América Latina*, ed. J. L. Martin del Campo. Mexico City: Siglo XXI.

______. 1988a. "Geografia de Gramsci na América Latina." In *Gramsci e a América Latina*, ed. C. Coutinho and M. Nogueira. São Paulo: Paz e Terra.

______. 1988b. *La Cola del Diablo: Itinerario de Gramsci en América Latina*. Buenos Aires: Puntosur.

Baierle, Sérgio Gregório. 1992. "Um novo principio ético-político: pratica social e sujeito nos movimentos populares urbanos em Porto Alegre nos anos 80." Master's thesis, Universidade Estadual de Campinas, São Paulo.

Barros, Robert. 1986. "The Left and Democracy: Recent Debates in Latin America." *Telos* 68:49–70.

Burgos, Raul. 1994. "As Peripécias de Gramsci entre Gulliver e o Pequeno Polegar." Master's thesis, Universidade Estadual de Campinas, São Paulo.

______. 1996. "Gramscismos e Gramscianos na Argentina." Universidade Estadual de Campinas, São Paulo. Unpublished manuscript.

Calderón, Fernando. 1987. "El Camino de la Transformación en Bolivia." *La Ciudad Futura* 6:17–18.

Canclini, Nestor G. 1984. "Cultura y Organización Popular, Gramsci con Bourdieu." *Nueva Sociedad* 71:75–82.

______. 1987. "Cultura y Politica, Nuevos Escenarios para America Latina." *Nueva Sociedad* 92:116–130.

______. 1988. "Culture and Power: The State of Research." *Culture and Society* 10:467–497.

Carvalho, José Murilo de. 1991. *Os Bestializados*. São Paulo: Companhia das Letras.

Castañeda, Jorge. 1994. *Utopia Desarmada*. São Paulo: Cia das Letras.

Chauí, Marilena. 1981. *Cultura e Democracia*. São Paulo: Editora Moderna.

Córdova, Arnaldo. 1987. "Gramsci y la Izquierda Mexicana." *La Ciudad Futura* 6:14–15.

Coutinho, Carlos Nelson. 1980. *A Democracia como Valor Universal*. São Paulo: Ciências Humanas.

______. 1981. *Gramsci*. Porto Alegre: L&PM Editores.

Coutinho, Carlos Nelson, and Marco Aurélio Nogueira, eds. 1988. *Gramsci e a América Latina*. São Paulo: Paz e Terra.

Dagnino, Evelina. 1972. "Cultural and Ideological Dependence: Building a Theoretical Framework." In *Structures of Dependence,* ed. F. Bonilla and R. Grilling. Stanford, Calif. Reprinted in *Transnational Enterprises: Their Impact on Third World Societies and Cultures,* ed. K. Kumar. Boulder: Westview Press, 1980.

______. 1994. "Os Movimentos Sociais e a Emergência de uma Nova Noção de Cidadania." In *Anos 90: Política e Sociedade no Brasil,* ed. E. Dagnino. São Paulo: Brasiliense.

______. 1995. "On Becoming a Citizen: The Story of D. Marlene." In *International Yearbook of Oral History and Life Stories,* ed. R. Benmayor and A. Skotnes. Oxford: Oxford University Press.

Doimo, Ana Maria. 1995. "A Vez e a Voz do Popular: Movimentos Sociais e Participação Política no Brasil Pós–70." Rio de Janeiro: Relume-Dumará/ANPOCS.

Garcia, Marco Aurélio, ed. 1986. *As Esquerdas e a Democracia.* São Paulo: Paz e Terra.

Gramsci, Antonio. 1971. *Selections from the Prison Notebooks.* Ed. and Trans. Quentin Hoare and Geoffrey Noel Smith. New York: International Publishers.

Ipola, Emilio de, and Juan Carlos Portantiero. 1984. "Crisis Social y Pacto Democrático." *Punto de Vista* 21:13–20.

Laclau, Ernesto, and Chantal Mouffe. 1985. *Hegemony and Socialist Strategy.* London: Verso.

Lechner, Norbert. 1986. "De la Revolución a la Democracia." *La Ciudad Futura* 2:33–35.

______. 1988. *Los Patios Interiores de la Democracia: Subjetividad y Política.* Santiago: Fondo de Cultura Economica.

Martin del Campo, Julio Labastida. 1985. *Hegemonia y Alternativas Políticas en America Latina.* Mexico City: Siglo XXI.

McCaughan, Edward. 1995. "Global Change and Paradigm Crisis: The Renovation of the Left Discourse in Cuba and Mexico." Ph.D. diss., University of California at Santa Cruz.

Mires, Fernando. 1984. "Cultura y Democracia." *Nueva Sociedad* 73:55–64.

Nogueira, M. Aurélio. 1988. "Gramsci, a Questão democratica e a esquerda no Brasil." In *Gramsci e a América Latina,* ed. C. N. Coutinho and M. A. Nogueira. São Paulo: Paz e Terra.

Nun, José. 1989. *La Rebelión del Coro.* Buenos Aires: Nueva Visión.

Oliveira, Francisco de. 1996. "O 'Reino' de 20 Anos," *Folha de São Paulo,* October 13.

Portantiero, Juan Carlos. 1977. "Los Usos de Gramsci." *Cuadernos de Pasado y Presente* 54:11–386.

______. 1981. "Lo Nacional-Popular y los Populismos Realmente Existentes." *Nueva Sociedad* 54:7–18.

______. 1988. "Gramsci em Chave Latino-Americana." In *Gramsci e a América Latina,* ed. C. N. Coutinho and M. A. Nogueira. São Paulo: Paz e Terra.

Riz, Liliana de and Emilio de Ipola. 1985. "Acerca de la hegemonia como producción histórica." In *Hegemonia y Alternativas Políticas en America Latina,* ed. J. L. Martin del Campo. Mexico City: Siglo XXI.

Sader, Eder. 1988. *Quando Novos Personagens Entraram em Cena.* São Paulo: Paz e Terra.

Sales, Teresa. 1994. "Raízes da Desigualdade Social na Cultura Brasileira." *Revista Brasileira de Ciências Sociais* 25:26–37.

Santos, Wanderley G. dos. 1979. *Cidadania e Justiça.* São Paulo: Editora Campus.

Scherer-Warren, Ilse. 1993. *Redes de Movimentos Sociais.* São Paulo: Loyola.

Tarcus, Horatio, and Blas de Santos. 1990. "Notas para una critica de la razón Burocrática." *Utopias del Sur* 4 (summer):12–14.

Teixeira, Ana Cláudia Chaves. 1995. "Movimentos Sociais e a Construção de uma Cultura Democrática." Universidade Estadual de Campinas, São Paulo. Mimeographed.

Telles, Vera da Silva. 1993. "Pauvretté et Citoyenneté, dilèmme du Brèsil Contemporaine." *Problèms de Amérique Latine* 9:73–85.

______. 1994a. "A Sociedade Civil e a Construção de um Espaço Público." In *Anos 90: Política e Sociedade no Brasil*, ed. E. Dagnino. São Paulo: Brasiliense.

______. 1994b. "Sociedade Civil, Direitos e Espaços Públicos." *Polis* 14:43–53.

Toledo, Caio Navarro. 1994. "As Esquerdas e a Redescoberta da Democracia." In *Anos 90: Política e Sociedade no Brasil*, ed. E. Dagnino. São Paulo: Brasiliense.

Vasconi, Tomás. 1990. "Democracy and Socialism in South America." *Latin American Perspectives* 65:25–38.

Weffort, Francisco. 1984. *Por que Democracia?* São Paulo: Brasiliense.

Wiener, Antje. 1992. "Citizenship, New Dynamics of an Old Concept: A Comparative Perspective on Current Latin American and European Political Strategies." Paper presented at the Seventeenth International Congress of the Latin American Studies Association, September, Los Angeles.

Williams, Raymond. 1977. *Marxism and Literature*. Oxford: Oxford University Press.

Chapter Three

Social Rights: Conflicts and Negotiations in Contemporary Brazil

MARIA CELIA PAOLI AND
VERA DA SILVA TELLES

Social movements are today at the core of Brazilian societal dilemmas. Indeed, they are at the center of the paradoxes that perplex those seeking to understand the uncertain trajectory of Brazil and the possibilities (all the more uncertain) of a future project capable of articulating modernization, equality, and social justice. During the 1980s, in claims for rights, social movements were organized, labor unions were strengthened, and aspirations for a more just and egalitarian society took shape. Movements projected their demands onto the public stage and left their imprint in important victories in the Brazilian Constitution of 1988. These victories were translated into the construction of plural spaces of representation of collective actors today who are recognized as valid spokespersons on the national political scene.

The 1980s were lived under the hope for democracy; yet the decade closed in a spectacle of poverty perhaps never before witnessed in Brazil's republican history, poverty engendered by the problematic convergence of an exclusionary tradition, prolonged economic crisis, and the perverse effects of economic modernization and economic restructuring. Brazil entered the 1990s with a consolidated democracy that formally recognizes social rights, civil guarantees, and citizens' prerogatives but that coexists at the quotidian level with violence and continual human rights violations, in a world that reveals the antithesis of citizenship and basic rules of civility, displaying what O'Donnell (1993) defines as a "truncated legality." This truncated system guarantees democratic political rights but is unable to enforce the law, civil rights, and justice in the heterogeneous terrain of social life. Democratic rights are compromised by other power circuits that obliterate the public dimension of citizenship, reestablishing violence and arbitrary power in the sphere of private relations, class, gender, and ethnicity, thereby rendering the state increasingly ineffective in enforcing its own regulations. Finally, the universalist agenda of rights—expressed by diverse social movements—reaffirms the urgency of equality and justice in a context of growing poverty while simultaneously being challenged by those who call into question well-known models of the welfare state (a model that was never realized in Brazil, one must remember). This contradiction reopens the tension between modernity and modernization; between the ethical requirement for rights and the imperative of efficacy in the economy; between a legal order that promises equality and the stark reality of existing inequalities, discriminations, and exclusions; between hopes for a world worth living in, as inscribed in movements' claims for rights, and the absence of future prospects for a majority afflicted by a form of modernization that destructures their way of life and leaves a precarious form of existence as their only possible destiny.

It is in terms of these paradoxes (among others) that the crisis of modern times is being processed. Beyond its more immediate economic and political circumstances, the crisis brings classic questions of rights, justice, and equality into focus. These questions address a social contract that must be refounded—not as a pledge of obedience to power, not reduced to the liberal syntax of legal rules ordering private relations, but as a document capable of affirming rights as the regulating principles of social life and of establishing the terms of negotiation and potential dialogue as rules of equity and justice that should prevail in social relations (Telles 1994). This is a possibility that exists, at least as a virtuality, on the horizon of Brazilian society, on account of an emerging civil society constructed on the conflictive terrain of social life, through practices of representation and negotiation, by collective actors recognized in the legitimacy of the rights they demand.

This is, we could say, the legacy of the 1980s: After years of arbitrary power and repression, under the historical horizon of an authoritarian, exclusionary, and hierarchical society, social struggles created an informal public space, both discontinuous and pluralistic, in which diverse demands circulated. A "consciousness of the right to have rights" was elaborated within this public space, an unprecedented experience in Brazilian history. Citizenship is pursued as a struggle and as a conquest, and the claim for rights interpolates society—in the form of exigencies that would open the way to a public recognition of specific interests and reasons that make plausible aspirations for more dignified work, a decent life, and a more just society. If in these last few years the script of Brazilian society has been modified, opening itself to the recognition of popular demands (even if in an ambivalent manner, as public opinion is always ready to undo legitimacy and evoke past images of chaos); if negotiation has become feasible in lieu of violence, which, although still present, is no longer the only available response; if the word "worker" is now received positively, no longer denoting inferiority; if all of this can happen, it is because, within the field of conflicts that animated the 1980s, a representative scheme has been constructed. Within this scheme, the claim for rights could circulate, creating identities where previously only undifferentiated men and women existed in their own deprivation. The ambiguities and ambivalence involved in this process, briefly suggested above, "merely" show that the path toward a more egalitarian and democratic society is a painful one. These ambiguities reveal that victories are won with difficulty against the backdrop of a social and political grammar that is constructed of exclusionary rules that reestablish old hierarchies and create new ones, thereby excluding the majority. But it is precisely with reference to these ambivalences and difficulties that one can situate the importance of social movements.[1] It is not that social movements are, in themselves, intrinsically politically virtuous. Rather, social movements are important because they constitute, in the conflictive terrain of social life, public arenas in which conflicts gain visibility and collective actors become valid spokespersons. In these arenas, rights structure a public language that delimits the criteria through which collective demands are problematized and evaluated in their exigency of equity and justice. This language is the source of the processes that mobilize aspirations to redefine social power by tying together different meanings and practices. As discussed in the Introduction to this book, these meanings and practices unsettle the dominant political culture by forcing it to confront other cultures and politics.

Constituted in a conflictive, plural, and decentralized terrain, these public arenas are created, re-created, or redefined at each moment, following the temporality of actual social conflicts. In these spaces of representation, negotiation, public representation, and public interlocution, workers, poor residents, homeless families, women, blacks, and marginalized minorities are the characters who have appeared on the Brazilian public stage in recent times[2]—they make themselves seen and recognized as subjects who address issues of justice and injustice in formulating their claims and demands and, in these terms, reelaborate the conditions of their existence with all that they carry in terms of values and traditions, necessities and aspirations, as issues that speak to ethical judgment and political deliberation. And this can mean various things.

In making themselves known on the political scene as subjects capable of public dialogue, these actors had the effect of destabilizing or even subverting symbolic hierarchies, which had held them in a subordinate position through a dense web of discrimination and exclusion. Raising issues and themes that were heretofore silenced or not considered pertinent to political deliberation, participants in these public arenas generated (and generate) a sense of enlargement of the political sphere via an extended and redefined notion of rights and citizenship. This redefined notion is not restricted to the institutional organization of the state but serves as a reference through which the ethical exigency of reciprocity and equality in social relations is elaborated, including the most prosaic and quotidian dimensions of social life where discrimination and exclusion are processed. It is in this redefinition of the notion of rights and citizenship that one can perceive the political meaning of the "democratic invention" (Lefort 1983) inscribed in these public spheres. These actors have the effect of modernizing, through dissent and conflict, the universal principles of equality and justice, since their presence on the political scene requires a permanent and continually renewed negotiation over the rules of equality and the measure of justice in social relations. It is under this prism, around these collective actors, that horizons of possibilities are opened that cannot be encapsulated in their singularities of class, gender, race, or ethnicity. The conquest and recognition of rights signifies the invention of *rules of public coexistence* and of *regulating principles of a democratic sociability* (Telles 1996). It is through this focus that we will discuss the democratic dynamic unleashed by the presence of collective actors on the Brazilian public scene.

The Construction of a Democratic Field of Conflict: Social Movements and Political Sociability

It is beyond our scope to provide an overview of the trajectory of Brazilian social movements during these last ten to fifteen years. But it is important to emphasize some aspects and events that mark this trajectory and help better qualify the issue we are addressing, namely the democratic and democratizing dynamic opened up by these public arenas of representation, negotiation, and interlocution.

First, the 1980s were marked by a notable associational and organizational dynamic that altered the political scene and introduced important fissures in the weighty authoritarian and exclusionary legacy of Brazilian history. The Workers' Party (Partido dos Trabalhadores, or PT), a party with strong roots in labor and popular movements, began to be structured at the beginning of the decade. Officially launched in 1980 at the initiative of leaders from a renewed and active labor movement, which had been a protagonist in the principal labor conflicts of the period, the PT had consolidated, by decade's end, its presence on the national political scene. The PT redefined the exclusionary and authoritarian terms and the oligarchical traces of Brazil's political system of representation and deliberation. It participated in the country's principal elections; conquered and expanded an important parliamentary base at national, state, and municipal levels; and won the mayoral elections in many municipalities, including some of Brazil's principal state capitals such as São Paulo (in 1988), Porto Alegre (1988, 1992, and 1996), and Belo Horizonte (1992).

During the 1980s, increases in worker and union conflicts agitated the country's principal urban centers. This decade witnessed the formation of three powerful labor union confederations, which stirred public debate on crucial questions regarding the conquest and expansion of rights and citizenship. Beyond the strictly political and labor movement arenas, social movements multiplied and diversified, bringing new themes and questions to the public debate. Movements organized around the most diverse themes of social life, such as questions of gender, racial and ethnic discrimination, ecology and the environment, and violence and human rights. Throughout the decade, these movements brought a deepened conception of rights and citizenship to public debate and the political sphere, incorporating demands for equity and justice in the social and cultural dimensions that affect identities, existence, and ways of life. As Sonia Alvarez has shown, an ample, multifaceted, and decentralized associative web developed around these movements, articulating grassroots associations, technical assistance groups, nongovernmental organizations (NGOs), churches, liberal professionals, labor unions, and even universities. Alvarez emphasizes that in this web made up of plural and heterogeneous public arenas, a capillarity of new themes and ethical exigencies of citizenship are produced, which traverse social groups, institutions, organizations, and parties, translating into a capacity, at times unexpected, to articulate and mobilize collective actors.

Second, in the recent political history of the country, the adoption of the 1988 Constitution was widely celebrated as the founding moment of democratic modernity, promising to bury once and for all the authoritarian legal order perpetuated by twenty years of military government. Granted, this promise has not been entirely fulfilled. Yet democratic legality, despite its limits and ambivalences, was negotiated after more than a year of efforts to influence Constituent Assembly deliberations and was influenced by the broad and diverse social mobilization prevalent during the first half of the 1980s. The recent trajectory of social movements was deeply implicated in an effort to inscribe new legal rights and influence the elaboration and implementation of a new constitutional order, first at the federal level and later at state and municipal levels (Silva and Saule 1993; Soares 1993).[3] Beyond incorporating a universalist rights and social protection agenda, the new legal text requires civic participation in public administration, opening up the possibility of a legality constructed through partnership and negotiation and capable of reconciling democracy and citizenship. These new possibilities are made explicit through the incorporation of legal instruments that redefine popular sovereignty beyond the practice of voting—through popular law initiatives, plebiscites and referendums, public audiences, and popular tribunes. This process led to a conquest of spaces of representation and negotiation in the formulation and implementation of diverse public policies; in the years following 1988, public forums—in which questions such as human rights, race, gender, culture, the environment, quality of life, housing, health, and the protection of children and adolescents are addressed as issues to be considered in a shared and negotiated administration of public assets—at the national, state, and municipal levels multiplied.[4]

This new institutionality—constructed in the convergence of social movements with the universe of institutions and the law—appears to reflect the very opposite of current government tendencies and proposals surrounding the role of the state. In the conservative redefinition of the state, social policies give way to industrial policies and the criteria of justice are abandoned in the name of efficacy. There is an "abandonment of the ethic of responsibility in favor of the ethic of efficiency as the foundation of compensatory social policies that are no longer redistributive" (Freitas 1995, 2).

This lack of synchrony between the conservative prescription and the new institutional reality forged by the constitution-building processes is a question undertaken by Ribeiro (1995). In analyzing the social rights and democratic procedures of public administration incorporated into the constitutions of Brazil's fifty largest municipalities, Ribeiro shows that these cases give institutional form to "a model of policy and city administration that is democratic, universalist, and redistributive of the benefits and costs of urbanization . . . a model of urban politics profoundly committed to the ideas of democracy, equality and social justice, the distinguishing features of a local welfare state" (108). If the municipal constitutions translate, at the local level, into a universalist agenda of rights, that agenda is not defined in terms of an abstract universality. Universal principals of equality and justice are affirmed as regulating the practices of representation and public interlocution, be it in the procedures foreseen for participatory democracy[5] or in instruments for the exercise of popular sovereignty.

We know that between the letter of the law and reality there is an enormous distance in which deeply rooted political traditions operate, conservatives obstruct the implementation of rights, and participatory practices are encapsulated by particularistic corporative interests. Nonetheless, this new institutionality translates into a historic experience, which has become a reference and parameter for new practices of active citizenship. These practices redefine the meaning of the law—not in the exclusive register of state juridical norms but rather as references through which claims for rights are formulated as demands for a democratic public order that incorporates substantive criteria of justice. These references realize what Habermas (1990) calls "decentralized and pluralized popular sovereignty," in multiple and differentiated public spaces in which collective rights and aspirations are affirmed as criteria for the judgment of public actions and circumstances that affect the lives of all. The experiments underway in various participatory forums constitute a practice—unprecedented in Brazilian history—of movements and organized groups appropriating laws and legal instruments consecrated by the new constitutional text and, in particular, in the municipal constitutions, to question the legitimacy of local executive decisions; denounce corruption and misuse of public funds; demand that public criteria be used in the formulation of local budgets; pressure local governments to regulate and implement rights guaranteed by law; and incorporate themes, questions, and demands formulated by movements and civic organizations into the public agenda.

In analyzing these experiences in municipalities in the interior of Bahia (a northeastern Brazilian state), Elenaldo Teixeira (1993) calls attention to the fact that, in the face of the traditional (and, in the case of these municipalities, scandalous) submission of the legislative to the executive branch—which sustains the oligarchical logic of the exercise of power in well-known practices such as nepotism, clientelism, and patronage—the liberal principle of separation of powers helped create a field of popular struggle through which to pressure the city council to fulfill its mandate in opposition to the arbitrary power and traditional predominance of the executive branch. The same is true, asserts Teixeira, at the judiciary level—the increasingly frequent legal actions against the state by popular organizations have obliged the judiciary to maintain greater autonomy, not only in relation to the executive but also in relation to local elites.[6]

Third, the early 1990s have been characterized by the redefinition of the state's role and the perverse social effects of modernization and economic restructuring. Yet recent experiences have called attention to democratic alternatives in a society undergoing crisis and facing an uncertain future. In the terrain of popular struggles, these democratic possibilities can be identified in the relations that organized movements have established with the state, dislodging the traditional practices of despotism *(mandonismo),* clientelism, and assistentialism through forms of public administration now being opened up to popular participation and new forms of negotiation. In this process, demands and claims establish an agenda of priorities and their relevance for the distribution of public resources, as well as the responsibilities of all involved actors (Telles 1994). This is what is happening, at least in some municipalities, in participatory budget processes (*orçamento participativo,* or OP) and in various forums of negotiation in which government officials, neighborhood associations, civic organizations, labor unions, and business associations negotiate alternatives for financial reform, the urbanization of *favelas,* the construction of affordable housing, administration and use of municipal public funds for urban development and social programs, proposals to defend or rehabilitate the environment, support of the so-called popular economy, possibilities of local development and income generation, as well as sectoral problems and specific or episodic issues.[7] The mechanisms of participation and public interlocution are varied, some prescribed in municipal constitutions, others constructed informally in response to circumstances and opportunities. The experiments are discontinuous and have varying results, some being episodic and others more permanent (Villas-Bôas 1994); they are created and re-created at each moment depending on local political circumstances. These experiences represent more than renovated forms of government. In the various forums of participation and representation that have emerged in the interface of state and society, new forms of political sociability are being constructed that open the way toward recognition and permit a new type of regulation capable of guaranteeing and creating new rights. We will address this question in greater depth below.

Alternative policies concerning housing and quality of life, racism and gender inequalities, violence and the guarantee of human rights, and the environment and sustainable development are elaborated and debated in diverse public arenas. These issues have inflamed debate in diverse forums that involve labor unions, grassroots movements, neighborhood associations, NGOs, technical assistance organizations, liberal professionals, and universities. Far from adhering to the "same old" complaints and accusations, this multiple and decentralized articulation has worked to elaborate alternative social policies in new spaces of action and intervention, whether in the formal political arena or in the cultural and societal arena (Alvarez 1995). Alternative policies for the construction of popular housing are discussed in diverse forums, at local and national levels, articulating popular organizations, NGOs, technical assistance groups, civil construction businesses, liberal professionals, and governmental representatives (A. Silva 1994); effective measures against racial and gender discrimination are similarly discussed, from social policies grounded in the principles of affirmative action to the elaboration of political and legal instruments that would ensure the implementation of rights guaranteed (and conquered) in the 1988 Constitution. NGOs, human rights groups, and even labor unions mobilize around various intervention programs for street children, searching for alternatives beyond the polarity of tutelage and repression that has historically characterized public policies toward this population. Labor unions, together with business owners and local government officials, elaborate and discuss alternative policies to address unemployment in political and labor forums. The alternative policies discussed range from the retraining of laid-off workers to the support of microenterprises operating at the fringes of the informal economy and the creation of workers' cooperatives designed to fill the cracks opened up by the process of industrial restructuring *(terceirização)*. In a context of deepening poverty and violence due to prolonged economic recession, the perverse modernization of the economy, and the lack of basic public services, this mobilization has the effect of reinventing politics, putting into focus the *play* of responsibilities involved in the various circumstances that shape the existence of social groups and even entire populations, pointing to innovative, effective, and at times unexpected possibilities for political action and public intervention.

To recognize the coming together of this democratic field entails the recognition that, in the circumstances of the current dilemmas, the struggle for rights circumscribes the dispute over different meanings of modernity, citizenship, and democracy. Between the burdensome legacy of Brazil's authoritarian and exclusionary tradition and the changes underway in the contemporary world, the Brazilian public is confronted by potentially antagonistic future alternatives. These alternatives counterpose, on the one hand, the possibilities of a democratic regulation of social life that recognizes and generalizes rights, and on the other, neoliberal proposals that represent an effort to privatize social relations through a rejection of the public mediation of rights and spheres of representation. The perspective of a broadened citizenship, open to public debate on pertinent questions and to democratic negotiation over the rules of social life, stands in contrast to the depoliticization inscribed in a conservative project that reduces civil society to the market, politics to technical-administrative rationality, and rights to the private autonomy of entrepreneurial individuals. The defense of rights mediated by universal categories of citizenship is thrown up against the course of a conservative restructuring of the state. This conservative project elides the question of public responsibility and is processed on an ideological terrain that renders meaningless the very notion of social rights, divesting them of parameters of justice and equality. Rights are thus relegated to a semantic field in which they are either associated with costs and burdens that thwart the modernization of the economy or equated with anachronistic corporatist privileges that must be overcome so that the market can fully realize its allegedly civilizing virtues.

In a context characterized by inequalities; growing poverty, discrimination, and violence; and the persistence of hierarchy and authoritarianism in social relations, this field of conflict and dispute is traversed by radical uncertainty and indetermination as to the possibilities, in Brazil, of augmenting the classic tasks of justice and equality, albeit in the new terms set forth by the contemporary world. But this uncertainty also provides a measure of the new possibilities available to an emerging Brazilian civil society. This is the question we will now address.

* * *

Rooted in a process, now many years old, of the organization of collective actors, of social struggles and claims for rights, this civil society can be understood as an articulation of associational practices, a universe of rights, and a democratic space of representation and public interlocution. Against the perverse automatisms of the market and contrary to the unitary character of the traditional space of the state (in the Brazilian case, exclusionary and authoritarian), this emerging civil society points to the possibility of new forms of democratic regulation of social life, with the purpose of enlarging mechanisms of representation. This democratic regulation is constructed through "rituals of negotiation," open to the plurality of emergent problems and themes that do not find a place in the unitary space of the state; it dislocates the arbitrary power of the state and extends the boundaries of rights beyond that defined by legal codes and formal legal rules. This civil society is being constructed in a convergence of processes that include a societal dynamic traversed by a multifaceted, decentralized conflictuality that surpasses traditional mechanisms of representation; the emergence of new themes, challenges, and problems (above all, the social question redefined by the economic restructuring of a globalized economy) that escape known political formulas; and the crisis of the state, namely the redefinition of its regulatory role and its relations with the economy and society (Telles 1994).

We are not denying the role of the state as a champion of entrepreneurial virtues (as in the liberal version) or libertarian virtues (as in the Left's version). Rather, we wish to stress the possibilities of constructing, between state and society, public arenas that make conflicts visible and that make demands resonate. Such arenas confer validity to the interests involved and entail the construction of public parameters that reinvent politics through the recognition of rights, measured by the negotiation and deliberation of policies that affect the lives of all.

The various forums of participation involving local governments have not emerged "all of a sudden." The proposal of popular participation forms part of a repertoire of political ideas that has been developing since the early 1980s and even before. Vocalized by popular movements and formalized in the platform of the Workers' Party, it is a repertoire that has gone through important changes. The very notions of "participation" and "popular" have been reelaborated in light of redefined political criteria over the years and even more so since the implementation of participatory experiences at the local government level.[8] However, these forums of participation are not simply an implementation of political principles and platforms. In practice, they have produced new political facts that have departed from established notions and unleashed a dynamic that poses unexpected challenges necessitating political invention and creativity.

In the first place, the opening of public forums of representation and participation had the effect of disseminating the conflictive dimension of social life. Something like a metamorphosis of social conflict occurs when such conflict enters public spheres that establish mediation between state and society. For it is here that the particularism of demands must redefine itself as a function of the public parameters of political administration in the cities. On one hand, this is where claims that are as diverse and particular as they are urgent for those who are struggling for survival are made. The political problem that emerges is how to define the priority criteria in the conflictive web that encompasses very localized and specific claims (such as for street paving), regional claims (such as for schools, day care, and health clinics), and other more generalized claims (such as for transportation and sanitation). This is what shapes the dilemma of a political scene traversed (and constituted) by the tension between scarce public resources and the multiplication of ethically founded, or at least socially just, claims.

But at the same time, this tension is what offers a measure with which to evaluate the democratic meaning of the political invention which has been occurring in various Brazilian cities. The participatory budget (OP) process of Porto Alegre is the best known and perhaps most successful case (see Baierle, in this volume). But it is not the only case. With different institutional formats and varying degrees of formalization, the previously unknown experience of "shared" public administration *(gestão partilhada da coisa pública)* is being realized in many cities, beginning with a public discussion of priorities in the distribution and use of public resources.[9] In a series of regional plenary sessions, popular organizations and community groups, together with representatives from other regions of the city, address the most pressing problems of their neighborhoods, defining priorities and establishing the agenda of demands and claims to be discussed in general assemblies. As Tarso Genro (1995, 22), former mayor of Porto Alegre (1992–1996), stated, the investments and public works of the municipality resulted from a type of negotiated public contract and were defined "through a regularization which determines basic rules of internal negotiation of each region and negotiation between the regions." But this process also requires a recognition that negotiation cannot be reduced to the materiality of what is demanded, for it is through negotiation that various collective actors are enjoined to construct the validity and legitimacy of their demands with reference to a notion in construction—and also in dispute—of what the "public interest" is at the local level. As Celso Daniel (1994a, 36), former mayor of Santo André (1988–1992), emphasized, in the OP forums what is at stake is the affirmation of a municipal project that "does not reduce itself to the sum of partial interests, or the aggregation of demands from a population of regions or social movements." The claims presented must gain legitimacy "in the quality of elements making up a municipal project." If it is true that these spaces are traversed by an uncompromising dispute among diverse interests, this dispute is resolved "not on the material level, but at the symbolic level of the public interest of the municipality."

After decades of accelerated urbanization, which constructed an urban network as large as it is differentiated and unequal, cities have gained a new centrality due to the convergence, virtually explosive and almost ungovernable in some cases, of problems, necessities, needs, and conflicts that escape resolution by centralized state policies.[10] Contrary to the traditional technocratic administration of cities, participatory forums of participation are open to a political invention capable of accommodating problems and conflicts in all their complexity. This was demonstrated, for example, in the recent experience of the Permanent Forum of Santo André, constituted in 1991. This forum included leaders from commercial and industrial business sectors; labor unions; cultural, political, and religious groups; and service clubs who met with the explicit purpose of debating and negotiating a broad public agenda. The issues addressed by the forum included alternative social policies, strategies to stimulate the region's economy, the environment, and the modernization of the public sector. In Pacheco's evaluation (1993), the Santo André forum was about negotiation, certainly difficult, that tried to reconcile sustainable economic development with the promotion of citizenship. The agenda of priorities addressed sought to confront the impact of the economic crisis and the already perceptible effects of economic restructuring, as well as to contemplate the identity of the region, which is at the center of Brazil's most modern industrialized pole and which had been the cradle of the new labor union movement and the Workers' Party.

Finally, the social crisis of the 1990s, in the wake of the processes of economic restructuring and globalization, has clearly indicated the importance of municipal public initiatives in expressing an articulation between economy and equality, development and quality of life—complicated equations that cannot be reduced to economic models and technical solutions, because they depend on social characteristics and local economies. Out of the conflictive web of interests involved, solutions must be constructed in democratic forums that articulate diverse social actors around a possible negotiation capable of initiating local development alternatives, job creation, and income generation. It is with this perspective that, at various levels, "development forums" have been created. Under different names and diverse institutional formats, these forums have become important spaces for articulation among local government officials, business executives, labor unionists, and workers.[11]

These experiments, among others, have been repeated in various municipalities using different institutional formats and, at times, have generated uncertain results. But together they have constituted an important political reference for the Brazilian public. The theme of popular participation has impacted debates in diverse arenas and already forms part of the political vocabulary beyond the narrow limits of activist groups.[12] More than one political procedure among many, the notion of participation, as well as of representation and democratic negotiation, defines the mode through which future dilemmas and possibilities are described and problematized.[13] It is the wedge through which differences and alternatives are defined in relation to the conservative proposals (and practices) advocated by the minimal state, which in practice result in the reduction of public space and the expansion of the sphere of private interest. Beyond the political or ideological rhetoric in which these questions are often formulated, the discourses register an emergent political sociability that affects the very rationality of power through the presence of collective actors who can no longer be ignored in the formulation of policies. One could say that these emergent forms of public sociability are a crucial element in the current redefinition of relations between state and society. Contrary to the traditional practice of defending corporatist interests from within the state apparatus, these spaces publicize conflicts through negotiations whereby rights become the normative reference that defines a new grammar in political life, thus preventing interests from being defended through brute force.

Constructed at the interface between state and society, these public arenas render state administrations permeable to the emergent aspirations and demands of civil society, removing from the state the exclusive monopoly of defining the agenda of society's priorities and pertinent problems. This implies another *mode of constructing a notion of public interest:* a plural and decentered notion, capable of transmitting the diversity and complexity of society, breaking therefore with the authoritarian version of society solidly rooted in Brazil's political history that is synonymous with the state and is identified with the authoritarian imposition of the law. This is the measure by which one can evaluate the democratic meaning of the experiences discussed here, which is why it is worth dwelling on this question.

It is necessary to clarify—and emphasize—that the public interest is not the direct, unmediated emanation of popular participation. Much to the contrary, the opening of spaces of representation and participation had the effect (among others) of demolishing the fiction that the popular sector is homogenous and unified. The democratic field of conflict that we are considering here is also the scenario from which the diversity of the popular sector emerges. The problems generated by this diversity are varied. First, as emphasized by Tarso Genro (1995) in commenting on his experience as mayor of Porto Alegre, social movements often espouse a "corporatist-geographic vision which tends to approach the city in a fragmented manner." Second, the dispute for public resources is often intransigent; it can internally divide the various popular organizations (Singer 1995) and mobilize old and new practices of clientelism and corporatism (Kowarick and Singer 1993). Third, urban struggles are often translated into so-called "conflicts of rights," as happened and as continues to happen in the city of São Paulo, where the struggle for housing (the right to housing) in areas of watershed protection (the right to a certain quality of life) brings to the fore the conflicts between residents, the homeless, environmental organizations, and government technicians over the meaning of public interest and the public good. These notions are always present in political discourse, but they have the peculiar quality of escaping a univocal definition, since a polysemy of meanings is also constitutive of conflict. Finally, the popular universe—or the city, to use a wider term—is traversed by different and not always convergent notions of law, rights, and justice. These different notions result in a varied and unequal sedimentation of historical experience as well as differentiated appropriations of political discourses and values that circulate in the contemporary public scene, representing a heterogeneity of methods of insertion and participation in urban life in general[14] and a synergy of these issues with cultural traditions.

Rather than taking these examples as evidence of the fragility of the popular sector or as proof of the inviolability of democratic city administrations open to the practices of participation and representation by supposedly old and new types of particularism, clientelism, and corporatism, as well as the traditionalism that often permeates popular culture, one could say that, to the contrary, it is this multifaceted and heterogeneous societal dynamic that helps qualify the meaning of the democratic construction in process in the experiments cited. These spaces of representation facilitate a negotiated construction of parameters that call for political deliberation and arbitration of conflicting interests.

In discussing the experience of OP, Tarso Genro describes the political dynamic in which the difficult "art of negotiation" requires the definition of rules establishing the criteria for the distribution of resources at the same time that they define public parameters delimiting local demands—"regulation is key because it hampers clientelism and obliges community leaders to think of their region in a more universal fashion" (Genro 1995, 22). Even if this is true, rhetoric is not unimportant, because it determines the way in which questions are problematized with reference to a democratic notion of public interest and the public good. It is in this mediation, constructed between the state and society, that one can perhaps see the dilemma posed by Marilena Chauí in commenting on the difficulties involved in constructing democracy in a society polarized by extreme need and privilege. If needs, by definition, cannot be universalized as rights, it is because they are so specific that "they are not able to transform demands of general interest of a particular social class, or much less, able to universalize and appear as rights" (Chauí 1994, 9). This antinomy can only be avoided through the enactment of a public measure that breaks the absolute hold of privilege and redefines the particularism of needs and the social movements that express them—*the democratic definition of this measure is the task of the public sphere.*

Finally, these experiences suggest that if it is true that democracy depends on the construction of the "rules of the game," then these rules cannot be reduced to the formal rationality of the constitutional order. The rules of the game are constructed through the mediation of public spaces in which circulates the logic that establishes the criteria of validity of that which is claimed as a right, and where questions pertinent to the public regulation of the institutional and legal spheres are negotiated (Habermas 1994). This is what is at stake in recent experiences in which the construction of these spaces is concomitant to the negotiated definition of rules that establish relevant criteria and priority of demands. An ethnography of the practices of negotiation in these spaces of representation would certainly offer valuable contributions to the understanding of how these rules are constructed and negotiated in terms of a *reinvention of the political contract.* It is in this sense that one can glimpse the possibility of a democratic legality that would be open to groups negotiating their differences around a *social pact of justice and equality.*

It is necessary to reaffirm here that these visions are virtualities. The dismantling of these spheres of representation through the deactivation of their power to formulate and implement public policies, or even the shrinking of these spheres into the corporative horizon of particular interests, are current possibilities. The so-called state "partnership with civil society" is an expression that has already become common. But its conservative version does not imply anything more than strategies that elide the question of public responsibility, generate a simulacrum of social policies devoid of equality and justice, reactivate local particularisms, and sanctify social and regional inequalities, when they don't outright reinforce the power of old and new local oligarchical politics (M. H. Castro 1995). But it is also possible to say that, beyond the immediate political circumstances, these experiments are anchored in a historical and societal terrain that makes them plausible, while at the same time the horizon of political debates is being defined around these experiences. It is precisely here that the virtuality of the democratic field constructed over these years can be seen as more than a mere supposition, indeed as a plausible political bet. This possible wager is evidenced in the recent history of a "classic" social movement, the labor movement.

Democratic Construction in Question: The Current Labor Movement

It might seem almost incongruous to speak of the promotion of citizenship and the enlargement of the democratic sphere of Brazilian society when we refer to the world of organized labor, especially in the 1990s. Workers who hold regular jobs in Brazil are, on the one hand, the subjects of rights consecrated in the five constitutions the country has witnessed since 1937. On the other hand, in recent years workers have become the preferential target of general policies that dismantle these rights.[15] These policies are eroding the historic victories in various spheres: the right to negotiate salaries, decent work schedules, paid weekends, advance job termination notice, the right to vacation time, access to technological education, workers' compensation, and, for women, maternity leave. They also threaten to destructure the social security system, which promises a dramatic deterioration of workers' standard of living. It is well known that this demolition of rights is a global process, occurring in countries that achieved industrial modernity through the constitution of expansive social rights as well as in those more recently industrialized countries that could perhaps aspire to a democratic regulation of labor relations. In fact, in the last decade, given that the condition of workers has begun to be seen as a condition of citizenship, the curtailment, if not destruction, of social responsibility (see Ewald 1986) for inequalities in labor has become absolutely visible. This erosion of social responsibility is evident in the already much analyzed impact of technological globalization, trade, and "financialization" of investments on the national economy. The insistent repetition of terms such as the need to "liberate productivity" and "reinvent" production to take advantage of a new "agile," "creative," or "flexible" economy are incessantly used in debates over new configurations of the economy, suggesting that workers' rights have become archaic and immobile, impeding and restraining a laudable world of new technology the implementation of which, it is admitted, will unfortunately and inevitably cause a laceration of society and the city.

At the level of values, the process of dismantling rights occurs by way of a discourse that is fundamentally antiegalitarian and destructive of workers' social guarantees—until now fundamental to social citizenship (Marshall 1967). It is argued that these uneconomical rights conspire against competitiveness, block productive and technological investment, and above all—on the level of values that interests us here—obstruct the true merit of individuals' energies and capacities, as they would tend to "accommodate" workers through social guarantees.

By depreciating social rights through an apolitical discursive construction that counterposes individual capacities in the "open market" and legally guaranteed social protection, the meaning of all institutions that make up the public patrimony of society is also undervalued; public services and public spaces are considered addictive activities with exorbitant costs with few returns. In Brazil at least, the attack on social rights is also a radical attack on public schools, hospitals, and public recreation areas, when not a direct attack on the public employees of this sector—spaces, things, and people tossed off as privileges of the past that do not fit in with the modernity that governments of the 1990s aspire to. Rights instituted in the public sphere, which shape the collective lifelong guarantees of workers, suddenly became archaic and retrograde. It is no exaggeration to assert that, in Brazil, these rights are historically the *only* base of social citizenship, embodied in systems of health, education, housing, family planning, minimum wage, jobs, elder care, access to cultural events, and so on. Rights migrate toward another so-called "modern" sphere, the sphere of the market. Seen primarily in terms of the rentability they can generate, rights are once again anchored without reference to politics.

It is almost frightening how much these arguments made by business executives, economists, and Brazilian government advisors recall the classic ideas of individualist liberalism of the nineteenth century—in an impoverished and decontextualized version. These new arguments reinterpret the conception of inequality as a matter of individual responsibility, in a disquieting return to the beginning of the Brazilian century, when social rights did not exist institutionally and were driven by conceptions of private philanthropy.

How can we speak of an enlargement of the democratic field of struggle for rights emerging from a deepened perspective on citizenship for workers in a country like Brazil, infamous for maintaining the most inequitable income distribution in the world and the lowest possible wage levels in relation to real and potential productivity? If the effects of globalization cause, even in what is considered a civilized, developed society such as pre-Thatcher Great Britain, a considerable deepening of inequalities—"the era of a new barbarism," as Hobsbawm (1995) calls it—how can one even imagine that a horizon of democratic social rights could still emerge in a society such as that of Brazil? Given that in Brazil a structure of social relations has always been radically heterogeneous and unequal and has never been able to produce even a liberal identity of citizen, such policies appear doomed from the start, promising only greater unemployment, increased precariousness in work conditions and labor relations, and growing inequity and exclusion. Would it not be more logical to conclude (as the facts increasingly seem to suggest) that it is impossible for such a democratic field to be introduced beyond the formal institutions of political power, and that the rooting of citizenship in the day-to-day sociabilities of this society, as has occurred since the 1980s, has only been an imagined possibility (Chauí 1994)? And, if so, is it necessary to conform ourselves to the "inevitability"—a word so often repeated today by those who judge themselves modern—of the end of universal values of equality, citizenship, and the idea of social rights?

In the second part of this chapter, we will try to show that this inevitability does not exist, not only because of the evident theoretical fragility on which it is premised—grounded in putative technological determinisms and modernizing economic imperatives—but because the implementation of massive social exclusion would depend today on an existing public space of conflict, composed of social subjects already constituted within this public space who are now recognized on the Brazilian political scene. What is at stake in such a space is the political and democratic meanings that the economic modifications might induce. This public space is also the place of action, debate, and critical political analysis, which has been constituting itself through the very expansion of workers' organized participation.[16] As a democratic field that was opened in the conflictive negotiations between social movements and local governments over living conditions, the labor movement of the 1990s—characterized by a relatively short yet spirited history of internal organizational changes and deep transformations of values—has been able to propose a civilized and democratic path for the political administration of the transformations underway in Brazilian society. The labor movement has taken on the task of balancing economic policy with the possibility of greater equity.

This path makes unprecedented use of a democratic notion of citizenship to lay the foundation for new actions on the part of workers and unions, thereby trying to reverse their relative loss of control and power over the regulation of a labor market shaped by what some have called the "passive insertion" of Brazil into the process of globalization (Mattoso 1995). The importance of this politically constructed notion of citizenship has been conspicuous, since the beginning of the 1990s, in the most organized segments of the labor movement, mobilized to dispute the cultural and political meaning of the regulation of labor relations.

A comparison between the modes of labor *confrontation* with employers and government in the early 1980s (consisting of frequent and effective strikes organized around industrial regulations and union intermediation [Noronha 1991]) and the posture and discourse of *negotiation* of the 1990s (when the professional unions and union confederations initiated and insisted in taking part in the construction of the regulations) clearly shows this transformation. It is further evidenced by the fact that a new conception of citizenship has begun to be supported by a strong union appreciation of the need for labor to participate in political institutions that make decisions affecting all of society, as these decisions also shape the labor market. The contrasts between the mode of *confrontation* of the 1980s and *negotiation* of the 1990s clearly attest to the working-class apprenticeship in citizenship, which distances workers from a dual tradition that places unions under either the unilateral dictates of the Labor Ministry (Ministério do Trabalho) or the ideologized space where the oppositionist elements tended to anchor themselves. This cultural and political trajectory also differentiates itself from the liberal notion of citizenship, as it is now conceived as active collective participation in dialogue and negotiation. Labor's new conception of citizenship also departs from the corporatist-state tradition[17] as it conceives of participation as involving the entire society: a participation in decisions that regulate a common existence.

When negotiating government social security policy in February 1996, Vicente Paulo da Silva, the president of CUT (Central Unica dos Trabalhadores), Brazil's most powerful labor federation, declared that one could not permit "CUT [to] become a ghetto," and that "a labor confederation which bases itself in the discourse of 'no' stands outside of social reality." On the same occasion, the press publicized that more than 80 percent of organized workers (principally steelworkers) supported negotiation as the best way to influence governmental policies,[18] once again illustrating the horizon that had been taking shape since 1991 in which the redefinition of an active citizenship of workers was turning toward the active construction of democratic forms of social regulation, in dramatic contrast to sedimented ways of thinking about unions in relation to institutions—a process that represents, undoubtedly, an alternative definition of politics.

By demonstrating how powerful a project of active citizenship can be—anchored in the continual constitution of subjects who can universalize their victories and break with institutional constraints through processes of permanent negotiation—this redefinition of the political practice of workers met a perhaps unanticipated obstacle: the limited disposition of democratic governments to construct partnerships with society or even to make concessions to the expansion of civic power. The formal postdictatorship democratic regime reproduces the classic pitfalls of self-defense of governmental power by protecting its monopoly of decisionmaking; such a monopoly historically has produced a legacy of exclusion and political demobilization of the population even stronger than that enforced by capital.

The Brazilian government's traditional conception of power as having "owners"—to evoke the expression of Raimundo Faoro—is deeply rooted. Regardless of the political regime, the Brazilian government has done whatever possible to distance itself from the republican ideal: It conceives of modernity as a society that marches in orderly fashion toward the future through governmental clairvoyance, thus rendering it immune to the destabilizing dangers of social conflict. Faithful to the authoritarianism through which society came to know so-called "modernity" in Brazil (Chauí 1985), a significant part of public opinion tends to delegate this precise role to public officials.

Since the late 1980s, however, it has been hoped that legitimately elected officials could take a step forward in creating a democracy spanning beyond the political regime to encompass society. Some local governments, who do not fear association with organized sectors of the city, have taken this step with some success. Just as a conservative version of this state-society "partnership" can reactivate local particularisms in the case of popular movements, the same can be seen in certain cases of labor negotiations. Undoubtedly, the perspectives opened up by the politicization of working-class citizenship displaces older dominant practices *assigning value to the working-class world* wherein the popular sectors are seen as good children, at times excessive or violent, at times docile, but whose needs have nothing to do with the public sphere.

Citizenship and Workers: Recent Studies

Three recent experiments demonstrate the real possibility of a democratic regulation of labor rights—and at the same time, the state's and capital's resistance to giving it a permanent institutional statute. The first and largest of these experiments occurred in the already much analyzed sectoral councils (1991–1994), most notably in the automobile sector, which resulted in a successful agreement.[19] This agreement—made possible by the efforts of labor unions to transform the council into a real decisionmaking forum—benefited business owners, workers, and the government alike and succeeded in creating unprecedented mechanisms for defining policy directions. As the literature points out, the sectoral council proved that it was possible for antagonistic actors to recognize the legitimacy of conflicting interests. An alternative to corporatist interests emerged, rooted in true labor union representation in which the state, workers, and employers came to perceive one another as equal agents with divergent interests. The act of negotiating would no longer occur through the mediation of the state, but through the recognition of the autonomy of all social agents involved. Above all, as Oliveira points out, this experience demonstrated that a "new contractuality" can give rise to the democratic regulation of labor relations. Actors are seen as capable of constituting, through negotiation, a common, more just, and legitimate measure of the responsibilities and rights of economic life. At the same time, as Cardoso and Comin point out, this new contractuality requires the strong politicization of relations between classes and interest groups, making them publicly responsible for decisions capable of affecting a large portion of the labor market. Along these lines, however, a third path between the extremes of the deregulation of workers' rights brought about by the oscillations of the market and the traditional legalistic and authoritarian regulation of the state appeared on the horizon.

A second experiment articulated by organized labor has far-reaching consequences; it proposes a new system of participatory labor relations that promotes shared responsibility for regulation and market relations. CUT, as well as other labor union confederations, has called for the national adoption and implementation of a collective work contract as the central instrument of this regulation. This contract would represent a new pact between state and society in which labor conflicts would find a terrain for the permanent collective negotiation of its own standards. Envisioned as stemming from the actual experiences of negotiation of the more representative unions, this instrument would take account of differences among labor situations in a very diverse market while treating different categories of workers under a common, although not unitary or abstract, conception of citizenship. This collective contract would have the power to end the currently obligatory interference of the labor courts in the "solution" of conflicts—that is, with the courts' legalistic normative and monologic power over labor disputes. If implemented, this model would require modifications in the functioning of labor unions to make them more representative; some "radical" versions of the proposal (around which there is little consensus) would eradicate reductionistic conceptions of labor organizations such as obligatory professional unity (unions organized through professional categories defined by law), the monopoly of representation within a given territorial base (one professional union for each municipality), and the imposition of the union tax (whereby each Brazilian worker is obliged by law to give one day's pay per year to the union, whether that worker is associated with the union or not; this tax is collected by the government and redistributed to the unions). The fact that the union confederations have initiated internal and external discussions and proposed an alternative jurisdiction for labor relations—which was first seriously considered by the Ministry of Labor in the Barelli administration—shows how much the notion of autonomy is sought as a basis of citizenship and political dialogue.[20]

The difficult question regarding the function of labor courts and their legalistic proceedings in the implementation of labor rights is a good example of this. The judicial regulation of labor relations in Brazil has been the mandate of a specific branch of the judiciary since the 1930s; any and all labor conflicts, individual or collective, must pass through its office, so that any direct negotiation has no legal contractual value. It would be impossible to show in the scope of this chapter the extent to which innovations in labor relations are impeded by this type of legalism, and the degree to which the bureaucratization of labor relations and contracts hinder the exercise of rights. The act of challenging labor courts' procedures and criteria in the 1990s bears a direct relationship to the stronger unions' consciousness of their autonomous capacity to create dialogue over diverging and conflictive interests. On the one hand, this points to a revitalization of historical rights—already consecrated worker protections—through new exigencies. On the other, unions and jurists involved in the quest for renovated labor rights are also conscious of the flip side of the coin: the existence of weak labor unions with little bargaining power, for whom this institutionalized labor courts system is a reference for the rights of the poorest workers—even if they are unable to understand the criteria this system uses, the language it speaks, its procedures, its bureaucracy, and its slow pace. The enormous distance between the meaning of equality lived in labor relations and the bureaucratized institutionalization of rights creates in the culture of the average worker a rupture between the existence of these rights and the form in which they experience the rights. Nothing illustrates this with as much eloquence as the common expressions "looking for my rights" *(procurar os direitos)* or, worse, "the hunt for rights" *(caçar os direitos),* rights that are hidden in some mysterious place in the law and that demand long procedures for recovery that true citizens could hardly be expected to endure (N. Sousa 1994; J. Sousa 1993; Caldeira 1984; Santos 1995).

Undoubtedly, workers' demonstrated desire and competence in proposing measures and acting at the institutional level completely changes the representations of state power that had previously pervaded the daily life of unions and their critics. A condition of citizenship that is conquered, and not (obligatorily) received, transforms the acceptance of the authority of government measures, since such measures must be subjected to profound modifications emerging from the heart of organized society. Certainly governments of the 1990s have considered this dynamic to be more than an inconvenience, and their appeals to the logic of the monopoly of decisionmaking has become ever more frequent. Not only have governments refused to institutionally strengthen these experiments in worker democracy, they increasingly evoke styles of power to contain the expansion of the processes and actors that might widen the democratic field. This governmental reaction brings to mind the description of the birth of modern politics as historians of the eighteenth century convey it: Modern politics seems to demand the banishment of common people from the proper space of politics, but combines during the transition with an ancient conception of the public as the captive audience of a performance offered to them by the state (Elias 1986; Habermas 1986).

The governments of the 1990s propose a different place for the workers' citizenship to be exercised, and this constitutes the third novel—even if ambiguous—experiment in labor regulation: firm-by-firm negotiations, said to be "free" because not subject to wider collective agreements. It seems counterintuitive that even this proposal for "free negotiation" involves detailed rules dictated by presidential decree and promotes a fragmented form of the corporatism so condemned by the government. It is perhaps even more contradictory when we consider, despite the professed democratic commitments of governing officials and business leaders, that public violence is still often used to deter social movements and strikes. The oil refinery strike (of April–June 1995) is emblematic of the contradictions of the realm of rights in Brazilian society, as the state resorted to an old public resource of control over labor relations to repress the strike—the military hand, which was permitted to intervene by the political manipulation of legal formalisms. The strike was described by the press, with justification, as an actual war carried out by the government against the strikers, in which careful strategies were implemented to impose a humiliating defeat followed by veritable bombardments on public opinion. Once again, Brazilian society returned to a time when workers appeared as the inverse of citizens and the reverse of modernity: Corporatist, insidious, backward, and arrogant, this reverted society sought to break workers' spines and portray them as people without virtue who could not possibly contribute to the future course of the public interest.

The recent and prodigiously rapid history of the dispute over the meaning of democracy produces important complexities enabling us to opt for either a happy or unhappy ending with respect to changes in the relationship between culture and politics since the early 1980s, when the democratic inventions emanating from social movements and the revitalized labor movement erupted as new actors on the political stage (Sader 1988). If the proposals for democratic negotiation of the 1990s demonstrate the maturity of those inventions, then nothing precludes the continued use of physical or symbolic violence (at all levels) in the dispute over who has the legitimate power of regulation. And more, nothing precludes the indifference of a large part of Brazilian society to the complete absence of rights in informal and illegal work situations, in double shifts endured by much of the female labor force, or in the horror of extreme situations of child labor and slave labor—all of which are illegal situations that are nonetheless tolerated in practice. To the contrary, it is within this traditional context of indifference to the absence of minimal social rights and guarantees for poor and miserable workers—mute witnesses to extreme Brazilian inequality—that the politics of pure and simple destitution of rights (or the threat to "flexibilize" those few rights remaining) is taking shape. It is worth reiterating that the social and political tolerance of the symbolic and physical violence of certain work conditions is also the fruit of years of legalistic and bureaucratic imposition of social rights—which led workers to forget the very meaning of having rights—and that this tolerance continues to reproduce the unequal context in which a revived liberalism is being implanted.

However, a transition occurred. A partnership in the definition and regulation of rights has already been experienced as something possible. Paths have been forged, in the world of labor, toward a new notion of citizenship based on widened social responsibility and the construction of a common measure for negotiating divergent interests from which violence and arbitrary power could be reasonably purged. This transition also includes a new union presence (of workers and also of some businesspeople) in larger spheres of citizenship, indicating that the expression "public classes" (utilized by Francisco de Oliveira) goes beyond its strict meaning in the professional world. For example, the constant presence of CUT in demonstrations and antiracist and antisexist struggles, as well as in environmental struggles, and the inclusion of these struggles in their worker education programs; the pledge of some business sectors to commit to children's rights by curtailing child labor; and campaigns against hunger all give these "public classes" a constitutive role in the definition of public responsibility for social inequalities. But it remains for the government to enter into forceful institutional dialogue with these sectors of civil society.

Produced by collective action ever in the process of transformation, the labor movement since the 1980s has modified the meaning and image of the relationship between the state and society in a democratic institutional context. From an almost archaic conception of governmental legitimacy—wherein the spectacle of power is personified by public officials who are the guarantors of order and around whom a heterogeneous, inequitable, and conflictive society is to be united while remaining confined to their proper social places—with the entrance of the labor movement into the public sphere, politics is unveiled as a space that can also be proximate and shared. Politics comes to be seen as a conjunction of decisions that, while regulating common existence, should welcome the organized participation of a divided society, which although unequal is capable of interacting through criteria constructed on understanding (Oliveira 1991).

The recognition that the union movement has constituted itself as one of the principal actors in a civil society unprecedented in Brazilian political history indicates that it is possible, although difficult, for democracy to also appear as a strong social force. From this angle, it doesn't matter that the impact provoked by the emergence of this side of the union movement—still poorly digested by society and by the government—has resulted in dramatic power struggles over the democratic and civilizational possibilities. In the end, it has already been demonstrated that it is the action of organized citizens that constructs a nation of citizens, and that this depends today on a field of complex and rapidly changing conflicts, which is far from being exhausted.

What has been demonstrated is not, obviously, the possibility of narrow and slightly corporatist pacts between unions, business, and the government, and even less the conception of "popular sovereignty" as a transference of political power from top to bottom. The significance of the recent history of the labor movement—as well as the trajectories of organized social movements—is that it allows us to envision a path that might transform values and conceptions of power and politically authoritarian social hierarchies through widened participation in the rules governing the common good. It is also a path through which different individuals, social groups, and citizens can begin to understand themselves as belonging to political society. And, for now, it is the only known path through which to arrive at a form of more genuine citizenship capable of combining the freedom to participate in public affairs with the legitimacy of a conflictive, yet shared, construction of democratic norms.

* * *

If it is through the lens of this emerging civil society that one can catch a glimpse of democratic utopia in contemporary Brazil, it is also true that it is through this lens that current dilemmas are concretized. On one hand, to what point will this emerging institutionality be capable of rooting citizenship in social practices, extending rights beyond the most organized groups, and rising above what Wanderley Guilherme dos Santos (1993) defines as the "regulatory confinement of citizenship"? Though this is a persistent question in Brazilian history, it is today redefined in the convergence of the country's long history of inequalities and exclusions, the new cleavages and differences produced by economic restructuring that challenges the classic agenda of universal rights, and the current dismantling of already precarious public services that further narrows the horizon of legitimacy of social rights.

The possibilities for the democratic field constructed over the last fifteen years seem today constrained between the weight of tradition and the force of a conservative project that is removed from the societal spheres of representation, negotiation, and dialogue and that neutralizes the ethical dimensions of justice and equality in the name of economic efficacy and technical rationality. The big question on the agenda in these times of change is how the future of Brazil is being decided at the very crossroads of these uncertain alternatives.

Notes

1. The notion of a "social movement" is here used in a broad and generic sense, as its definition, or at least its contextualization, is not among the objectives of this text. In regard to the notion of social movements, see Alvarez 1997; Doimo 1995; Paoli 1995.

2. These are groups of people who have made a political appearance in the urban centers of the country. In discussing the formation of the recent political scene, it is also important to note the struggles of rural workers, especially landless populations, which have been protagonists in conflicts in various regions of the country. Also, indigenous populations, since the 1970s, have been occupying the Brazilian public scene in defense of their ethnic traditions and in their claims for solutions to the land conflicts surrounding their territories.

3. As soon as the constitutional process was inaugurated in 1985, social movements, church groups, and technical assistance groups launched the National Movement for the Constitution, which articulated, in various regions and cities of the country, the Popular Pro-Participation Plenary Sessions for the Constitution. As Ana Amélia Silva notes, these plenary sessions synthesized and articulated a wide range of popular claims, simultaneously estab-

lishing a new relationship between the legal institutional camp and social movements: "In giving a new importance to the practices of negotiation, popular forces were represented at a high institutional level, articulating their demands together with elected officials dedicated to popular interests, which led to the creation of new rights. On the other side, the political learning of this experience also occurred in confrontations with powerful lobbies that articulated their interests together with conservative elected officials at the same time as popular pressure was put on the Congress, transforming the constituent assembly deliberations into a large space of political struggle. The big qualitative jump for popular participation . . . appeared in March of 1987, when the internal administration of the constituent assembly deliberations opened the possibility, through mechanisms of legislative popular initiatives . . . of elaboration and defense of popular amendments to the Constitution. The fruit of these mobilization efforts was translated into Popular Amendments on diverse subjects, which gathered more than 12 million signatures which were delivered to the federal constituent assembly" (1991, 5–6). This same process was undertaken and continued in state general plans and was even further replicated at the municipal level, with the elaboration and promulgation of municipal constitutions and also with the constitutional requirement that cities of over twenty thousand inhabitants had to design municipal general plans. For more information, see Silva and Saule 1993; Ribeiro 1995; Soares 1993; Baierle 1992.

4. With different levels of representation and power, diverse "consultative" and "deliberative" councils were established at the federal, state, and municipal levels; these legally sanctioned councils were created alongside public forums that had not been legally specified, but that were driven by the principals of participatory democracy blessed by the new constitution. On the social policies related to housing and "urban reform," see A. Silva 1994.

5. "There was a relatively widespread occurrence of municipal budgets being created with societal participation. In eighteen municipalities (among the fifty researched), municipal constitutions instituted this process, and only in three cases were no participatory structures established, whereby participation was vaguely defined as only consultative" (Ribeiro 1995, 120). Whether the type of council is representative, deliberative, or consultative, "of the fifty city laws studied, only three did not create councils, which represents an extraordinary multiplication of this form of mediation between society and local government" (127). These councils are envisioned to play a role in the areas of health, education, the environment, economic development, issues involving children and adolescents, and others.

6. Despite oligarchical control over judicial decisions in these municipalities, Teixeira notes that there has been a more rigorous fiscalization of the municipalities by the State Audit Office (Tribunal de Contas), the agency that decides the validity and legality of municipal expenditures; and that the number of rejected expenditures has grown, leading to many criminal investigations being brought to the courts (Tribunal de Justiça).

7. Various descriptions of these experiences can be found in Daniel 1994a, 1994b; Baierle 1992; Kowarick and Singer 1993; Pacheco 1993, 1995; Caccia-Bava 1995; Ferreira Netto 1995; Villas-Bôas and Telles 1995.

8. See Daniel 1994a; Ribeiro 1995; Doimo 1995; Alvarez 1997.

9. These experiences are not exclusive to the municipal administrations of the Workers' Party. Cities under the administration of other parties are becoming important references for mayors and political officials of diverse political orientations. For a description of some of these experiences outside of Porto Alegre, see Villas-Bôas and Telles 1995.

10. In the precise words of Dowbor (1993), "this situation means the emergence of millions of local dramas, reflecting serious problems related to housing, health, pollution,

schools, water supply systems, special programs needed to address extreme poverty, sanitation projects, etc. Thus, the municipalities begin to encounter an explosive situation which demands agile intervention which goes beyond the traditional routines of urban cosmetics—these problems demand large infrastructure projects, social policies and job-creation programs, involving local strategies and the stimulation of economic activities" (6). See also Pacheco 1995 and Rocha 1995.

11. Descriptions of these experiences can be found in Pacheco 1993; Caccia-Bava 1995; Ferreira Netto 1995; Paiva 1993; Ferreira et al. 1994. For a more general discussion, see Dowbor 1993; Coelho 1995; Pacheco 1995.

12. This is illustrated by the creation of the National Forum of Popular Participation in Democratic Municipal Administrations in 1990. With the objective of promoting the exchange and systematization of experiences in progress in municipal administrations, department heads, municipal consultants, researchers, and representatives of social movements, political parties, and technical assistance organizations meet in the forum. Since 1992, conferences and meetings have been organized in various regions of the country, bringing together city council members, mayors, and local political representatives to debate questions about the mechanisms of popular participation, local development alternatives, and the participatory budget process. On the theme of popular participation, see Villas-Bôas and Telles 1995.

13. See Daniel 1994a; Genro 1995; Caccia-Bava 1995; Dowbor 1993. For an outline of the discussion in the Latin American context, see Cunill 1991.

14. The conflict that arose around street vendors in the first months of the Workers' Party administration in São Paulo (1988–1992) was paradigmatic. The conflict involved the use of city spaces by merchants, pedestrians, and a myriad of street vendors who, in the context of social crisis and unemployment, had begun to occupy the downtown sidewalks, selling a variety of products. There were enormous differences among the street vendor groups as to the way in which they should defend their right to the use of the city, mobilizing different and not always convergent criteria of legitimacy and justice; these groups included "historical" street vendors, seniors and the disabled, recently unemployed moonlighters, and workers who sought to supplement their low wages in the formal economy. Arbitration was difficult between the notion of "acquired privileges" derived from the clientelist practices of previous administrations and the wider criteria of social justice, leading to exclusive and corporatist versions of the right to work and, in this case, the right to have access to the city's public spaces.

15. In Brazil, since 1942, labor legislation has required that a standard work contract with a firm respect the following principal social rights guaranteed by the constitution: minimum wage, extra pay for overtime work, paid weekends, vacation time, advance notice of job termination, an extra month's salary at the end of each year, additional payment for dangerous or unhealthy working conditions, higher pay for night work, fully paid pregnancy leave, and social security benefits. See Gomes 1979 and Paoli 1987 on the historical context of the building of these rights.

16. Relying on popular participation, this process differentiates itself from the formation of the modern bourgeois public space of the European eighteenth century, described by Habermas, which excluded any type of popular participation in the debate of political criticism (cf. Habermas 1986).

17. On the original meaning of Brazilian corporatism, see the clarifying work of Ângela Maria Carneiro de Araújo (1994).

18. *Journal do Brasil,* January 28, 1996; *O Estado de São Paulo,* February 4, 1996.

19. Brazil's tripartite sectoral councils were concerned with negotiating industrial sector policies. Labor union representatives, business owners from all segments of the industrial sector, and government officials met to define a whole conjunction of measures and policies for the productive sector. It is important to note that these meetings occurred not only to define policies of work relations but also industrial sector policy as a whole. The most successful sectoral council initiative was in the automobile industry; in a moment of crisis, negotiators redefined production levels, investments, jobs, car prices, and taxes. See Oliveira et al. 1993; Cardoso and Comin 1995; N. A. Castro 1985.

20. On the proposal of this "national system of labor relations" see Siqueira Neto 1991, 1994; Ministério do Trabalho 1994; V. Silva 1994.

References

Alvarez, Sonia E. 1997. "Reweaving the Fabric of Collective Action: Social Movements and Challenges to 'Actually Existing Democracy' in Brazil." In *Between Resistance and Revolution: Cultural Politics and Social Protest,* ed. R. Fox and O. Starn, 83–117. New Brunswick, N.J.: Rutgers University Press.

Araújo, Ângela Maria Carneiro de. 1994. "Construindo o Consentimento: Corporativismo e Trabalhadores no Brasil dos anos 30." Ph.D. thesis, Universidade Estadual de Campinas, São Paulo.

Baierle, Sérgio Gregório. 1992. "Um Novo Princípio Ético-Político: Prática Social e Sujeitos nos Movimentos Populares Urbanos em Porto Alegre." Master's thesis, Universidade Estadual de Campinas, São Paulo.

Braga, Elza M. F., and Irlys A. Barreira, eds. 1993. *A Política da Escassez: Lutas Urbanas e Programas Sociais Governamentais.* Fortaleza: Fundação Demácrito Rocha.

Caccia-Bava, Sílvio. 1995. "Dilemas da Gestão Municipal Democrática." In *Governabilidade e Pobreza no Brasil,* ed. L. Valladares and M. Coelho. Rio de Janeiro: Civilização Brasileira.

Caldeira, Teresa. 1984. *A Política dos Outros.* São Paulo: Brasiliense.

Cardoso, Adalberto, and Alvaro Comin. 1995. "Câmaras Setoriais, Modernização Produtiva e Democratização nas Relações de Trabalho no Brasil: a Experiência do Setor Automobilístico." In *A Máquina e o Equilibrista,* ed. N. Castro. São Paulo: Paz e Terra.

Castro, Maria Helena. 1995. "Reforma do estado e democratização do poder." In *Poder Local, Participação Popular e Construção da Cidadania,* ed. R. Villa-Bôas and V. da Silva Telles. São Paulo: Pólis, Fórum Nacional de Participação Popular.

Castro, Nadya Araújo, ed. 1985. A Máquina e o Equilibrista. São Paulo: Paz e Terra.

Chauí, Marilena. 1985. *Cultura e Democracia.* São Paulo: Editora Moderna.

______. 1993. "Uma Opção Radical e Moderna: Democracia Cultural." In *Experiências de Gestão Cultural Democrática,* ed. H. Faria. São Paulo: Pólis, Publicação Pólis no. 12.

______. 1994. "São Paulo: Violência, Autoritarismo e Democracia." *Revista Caramelo* 7:34–45.

Coelho, Franklin Dias. 1995. "Reestruturação Econômica e as Novas Estratégias de Desenvolvimento Local." Mimeographed.

Cunill, Nuria. 1991. *Participación Ciudadana: Dilemas y Perspectivas para democratización de los estados latinoamericanos.* Caracas: CLAD.

Daniel, Celso. 1994a. "Gestão Local e Participação da Sociedade." In *Participação Popular nos Governos Locais,* ed. R. Villas-Bôas. São Paulo: Pólis, Publicação Pólis no. 14.

______. 1994b. "Governo Local e Reforma Urbana num Quadro de Crise Estrutural." In *Globalização, Fragmentação e Reforma Urbana: O Futuro das Cidades Brasileiras na Crise,* ed. L. Ribeiro and O. Santos, Jr. Rio de Janeiro: Civilização Brasileira.

Doimo, Ana Maria. 1995. *A Vez e a Voz do Popular: Movimentos Sociais e Participação Política no Brasil pós–70.* Rio de Janeiro: Relume-Dumará.

Dowbor, Ladislau. 1993. "Governabilidade e Descentralização." Mimeographed.

Elias, Norbert. 1986. *A Sociedade da Corte.* Lisbon: Estampa.

Ewald, François. 1986. *L'État-Providence.* Paris: Bernard Grasset.

Ferreira, Ana Luiza, et al. 1994. *O desafio de ser governo.* São Paulo: Pólis, Publicação Pólis no. 18.

Ferreira Netto, Lino. 1995. "A Atuação do Município no Combate à Pobreza: Possibilidades e Limitações." In *Governabilidade e Pobreza no Brasil,* ed. L. Valladares and M. Coelho. Rio de Janeiro: Civilização Brasileira.

Freitas, Antônio Rodrigo. 1995. "Direitos dos Trabalhadores: Regulamentação x Desregulamentação." Mimeographed.

Genro, Tarso. 1995. "Reforma do Estado e Democratização do Poder Local." In *Poder Local, Participação Popular e Construção da Cidadania,* ed. R. Villas-Bôas and V. Telles. São Paulo: Pólis, Fórum Nacional de Participação Popular.

Gomes, Angela Castro. 1979. *Burguesia e Trabalho.* Rio de Janeiro: Campus

Habermas, Jürgen. 1986. *L'Espace Public: Archeologie de la Publicité Comme Dimension Constitutive de la Société Bourgeoise.* Paris: Payot.

______. 1990. "Soberania Popular como Procedimento." *Novos Estudos* 26:100–113.

______. 1994. "Struggles for Recognition in the Democratic Constitutional State." In *Multiculturalism: Examining the Politics of Recognition,* ed. A. Gutmann. Princeton: Princeton University Press.

Hall, Michael. n.d. "On Widening the Scope of Latin American Working-Class History." Mimeographed.

Hall, Michael, and Paulo Sérgio Pinheiro. 1979. *A Classe Operária no Brasil, 1889–1930.* São Paulo: Brasiliense.

Hobsbawm, Eric J. 1995. *A Era dos Extremos: O Breve Século XX.* São Paulo: Companhia das Letras.

Kowarick, Lúcio, and André Singer. 1993. "A Experiência do Partido dos Trabalhadores na Prefeitura de São Paulo." *Novos Estudos* 35:195–216.

Lefort, Claude. 1983. "Direitos do Homem e Política." In *A Invenção Democrática.* São Paulo: Brasiliense.

Marshall, Thomas Humphrey. 1967. *Cidadania, Classe Social e Status.* Rio de Janeiro: Zahar.

Mattoso, Jorge. 1995. *A Desordem do Trabalho.* São Paulo: Scritta.

Ministério do Trabalho. 1994. *Forum Nacional sobre Contrato Coletivo e Relações de Trabalho no Brasil.* Brasília: Ministério do Trabalho.

Noronha, Eduardo. 1991. "A Explosão das Greves na Década de 80." In *O Sindicalismo Brasileiro nos Anos 80,* ed. A. Boito. São Paulo: Paz e Terra.

O'Donnell, Guillermo. 1993. "Sobre o Estado, a Democratização e Alguns Problemas Conceituais." *Novos Estudos* 36 (July):123–146.

Oliveira, Francisco de. 1991. "Uma Alternativa Democrática ao Liberalismo." In *A Democracia como Proposta.* Rio de Janeiro: Ibase.

______. 1994. "A Prova dos Nove: Conflitos de Classe, Publicização e Nova Contratualidade." In *O Brasil no Rastro da Crise,* ed. E. Diniz et al. São Paulo: Hucitec.

Olivieira, Francisco de, et al. 1993. "Quanto Melhor, Melhor: O Acordo das Montadoras." *Novos Estudos* 36:3–8.

Pacheco, Regina Sílvia. 1993. "Iniciativa Econômica Local: A Experiência do ABC." In *Parceria Público-Privado,* ed. E. Lodovici and G. Bernareggi. São Paulo: Summus.

______. 1995. "Gestão Metropolitana no Brasil: Arranjos Institucionais em Debate. In *Governabilidade e Pobreza no Brasil,* ed. L. Valladares and M. Coelho. Rio de Janeiro: Civilização Brasileira.

Paiva, Andrade E. 1993. "Geração de Emprego e Renda na Gestão Popular da Prefeitura de Volta Redonda." *Proposta* 59 (December):45–48.

Paoli, Maria Célia. 1987. "Labour, Law, and the State in Brazil." Ph.D. thesis, University of London.

______. 1992. "Citizenship, Inequalities, and Democracy: The Making of a Public Space in Brazilian Experience." *Social and Legal Studies* 1:143–159.

______. 1995. "Movimentos Sociais no Brasil: Em Busca de um Estatuto Político." In *Movimentos Sociais e Democracia no Brasil,* ed. M. Hellmann. São Paulo: Marco Zero.

Ribeiro, Luiz Cezar Queiroz. 1995. "A (In)governabilidade da Cidade? Avanços e Desafios da Reforma Urbana." In *Governabilidade e Pobreza no Brasil,* ed. L. Valladares and M. Coelho. Rio de Janeiro: Civilização Brasileira.

Rocha, Sonia. 1995. "Governabilidade e Pobreza: O Desafio dos Números." In *Governabilidade e Pobreza no Brasil,* ed. L. Valladares and M. Coelho. Rio de Janeiro: Civilização Brasileira.

Rodrigues, Iram J. 1990. *Comissão de Fábrica e Trabalhadores na Indústria.* São Paulo: Cortez/Fase.

Sader, Eder. 1988. *Quando Novos Personagens entram em Cena.* São Paulo: Paz e Terra.

Santos, Boaventura de Sousa. 1995. "O Estado e o Direito na Transição Pós-Moderna." In *Pela mão de Alice.* São Paulo: Cortez/Fase.

Santos, Wanderley Guilherme dos. 1993. "Fronteiras do Estado Mínimo." In *Razões da Desordem.* Rio de Janeiro: Rocco.

Silva, Ana Amélia. 1991. *Reforma Urbana e o Direito à Cidade.* São Paulo: Pólis, Publicação Pólis no. 1.

______. 1994. "Dimensões da Interlocução Pública: Cidade, Movimentos Sociais e Direitos." In *O Brasil no Rastro da Crise,* ed. E. Diniz et al. São Paulo: Hucitec.

Silva, Ana Amélia, and Nélson Saule. 1993. *A Cidade faz a sua Constituição.* São Paulo: Pólis, Publicação Pólis no. 10.

Silva, Vicente Paulo da. 1994. "Contrato Coletivo de Trabalho." *Folha de São Paulo* (October 12).

Singer, Paul. 1995. "Poder Público e Organizações Populares no Combate à Pobreza: A Experiência do Governo Luiza Erundina em São Paulo." In *Governabilidade e Pobreza no Brasil,* ed. L. Valladares and M. Coelho. Rio de Janeiro: Civilização Brasileira.

Siqueira Neto, José Francisco. 1991. *Contrato Coletivo de Trabalho: Perspectiva de Rompimento com a Legalidade Repressiva.* São Paulo: Ltr.

______. 1994. "A Modernização Necessária." *Teoria e Debate* 23:18–23.

Soares, José Arlindo. 1993. "Lei Orgânica e Plano Diretor. Limites Políticos e Novos Reconhecimentos." In *Brasil Urbano: Cenários da Ordem e da Desordem,* ed. E. Nascimento and I. Barreira. Rio de Janeiro: Notrya.

Soler, Salvador. 1992. "Estado e Movimentos Sociais: Entre a Conquista e a Concessão." *Cadernos do CEAS* 136:59–69.

Sousa, José Geraldo de, Jr. 1993. "Movimentos Sociais: O Sujeito Coletivo do Direito." In *Lições de Direito Alternativo,* ed. E. Arruda. São Paulo: Ltr.

Sousa, Nair Heloísa Bicalho de. 1994. "Trabalhadores Pobres e Cidadania: A Experiência de Exclusão e da Rebeldia na Construção Civil." Ph.D. thesis, University of São Paulo.

Teixeira, Elenaldo. 1992. "Cidadania e Poder Local." *Cadernos do CEAS* 136:46–58.

______. 1993. "Participação Popular e Poder Local: Um Exercício de Cidadania." *Cadernos CRH* 18:49–76.

Telles, Vera da Silva. 1994. "Sociedade Civil e os Caminhos (Incertos) da Cidadania." *São Paulo em Perspectiva* 8 (2):7–14.

______. 1996. "As Novas Faces da Cidadania: Uma Introdução." In *Novas Faces da Cidadania: Identidades Políticas e Estratégias Culturais,* ed. CEBRAP, Cadernos de Pesquisa no. 4. São Paulo: Editorial Entrelinhas.

Villas-Bôas, Renata. 1994. "Os Canais Institucionais de Participação Popular." In *Participação Popular nos Governos Locais,* ed. R. Villas-Bôas. São Paulo: Pólis, Publicação Pólis no. 14.

______. 1995. "Conflitos e Negociações com o Comércio Ambulante na Gestão Municipal de Luiza Erundina em São Paulo." Mimeographed.

Villas-Bôas, Renata, and Vera da Silva Telles, eds. 1995. *Poder Local, Participação Popular e Construção da Cidadania.* São Paulo: Pólis, Fórum Nacional de Participação Popular.

Chapter Four

New Subjects of Rights? Women's Movements and the Construction of Citizenship in the "New Democracies"

VERÓNICA SCHILD

Vast networks of professionals and activists who are feminists, or who are at least sensitive to women's issues, are at work today in Chile and other Latin American countries. These networks are not only responsible for sustaining the work of grassroots organizations and nongovernmental organizations (NGOs) but are also engaged in the production of knowledge, including categories that become part of the moral repertoires used by the state. In other words, government agencies and nonprofit, party-based initiatives working on behalf of women rely heavily on the efforts of women positioned in these networks. Focusing on these vast and influential—though largely overlooked—networks makes the distinction between state and civil society increasingly problematic. Although Alfred Stepan has correctly reminded us that the state "structures relationships *between* civil society and public authority in a polity" in addition to structuring "many crucial relationships within civil society as well,"[1] to address the problem simply in these terms is unhelpful, since this structuring relies on important cultural resources from civil society itself.

In this chapter I will explore the dialectical relation between state forms and social movements in the construction of the new hegemonic projects of neoliberal

---

I wish to acknowledge the financial support of the International Development Research Centre of Canada (IDRC) and of the Social Sciences and Humanities Research Council of Canada, as well as of the University of Western Ontario, that allowed me to conduct the research in Chile on which this chapter is based. I also am very grateful to Ted Schrecker, Evelina Dagnino, Jeffrey Rubin, Arturo Escobar, Philip Corrigan, and Malcolm Blincow for their suggestions and comments.

"modernization," by addressing the women's movement in the context of this particular configuration of state–civil society relations taking shape in present-day Chile. The focus of the discussion is on the articulation of the multiplicity of experiences, discourses, and practices of development NGOs, feminists, popular organizations, and government institutions by the state.[2] My analysis is, in part, grounded in recent interviews with a number of women activists and professionals working in Santiago's many NGOs, research centers, foundations, and government agencies, as well as in grassroots organizations, neighborhood councils, and local municipal agencies. Furthermore, I draw from what is by now a lengthy contact with organized women from the popular sectors, particularly from the most populous southern periphery of Santiago. This contact, which I first established during extensive fieldwork in 1987, has given me a particular insight into the conditions that enable women to differentially position themselves, and be differently positioned, in the present political process.

Judging from the scope of the transformations under way throughout the world and from the massive forms of dislocation and anxiety these transformations are unleashing, recent neoliberal projects are nothing short of "revolutionary."[3] Such projects are clearly not only economic and institutional but also, most crucially, cultural-political. Taking a cue from Rob Watts, I suggest here that in the specific context of neoliberal modernizing projects, the distinction between state and civil society appears increasingly blurred (1993/1994, 108). In short, what Philip Cerny (1990) refers to as the robustness of states in the late twentieth century is all too apparent. Under the guise of limited intervention or nonintervention, an aspect of the dominant neoliberal discourse with its commitment to a market-driven model of development, states are intervening in important ways that have significant cultural effects. States, in other words, are at the center of the present modernizing project, the so-called neoliberal project.

Transitions to civilian rule in Latin America today thus involve a reconfiguration of state–civil society relations along the lines of the neoliberal modernizing project, with powerful cultural effects. Central to this modernizing project is the redefinition of citizenship as the active exercise of responsibilities, including economic self-reliance and political participation. Implicit in this redefinition is a dismantling of the ostensibly "passive" citizenship associated with the postwar, so-called "statist," period.[4] This undoing of the postwar meaning of citizenship has been preceded by an assault on those institutions and practices that, albeit imperfectly, held out for generations the hope of membership.[5] In his suggestive piece "Democracy and Modernization, Thirty Years Later," José Nun recently reminded us that in the course of these projects we are presented with imaginary discontinuities, "as if Latin America had never experienced capitalist penetration, its economies had never been open to the world market, as if the early-1960s doctrine of modernization had never existed" (1993). Indeed, the apparent democratization of interventionist states of yore has presented an additional discontinuity, as if all modern Latin American states had exercised predominantly coercive power over their citizens. Thus the brush of recent modernization also tars with amnesia, as it were, those other cultural projects of modern Latin American states such as the liberal state forms of the late nineteenth century and, more recently, the Estados Populistas.[6]

The restructuring process presently under way is shifting the terms under which people live their lives from day to day. This is necessarily transforming the "common material and meaningful framework" in which the contestations, resistance, and struggles of subordinate groups are embedded.[7] In Chile, redefining the terms of citizenship is one crucial element of this transformation, and it is being done without a trace of memory or regret on the part of many.[8] In this chapter I pursue the questions of cultural-political restructuring and more specifically of the redefinition of citizenship, in a deliberately one-sided manner, by highlighting the paradoxical processes through which state institutions and organizations as well as civil society rearticulate already existing, indeed often contestational or outright oppositional, forms to bring about the transformations associated with such redefinitions. My main focus, then, is primarily on the various ways in which cultural and material resources are recruited for the construction of new state forms.[9] This focus, I argue, throws light on the ambiguous and contradictory character of social movements. Although social movements may, in one conjuncture, challenge domination as a particular "congealed" structure of power relations (Slater 1994, 27) and of oppressive and exclusionary identities, in another they may themselves contribute to the emergence and development of new forms of domination. In the following pages I trace the processes whereby the efforts of feminist activists and professionals in Chile who are concerned with women's meaningful participation are being transformed into resources through which the state defines both the appropriate behaviors of citizens and the spaces for the practice of citizenship.

I begin with a critical examination of recently established agencies—both governmental and nongovernmental—that since 1990 have been in the business of resolving the "real" problems of Chilean women. Certainly the attention to the discursive constitution of women's problems, and more generally the efforts to integrate different categories of women "excluded" from the national community, have not materialized out of thin air, and must be linked to the struggles of the women's movement. But more concretely, I argue that there is a convergence between, on the one hand, the concerted actions of the networks of women activists and professionals that make up a large segment of the women's movement and, on the other, the renewed efforts of the Chilean neoliberal state to redefine the nature of the "national community" and the appropriate behaviors of its constituent members (including those activists and professionals working with women at the grassroots level).[10] More specifically, the terms of gendered citizenship and community, then, are increasingly being established by some women in the name of all. This ought to be a reminder that the emancipatory potential of social movements must always be understood in context. In the case of the women's movement, its accomplishments and impacts must be understood in connection with the latest phase of Chilean state formation. This phase is characterized by the renewed attempts of dominant groups to construct a hegemonic project that articulates elements of socioeconomic "modernization" with a particular conception of citizenship—one based on individual subjects as bearers of rights who must entrepreneurially fashion their overall personal development through wider relations to the marketplace.[11]

Social Movements and the Problem of State–Civil Society Relations in Neoliberal Modernizing Projects

Studies of Latin American social movements have for some time underscored these movements' important contribution to cultural transformations and the democratization of everyday life, as well as their significant consequences for the broader processes of political transformation in the region (Escobar and Alvarez 1992; Slater 1991, 1994; Foweraker and Craig 1990). In the aftermath of authoritarian rule, therefore, it could be confidently assumed that social movements had left indelible marks on democratization processes in Latin America; and yet the "democracies" that are unfolding in countries like Uruguay, Argentina, and Chile bear some very old, familiar features.[12] They continue to be embedded in contexts of gross social and economic inequalities and to be characterized, among other things, by a return to politics as usual and by a loss of visibility of many social movements. These developments, along with the political transformations that have occurred in Mexico, have dampened many scholars' initial optimism about the wider democratizing potential of social movements and have led to caution or outright pessimism (Slater 1994; Canel 1992; Hellman 1992).

An important supposition in much work on social movements is the rediscovery of "the political" as a realm in its own right, which, via a revaluation of liberal democracy, is viewed as a potentially pluralist space.[13] This identity-centered, antistatist—or poststatist—view of the emancipatory role of social movements has also been linked, often implicitly, with the rediscovery of civil society manifest in many recent theoretical writings (e.g., Arato and Cohen 1992; Keane 1988, 1995; Held 1991). Ultimately, a revenge of "civil society" seemed to take hold in the purged discourse of still-leftist social movement analysts in the 1980s. This is symbolized most significantly by the view of social movements as disrupters of sedimented, limiting social identities and of narrow understandings of the political, and hence as capable of opening up new spaces of democratic practice and, often, of even bypassing the state altogether (Rowe and Schelling 1991; Evers 1985).

But do the democratizing struggles of social movements offer such open-ended possibilities? Could it be that those who announced the autonomy of the political with infectious enthusiasm and placed their hopes in the radical potential of liberal democracy did so by unnecessarily underplaying the continuing significance of the state?[14] The massive transformations associated with economic, social, and political restructuring that have been taking place throughout the world, and the crucial role of states in them, suggest that this is in fact the case. Increasingly, these changes, which in Latin America and most recently in eastern Europe are linked with so-called transition and democratization processes, today give the much celebrated "moment of civil society" a seemingly ephemeral character.[15] Given these global capitalist transformations, how effective is it to pose the question of the political relevance of social movements in a context that privileges a state-society split?

Consequently, I suggest a rethinking of the impact of social movements that defends the notion that states have fundamental cultural effects on societies and that therefore challenges the current conceptual dichotomy that seems to set the state unambiguously against a sphere of action outside the state, in civil society. I propose an analysis sensitive to the changing, broader context of power relations in which social movements are embedded. This broader context refers explicitly to the cultural processes associated with state formation. Following recent conceptions of the state influenced by the work of Foucault (Corrigan and Sayer 1985), my analysis begins with the assumption that a state is not a monolith with intentions—such as, for example, to "co-opt"—but rather an abstraction that refers to ensembles of institutions and practices with powerful cultural consequences.[16] Moreover, these cultural consequences stem from the precise, concrete manner in which institutions and practices rule—the "forms of rule and ruling." Central to this ruling are not the intentions of the bureaucrats and professionals housed in institutions, but the texts (policy documents, position papers, memos, and the like) that these bureaucrats produce as a matter of routine in the course of their ongoing activities.[17] Knowledge that is central to the ordering of social life is produced through these "textually mediated practices," to borrow Dorothy Smith's apt formulation. Foucault proposed the term "governmentality" to refer "generally to all projects or practices intending to direct social actors to behave in a particular manner and towards specified ends in which political government is but one of the means of regulating or directing action" (Watts 1993/1994, 109). Power, in this sense, is not exercised exclusively as violence through coercive organs but as the regulation of people's behaviors and subjectivities. Foucault, using a Christian metaphor, referred to this dimension as "pastoral" power (1983, 1991). This notion of power as "pastoral" allows us to make sense of the fundamentally moral dimension of projects of domination implicated in the processes of state formation. Corrigan and Sayer (1985) capture this notion best by highlighting how the interest of states in determining how social life should be conducted translates into an interest (often "forcibly encouraged") in regulating the behavior of individuals. In this context, states play a central orchestrating role in the constitution of new identities. They "define, in great detail, acceptable forms and images of social activity and individual and collective identity; they regulate, in empirically specifiable ways . . . social life. In this sense, 'the State' never stops talking" (Corrigan and Sayer 1985, 3). I use the term "orchestrating" in this context to highlight the point that the role of the state is not to determine or fix forms of sociality and subjectivities but rather to "lay down" a structure of possibilities that sets the parameters for people's actions.[18]

In particular, capitalist state projects of domination entail powerful discourses of belonging that aim to construct a totality through individualizing strategies. These have characteristically hinged on an appeal to "citizenship," an identity that locates us as members of national and—to paraphrase Benedict Anderson—ultimately "imagined" communities (1983). In other words, state projects are integrative projects, and citizenship is, in one very significant and all too often underestimated sense, a powerful mechanism of integration. The crucial quality of citizenship is that its meaning is never fixed. Not only are there different *types* of citizenship in liberal democratic regimes; there are also *changes* that occur within each type over time. Thus, being a citizen of a welfare state is different from being a citizen of a newly emerging neoliberal state. As Janine Brodie reminds us, "different state forms, whether they be laissez-faire, welfare, or neoliberal, weave different meanings into our everyday lives" (1995, 27).

Clearly, today, just as before, states are very much involved in defining both national communities and appropriate social and political behaviors. Citizens, with their qualities and behaviors, are central to the current modernizing projects. It is not surprising, for example, that "welfare dependency" in North America and Europe and "state dependency" in Latin America should be such prominent topics at this moment. The all-consuming focus of the discourse of the right—both in and out of government in Great Britain, the United States, and increasingly Canada—on categories of people such as single mothers and welfare "bums," and more generally on the moral imperatives of restructuring social programs, illustrates the degree to which the identities and conduct of individuals matter to the state. Moreover, this period of intense debate over the meaning of citizenship powerfully underscores the degree to which the terms of belonging have always been, if not defined, then ultimately enforced by the state. "Citizenship" is a pivotal category in this redefinition of collective and individual identities.

In places like Chile and other countries of the Southern Cone, military dictatorships brutally severed the links that had held together states and civil societies in the post–World War II period. Increasingly, these links are being rebuilt, but in the framework of historical amnesia previously referred to, so that the pattern is no longer that inspired by the Economic Commission for Latin America (ECLA) and in use beginning in the 1940s.[19] Instead, "economic liberalism" is being used to reconnect the fabric of state–civil society relations. In the context of the imaginary discontinuities in previous modernization projects, citizenship now holds the hope of the recognition and self-recognition that we are not modern yet—but that we are potentially capable of becoming modern, if and only if we rely on ourselves.

Citizenship and civil society have thus become key words in the political grammar of many practitioners and observers of political liberalization processes in Latin America. This political grammar suggests a convergence, in form and content, of different practices. First, an important legacy of the practices of social movements during the last two decades has been the tendency to highlight the centrality of the question of identity in politics; the meanings and practices of citizenship suddenly mattered. A second strand refers to the activities of newly minted civilian governments in Latin America. These civilian governments are increasingly legitimizing their public and social policies in terms of a discourse of modernity pivoting on the key issues of autonomy, accountability, and responsibility. These refer to the qualities expected not only of bureaucracies but also of citizens and of civil society in general. A third strand refers to the growing trend in international aid to bolster democratic politics in the region by emphasizing decentralization and active (economic) citizenship.[20] For example, a cursory exploration of recent funding for national governments and NGOs provided by philanthropic European and North American agencies, as well as by multilateral agencies such as the World Bank, suggests an increasing commitment to projects that aim to strengthen "civil society" and promote "citizen participation."[21]

I want to draw attention to this "convergence" as an active process of articulation of existing discourses, experiences, and quite literally of bodies, the outcome of which is a shifting of the matrix, or material and discursive framework, that "define[s] the quotidian world in which we are constrained to live" (Sayer 1994, 375). It is important to keep in mind, however, that although state forms define and impose, what people and groups do with these forms is another matter. There is no telling beforehand, for example, what form the identity of today's "marketized" citizen may take, or in what contexts such an identity may be deployed by different social groups. The point, however, is that the terms in which citizenship may be adopted, contested, and struggled over are predetermined. This is another way of restating the point that although people obviously contest and struggle, their struggles are not entirely of their own making. A crucial step, then, in coming to terms with the "revolutionary" dimension of changes associated with neoliberal modernizing projects is understanding the construction of new state forms. It is this process of "laying down" the new forms, as it were, that relies on what is already there, to which I now turn. I argue in the following pages that, in the Chilean case, a confluence seems to have been established between the activities of women's movements, namely women's struggles to define new political identities and thus to expand the notion of citizenship, and the project of constitution and regulation of identities and subjectivities by a neoliberal state form. Indeed, this Chilean modernizing project has come to *depend* on the many activities of professionals and activists working for NGOs, universities, and independent research institutes, a majority of whom are women.

From the Margins to the Center? Women in the New Chilean Democracy

Since the elections of 1990 and the apparent general demobilization of Chilean social movements, the women's movement seems to have lost its visibility and has, in fact, been pronounced transformed, paralyzed, or even dead.[22] The end of dictatorship has eliminated the obvious enemy that once united myriad, heterogeneous groupings and organizations. Indeed, the transition to "democracy," or to normal politics, has exposed the real differences and tensions among women that were latent in the past. A fundamental divide exists today between those feminists who feel that the struggle for women's greater equality must be fought from within party politics and the state (informally known as the *"politicas"*), and those who insist that this stance will lead to a loss of autonomy and hence of the transformative-emancipatory potential of the movement (the *"autónomas"*). Already in late 1988, the creation of two new coordinating bodies with very different goals, the Concertación de Mujeres por la Democracia and the Coordinación de Organizaciones Sociales de Mujeres, heightened the tensions between these two basic positions palpably. The Coordinación de Organizaciones Sociales de Mujeres brought together feminists who chose a strategy of action beyond what the parties and the state were capable of, in the name of preserving the autonomy of the women's movement. On the other hand, those well-known feminists who joined the Concertación de Mujeres por la Democracia belonged to the center and leftist parties that formed the Concertación por la Democracia, the first civilian government after 1989. This women's coalition was formed with the express purpose of presenting women's demands to the new civilian government.[23] Those women who took part in this initiative insist, no doubt accurately, that, without the pressure they exerted as a group and without the pressure exerted subsequently by the few feminist parliamentarians and politicians elected in 1989, the Concertación government would not have had a women's program (Programa de la Mujer).[24] Clearly, the Concertación de Mujeres por la Democracia represented the *doble militancia* (feminists who are also members of political parties), who chose to work for change within the parameters established by the political mainstream. As such, it excluded those who, while not choosing to marginalize themselves from this process, opted instead to play out their "double-militancy" in the Communist Party and the Movement of the Revolutionary Left (MIR).[25]

Despite ongoing debates among feminists about the status of the women's movement, a cursory exploration of the perpetual networks that constitute the movement reveals important continuities and changes. A number of independent women's research institutes—for example, Centro de Estudios de la Mujer (CEM), its splinter group Instituto de la Mujer (CEDEM), and ISIS Internacional—continue to operate, as do a number of NGOs working with women's issues as well as women's centers (including the first center to have opened in Santiago during the dictatorship, Casa de la Mujer la Morada). In addition, the women's radio station, Radio Tierra, and a number of feminist bulletins, journals, and a newspaper continue to inform and educate the Chilean population about women's issues.

Yet recent developments suggest that whereas the Chilean women's movement continues to operate, its strategies are changing. Two recent examples of new mobilizations come to mind: the campaign to vote more women into Parliament, mounted during the last parliamentary elections; and the widespread discussions and meetings organized in preparation for the Beijing Conference on Women in September 1995.[26] Furthermore, two *redes de mujeres* (women's networks) have been created; one mobilizes women around issues of health and reproductive rights and the other focuses on issues of male violence against women. These networks are sustained by NGOs and women's organizations, and their achievements to date suggest that, at least so far, the former has been more successful than the latter. For example, the health-related network has successfully organized public discussions on abortion; inaugurated the International Day of Women's Health; and, as a consumer watchdog, conducted an exposé of the widespread use in hospitals of an unauthorized, experimental drug to treat women.

Beyond these questions of strategy and practice, however, there is the question of the cultural impact of the women's movement on Chilean society. The movement's important legacies are evident in the sociopolitical transformations that have taken place since 1990. Perhaps the most conspicuous achievement is the creation of the Servicio Nacional de la Mujer (National Women's Bureau), or SERNAM. The creation of this government agency in January 1991 was in response to the demands expressed by the Concertación de Mujeres por la Democracia during the negotiations among various opposition groups for a coalition, eventually resulting in the Concertación por la Democracia and paving the way for the elections of 1990.[27] SERNAM has a limited operating budget, and, in fact, it relies heavily on foreign funding to develop and implement its programs.[28] It has a director with the rank of minister of state who is directly accountable to the president. In addition, SERNAM has directors in each of the country's thirteen regional governments, and within these regions it is represented in a number of local and municipal governments, often through Oficinas Municipales de la Mujer (Municipal Women's Bureaus) or OMMs. SERNAM's explicit aim is to "design and coordinate public policies at sectoral and interministerial levels."[29] In other words, this ministry-like institution acts primarily as a watchdog; it was created to oversee all other ministries' policymaking activities in areas directly affecting women. Beyond this advisory role, SERNAM has the power to propose legislation to Parliament, to promote society-wide educational campaigns, and to design and implement specific social programs.

How much SERNAM is actually able to accomplish obviously depends on the broader context in which it operates. Two major factors limit the institution's range of actions. First, there is often a considerable amount of resistance to SERNAM on the part of government ministers and their teams of experts. It would be naive, therefore, to assume that just because this institution was established, all other ministries would follow SERNAM's mandate and start implementing programs that favor women. A refusal on the part of male ministers and their policy experts to consider the gendered dimension of key policy areas like health, education, and particularly labor is often cited as a limiting factor for SERNAM, and it is something that women at all levels in and out of government simply refer to as the "high degree of *machismo*."

A second limitation originates in the composition of the institution. SERNAM reflects the proportional strengths of the different political parties that make up the Concertación government. The Christian Democratic Party is the strongest of the parties in the ruling coalition. Thus, SERNAM operates under what some critics dub a "straitjacket," because the strong links between the ruling party and the Catholic Church render certain areas of legislation and policy difficult, if not impossible, to address. In a context in which the Catholic Church rules de facto over issues that are presumed to directly affect the moral life of the national community, including sexuality and family issues, the Concertación government, and SERNAM by extension, will in all likelihood not propose legislation on, for instance, divorce[30] or abortion.[31]

Despite these limitations, SERNAM has succeeded in pressuring Parliament to consider gender-specific issues such as changes to the civil code (which has not been revised since the nineteenth century), including legislation that discriminates against women in areas such as marriage, property rights, and labor. Some of these initiatives have, in fact, resulted in new legislation. For example, the new Ley de Violencia Intrafamiliar (Law against Family Violence) now makes spousal physical abuse a punishable act. Effective implementation of such laws such is, of course, another matter. Recent rulings in family violence cases suggest that judges continue to emphasize the integrity of the family, not the rights of abused women. In one case heard in a Santiago court, for example, a woman who withheld sexual relations from an abusive husband was deemed by the judge to be suffering from a "sexual dysfunction" and was ordered to undergo sex therapy. The husband got off scot-free.[32]

Another important organization, as far as poor women are concerned, is PRODEMU (Fundacion para la Promoción y Desarrollo de la Mujer). PRODEMU was established in 1990 as a private foundation created and controlled by the Christian Democratic Party, and works for women's promotion and development; it is headed by the president's wife and a seven-member National Council. In effect, the executive vice president directs and administers the institution with the help of a team of professionals. PRODEMU operates throughout the country, working in coordination with different levels of government—municipal *(municipalidades)*, governates *(gobernaciones)*, and intendancies *(intendencias)*—as well as with other public and private institutions. The work is carried out by professionals and volunteers, as well as by a sizable group of *monitoras*, or workshop instructors, who are paid a nominal sum. The explicit targets of PRODEMU are women living in conditions of poverty or "extreme" poverty, whether organized or unorganized, homemakers or participants in informal economic activities.

PRODEMU was established to fill the vacuum created during the transition to civilian rule in the area of volunteer work helping poor women. Central Relacionadora de los Centros de Madres (CEMA) in Chile, the institution inherited by Pinochet's wife from earlier incarnations, which coordinated and oversaw mother's centers, was not dismantled at the time of the transition. In fact, through a legal maneuver introduced at the eleventh hour, military wives maintained their control of CEMA-Chile. A great number of centers opted out of CEMA-Chile and were thus left in search of a new coordinating organization. It is as such a coordinating agency that PRODEMU feels it can most effectively address women's programs and activities. In fact, the leaders of grassroots women's organizations who are associated with PRODEMU, and even those who are not and who cannot distinguish this coordinating body from CEMA-Chile, typically refer to PRODEMU as a *CEMA democratico* (PRODEMU 1993, 48).

Since 1990, the organization has been heavily involved in providing technical and educationai support to neighborhood-based organizations of women who are predominantly homemakers. The institution relies heavily on the contribution of its virtual army of workshop instructors. These *monitoras* are a group of poorly-paid, mostly poor, lower-middle-class women with an exceptional degree of commitment to their work. Many of these women taught handicrafts in workshops during the dictatorship, either for CEMA-Chile or for opposition NGOs working with women in poor neighborhoods.[33] They are required to travel long distances to the poor communities where workshops are held, often at considerable personal risk.

Presently, PRODEMU is in the process of redefining its areas of action. This development coincides with the inauguration of a second Concertación government, this time with the majority presence of the Christian Democratic Party. In this context, PRODEMU has officially identified two broad national objectives in relation to which it aims to frame its own programs. These are the Programa Nacional de Superacion de la Pobreza and the Plan de Igualdad de Oportunidades para las Mujeres. Initially, PRODEMU'S collaboration with SERNAM was tenuous, although such collaboration seems increasingly to be at least a goal of the organizations. In fact, SERNAM officially recognizes coordination in some activities.

The overall goal of PRODEMU to date has been to teach handicraft skills to women that they can use in "strategies of self-consumption" *(autoconsumo)* as well as for the benefit of their families. To this end it has developed a number of programs and enlisted the services of approximately 2,500 *monitoras*. This stated goal of PRODEMU, not to mention the work that flows from it, reveals that the institution has learned important lessons from the activities of NGOs sensitive to women's conditions. Emphasizing "self-consumption" over family concerns in the context of a Catholic-based institution is an interesting undertaking. It suggests a recognition of women as independent subjects rather than as mere appendages of their families. In this appropriation, and transformation, of the link made by earlier feminist-inspired activities between economic necessity and empowerment, PRODEMU has achieved a happy marriage between women's autonomy and the market. Its handicraft workshops aim to empower women as economic subjects.

The Expanding Networks of the Women's Movement in Chile

Understanding both the state and civil society, and the relation between them, entails first and foremost making sense of what people who work in settings such as government agencies, institutes, NGOs, and grassroots organizations actually do.[34] Even a cursory exploration of what has happened among feminist professionals in Chile in the past five years reveals an important trend.[35] Many social scientists—sociologists and economists as well as social workers and educators—mostly employed in NGOs during the dictatorship, have joined the various ministries and agencies such as the Instituto Nacional de Estadística or the INE (National Statistics Institute). A significant number of them have moved to middle-level positions in SERNAM. In addition this government presence, feminist professionals continue to be found in NGOs and independent research institutes. They are increasingly also found in universities, where in some cases they have succeeded in establishing courses in women's and gender studies. These moves should not be seen as permanent, as there appears to be a constant migration of professionals in and out of government agencies and more generally between the nongovernmental and governmental sectors. An important reshuffling of personnel, affecting the positions of women professionals, took place after the election of the Christian Democrat Eduardo Frei in 1994. However, such movements often result from microphenomena, such as disagreements over certain programs or policies, at times leading to the resignation of entire teams or simply the termination of a limited contract at the end of a specific project.

The nature of the work of professionals at NGOs is also changing.[36] Since the late 1980s much of the aid from bilateral, mostly European, agencies and private foundations has declined. Ostensibly this aid has been diverted to other, presumably needier, parts of the world. Although this may be so in some cases, a more plausible explanation can, no doubt, be found in the changing relations of these agencies to their own national governments. European governments are in the throes of a restructuring process—in response to global restructuring—and are steadily withdrawing support from their official and voluntary aid sectors. In addition, the events of 1989 and afterward in Europe—namely, the emergence of eastern Europe as a target area—are no doubt contributing to the diversion of funds away from countries like Chile.[37]

Most of the remaining funding from European donors has been redirected to support the social programs of the civilian governments. The first Concertación government, headed by Patricio Aylwin, was instrumental in insisting that all funds be channeled through the government. Funds are still reaching the NGOs, but the direction of funding is firmly in the hands of the government, and the nongovernmental beneficiaries are those organizations who increasingly act as the executors or evaluators of government social programs.[38] One prominent example is FOSIS (Fondos de Solidaridad e Inversion Social), the experimental program of social assistance initiated during the Aylwin government, which relies extensively on the work and knowledge base of NGOs. FOSIS is the Chilean version of similar solidarity investment funds found in other parts of Latin America, whose aim is to soften the extreme social effects of structural adjustment policies, and of the neoliberal development model more generally. The goal of these projects is to help the poor and marginalized access the market by financing small social and economic infrastructure programs. Hence they represent a sort of "social adjustment" strategy that, as the World Bank readily admits, are politically motivated because they seek to guarantee political support for neoliberal economic reforms. FOSIS relies heavily on foreign funding.

In this respect, the predicament of Chilean, and more generally Latin American, NGOs parallels that of NGOs in Europe and in North America. Canadian NGOs, for example, are being wooed by provincial governments for innovative forms of program delivery, or what critics call the "downloading" of government responsibilities. In all cases, an emphasis on the responsibilities of citizenship, as opposed to "mere" rights, is the new ideological linchpin. A key difference between the cases of Chile and Canada is that in the former, although some NGOs seem reluctant to follow the trend, the majority have either acquiesced to, or willingly embraced, their new roles. This has led critics to refer to these NGOs as "para-statal" organizations. In Canada, however, the NGOs' reluctance to transform themselves into agents of government restructuring programs still seems to predominate.[39]

SERNAM's programs are almost entirely funded from abroad. For example, the Women's Resource Centers (CIDEMs), a centerpiece SERNAM program and presumably the initiative through which the institution keeps an "ear to the ground," are heavily funded by a grant from the Swedish Development Agency. Often, NGOs are put in the position of having to compete directly with SERNAM for funding, as occurred recently with money from the Swedish Development Agency earmarked for "strengthening civil society" by sponsoring the activities of approximately 500 women's NGOs. The money, it turns out, was given to SERNAM for "administration." When the director of the agency turned down this responsibility, another government agency undertook it, much to the discontent of the NGOs. As a result of these changing priorities of foreign and domestic funding agencies, most women's NGOs, and indeed most local or community-based NGOs, are either scrambling to survive or disappearing altogether. Those that remain are increasingly dependent on government-funded projects to survive.

More generally, government agencies actively recruit professionals from NGOs to develop and implement, as well as evaluate, social programs. Needless to say, theirs is not an easy relationship. A common complaint on the part of the NGO professionals is that their approach to social programs highlights "process," while the agencies emphasize "outcomes" and "products" (for example, the number of streets paved, or the number of women trained in a particular skill). Ultimately, however, to survive, NGOs must adapt to this commodification of their purposes and to the impact of these changes on society.

Winners and losers are emerging from this scramble to survive. Among the winners are those NGOs that can retool themselves to offer either unique expertise in specific areas of work with the poor or alternatively a knowledge base that can be tapped for the design, implementation, and evaluation of projects. For many women's NGOs, this means having to abandon the kinds of projects they closely associated with their feminist commitments—for example, projects that promote consciousness raising through a "feminist curriculum" (the various workshops on topics such as sexuality, women's rights, and leadership training). The big losers are activist NGOs that are closest to the grass roots. These organizations, predominantly run by working-class women, may have neither the professional skills—such as general expertise or specific skills in project writing or bidding—nor the certification increasingly required of them. It is through these transformations that class becomes relevant in NGOs. Often, demands for professionalization and certification are acting to exclude individual working-class women or entire groups. In one instance, an NGO that has managed to retool itself and act as an executor of government social programs in poor communities is running into difficulties because its most experienced and skilled community organizer is a working-class woman without a professional certificate. This NGO is increasingly under pressure to address this irregularity in its personnel composition. Sometimes entire groups lose out in the bid for projects because of the members' lack of professional credentials. Such was the fate of the Coordinadora de Mujeres of San Joaquín. This long-standing local organization is made up of leaders of women's groups from a number of poor neighborhoods *(poblaciones)* in the commune of La Granja, in the southern periphery of Santiago. The *coordinadora* presented a proposal for a small-scale women's leadership training school to the local Municipal Women's Bureau. This proposal included the by now recognizable "feminist curriculum": handicraft workshops, workshops in personal development *(desarrollo personal),* and a number of leadership training workshops. The women relied on their own experiences over a period of ten years as volunteer workshop instructors and developed the proposal in consultation with Tierra Nuestra, a locally based women's NGO. Their proposal was turned down by the Municipal Women's Bureau because the group did not meet the professional certification criteria. Moreover, the person in charge of the bureau subsequently designed a similar project—the women from the San Joaquín *coordinadora* insist that it was a copy of their plan—and invited the organization to teach the handicraft workshops. According to the rules governing these funds, only qualified professionals were considered competent to teach leadership and personal development workshops sponsored by the local government.[40]

NGOs and local organizations run by working-class women also lack the longstanding contacts with the smaller network of professional women regularly tapped by government agencies. The urgency of having the right connections is made evident by the descriptions of women in NGOs of their relations with SERNAM. Typically, project ideas and evaluations of existing projects are commissioned by the agency not by inviting NGOs as organizations, but rather by inviting individuals within them. Often, those who are outside the known circles, like women from NGOs based in the *poblaciones,* are not even aware of the projects in question. Thus, vital information circulates in a network that is highly stratified and that has expanded to include women in government ministries and other agencies, at the same time marginalizing others who are closer to the grass roots. These "popular" women's NGOs are quite literally struggling to survive.

Despite the tensions generated by its heterogeneous composition, a broadly based women's movement flourished during Pinochet's regime. Its demands were summarized in the slogan "Si la mujer no esta, la democracia no va!" (Without women democracy won't happen!).[41] With the return to "normal" politics, however, superficially solid alliances among women in their struggle for an inclusive conception of democracy are coming undone. The lesson taught by these recent years is that class does matter as far as women and their struggles are concerned. In a capitalist, liberal democratic context, the political integration of some women is occurring at the cost of the marginalization of others. Struggles for the articulation of women's rights within the state involve women differently, and empowerment and autonomy, two key elements associated with an active, liberal citizenship, are not translating into equality for different women. Poor and working-class women—who were at the forefront of struggles against the Pinochet dictatorship—are losing their public visibility.

The much-reduced public visibility of organized poor and working-class women is widely recognized, although the view that this change can be explained by women having returned to their homes is not. One explanation equates this loss of visibility with the recent economic gains of the poor in general, and of poor women in particular. Having succeeded in correcting the conditions that led them to organize in the first place, poor women, according to this explanation, are "returning to their homes" (a phrase that came up frequently in my discussions with feminists). This takes for granted Maxine Molyneux's model of women's politics based on different kinds of needs; Molyneux distinguishes between those needs that lead women to organize around their "practical" needs and those that lead them to organize around their "strategic" needs, involving a more general, gender-based (i.e., feminist) analysis of the roots of their oppression (1986, 283–285).

The reduced visibility of poor and working-class women is clearly evident in the activities of SERNAM. The grass roots—organized through what one popular women's NGO worker refers to as a "veritable ant's work"—are being tapped by the Municipal Women's Bureau and other state institutions in their efforts to implement an array of social programs for poor women. The official view of poor women is that they are potential economic subjects in need of help in accessing the market. Thus, they are being invited through programs appealing to specific, newly created categories of persons such as *jefas de hogar* (women heads of households) and *empresarias* (women engaged in so-called self-help economic activities). These programs are, in effect, reorganizing the relations between women at all levels. Although the programs may be designed by women professionals attached to government agencies like SERNAM as well as to NGOs, they are being implemented at the local level, with the collaboration of women working both in the local government and in the neighborhoods themselves. Indeed, it is ultimately those working in neighborhood councils who must attempt a fit between their needier neighbors and the categories of a particular program. Clearly, there is also room for creative manipulation of such categories at the grassroots level. As two women leaders of neighborhood councils from adjacent neighborhoods in a *población* of Santiago's southern periphery confided, when they consider women heads of household in their neighborhoods, they include not only those who are "visibly alone and in charge of their families," but also those with "good-for-nothing" husbands—usually meaning alcoholics—who do not contribute a cent to the household. Having said this, the two leaders also pointed out that privileging some women and not others, in a condition of generalized poverty and lack of opportunities for women, creates tensions and anger among those who are excluded.

This reorganization of the relations among different women, and more specifically the new content being given to the "clientelization" of only certain poor and working-class women by state agencies including the Municipal Women's Bureau, is shaping the parameters of these women's political practices. As I have argued elsewhere, being a client of "feminist" inspired programs is a double-edged process leading to unintended consequences. This process is expressed in the declaration presented by the Movimiento de Mujeres Populares (Movement of Popular Women), or MOMUPO, at the National Feminist Encounter in Valparaiso in November 1991:

> In these past years we learned to appropriate feminism as an approach to make sense of our lives. We know and understand the discrimination which we suffer, and this leads us to feel an internal strength and solidarity, a rebellious need to be women who want to liberate ourselves from this structure of power concentrated in men which is patriarchy. We assume our struggle against gender injustice, in solidarity with all women, without distinctions of race or class.
>
> However, in these years we have also learned to assume that feminism entails different processes depending on one's class. In the case of *pobladoras* this process generated a number of doubts, conflicts and discussions over the feminist discourse. (MOMUPO 1991)

The same document identifies the dilemmas faced today by "popular feminists," as working-class Chilean feminist activists identify themselves: "We see a great danger in social policies aimed specifically at the so-called extremely poor sectors being implemented by treating women as isolated individuals, without allowing for the creation of collective spaces where women can articulate and present their own demands" (MOMUPO 1991). This concern highlights a central issue in the transformations taking place in women's politics in Chile today. The clientelization of some poor and working-class women, carried out by others in the name of advancing the cause of women, is in effect undermining the possibility that poor and working class women will come together to articulate their own needs. The ultimate question is: Who has the right to define the terms of women's struggles?

The Chilean women's movement's challenge to traditional femininities and its struggle to promote new forms of citizenship for women has taken the very concrete form of working with women in neighborhood-based organizations and offering a "feminist curriculum" aimed at consciousness raising on matters such as female sexuality, women's rights under Chilean law, parent-child relations, and leadership potential.[42] That feminist curriculum resolved to subvert dominant forms of sociality and promote alternative female subjectivities. More broadly, it sought to "empower" women—here workshops on rights and on leadership training were crucial—as political actors. Thus, without calling it such, the women's movement was engaged in undermining Chile's authoritarian political culture by promoting a redefinition of citizenship and more generally the concept of the political. Given the important feminist dictum that the personal is political, it is fair to say that in Chilean society, where acceptable forms of collective and individual identity traditionally positioned women as extensions of their families, incursions into the private, such as those embodied by the feminist curriculum of NGOs during the dictatorship, have made a difference, if not in how most women live their lives then at least in what they desire for themselves.

Consequently, the days when women could be appealed to by political parties and government programs alike as homemakers, wives, and mothers—and their votes bought with a kilo of sugar, some tea, and cooking oil, a practice still prevalent three decades ago—are gone. Women in Chile today are appealed to as individuals, selves with their own needs and rights. To this extent, the dominant discourses of exclusionary political forms have been transformed.[43]

A measure of this cultural effect of the women's movement is that, as many politicians and practitioners readily admit, they can only appeal to women directly as individuals rather than as members of, or extensions of, their families. The offers to women by government programs, party-based foundations, and other related initiatives all contain a version of the curriculum first developed by NGOs. A cornerstone of this curriculum is the concern with female selves and female bodies captured by the category *personal development.* Needless to say, the content of *personal development* varies from program to program, but the call embodied in it to change and/or improve the "individual self" does not.

More indirect legacies of the women's movement have been taken up. The distinctive methods of consciousness raising that emerged and evolved during the period of dictatorship in Chile have come to be recognized as a central component of work with women. SERNAM identifies these methods as a key first step in the project of "integrating women into development" (Servicio Nacional de la Mujer 1994). Even Christian-based foundations like PRODEMU have identified methods of consciousness raising as a fundamental element in their work with women. The key component of this curriculum is *personal development,* here defined with reference to a series of workshops that supposedly tap directly into women's senses of self. Through these forms of social intervention, in the name of "active citizenship" and through the implementation of strategies to *improve the self,* attempts are being made to hierarchically integrate poor and working-class women. These women are, in effect, being repositioned, and are repositioning themselves, as new types of *clients* of administrable "needs"—as people who are being fashioned into certain kinds of individual subjects who will develop their individualism through the marketplace.[44]

The degree to which these attempts succeed in integrating women is, of course, another matter. For example, many women are making sure to qualify for, and are entering into, the new programs with the express purpose of gaining access to the goods offered. Women are also deliberately using (or "abusing") the programs for their own purposes. Thus, examples such as that offered by the two neighborhood council leaders discussed above suggest that some women may indeed be empowered by the new forms, that they are creatively adapting to them and using them. Moreover, it is undeniable that some individual women are faring well through these programs. They may in some cases, thanks to day-care centers built in their neighborhoods with the support of new funds, be enabled to work as *temporeras* in nearby fields without worrying about the fate of their children. Alternatively, they may, for the first time in their lives, have access to dental and other health services offered to them in connection with new employment training programs. At the same time, however, the concern expressed by MOMUPO leaders seems to be borne out in practice. While women who were active in organizations during the dictatorship may "not be returning home" as some would want us to believe, neither do they seem to be participating in neighborhood-based women's organizations. Instead, when they are not leaving the neighborhoods to work—many as *temporeras* in nearby fields and in other forms of "flexible" work—or to pursue job training through one of the many schemes that are offered, increasing numbers of women are busy in their neighborhoods taking part in a plethora of social programs designed to teach them individually and collectively to pull themselves out of their own condition of poverty. Thus, the power of new state forms works in the case of individual poor and working-class women in the way it "forcibly organizes, and divides, subjectivities, and thereby produces and reproduces quite material forms of sociality" (Sayer 1994, 374).

Conclusions

One could argue, with the Chilean case in mind, that what we are witnessing today is the positioning of some women in emerging neoliberal democracies as successful players, committed to making the identity of liberal citizenship, as "a subject of rights," available to all women.

The conceptual forms being produced by the network of professional women in NGOs, research institutes, and government agencies like SERNAM are defining a political identity for all women. Those who fail to see themselves as belonging to this community, but are nevertheless included, resent this. Among them, some have conceptualized their own versions of what women need. These alternative versions are informed by finer distinctions differentiating them from, for example, middle-class feminist others. Such women recognize the specificity of class, for example, as a determinant of community. Yet, paradoxically, these cleavages are manifested through what seems like a common language of rights. The process through which this became possible is linked to the legacy of the activities of the women's movement during the authoritarian regime.

In critically exploring the ambiguous and contradictory legacy of the Chilean women's movement, I have questioned the neat separation between state and civil society that is made, or implied, in much of the literature on social movements that focuses on cultural questions. I have also argued that it is very difficult to determine once and for all either the "proper" terrain for assessing the cultural-political legacies of social movements or the character of such legacies. In short, we must beware of a tendency to fix the gains of social movements in time.

Notes

1. Alfred Stepan, quoted in *Bringing the State Back In,* ed. Peter Evans, Dieter Rueschemeyer, and Theda Skocpol (Cambridge: Harvard University Press, 1985), 7.

2. I make this distinction between government institutions and the state quite deliberately. Government institutions have a materiality, manifested in the vast array of policies and regulations emanating from them, that is absent in "the state." In my use of "the state" I follow the influential reconceptualization begun in historical sociology, and most compellingly developed in Corrigan and Sayer 1985. Philip Corrigan (1990), following the important work on the state by Philip Abrams, puts it succinctly: The state is *not* a "thing." For Abrams, this means quite simply that we should not take the state itself as an object of study. He suggests instead that "the state" is "a *claim* that in its very name attempts to give unity, coherence, structure, and intentionality to what are in practice frequently disunited, fragmented attempts at domination" (Sayer 1994, 371).

3. The term "revolution" is used here in its older, pre–1789 sense, which, as Peter Starr reminds us, signified "a great sea change in political affairs, without significant prejudice as to its 'progressive' or 'regressive' nature" (1995).

4. The earlier emphasis on universal rights as entitlements was, of course, restricted in practice in what I call Chile's "limited welfare state." The present drastic restructuring of the Chilean state is but an extreme version of processes under way in full-fledged welfare states, for example Great Britain in the 1970s, the United States in the early 1980s, and most recently France and Canada. Thus the redefinition of citizenship is at the eye of the storm. Will Kymlicka and Wayne Norman (1994) do an admirable job of surveying the conceptual battlefield of citizenship. It is a pity, however, that they have chosen not to address the integrative function of citizenship, for in my view it is precisely here that the cultural consequences of the battle over citizenship are manifested *in practice.*

5. In Chile, for example, economic and political repression, followed by a frenzy of privatization and more general economic and social restructuring begun under Pinochet's dictatorship, has paved the way for cultural-political restructuring under civilian rule. Evidently the decline of the postwar order and the ascendancy of a neoliberal orthodoxy as the

matrix of recent modernizing projects is not exclusive to Chile or to Latin America, but is a worldwide phenomenon.

6. The degree to which previous modernizing projects have ultimately succeeded in becoming inclusive and sustained over time has been, as we know, the topic of much debate, perhaps best exemplified in the writings on the democratic breakdown and authoritarianism of the 1970s (e.g., O'Donnell 1973; Linz and Stepan 1978).

7. I borrow this from William Roseberry's discussion of hegemony (1994, 361).

8. Judging from the many informal discussions I had in the late 1980s with many intellectuals of the so-called "critical Left," huddled in the offices of NGOs and research institutes, it was fashionable even then to criticize "state dependency" and to attribute the failure of NGO activities at the grassroots level to the poor people's "culture of dependency." Clearly, the conceptual shift had already begun. Today, in a seemingly happy marriage of historical amnesia and modernization discourse, the shift in the official discourse is complete. Citizenship, and state–civil society relations in general, are discussed as if there never had been other modernizing projects or as if citizenship had been, until this anticipatory moment—best characterized as the preamble to modernity—been nothing more than a mere legal status on paper.

9. This deliberate focus on the construction of new state forms is embedded in a broader set of assumptions about the relation between culture and politics, which I share with other recent approaches to Latin American politics. See, for example, Rubin forthcoming; see also Rubin's piece in, and the Introduction to, this volume.

10. In a recent piece I attempted to come to terms with this new configuration by examining the fate of women's NGOs in the post-1989 election period, which saw the transfer of foreign funding from "civil society" to "the state" (see Schild 1995).

11. See Macpherson 1962 for a pathbreaking discussion of the link between liberal democracy and market-based individualism.

12. Witness the discursive scramble afoot to find new classifications for these democracies, which are not quite what they were expected to be (see, e.g., O'Donnell 1992). Parallel efforts to elaborate ideal types against which to measure the "new" democracies, which read like renewed articles of faith, are most recently illustrated by the work of the group directed by Adam Przeworski et al. (1995).

13. The self-critical revision of the socialist project offered by Ernesto Laclau and Chantal Mouffe (1985), and especially Mouffe's teasing out of the radical potential of liberal democracy (1992), have been important theoretical *points d'appui* here. This move corresponds to a wider disenchantment with the structural, state-based analyses that had dominated the discourse of Marxist and *marxisant* social scientists alike. In political studies, this disenchantment has led to the euphoric rediscovery of the conceptual toolbox of the 1950s, a.k.a. "political modernization" (critiqued, for example, in Nun 1993; Schild 1992; Munck 1990).

14. The work of Chantal Mouffe (1988, 1992) on radical democracy is paradigmatic of this reappropriation of the emancipatory potential of liberal democracy.

15. How ephemeral this moment has been is illustrated not only by the demobilization of many Latin American social movements during the period of transition but also by many eastern European movements that seem to be suffering a similar fate (see, e.g., Bozoki and Sükösd 1993).

16. Culture, in this context, refers to the "constant process of producing meanings of and from our social experience and such meanings necessarily produce a social identity for

the people involved" (Fiske 1989). For a more extensive discussion of the concept of culture in relation to politics, see this volume's Introduction.

17. Here I follow Dorothy Smith's suggestive and important conceptualization of organizational activity, and of practices of ruling in general, as textual practices. According to Smith: "Our knowledge of contemporary society is to a large extent mediated to us by texts of various kinds. The result, an objectified world-in-common vested in texts, coordinates the acts, decisions, policies and plans of actual subjects as the acts, decisions, policies and plans of large-scale organizations" (1990, 61).

18. In this context, William Roseberry's point—that while the state never stops talking, what different audiences do with this talk is a different matter—is well taken. Having said this, however, it is equally important to remember that this talk does not constitute a potentially endless field of possibilities. State talk, that is, structures possibilities.

19. The transformations that have taken place since the 1970s in other parts of the world associated with the dismantling of the welfare state, and more generally with a rejection of Keynesian economics in favor of laissez-faire economic liberalism, are, of course, parallel processes.

20. These transformations in the aims of donor agencies, particularly those in the voluntary sector, mirror changes linked to restructuring in the donors' own countries. Increasingly, the notion of philanthropic, voluntary sector agencies acting as the necessary substitutes for the "unavoidable" decline of state sources is gaining popularity.

21. The World Bank's interest in and support of so-called "innovative social programs" such as the Fondos de Inversion Social, which have been introduced in a number of Latin American countries, is one example of this shift. Others are the recent projects financed by the Swedish International Development Agency (SIDA) and the Ford Foundation in Chile that aim to "strengthen civil society."

22. For a recent interpretive account of the evolution and present fate of the Chilean women's movement, see Gaviola, Largo, and Palestro 1994. For more comprehensive accounts see, for example, Chuchryk 1984; Gaviola et al. 1986.

23. For a discussion of the demands of the Concertación de Mujeres por la Democracia, see Montecino and Rossetti 1990.

24. Antonieta Saa, interview, in Hola and Pischedda 1994.

25. Many feminists felt marginalized from active participation in the so-called "reconstruction of democracy." For a critical appraisal of this initiative and its outcomes, see Gaviola, Largo, and Palestro 1994.

26. See Jean Franco in this volume for an account of the often virulent debate centered on the category "gender" in connection with the official document prepared by the Servicio Nacional de la Mujer (SERNAM) for the Beijing summit.

27. The *decreto de ley* that established SERNAM was passed after a seven-month long parliamentary discussion. SERNAM's precursor was the still-born Ministerio de la Familia, proposed during the Popular Unity period, 1971–1973.

28. Since its inception, SERNAM has received funding from a variety of international agencies, including the World Bank, the Food and Agriculture Organization of the UN (FAO), UNICEF, the Pan-American Health Organization, and various NGOs, as well from the European Union and the governments of Sweden, Spain, the Netherlands, and Denmark (Servicio Nacional de la Mujer 1994, 19).

29. See Servicio Nacional de la Mujer 1994, 15.

30. According to a nationwide opinion poll conducted by the Chilean polling agency Adimark, up to 72.8 percent of Chileans over 18 years of age favor some form of legislation permitting abortion, 46 percent favor a law granting divorce in some circumstances, and 27 percent favor granting divorce on demand (Servicio Nacional del la Mujer 1994, 48).

31. Approximately 150,000 abortions are performed in Chile each year. Most of these are performed illegally and in high-risk conditions (Claro, n.d.). Therapeutic abortions were allowed in the country until 1989, when the Junta introduced legislation eliminating even this option. Needless to say, in Chile as in other places where abortion is illegal, those who suffer the worst consequences of high-risk procedures are poor women.

32. Paulina Weber, director of Movimiento Pro Emancipación de las Mujeres de Chile (MEMCH), interview by author, Santiago de Chile, July 1995.

33. The role of *monitoras* in what I call "women's work with women" over many decades in Chile has never been studied. Quite clearly, this group of foot soldiers is crucial in the struggle for women's hands and minds.

34. I paraphrase Rob Watts paraphrasing B. Frankel's insistence that we do not anthropomorphize the state (1993/1994, 107) and more generally, of course, Dorothy Smith (1990), who has been insisting on this for decades.

35. A careful study of feminist professionals in Chile in the mid-1990s remains to be done. My observations, which are based on discussions conducted since 1991 with feminists found in the myriad organizations and agencies at work in Chile, reveal very strong trends but, obviously, these observations are not conclusive.

36. See Schild 1995 for a discussion of the transformations in NGOs working with women during Chile's transition to civilian rule.

37. My conversations with certain representatives of European foundations in Santiago in the early 1990s, and more recently in July 1995, revealed a generalized sense of frustration on their part. They opposed the shift in funding priorities taking place in their own national organizations, which, they claimed, was forcing them to favor projects offering narrowly conceived economic "empowerment" schemes to the poor.

38. The government agency that controls the flow of funding from abroad is the Agencia de Cooperación Internacional. Soon after the Aylwin government came to power, representatives of international agencies stationed in Chile were called to a meeting and told that the government was not interested in "co-government."

39. Deficit restructuring by the Canadian federal and provincial governments has resulted in massive cutbacks in the country's entire social welfare sector, including funds previously transferred to a large segment of the voluntary or nonprofit sector. In effect, the state is increasingly devolving its responsibility for the social rights of citizenship to the decentralized, local level, under the guise of an appeal to community and individual empowerment. At the same time, the voluntary or nonprofit sector is itself being pushed to transform its activities into conformity with a market-like framework. For example, the United Way of Metropolitan Toronto, the largest charitable fund-raising umbrella group in Canada, which funds numerous nonprofit agencies, has increasingly insisted that larger proportions of its funding allocations to programs be used as a basis for providing entrepreneurial services at cost to other nonprofit agencies (Malcolm Blincow, personal communication).

40. This history is based on a discussion I had with the women of the Coordinadora de Mujeres of San Joaquín in July 1995. In fact, I visited them during a meeting in which they were preparing a formal letter of complaint to be presented to the mayor of San Joaquín.

As they put it, they would not be "pushed around just like that." In the end, however, it was clear to them that under the circumstances they could do little more than complain.

41. For a discussion of the Chilean women's movement, see Chuchryk 1991, 149–184.

42. I have discussed this project of the Chilean women's movement at length in earlier publications; see Schild 1991, 1994.

43. Now that the Pope has both acknowledged and recognized, within limits, the contributions of feminists, even the conservative right will have to adapt.

44. In an earlier publication (Schild 1995, 143), I linked this positioning of poor and working-class women as clients of administrable needs to Nancy Fraser's discussion of the development of "expert needs discourses" within feminist practice and its impact on feminist politics. See Fraser 1989.

References

Anderson, Benedict. 1983. *Imagined Communities: Reflections on the Origin and Spread of Nationalism*. London: Verso.

Arato, Andrew, and Jean Cohen. 1992. "Civil Society and Social Theory." In *Between Totalitarianism and Postmodernity*, ed. P. Beilharz, G. Robinson, and J. Rundell. Cambridge: MIT Press.

Bozoki, András, and Miklós Sükösd. 1993. "Civil Society and Populism in Eastern European Democratic Transitions." *Praxis International* 13 (3):224–237.

Brodie, Janine. 1995. *Politics on the Margins: Restructuring and the Canadian Women's Movement*. Halifax: Fernwood.

Canel, Eduardo. 1992. "Democratization and the Decline of Urban Social Movements in Uruguay: A Political-Institutional Account." In *The Making of Social Movements in Latin America: Identity, Strategy, and Democracy*, ed. A. Escobar and S. Alvarez. Boulder: Westview Press.

Cardoso, Ruth Corrêa Leite. 1992. "Popular Movements in the Context of the Consolidation of Democracy in Brazil." In *The Making of Social Movements in Latin America: Identity, Strategy, and Democracy*, ed. A. Escobar and S. Alvarez. Boulder: Westview Press.

Cerny, Philip G. 1990. *The Changing Architecture of Politics*. London: Sage.

Chuchryk, Patricia. 1984. "Protest, Politics, and Personal Life: The Emergence of Feminism in a Military Dictatorship, Chile 1973–1983." Ph.D. diss., York University.

______. 1991. "Feminist Anti-Authoritarian Politics: The Role of Women's Organizations in the Chilean Transition to Democracy." In *The Women's Movement in Latin America*, ed. J. Jaquette. Boulder: Westview Press.

Claro, Arparo. n.d. "El Aborto Inducido." *Mujer/Fempress*, special issue.

Corrigan, Philip. 1990. *Social Forms/Human Capacities*. London: Routledge.

Corrigan, Philip, and Derek Sayer. 1985. *The Great Arch: English State Formation as Cultural Revolution*. Oxford: Blackwell.

Escobar, Arturo, and Sonia E. Alvarez, eds. 1992. *The Making of Social Movements in Latin America: Identity, Strategy, and Democracy*. Boulder: Westview Press.

Evans, Peter, Dieter Rueschemeyer, and Theda Skocpol, eds. 1985. *Bringing the State Back In*. Cambridge: Harvard University Press.

Evers, Tilman. 1985. "Identity: The Hidden Side of New Social Movements in Latin America." In *New Social Movements and the State in Latin America*, ed. D. Slater. Amsterdam: CEDLA.

Fiske, John. 1989. *Understanding Popular Culture.* Boston: Unwin Hyman.

Foucault, Michel. 1983. "The Subject and Power." In *Michel Foucault: Beyond Structuralism and Hermeneutics,* ed. H. Dreyfus and P. Rabinow. 2nd ed. Chicago: University of Chicago Press.

______. 1991. "Governmentality." In *The Foucault Effect: Studies in Governmentality,* ed. G. Burchell, C. Gordon, and P. Miller. Chicago: University of Chicago Press.

Foweraker, Joe, and Ann L. Craig, eds. 1990. *Popular Movements and Political Change in Mexico.* Boulder: Lynne Rienner.

Fraser, Nancy, ed. 1989. *Unruly Practices: Power, Discourse, and Gender in Contemporary Social Theory.* Minneapolis: University of Minnesota Press.

Gaviola, Edda, Eliana Largo, and Sandra Palestro. 1994. *Una Historia Necesaria: Mujeres en Chile, 1973–1990.* Santiago: Aki & Aora.

Gaviola, Edda, et al. 1986. *Queremos Votar en las Proximas Elecciones: Historia del Movimiento Femenino Chileno 1913–1952.* Santiago: Coedicion.

Held, David. 1991. "Democracy, the Nation-State, and the Global System." In *Political Theory Today,* ed. D. Held. Cambridge, England: Polity Press.

Hellman, Judith Adler. 1992. "The Study of New Social Movements in Latin America and the Question of Autonomy." In *The Making of Social Movements in Latin America: Identity, Strategy, and Democracy,* ed. A. Escobar and S. Alvarez. Boulder: Westview Press.

Hola, Eugenia, and Gabriela Pischedda. 1994. *Mujeres, Poder y Politica: Nuevas Tensiones Para Viejas Estructuras.* Santiago: Centro de Estudios de la Mujer (CEM).

Joseph, Gilbert M., and Daniel Nugent, eds. 1994. *Everyday Forms of State Formation: Revolution and the Negotiation of Rule in Modern Mexico.* Durham, N.C.: Duke University Press.

Keane, John. 1988. *Civil Society and the State.* London: Verso.

______. 1995. *Tom Paine: A Political Life.* London: Bloomsbury.

Kymlicka, Will, and Wayne Norman. 1994. "Return of the Citizen: A Survey of Recent Work on Citizenship Theory." *Ethics* 104:352–381.

Laclau, Ernesto, and Chantal Mouffe. 1985. *Hegemony and Socialist Strategy: Towards a Radical Democratic Politics.* London: Verso.

Linz, Juan J., and Alfred Stepan, eds. 1978. *The Breakdown of Democracy in Latin America.* Baltimore: Johns Hopkins University Press.

Macpherson, C. B. 1962. *The Political Theory of Possessive Individualism.* Oxford: Clarendon Press.

Molyneux, Maxine. 1986. "Mobilization Without Emancipation?" In *Transition and Development: Problems of Third World Socialism,* ed. R. Fagen, C. Deere, and J. Coraggio. New York: Monthly Review Press.

MOMUPO. 1991. "Planteamiento de MOMUPO al Encuentro Nacional Feminista." Valparaiso, November. Mimeographed.

Montecino, Sonia, and Josefina Rossetti, eds. 1990. *Tramas para un Nuevo Destino: Propuestas de la Concertación de Mujeres por la Democracia.* Santiago: Arancibia Hinnos.

Mouffe, Chantal. 1988. "Hegemony and New Political Subjects: Toward a New Concept of Democracy." In *Marxism and the Interpretation of Culture,* ed. C. Nelson and L. Grossberg. Champaign-Urbana: University of Illinois Press.

Mouffe, Chantal, ed. 1992. *Dimensions of Radical Democracy.* London: Verso.

Munck, Gerardo L. 1990. "Identity and Ambiguity in Democratic Struggles." In *Popular Movements and Political Change in Mexico,* ed. J. Foweraker and A. Craig. Boulder: Lynne Rienner.

Nun, José. 1993. "Democracy and Modernization, Thirty Years Later." *Latin American Perspectives* 20 (4):7–27.
O'Donnell, Guillermo. 1973. *Modernization and Bureaucratic-Authoritarianism: Studies in South American Politics.* Berkeley: Institute for International Studies, University of California.
______. 1992. "Delegative Democracy?" Working paper no. 21, East-South Systems Transformation, University of Chicago.
PRODEMU. 1993. *Evaluación Impacto de Programas.* Santiago. Unpublished document.
Przeworski, Adam, et al. 1995. *Sustainable Democracy.* Cambridge: Cambridge University Press.
Roseberry, William. 1994. "Hegemony and the Language of Contention." In *Everyday Forms of State Formation: Revolution and the Negotiation of Rule in Modern Mexico,* ed. G. Joseph and D. Nugent. Durham, N.C.: Duke University Press.
Rowe, William, and Vivian Schelling. 1991. *Memory and Modernity: Popular Culture in Latin America.* London: Verso.
Rubin, Jeffrey W. Forthcoming. "Decentering the Regime: Culture and Regional Politics in Mexico." *Latin American Research Review.*
Sayer, Derek. 1994. "Everyday Forms of State Formation: Some Dissident Remarks on 'Hegemony.'" In *Everyday Forms of State Formation: Revolution and the Negotiation of Rule in Modern Mexico,* ed. G. Joseph and D. Nugent. Durham, N.C.: Duke University Press.
Schild, Verónica. 1991. "Gender, Class, and Politics: Poor Neighbourhood Organizing in Authoritarian Chile." Ph.D. diss., University of Toronto.
______. 1992. "Jenseits der 'Zivilgesellschaft': Unsichtbare Aspekte des Übergangs von der Diktatur in Chile." *Peripherie: Zeitschrift für Politik und Ökonomie in der Dritten Welt* 47/48:31–48.
______. 1994. "Recasting 'Popular' Movements: Gender and Political Learning in Neighbourhood Organizations in Chile." *Latin American Perspectives* 21 (2):59–80.
______. 1995. "NGOs, Feminist Politics, and Neo-Liberal Latin American State Formations: Some Lessons from Chile." *Canadian Journal of Development Studies,* special issue: 123–147.
Servicio Nacional de la Mujer. 1994. *Memoria: Servicio Nacional de la Mujer, 1990–1994.* Santiago: Editorial Antártica.
Slater, David. 1991. "New Social Movements and Old Political Questions." *International Journal of Political Economy* 21 (1):32–65.
______. 1994. "Power and Social Movements in the Other Occident: Latin America in an International Context." *Latin American Perspectives* 21 (2):11–37.
Smith, Dorothy E. 1990. *The Conceptual Practices of Power.* Toronto: University of Toronto Press.
Starr, Peter. 1995. *Logics of Failed Revolt.* Stanford: Stanford University Press.
Watts, Rob. 1993/1994. "Government and Modernity: An Essay in Thinking Governmentality." *Arena Journal* 2:103–157.

Chapter Five

The Explosion of Experience: The Emergence of a New Ethical-Political Principle in Popular Movements in Porto Alegre, Brazil

SÉRGIO GREGÓRIO BAIERLE

Urban Popular Movements in the Changing Landscape of Brazilian Politics

In this chapter, I will analyze the relationship between political culture and citizenship, based on the recent experiences of urban popular movements in Porto Alegre as well as in other Brazilian cities. My objective is to contribute to a revised analysis of these movements as strategic spaces wherein different conceptions of citizenship and democracy are debated. Urban popular movements are understood here as the conjunction of forms of action and the construction of collective identities involved in struggles for access to the city and to citizenship.

Although recent Brazilian political history reveals a growing representation of organized workers in the formal political arena (legislative and executive), as well as a more complex associational fabric, there has been a growing perception, especially in the academic sphere, that social movements have lost their dynamism. The facility with which urban popular movements have gravitated toward the arena of government action is notable. Thus, since the inception of the so-called New Republic in Brazil in 1985, many scholars of social movements have focused on institutional and technical levels of political action as key spaces for social transformation, generating studies, projects, and "miraculous" plans within what has come to be called the field of "institutional engineering" (Jacobi 1989). In the most extreme interpretation, one could not hope for active citizenship among sectors that have been traditionally segregated from mainstream economic and political life. These sectors must be transformed by the power of the state, first as clients, so that they might then become citizens (Reis 1990). Along a slightly more sophisticated line, some scholars maintain that capitalist modernity has rendered the utopia of participatory democracy impossible. The basic argument here is that organized popular sectors represent a very small parcel of the population, which is flawed by internal contradictions. Even these organized sectors are unable, due to their corporatist characteristics, to reach a level of action aimed at society as a whole and to propose objective and effective solutions to the problems afflicting large metropolitan areas such as São Paulo (Kowarick and Singer 1993).

Despite the appraisal that social movements now find themselves in crisis due to their "militaristic-instrumentalist" profile *(perfil aparelhista-militar)* (Abreu 1992), their "reducibility" that makes them "to-be-in-order-not-to-be" (Oliveira 1991), their inability to find their niche, their entrapment between "Leninist" and "movementist" logics, their rejection of political and party mediations (Castagnola 1987), their reproduction of contradictions they had sought to overcome (Cardoso 1987), or, still yet, the endurance of a process of "deconstruction" (Telles 1988), an alternative paradigm must be proposed. "In spite of the academic massacre sealed by the *postmortem* of many analysts, Brazilian popular movements are alive and constitute an important element in the configuration of democratic processes in Brazil. Popular movements, especially when one takes into account their enormous conceptual limitations, are moving Brazil toward a political model of participatory democracy" (Ottmann 1995, 188). From the perspective of urban popular movements, this process is revealed through an expansion of their "web" of actions and mediations (Alvarez 1997) and by the construction of a "public non-state sphere of social control or accountability" for the production and management of certain social policies (Genro 1995). This new political culture is guided by a new ethical-political principle, collectively constructed by breaking with the authoritarian-paternalist tradition of appropriating popular demands. Neighborhood associations, which had a pivotal role in organizing these movements, have progressively given way to broader chains of mediation. This trend is apparent in the construction of thematic movements (organized around health, housing, education, and so on); movements with a focus on issues beyond their relationship with the state (such as gender, ethnicity, religion, and sexual orientation); and, more recently, institutions that monitor state activities (such as neighborhood unions, popular councils, municipal and state councils, centralized coordinations of movements *(centrais de movimentos),* and national forums). The definition of rights begins to find spaces and languages for its institution through practices legitimized by this emerging civil society (Telles 1994).

The tendency toward pragmatism, still predominant among urban popular movements, has been interpreted in most of the academic and activist literature as an expression of fragility ("neighborhoodism," "demandism," or "immediatism"). Nevertheless, if one attempts to "de-ontologize" social movements (Melucci 1986), one can interpret this tendency as the essence of common sense given the recurrent history of clientelist traditions in Brazil. In my view, the tendency toward pragmatism is a political phenomenon with a more complex significance: the absence of hegemony. Here I use the term "hegemony" in a Gramscian sense, as a specific mode of the exercise of power that is based on active consent (Dagnino 1989; see also Dagnino, in this volume).

The absence of hegemony does not imply a classic case of revolutionary rupture from societal domination through increasingly frequent outbreaks of urban violence. Instead, I am referring to a crisis of alternatives, which leads to an ethical-political crisis. This crisis generates both a civic movement to redefine public spaces with new bases of support (such as the movements for direct elections, constitutional forums, ethical politics, the impeachment of President Collor, and the creation of sectoral councils) as well as a "predatory culture" that "sustains and legitimizes privatist and violent policies of sociability and social protection, subcultures and micro-societies of more or less open crime, on one side, and a conjunction of privilege and favoritism in the distribution of public benefits on the other" (Ribeiro 1994, 277). This is the paradox of the present conjuncture: the growing inconsistency or even the abandonment of socially integrative projects on the part of dominant classes in a context in which formal democratic institutions are being rebuilt (an increased voter base, regular elections, the liberty to organize and demonstrate, competition among political parties, and parliamentary and voter-elected governments) and in which the civic associational fabric, especially in the large urban centers, is growing.

In a certain sense, we can say that politics, beyond constituting a struggle to realize interests, consists of processing conflicts generated around the construction of identities and the definition of spaces for the expression of these conflicts. Defined as such, politics incorporates, in its paramount moment, the social construction of interest, which is never given a priori. For example, although mainly a project organized by the discourse of liberal democracy, the transition from military-authoritarian rule in Brazil cannot be read as merely a slow and gradual restoration of the democratic rules of the game, as the unidirectional reading of neoliberals and social democrats of the recent past would suggest. The transition revealed a conjunction of conflicts concerning the very definition of the quality of citizenship and of the democracy to be reconstructed. Not only did these conflicts reveal different options for a resolution of civil society–state relations; they were developed through recurrent political and social crises. That is, these conflicts occurred in a terrain that was relatively open to experience *(a experiência)*.

If we break with the militaristic notion that social movements are teleologically geared to grow and overturn the capitalist state, it is possible to understand—within the networks in which the movements operate—the struggle over diverse meanings of citizenship, established in the practices and structures wherein the collective identity of subaltern classes is constructed. On the one hand, this implies a historical-political conception of movements, in which they cease to be a given fact and constitute themselves as trajectories of options and reactions within fabrics or networks of political interaction and through structures that are revealed in their practices. This conception diverges from the idea of an inherent purity to social movements (Evers 1984) as well as from a structural-determinist conception (Castells 1983; Lojkine 1981). On the other hand, this interpretation opens the way for a strategic conception of citizenship, "which recognizes and emphasizes the intrinsic character of cultural transformation in democratic construction" (Dagnino 1994, 13).

Political Crisis and New Notions of Citizenship

In Brazil, the Proclamation of the Republic (November 15, 1989) did not establish a republic of citizens. To the contrary, during the military coup, "the people, bestialized, looked on" ("o povo assistiu a tudo bestializado") (Carvalho 1989). As a reaction to social tensions, which accumulated in the post-slavocratic order, the appropriation of liberalism did not alter the logic of excluding the subaltern classes from the political process. The nature of the relationship between the subaltern classes and the formal world of politics alternates between indifference, pragmatism, and violence, if not debauchery and carnivalization. This is not about rupture from, or legitimization of, order but is perhaps an articulation of both on another level. A "logic of ruffianism" *(lógica de malandragem)* seems to prevail, in which parody on one hand and "aptness" *(jeitinho)* on the other generate a strong sense in the popular imagination that formal public spaces are not public at all. The neighborhood, the market, the church, and the tavern are public. The formal spaces of politics (government and parliament) appear as the private spaces of the educated and privileged *(os doutores)*.

The significance of this popular perception of what constitutes the "public" is that, although subaltern classes have been identified as part of the "irrational" side of Brazilian city making, they remain the undeniable face of the character of urban society. While the logic of profit prevails in urban settings, it is obliged to coexist with and adapt to land occupations and to political pressure from inhabitants of substandard housing for more space and for the recognition of their organizations. Despite half a century of government action to repress and eradicate illegal housing settlements in all large Brazilian cities, these settlements have only increased. In Porto Alegre, for example, almost 30 percent of the population today lives in substandard housing (compared to 10 percent in 1970 and 15 percent in 1980) due to the absence of basic services and the poor quality of construction—that is, due to the skewed nature of land and property.

In a substantial effort to address this situation, the municipal government of Porto Alegre has increased its public infrastructure investments in recent years (1989–1996). The municipality has expanded urban services such as water (which now reaches more than 90 percent of the population), trash collection, sewage, street paving, public transport, and education. Overall, this effort has occurred in a context of recurrent economic crisis, with the concomitant deterioration of salaries and job opportunities, and has less than compensated for the growing impoverishment of the urban working class.

Policies of forced displacement, intensified in the years immediately following the military coup of 1964, and the effort to create a "European" city through legal mandate—as proposed by the Urban Development General Plan of Porto Alegre (with wide streets, evenly spaced lots, and artificial planning), elaborated in 1979—were unable to impede or control the various logics with which the subaltern classes interfered in this development of the city. There was a very simple reason for this: subaltern classes also are subjects; they occupy spaces, move, and speak. And they have been demonstrating this for more than a century. Today, these subjects, so often cursed and silenced, have begun to reelaborate part of their subaltern logics and penetrate some arenas of public policymaking, no longer accepting equal rules for the unequal, or the official separation between the real city and the legal city.

After 1930, the citizenship of the subaltern classes in Brazil gradually ceased to be a police matter but continued to be bargained with the state, which offered social protection on the one hand and political subordination on the other. Eradicating the political autonomy of the working classes in exchange for social rights, the state managed the concession of such rights in a hierarchical and clientelistic fashion (Santos 1979). It is important to recall that, until recently, only formal sector workers with signed work cards *(carteira de trabalho assinada)* had the right to public health services. Curiously, the universalization of the right to health (which does not guarantee its implementation), social security, and education was to happen only under the shield of the military regime (1964–1985) within a quasi-social-democratic conception. Yet the governance of social policies occurred in a technocratic, statist manner that excluded any possibility of autonomous participation in the administration of these policies by their putative beneficiaries.

After 1980, this entire framework began to be redefined in the wake of a twofold crisis: on the one hand, a "crisis of the expansion of the political arena" (O'Donnell 1982), sparked by the emergence of sectors previously excluded from the game of alliances played by the military regime; and on the other hand, a "crisis of the mode of regulation" (Boyer 1985), triggered by the external stranglehold on the economy and the state's inability to maintain investments and absorb the costs of the external debt. The adoption of the "Washington Consensus" (Fiori 1993) by the dominant classes, in the faith that no salvation outside of structural adjustment is possible, was consolidated by the election of Fernando Henrique Cardoso in 1994. Although the triumph of the Washington Consensus within the transnationalized corporate arena was supported by the mass media, the question regarding the lack of expansion of the system's social-political base remains unresolved. From the point of view of the question of citizenship, different alternatives emerge and compete in this field open to experience.

The organic conception of citizenship, identified with "State trade unionism," has endured since the "Vargas Era" (Boito 1982). In this alternative, society is partially absorbed by the state apparatus, and access to social rights is structured in a way that privileges workers in the formal economy.

In a competing, residually social-democratic conception, by contrast, the "citizen" is confused with the consumer, who seeks to satisfy particular needs. This view of citizenship implies that demands become collective only from the vantage point of individual cost-benefit analysis through the market, through the sale of individual labor, and through the periodic exercise of voting rights. The public obligation to provide social services or the state's role in their administration is only justified for sectors of the population pushed beneath the poverty line (Draibe 1988). An example of this conception is the current reform proposed for the federal social security system, which eliminates an entire hierarchy of rights and replaces it with only minimal guarantees and which remains tied to the level of individual contribution. This kind of legislation reveals a reemergence of populism, only now of a "neoliberal" kind. "In this context, the proposal that the government dismantle the State could end up by adopting the seemingly progressive feature of redistribution, even though subsequent facts (that is, the concrete results of neoliberal administrations) reveal the falsity of this appearance" (Saes 1994, 48).

In yet another competing vision, which we could classify as Christian democratic, citizens are people who need to have their social rights redeemed. Participation is identified mainly through collective projects *(o mutirão)*—that is, by the volunteer efforts of organized civil society to integrate the marginalized, such as through the creation of programs to supplement income, and through the provision of services for the "needy population." The most recent example of this vision is the campaign for "Citizen Action For Life, Against Hunger and Misery," led by the sociologist Herbert de Souza (Betinho).

Questioning the distinction between the citizen who is a bearer of civic and political freedoms and the citizen who has social rights, there is a fourth conception of citizenship that also struggles for space in Brazilian society. Understood as the "right to have rights," citizenship is here constructed by the direct and indirect participation of citizens, as political subjects, not only in solving their problems in public spaces where collective decisions can be made but also by engaging in a process of democratic radicalization aimed at transforming the very order in which they operate. In the federal realm, examples of the foundational role played by popular movements would include the health councils tied to the federal health care system, which have most influence at the local level, and the sectoral councils in the production sphere. Obviously the more revolutionary experiences, which have generated a new political culture, have been limited due to the balance of forces at the local level. Examples include the Forum do Prezeis, forums created in the first administration of Jarbas Vasconcelos in Recife (1986–1988), which permitted popular participation in the administration of urbanization projects in "special zones of social interest"; Funaps Comunitário, a fund redefined in the administration of Luiza Erundina in São Paulo (1989–1992), which supported self-built cooperative housing initiatives; and the participatory budget process *(orçamento participativo),* which encouraged popular participation in the definition of priorities and criteria for municipal budgeting in cities administered by popular coalitions including the Workers' Party. It is irrefutable that these examples represent a rich historical accumulation of experience with an articulation of popular identities. These examples challenge the dominant model of development, with its "social" policies that have produced—with or without a stable currency—nothing more than an expansion of *social apartheid.*

The Participatory Budget Movement in Porto Alegre: 1989–1996

In the principal urban centers in Brazil, urban popular movements began to assert demands through organized actions in the mid-1970s, which pivoted around land occupations and demands for access to urban services. These actions would ultimately translate into an affirmation of a culture of rights (Telles 1984), the consciousness that responding to these demands is not a favor on the part of the state but a state responsibility according to the basic rights of citizenship. This consciousness entails a fundamental change in the relationship with the state. In place of a submissive beggar, a new character emerges (Sader 1988) who challenges the traditional order, who is capable of initiating collective land occupations, barricades in the streets, physical confrontations with the police, and demonstrations in front of public buildings. These kinds of actions, which occurred from 1975 to 1985, had an immediate repercussion in the mass media and were integrated by the political opposition as acts of protest against the military regime. The movements of this period did not, however, radically question the prevailing delegative and clientelistic institutional and organizational formats, which historically had informed the dynamics of neighborhood associations (Associações de Moradores) and Societies of Friends of the Neighborhood (Sociedades de Amigos de Bairro).

The emerging culture of rights, although incipient and limited, contrasted with the tradition of neighborhood associations in Porto Alegre. In Rio Grande do Sul, and also apparently in Rio de Janeiro, the surge of neighborhood associations was preceded by the formation of state federations. In Porto Alegre, this process was based on the populist labor party administrations of the 1950s, especially during the administration of Leonel Brizola. The process involved state efforts to articulate and politically mobilize the movement in order to radicalize the national-developmentalist political block. Preventing the construction of autonomous social movements, the state appeared as a potential protagonist of social transformation, as an instrument in the struggle against "imperialism," or as the guardian of the subaltern classes. The clientelist distribution of keys in housing projects, as occurred in Vila dos Industriários (IAPI) in Porto Alegre (Schnorr 1990), was accompanied by the organization of neighborhood organizations, the principal role of which was to provide links to the government.

It is worth noting, however, that the ties to the populist administrations, constructed under a vision in which the state was to organize society and establish criteria of access to citizenship, constituted an effective tradeoff with the popular sectors. In opening pathways for permissible participation and the satisfaction of basic urban needs, spaces were also created for the attribution of alternative meanings to the marching orders coming from above. These pathways would become particularly important when clientelistic chains of command were broken by force (after 1964). In the climate of opposition to the military regime, neighborhood associations became a refuge for persecuted militants and subsequently a space of political reaffirmation. Given the violence with which the military regime descended upon the urban shantytown populations, banishing thousands of people to distant peripheries with no infrastructure (in Porto Alegre the program was entitled "Eradicate to Promote"), it is not difficult to understand urban movements' sympathy for the opposition.

A more explicitly political response from the military regime took shape only after the mid-1970s, due to the regime's need to effectively compete in elections (Fruet 1991). Thus, a series of social and housing programs were created to depoliticize the neighborhood associations, which were proliferating rapidly by the late 1970s and early 1980s. In Porto Alegre, the primary tactic utilized to depoliticize the burgeoning organizations was a designation of disputed urban lands as "public domain" in areas that were illegally occupied. As these areas, in general, were in locations unsuitable or improper for housing (along streams, nestled against hillsides, or in environmentally protected areas) and had insignificant market value due to urban zoning prohibitions, their subsequent purchase by the state proved quite profitable for all parties concerned. At the same time, the populations living in these areas began to encounter in the municipal administration either a great ally or a great enemy, with the threat of eviction riding on good "electoral behavior." With a large number of neighborhood associations gravitating toward opposition parties, municipal authorities sought to create a base of support (mayors began to be elected again only after 1985), operating in a mode similar to even the populist labor parties of the 1950s, distributing much land and agreeing to negotiate only with neighborhood associations created by them or tied to them. These were different times, however.

In most large Brazilian cities, by the late 1970s and early 1980s an intense process of popular mobilization had evolved, which we denominate here as the "practice of confrontation"—a process that systematically questioned the authoritarian model of the relationship between the state and popular organizations. This period was rich in experiences of articulation between workers' organizations and neighborhood organizations. The civil construction workers' strike in Porto Alegre in 1979, for example, brought entire families to the downtown streets to participate in the collection of a strike support fund, publicly revealing situations of poverty that usually remained hidden (Guareschi 1980). The return of multiparty competition in 1979 permitted the construction or renewal of links between popular organizations, uniting them in struggles against the military regime and in massive protest demonstrations. It seemed to many observers that a significant social transformation was within arm's reach. As Vinicius Fagundes Almeida, from the Estrada dos Alpes Neighborhood Association in Porto Alegre, recalled: "The meetings took place in the Catholic Church, in the chapel, but we invited evangelicals, people from all religions, so that they would participate. It was one of the most beautiful moments of our community struggle, because we knew that we were fighting, we had an enemy in common, and we visualized that enemy. So, we combated it: it was the dictatorship" (interview with author, 1991).

The Left's enthusiasm for the growth of popular mobilizations led many activists to work directly to construct "the movement": a unitary subject under a vertical hierarchy of command, whose priority would be to overthrow the military regime. The field of urban popular movements was thereby articulated through a contradictory conception: It was oriented, on the one hand, toward the idea of "dual power" (in the creation of popular "soviets" in the various regions of the city) and, on the other, toward communitarianism, with the remaining differences between these orientations being hidden under the dusty carpet of backroom deals and tactical alliances.

The founding of the Municipal Union of Neighborhood Associations of Porto Alegre (União Municipal de AMs de Porto Alegre, or UAMPA) in 1983 was a primary example of the effort to reconcile these apparently antagonistic conceptions of popular mobilization. The break in the traditional "monogamous" relationship between the neighborhood associations and the state occurred principally within an instrumental conception of demands for access to the city and to citizenship. This new conception of citizenship led to a series of emerging themes such as the construction of alternative proposals for public policies, the development of cooperative enterprises, the formation of women's groups, the alliance with labor movements, the dissemination of cultural groups, and political education.

All paths were to lead to the overthrow of the military regime, but what would happen after it was overthrown was left to the imagination of each component of the antiauthoritarian block. For business sectors, generally organized around the media, room for dissent would not extend much beyond the reconstruction of formal democratic institutions, ensuring that the political and economic crisis would be handled under their close supervision. For social movements, the meanings of the transition were multiple, ranging from the pragmatic belief that the overthrow of the regime would immediately improve living conditions to the more idealistic notion that it would lead to the utopia of a revolution commandeered by organized workers.

As the Left's "democratic centralism" was melded onto traditional organizational and representational forms, a delegative conception of power and a pattern modeled on trade unions were largely preserved in the neighborhood associations—as reflected by the monopoly of representation by place of residence and the tendency toward legalism. Given the urgent need to expand the opposition's popular base, the definition of who represents whom and what—stemming more from a bureaucratic conception than an organic one—ended up generating a series of semiartificial federative structures without real power of representation, functioning more as "firemen" running after "fires" and seldom able to take a leading role as organizer or constructor. The popular organizational results were, in the neighborhood, the neighborhood association; in the municipality, the Union; in the state, the Federation; and at the federal level, the Confederation. It was as if "territories" could be occupied by being named and as if the proper name, ad hoc, would forge the framing of the subjects subordinated to it. UAMPA embodied, in truth, the apex of the "practice of confrontation" among diverse Leftist political tendencies, and two years later an identity crisis began to plague this "federative" organization. If the command was supposed to be unitary, which tendency would exercise control? And how could that tendency be made to prevail? How could association members live with political differences without translating those differences into diverse practices and institutions?

With the end of the military regime in 1985, the ties that had sustained the antiauthoritarian bloc were dissolved. Often considered a school for Leftist political activists, the urban popular movements were torn apart by the different articulations of forces that had constituted them, finally breaking the enchantment of "common unity." To the extent that opposition parties began to assume positions within the formal political arena, their differing proposals for the reconstruction of democratic institutions and for social transformation became more explicit. In Porto Alegre, for example, with the Democratic Labor Party (Partido Democratico Trabalhista, or PDT) holding the mayorship from 1986 to 1988, a new effort to redefine the populist-labor organic conception of citizenship was revealed. Certain municipal agencies attempted to constitute themselves as the cupola of popular organizations. The proposal to create a popular council tied to each municipal department (always promised and never put into practice), with the participation of representatives from neighborhood associations, collapsed the roles of political parties, the state, and social movements into a single role. For example, the PDT administration employed "neighborhood inspectors" who were in fact nothing more than the PDT's neighborhood political brokers *(cabos eleitorais)* and who were contracted by the Municipal Department of Urban Maintenance to "represent" neighborhoods vis-à-vis the government, seeking to annul the region's own representative mechanisms.

At the state and federal levels, the Party of the Brazilian Democratic Movement (Partido do Movimento Democratico Brasileiro, or PMDB) deployed a residual conception of citizenship that fused social-democratic and Christian-democratic conceptions. Social services were selectively offered to poor sectors of the population and at the same time their participation was encouraged—but only at the level of policy implementation and not in the formulation of policies or in the distribution of resources. The most explicit example of this was the distribution of milk coupons during the Sarney government. The coupons were generally allocated, in insufficient quantities, to neighborhood organizations, which in turn assumed responsibility for directly distributing the coupons to the needy population.

This "school of hard knocks" *(educação pela pedra)* experienced by the urban popular movements translated, on the one hand, into the growth of pessimism and pragmatism with regard to their relationship with the state but, on the other hand, created opportunities for the strategic reconstruction of urban struggles. This reconstruction entailed the development of innovative practices—such as participation in national, state, and local constitution-drafting processes—as well as a redefinition of the advisory role of NGOs, the eschewal of a unitary conception of "the movement," and the expansion of the banner for urban reform. From this new emphasis on the instruments of urban intervention, an emphasis on democratic administration evolved, breaking with the statist and technocratic conception of planning. This emphasis entails the acknowledgment that no single vision of the future can prevail in a city produced by a multiplicity of subjects with differentiated interests. "Because of this, planning should be more than a model of the 'good city'; it should be an institutional space in which movements of transformation can be interpreted by society" (Rolnik 1990, 18).

The administrations of the Popular Front (1989–1996) in Porto Alegre were in principle oriented toward popular participation; the idea to govern in partnership with the popular councils (understood as autonomous instances of the articulation of diverse popular movements by city region) initially expressed a conflict between the soviet model and populist appeal, between the conceptions of "a government of the workers" and "a government for all of the city," which was in part resolved by the following formula: Govern with the workers, but for all of the city (Harnecker 1993).

A product of multiple subjects, the participatory budget process (*orçamento participativo,* or OP) was constructed in a period of permanent tension between the municipal government's degree of openness to civil society's projects and the degree of society's institutional learning, especially among the urban popular movements. This does not mean that some optimum balance cannot be reached, but rather it implies that the process is a game, the permanence and quality of which always depend on the will of both sides to continue playing.

The OP process began in 1989 as an immense participatory research project, involving the municipal administration and organized communities in the sweeping consolidation of popular demands and priorities. The first difficulty encountered was the representational structure of the urban popular movements. The city's general plan divided it into only four zones, and these zones did not coincide with the divisions in the organizational structure of the urban popular movements. Therefore, it was necessary to augment the number of regions to arrive at the current number of sixteen, some of which are now also subdivided into microregions. This new organizational structure implied a radical redefinition of representation of the community leaders. Forced by successive authoritarian and populist governments to conform to the definitions of official acknowledgment and political clientelism, community organizations succeeded in obtaining a space of legitimacy no longer dependent on the strength of their connection to the state apparatus but based on their effective capacity to mobilize and persuade. It was no longer enough to be president of a neighborhood association; it had now become necessary to debate proposals in plenary session assemblies open to participation by the most varied types of organizations and by individual citizens.

The second problem encountered was one of method; although the OP was oriented toward determining priorities by region, the process generated a volume of demands far greater than the municipal administration could meet—either financially or operationally. Under political pressure, the government was forced to carry out fiscal reforms in order to increase revenues and reduce its debt to a level of less than 10 percent of the annual budget. This reform liberated funds for new investments. Concomitantly, to ensure that the investment decisions were made via the Council of Participatory Budgeting (Conselho do Orçamento Participativo, or COP), the government—through the creation of the Planning Cabinet (Gabinete de Planejamento, or GAPLAN) and the Coordination of Communitarian Relations (Coordenação de Relações Comunitárias, or CRC)—tied the execution of planning and investment decisions directly to the mayor's office. This strategy partially breaks with the traditional prominence of municipal department heads *(secretários)* and the formation of clientelist fiefdoms centered in those departments. The COP—currently comprised of forty-six members (two from each region, two from each of five thematic plenary sessions, one from UAMPA, one civil service employee, and only two from the government, who do not have the right to vote)—established a systematic criteria for establishing budgetary priorities such as the level of poverty of each region, the number of people who would benefit from a particular budgetary allocation, and the level of participation in a regional assembly.

These systematic criteria enable participants to accompany and discuss even the calculations by which particular resources are allocated to meet specific demands. For example, as illustrated in Table 5.1, the COP can verify, for the year 1995, the distance in meters of asphalt that is due to each of the city's regions. After 1994, with the goal of involving people and organizations tied to other movements (such as cultural, trade union, women's, black, and other movements), thematic plenary sessions were created (focusing on transportation, health and social assistance, education, culture and recreation, economic development and taxation, and urban development).

Although the OP has become a central axis of popular grassroots participation in Porto Alegre, there is an interrelation between its dynamic and the whole fabric

TABLE 5.1 Asphalt Appropriations for Porto Alegre's Municipal Regions, 1995

Region	Need[a]	Proportion Affected[b]	Population[c]	Priority[d]	Total		Meters of Asphalt
01	3	4	2	3	12	(4.3%)	1,004
02	(This region was not considered for this category in 1995)						
03	3	6	3	6	18	(6.5%)	1,505
04	9	2	1	12	24	(8.7%)	2,007
05	3	4	2	12	21	(7.6%)	1,756
06	6	4	1	9	20	(7.2%)	1,673
07	3	4	3	12	22	(8.0%)	1,840
08	3	2	1	6	12	(4.3%)	1,004
09	6	2	1	12	21	(7.6%)	1,756
10	3	4	2	6	15	(5.4%)	1,255
11	3	2	1	9	15	(5.4%)	1,255
12	6	2	3	12	23	(8.3%)	1,924
13	12	2	1	12	27	(9.8%)	2,258
14	3	2	3	6	14	(5.0%)	1,171
15	3	2	2	12	19	(6.9%)	1,589
16	3	2	4	3	12	(4.3%)	1,004
Total					275	(100.0%)	23,001

[a]Lack of services and/or public infrastructure.

[b]Proportion of the region's population living in areas with an extreme lack of services or infrastructure (criteria no longer used after 1995) (weight 2).

[c]Total population of the area (weight 1).

[d]Priorities chosen by the region (weight 3).

SOURCE: Municipal Planning Department of Porto Alegre.

of other open spaces for direct and indirect participation in the sphere of municipal public power. To contemplate the future of the city, for example, the "Constituent City" *(Cidade Constituinte)* was created in 1993—an assembly with annual publications that articulates the most diverse social sectors with the aim of collectively establishing future directives for city planning. Some of these directives are being incorporated in the reformulation of the general plan (including participatory planning with respect to popular territorialities; decentralization, including urban administration; the struggle against real estate speculation and spatial segregation, with an incentive to construct popular housing; and the articulation of the city as a technological pole). This effort to think of the city as a whole has as its foundation the participation of citizens, based on sectoral councils that were institutionalized in the early 1990s. Examples of these sectoral councils include the Councils on Education; Health; Housing and Access to Land; Transportation; Children and Adolescents; and Women. The councils facilitate a decentralized approach to the administration of specific public policies. Councils that address children's issues—in which the council members are chosen by direct vote of the population and are responsible for proposing policy alternatives to problems involving street children and instances of violence against children—have also been established in the city's regions. Similarly, in partnership with the courts, a grassroots paralegal program has been created by a feminist NGO (Themis)—in collaboration with municipal authorities—to train poor and working-class women to advise neighborhood women on issues that concern them. Local health commissions (Comissões Locais de Saúde) have also been established, involving the direct participation of beneficiaries and health professionals. School councils (Conselhos Escolares) involve the participation of students, parents, teachers, and state employees and are engaged in selecting school administrators and setting local educational priorities.

Although dynamic and ever changing, the structure of the OP involves an annual cycle constituted by four basic movements: two rounds of regional and thematic plenary sessions promoted by the municipal administration in conjunction with delegates and council members, the elaboration of the actual budget, and its approval by the city council.

In the first-round plenary sessions, the previous year's investment plan is subjected to citizen scrutiny in a public rendering of accounts. What was and was not accomplished is evaluated, and the principal problems in the fulfillment of the agreed-upon timeline are identified. This evaluation is the culmination of a series of previous discussions carried out in the citizen forums described earlier, assembled by regional and thematic OP representatives and by interested citizens to monitor a given public work or service. In these forums, government employees responsible for the works or services in question are obliged to clarify or reexamine specific projects in that area.

Also in this first round, regional and thematic delegates are chosen, in accordance with the number of participants present respecting criteria of proportionality, which are in turn reconsidered each year. This continuous discussion of criteria has the objective of avoiding, as much as possible, the occurrence of "stacking" *(inchaços)*, or of bringing people to the meetings to simply vote with "so-and-so" *(fulano)* and not to effectively participate in the debates. It is in these intermediate plenary sessions that organized segments of the population identify and define their most pressing needs and select the demands and themes to be prioritized in the municipal budget (such as street paving, sanitation, land regularization, housing, education, health, public transit, and culture).

In the second round of the OP, participants of each plenary session deliver their budgetary priorities to the government and choose council members for the COP. After this process, regional and thematic Forums of Delegates of Participatory Budgeting (FROPs) are also formed.

The elected council members are charged with proposing, monitoring, and deciding on all subjects related to the municipal budget—from discussions about revenue and spending, the long-range plan, and the Law of Budgetary Directives (Lei de Diretrizes Orçamentárias) to the actual execution of the budget. The COP is coordinated by a commission made up of the two government representatives in the council and two representatives from among the popular council members, elected by their peers. Beyond this commission, there is also a tripartite commission made up of six members (two from the government, two from the COP, and two public servants), which deliberates the contracting of municipal employees. Council members cannot be reelected to the COP for more than two consecutive years. Also, councillors are not remunerated for their activities.

The regional and thematic delegates, in turn, demand responsiveness from COP council members, disseminate discussions about investments under way in their particular area of thematic interest, and maintain the power to dismiss council members from plenary sessions if they are found to disregard the decisions of the FROP.

The third step of the cycle entails the production of the budget itself. In this phase, all the municipal secretaries and government representatives who previously met with the COP are involved in discussing the policies pursued by their sectors, the public works and services proposed, and the cost as well as technical and juridical viability of particular policies. These debates also have repercussions in the FROPs, which are thereby able to better prioritize their demands. On the basis of COP and FROP inputs, the government creates a detailed draft budget proposal and submits it to the COP for evaluation before drawing up the final version. Although there has been no instance in which a COP decision was not respected by the government, the mayor, according to the COP's internal guidelines, has final veto power. Because the mayor depends on the support of the COP in seeking the city council's approval for the budget, he has a built-in incentive to reach consensus with the COP.

After COP approval, the municipal budget is sent to the city council for a vote. Although this moment is always tense—as many council members have their own projects they wish to see deliberated—the pressure from the OP delegates and COP members is very strong, which generally results in almost the entire budget proposal being approved. COP members have begun to use cameras and tape recorders to register the opinions of the city council members, threatening to reproduce any damning evidence in working-class neighborhoods *(vilas populares)*. Although this tension can be read in different ways, it is not exactly a zero-sum game but is rather more of a dispute between blocks of forces that is articulated both inside and outside the legislative arena.

No longer able to function as privileged dispatchers, many city council members are perplexed by the OP process. In 1996, for example, some of these members attempted to amend the COP bylaws. Although popular participation in the elaboration of the municipal budget was enacted into law in 1990, considerable polemics continue regarding the advantages and disadvantages of regulating the functioning of the COP. Some city council members believe that only a percentage of resources (say, 50 percent) should be allocated by the OP process. Others believe that the COP should only be assigned decisionmaking power over investments in the peripheral, poor neighborhoods, while the city council should decide on questions of more "global" interest to the city as a whole. In fact, city council members retain these prerogatives in approving the budget. Still, some opposition members feel constrained by the power and participation of organized segments of the population.

The experience of the Popular Front government has triggered a fundamental learning process. This learning did not occur because the state imposed a particular vision of democratic participation on society. Rather, learning was possible because the state opened up the public space in which organized popular sectors could appropriate local policymaking, revealing that the process of appropriation could be enacted by multiple (rather than unitary) subjects representing a wide array of social and political forces. The municipal government no doubt played an active role in constituting this multiple subject, but the government's actions were themselves shaped by the popular sectors' autonomously constructed "interests," now articulated in their own spaces of civic action.

The type of "social contract" established by the OP (Pozzobon 1995)—with its roots in the political culture of the citizens of Porto Alegre (it is estimated that more than one hundred thousand people are directly or indirectly affected by the OP process, although only ten thousand people involve themselves annually in the plenary sessions)—has begun to transform itself into a "public, non-state sphere of control," wherein public power (the state) establishes a space of coadministration, debating its proposals for the city with organized sectors of the population. This concept serves as an important instrument for the analysis both of neoliberal proposals to shrink the state apparatus as well as of the statist tradition of historical socialist experiences. This "non-state" public sphere has to do with establishing respect for a collectively constructed will by reconstructing the role of the state on grounds clearly distinct from the authoritarian tradition that has historically characterized the presence of the state in Brazilian society. Even the congress, for example, did not emerge in Brazil as an effective public space that was open to societal participation. To the contrary, its configuration as a type of "club of notables" only very recently has begun to be transformed. The OP process begins to approximate a more genuinely democratic conception of the public sphere. Although constituted as a sphere of municipal public control, and therefore still limited by the boundaries of municipal public actions, the OP enables the emergence of popular sectors as active subjects of citizenship, as producers of opinions and public decisions.

The success of this experience and its rapid transformation as an international reference implies, however, important strategic challenges for urban popular movements. In truth, urban popular movements in Porto Alegre remain contradictory today. Although these movements are now structured within a network of organizations and people with the power to intervene in multiple spaces of municipal government, they have difficulty moving or articulating their demands beyond the guidelines and parameters of this governmental sphere.

For example, with the establishment of OP plenary sessions in the regions, the space of the OP began, in a certain sense, to be confused with the actions and efforts of neighborhood-based popular councils. What is the difference between a meeting of FROP and a popular council when the leaders present are often one and the same? The popular council meets autonomously, while a Regional Coordinator of Participatory Budgeting (CROP), an employee of the municipal administration charged with coordinating each plenary session with diverse governmental sectors, is always present in the FROP plenaries. In many regions, one no longer speaks of "popular councils," and these differences are diluted. Thus, the construction of popular interests has begun to occur in some regions mostly in the spaces of coadministration, in the public sphere of control of the municipal budget. This does not mean that popular subjects have lost their autonomous critical perspective, as evidenced by the militant tone of demands articulated in regional plenaries of the OP, wherein CROP takes on a role subordinate to the collective. Yet the absence of differentiation certainly represents a problem for the urban popular movements' organizational autonomy. On the one hand, the questions debated tend to concentrate almost exclusively on the actions of the municipal administration. On the other, because the development of this new political culture implied in the democratic structure of the OP has not been consolidated strategically, it has also not been translated into practices that would more effectively and systematically confront the many existing tensions within and among popular movements. There is a certain consensus among the leaders of the sixteen regions of Porto Alegre on the limits of UAMPA to fulfill this articulatory role, but other alternatives have yet to emerge.

Furthermore, with the increasingly complex structure of representation of the OP, difficulties are emerging in the relationships among the multiple spaces for participation that today are involved in the OP process. The greatest difficulty today is how to encourage the COP and the FROPs to effectively address questions of more global interest, such as the reform of the city's general plan. The demands of council members' local constituencies continue to focus on localized region-specific interests. This situation enhances the relative autonomy of the council members when they have to vote on more global policy questions. Individual autonomy can promote a learning process but always runs the risk of not adequately translating the interests of the members' constituencies.

Here resides another conundrum. The fact that a channel of participation has been opened does not eliminate, in itself, the social division of labor or the unequal appropriation of strategic information. In a context in which the government sector can withhold prime information, even a council member may feel uncomfortable voting on certain proposals, but it is difficult to vote against the government position if the member cannot construct a consistent counterargument. As council members only meet in the official spaces of the COP and have little contact with one another in other spaces of negotiation or even in seminars, educational events, or parallel debates, their positions on "global" planning issues tend to be all the more fragile the further a particular policy in dispute is removed from the specific demands of their regional or thematic plenary sessions.

Social Movements and the Emergence of a New Ethical-Political Principle

Despite the embryonic character of urban popular movements in Porto Alegre, their unequal distribution of experience, and the gap in strategic information, the experience of the OP points to the emergence of a new ethical-political principle. What is fundamental is the emergence of a new type of citizen, a new relationship between the public and the private, constructed as a countercurrent to the capitalist modernization of Brazil, which for its part is creating deprivation, massification, exclusion, and the privatization of social life and the public sphere. The rupture from state tutelage and the remaking of processes of representation and construction of interests express a demystification of politics and a qualification of democracy. Citizenship ceases to be looked at by the state only in terms of public works and services, because more than responses are at play here. What is at stake is a redefinition of politics itself and of the institutions that formulate "responses." More than "taking power," what these new citizens question, radically, is the mode in which power is exercised.

It is imperative to consider critically the alleged incapacity of the urban popular movements to think more "globally," to move beyond fragmentary, particularistic, localized, and parochial conceptions of the city. We must also understand that the capacity to view the public interest more globally, although empirically relevant, entails a learning process. It is part of the history of the dominant classes, but it is a novelty for the subaltern classes. In Porto Alegre, through the OP, an important change is occurring in this regard. If in the first years of the OP the principal problems addressed were centered on regional demands and criteria, more recently, in thematic discussions, key questions such as land regularization, changes in the city's general plan, and the construction of economic alternatives have begun to be debated. Furthermore, in the FROPs as well as the COP, proposals directed at other governmental levels (federal and state) are also now emerging, such as ballot initiatives to approve state and federal budgets with the goal of expanding the available resources for health and education in the city.

In sum, I are not speaking here of an abstract citizenship ruled by moral imperatives. The ethic that has developed, understood as a radical democratic rationality, is the fruit of political education over very concrete policy issues. The people do not meet just because they like to gather together in a gesture of Christian solidarity, although this is in itself a valid reason. They meet because they need to, because they have needs and it is in discussing their needs that they construct collective interests, discover causes and consequences, learn to speak, to listen, to plan. Their actions produce concrete changes that improve their lives. The collective consciousness of knowing how to be the author of transformation in their streets, in their neighborhoods, and in their city is a fundamental tool through which this new ethical-political principal is forged, structuring a social and rationally designed solidarity.

This is nothing magical or unprecedented in the contemporary world, and much less does this text have the pretension that it contributes to a new myth, but experiences such as those of Porto Alegre, in Brazil, can only emerge at the eve of the turn of the millennium.

The election and the reelection of the Popular Front (1988, 1992, and 1996) were not "electoral accidents" but a continuing expression of a need for political space by the urban popular movements and other sectors. The Workers' Party, which leads the Popular Front, is itself a type of social movement, composed of thousands of militants with active political lives who learned, through the construction of the party, to elaborate their internal differences through democratically constructed rules.

The experience of the OP enables us to begin to deconstruct what we can call the "state paradigm" (with the aim of exhausting and defeating it)—a paradigm informing both the technocratic environment that produced capitalist modernization in Brazil before and after the military regimes, as well as many sectors of the Left, which are still wedded to the notion that the solution to social questions can only be found in an increase in the regulatory capacity of the state apparatus. The very notion of the state separated from society is in question here, to the extent that the public debate around societal interests impedes the conception, for example, that the economy is a sphere with no subject, or the subject of which is entirely determined by capitalist logic.

The conservative project is characterized by an effort to reduce or impede a politicization of traditionally neutralized areas of the social (Offe 1985). If, in the "postindustrialized" countries, the question facing social movements is the politicization of private spheres of life and of economic civil society, then in countries like Brazil these new perspectives of action and collective identity are founded in the necessity of the political construction of the nation. In this sense, the idea of citizenship acquires a dual significance in the present conjuncture. This dual significance of citizenship includes both the exercise of rights from the state and the self-governance and autonomy of society. Drawing on Touraine (1989), one can perceive that urban popular movements join historical movements with movements that are also increasingly more social; they not only search for their integration into a given societal project but seek to critically interact with this process, developing a foundational practice and identifying allies and enemies in the process of gaining knowledge and consciousness about *lived* social relations.

References

Abreu, Haroldo. 1991. "Movimentos Populares Urbanos." Rio de Janeiro: FASE.

______. 1992. *Movimentos Sociais: Crise e Perspectivas*. Porto Alegre: FASE/CIDADE.

Alvarez, Sonia E. 1997. "Reweaving the Fabric of Collective Action: Social Movements and Challenges to 'Actually Existing Democracy' in Brazil." In *Between Resistance and Revo-*

lution: Cultural Politics and Social Protest, ed. R. Fox and O. Starn, 83–117. New Brunswick, N.J.: Rutgers University Press.

Boito, Armando, Jr. 1982. *A burguesia contra Populismo.* São Paulo: Brasiliense.

Boyer, Robert. 1985. "Accumulation, Regulation et Crise: Quelques Definitions et Problème de Méthode." Paris. Mimeographed.

Cardoso, Ruth Corrêa Leite. 1987. "Movimentos Sociais na América Latina." *Revista Brasileira de Ciências Sociais* 3 (1):27–37.

Carvalho, José Murilo de. 1989. *Os Bestializados.* São Paulo: Cia. das Letras.

Castagnola, José Luís. 1987. "Problemática y Alternativas de los Nuevos Movimientos Sociales." *Cadernos del CLAEH* 42:154–167.

Castells, Manuel. 1983. *A Questão Urbana.* São Paulo: Paz e Terra.

Dagnino, Evelina. 1989. "A Contribuição de Antonio Gramsci para a Teoria da Ideologia." Universidade Estadual de Campinas, São Paulo. Mimeographed.

______. 1994. "Apresentação." In *Anos 90: Política e Sociedade no Brasil,* ed. E. Dagnino. São Paulo: Brasiliense.

Draibe, Sonia Miriam. 1988. *O Estado do Welfare Brasileiro.* Campinas: NEPP–Universidade Estadual de Campinas.

Evers, Tilman. 1984. "Identidade, a Face Oculta dos Novos Movimentos Sociais." *Novos Estudos CEBRAP* 4:11–27.

Fiori, José Luís. 1993. "Ajuste, transição e governabilidade: O enigma Brasileiro." In *Desajuste global modernização conservadora,* ed. M. Tavares and J. Fiori. Rio de Janeiro: Paz e Terra.

Fruet, Genoveva Maya. 1991. "Conflict, Continuity, and Community Interaction in a City Public Housing Agency, Porto Alegre, Brazil." Master's thesis, Massachusetts Institute of Technology.

Genro, Tarso. 1995. "Experiências Democráticas de Participação Popular nas Prefeituras: Porto Alegre." In *Poder Local, Participação Popular, Construção da Cidadania,* ed. R. Villas-Bôas and V. Telles. São Paulo: Pólis, Fórum Nacional de Participação Popular.

Guareschi, Pedrinho. 1980. "Urban Social Movements in Brazilian Squatter Settlements." Master's thesis, University of Wisconsin.

Harnecker, Marta. 1993. *De Armonia y Conflitos.* Havana: MEPLA.

Jacobi, Pedro. 1989. "Atores Sociais e Estado." *Espaço e Debates* 26:10–21.

Kowarick, Lúcio, and André Singer. 1993. "A Experiência do Partido dos Trabalhadores na Prefeitura de São Paulo." *Novos Estudos CEBRAP* 35:195–216.

Lojkine, Jean. 1981. *O Estado Capitalista e a Questão Urbana.* São Paulo: Martins Fontes.

Melucci, Alberto. 1986. "Il Conflito come Teatro, dai Personaggi ai Segni." In *Fine della Politica? La Politica tra Decisione e movimenti,* ed. A. Bolaffi and M. Ilardi. Rome: Riuniti.

O'Donnell, Guillermo. 1982. *1966–1973, El Estado Burocrático-Autoritario: Triunfos, Derrotas y Crises.* Buenos Aires: Belgrano.

Offe, Claus. 1985. "New Social Movements: Challenging the Boundaries of Institutional Politics." *Social Research* 52 (4):817–868.

Oliveira, Francisco de. 1991. "Os Protagonistas do Drama: Estado e Sociedade no Brasil." In *Classes e Movimentos Sociais na América Latina,* ed. S. Laranjeira. São Paulo: Hucitec.

Ottmann, Götz. 1995. "Movimentos Sociais Urbanos e Democracia no Brasil." *Novos Estudos CEBRAP* 41:186–207.

Pozzobon, Regina. 1995. "A Cidadania com Igualdade Plena: um Caminho em Construção na Cidade de Porto Alegre." *De Olho no Orçamento* 2 (3):4.

Reis, Fábio Wanderley. 1990. "Cidadania Democrática, Corporativismo e Política Social no Brasil." In *Década Perdida de Noventa: Prioridades e Perspectivas de Políticas Públicas,* vol. 4, ed. F. W. Reis et al. Brasília: IPEA.

Ribeiro, Luiz Cesar de Queiroz. 1994. "Reforma Urbana na Cidade da Crise: Balanço Teórico e Desafios." In *Globalização, Fragmentação e Reforma Urbana,* ed. L. Ribeiro. Rio de Janeiro: Civilização Brasileira.

Rolnik, Raquel. 1990. "Morar, Atuar e Viver." *Teoria e Debate* 9:18–23.

Sader, Eder. 1988. *Quando Novos Personagens Entraram em Cena.* São Paulo: Paz e Terra.

Saes, Décio. 1994. "A Reemergência do Populismo." In *Anos 90: Política e Sociedade no Brasil,* ed. E. Dagnino. São Paulo: Brasiliense.

Santos, Wanderley Guilherme dos. 1979. *Cidadania e Justiça.* Rio de Janeiro: Campus.

Schnorr, Pedro Rudimar. 1990. "Vilas Populares: do IAPI à Periferia." CIDADE, Porto Alegre. Mimeographed.

Telles, Vera da Silva. 1984. "A Experiência do Autoritarismo e Práticas Instituintes." Master's thesis, FFLCH, University of São Paulo.

______. 1988. "Anos 70: Experiências, Práticas e Espaços Políticos." In *As Lutas Sociais e a Cidade,* ed. L. Kowarick. São Paulo: Paz e Terra.

______. 1994. "Sociedade Civil e a Construção de Espaços Públicos." In *Anos 90: Política e Sociedade no Brasil,* ed. E. Dagnino. São Paulo: Brasiliense.

Touraine, Alain. 1989. *Palavra e Sangue: Política e Sociedade na América Latina.* Campinas: Universidade Estadual de Campinas/Trajetória Cultural.

Part Two

The Cultural Politics of Ethnicity, Race, and Gender

Chapter Six

Ambiguity and Contradiction in a Radical Popular Movement

JEFFREY RUBIN

In discussing contemporary leftist movements in Mexico and Latin America, scholars and activists often criticize Leninist strategies and praise the less hierarchical, more identity-based politics of recent social movements. At the same time, observers of social movements often wonder whether such decentralized, autonomous, and plural efforts can forge successful challenges to broad structures of domination (Calderón, Piscitelli, and Reyna 1992, 27). For example, in contrast to expectations of broadening alliances and increasing political clout on the part of Colombian social movements a decade ago (Fals Borda 1986), observers paint a bleak picture of the Colombian Left in the 1990s. Marc Chernick and Michael Jiménez document the simultaneous failures of Colombian guerrilla movements, characterized by "unambiguous vanguardism" and an unarmed left weakened by fragile mobilization and violent repression (1993, 73–74). In another context, Amrita Basu contrasts the weaknesses of radically democratic grassroots organizing in the Indian state of Maharashtra with those of the Leninist politics of the Communist Party of India (Marxist), which governed the state of West Bengal.

This chapter is based on field research carried out in Juchitán, Mexico, in 1983, 1985, 1986, and 1993 and funded by the Social Science Research Council, the Doherty Foundation, the Inter-American Foundation, the Tinker Foundation (through a grant to the Committee on Latin American and Iberian Studies at Harvard University), and Amherst College. I am grateful for the close readings and thoughtful comments provided by Amrita Basu, Vivienne Bennett, Leslie Salzinger, and Austin Sarat. Earlier versions of this paper were presented at the Latin American Labor History Conference, SUNY at Stony Brook, in April 1992 and at the seventeenth International Congress of the Latin American Studies Association in Los Angeles in September 1992. Parts of the current version were presented at the Ethnic Studies Seminar at the University of California at San Diego in January 1994 and at the Cultures of Politics/Politics of Cultures Conference at the State University of Campinas, Brazil, in March 1996. I am indebted to the participants at all of these meetings for their thoughtful comments.

After promising beginnings for each form of opposition, grassroots organizing in Maharashtra could not sustain itself and splintered over issues of gender and political strategy, while the communists in West Bengal promoted only very limited reforms. As a result, Basu argues, "if a political strategy is to be radical, it must maintain a creative tension between 'guided spontaneity' and organizational discipline" (1992, 237).

This chapter will examine the internal characteristics of a radical grassroots movement, the Coalition of Workers, Peasants, and Students of the Isthmus, or COCEI,[1] which has successfully mobilized peasants and workers on the basis of just such creative tension in the Zapotec city of Juchitán, in southern Mexico. COCEI sustained militant grassroots activism and electoral participation in Juchitán through fifteen years of regime-sanctioned killings and military occupation, eventually gaining the right to govern the city of 100,000 in 1989. In contested and changing ways, the path from polarization to democratization brought fair elections, opposition government, new opportunities for alternative linguistic and cultural elaboration, spaces for dissent and democracy in labor unions and community associations, and protection for small-scale agriculture. In describing COCEI, I will argue that its endurance and strength derived from the "creative tension" Basu recommends and that the source of this creativity lay in the numerous axes of ambiguity and contradiction within the movement itself.

COCEI's success in mounting continual challenges to local and national authorities in the face of violence occurred in large part because Juchitecos transformed their neighborhoods, workplaces, and fiestas into sites of intense political discussion, redefining the meanings and alliances of their culture in the course of recurring daily activities. It was this fostering of a new and hybrid political culture (see this volume's Introduction, 8–9) that enabled COCEI to secure its power even as neoliberal economic restructuring and the demobilization of popular movements dominated policymaking elsewhere in Mexico and Latin America. Like the Zapotec political movements and cultural practices that preceded it in Juchitán, COCEI forged alternatives to the discourses of nationalism and economic development through which outsiders characterized the city and sought to intervene there. By making use of these local capacities for cultural resistance and appropriation to construct an organized movement and gain formal political power, COCEI brought about an enduring form of regional democratization.

This democracy includes, but is not limited to, free and fair electoral competition and the transfer of municipal power. In addition, COCEI's cultural politics "mobilize[d] constructions of individuals, rights, economies, and social conditions that cannot be strictly defined within standard paradigms of Western modernity".[2] As a result of these alternative constructions, poor Juchitecos in the 1990s had greater voice, and could hold those with power more accountable, in more arenas of their lives, than they could in the 1960s and 1970s. Furthermore, the militancy and disruption that fostered democracy in Juchitán were themselves facilitated by difference. Democracy occurred in Juchitán not because Western practices had proceeded apace there but because Juchitecos exercised control over the cultural and economic borders linking them to the outside.[3] As a result, much of the normalization characteristic of Western development was avoided in Juchitán, and the intersection of Zapotec and Mexican cultures produced a hybrid form of modernity (García Canclini 1989) unusually open to innovation as well as to dialogue with Western discourses of democracy.

The success of COCEI's activism shows that the process of "unsettl[ing] dominant cultural meanings" (see this volume's Introduction, 8) through collective action is simultaneously one of constructing and reconstructing unstable meanings within movements. Thus, rather than portraying a social movement as an internally coherent set of beliefs and practices, I make use of my experiences of daily life among COCEI supporters to focus on "the blurred zones in between" what were once seen as "the crystalline patterns of a whole culture" (Rosaldo 1989, 209). These blurred zones within COCEI include *ambiguity* with regard to social and political forms (such as violence, democracy, and gender) and *contradictions* concerning people's claims about their own and others' experiences (such as between the accounts of COCEI leaders and ordinary Juchitecos, and between those of men and women). Both of these phenomena illustrate the ongoing presence within COCEI of different and at times opposing forms of discourse and practice. In addition, COCEI's experiences demonstrate that a politics based on vanguard leadership, dogmatic Marxist analysis, and often confrontational stances can be successful and also contain spaces for the production of meaning by ordinary people, for alliance and accommodation, and for internal contestation over representation and mobilization.

What Michel de Certeau calls "tactics and strategies" (1984, xix) coexist in COCEI. As a result, the improvised, "tactical" manipulations that people perform in their daily lives can take on, through COCEI's own actions, the more coordinated, "strategic" power of the regime. However, as a result of the hierarchical process through which COCEI determines its strategies, ordinary Juchitecos experience impositions not only from the state but from their own movement as well. These forms of control occur through what Néstor García Canclini has called "deductivist" economism and "inductivist" folklore (1988). COCEI leaders and intellectuals assume both homogeneous class interests—that Juchiteco peasants and workers share a common class position and corresponding material interests—and inherent Zapotec identity—that all Juchitecos are and know themselves to be members of an indigenous culture the attributes of which remain fixed through time. García Canclini argues that the prevalence of such essentialist assumptions explains "why so many popular projects for transformation do not manage to alter the social structure" (1988, 484). However, COCEI's experiences indicate that García Canclini overemphasizes the extent to which essentialist discourses necessarily constrain collective action and social transformation.[4]

Indeed, COCEI's successes demonstrate that the transformative potential of collective action lies in its balancing of different sorts of internal practices rather than in the prevalence of one or another set of relatively homogeneous practices. The ambiguities and contradictions within COCEI show how characteristics praised by new social movement theorists such as internal democracy, nonviolence, and participation by women appear in complex interaction with other, less obviously praiseworthy attributes.[5] In the case of COCEI, these include "threads of violence" in imagery and action, militant and hostile stances toward a variety of "others," and the relative absence of internal democracy. In addition, many of COCEI's historical claims contradict the experiences of ordinary Juchitecos, and, despite COCEI's extensive promotion of images of women's activism, women are excluded from positions of political leadership and artistic innovation in the movement.

My understanding of COCEI and the sorts of contradictions to which I am most sensitive grew out of my own position between COCEI leaders and supporters during my fieldwork. Although COCEI leaders treated me cordially for the most part and tacitly accepted my presence in Juchitán, they refused interviews, except during my two visits to Juchitán with reporters, before the initiation of my fieldwork. My fieldwork, in contrast, consisted primarily of participation in daily activities and rituals, along with much discussion and questioning, in extended family courtyards in Juchitán's poor neighborhoods as well as in the central market.[6] From this position, it was apparent that COCEI's internal characteristics differed from those of conventional portraits of leftist grassroots movements, including many portraits of COCEI itself. Such conventional descriptions, which emphasize congruence between the claims of leaders and the experiences of supporters, are captured in straightforward representations of COCEI leaders and members as children of the *pueblo* fighting against oppression. In contrast, COCEI in its daily functioning and Juchitecos in their daily lives exhibit multiple and conflicting representations and strategies with regard to violence, militancy, internal democracy, economic change, disorganization, gender, and culture.[7]

Leaders as Children of the Pueblo

One of the primary sources of COCEI's power was the way in which COCEI leaders and the movement itself were consistently viewed, across classes, as having grown from within the *pueblo*. Straightforward representations of this relationship appeared repeatedly in the speeches and writings of COCEI leaders, in journalistic and scholarly accounts, and in the responses of COCEI supporters to questions about the movement. Writers in *El Satelite,* the local newspaper, made such claims throughout the 1970s: "Thus the combative and nonconformist spirit of the Juchitecos has awakened in the Coalition." And it was the children of the pueblo who led this process, beginning at "the moment when its youth broke the silence to raise the banner of total liberation" (*El Satelite* [hereafter *ES*], October 27, 1974; May 9, 1976; February 12, 1978). Furthermore, COCEI was consistently perceived as paying close attention to what people needed and as acting strictly in the interests of the poor (*Por Esto,* July 16, 1981, p. 50). COCEI achieved this by combining radical goals with practical short-term objectives and by interweaving processes of consciousness raising and mobilization (COCEI 1983, 4).

This description of the origins and practice of radical politics, which resembles many portraits of popular movements in Latin America, suggests a one-dimensional notion of mobilization: Poor people rallied in support of a radical movement with which they identified, and which fought to rectify commonly perceived oppressions and injustices. The complexity of Juchitán's regional history demonstrates why this view of politics oversimplifies the connections between past and present (Rubin 1994). The discussions of COCEI's internal characteristics that follow will similarly complicate and modify the notion of unified, self-sustaining mobilization as a response to oppression. However, the explanations presented by political leaders and observers correspond to the ways in which most poor Juchitecos described their relationship to COCEI. Along with many other things, poor Juchitecos understood and experienced politics in this way, and as a result acted to transform the world around them.

Regime Violence and the Threat of Indigenous Explosiveness

Violent repression contributed directly to the development of class consciousness and to the rootedness of COCEI in peoples' daily lives, as ordinary Juchitecos experienced and recounted instances of harassment, shootings, and massacres of their family members and neighbors. COCEI made this connection explicit in its public images and speeches, and writers in *El Satelite* observed the link between violence and mobilization as well: "In this city, with the direct and indirect intervention of the authorities imposed by the PRI, many of our fellow Juchitecos have been assassinated" (*ES*, May 13, 1979; October 23, 1977). In this context, the manipulation of boundaries between violence and nonviolence constituted a key element in COCEI's own (predominantly nonviolent) political strategy. A national PRI official in Juchitán, interviewed by reporters in August 1983, used the phrase "threads of violence" to characterize what he interpreted as COCEI's quasi-savage nature. In virtually all of its mobilization activities, COCEI made explicit use of such "threads of violence"—forms of the Zapotec language perceived as violent or inciting violence, explicit threats of violence, the selective use of violence, and references to an inherent potential for violence on the part of Juchitecos. Indeed, it was by appearing to threaten the existing order that the movement was able to pressure authorities to grant concessions.

When it formed in 1973, COCEI explicitly rejected guerrilla tactics, which had been employed by opposition movements in other southern regions of Mexico since the 1960s. COCEI's mass activities operated in the area of the illegal but politically tolerated, and at the margins of nonviolence. In practice, this meant impassioned, angry demonstrations, occupations of buildings, the sequestering of buses, the painting of slogans on walls, and occasional looting, in addition to strictly legal activities through official channels. Threatening the existing order meant not only pressing the borders of nonviolence but doing so in a way that made use of beliefs about the dangerous character of Indians. When COCEI supporters occupied public buildings or blocked highways, they were not just poor Mexicans, but fierce Indians whose tempers could not wholly be trusted to respond appropriately to the unwritten rules and language of secular Mexican politics. Indeed, COCEI leaders inspired Juchitecos in demonstrations and marches in a language (Isthmus Zapotec) that state and national officials, as well as some prominent local businesspeople, could not understand.

Even politically moderate members of Juchitán's middle and upper classes, most of whom could understand this language, feared the violence to which COCEI leaders referred. These moderates insisted that violence would lead to chaos and the end of family stability, and they observed that some COCEI supporters chose language that was "out of the ordinary" (*ES,* March 10, 1974). In seeking to keep COCEI within the realm of the acceptable, moderates counseled the movement to avoid extremes and proceed with care: "You are fighting in the middle of a lagoon where there are thousands of poisonous animals that from one moment to the next can jump out, and you won't know from where. Use your intelligence and don't go crazy. Because the extremes are disastrous" (*ES,* March 10, 1974).

COCEI's ability to manipulate its stance just inside or outside the cultural border between "the ordinary" and "disastrous extremes" enabled the radical movement alternately to gain support from moderates and threaten them. In the face of the elite's perception of the proximity and danger of extremes, it was precisely COCEI's threats and threads of violence, including its real ability to bring together angry crowds, that complemented COCEI's identity as the legitimate children and champions of the pueblo. The fears and angers that made possible such a politics, furthermore, were not simply turned on or off as a political tactic. Rather, the very unruliness and complexity of emotion that empowered radical politics and that originated in large part outside COCEI were consistently central to the nature of the movement itself and the context in which it operated. In describing the practice of liberation theology in Nicaragua, Roger Lancaster observed that ordinary people's visions of radical politics were "tormented by demons and motivated by dreams," and that "the Jehovah of the Poor . . . is the wrath of the people incarnate" (Lancaster 1988, xxi). COCEI's discourse of violence, along with its practices of militancy and hostility, indicate that such demons and wrath were an integral part of mass mobilization in Juchitán.

Militancy

Along with its "threads of violence," COCEI adopted a militant public posture that engendered considerable criticism on the part of some middle-class and elite sympathizers as well as opponents of all classes. Despite instances of flexibility in their private negotiations with regime officials, in public COCEI leaders consistently employed radical Marxist rhetoric, derogated leftist political parties, expressed extreme hostility to outsiders, and dealt with local opponents in confrontational rather than conciliatory ways.[8] In several of these areas, the public positions and private beliefs of leaders differed from the language and experiences of COCEI's peasant and worker supporters. This did not elicit comment or criticism from most of these supporters, however, as different conceptions of politics and daily life appear to have coexisted easily and fluidly. Rather than weakening the movement, COCEI's militancy, like its manipulation of violent action and imagery, strengthened the movements' ability to rally supporters and challenge the Mexican regime.

Political Ideology and Political Parties

COCEI leaders explained international relations, Mexican politics, and regional economic development in parsimonious Marxist terms, though with an explicit cultural component: U.S. imperialism dominated Latin American economies and politics; the PRI ruled Mexico in the interest of the Mexican economic oligarchy and international capital; and the state promoted economic development in the isthmus in order to achieve large-scale, capitalist production and marginalize or destroy indigenous culture. In the words of Daniel López Nelio, a COCEI leader: "The Zapotec race is oppressed by a whole economic system, the same as the working class"; and "the Benito Juárez dam . . . was meant to systematically destroy Zapotec culture (López Nelio 1993, 235, 233).[9]

In defending this culture, COCEI leaders opposed political parties throughout the 1970s, characterizing them as corrupt and dedicated to their own institutional needs (*ES*, October 6, 1974). In the COCEI leaders' view, direct mobilization of the people in acts of protest was always the central and most important activity of an opposition movement (Punto Crítico 1977; Martínez López 1985). During the Ayuntamiento Popular, the period of militant COCEI government between 1981 and 1983, COCEI leaders reaffirmed that theirs was not an electoral organization, that there could be no viable opposition through parliamentary means, and that radical goals necessitated demonstrations and popular mobilizations, including illegal acts (Waterhouse 1983, 87–92). COCEI opposed the national electoral strategies of the Mexican Communist Party and the Unified Socialist Party of Mexico, as well as those parties' criticisms of COCEI for not establishing internal democratic procedures and for not distinguishing between COCEI as a political movement and COCEI in office. According to Howard Campbell, COCEI leaders responded to his questions about "downplaying ethnicity and regionalism in order to forge larger political alliances" by mentioning their local accomplishments and by asking the question: "Why shouldn't the national left conform to our way of doing things?" (Campbell 1990, 350).

Outsiders

COCEI's militancy included ongoing hostility to most outsiders, a category that in practice applied to people who had not been raised in Juchitán. This hostility was not uniform, and where it existed it often originated in the behaviors of the outsiders themselves (de la Cruz 1993). However, in contrast to a position of openness exhibited by grassroots movements elsewhere, COCEI chose a public and private position of hostility and harassment toward even sympathetic outsiders that paralleled its ongoing, public condemnation of political parties.

COCEI's stance toward the Juchiteco middle class and elite is another, and probably the most consequential, example of the movement's confrontational political style. Despite the presence of a discernible moderate discourse in support of COCEI, and despite the commonly held beliefs that many *priístas,* fed up with corrupt government, had voted for COCEI in the 1980 and 1981 elections, Juchitecos who did not identify with COCEI felt themselves to be harassed and mistreated throughout the Ayuntamiento Popular. They cited patronage practices on the part of the COCEI municipal government, protested the harassment of opposition supporters in the streets,[10] and complained of the transformation of the symbolic center of the city into a center of radical political culture.[11] In addition, businesspeople as well as Communist Party members who claimed to be supportive of COCEI complained of the organization's refusal to seek accords with the private sector. This does not mean that critics would have supported COCEI if the movement had pursued its radical demands in conciliatory language or through democratic procedures. Rather, it demonstrates that COCEI leaders repeatedly chose to advance a dogmatic political ideology and to maintain hostile public and private stances toward leftist political parties, outsiders, and local *priístas.* Such a practice contrasts with the more tolerant and open stance attributed to contemporary popular movements generally and indeed exhibited by some.

Militancy and Ordinary Juchitecos

COCEI's militant stance also contrasted in a number of ways with the political language and approach of ordinary Juchitecos. Little of the dogmatic analysis used by the leadership appeared in popular political discussion, which was much more grounded in description of local experience. In addition, COCEI supporters generally did not advocate a return to subsistence agriculture or speak nostalgically about a past (and present) of unpaved roads and oxen, despite the glowing terms with which a variety of COCEI leaders and intellectuals described these matters (López Nelio 1993).

COCEI's militancy toward the local middle class and elites also diverged from the attitudes and behavior of ordinary Juchitecos. In part, there was common ground—COCEI supporters rallied behind the movement's attacks on local landowners and businesses and generally approved of the harassment and biased treatment about which *priístas* complained. On the other hand, COCEI supporters were members of family networks that generally included some *priístas,* poor or not so poor, and ritual events tended to bring COCEI and PRI activists into the same courtyards. Both groups found ways to bridge the political hostility and establish cordial and even respectful relations, at least in some contexts.

Some families made banter and disagreements about politics a form of daily interaction and pleasure. The members of one COCEI family, for example, gleefully provoked their Tía Ramona nightly for her allegiance to the PRI, and she responded, in stereotypical Juchiteca fashion, with robust tales of her zealous activity in support of her party. In the midst of heated argument, they nevertheless all agreed that "people join together with those they like to hang around with" and that "one is at home in one's party" (interview, summer 1986). In another case, a family of PRI-supporting moderates expressed interest in and respect for the way in which COCEI had won over their schoolteacher aunt through union activities. Doña Mariana, an elderly midwife, attended equally to the deliveries and overall health of PRI and COCEI women in Juchitán, despite her overt skepticism of COCEI's intentions and competence. Revealingly, it took a year and a half of relatively close relations before Doña Mariana revealed to my wife and me that she had come to see value, late in life, in a habit she had often roundly criticized—the habit on the part of many poor Juchitecos of eating with their hands. In a similar fashion, I suspect that Doña Mariana may also have had some understanding and sympathy for the political behaviors she criticized.

These examples indicate that Juchitecos, through their complex and close-knit personal interactions, developed understandings and relationships considerably more nuanced than those expressed in the public stances of their leaders toward a variety of "others": foreign political groups, Mexican political parties, outside visitors, and local PRI supporters. COCEI's strength derived not only from its ability to evoke emotions of anger and fear, acting politically at the margins of violence, but also from its leaders' success in fostering hostile and militant actions that were at odds with key aspects of Juchitecos' daily experience.

Democracy

In the minds of both COCEI leaders and supporters, the advance of peasants' and workers' interests did not require procedural democracy. Rather, it required the kind of attentiveness and trustworthiness that was demonstrated repeatedly in the direct-action campaigns of the 1970s. Although COCEI participated in a variety of elections, pressing for adherence to formal procedures and seeking to gain control of local associations and government through votes, the ideology of the organization did not favor democratic procedure over other forms of organization and decisionmaking. COCEI activist Carlos Sánchez offered a view of democracy in keeping with Leninist and Maoist practices of democratic centralism: The leadership of COCEI did not change by way of democratic elections but through the incorporation of new leaders from among those who participated. This, according to Sánchez, was a democratic process not because of elections but because it naturally produced a vanguard to lead the struggle of the *pueblo* (interview, August 1983).

COCEI supporters understood "democracy" to mean participation and responsiveness, with electoral procedures constituting one useful means of participation among several. Families in Juchitán's poor neighborhoods emphasized repeatedly that COCEI leaders knew them, listened to them, helped them, and acted faithfully in their interest. From this perspective, measuring democracy in terms of shifting combinations of responsiveness, accountability, and elections (Fox 1992), COCEI can be characterized as exhibiting a significant but limited degree of internal democracy. However, in terms of allowing and promoting expression, recognizing difference, establishing spaces and procedures for autonomy and debate, and indeed incorporating voices and suggestions, my observations and interviews in Juchitán suggest that COCEI leaders, despite their responsiveness and despite instances of accountability, exhibited considerable disregard for internal democracy in theory and practice.[12]

Nonetheless, COCEI's most innovative strategic move in the 1970s, in terms of its interaction with both Juchitecos and the regime, was its decision to participate in municipal elections and to place considerable rhetorical emphasis on its democratic claim to municipal sovereignty. Beginning in 1974, soon after its formation, COCEI fielded independent candidates with little chance of officially recognized victory at a time when virtually all Mexican radical movements rejected such participation (Haber 1993, 218). In 1979, COCEI leaders debated whether to participate in the first national elections following a much heralded political reform, as well as whether to gain legal status in the 1980 municipal elections by allying with a national political party. Emphasizing the dangers of party politics and ignoring COCEI's own immersion in municipal elections, the dominant elements within COCEI insisted that the important work of radical politics could occur only "at the margins of elections" (*ES,* July 22, 1979). The debate, however, illustrated the ambiguous location of these margins and itself represented a dividing line between two different leftist positions. Before 1979, COCEI participated in elections in practice but rejected them in theory, and its participation occurred overwhelmingly in the regional context. Beginning in 1980, COCEI not only participated in municipal elections but engaged directly with national political actors in the process—allying with a national party, competing in national and state legislative elections, and, later in the decade, advocating such engagement as a leftist strategy. By changing its electoral discourses and practices on the ground, COCEI thus forged a path that would be recapitulated by much of the Mexican and Latin American Left—from grassroots politics "at the margins of elections" to grassroots politics directly engaged with national electoral processes.

In the 1980s, when it participated in elections, governed, opposed military occupation and repression, and governed again, COCEI relied on the rules of democratic procedure in advancing its claims. In so doing, COCEI constructed what Evelina Dagnino characterizes as new and broad forms of citizenship, including "the invention and creation of *new* rights" (Dagnino, in this volume). In the course of the 1980s, Juchitecos gained the rights to speak out in agrarian agencies and labor courts, solve local problems by local means, use their own language in official proceedings, gain access to complex networks of information, and maintain their own ritual practices and standards of beauty. However, COCEI leaders did not describe these capabilities in terms of citizenship. Rather, like activists in the Organization of Black Communities of the Pacific Coast of Colombia (Grueso, Rosero, and Escobar, in this volume), they "emphasiz[ed] cultural autonomy and the right to be who we are and have our own life project."[13]

COCEI's lack of internal democracy, the changing nature of its participation in elections, and the multifaceted rights it achieved for Juchitecos demonstrate that powerful electoral and nonelectoral political practices coexisted in the movement, with neither leaders nor supporters appearing to find this situation problematic. Like the coexistence of divergent approaches to Marxist ideology, to outsiders, and to local *priístas* on the part of COCEI's leaders and supporters, and like the movement's alternating strategies of nonviolence and violence, the issues of democracy and citizenship illustrate COCEI's multiple and even contradictory political understandings and approaches. Furthermore, the convergence between the views of COCEI leaders and moderates within the PRI about the limited value of procedural democracy suggests that COCEI's nondemocratic beliefs and practices did not necessarily arise from democratic centralist convictions, as critics often claimed, but rather from the history of beliefs and practices about democracy in Juchitán. In the course of this history, procedural democracy was one strand among many political forms that safeguarded or endangered different people's interests and goals.

Economic Change and Political Activism

Juchitecos' clear sense of themselves as exploited, together with the absence of descriptions of economic threats to their physical survival, suggest that the relationships between the process of economic transformation, the development of consciousness, and the formation of a radical political opposition were less direct than COCEI leaders and outside observers suggested. This is another, and perhaps the most striking, example of the coexistence within COCEI of contradictory understandings about the experiences of Juchitecos. COCEI leaders claimed that their coalition had originally formed in response to a direct threat to peasant survival, because of the construction of the Benito Juárez dam and the adjacent irrigation district. Scholars and COCEI leaders alike attributed this result not only to land monopolization but to an oil-led, dual economy and the untrammeled expansion of capitalism and the central state (Binford 1983; Campbell 1994; COCEI 1983; Prevôt-Schapira and Rivière-d'Arc 1986). In this view, faced with losing their land, their income, and their way of life, peasants rebelled.

One of the most interesting and perplexing aspects of my fieldwork in Juchitán was the fact that a wide range of ardent COCEI supporters did not describe their families' economic histories or their present lives in terms compatible with those of the researchers. They spoke, rather, of gradual changes and piecemeal adaptation, of changes in family economies, not of threats to survival. These included politically active and committed COCEI supporters who were astute at describing instances of economic exploitation and evaluating the political interaction between regime and opposition. Although it may be the case that many people did not perceive the whole picture, as it was understood by leaders and researchers, Juchitecos' descriptions of their family situations indicate that matters were considerably more heterogeneous than observers claimed and that economic transformation was not a uniform or life-threatening process. People continued to have land twenty years after the construction of the dam, just less of it, and jobs were available in the urban economy to make up for lost agricultural income.

Furthermore, although COCEI spokespeople presented peasant life in the mid-1980s as a uniform continuation of past oppressions, COCEI supporters often expressed satisfaction with aspects of their present economic lives. In 1985, for example, Antonio Rodríguez and Ana María Díaz, two articulate and committed COCEI activists, commented with satisfaction on the recent sorghum harvest and the prices for the crop, as well as on the sugar crop and the functioning of the nearby state-run sugar mill. According to Aníbal, a young COCEI-supporting farmer, agricultural credit was helpful in securing machinery and insurance, and it was readily available. In addition, though he grew corn at the time, Aníbal said that friends had been trying to convince him to plant sugarcane, and that this sounded like a reasonable idea to him. In contrast, COCEI was at this time particularly critical of pressures on farmers to grow alternative crops such as sorghum and sugar, and the movement also censured the exploitative and inefficient functioning of the sugar mill. In this discussion of his agricultural experiences, Aníbal mentioned neither COCEI's role in securing credit for peasants nor the organization's critique of the sugar mill.

How can these apparent discrepancies be explained? For one thing, it is likely that poor peasants and workers were relatively satisfied with aspects of their economic lives in 1985 precisely because COCEI had fought so successfully to defend and support local family economies. In addition, it is not necessarily contradictory to express satisfaction *and* identify exploitation; Juchitecos may well have been pleased, in a context of extreme exploitation, to be doing as well as they were. However, there still appears to be a contradiction between the kinds of views expressed by Juchitecos and the explicit and militant claims of COCEI leaders and intellectuals, as well as of outside observers. The Juchitecos I have quoted actively supported one of the strongest and most radical grassroots movements in Mexico, and they had done so, at the time of my discussions with them, over the course of the preceding thirteen years. However, these same Juchitecos did not remember the *ejido* land conflict on which many of COCEI's early mobilizations, and most of the coalition leaders' claims to early legitimacy and success, were based. These Juchitecos did not speak of their survival as having been threatened by economic transformation in the 1960s and 1970s; they expressed some satisfaction in the 1980s with the agricultural institutions that COCEI harshly and uniformly condemned; and they did not qualify their satisfaction by observing that these institutions dealt with them fairly *because* of COCEI's mobilizations.

These contradictions, like those regarding violence, militancy, and recent economic changes, demonstrate that COCEI's leaders and intellectuals made use of, and perhaps themselves held, a uniformly critical understanding of local political and economic history that was at odds with many of the experiences of COCEI's peasant and worker supporters. COCEI's success in confronting the Mexican government suggests that its militancy, in analysis and action, was an extraordinarily powerful means of threatening the regime, withstanding repression, and achieving sustained negotiation over a period of twenty years. Furthermore, COCEI's success in maintaining steadfast mass support among poor Juchitecos—and the absence of comment or criticism regarding the apparent discrepancies between the supporters' and their leaders' representations of recent economic experiences—indicate that ordinary Juchitecos did not find these discrepancies troubling. This may be because they understood their leaders' beliefs and claims to be political strategies, and in fact extraordinarily effective ones. It may also be the case that Juchitecos *agreed* with the statements of COCEI leaders, even when those statements contradicted some of the details of their own daily lives. Either way, the economic experiences of COCEI supporters indicated not only that exploitation was uneven and contradictory but that the multiple discrepancies between the discourse of COCEI leaders regarding economic change, the experiences of ordinary Juchitecos, and the ways in which Juchitecos speak of these experiences—like other contradictions regarding the movement's violence, militancy, and democratic practices—constituted a prominent characteristic of radical political mobilization in Juchitán.

Disorganization and Backward Vision

In addition to its use of violent imagery, its militant stance, and the multiple discrepancies between the views of leaders and supporters, another prominent characteristic of COCEI was its lack of institutionalization. COCEI was very well organized in the sense that it had identifiable leaders and supporters, participated in elections, negotiated with regime officials, and carried out numerous local projects such as the creation of health centers, squatter settlements, and markets. In addition, one of COCEI's most important strengths was its ability to coordinate mass rallies involving thousands of people from diverse neighborhoods and towns.

Yet there was also a disorganized side to COCEI. For example, many COCEI supporters didn't vote, even in the most important elections. Voting had multiple meanings in Juchitán, and COCEI leaders made only limited efforts to shape these meanings in the direction of widespread participation. The young women in one family spent hours getting dressed up to vote and then cast multiple votes. Voting in this case was simultaneously an important social activity and a strategic effort to combat fraud with fraud. In other families, in contrast, COCEI supporters commented that they lacked voting identification cards or simply did not intend to vote, and COCEI did little to change these decisions. In another example of disorganization, COCEI supporters in one town who began campaigning for a local health center knew little of the coalition's successful efforts to establish the same sort of facility in another town several years earlier. Sympathetic critics in Juchitán argued that COCEI had not established vehicles for discussion and education that could have kept its supporters informed. Critics also blamed COCEI's disorganization for what they saw as an even more significant flaw in the coalition's approach: the absence of what they called a "forward-looking plan" for regional economic development (Zermeño 1987, 79–88). Instead of developing such a plan, COCEI rhetorically praised the subsistence maize economy, took steps to ensure the survival of small-scale production through credit and insurance, and acted to defend peasant and worker claims within existing economic arrangements.

COCEI leaders appear to have chosen a flexible style of mobilization, promoting centers of activity without necessarily coordinating them. They chose to let the movement follow ebbs and flows of political intensity; to accept that sometimes radical politics would "disappear" whereas at other times it was everywhere, in people's greetings, words, and daily affairs. Alberto Melucci describes grassroots organizing in this fashion when he states that collective action "assumes the form of networks submerged in everyday life. . . . The 'movements' emerge only in limited areas, for limited phases and by means of moments of mobilization" (1988, 248). Such an understanding of collective action coincided with the ways in which ordinary people were willing to become involved in politics, with COCEI leaders learning this aspect of grassroots mobilization in part from Juchitecos themselves.

COCEI's rootedness in Zapotec history, art, and daily life fueled the "disorganized" and "insurgent" aspects of the movement.[14] COCEI was strong because it indeed responded directly to the needs people felt, to the language they spoke and the humor and puns with which they spoke it, and to the varying rhythms of their lives. In its strategic battles, COCEI was able to draw on fierce tempers, on the unpredictability and changing locations of political passions, on the quick movement and militancy enabled by the absence of internal democracy, and on the fear of insurgency that could be elicited by images of indigenous violence. Furthermore, COCEI's "disorganization amidst organization," in the way it respected people's own preferences and the changing demands of their lives, provided a protection from the dangers to grassroots activism posed by people's exhaustion. It made possible what Melucci characterizes as "experimentation with and direct practice of alternative frameworks of meaning . . . on which the networks [of collective action] themselves are founded and live from day to day" (Melucci 1988, 248). Rather than imposing a set of demands and an ideology, COCEI's looser relationship with individual Juchitecos enabled people to live in partial autonomy from formal politics, an autonomy from which people could be rallied, or could rally others, time and again in the course of twenty years.

Thus, despite discrepancies between public ideology and local belief, COCEI was strong precisely because it indeed took popular experience and popular culture seriously. Instead of promoting a particular economic project, COCEI responded continually to people's economic lives as they existed. Instead of sponsoring campaigns for cleanliness, as did reformist members of the PRI, COCEI celebrated local cultural practices. COCEI did not challenge people's commitment to their work as small agricultural producers, market vendors, artisans, fishermen, or midwives. Nor did the movement challenge people's ability to be successful in these activities. At the same time, in defending the rights of peasants and workers to the guarantees provided by the Mexican Constitution and Mexican law, COCEI indeed undertook the radical act of constructing new forms of citizenship.

Ethnicity, Gender, and Cultural Projects

From its inception, COCEI conducted its activities in Zapotec, speaking to people in their courtyards and addressing meetings, demonstrations, and marches in the local language. During the years of the Ayuntamiento Popular, Zapotec became the language of schools and government offices (Campbell 1990, 358), differentiating COCEI's administrative practices from those of the PRI. According to COCEI intellectual Victor de la Cruz, "The young [COCEI] administrators begin to feel that the pressure of Zapotec is much stronger when they have municipal power. Up in City Hall, they yell, tell jokes, collect taxes, and administer justice in Zapotec" (de la Cruz 1984, 23; quoted in Campbell 1990, 365). Humor was an important aspect of the Zapotec character of COCEI speech and was one of the ways in which COCEI leaders established intimate forms of communication with supporters.

Also from the beginning, COCEI carried out its public activities with the customs and adornments of Zapotec ritual. These ceremonial practices involved the active participation of women, who attended demonstrations in the embroidered blouses and long skirts reserved for fiestas and distributed food and gifts much the way this was done in ritual celebrations. In addition to playing a role in public events, ethnic identity contributed to the content of popular thinking and provided specific pathways of language and social life through which people could respond to the ideas and activities of COCEI. Juchitecos brought to their politics shared memories of nineteenth- and early-twentieth-century rebellions, when Juchitecos took up arms to resist the political and economic encroachments of the state capital. In the 1970s, they began to connect the present to this rebellious past in new ways. They not only characterized themselves as poor but identified the individuals, private enterprises, and state agencies that exploited them economically and denounced the political impositions that denied them self-government. These discussions, conducted almost exclusively in Zapotec, occurred in market stalls, local bars, and family courtyards, the physical and social locations that had been constructed by, and in turn contributed to the reelaboration of, local cultural beliefs and practices.

Family courtyards were particularly important places for discussion and mobilization, and their gender and class characteristics provided fertile ground for rethinking politics and getting people out into the streets. Such courtyards generally included several branches of the same extended family. As a result of the economic changes of the previous twenty years, the members of these families frequently did different types of work. In contrast to many other urban environments in Mexico, however, an increase in a family's economic resources in Juchitán did not usually lead to leaving the family courtyard or abandoning Zapotec identity and ritual. For this reason, COCEI's attention to the needs of any one occupational group, in the context of its championing of Zapotec identity and political sovereignty, was generally seen as support for all.

Gender, Cultural Elaboration, and Radical Organizing

Through their control of family courtyards, the central market, and neighborhood marketing networks, Juchiteca women played a key role in the development of political consciousness and grassroots mobilization. This process often began in the market in the early morning, where the previous day's news would be disseminated, and continued throughout the day during the preparation and selling of foods and goods in the central market and in casual discussions in the streets and family courtyards. The market itself was a crowded, expanding, "disorderly" place. Though its two-story structure occupied an enormous city block, vendors crowded into the surrounding streets, and women with their wares in baskets or on blankets found places in front of or between the larger stalls or circulated through the market on foot. In addition to providing multiple, mobile public spaces, the market offered the still fully visible but more private spaces behind the tables on which the products were displayed. This area behind the tables was where the vendors stood or sat as they sold their wares, talked with each other or with family members when business lagged, and ate meals. In my own work, I was introduced to the difference between the spaces in front of and behind the market stalls in a dramatic way. In front of the stalls, I casually engaged in banter about prices and gossip and caught up on the events of the day. Six months later, seated on the vendors' side of the stall, I was told, as a prelude to a detailed interview: "People came by here and said you were a spy. Are you a spy?"

The circulation of information in Juchitán also occurred during communal planning and preparations for fiesta activities, which brought women and their families across the city from one neighborhood to another. Juchitán's urban character ensured that this communication took place within dense personal and occupational networks that relied not only on gossip but also on local and national newspapers, magazines, and radio stations, many of which routinely repudiated official government positions. Juchitecas used this information and their convictions about the events of the day literally to get their families out into the streets—to attend neighborhood meetings, participate in demonstrations in the center of the city, and register and vote.

Men and women played distinct roles in perpetuating the vibrant Zapotec culture that was arguably the single factor most responsible for COCEI's power. Men monopolized formal artistic culture in Juchitán—painting, poetry, and songwriting—along with certain forms of craftsmanship and the less-formal singing and philosophizing that occurred in local cantinas. Campbell (1994, 179–189) has shown these activities to be essential components of COCEI's elaboration of culture and dissemination of ideas. However, the success of COCEI's radical political efforts hinged as much or more on the production of an engaged, creative culture of daily life—in courtyards, neighborhoods, and markets—by women. The activities of women in Juchitán have focused more on shaping and contesting aspects of life in these daily domains, whereas men have been more involved in establishing a formal narrative of that life. In this sense, men's cultural activities are closer to the ideological, militant stances that have been described above as characteristics of COCEI's public politics—and that have been developed and practiced by COCEI's young male leaders—whereas women's cultural activities are more directly related to the daily experiences that have been shown to contradict or modify those public stances.

Shoshana Sokoloff's research (1993) on the relationship between midwives and doctors in Juchitán supports this observation. Sokoloff notes that male COCEI leaders, in accord with their essentialist representations of Zapotec culture, portrayed midwives as native to Juchitán's poor neighborhoods, practicing an art that had been passed down for generations. In contrast, Sokoloff found a variety of backgrounds, linguistic abilities, and types of training among midwives. Doña Mariana Galán, for example, who was known throughout Juchitán as "the mother of us all," was born of Spanish parents in another part of the state; had been trained to deliver babies by her brother-in-law, a Japanese doctor (to spite her mother!); and spoke only rudimentary Zapotec. In contrast to most Third World encounters between midwives and Western doctors, Sokoloff found that Juchitán's midwives had not been replaced by outside practitioners but had interacted with them on very much their own terms. Whereas male narratives about midwifery reinforced COCEI's cultural project and militant stance, it was the daily activities of women, as mothers and midwives, that achieved the practical work of keeping Zapotec cultural practice alive and strong by achieving a trustworthy, *Zapotec* way of delivering babies in an urban setting.

As with their romantic view of local midwives, COCEI's male leaders adopted a view of feminism that was at odds with women's actual social and political roles. COCEI leaders spoke repeatedly about Juchitán's egalitarian gender relations and about the equal participation of women in the movement. In political events and widely disseminated photographs, COCEI featured proud-looking women in festive Zapotec attire, and COCEI artists and writers highlighted the strength and exoticism of local female sexuality.[15] However, despite women's central role in the work of cultural adaptation, as well as in developing political consciousness and mobilizing family members, women did not hold positions of leadership within COCEI and generally did not participate in the artistic and literary activities that were central to the movement's cultural project. Furthermore, Juchitecas suffered enduring forms of exploitation and subordination on a day-to-day basis, including sexual double standards, limited educational opportunities, responsibility for both household and money-earning activities, and domestic violence.

Zapotec culture in Juchitán exhibited forms of ambiguity regarding male gender roles that were also absent from COCEI's artistic and political narratives. Males who were publicly identified in both Zapotec and Spanish by the Zapotec word *muxe* played a prominent role, distinct from those of both women and other males, in economic and ritual activities. Boys often took up this identity in adolescence and went on perform economic roles associated with women. *Muxe* also played specific public roles in the division of labor at fiestas, where they sat among women and danced as women while exhibiting body forms, dress, and adornment that mixed common "male" and "female" characteristics. The public prominence of an alternative male gender role in Juchitán illustrates in yet another way the richness and inventiveness of the Zapotec culture that supports political radicalism, as well as the prominence of ambiguity within that culture. This characteristic also underscores the fact that in its depictions of women and sexuality, as in its militancy, its claims about the origins of political activism, and its "disorganization," COCEI promotes representations of local life that correspond to some aspects of the worldviews of Juchitecos, while at the same time coexisting with, and relying on, quite different, less homogeneous, and far more contested daily practices. Despite the harms and costs of its misrepresentations—such as the continuing exclusion of women from positions of political power, the lack of attention to women's domestic and occupational subordination, and the exclusion from artistic discourse of a prominent form of male social life—COCEI achieved its ongoing strength, including gains valued by women and *muxe*, through its ability to balance these (mis)representations with respect for the autonomy of daily practice.

COCEI's Cultural Project

In the course of its twenty-year history, COCEI has developed a unique and far-reaching cultural project. This project includes an influential role in the activities of the government-funded Casa de la Cultura (Cultural Center); the promotion of painting, music, poetry, and Zapotec language studies among young Juchitecos from all classes; and the nurturing of a prominent group of young male artists. These artists formed the nucleus of what Campbell describes as an active local bohemian subculture (1990, 377–385). As a result of these efforts,

> large numbers of Juchitecos began to compose ballads and poems in honor of COCEI martyrs, revive disappearing arts and crafts, collect oral histories, write their memoirs, photograph local sites, and improve their ability to speak Zapotec. Additionally, Juchitán became a town where 19 year old indigenous youths discussed political philosophy and new trends in the art world as well as the fine points of their own historical and cultural traditions. (389)

COCEI's cultural project involved the elaboration of a narrative of Juchitán's history in political speeches and newspapers. This discourse also developed through the production of literary texts and artistic representations, historical and political analyses, and posters and T-shirts. Since 1975, COCEI intellectuals have published a sophisticated literary magazine, *Guchachi' Reza* (Zapotec for "sliced-open iguana"), whose title evokes Juchitecos' sense of identity and distinctiveness: "Now, what is our concern? That our children know how to speak Zapotec and play in Zapotec. This is our concern. Why? For the continuity of our history and so that in one hundred years or three centuries, we can continue eating iguana" (López Nelio 1993, 235).

COCEI's cultural project bridged cultural and class distances with fluidity and eclecticism, while at the same time its public stances reinforced class divisions and sought to keep various outsiders out. COCEI thus maintained control of its cultural borders by combining essentialist representations with boundary-crossing restrictions. COCEI not only revived and recreated a Juchiteco Zapotec identity and history but did it in a way that connected young people in poor neighborhoods to a local cultural institution, to the imagery and practice of radical politics, and to national artists and intellectuals. These connections encouraged Juchitecos to look outward, much as the midwives looked outward, not to embrace the foreign as different and better but to make appropriate use of that which came from outside in elaborating the local. Juchitán's artistic connections to the outside also attracted outsiders in, reinforcing Juchitecos' own sense of autonomy and importance as well as developing allies at the national level.

COCEI's cultural project, like other aspects of the coalition's ideology and political practice, was based on numerous discrepancies between pasts claimed and pasts experienced. COCEI's historical account ignored such phenomena as the subordinate position of women in Juchitán, the mistreatment of neighboring ethnic minorities, long periods of accommodation to outside authorities, critiques of local power relations from within the PRI, and unpublicized meetings in which COCEI representatives negotiated several of the terms of its existence with state and national authorities. COCEI's cultural representations also ignored the ambitions of poor Juchitecos to advance economically and participate in the national consumer culture that surrounded them, as well as the continuing presence in Juchitán of peasants and workers who supported the official party rather than COCEI.

Yet COCEI's strategic essentialism enabled the movement to wrest control over public cultural display and experimentation from local elites and make use of its own sources of energy and talent to establish a new artistic arena and reinvigorated historical narrative.[16] COCEI's cultural project went beyond making use of existing historical memories or ethnic mechanisms for the purposes of political mobilization. Rather, the coalition succeeded in developing a powerful regional presence and keeping the Mexican regime at bay in part by claiming cultural activities for a poor people's movement and making use of them not only to represent and define but to empower and give pleasure. Such an explicit cultural project is without parallel in contemporary Mexico. It is a rare affirmation not only of the value of indigenous life and culture but of that culture's ability to sustain and reinvent itself and to appropriate the outside from a position of equality and power.

Conclusion

COCEI exhibited ambiguity with regard to violence, political division within families, electoral practices, levels of organization, and gender roles. Similarly, the claims of its political and intellectual leaders contradicted those of ordinary Juchitecos with regard to outsiders, past and present economic experiences, and the social experiences of women. Together, these ambiguities and contradictions suggest that it is the coexistence of multiple forms of difference that animates a radical social movement. This coexistence of differences in Juchitán has significant negative consequences, such as the continuing violence toward and exclusion of women, the rejection of political moderates, the inability of COCEI leaders to speak the language of groups outside Juchitán and thereby make alliances, and the absence of internal democracy. However, the coexistence of differences also provides "new spaces for the production of meanings" (Escobar 1992a, 82) that mobilize, impassion, and threaten and thereby create new political forces and transform formal politics and daily life.

This understanding of radical politics calls into question portrayals of leftist movements as consisting of, or moving toward, unified and homogeneous consciousness and action. It supports Mary Louise Pratt's call for ways of theorizing heterogeneity as well as for recognizing that what looks like fragmentation to those in dominant positions can be both integrating and empowering to subordinate actors in social movements. Indeed, COCEI's internal characteristics and the multifacetedness of democracy in Juchitán in the 1990s indicate, as Pratt suggests, that democratic processes *produce* heterogeneity (Pratt, in this volume).

The ambiguity and contradiction within COCEI challenges claims about the presence of internal democracy, gender equality, and other praiseworthy characteristics in grassroots movements. In his work on Nicaragua, Roger Lancaster argues that popular religion played a central role in the radical consciousness of Sandinista supporters. The contradictions Lancaster identifies within popular religion and the distances between religion and the formal aspects of Sandinista politics parallel the discrepancies in Juchitán between practices of daily life and COCEI's public positions. In Lancaster's analysis, radical consciousness in Nicaragua was in significant part a place of hidden spaces and semiprivate discourses absent from the official voices of Sandinismo and liberation theology (1988, 143–144, 162). Power, in this context, "is an ongoing negotiation between macro- and micro-discourses, between official narratives and private rumors" (Lancaster 1988, 162), much as COCEI's power resulted from negotiations between Juchitecos' own understandings of their experiences and COCEI's public claims, and between women's reshaping of daily procedures and men's formal artistic narratives. The resulting social movement "can successfully reproduce itself, not only *despite*, but *because of*, the pervasiveness of complaint and conflict" (Lancaster 1988, 162–163, emphasis in original).

COCEI illustrates a radical politics characterized by flexible and changing mixtures of Leninist and new social-movement political practices. COCEI's leaders chose over the course of twenty years to maintain and elaborate the distances between the discourses of the movement and those of its supporters because the resulting political strategies were extraordinarily effective in wresting concessions from the state and maintaining organizational cohesion. Similarly, ordinary Juchitecos' tactics for describing and adapting the practices of daily life were effective in fostering survival and pleasure in workplace and courtyard, as well as in the more formal locations of radical politics. In its mixture of these two sets of activities, COCEI maintained multiple locations of "complaint and conflict" and indeed reproduced itself in the face of formidable opposing powers.

COCEI's striking success in fostering cultural autonomy and in creating a political voice for indigenous people suggests that essentialist class and ethnic discourses, when combined in ambiguous ways with other forms of belief and action, can simultaneously reflect people's experiences and be of considerable strategic use. It is precisely within such spaces of ambiguity, the distances between militant confrontation and neighborhood accommodation, between Marxist analysis of development and daily work experience, between nonviolence and violence, that ordinary people act as "agent[s] of culture in process" (Fiske 1990, 86), reforming and adapting their own practices and beliefs to those invented by others. This is where ordinary Juchitecos as well as their leaders—at times in tension with one another—perform "an 'art of making' that proceeds by manipulating imposed knowledges and symbols at propitious moments" (Escobar 1992a, 74, drawing on de Certeau). In family courtyards, neighborhood committee meeting places, cantinas, and schools as well as in the many activities of the city's Casa de la Cultura, Juchitecos forge justifications for and limits to violence, reinterpret the meaning of their labor, cajole and defy political opponents, and reinvent ritual and art through a discourse of political opposition. In this way, they give life to a political movement that can challenge existing relations of power.

Notes

1. Pronounced *ko-sáy*.

2. See this volume's Introduction; see also Dagnino and Slater, in this volume.

3. Several chapters in this book illustrate the centrality of cultural borders with the outside—how they are constructed and maintained, how fluid they are, who controls them—to the cultural politics of social movements (Yúdice; Slater; Díaz Barriga; Grueso, Rosero, and Escobar; Warren; da Cunha; and Pratt).

4. For other examples of strategic essentialism, see the chapters (in this volume) by Grueso, Rosero, and Escobar; and Warren. For a less essentialist position, see the chapter by da Cunha.

5. New social movement theorists in the 1980s tended see the praiseworthy, "new" characteristics as predominant in emerging social movements (Fals Borda 1986; Slater 1985). In contrast, more recent writers have emphasized the coexistence of opposing "old" and "new" forms (Lancaster 1992; Starn 1992).

6. My fieldwork also included interviews in Juchitán with COCEI activists, members of other leftist organizations, reformists within the Institutional Revolutionary Party (PRI), and other politicians and public officials, as well as journalists, businesspeople, teachers, and midwives. I consulted published accounts of politics, economic development, and cultural activities in the region, as well as government data and studies. I found a particularly rich source in the Juchitán weekly newspaper, *El Satelite*, published from 1968 to 1979. I also interviewed politicians, officials, and grassroots activists in Oaxaca and Mexico City.

7. I should say at the outset that I take up issues of complexity and ambiguity in only a handful of the many ways they might fruitfully be explored. While focusing on the abovementioned categories, for example, this chapter will not examine differences and tensions among different groups of poor Juchitecos. Thus, I will make use of broad categories of "ordinary Juchitecos" or "Juchiteca women" that in themselves embody the sort of essentialism of which I am otherwise critical. These overgeneralized categories enable me to identify areas of ambiguity and contradiction, while at the same time suggesting the need to explore differences considerably further.

8. COCEI leaders began to modify this stance in 1986, when they agreed to join the coalition municipal government arranged by Governor Heladio Ramírez.

9. COCEI's emphasis on the centrality of a cultural project to political contestation provides a Latin American illustration of the control of historicity that Alain Touraine locates at the center of European social movements (1988).

10. These critics acknowledged or ignored, but did not deny, that similar patronage and harassment had generally been practiced by the PRI.

11. Like many other Latin American social movements, COCEI sought "the appropriation of the city by the urban poor not only as an economic but as a cultural space" (Escobar 1992a, 80).

12. There have been recent pressures within COCEI to change this approach and institute democratic procedures for leadership selection and decisionmaking.

13. Libia Grueso, Leyla Arroyo, and Carlos Rosero (Escobar 1995, 212). Verónica Schild (in this volume) also cautions against defining social-movement goals in terms of citizenship, pointing to the negative effects of neoliberal discourses of citizenship in Chile.

14. Since 1986, and especially since COCEI's participation in *concertación social* under President Salinas, the coalition has also been moving in a direction that could prove to be demobilizing. Some of COCEI's past critics have praised the movement for putting aside its militancy, for governing impartially, and for making good use of newly acquired economic resources. Others fear that such moderation and cooperation with the regime will lead to a weakening of COCEI's oppositional stance.

15. Most commentary on Juchitecas, dating at least from nineteenth-century European travelers, exaggerated their power and erroneously portrayed them as the real power holders in a matriarchal society. Nevertheless, more than women of most other indigenous groups, Juchitecas possessed a margin of economic, social, and sexual autonomy that both motivated and enabled them to maintain Zapotec culture and their own position within it.

16. For a discussion and bibliography concerning strategic essentialism, see Krishna 1993, esp. 402, 415.

References

Basu, Amrita. 1992. *Two Faces of Protest: Contrasting Modes of Women's Activism in India.* Berkeley: University of California Press.

Binford, Leigh. 1983. "Agricultural Crises, State Intervention, and the Development of Classes in the Isthmus of Tehuantepec, Oaxaca, Mexico." Ph.D. diss., University of Connecticut.

Calderón, Fernando, Alejandro Piscitelli, and José Luis Reyna. 1992. "Social Movements: Actors, Theories, Expectations." In *The Making of Social Movements in Latin America: Identity, Strategy, and Democracy,* ed. A. Escobar and S. Alvarez. Boulder: Westview Press.

Campbell, Howard. 1990. "Zapotec Ethnic Politics and the Politics of Culture in Juchitán, Oaxaca (1350–1990)." Ph.D. diss., University of Wisconsin.

______. 1994. *Zapotec Renaissance: Ethnic Politics and Cultural Revivalism in Southern Mexico*. Albuquerque: University of New Mexico Press.

Chernick, Marc W., and Michael F. Jiménez. 1993. "Popular Liberalism, Radical Democracy, and Marxism: Leftist Politics in Contemporary Colombia, 1974–1991." In *The Latin American Left: From the Fall of Allende to Perestroika,* ed. B. Carr and S. Ellner. Boulder: Westview Press.

COCEI. 1983. "La Tenencia de la Tierra y el Movimiento Campesino en el Istmo de Tehuantepec." Paper presented at the Primer Congreso Sobre Problemas Agrarios, 1982, in Chilpancingo, Guerrero. Published in *COCEI: alternativa de organización y lucha para los pueblos del istmo,* ed. COCEI. Juchitán, Mexico: COCEI.

Covarrubias, Miguel. [1946] 1986. *Mexico South: The Isthmus of Tehuantepec.* London: KPI Limited.

de Certeau, Michel. 1984. *The Practice of Everyday Life.* Berkeley: University of California Press.

de la Cruz, Victor. 1984. "Hermanos o ciudadanos: dos lenguas, dos proyectos políticos en el Istmo." *Guchachi' Reza* 21:18–24.

______. 1993. "Social Scientists Confronted with Juchitán: Incidents of an Unequal Relationship." In *Zapotec Struggles: Histories, Politics, and Representations from Juchitán, Oaxaca,* ed. H. Campbell et al. Washington, D.C.: Smithsonian Institution Press.

Escobar, Arturo. 1992a. "Culture, Economics, and Politics in Latin American Social Movements Theory and Research." In *The Making of Social Movements in Latin America: Identity, Strategy, and Democracy*, ed. A. Escobar and S. Alvarez. Boulder: Westview Press.

______. 1992b. "Culture, Practice, and Politics: Anthropology and the Study of Social Movements." *Critique of Anthropology* 12 (4):395–432.

______. 1995. *Encountering Development: The Making and Unmaking of the Third World.* Princeton: Princeton University Press.

Escobar, Arturo, and Sonia Alvarez, eds. 1992. *The Making of Social Movements in Latin America: Identity, Strategy, and Democracy*. Boulder: Westview Press.

Fals Borda, Orlando. 1986. "El Nuevo Despertar de los Movimientos Sociales." *Revista Foro* 1:76–83.

Fiske, John. 1990. "Ethnosemiotics: Some Personal and Theoretical Reflections." *Cultural Studies* 4 (1):85–99.

Fox, Jonathan. 1992. "Democratic Rural Development: Leadership Accountability in Regional Peasant Organizations." *Development and Change* 23 (2):1–36.

García Canclini, Néstor. 1988. "Culture and Power: The State of Research." *Media, Culture and Society* 10:467–497.

______. 1989. *Culturas hibridas: Estrategias para entrar y salir de la modernidad.* Mexico City: Grijalbo.

Haber, Paul. 1993. "Cárdenas, Salinas, and the Urban Popular Movement." In *Mexico: Dilemmas of Transition*, ed. N. Harvey, 218–248. London: Institute of Latin American Studies (University of London) and British Academic Press.

Krishna, Sankaran. 1993. "The Importance of Being Ironic: A Postcolonial View on Critical International Relations Theory." *Alternatives* 18:385–417.

Lancaster, Roger. 1988. *Thanks to God and the Revolution: Popular Religion and Class Consciousness in the New Nicaragua*. New York: Columbia University Press.

______. 1992. *Life Is Hard: Machismo, Danger, and the Intimacy of Power in Nicaragua*. Berkeley: University of California Press.

López Mateos, Manuel. 1993. "When Radio Became the Voice of the People." In *Zapotec Struggles: Histories, Politics, and Representations from Juchitán, Oaxaca*, ed. H. Campbell et al. Washington, D.C.: Smithsonian Institution Press.

López Monjardin, Adriana. 1983. "Juchitán, las historias de la discordia." *Cuadernos Políticos* 38:72–80.

López Nelio, Daniel. 1993. "Interview with Daniel López Nelio." In *Zapotec Struggles: Histories, Politics, and Representations from Juchitán, Oaxaca*, ed. H. Campbell et al. Washington, D.C.: Smithsonian Institution Press.

Martínez López, Felipe. 1985. *El Crepusculo del Poder: Juchitán, Oaxaca 1980–1982*. Oaxaca: Universidad Autonoma Benito Juarez de Oaxaca, IIS.

Melucci, Alberto. 1988. "Social Movements and the Democratization of Everyday Life." In *Civil Society and the State: New European Perspectives*, ed. J. Deane. London: Verso.

Prevôt-Schapira, Marie-France, and Hélene Rivière-d'Arc. 1986. "Poder y Contrapoder en el Istmo de Tehuantepec." In *Poder Local, Poder Regional*, ed. J. Pádua N. and A. Vaneph. Mexico City: El Colegio de México.

Punto Crítico. 1977. *Punto Crítico* 83 (November 15).

Rosaldo, Renato. 1989. *Culture and Truth: The Remaking of Social Analysis*. Boston: Beacon Press.

Rubin, Jeffrey W. 1994. "COCEI in Juchitán: Grassroots Radicalism and Regional History." *Journal of Latin American Studies* 26 (January):109–136.

______. Forthcoming. *Decentering the Regime: History, Culture, and Regional Politics in Juchitán, Mexico*. Durham, N.C.: Duke University Press.

Slater, David, ed. 1985. *New Social Movements and the State in Latin America*. Amsterdam: CEDLA.

Sokoloff, Shoshana. 1993. "The Proud Midwives of Juchitán." In *Zapotec Struggles: Histories, Politics, and Representations from Juchitán, Oaxaca*, ed. H. Campbell et al. Washington, D.C.: Smithsonian Institution Press.

Starn, Orin. 1992. "'I Dreamed of Foxes and Hawks': Reflections on Peasant Protest, New Social Movements, and the Rondas." In *The Making of Social Movements in Latin America: Identity, Strategy, and Democracy*, ed. A. Escobar and S. Alvarez. Boulder: Westview Press.

Touraine, Alain. 1988. *Return of the Actor: Social Theory in Postindustrial Society*. Minneapolis: University of Minnesota Press.

Waterhouse, Isabelle. 1983. "Co-optation and Control: The Case of the Mexican Communist Party." M. Phil., Oxford University.

Zermeño, Sergio. 1987. "Juchitán, la Cólera del Régimen." In *Juchitán: Límites de una Experiencia Democrática*, ed. M. J. Bailón Corres and S. Zermeño. Mexico City: Instituto de Investigaciones Sociales, UNAM.

Chapter Seven

Indigenous Movements as a Challenge to the Unified Social Movement Paradigm for Guatemala

KAY B. WARREN

Chantal Mouffe and Ernesto Laclau argue that the urgent political work for this historical moment is the quest for "radical and plural democracy." They advocate diverse routes for individuals to pressure democracies for wider social, economic, and environmental justice. In their view, this is a post-Marxist project. The dramatic collapse of state socialism and the apparent exhaustion of its appeal in much of the world painfully confirms the limits of ideologies that construct a political subject focused primarily on the politics of class conflict or on universalized revolutionary struggle.

My thanks go to Arturo Escobar, Sonia Alvarez, and Evelina Dagnino for the invitation to join their international research group on social movements. From the onset, I want to make clear that I alone assume sole responsibility for the final line of analysis in this essay. This analysis is based on research I have pursued on indigenous issues in Guatemala since 1970, on discussions with Pan-Mayanists about their movement since 1989, and on encounters with their critics over the same time period. More of my work on the Pan-Mayan movement can be found in Warren 1992, 1993, 1995, 1996, forthcoming(a), and forthcoming(b), and in *Indigenous Movements and Their Critics: Pan-Mayanism and Ethnic Resurgence in Guatemala* (forthcoming[c]).

The essay has also been energized by generous feedback from Charles Hale, Judith Maxwell, June Nash, Diane Nelson, Abigail Adams, and Miguel Centeno; debates with Deborah Levenson-Estrada (1994; forthcoming); and stimulating seminars at the University of Michigan and Johns Hopkins University. Jeff Himpele introduced me to the concept of parallel middle classes and to comparative insights from Bolivia, which have proven very valuable in this analysis (see Himpele 1995).

Yet these theorists would not for a moment free democracy from criticism, given liberal capitalism's crisis with growing gaps between the rich and poor and the persistence of systems of "rights [that] have been constituted on the very exclusion or subordination of rights" of others (Mouffe 1993, 70). The proliferation of "progressive" social movements in many countries signals the unfinished business of politicizing these economic and jural tensions and reflects the panoply of issues and identities salient to individuals in their daily lives.[1] As this analysis will show, however, the definition of what is progressive is highly contested in Guatemala, given alternative framings of community and participation.

As in much of Latin America, Guatemala is involved in its own blend of transitions. Three decades of military rulers who repressed social movements have given way since 1985 to a series of civilian governments that have struggled with the legacy of a highly militarized nation-state. After the failure of the armed insurgency to topple the state in the 1980s, grassroots organizations such as Comité de Unidad Campesina (Committee for Campesino Unity, or CUC); Coordinadora Nacional de Viudas de Guatemala (National Coordinator of Guatemalan Widows, or CONAVIGUA); and Grupo de Apoyo Mútuo (Mutual Support Group, or GAM)—all with strong ties to the Left—rededicated themselves to press for a substantial role in national politics and, more recently, for wide-ranging reforms during the peace negotiations, which have involved the government, military, guerrillas, elites, and many national interest groups.

This essay argues that, over the last twenty years, the movement of oppositional politics from the class-antagonism paradigm—the struggle of labor versus capital that informed the insurgency and diverse leftist movements with their own histories of organizing specific sectors of the population in Guatemala—toward a more heterogeneous politics of social movements has been complicated by widespread intolerance of indigenous activism and its distinctive political agenda.[2] What has been the character of this ambivalence? What does it reveal and obscure about the practices of indigenous activists (and those of its antagonists)? How are critiques of indigenous mobilization deployed by a variety of political interests?

Specifically, this analysis pursues the strong reactions that different political sectors have to the ethnic-based goals of the Pan-Mayan movement—which seeks culturally to unify indigenous Guatemalans across language divides—and the alternative it presents to what I will call the "unified social movement paradigm," which guided important elements of the grassroots Left through the early 1990s.[3]

The goals of this essay are fourfold. First, I will introduce a Guatemalan movement that does not fit the dominant grassroots paradigm in order to argue for a widening of the range of movements social observers see as progressive in the face of Guatemala's social inequities and injustice. The Pan-Mayan movement seeks recognition of cultural diversity within the nation-state, a greater role for indigenous politics in national culture, a reconsideration of economic inequities, and a wider distribution of cultural resources such as education and literacy in indigenous languages. Second, I will challenge the proponents of the unified theory of oppression by exposing some of the assumptions that guided their early dismissal of other forms of dissent and alternative struggles for social change. Third, I will describe the ways in which movements with antagonistic histories nevertheless continue to influence each other's sense of purpose and to collaborate on issues of common concern. This has certainly been the case through the period of the peace negotiations and has caused some analysts to argue that the recent convergence transcends these movements' divisive histories. Finally, I will consider the ways in which Pan-Mayanism raises important issues for how social scientists conceptualize class, capital, and politics.

My argument is that a practice-oriented and relational view of social movements reveals a more textured sense of struggle and addresses participants' subjectivity—what they find critical to confront in their lives both on and off the official agendas. A cultural framing of social movements, rather than a linear sense of struggle against an external monolith, is the goal of this inquiry. As will become evident, cultural framings of research on social movements add new dimensions to analysis: a concern with the interplay of class, ethnicity, and culture in ongoing movements; an examination of the specific sorts of "cultural capital" produced by social movements; and a scrutiny of the choices different analysts make when they include certain movements under the progressive umbrella and exclude or mute others.

Fissures in the "Popular" Model for Grassroots Organizing

The 1991 Segundo Encuentro Continental de Resistencia Indígena, Negra y Popular—which was held at the dusty fairgrounds just outside Guatemala's second city, Quezaltenango—was an example of the assertion by the Latin American *popular* Left that diverse social movements (including class-based, indigenous, Afro–Latin American, women's, and human rights) could be successfully encompassed by the reigning *popular* paradigm that called for the grassroots organization of the masses by sectors.[4] Through its leadership and working documents, the international congress argued for a unified theory of oppression, the continued relevance of class as the master inequity, and the capitalist world in the guise of Western neoliberalism as the prime engine of oppression. Some indigenous participants, however, found personal and political dilemmas in this framing of social conflict.

North American anthropologist Charles Hale captured the double bind for some of the Mayan participants in the following terms:

> Indians who identify as *populares* generally have chosen to emphasize the demands that unify them with subordinate Mestizos. This does not imply a "loss" of Indian identity ("culture loss" is a problematic term in any case) but it does tend to involve either a shift in priorities away from demands specific to Indian cultural roots, or to a difficult commitment to struggle for those demands from within a predominately non-Indian political movement. (1994, 36)

Some indigenous Guatemalans have made their peace with this model and have pursued long careers of activism. Others have found elements of the *popular* movement unresponsive to their personal politics.

One could not fault the courage of those attending these meetings, which took place in a highly militarized Guatemala, where the severe repression of political activists continued in the early 1990s. From countries throughout the Americas, some three hundred delegates—all with impeccable political credentials, as one participant assured me—attended small work groups and plenary sessions that were held in a huge hall. An estimated thirty thousand community activists—the majority of whom were impoverished rural women who did not participate in the congress itself—marched for hours through the city's streets in the final public demonstration of support for the grassroots Left and the goals of the congress. Rigoberta Menchú, who was yet to be awarded the Nobel Prize, sought to guarantee the safety of the participants through the international monitoring generated by her press conferences at the meetings, and by all accounts she was successful in heading off government reprisals.

As many observers noted, however, the Segundo Encuentro was only partially successful in channeling culturally based dissent. Nationally prominent Mayan leaders shared their complaints with me in conversations between sessions: They had been invited as observers only at the last minute and found themselves marginalized by the rigid structure of the meetings, which allowed only two official representatives of Pan-Mayan organizations in a national delegation of forty representatives. Nevertheless, around the edges of the official program, Pan-Mayanists met privately with indigenous representatives from other countries, and, after the congress, some went out of town for an indigenous retreat, closed to others. This was not the first time indigenous leaders from across the Americas had created opportunities to discuss common concerns and compare strategies. Rather, it was another moment in what some have termed "the Indian awakening in Latin America."[5]

Skeptics of the congress suggested that the *popular* left included the word "indigenous" in the conference title and documentation largely for pragmatic reasons—that is, to tap into the anti-quincentenary fervor throughout the Americas in order to reassert the viability of *popular* movements after the cold war. Although *popular* politics may need renewed support elsewhere in Latin America, in Guatemala activism has been diverse, successful, and championed by the international solidarity community in the face of continuing repression in the 1980s and 1990s. Cultivators, migrant workers, students, urban workers, widows, families of the disappeared, and refugees have been organized by the movement. *Popular* leaders have been highly supportive of the ongoing negotiations to bring the guerrilla-counterinsurgency conflict to a formal end and to spur reforms such as the dismantling of the system of civil patrols in rural communities and the return of refugees displaced by the war. In 1995, *popular* leaders directly participated for the first time in national elections through their new coalition party, the New Guatemala Democratic Front (FDNG, or *el Frente*), and won six congressional seats.

Who were the dissenters at the Segundo Encuentro, the indigenous leaders who were alienated by an international congress intended to include their interests? Why do they now find themselves uncertain whether *el Frente* is the solution to the absence of indigenous issues in national politics? How have dissenters and *populares* been incorporated into the peace process through the Asemblea de la Sociedad Civil?

The Pan-Mayan Movement in Guatemala: An Overview

Since the mid-1980s, educated Mayas have worked to create a social movement focused on indigenous cultural revitalization. Mayan teachers, development workers, linguists, social scientists, and lawyers—combinations of professions and cultural identities that rarely existed before the early 1970s—have been involved in their own research centers for the production and dissemination of materials for a variety of education projects. Most have been schooled in Guatemala; a handful studied in the United States or Europe.

Over the years, Mayan intellectuals and writers have circulated counterhistories denouncing the racism of national histories, searing critiques of foreign research practices and scholarship, texts to promote Mayan language retention, criticisms of Western models of development, and political psychology to counteract internalized racism. Through this activist research, Mayan intellectuals condemn colonialism and racism as an ongoing situation rather than a moment of sociogenesis that occurred five centuries ago during the Spanish invasion.

Mayan studies scholars assert that there is a Mayan way of knowing: a subject position no one else can occupy and political interests no one else has to defend. This essentialism is tactical and situational: Mayas are arguing the essentialist position to claim their own unique authority as social critics. Their goal is clear: to undermine the authoritativeness of *kaxlan* (non-Mayan) accounts—put forward by Guatemalan Ladinos or foreigners—which until their recent activism and resistance had monopolized the representation of Mayan culture and national history.

The early years of the movement were focused on issues of cultural origin and self-definition—"Who are we if we are not the negative stereotypes we have been taught?"—in short, on essentialist issues. One activist put it such that Indians were like street children who did not know their parents and therefore could not plan for the future. Echoing these sentiments, a recent Pan-Mayanist poster, showing Guatemala's verdant hills in the background and a Mayan couple in the foreground, is remembered for the following message: "Un pueblo que desconoce su pasado no tiene un futuro" (A community/people that doesn't know its past doesn't have a future). In the late 1980s and early 1990s, publications in Mayan studies by Demetrio Rodríguez Guaján (1989), Demetrio Cojtí Cuxil (1991), and Luis Enrique Sam Colop (1991) were preoccupied with these issues.

By the mid-1990s, however, debates in the movement had refocused on future directions for Mayan nation building and concrete priorities in education, legal issues, and self-administration. Along these lines, conference proceedings and collaborative projects on Mayan schools and customary law have been published by the Centro de Estudios de la Cultura Maya (CECMA 1992, 1994; Esquit and Ochoa García 1995). Cojtí Cuxil's publications on Mayan rights culminated in his volume *Políticas para la Reivindicación de los Mayas de Hoy* (1994), which summarized explicit demands on the state for reforms in language policy, regional administration, the military, economics, education, communication, and respect for Mayan ceremonial centers. Víctor Rancanoj (1994) has used Mayan hermeneutics to generate a revisionist history of precolonial society and to argue for the revitalization of early models of authority and leadership in the new social order he hopes will be established. The issue at hand for Mayan leaders is now longer-term planning of their agendas—prepared in twenty-year increments to reflect the Mayan calendrics—rather than the year-to-year planning called for by development funding agencies.

The production and circulation of Mayan studies is not an ivory-tower enterprise, given that virtually all Pan-Mayanists come from rural backgrounds. Some have stayed in their home communities working as farmers, teachers, or extensionists in development organizations. Often, they are regional and grassroots leaders in the agricultural cooperative movement, religious groups, or local development efforts. Others have relocated to urban centers to pursue professional training and higher education, working as academics, bookstore owners, publishers, social workers, administrators, teachers, and professionals for nongovernmental organizations (NGOs), the United Nations Children's Fund (UNICEF), and government development programs. On weekends, during vacations, and for major events, professionals often return to their home communities, where some maintain their own immediate families and work on local development projects.

Over the last twenty years, Pan-Mayanism has emerged institutionally. Pan-Mayanists analyze indigenous languages, produce educational materials, host workshops for teachers, organize grassroots language committees, establish Mayan schools, and support Mayan community leaders (from mayors to midwives to Mayan priests) through groups such as the Proyecto Lingüístico Francisco Marroquín (PFLM),[6] Academia de Lenguas Mayas de Guatemala (ALMG), Centro de Documentación Maya (CEDIM),[7] Centro de Estudios de la Cultura Maya (CECMA), Oxlajuuj Keej Maya' Ajtz'iib',[8] and the Asociación de Escritores Mayances.[9] Through the Coordinadora Cakchiquel de Desarrollo Integral (COCADI),[10] activists promote Mayan calendrics, elders, and ecologically sensitive strategies for development, and critique Western development ideologies as neocolonialist. Survey research has been conducted at the Centro de Investigaciones Sociales Mayas (CISMA); research findings are exchanged through the Seminario Permanente de Estudios Mayas (SPEM)[11] and the widely attended annual Taller Maya[12] conferences. A variety of educational materials have been published and distributed through Mayan presses such as Editorial Cholsamaj and Nawal Wuj.[13] Textbooks and teaching guides have been produced through Mayan-Ladino collaborations at the Instituto de Lingüística[14] of the Universidad de Rafael Landívar. The Consejo de Organizaciones Mayas de Guatemala (COMG) was created in the late 1980s as an umbrella group to facilitate communication among Mayan organizations and publicize cultural rights demands.[15] Other less formal groups of students and community members constitute themselves for particular activities and then disperse to their home communities.

While diverse in histories, agendas, and politics, research and educational centers share a common concern with promoting Pan-Mayan loyalties and revealing the ways in which Guatemalan racism and U.S. neocolonialism have politically marginalized and impoverished indigenous populations. The resulting scholarship constitutes a field of cultural studies that crisscrosses Western disciplines and social theories as it seeks to create its own paradigmatic understanding of social life with its own hermeneutics.[16] Cultural centers are attempting to unite Mayas across language groups and communities to build a national movement. To do so, scholars and activists have sought to transcend internal differentiation and localized identifications to create, through their informal educational efforts and other activities, an encompassing "imagined community" of *Maya*'.[17]

It would be shortsighted to dismiss this cultural revival as primordial or marginal to modern politics. Social analysts such as Hobsbawm and Ranger (1983) have pointed to the reemergence of tradition precisely at times of discontinuity. Wallace's early historical work (1972) and Clifford's postmodernism (1988) have taught us that revitalization is a process of political articulation and cultural hybridizing, not inevitably a nostalgic escape to the past. Gellner (1983), Fox (1990), Chatterjee (1993), and others have noted the important role that public intellectuals play in social movements and raise important questions about the class composition, culture, and politics of nationalist movements. Mouffe (1993) has warned against essentialism, against the positing of unitary constructions of identity politics. The following analysis touches on these issues for the Pan-Mayan movement.

Mayan indigenous identity has always had local and translocal manifestations and transformations, from its diverse Olmec roots over 3,000 years ago to the present. The resulting transcultural formation has striking regional continuities, local variations, and very different colonial and contemporary histories in Mexico, Guatemala, Belize, Honduras, and El Salvador. Today the lived reality in local communities echoes the heterogeneous *interplay* of cultural continuities and local elaborations, divergent state histories, regional economic specialization, migration flows, waves of Catholic and Protestant evangelism, and political movements that have challenged the status quo.[18]

Public Intellectuals: Historical Continuities and Transformations

By publicly seeking to represent the collective interests of all Mayas and speaking out on national politics, Mayan public intellectuals represent an astounding change in Guatemala. The presence of intellectual activist leaders is best understood, however, as a variation on a theme that has its own social and political history.[19] Since the breakup of prehispanic states and the colonial resettlement of indigenous populations, traditionalist intellectuals—the *kamol b'ey* of the civil religious hierarchy and the *ajq'ij* shamans—focused their efforts on the creation of *localized* moral spaces for the celebration of the unique connection of individuals with their local community, their ancestors, and their indigenous religion, which worshiped the Earth-World *(ruwach'ulew)*—Nature—and the wider cosmos as sacred.[20] Through a subversive syncretism of Mayan religion and sixteenth-century Catholicism, these leaders promoted a view of the world not wholly shared by Ladino neighbors and their Christ-centric theology, which was simply unaware of Mayan spiritual transcendence in the sacred Earth-World. They were also unaware of the hidden transcript of denunciations of racism and complicity kept alive in veiled religious language in localized saint societies *(cofradías)*, which had been introduced by the colonizers.[21]

Newer generations of public intellectuals are the legacies of this cultural formation and the transgenerational struggle of Mayan families to seek education for their children. In the 1950s and 1960s, religious groups such as Catholic Action and U.S.-supported development projects such as cooperative federations offered nonformal adult education and urged parents to keep their children in school. The Catholic Church created high schools and short-term educational programs in urban centers for indigenous students. Many of the Pan-Mayanists in their 40s and 50s working in the fields of development and linguistics received at least some of their education through these programs for indigenous youths.

The growing numbers of Mayan leaders and their involvement in a variety of local struggles was overwhelmed in the late 1970s and early 1980s by a catastrophic war between the Guatemalan army and the leftist guerrilla forces that had united under the umbrella of the Unidad Revolucionaria Nacional de Guatemala (Guatemalan National Revolutionary Party, or URNG).[22] State terrorism was directed at civilian populations to punish any incipient interest in oppositional politics; guerrillas sought recruits and civilian support and punished class enemies and government collaborators. Mayan organizational leaders—traditionalists, Catholic catechists, development workers, teachers, secular youths, and grassroots sympathizers—became suspect just for being in positions of authority or influence. Many were hunted down and killed. *Popular* groups, such as CUC, were forced to operate clandestinely in the countryside. Whole communities were slaughtered during this genocidal violence, which left eighty thousand dead, one-fifth of the national population displaced from their homes, and hundreds of thousands of refugees outside the country (Montejo and Akab' 1992; Manz 1988).

The guerrilla-counterinsurgency war created a sorrowful conjuncture for new political possibilities. It exposed the broken promises of a guerrilla movement unable to take over the state in the name of socialism and the limits of existing ideologies—revolutionary Marxism, liberal Catholicism, radicalized Theology of Liberation, or economic development through agrarian cooperatives—to chart the next step. Since the de-escalation of widespread warfare in the mid-1980s, the challenge has been to democratize Guatemala in the face of the continued intervention of the armed forces in civilian life and the corruption it has engendered, the internalized violence of communities where individuals war against each other to establish who is most powerful, and the displacement of so many people from their homes and fields. Another challenge has been to turn national attention to urgent development problems—demographic pressures, poverty, illiteracy, the lack of schools and health facilities, unemployment, and the land crisis.

Popular groups became active at this juncture to protest forced military recruitment, to meet the needs of widows and families searching for the disappeared, to protest continuing human rights abuses, and to aid internal and international refugees. Religious groups, particularly the evangelical missions, intensified their efforts in congregation building. And the Pan-Mayan movement emerged to articulate demands for the recognition of collective cultural rights for indigenous Guatemalans, who by some estimates make up 60 percent of the population (Tzian 1994).

To disseminate their concern for self-determination in the democratic opening of the late 1980s, Pan-Mayanists created educational programs and rural-urban networks through which public intellectuals inspired leaders to work for cultural resurgence in hundreds of communities. Behind these demands was a sense of a genocidal dimension to the war, that indigenous communities were singled out for destruction and that indigenous teachers and community leaders were tortured and killed because they were culturally (and even ethnically or racially) different. Many indigenous leaders felt that local Ladinos were shielded from military violence because they were automatically identified with the state.

The Pan-Mayan Movement and Its Educational Projects

As one nationally prominent Mayan leader put it, "This wave is not granite; rather, it defines a certain tendency. There is great variation within the *movimiento maya*. Some are more radical in Mayan religion, others in language, others in politics." It is difficult to characterize a movement as institutionally diverse, polycentric, and dynamic as this one; and it is impossible to capture its variegated practices in an overview. On the cultural revitalization and education fronts, however, Pan-Mayanists have given priority to the following projects:

1. Language revitalization, literacy training in Mayan languages, and local language committees.[23]
2. The revitalization of Mayan chronicles of culture, history, and resistance to the Spanish invasion—such as the *Popol Vuj* and the *Anales de los Kaqchikeles*. One of the most striking characteristics of the movement is its historical consciousness—its multiculturalist sense of the ways Mayas were written out of national history and its urgency to imagine new histo-

ries.[24] Eurocentric histories of Guatemala and school textbooks have been critically reexamined. There is great cosmological interest in the Mayan shape of time; including Mayan calendrics and numerics and their profound associations with historical astronomy. Glyphic texts have also been studied.

3. The production of school texts and teacher training materials for use in special programs for high school students and in Mayan elementary schools.[25]
4. The revitalization of Mayan leadership norms, specifically councils of elders in rural communities and Mayan shaman-priests on local and regional levels.[26]
5. The development and dissemination of a discourse of indigenous rights, focusing on recognition and self-determination, which gives shape and international legitimacy to Mayan cultural revitalization. The movement envisions a transformation of Guatemalan politics to accommodate a *pluricultural* nation with decentralized state services such as courts, schools, and local administration run by Mayas in regional languages.[27] Early on, the movement sought to make candidates for national office more accountable to indigenous voters by holding public candidate forums before elections. The movement seeks cultural autonomy, yet the full extent of this quest for self-determination is still an open-ended issue.

Pan-Mayan projects that flow from these priorities currently operate throughout the western highlands where most of the country's indigenous population resides. Although the movement has received support for particular projects from diverse sources—including European NGOs, UNICEF, U.S. foundations, universities, and the Guatemalan government[28]—it has also attracted intense skepticism. Now it is time to turn to Pan-Mayanism's detractors, who in the 1990s have increasingly made their opinions known through the mass media.

Critics of the Pan-Mayan Movement

Almost from its inception, the Pan-Mayan movement has been disparaged by the Right and Left in Guatemala and beyond. Critics, including Latin Americanists at U.S. universities, were quick to dismiss the movement in the 1980s, despite the paucity of information on its goals or activities. The U.S. Agency for International Development (USAID) and Guatemalan business elites have been highly critical of the movement, which, although market oriented, stresses collective as opposed to individual rights to development resources. The Summer Institute of Linguistics, an arm of the Wycliffe Bible Translators, repeatedly clashed with the movement over language issues and control of the dissemination of publications in indigenous languages. Ladino intellectuals, many of whom were deeply invested in anti-imperialist struggles, were militantly opposed to ethnic-based organizing.

Local Ladinos have generated their own charges of reverse racism and fears of Indian rebellion.[29] European and Latin American development professionals working in UN-sponsored human rights projects have also expressed serious reservations about the movement.

Regardless of their politics, detractors of the Pan-Mayan movement have tended to draw from a common pool of images:

1. The movement is accused of separatism, ethnic polarization, and the creation of a potential for violence, in light of examples of ethnic nationalist movements elsewhere in the world.
2. The movement is accused of violating the local grounding of identity in place and community. The very attempt to create a transcendent sense of indigenous identity is seen as an inauthentic act culturally and a manipulative act politically.
3. The movement is seen as not appropriate for the country because some regions are populated predominately by a single indigenous language group, some regions are mixed with different proportions of indigenous groups and Ladinos, and other regions are predominately nonindigenous. Return refugee communities are not infrequently a mixture of a variety of cultural backgrounds and may speak of themselves as *campesinos,* not Mayas or indigenous peoples.
4. That Ladino culture includes indigenous elements, Mayan culture has been "ladinoized," and all of Guatemala has been drawn into the globalization of popular culture is seen as further erasing the relevance of ethnic-based organizing in favor of *mestizaje* and hybridity.
5. Building on language as a key basis of revitalization, activists are seen as stressing language group endogamy and seeking to prohibit marriage across language groups.
6. Mayan leaders and participants are seen by some critics as neither indigenous nor Ladinos but rather as a third ethnicity because these Mayas are not agriculturalists. As such they are seen as not rightfully representing their people.

In addition to the foregoing, criticism from the *popular* as well as the U.S. Left has added the following issues:

1. The movement is condemned for dealing with cultural issues rather than with more urgent, material concerns such as poverty and access to land for farmers, which are serious concerns given the rapidly growing rural population and the skewed ownership of farmlands that leaves many agriculturalists virtually landless.
2. The movement, which has decided not to label itself "political" and avoids the term "activist," is devalued for dodging the real politics of Guatemala.

3. The measure of success of a social movement is its ability to achieve mass mobilizations and public protests. Pan-Mayanism, with its focus on education and scholarship, is judged as not passing this basic test of demonstrating mass appeal.

Pan-Mayanists dispute these criticisms, which they see as tactical mischaracterizations designed to disempower the movement and attack the intentions and legitimacy of its leadership.[30] From their point of view, the Right and the Left in Guatemala have either wanted to absorb Mayas nationally or to use Mayas as shock troops, as facades for their particular political agendas.[31] While they are willing to work with both sets of structures, Pan-Mayanists are clear about having their own distinct agenda, which in their view is simply not translatable into the agendas of other groups.

In the 1990s, critiques of Pan-Mayanism have received intensive coverage in all major Guatemalan newspapers. The pressure has been relentless, especially recently, with opinion pieces by prominent commentators appearing almost every week. Among the most prolific and controversial of these journalists is Mario Roberto Morales, who has written for *Siglo Veintiuno* and *Prensa Libre*. He is currently finishing his Ph.D. in literature at the University of Pittsburgh. Morales's tactic is to use strategies from cultural studies to deconstruct and delegitimize Pan-Mayanism. Although his academic advisers may not know this, he has cleverly appropriated a method associated with the cultural Left in the United States to provide conservative and other readers with political ammunition in Guatemala. His pieces employ images of globalized popular culture, hybridity, mimesis, culturally fabricated otherness, and *mestizaje* to argue against the existence of separate cultural groups in Guatemala. In a theoretical vein, this is a provocative, contemporary argument, elements of which many cultural observers would agree with, at least aesthetically. Latin America is a dynamic and fluid cultural field in which identities are being continually reconstituted and international mass media and many foreign consumer products are now taken for granted in even remote areas. Morales adds a political-economic dimension to this argument by asserting that Pan-Mayanism is not a local creation but rather is being externally promoted by outside forces, international bankrollers whose agenda is to expand global markets, inequities, and exotic "others" for tourist consumption. Once again, one might agree at least in principle with the importance of interrogating the interests of foreign support for national development initiatives. However, Morales's reductionism and polemicism become apparent when he argues that cultural resurgence is only playacting by ladinoized Mayan intellectuals serving as willing, if cynical, facilitators for those seeking to widen their markets. My problem with this argument is not that Morales wants to question the personal motivations of Pan-Mayanists but rather that his framing of the issue simply avoids engagement with the politics within Guatemala to which this movement is responding as it struggles for rights that have been denied much of the national population.

Morales began his career on the Left as a teacher at the University of San Carlos and a supporter of the Fuerzas Armadas Rebeldes (FAR) guerrilla group before leaving to join another splinter group.[32] He presently configures himself as a Leftist critical of the URNG, the guerrilla umbrella group active since the late 1980s in the peace negotiations, the Pan-Mayanists, and the current governing party, the PAN; Morales has written extensively about social issues in Guatemala. Other commentators, such as Carlos Manuel Pellecer, who writes for *La Hora,* are also former Leftists, though Pellecer is from the generation of the 1950s revolution. By contrast, Mario Sandoval, a Pan-Mayan critic who contributes to *Prensa Libre,* has been a leading organic intellectual on the Right, associated with the Movimiento Nacional de Liberación (MLN) political party. The lack of Ladino columnists from the intellectual Left who might offer positive readings of Mayan resurgence has resulted in ethnically polarized criticism of the movement.[33]

Mayas have not been left defenseless in this public war of words. Estuardo Zapeta has been a steady contributor on a range of subjects to *Siglo Veintiuno;* Demetrio Cojtí Cuxil writes for *Siglo Veintiuno* and *El Regional;* Luis Enrique Sam Colop writes regular columns for *Prensa Libre;* Miguel Angel Velasco Bitzol is one of several members of CECMA who contributes to *La República;* and the novelist Gaspar Pedro Gonzáles is a columnist for the magazine *Tinamit.* This is a highly educated, well-published group of Mayan intellectuals, several of whom have pursued advanced studies outside Guatemala.[34] Cojtí Cuxil, Sam Colop, and Gonzáles are elder statesmen of the movement and have published widely in their own right. Their journalism has a secondary circulation to Mayan organizations through Rutzijol, the Mayan newsclipping service, which reprints in bimonthly collections national news stories about Mayas from a variety of political perspectives and which includes its own collective editorial responses to political issues.

During 1996, as the hostility of Ladino columnists escalated and as newspaper editorials began to reflect this negative perspective, the heads of Mayan organizations met privately to decide whether they should respond in print. Their tactic in 1996 was *not* to denounce these critics directly and, instead, to continue the process of interpreting Pan-Mayanism and Guatemalan politics for the public.[35] For their part, nationally prominent Ladino intellectuals, who have long histories of *popular* support, grew alarmed with the crescendo of hostility and worried that it would only fuel ethnic antagonism and complicate dialogues for social reconstruction after the peace accords. That summer, progressive Ladino intellectuals began to meet privately to explore their personal views of identity and cultural difference and to pursue opportunities for off-the-record dialogues with Mayan leaders.

Revisiting Material Versus Cultural Dilemmas: Thoughts on Cultural Capital

What does this critical discourse reveal about the hopes of the movement and the fears of its critics? Implicit in the criticisms of Pan-Mayanism is a Guatemalan version of the "race versus class" debate about the real sources of unequal opportunities in ethnically plural, class-stratified societies. Rather than seeing class and ethnicity as politically and culturally interactive, critics from a variety of positions on the Left have long argued that Pan-Mayanists have made the wrong choice in stressing their cultural identity.

One can also see in these debates a reproduction of the material-cultural divide that continues to plague the social sciences despite the paradigm blurring of the past several decades. In this instance, material conditions are seen as more autonomous, real, and basic than anything else. "But what about exploitation?" is the critics' common reply, through which they seek to convey a materialist urgency that trumps cultural issues, no matter how worthy. The material world, in terms of land, labor, class structures, and ethnicity itself, is often conceptualized as if it were transparently free from cultural and social mediation by *popular* movements. There is little sense that these material demands are in practice politically advanced selective constructions, conveyed in fields of social relations that also define their significance. The alternative I wish to pursue would confront the cultural issues (and political interests) infused in the construction of materialist politics as well as the materialist concerns (and political interests) infused in cultural framings of politics.

Furthermore, this paradigm blurring allows us to ask important questions of social movements, whatever their politics. How do activists structure the production and circulation of the social meanings crucial to their movement? How does the political vision advanced by activists organize the production, distribution, and consumption of the movement? How in practice do other participants consume this culture and produce their own meanings in the process? Movements may seek to adjust access to a variety of resources, both to attract participants and to pursue their political vision. The creation and redistribution of "cultural capital"—which in this setting includes the media, education, knowledge of the past and present, languages with which to interrogate the status quo, cosmological knowledge, models of community authority, experience in organizational cultures, and skills to communicate across language communities and through various technologies—are other resources, differential access to which makes a material *and* cultural difference in peoples' lives.

In this context, scholars of social movements might consider the utility of an *anthropological* notion of "cultural capital." Unfortunately for the case at hand, analysts have conventionally understood cultural capital to be a monopoly of the mainstream. In an early psychological approach, Oscar Lewis's notion of the "culture of poverty" (1966) condemned the underclasses for the poverty of their lived culture, by which he meant their lack of idealized mainstream norms (many of which, in fact and in practice, ironically elude the middle class as well). In a more sociological and structural vein, Pierre Bourdieu (1977, 1984) presented a formulation of symbolic capital and status hierarchies as singular ladders with high-status culture at the apex. More recently, Phillipe Bourgois (1995), by noting how inner city entrepreneurs mobilize their own cultural and social capital in highly segregated social settings, has urged that the notion of cultural capital be historicized and made interactive. He remains astutely aware of the political and economic contexts in which this occurs. But although Bourgois acknowledges the local deployment of different kinds of cultural capital, he largely dismisses their salience and impact on the wider society.

Such approaches—especially when they are structurally generalized—tend to portray culture as bounded groups and communities rather than to pursue the polyculturalism that individuals in some marginalized communities have used to manipulate status hierarchies and widen their access to resources at the center and the margins. Along these lines, I would argue for a concept of cultural capital that identifies the ways in which specific cultural formations in their larger contexts give distinctive shapes to the cultural capital they find relevant; recognizes the circulation and distribution of nonmaterial and nonquantifiable cultural resources as an additional issue for social movements; and draws our attention to the changing forms of capitalist production—in this moment of transnational intensification and the global flow of knowledge, information, and people—that make transculturalism and certain media especially important and powerful.

Note that in this formulation there is no simple link between cultural capital and economic capital; rather, specific links need to be problematized in particular situations.[36] In fact, many Pan-Mayanists have access to a great deal of cultural capital—from fluency in indigenous languages and shamanism to knowledge of the high-tech tools of the electronic age—yet the overwhelming majority live in modest economic circumstances. At work, for instance, Pan-Mayanists have been quick to push development donors for access to computer technology for their research and publication efforts. Specialized computer programs now facilitate their publication of educational materials and research on prehispanic Mayan calendrics, historical astronomy, and glyphs. Public intellectuals have mastered the conventions of national and international meetings as public forums for their work. In sum, Pan-Mayanists have internationalized and hybridized Mayan culture to intensify and repoliticize the cultural differences between indigenous and Ladino communities at home.[37] How, then, are cultural capital and economic class related in the practice of Pan-Mayanism?

The problem of culture and class remains a challenge for analysts, given the prominence in Latin American studies of structuralist frameworks such as historical materialism, internal colonialism, and world systems theory. Most analysts would agree, however, that classes are not theoretical abstractions—they are culturally and materially constructed in particular situations, as are other forms of stratification. High theory aside, class is not a separable domain but rather a multidimensional form of stratification that is in practice often gendered, racialized, and saturated with cultural difference. For instance, as a result of the genocidal civil war in Guatemala, impoverished rural widows became a distinctive political-economic class—the result of Mayan family structure, agrarian sexual divisions of labor, and the violent repression that killed their husbands and left these women without a subsistence base. Courageously, CONAVIGUA, the *popular* movement's widows' organization, brought women from this existentially gendered class together for crucial psychological, political, and material support.

Thus, the forging of identification with a particular "class-based" identity—by mobilizing groups around it—is also a process of construction. It is a political process fraught with some of the same dilemmas, such as the standardization and displacement of local culture, that critics see in Pan-Mayan identity. The constructed nature of this identification does not diminish the vital way in which CONAVIGUA has come to meet the needs of women and children who were scarred by the war's violence.

When Mayan leaders assert that "class conflict is *not* our issue" but Western neocolonialism and racism are, one sees the heterodoxy and originality of the movement. On the one hand, they seek to build a cross-class movement—a new sort of Mayan solidarity—that would include middle-class professionals and businesspeople as well as cultivators, students, teachers, development workers, and rural shopkeepers. In fact, urban migration for reasons of employment or physical safety and new organizational involvements compel members of many extended families to have multiple class-ethnic identifications, localized in different ways in rural and urban space.

When Pan-Mayanists make charges of widespread racism in Guatemala instead of focusing on class conflict, they seek radically to reframe who is accountable to social criticism. For them, Ladino peasants, urban migrants, and the working classes are complicit along with others in the reproduction of prejudices that have destructive effects in everyday life. A wide array of "public" institutions are also implicated. The signal problem for social action—as the labor-capital analysts would have it—is not limited to Guatemala's tiny economic elite, which shockingly owns 75 percent of the country's agricultural land. The problem also involves the more diffuse persistence of racism in national culture, where everyday life and the media are untroubled by open discussions that characterize indigenous people as not rightful participants in civil society and as not ready for jobs and education because of their ethnic inferiority. Moreover, antagonism is racialized in Guatemala for Ladinos, who resent the mobility of Mayas and their demands for political space (Hale 1995, 1996).

So far, this analysis has juxtaposed the language of movement critics with the social analysis generated by the movement. Now it is time to reorient the analysis in order to engage the movement from the perspective of the practices and the personal stakes of the Pan-Mayan leadership.

Pan-Mayanists, Upward Mobility, and Different Ways of Being "Middle Class"

Is Pan-Mayanism a social movement or is it instead an emerging class-ethnicity seeking to consolidate its power and privilege? If one widens the notion of class beyond models of agrarian and industrial production—something that is increasingly important in this age of information, communication, and dislocation—it becomes clear that Pan-Mayanists are attempting to design a novel social formation. They want the alternative of asserting a "Maya-ness" that, while valuing agrarian work and spirituality, also opens employment options transgressing the mental-manual divide that was colonially established through forced labor policies and maintained by commercial interests and Guatemala's oligarchy into the twentieth century.

To undertake development projects engaging indigenous adults and schoolchildren in the highlands, movement activists have created rural-urban networks of development professionals who share access to cultural and material capital far beyond Guatemala's borders. Educational pamphlets, books, videos, audiotapes, and computer disks that are locally produced circulate widely through these networks; participants are continually on the move to attend and organize meetings to keep current with information and new organizational strategies; and international groups are tapped for financial assistance and external leverage in struggles for rights and cultural capital.

From both the cultural capital *and* materialist points of view, a parallel middle class of educated indigenous employees has crystallized.[38] These individuals are proud of their achievements, which have been built on an older generation's commitment in the 1950s and 1960s to see their children and grandchildren get ahead *(superarse)* and escape grinding poverty. The discourse of self-improvement and mobility was promoted by groups such as Catholic Action and the cooperative movement, which were trying to head off radical politics in the process. The achievement of this goal was a great challenge in communities where most indigenous workers were impoverished subsistence farmers or day laborers. Since there were few nonfarming jobs in rural communities, and these were often monopolized by Ladinos, the educated children of these families have been quick to pursue jobs in local and regional development organizations and the schools. Many have realized that nonmanual employment calls them away from their agricultural communities to regional and urban centers.

On the whole, today's Pan-Mayanists are not a class of petty merchants in the informal economy but are rather individuals employed by development NGOs and state bureaucracies including the school system, extension services, and the government-supported national research center, the *Academia de Lenguas Mayas de Guatemala*. In terms of cultural capital—that is, education, organizational access, ties to the production of culture, and status as bicultural knowledge brokers—these activists have consolidated an ethnic-class blend that gives them access to specialized jobs, contacts, and transnational flows of communication.[39] Many of these Mayas are recognized as "professionals" in the sense that they are salaried workers with technical knowledge. Some have only six years of formal education but have become experts on the job through their own intellectual efforts and participation in nonformal education programs. Many are high school graduates who hoped to be teachers; others have begun college, a long-term process for students who generally have young families to support. A small but growing number have college degrees, law degrees, and doctorates.

Economically, most Pan-Mayanists who work for NGOs, research organizations, universities, and government agencies have lower-middle-class or middle-class wages and poor job security. Changes in international development priorities or in national ruling parties can sweep away jobs in development fields. Development organizations are perennially in search of funding for new projects in order to support their professional and administrative staffs, overhead, and project development efforts. Many development experts are hired on a project-by-project basis by international organizations, which are under some political pressure to include national professionals and, following the dictates of neoliberal economics, under greater economic pressure to subcontract work to save money rather than to expand their permanent staffs. Universities operate under similar constraints, so most academic positions are part time and poorly paid.

The salaries paid by international NGOs and the UN are highly stratified and thereby reproduce the status hierarchy of international, national, and local spheres. International professionals—from Europe, the United States, and Latin America—earn five times what high-ranking national professionals receive from the same employers, while local office personnel receive conventional subsistence wages.[40] In practice, development work, even at its most lucrative, is short term. Some international projects offer six months of excellent salaries for professionally credentialed principals (who thus are able to survive periods of unemployment between jobs), others only a month or two of part-time employment. Although a very few elite Pan-Mayanists have achieved the financial success that would allow them to own urban homes and cars, most Pan-Mayanist professionals live in marginal, overcrowded rental housing. In fact, their extended family residences back home may offer more space and better facilities.

Thus, a singular materialist definition of "middle class," which emphasizes consumer prosperity, does not fully capture the parallel middle class's standard of living, which in some respects is not much different from that of rural teachers, community development workers, general store owners, and small farmers with their own land. Furthermore, many urban-based Pan-Mayanists must disperse their higher earnings among their own extended families of farmers, students, and urban migrants. These obligations are reinforced by Mayan kinship structures, which Pan-Mayanists value highly.

The Pan-Mayanist emphasis on education makes sense given their commitment to home communities and rural development. The illiteracy rates for Guatemalans, which range up to 75 percent for rural Mayan women, demonstrate how much work there is to be done. The Pan-Mayanist concern with racism reflects their difficult family histories of plantation labor and their current experiences with economic mobility and ethnic divisions of labor in the development industry, which rarely gives Mayas positions of authority over Ladinos or international professionals.

Doubtlessly, one source of negative feelings toward Pan-Mayanism is the growing competition for jobs in urban areas between the parallel middle classes. Middle-class Ladino intellectuals in the social sciences are caught in the same employment dilemmas as educated Mayas and now face a new source of direct competition for development work, academic positions, and state jobs. Interestingly, while Mayan professionals are aware of job competition, they argue that indigenous professionals bring to these positions specialized knowledge, especially fluency in indigenous languages, which few Ladinos have invested time in learning. What especially puzzles Mayan intellectuals is the ambivalence—which they see as hypocritical—of some international scholars and international development workers toward their achievements.[41] Clearly there is little direct competition in these cases.

Like their counterparts in *popular* organizations, however, Pan-Mayan public intellectuals can be legitimately asked questions about the internal politics of the movement—who speaks for whom, how hybrid class and cultural identities are constructed and standardized, what is taught as Mayan culture, who is being educated, and whose knowledge is authoritative. Pan-Mayanists cannot escape exerting power as they decide what is published; how dialects within languages are standardized in written form; how one deals with issues of gender, class, religion, and locality; and which dimensions of self-determination are promoted or are sidelined for a later date. As one would expect, internal cleavages—heterogeneities of religion, gender, generation, and locale—have not been left unaddressed by participants who, regardless of their common commitment to revitalization and rights, feel marginalized within the movement.

For all the reverence expressed toward rural culture, indigenous cosmology, consensus politics, and Mayan elders, Pan-Mayanists operate with their own internal hierarchies, ideologies of difference, and plural identities. For instance, Mayan youths—who see Christianity as a form of colonialism—are ambivalent about the antiracism struggles of their parents, who continue to teach and worship in Christian groups such as Catholic Action. Educated Mayas who revere shamanic rituals at their conferences wonder if neotraditionalist shamans should be officially credentialed, as other experts are. And the older generation of Mayan leaders harbor complicated feelings about educating daughters who, in their view, should stay at home to reproduce Mayan culture in the next generation.

Coalitional Possibilities: Defining Common Purpose Across Cleavages

Pan-Mayanists are making decisions about their movement among a field of other powerful actors—which includes national authorities and elites, the *popular* movement with its international sources of support, the international development community, and the international indigenous rights movement—each with its own programs and politics. To create Mayan elementary schools, Pan-

Mayanists pragmatically collaborate with Ladino universities, USAID, the UN, the European Union, and Norwegian NGOs.

These accommodations are strategic. On the one hand, they have pressured the movement to stress decentralization as a tactic of self-determination for education and self-administration. In fact, decentralization—which is part of the package of neoliberal reforms promulgated by the international development community in the face of cuts in government bureaucracies and services mandated by the International Monetary Fund (IMF)—appears to have become an alternative route to the movement's dream of a Mayan nation made up of regional language groups within the Guatemalan state. At this point, movement leaders imagine federalist models of cultural autonomy as the institutional vehicle for their cultural vision. Perhaps it is ironic that the Pan-Mayan movement, which has sought unification and standardization in the face of community microvariation, has embraced decentralization. But this may be inevitable given the regional character of indigenous languages, economies, and community leadership and the decentralized international development policies currently in vogue.

On the other hand, one would expect continuing tensions between decentralization and centralization, and further debates about the significance of these terms in national politics and local communities. This has become the case since the December 1996 signing of the peace accords. European donors have demanded that Pan-Mayanists create broader organizations and a consensus on project priorities, or these NGOs will look to other groups.

The divide between Pan-Mayanism and the *popular* movement, which some commentators have portrayed as unbreachable or irreconcilable because of ideological or class differences, is bridged quite frequently by individuals who are active in both camps or who borrow ideas from each other for their own uses. Thus, in practice there are many instances of cross-fertilization and frequent moments of common purpose between the Pan-Mayan and *popular* movements. Not all are convinced, however, that *el Frente,* the new grassroots coalition party, which has courted Mayan voters and has strong *popular* ties, will shed its leftist roots, push for the implementation of Pan-Mayanist reforms over other priorities, or develop wider electoral appeal. But most agree that the time is not right for a Mayan political party.

Pan-Mayanists have widened their class analysis over time. They now see Ladino poverty as an important issue that needs to be addressed and recognize that the racism of the Ladino underclass is economically fueled. In their reflections on the multiple meanings of racism, they have drawn on Ladino scholars such as Carlos Guzmán Bockler and Jean-Loup Herbert (1995), who used an internal colonialism model to conceptualize domination and who discussed the unstable nature of Ladino identity. They have turned recently to the work of Marta Elena Casaús Arzú (1992), who wrote a powerful social history of Guatemala's oligarchy. Of special interest is her documentation of the genealogical reproduction of Guatemala's microelite, lineage by lineage, since the sixteenth century through tactical endogamy, intermarriage between these lineages (which controlled vast private resources and public powers), and the racist ideology of *limpieza de sangre*. In fact, many of these elite lineages see themselves as whites who stand totally apart from and above the indigenous-Ladino divide; none regard themselves as having indigenous blood.

For their part, many intellectuals on the Left have changed their views on indigenous issues over the years and moved away from total assimilation as the only future for indigenous communities.[42] Pan-Mayanists admire the courageous work of *popular* human rights activists who publicize human rights abuses at great risk to themselves. They agree on the importance of demilitarizing civilian life and disbanding civil patrols, which parents feared would socialize their sons into violence, corruption, and disrespect for the moral authority of their families. The activities of the grassroots organization Majawil Q'ij and the widespread use of Mayan priests in public events—from the Segundo Encuentro to the regional meetings of grassroots organizations—are among the *popular* movement's contributions to activism in the name of Mayan culture. Moreover, Rigoberta Menchú's hosting of indigenous conferences and her collaboration with Demetrio Cojtí Cuxil at the 1995 Taller Maya conference, where they jointly delivered a paper on Mayan languages, are high-profile instances of common concern.

There have been important recent experiments in institution building across the Pan-Mayan–*popular* divide. In 1995, before the elections, a low key group called K'amol B'ey was formed to begin discussions about developing a "vía maya de política electoral." The idea was not to create a political party but rather a dialogue in which indigenous leaders from *popular* groups and the Pan-Mayan movement would play more than a token role and Ladinos would listen to their concerns. These discussions appear to have generated concrete results on both sides. For instance, the Fundación Rigoberta Menchú, which despite its name is primarily a Ladino-run institution, is now funding projects in Mayan education. Also, Demetrio Cojtí Cuxil has published with the Asociación para el Avance de las Ciencias Sociales en Guatemala (Association for the Advancement of Social Sciences in Guatemala, or AVANCSO), an important research center long associated with *popular* issues.

Most significantly, the inclusion of indigenous cultural rights in the 1995 peace-accord process—through negotiations involving the government, the guerrillas, the military, and representatives of other sectors in meetings of the civil assembly—marks the public recognition of Mayan culture by a variety of interests. A coalition of Pan-Mayan and *popular* activists came together for the accord process, working to voice Mayan concerns. The resulting organization, Coordinación de Organizaciones del Pueblo Maya de Guatemala (Coordinator for the Organizations of the Mayan People of Guatemala, or COPMAGUA), commissioned position papers from fourteen sectors and through sustained discussion created a consensus about key issues in order to influence the deliberations of the Asemblea de Sociedad Civil.

From the time of the Segundo Encuentro to the present, Mayas active in the grassroots Left have become increasingly engaged culturally and ethnically, leaving some of their Ladino colleagues wondering about the impact of Mayan resurgence on the Left and the possibility of new Mayan alignments across old political cleavages. In 1996, some Ladino leaders felt that indigenous *populares* could go toward a cross-movement alliance that would either include Ladinos or perhaps lead in an independent direction with other Mayas.

In 1996, the missing Ladino voice, one that would publicly condemn Ladino racism and affirm Mayan cultural existence, was added to the calculus. Casaús Arzú, the critic of elite hegemony and a member of one of the country's most prominent families, returned to Guatemala after years of exile for her radical politics in the 1970s. For her, this is a crucial historical juncture, an opportunity for Ladino-Mayan dialogue to work toward intercultural understanding and the dismantling of racism. Casaús Arzú has worked with Demetrio Cojtí Cuxil to promote these dialogues. She argues that Guatemala must avoid perpetuating either the "nación étnica," in which Ladinos continue to rule a homogenous national culture, or the "nación étnica maya," in which Mayas seek a separate nation. Instead, her goal is the "nación política," which would recognize cultural difference and tackle racism but rule out the formation of separate ethnic nations. In her mind, these dialogues are absolutely crucial to avoid future violence.

Do these lines of mutual influence and collaboration point toward a new unified paradigm, a new synthesis of movements? Or will a division of labor continue between cultural rights and education on the one hand and agrarian issues and human rights abuses on the other? The notion of a variety of social movements pursuing their own projects and coalitional opportunities is closer to some European, South Asian, and South African notions of social activism than to the unified paradigm approach which guided the Guatemalan *popular* movement through years of repression and the beginnings of a transition to a yet unfinished democracy.[43] The issues of forging wider unities and identifications, determining how they would be labeled, and deciding at whose expense they would be established has been very much on the minds of radical democracy theorists. Interestingly, there is still great nostalgia for the past in much of this political theorizing. As in the *popular* movement, it is marked by the dream of a radical and plural democracy as an enduring project of the Left rather than as a novel set of struggles that are the legacies of many different histories.

At this point, the Pan-Mayan movement uses a different language for transcendence—one that would promote ethnic politics as the highest measure by seeking an institutionalized voice for Mayas and structural reforms in power relations. In practice, the impulse toward separatism has been moderated by alliances with other groups to reform state and society: to transform the conventional processes of society, renegotiate the terms by which people live, and reorganize the cognitive structures that shape meanings and identities (see Trend 1996, 105, 110, 161). It is evident that Mayas want official recognition for their languages as part of the routine operation of the state rather than treated as special characteristics of minorities.

This will involve raising issues such as the training of legal translators in different languages so that indigenous Guatemalans can understand court proceedings and act in their own best interests. It will also involve the production of government documents, such as marriage licenses, so that they will be available in the languages (common or distinctive) spoken by the newlyweds as well as in Spanish.

Conclusions

The reaction in Latin America to ethnic- and race-based organizing has often been highly charged. For example, Brazilian scholars have been critical of recent investigations of racism and race-based mobilization in their country.[44] Why, some critics ask, find racism where Brazilians—including many Afro-Brazilians—deny it? Guatemala would seem to provide a complicated contrast: Why deny indigenous populations, including an emerging parallel "middle class," the chance to pursue the relevance of indigenous culture and racism in their social struggles and movements? This chapter has argued that taking a cross-class ethnic movement seriously will help broaden the understanding of culture and politics in countries seeking to institute participatory democracy. It might also undermine analyses that divide social movements into two streams: those that seek cultural affirmation and those that seek wider access to resources. By seeing the importance of recognizing and redistributing cultural capital, the Pan-Mayan movement reveals the real-world limits of such formulations.

For the radical democracy theorists discussed in this essay, there are constructive possibilities in adversarial relations. To these debates, Pan-Mayanists contribute their critiques of the essentialisms of class identity and class conflict in *popular* discourse. Nevertheless, thinkers such as Mouffe (1993) would be quick to condemn Pan-Mayanists for their ethnic essentialism—its foregrounding of a singular and fixed "Maya-ness" and its elevation of a Mayan way of knowing above other viewpoints. Her comments about feminism parallel her thinking about ethnicity:

> Feminism, for me, is the struggle for the equality of women. But this should not be understood as a struggle to realize the equity of a definable empirical group with a common essence and identity—that is, women—but rather as a struggle against the multiple forms in which the category 'women' is constructed in subordination. However, we must be aware of the fact that those feminist goals can be constructed in many different ways, according to the multiplicity of discourses in which they can be framed: Marxist, liberal, conservative, radical separatist, radical democratic, and so on. . . . Instead of trying to prove that a given form of feminist discourse is the one that corresponds to the 'real' essence of womanhood, one should aim to show how it expands the possibilities for an understanding of women's multiple forms of subordination. (1993, 88)

In the Pan-Mayan dialogue with the *popular* movement since the Segundo Encuentro, both parties appear to have expanded the possibilities of understanding the multiple forms of Mayan subordination. Further discursive theorizing may well occur in the new communities of dialogue between Ladino intellectuals and

Pan-Mayan leaders. But for Pan-Mayans, the outstanding issue is taking effective action toward their agendas for change. Clearly the post–peace accord period is crucially important to all these parties.

In this analysis, I have argued that we need processual studies of social ideologies that treat the circulation of knowledge and culture as an issue not of formal ideology but rather of contextualized social practice. Anthropology's contribution is not to reproduce images of bounded essentialized cultures or ethnicities but rather to assist in understanding the production, distribution, and reappropriation of culture by all parties.

It is too early to know what sort of impact the Pan-Mayan movement, based on education, language, cultural reaffirmation, and collective rights, will have on the regions of Guatemala where it is most active. There will be no demonstrations to count because this is not a mass movement that generates protest. But there will be new generations of students, leaders, teachers, development workers, and community elders who have been touched in one way or another by the Pan-Mayan movement and its cultural production. Knowing how important local and regional identities continue to be in the countryside, we can expect that rural Guatemalans will consume the cultural production of this and other movements in different ways. Local groups will continue to generate their own development agendas and projects independently of the Pan-Mayan movement—yet now in the name of Mayan culture and the language of rights. Clearly it will be important to watch regional organizations and communities reweave the knowledge and social forms of both movements into local material-cultural agendas.

Perhaps the Pan-Mayan movement is like the Black Consciousness (BC) movement in South Africa—that is, a form of cultural production crucial to inventing a language that names and challenges the corrosive consequences of structural discrimination and diffuse racism. The BC movement's leaders argued that personal and collective affirmation was crucial to defeat the internalized racism of apartheid. Other groups criticized its cultural focus, and yet the movement served as a vital bridge to grassroots participation in a range of organizational structures and projects—some multiracial and others predominately black South African (Marx 1992). Perhaps the Pan-Mayan movement foreshadows a successful turn to education as a form of rural-urban grassroots activism and community involvement that will make the best of the national move to decentralized development initiatives. What is certain as the movement continues to take shape is that the cultural issues and rights Pan-Mayanists have defined as critical and the controversies they have unleashed will be extraordinarily important for Guatemala's future.

Notes

1. For more on radical democracy, the contested place of Marxism in this transformation, and the heterogeneity of Marxist approaches themselves, see Laclau and Mouffe 1985; Mouffe 1992, 1993; Trend 1996.

2. Most of my information comes from public events, from specialized conferences, and from interviews with grassroots leaders, intellectuals, U.S. Agency for International Development (USAID) officials, others in the development community, and townspeople in San Andrés. Another source has been the very public airing of these disputes in the Guatemalan press. In some cases, members of the international *popular* left have met with me to explain their views. Pan-Mayanists have also shared press clippings and discussed their critics with me in interviews and in private conversations at events such as the Segundo Encuentro. I have decided not to mention individual names from personal discussions. Some critics have moderated their opinions over time, while others have intensified their intolerance. Particular lines of criticism continue to travel between Guatemala and the United States along the conference circuit. In contrast to the evasiveness of other foreigners, Levenson-Estrada (forthcoming) and Stoll (1993) have published critiques of Pan-Mayanism from politically distinctive points of view.

3. Whether or not there is a unified Left in current political practice—or how current politics relates to the history of the Left's internal divisions—is not the task of this essay. Congresses like the Segundo Encuentro argued forcefully that the grassroots Left, in all its diversity, has come to share a common international political paradigm.

4. For more on the *encuentro,* see the final report of the congress in Segundo Encuentro Continental 1991, Hale's analysis (1994), and Smith's overview (1991). In their early writings, Mayan intellectuals did not make more than oblique references to the meetings.

5. See, for example, Materne 1976. In fact, there have been a series of international indigenous meetings in Guatemala, including Rigoberta Menchú's Indigenous Summit in 1993 and CECMA's conference, which resulted in the volume on *Derecho Indígena* (1994).

6. See López Raquec 1989.

7. CEDIM has just begun publishing *IXIM,* a newsletter of commentary and announcements.

8. See their work in England and Elliot 1990 and Oxlajuuj Keej 1993.

9. See Cojtí Cuxil 1991.

10. See COCADI 1985, 1988, 1992a, 1992b and Rodríguez Guaján 1989.

11. See Sam Colop 1991 and Pop Caal 1992.

12. Collections of papers presented at these meetings are available through the Academia de Lenguas Mayas de Guatemala. See Taller Maya 1992, 1993.

13. See England and Elliot 1990.

14. Titles include Ajquijay and Rodríguez 1992 and Dávila 1992.

15. See COMG 1991, 1995.

16. On the issue of Mayan hermeneutics, see Watanabe 1992; B. Tedlock 1982; D. Tedlock 1983; and Warren 1995, 1996.

17. Benedict Anderson (1983) gives us this language, and the Mayas remind us of how diversified the grassroots process is. Although many anthropologists have rightfully criticized Anderson's top-down image of cultural production, his stress on media is important for the Mayan case. Significantly, Pan-Mayanism calls our attention to diversifying what counts as media in the project of nation and community building. Dress—especially for Pan-Mayan men—turns out to be a very important medium for creating new levels of ethnic identification. Women's clothing is both locally inflected and regionally keyed to language groups.

18. See Smith's important argument (1993) about Mayan commerce as a form of agency for the Totonicapan region.

19. See Carmack 1973 for a discussion of the continuity of these positions with prehispanic power structures.

20. See Watanabe 1992; Warren 1989; and B. Tedlock 1982. See Warren 1995 for an argument about the separation of knowledge and power in community authority and Warren 1992 for a discussion of variations in community versus national leadership in the Pan-Mayan movement.

21. For Mayan chronicles of their religion and conquest, see Recinos 1950 and D. Tedlock 1985. On the subversiveness of the *cofradías,* see Warren 1989.

22. For details, see Carmack 1988, 1995; Falla 1994; Montejo and Akab' 1992; and Warren 1993.

23. See, for example, Taller Maya 1992, 1993; CECMA 1992; CEM-G 1994; Oxlajuuj Keej Maya' Ajtz'iib' 1993; and England and Elliot 1990.

24. See Sam Colop 1991 and Warren 1996, forthcoming(c).

25. See Ajquijay On and Rodríguez 1992 and Dávila 1992, among many others.

26. See COCADI 1992a, 1992b and CECMA 1994.

27. See CECMA 1994; COMG 1991; and Cojtí Cuxil 1991, 1994, 1996.

28. For example, funders of projects include the European Union; Norwegian groups such as Redd Barna, NORAD, FAFO, and APN; the Canadian Center for Human Rights, Development, and Democracy (CIDHDD); and the United Nations through a variety of programs such as UNESCO and PRODERE. U.S. funders include USAID, the Plumsock Foundation, and, for scholarly exchanges, the Guatemalan Scholars Network and the Latin American Studies Association (LASA). University supporters include the Universidad Rafael Landívar through the Instituto de Lingüística and the Universidad Mariano Galvez.

29. See Charles Hale (1995, 1996) for important ethnographic work on Ladino reaction to Mayan mobilization.

30. A sustained reply to each of these lines of criticism to weigh their accuracy is a task that belongs to the Pan-Mayanists themselves.

31. Pan-Mayanists believe that foreign and national academics have their own agendas in publishing on Guatemala, which differ from the research agenda of Mayan public intellectuals.

32. His disenchantment is said to date from a period when he lived in Nicaragua and was jailed, apparently for reasons of internal politics.

33. Ladino intellectuals, however, have published scholarly work on Mayan resurgence. See Bastos and Camus 1995, 1996 and Solares 1993.

34. Cojtí Cuxil has a doctorate in communications from a Belgian university and works for UNICEF; Sam Colop pursued a doctorate in Mayan linguistics at the State University of New York at Buffalo after obtaining a Guatemalan law degree and works on legal issues in Mayan development. Estuardo Zapeta is a doctoral student in anthropology at the State University of New York at Albany.

35. Pan-Mayanists have responded in print from time to time. See Cojtí Cuxil 1996 on the charge of separatism and Sam Colop 1991 on specific notorious journalists in the national press.

36. Relevant to any sustained discussion of Guatemala would be larger issues of political economy such as the country's place in the North American Free Trade Agreement (NAFTA) regionalization and the continuation of *maquiladora* production as one national development strategy among others.

37. This is not the first instance of ethnic intensification on either side of the divide. See Brintnall 1979 for an argument that the activities of Catholic Action and Protestant groups in the 1950s and 1960s intensified indigenous identity and anti-Ladino sentiment by cross-cutting cleavages that had subdivided communities.

38. See Jeffrey Himpele's work (1995) on the Aymara parallel middle-class formation in Bolivia, which challenges the unified or single-class hierarchy model and its evolutionary subtext. Actually, Guatemalan historians working on Quezaltenango note an earlier period of indigenous florescence, including language revival and political power, so the current movement may not be as "new" as anthropologists cast it.

39. It is difficult to come up with hard estimates of the numbers of participants in these diverse networks, especially now that hundreds of highland communities have their own language committees that are associated with the Academy of Mayan Languages of Guatemala (ALMG). National conferences on specialized topics routinely draw hundreds of leaders, some local (depending, of course, on the venue) and others national. That President Vinicí Cerezo, Minister of Education Alfredo Tay Coycoy, and Rigoberta Menchú addressed the 1994 Primer Congreso de la Educación Maya, for example, indicates the growing importance of the Pan-Mayan movement. More than two hundred educators from throughout the country attended this three-day event. The Primer Congreso de Estudios Mayas in August 1996 drew several hundred participants, including Ladino intellectuals, Mayan leaders, North American scholars, and community activists.

40. This information was provided by foreign and Mayan professionals who have worked for these organizations at various levels.

41. They are right that many foreign professionals come from working-class and impoverished rural backgrounds a generation or two ago and have used education and employment to consolidate comfortable middle-class lives. This writer certainly fits the profile.

42. For example, compare Jonas and Tobis 1974 with Jonas 1991 and Jonas and Stein 1990.

43. The social-historical reasons for the hegemonic and often intolerant nature of the *popular* movement and its scholars are beyond the scope of this chapter. But the punishing reactions at the 1992 Latin American Studies Association (LASA) conference to Carol Smith's historical analysis of racism in the work of nationally prominent academics on the Left and to my own early work on the Segundo Encuentro show how hard it may be to reconstruct this history. A social history of the full scope of the Left and its views of other political currents might go far toward showing how this political vision has been reproduced over time.

44. See Hanchard's provocative study (1994).

References

Ajquijay On, Adela, and Demetrio Rodríguez. 1992. *Cultura Maya: Pasado y Futuro*. Guatemala: Universidad Rafael Landívar.

Anderson, Benedict. 1983. *Imagined Communities: Reflections on the Origin and Spread of Nationalism*. London: Verso.

Bastos, Santiago, and Manuela Camus. 1995. *Abiendo Caminos: Las Organizaciones Mayas desde el Nobel hasta el Acnerdo de Derechos Indígenas*. Guatemala: FLACSO.

______. 1996. *Quebrando el Silencio: Organizaciones del Pueblo Maya y sus Demandas*. Guatemala: FLACSO.

Bourdieu, Pierre. 1977. *Outline of a Theory of Practice*. Cambridge: Harvard University Press.

______. 1984. *Distinction: A Social Critique of the Judgement of Taste*. Cambridge: Harvard University Press.

Bourgois, Phillipe. 1995. *In Search of Respect: Selling Crack in El Barrio*. Cambridge: Cambridge University Press.

Brintnall, Douglas E. 1979. *Revolt Against the Dead: The Modernization of a Mayan Community in the Highlands of Guatemala*. New York: Gordon and Breach.

Carmack, Robert. 1973. *Quichean Civilization: The Ethnohistoric, Ethnographic, and Archaeological Sources*. Berkeley: University of California Press.

______. 1995. *Rebels of Highland Guatemala: The Quiche-Mayas of Momostenango*. Norman: University of Oklahoma Press.

Carmack, Robert, ed. 1988. *Harvest of Violence: The Maya Indians and the Guatemalan Crisis*. Norman: University of Oklahoma Press.

Casaús Arzú, Marta Elena. 1992. *Guatemala: Linaje y Racismo*. San José: FLACSO.

CECMA (Centro de Estudios de la Cultura Maya). 1992. *Hacia una Educación Maya: Encuentro Taller de Escuelas con Programas de Cultura Maya*. Guatemala: Cholsamaj.

______. 1994. *Derecho Indígena: Sistema Jurídico de los Pueblos Originarios de América*. Guatemala: Serviprensa Centroamericana.

CEM-G. 1994. *Logros y Experiencias de la Educación Bilingüe Intercultural en Guatemala*. Guatemala: PRONEBI.

Chatterjee, Partha. 1993. *The Nation and Its Fragments: Colonial and Postcolonial Histories*. Princeton: Princeton University Press.

Clifford, James. 1988. *The Predicament of Culture: Twentieth-Century Ethnography, Literature, and Art*. Cambridge: Harvard University Press.

COCADI (Coordinadora Cakchiquel de Desarrollo Integral). 1985. *El Idioma, Centro de Nuestra Cultura*. Guatemala: COCADI.

______. 1988. *Maya Kaqchikel Ajlab'al: Sistema de Numeración Maya Kaqchikel*. Guatemala: COCADI.

______. 1992a. *Agenda 1992*. Guatemala: COCADI.

______. 1992b. *Conclusiones Generales, Primera Reunión en Consejo de Principales Kaqchikeles*. Guatemala: COCADI.

Cojtí Cuxil, Demetrio. 1991. *Configuración del Pensamiento Político del Pueblo Maya*. Quetzaltenango, Guatemala: Asociación de Escritores Mayances de Guatemala.

______. 1994. *Políticas para la Reivindicación de los Mayas de Hoy*. Guatemala: Cholsamaj.

______. 1995. *Ub'aniik Ri Una'ooj Uchomab'aal Ri Maya' Tinamit; Confirguración del Pensamiento Político del Pueblo Maya*. Vol. 2. Guatemala: SPEM/Cholsamaj.

______. 1996. "The Politics of Mayan Revindication" In *Mayan Cultural Activism in Guatemala*, ed. E. Fischer and M. Brown. Austin: University of Texas Press.

Cojtí Macario, Narciso. 1988. *Mapa de los Idiomas de Guatemala y Belice*. Guatemala: Piedra Santa.

COMG (Consejo de Organizaciones Mayas de Guatemala). 1991. "Derechos Específicos del Pueblo Maya / Rujunamil Ri Mayab' Amaq'." Guatemala: Cholsamaj.

______. 1995. *Construyendo un Futuro para Nuestro Pasado; Derechos del Pueblo Mayan y el Proceso de Paz*. Guatemala: Cholsamaj.

Curruchiche Gómez, Miguel Angel. 1994. *Discriminación del Pueblo Maya en el Ordenamiento Jurídico de Guatemala*. Guatemala: Cholsamaj.

Dávila, Amílcar. 1992. *Educar, No Alienar; Identidad, Etnias y Educación en Guatemala.* Guatemala: Universidad Rafael Landívar.

de Paz, Marco Antonio. 1993. *Maya' Amaaq' xuq Junamilaal; Pueblo Maya y Democracia.* Guatemala: SPEM/Cholsamaj.

England, Nora, and Stephen Elliot, eds. 1990. *Lecturas sobre la Lingüística Maya.* Guatemala: CIRMA.

Esquit Choy, Edgar, and Carlos Ochoa García, eds. 1995. *Yiqalil q'anej, kunimaaj tziij, niman tzij; El respeto a la palabra.* Guatemala: CECMA.

Falla, Ricardo. 1978. *Quiché Rebelde: Estudio de un Movimento de Conversión Religiosa, Rebelde a las Creencias Tradicionales, en San Antonio Ilotenango, Quiché (1948–1970).* Guatemala: Editorial Universitaria de Guatemala.

______. 1994. *Massacres in the Jungle: Ixcán, Guatemala (1975–1982).* Boulder: Westview Press.

Fischer, Edward, and McKenna Brown, eds. 1996. *Mayan Cultural Activism in Guatemala.* Austin: University of Texas Press.

Fox, Richard. 1990. "Hindu Nationalism in the Making, or the Rise of the Hindian." In *Nationalist Ideologies and the Production of National Cultures*, ed. R. Fox, 63–80. Washington, D.C.: American Anthropological Association.

Gellner, Ernest. 1983. *Nations and Nationalism.* Ithaca: Cornell University Press.

Guzmán Bockler, Carlos, and Jean-Loup Herbert. 1995. *Guatemala: Una Interpretación Histórico-Social.* Guatemala: Cholsamaj.

Hale, Charles. 1994. "Between Che Guevara and the Pachamama: Mestizos, Indians, and Identity Politics in the Anti-Quincentenary Campaign." *Critique of Anthropology* 14 (2):9–39.

______. 1995. "El discurso ladino del racismo al revés en Guatemala." Paper presented at the Nineteenth International Congress of the Latin American Studies Association, September, Washington, D.C.

______. 1996. "Maya Effervescence and the Ladino Imaginary in Guatemala." Paper presented at the American Anthropological Association meeting, November 11.

Hanchard, Michael. 1994. *Orpheus and Power.* Princeton: Princeton University Press.

Himpele, Jeffrey. 1995. "Distributing Difference: The Distribution and Displacement of Media, Spectacle, and Identity in La Paz, Bolivia." Ph.D. diss., Princeton University.

Hobsbawm, Eric, and Terence Ranger, eds. 1983. *The Invention of Tradition.* New York: Cambridge University Press.

Jonas, Susanne. 1991. *The Battle for Guatemala; Rebels, Death Squads, and U.S. Power.* Boulder: Westview Press.

Jonas, Susanne, and Nancy Stein, eds. 1990. *Democracy in Latin America: Visions and Reality.* New York: Bergin and Garrey Publishers.

Jonas, Susanne, and David Tobis, eds. 1974. *Guatemala.* Berkeley: North American Congress on Latin America.

Laclau, Ernesto, and Chantal Mouffe, eds. 1985. *Hegemony and Socialist Strategy: Towards a Radical Democratic Politics.* London: Verso.

Levenson-Estrada, Deborah. 1994. *Trade Unionists Against Terror: Guatemala City 1954–85.* Chapel Hill: University of North Carolina Press.

______. Forthcoming. "Commentary." In *Issues in Self-Determination*, ed. J. Waterbury and W. Danspeckgruber. Boulder: Westview Press.

Lewis, Oscar. 1966. "The Culture of Poverty." *Scientific American* 215:19–25.

López Raquec, Margarita. 1989. *Acerca de los Alfabetos para Escribir los Idiomas Mayas de Guatemala*. Guatemala: Ministerio de Cultura y Deportes.

Manz, Beatriz. 1988. *Refugees of a Hidden War: The Aftermath of Counterinsurgency in Guatemala*. Albany: State University of New York Press.

Marx, Anthony. 1992. *Lessons of Struggle: South African Internal Opposition, 1960–1990*. New York: Oxford University Press.

Materne, Yves. 1976. *The Indian Awakening in Latin America*. New York: Friendship Press.

Menchú, Rigoberta. 1984. *I Rigoberta Menchú: An Indian Woman in Guatemala*. Ed. Elisabeth Burgos-Debray. London: Verso.

Montejo, Victor, and Q'anil Akab'. 1992. *Brevísima Relación Testimonial de la Continua Destrucción del Mayab' (Guatemala)*. Providence, R.I.: Maya Scholars Network.

Mouffe, Chantal. 1993. *The Return of the Political*. London: Verso.

Mouffe, Chantal, ed. 1992. *Dimensions of Radical Democracy: Pluralism, Citizenship, Community*. London: Verso.

Oxlajuuj Keej Maya' Ajtz'iib' [Ajpub', Ixkem, Lolmay, Nik'te', Pakal, Saqijix, and Waykan]. 1993. *Mayab' Chii'; Idiomas Mayas de Guatemala*. Guatemala: Cholsamaj.

Pop Caal, Antonio. 1992. *Li Juliisil Kirisyaanil ut li Minok ib'; Judeo Cristianismo y Colonización*. Guatemala: SPEM/Cholsamaj.

PRONEBI. 1994. "Logros y experiencias de la educación bilingüe intercultural en Guatemala." Primer Congreso de Educación Maya en Guatemala, August 8–11, 1994.

Rancancoj A., Víctor. 1994. *Socioeconomía Maya Precolonial*. Guatemala: Cholsamaj.

Recinos, Adrián, trans. 1950. *Memorial de Sololá. Anales de los Cakchiqueles*. Mexico City: Fondo de Cultura Económica.

Rodríguez Guaján, Demetrio [Raché]. 1989. *Cultura Maya y Políticas de Desarrollo*. Guatemala: COCADI.

Sam Colop, Luis Enrique. 1991. "Jub'aqtun Omay Kuchum K'aslemal: Cinco Siglos de Encubrimiento." Seminario Permanente de Estudios Mayas, Cuaderno No. 1. Guatemala: Cholsamaj.

Scott, James. 1990. *Domination and the Arts of the Resistance*. New Haven: Yale University Press.

Segundo Encuentro Continental. 1991. *Documentos y conclusiones*. Guatemala: Secretaria Operativa del Segundo Encuentro Continental.

Smith, Carol. 1990. *Guatemalan Indians and the State: 1540–1988*. Austin: University of Texas Press.

______. 1991. "Maya Nationalism." *NACLA* 25 (3):29–34.

______. 1993. "Local History in Global Context: Social and Economic Transitions in Western Guatemala." In *Constructing Culture and Power in Latin America*, ed. D. Levine, 75–118. Ann Arbor: University of Michigan Press.

Solares, Jorge. 1993. *Estado y Nación: Las Demandas de los Grupos Etnicos en Guatemala*. Guatemala: FLASCO.

Stoll, David. 1993. *Between Two Armies in the Ixil Towns of Guatemala*. New York: Columbia University Press.

Taller Maya. 1992. *Proceedings of the Thirteenth Annual Conference*. Guatemala: ALMG.

______. 1993. *Proceedings of the Fourteenth Annual Conference*. Guatemala: ALMG.

Tedlock, Barbara. 1982. *Time and the Highland Maya*. Albuquerque: University of New Mexico Press.

Tedlock, Dennis. 1983. *The Spoken Word and the Work of Interpretation*. Philadelphia: University of Pennsylvania Press.

Tedlock, Dennis, trans. 1985. *Popol Vuh: The Definitive Edition of the Mayan Book of the Dawn of Life and the Glories of Gods and Kings*. New York: Simon and Schuster.

Trend, David. 1996. *Radical Democracy: Identity, Citizenship, and the State*. New York: Routledge.

Tzian, Leopoldo. 1994. *Kajlab'aliil Maya'iib' Xuq Mu'siib': Ri Ub'antajiik Iximuleew; Mayas y Ladinos en Cifras: El Caso de Guatemala*. Guatemala: Cholsamaj.

Wallace, Anthony F. C. 1972. *The Death and Rebirth of the Seneca*. New York: Vintage.

Warren, Kay B. 1989. *The Symbolism of Subordination: Indian Identity in a Guatemalan Town*. 2nd ed. Austin: University of Texas Press.

______. 1992. "Transforming Memories and Histories: The Meanings of Ethnic Resurgence for Mayan Indians." In *Americas: New Interpretive Essays*, ed. A. Stepan, 189–219. New York: Oxford University Press.

______. 1993. "Interpreting la Violencia in Guatemala: Shapes of Kaqchikel Silence and Resistance in the 1970s and 1980s." In *The Violence Within: Cultural and Political Opposition in Divided Nations*, ed. K. Warren, 25–56. Boulder: Westview Press.

______. 1995. "Each Mind Is a World: Dilemmas of Feeling and Intention in a Kaqchikel Maya Community." In *Other Intentions: Culture and the Attribution of States of Mind*, ed. L. Rosen, 47–67. Seattle: University of Washington Press for the American School of Research.

______. 1996. "Reading History as Resistance: Mayan Public Intellectuals in Guatemala." In *Mayan Cultural Activism in Guatemala*, ed. E. Fischer and M. Brown. Austin: University of Texas Press.

______. Forthcoming(a). "Enduring Tensions and Changing Identities: Mayan Family Struggles in Guatemala." In *History in Person: The Mutual Construction of Endemic Struggles and Enduring Identities*, ed. D. Holland and J. Lave. Santa Fe, N.Mex.: SAR Press.

______. Forthcoming(b). "Mayan Self-Determination: Multicultural Models and Educational Choice in Guatemala." In *Issues in Self-Determination*, ed. J. Waterbury and W. Danspeckgruber. Boulder: Westview Press.

______. Forthcoming(c). *Indigenous Movements and Their Critics: Pan-Mayanism and Ethnic Resurgence in Guatemala*. Princeton: Princeton University Press.

Watanabe, John. 1992. *Maya Saints and Souls in a Changing World*. Austin: University of Texas Press.

______. Forthcoming. "Neither as They Imagined nor as Others Intended: Mayas and Anthropologists in the Highlands of Guatemala Since 1969." In *Supplement to the Hand Book of Middle American Indians*, vol. 6, ed. J. Monaghan. Austin: University of Texas Press.

Wilson, Richard. 1995. *Mayan Resurgence in Guatemala*. Norman: University of Oklahoma Press.

Chapter Eight

The Process of Black Community Organizing in the Southern Pacific Coast Region of Colombia

LIBIA GRUESO, CARLOS ROSERO, AND ARTURO ESCOBAR

Ethnicity, Territory, and Politics

Since the end of the 1980s, Colombia's Pacific coast region has been undergoing an unprecedented historical process: the emergence of collective ethnic identities and their strategic positioning in culture-territory relations. This process is taking place in a complex national and international conjuncture. At the national level, the conjuncture is marked by two events: the radical opening of Colombia's economy to world markets after 1990, particularly in the ambit of the country's integration into the Pacific Basin economies; and a substantial reform of the national Constitution in 1991, which, among other things, granted the black communities of the Pacific region collective rights to the territories they have traditionally occupied. Internationally, tropical rain-forest areas, including Colombia's Pacific coast, have acquired a certain specificity in light of the fact that they are home to most of the planet's biological diversity. Confronted with the rapid destruction of these areas, the concomitant loss of species, and the potential impact of this loss on the future of humanity, scientists, environmentalists, governments, and nongovernmental organizations (NGOs) have thrown themselves with fervor into the task of "preserving biological diversity."

The emergence of collective ethnic identities in the Colombian Pacific region and similar regions in other parts of the world thus reflects a double historical movement: the irruption of the biological, the continuity of life as we know it, as a global problem; and the irruption of the cultural and the ethnic, as highlighted by the Colombian government's decision to recognize these concepts in its desire to construct a pluriethnic and multicultural society. This double irruption of the biological and the cultural takes place in the changing contexts of capitalism and modernity that scholars have attempted to explain in terms of globalization (Robertson 1992; Gonzáles Casanova 1994), postfordism (Harvey 1989), or ethnoscapes (Appadurai 1991); and in which the multiple intersections of the local and the global are no longer analyzed in terms of polarized space-time categories—such as tradition and modernity, center and periphery—but in terms of cultural hybridizations (García Canclini 1990), the local processing of global conditions (Pred and Watts 1992), alternative modernities, and postdevelopment (Escobar 1995).

The Colombian Pacific coast region, as we shall see, is defined by the local black and indigenous movements as a region-territory of ethnic groups. Based on cultural differences and the rights to identity and territory, these social movements challenge the Euro-Colombian modernity that has become dominant in the rest of the country. Black and indigenous cultural politics, in this way, challenge the conventional political culture harbored in the practices of the traditional political parties and the state, unsettle the dominant project of national identity construction, and defy the predominant orientation of development. Forces opposed to the movement—from local black elites to new agribusiness capitalists and narco-investors—continue to adhere to the same definitions of capital, development, and the political that have become entrenched in the last fifty years with disastrous consequences on the social, environmental, and cultural reality of the country. Through their appropriation of the territory and their cultural affirmation, the social movements seek to resist the onslaught of capital and development on their region.

This chapter describes and analyzes the emergence of the social movement of black communities in the southern Pacific coast region of Colombia.[1] First, we analyze the national conjuncture of the constitutional reform of 1991 that propitiated the structuration of the movement, focusing on the negotiated elaboration of the law of cultural and territorial rights for the black communities (Ley 70 of August 1993). Next, we examine the movement as an ethno-cultural proposal, emphasizing the politico-organizational principles developed as a result of massive collective mobilization around Ley 70. These principles reflect important processes of black identity construction as well as novel practices and theoretical formulations concerning the relation between territory, biodiversity, culture, and development that we later analyze from the perspective of the intersection between the cultural politics of the movement and established political cultures. We conclude the chapter by suggesting ways of thinking about the political from the perspectives of territory, nature, and culture.

The Constitutional Reform of 1991 and the End of the Invisibility of Black Cultures

From the times of conquest and slavery to today's rampant capitalism—including historical boom and bust periods of gold, platinum, precious woods, and rubber—Colombia's Pacific coast region has been affected by the forces of capitalist modernity (Whitten 1986; Leyva 1993; Aprile-Gniset 1993). Since time immemorial, this region has been seen primarily as a source of raw materials and a depository of allegedly inexhaustible natural riches, and its inhabitants have been subjected to systematic invisibility and ethnocentric representations. Perhaps because Colombia's majority Andean population sees in the Pacific region and its people an example of ineluctable cultural and economic backwardness, the social sciences have paid scant attention to the vibrant black cultures that have developed there throughout the centuries (Friedemann and Arocha 1984; Arocha 1991; Wade 1993).

This region covers a vast area (about 70,000 square kilometers) stretching from Panama to Ecuador and from the westernmost chain of the Andes to the ocean. It is a unique rain-forest region, one of the world's wettest and most diverse. About 60 percent of the region's 900,000 inhabitants (800,000 Afro-Colombians; about 50,000 Embera, Waunana, and other indigenous people; and another 50,000 mestizo colonists) live in the few larger cities and towns; the rest inhabit the margins of the more than 240 rivers in the region, most of which flow from the Andes toward the ocean. Black people have maintained distinct material and cultural practices—such as multiple subsistence and economic activities involving agriculture, fishing, hunting and gathering, and small-scale gold mining and timber collecting; extended families and matrilocal social relations; strong oral traditions and religious systems; and particular forms of knowledge and use of the diverse forest ecosystems—which are too numerous and complex to summarize here.[2] What is important to emphasize is the continued existence of important, different cultures in a region that is finally attracting the attention of the national government in its ambitious effort to participate in the alleged economic bonanza accompanying the development around the "sea of the twentieth-first century"—the Pacific Ocean.

This renewed interest on the part of the state takes place in a climate significantly different from the invisibility that characterized the region's biological and cultural reality even a decade ago. On the biological side, the debut of the discourse of biodiversity conservation in the theater of international development has substantially modified the perception of the region in the eyes of many. Culturally, the constitutional reform of 1991 transformed forever the economy of ethnic visibilities in the country. The new Constitution reversed a long-standing project of nation building; no longer the building of a racially and culturally homogeneous society (a mestizo people coded as "white"), the new goal—enshrined in the 1991 Constitution—is presented as the construction of a pluriethnic and multicultural nation.

For many sectors of society, including the black communities, the Asamblea Nacional Constituyente (ANC)—the seventy-member body entrusted with the reform of the Constitution, popularly elected in December 1990—represented the hopes of finding a way out of the deep social and political crisis in which the country was immersed at the beginning of the decade. In the period preceding the formation of the ANC, a number of black initiatives with diverse political orientations, mostly local in character, had already been organized. These groups—which included individuals and organizations linked to Christian communities, the Left, traditional parties, government programs, and NGOs, all with experience in black issues and with a greater or lesser degree of awareness about the demands of the black communities[3]—convened in the Preconstituent Conference of Black Communities in Cali in August 1990 with the purpose of working out a proposal for action in the current conjuncture. From this conference emerged the Coordinadora Nacional de Comunidades Negras (CNCN) as a mechanism to coordinate and implement the actions agreed upon at the conference. However, the profound divisions and the wide range of perspectives represented at the CNCN—from peasant, urban, popular, and traditional party-oriented groups to leftist and ethno-cultural movements—ensured that the CNCN was to be a short-lived experiment. When the ANC convened, each of these black sectors assessed the situation according to their own sets of interests and modes of historical insertion in the country.[4]

There was no black representation in the ANC; the plight of the black communities was brought before the assembly by one of the indigenous representatives and was finally addressed by Artículo Transitorio 55, or AT 55 (Transitory Article 55). This was not easily achieved. From the very beginning, the demands for recognition of territorial and ethnic rights for the black communities were opposed by many of the sectors represented in the ANC, even democratic sectors such as the M-19 Alliance.[5] Black communities, it was argued out of ignorance, did not conform to the definition of an "ethnic group" since they lacked their own language and forms of right and authority; they were fully integrated as citizens into the mestizo life of the country; and they had adopted alien cultural elements. Some asserted that the demand for territorial rights was a separatist position best dealt with within the framework of decentralization promoted by the new Constitution. The inclusion of AT 55 was thus possible only after a massive lobbying campaign that even included the takeover of buildings.[6]

The constitutional reform is, in this way, the first important space of black community organizing on the basis of cultural, ethnic, and territorial demands; it entailed the construction of an alternative proposal by the black communities centered on ethnic and cultural rights. Once the 1991 Constitution went into effect, a number of black organizations came together to evaluate the results of the ANC and to discuss their participation in the election of representatives of ethnic groups to Congress, as stipulated by the Constitution. From then on, a rift grew between those who favored the construction of a movement for political participation in the established institutions and those who believed in a social movement in which electoral participation was only one possibility and not the central element.

This difference marked the definitive distancing between the nucleus of activists who remained within the CNCN and the black sectors closer to the traditional Liberal and Conservative Parties. CNCN members dedicated their efforts from then on to regulating AT 55 (the negotiated process of specifying its contents until its enactment into law, which took place in August 1993); to strengthening community organizing; and to reaching out to peasant organizations in Chocó Province. From this dynamic there emerged in October 1993, as a national organizational response, the Proceso de Comunidades Negras, or PCN (Process of Black Communities), a network of more than 120 local organizations that assumed the regulation of AT 55 and the consolidation of responses from local organizations. The distance from those who emphasized political or bureaucratic representation deepened.[7] At the same time, the collective construction of mechanisms and forms of participation in the interior of the movement made possible the consolidation of at least minimal political and ideological agreements and halted the organizational dispersal that had been occurring previously.

The ethno-cultural character of the movement that surfaced during the ANC; the promulgation of AT 55, with its recognition of collective rights to traditional territories; and the ensuing threats to the black people of the Pacific region and their territories were the main factors determining the nature of the organizing work being done in rural areas. This emphasis reflected the importance attributed by the PCN to maintaining social control of territory and natural resources as a precondition for the survival, re-creation, and strengthening of culture. Among the riverine populations, activists geared their efforts toward advancing a pedagogical process with and within the communities on the meaning of the new Constitution; reinforcing the fundamental concepts of territory, development, traditional production practices, and use of natural resources; and strengthening the organizational capacity of these communities. This sustained effort during the 1991–1993 period served to lay down the basis for the elaboration of a proposal for the law called for by AT 55 and also to firm up a series of politico-organizational principles, as we will discuss later in this chapter. It also helped PCN activists recognize the various tendencies, trajectories, and styles of work found among the array of black organizations involved with the debate on, and regulation of, what was to become Ley 70.

The collective elaboration of the proposal for Ley 70 was another decisive space for the development of the movement. This process was advanced at two levels, one centered on the daily life and practices of the black communities of the Pacific, the other on the ideological and political reflections of the activists. The first level—carried out under the rubric of what was referred to as "the logic of the river"—relied on the broad participation of local people in the articulation of their own rights, aspirations, and dreams. The second level, although using the rivers and their settlements as referents, sought to transcend the rural domain and raise the broader issues involving black people as an ethnic group, even beyond what could be granted by the law. This level entailed a rearticulation of the notions of territory, development, and the social relations of black communities with the rest of Colombian society. Despite differences and the manipulation of the process by black politicians linked to the Liberal Party, an agreement was reached on the text of the law to be negotiated with the government.[8]

In this context, negotiations with the government entailed a double effort of constructing agreements between, on the one hand, organizations and communities, and on the other, these groups and the government. Given the forceful implementation of the neoliberal opening of the economy and the growing currency of discussions on biodiversity and genetic resources, these negotiations became ever more tense; while the government became more intransigent as its awareness of the capacity of their black interlocutors grew, the black organizing groups grew stronger in structure, experience, coordination, and awareness of their rights. Government officials realized that the demands of the organizing process went well beyond the desire for integration and racial equality, as had been maintained until then by other sectors of the black community. Besides, black organizations mounted a strategy of persuasion and consciousness raising among the delegates to the special high commission appointed by the government for the regulation of AT 55. The entire process constituted a veritable social construction of protest (Klandermans 1992) that was to culminate in the approval by the Senate of the version of the law (Ley 70) negotiated with the communities. However, it is important to recognize that during and after the convening of the ANC, there were a variety of ideological and political tendencies among black organizations. It was for this reason that the black communities' proposal was presented by an indigenous representative.[9]

The Social Movement of Black Communities and the Ethno-Cultural Proposal of the Process of Black Communities

Black communities in Colombia are far from being homogenous—culturally, historically, or politically. There are at least six sociocultural regions with an important black presence: the Caribbean coast, the Pacific coast, the Magdalena, the Cauca and Patía river valleys, and the Archipelago of San Andrés and Providencia. These communities comprise a vast spectrum of political positions, experiences of mobilization, and conceptions of the struggle that motivate, in turn, continuous tensions, alliances, and realignments of forces, depending on the particular situation. Historically speaking, there have been periods of black convergence and unification; the construction of a movement on the basis of ethno-cultural rights in the wake of the ANC is one of these exceptional experiences.

The first Asamblea Nacional de Comunidades Negras, or ANCN (National Conference of Black Communities) took place in July 1992 in the predominantly black city of Tumaco (100,000 inhabitants) with representatives from all over the Pacific, the Caribbean and the Norte del Cauca regions. Its principal conclusions were geared toward laying down a framework for the regulation of AT 55 and building the necessary organizational and operational mechanisms to this end. At the ANCN's second national conference in May 1993, delegates revised and approved the law's text as negotiated by government and black community representatives in the ambit of the High Commission created for this purpose by the Constitution.

The third national conference was convened in September 1993 in Puerto Tejada, another predominantly black town, south of Cali in the Norte del Cauca region. With more than 300 delegates attending, the conference debated the politico-organizational situation of black communities in 1993. At that time, black sectors linked to the traditional liberal and conservative parties—eager to capitalize on the unprecedented legal mechanisms favorable to black communities that had been achieved by the mobilization and social construction of protest—had begun to adopt a confused and opportunistic discourse on "blackness" that usually did not go beyond the question of skin color. Recognizing the existence of these sectors and the diversity among the social movements of black communities, the conference proposed to characterize its own identity as "a sector of the social movement of black communities composed of people and organizations with diverse experiences and goals, but united around a set of principles, criteria and objectives that set us apart from other sectors of the movement. In the same vein, we represent a proposal to the entire black community of the country, and aspire to construct a unified movement of black communities able to encompass their rights and aspirations."[10]

The objective of the organizing process was stated as "the consolidation of a social movement of black communities for the reconstruction and affirmation of cultural identity," leading to an autonomous organizing strategy "for the achievement of cultural, social, economic, political and territorial rights and for the defense of natural resources and the environment." A central feature of the conference was the adoption of a set of politico-organizational principles formulated out of the practice, lifeworld vision, and desires of the black communities. These principles concern the key issues of identity, territory, autonomy, and development:

> 1. *The reaffirmation of identity* (the right to be black). In the first place, we conceive of being black from the perspective of our cultural logic and lifeworld in all of its social, economic, and political dimensions. This logic counters the logic of domination that intends to exploit and subject our people. Our cultural vision opposes a model of society that requires uniformity for its continued dominance. Being black thus cannot be restricted to particular moments but should encompass our entire lives. Second, our cultural affirmation entails an inner struggle with our consciousness; the affirmation of our being is not easy, since we are taught in many ways and through multiple media that we are all equal. This is the great lie of the logic of domination.

This first principle clearly identifies culture and identity as the organizational axes of both daily life and political practice. As we will see later in this chapter, despite its seemingly essentialist tone, this principle also partakes of a conception of identity as constructed.

2. *The right to territory* (the right to space for being). As a vital space, territory is a necessary condition for the re-creation and development of our cultural vision. We cannot be if we do not have a space for living in accordance with what we think and desire as a form of life. It follows that we see territory as a habitat and space where black people develop their being in harmony with nature.

3. *Autonomy* (the right to the exercise of being-identity). We understand autonomy in relation to the dominant society, other ethnic groups, and political parties. It arises out of our cultural logic. Thus understood, we are autonomous internally in the political realm and aspire to social and economic autonomy.

4. *Construction of an autonomous perspective of the future.* We intend to construct an autonomous vision of economic and social development based on our culture and traditional forms of production and social organization. The dominant society has systematically imposed on us a vision of development that responds to their own interests and worldview. We have the right to give others the vision of our world, as we want to construct it.

5. *Declaration of solidarity.* We are part of the struggle for the rights of black people throughout the world. From our own particularity, the social movement of black communities shall contribute to the efforts of those who struggle for alternative life projects.

This declaration of principles constituted a rupture with the political and developmentalist formulations of the Left, including black urban organizations and traditional liberal political sectors. It responded to the specific situation of the black communities of the Pacific and, while demanding a solution to their pressing problems, placed greater emphasis on the nature and content of the possible solutions. The declaration also cast into relief the growing gap between the PCN and other organized black sectors. These differences arose over four main issues: (a) the perception of history and identity; (b) the views and demands concerning natural resources, territory, and development; (c) the types of political representation and participation of the communities involved in black mobilization, and the relationship between the latter and the rest of society; and (d) the conception of organizational strategy and modes of construction of the movement.

With this strategy, the PCN sought to pursue various goals: to become a source of power for black communities vis-à-vis the state and other social actors; to advance the social movement of black communities; and to contribute to the search for more just and viable societal options for the country as a whole. From then on, the PCN strategy and its successive transformations were to depend on the activists' investigation and assessment, on the one hand of the historical and cultural reality of the communities and on the other of the balance of forces—from the local to the international level—between the communities, the social movement, and other social sectors, economic groups, and centers of power.

As a result of this new situation, the basic agreement that existed with the organizations of Chocó Province broke down shortly after the approval of Ley 70. Article 66 of the law created a special electoral district for black communities, reserving two seats for black candidates in the chamber of representatives. The ensuing electoral process also divided the organizations of Chocó itself and spurred a national explosion of candidate lists. Article 66 had been regulated by the High Commission without taking into account the proposal of the organized communities, thus favoring black traditional party politicians and their clientelistic networks. In the end, one of the seats was occupied by a politician from the conservative party who usurped the name "social movement of black communities" for his campaign, confusing public opinion, and who declared thereafter that the time of grassroots organizing was over. The second seat went to a representative of the Chocó organizations who had participated in the regulation of Ley 70 and who was elected with the support of factions of the indigenous, socialist, and women's movements and of some government institutions. Although this candidate had participated actively in ethno-cultural organizations, once elected she shifted her position from the ethnic approach to emphasizing the country's marginalized peoples as a whole.

Conveniently, the government began to question the PCN's representation, legitimacy, and achievements by arguing that there were other organized sectors of the black community. Depending on the specific situation and its interests at the moment, the government would lend support to the positions of the two black Congress members as "legitimate representatives" of the black community. The political practices of these members did indeed conform to the conventional clientelistic scheme so characteristic of Colombian party politics, to the extent that their efforts focused on public jobs for their constituencies, bureaucratic representation, the creation of institutional spaces, and the use of public funds to ensure their reelection and political survival. Coupled with the government's accommodating manipulation of the situation, their actions distorted the meaning of the demands raised by the black communities and constrained the role of ethno-cultural organizations in negotiations with the state on vital matters such as territory and natural resources.

For some activists, the election of the black candidates to Congress represented a step backward for black communities. Nevertheless, and even if the traditional black politicians succeeded in permeating wide sectors of the black community, the ethno-cultural movement remained as an important organizational dynamic at the national level. Its assessment of the Pacific coast region as Colombia's most significant black region and as a strategic ethnic and ecological unit—with the concomitant emphasis placed on the defense of the territory—was one of its most pertinent accomplishments. In a similar vein, it has been the ethno-cultural sector of the movement that has trained the majority of activists to effectively carry out a critical dialogue and collective negotiations with the state, and that has attempted to endow river communities with a tool kit for the defense of their rights within the framework of Ley 70 and Ley 121 of 1991. These accomplishments have become key components of the political practice of the entire black community.[11]

The 1995–1996 period saw the appearance of new organized black sectors with different, and at times conflicting, agendas, seeking to capitalize on the space earlier created for black people's rights. During these two years, the number of organized sectors of black communities increased significantly.[12] The conflicts and contradictions among all of these groups have impinged upon important issues such as the composition and work of the High Commission, the formulation of the National Development Plan for Black Communities, and the regulation of Ley 70, weakening the bargaining position of communities vis-à-vis the government. Given that many of these groups do not have a developed political or ideological position, and considering that their actions focus on gaining access to institutional and bureaucratic spaces, it is still difficult to attempt a characterization or assessment of the groups that exist at present.

Territory, Identity, and Strategy: From Cultural Politics to Political Culture

The social movement of the Pacific black communities is endowed with very particular features arising from the historical, cultural, ecological, and economic specificity of the region. The movement constitutes a complex process of construction of ethnic and cultural identity in relation to novel variables such as territory, biodiversity, and alternative development. In this section, we will highlight some of these complexities from the perspective of the effect that the cultural politics set into motion by the movement is having or might have on notions and practices of collective identity, political culture, biodiversity, and alternative development.

The Construction of a Collective Identity

For many years, the approach to the reality of black people in Colombia was shaped by three basic concepts: marginality, discrimination, and equality. Black identity was largely conceived in terms of equality before the law. The ambiguous character of this formulation has been pointed out by many, to the extent that the assertion "we are all equal before the law"—which denies the existence of discrimination and promulgates the elite ideology of "racial democracy" prevalent in most of Latin America—makes impossible the articulation of an oppositional ethnic discourse (Wade 1993). Until recently, black opposition emphasized a common past grounded in slavery and in the forms of resistance to it, especially in the *palenques*. In this vision, history was chiefly commemorative and was indelibly tainted by the representation of a past always diminished by domination.[13] In contrast, the PCN adamantly asserts that the invocation of a common past must be accompanied by a parallel identification of lessons for the present and a project for the future. This emphasis constitutes a rupture with black organizing efforts of the 1970–1990 period that called for integration as a way to overcome racial discrimination and oppression. This earlier theory of the struggle arose out of the economic and political marginalization of the region and shared some similarities with black civil rights struggles in other parts of the world, particularly in the United States.

In the late 1970s, the state itself began to foster the process of the "integration" of the Pacific region into the rest of the country, particularly through ambitious development plans (Escobar and Pedrosa 1996). These attempts at integration into national culture and economic markets have had devastating effects on the values and aspirations of local cultures. It is for this reason that the ethno-cultural approach highlights the importance of reconstructing and exercising cultural differences as a mechanism for eradicating socioeconomic and political inequality. The new focus entails a significant redefinition of the relationship between the black communities and the rest of society and reflects an important trend in the black movement. For the activists who share this vision, the historical resistance of black communities in the Pacific and other parts of the country suggests a certain intentional distancing on the part of these communities as a way of constructing their own social and cultural forms of organization. This would explain the persistence of distinct cultural features in the Pacific and other regions such as the different sense of time, the lack of interest in accumulation, and the social and economic role of kindred and extended family. Some of these cultural practices are recovered and invoked by activists as basic elements of the organizing process. Even if the Pacific coast region has been integrated into the world economy for centuries as provider of raw materials (Whitten 1986), the river communities never strove for a full integration into Colombia's economy.[14]

In sum, if integrationist approaches seek the incorporation of black communities into national life, ethno-cultural approaches construct the relation between national and minority cultures and their corresponding projects as problematic. These overall approaches reflect diverging readings of the history, living conditions, and cultural expressions of the black communities of the Pacific; they maintain a tension that shapes organizing processes to this day. According to the ethno-cultural process, the movement must be constructed on the basis of broad demands for territory, identity, autonomy, and the right to its own vision of development and the future. Similarly, ethno-cultural activists espouse a view of blackness that goes well beyond issues of skin color and the racial aspects of identity.

The black communities' social movement is embarked on a process of collective identity construction that bears similarities to the construction of Caribbean and Afro-British identities analyzed by Stuart Hall (1990). For Hall, ethnic identity construction entails cultural, economic, and political negotiations characterized by a certain "doubleness." On the one hand, identity is thought of as rooted in shared cultural practices, a collective self of sorts; this conception of identity has played an important role in anticolonial struggles and involves an imaginative rediscovery of culture that lends coherence to the experience of fragmentation, dispersal, and oppression. On the other hand, identity is seen in terms of the differences created by history; this aspect of identity construction emphasizes becoming rather than being, positioning rather than essence, and discontinuity as well as continuity at the cultural level. In this way, the coexistence of difference and sameness constitutes the doubleness of identity today; it recognizes the dialogues of power and resistance generated by the various encounters between European modernity and other cultural forms and—in the context of the "New World"—the fact that cultural identity is always creolized and characterized by difference, heterogeneity, and hybridization (see also García Canclini 1990).

The doubleness of identity can be seen at play in the ethno-cultural approach of the Pacific coast black movement. For the activists, the defense of certain cultural practices of the river communities is a strategic question to the extent that these communities are seen as embodying not only resistance to capitalism and modernity but also possibilities for alternative constructions. Although often couched in culturalist language, this defense is not intransigent or essentializing to the extent that it responds to an interpretation of the challenges faced by the communities and the possibilities presented by a cautious opening toward forms of modernity such as biodiversity conservation and alternative development. Identity is thus seen in both ways: as an anchor of "traditional" practices and forms of knowledge and as an ever changing project of cultural and political construction. In this way, the movement builds upon the river communities' submerged networks of cultural practices and meanings as well as their active construction of lifeworlds (Melucci 1989); it sees such practices in their transformative capacity of the biophysical and social environments; and it attempts to articulate, as we shall see in the following sections, a practical project of territorial defense and alternative modes of development.

To the fixed, static, and conventional notion of identity implicit in the new Constitution, the movement thus opposes a more fluid notion of identity as political construction. Although this identity is constructed in novel terms of culture and ecology, it is also traversed by class. Most black elites of the Pacific coast, in fact, resent Ley 70 not only because they feel that the law treats them like "Indians" but because they want to integrate and be treated as regular Colombians—that is, they do not want to be singled out as an "ethnic minority" at all.[15]

As an important aspect of identity construction, gender is also progressively becoming a salient aspect in the agenda of ethno-cultural organizations, although it is still given insufficient attention. The fact that many of the top leaders and activists of the movement are women who are committed to the ethno-cultural approach and who are increasingly interested in advancing gender questions is acting as a catalyst for the articulation of gender issues. These leanings were already felt in 1994, when the need to embrace gender as an integral part of the movement—as opposed to promoting the creation of separate women's organizations—was recognized.[16] The organization of black women is beginning to overflow the boundaries of the larger movement and to take on a dynamic of its own. In 1992, the first meeting of black women of the Pacific coast already attracted over 500 participants; a network of black women's organizations exists and is gaining visibility in various domains of activity particularly since 1995 (Rojas

1996); and discourses of gender and biodiversity are also slowly emerging (Camacho 1996). Although most of these efforts are still couched in conventional "women in development" terms (Lozano 1996), the number of activists committed to gender mobilization is increasing. Studies of the black women's mobilization are already under way, particularly from the perspective of the intersection of gender and the ethnic constructions of identity and political strategy that have been dominant until now.[17]

Reformulating the Political

One may think that the biophysical, social, and cultural characteristics of the Pacific coast region would lend themselves to a nontraditional approach to politics; however, this has hardly been the case. Until recently, conditions in the region have been used to strengthen a conventional system based on political *clientilismo* that articulates with traditional social relations—established on the basis of extended families and kinship groups—and with particular geographical spaces. Votes and favors are exchanged and circulate, budgets are negotiated, and regional and local bureaucracies and programs are enacted, all on the basis of these articulations. As in many other parts of the country, local bosses control political groups and participate, in turn, in wider political clientelistic networks controlled by more important bosses. Coupled with the fact that the Pacific region is composed of four provinces, three of which have capitals that lie in the Andean region (the exception being the northern Chocó Province), this clientele-based system ensures that decisions are made outside the region. These two factors—the difference between the northern Chocó and the central and southern provinces, and the clientelistic system—have militated against the political construction of the Pacific as an ecological and cultural region and against the emergence of significant social movements.

As in other parts of Latin America, the absence of black movements is related to racial miscegenation, democracy, the political control mechanisms initiated during colonial times, and elite ideological constructions of various kinds, such as notions of racial democracy (Serbin 1991). Black demands have generally been tied to those of economically subordinate sectors and channeled through their political organizations without any ethnic specificity. Blacks' attempts at organizing in racially defined terms have not been completely absent in Colombia.[18] However, ethnic organizing remained latent until 1991, when black groups of all persuasions—whether linked to community organizations or to conventional political parties—began to see black identification as a means to access spaces from which they were previously excluded.

Few of these efforts have succeeded in breaking away from traditional political practices. For the PCN, it was a question of convincing communities of their right to participate in a gamut of mechanisms of representation and negotiation with the state, such as the electoral process. In contrast to traditional *clientilismo,* PCN activists have sought to foster more daring proposals along with broad mechanisms of decisionmaking and degrees of political consciousness that go well beyond each individual group or river community. At the basis of this strategy is the conviction that the link between the ethnic and the political must be constructed. In this way, for instance, electoral processes are geared to the formulation of ideals and the elaboration of lists of candidates who represent community needs and aspirations, in contradistinction to the usual strategy of exchanging votes for favors or state programs. Traditional politicians have responded angrily to this strategy by blocking community initiatives, reinforcing elite coalitions, and pointing their fingers in accusation at movement activists.

The PCN's strategy of constructing the political, in sum, seeks to irrupt in a field that was previously off limits to nonconventional actors and to provide—at the same time that it chips away at the power base of traditional politicians—alternative political nuclei. This strategy was first attempted in 1992 (after the ANC) in the black city of Buenaventura and was implemented on various other occasions, such as during the 1992 and 1994 elections. Even if Ley 70 fostered an explosion of candidate lists for black representatives in Congress, the lists themselves and the bulk of the mobilization for the electoral process did not correspond to the ethno-cultural orientation of the movement but to political forces linked to the traditional political parties, who eagerly seized these unprecedented electoral opportunities. Despite this outcome, it is possible to assert that the ethno-cultural movement of black communities, with its alternative participatory practices articulated on the notion of cultural difference, has begun to transform the conventional political culture in Colombia's Pacific region and beyond.

Cultural Politics, Territory, and Biodiversity

Because of its rich natural resources, Colombia's Pacific coast region is currently in the mire of both the national and the international development establishment. It is also a territory of ethnic groups, who constitute 93 percent of its population and whose active mobilization in recent years has become a preoccupation for government agencies and politicians alike. An important aspect of this mobilization is the involvement of black and indigenous groups in discussions about biodiversity conservation, genetic resources, and the control and management of natural resources. For the social movement of black communities, these issues cannot be dissociated from the question of territorial control. In fact, the relationships between culture, territory, and natural resources constitute a central axis of discussion and strategy building both within movement organizations and in their dealings with the state. Conversely, disagreements in the conceptualization of the culture/territory/natural resource relationship have created tensions among community organizations and between some community sectors and ethno-cultural organizations.

These tensions are related to the overall intensification of development, capitalism, and modernity in the region (Escobar and Pedrosa 1996). First, the growing migration to the Pacific of peasants, proletarians, and entrepreneurs displaced from the interior of the country is having a visible socioeconomic, ecological, and cultural impact arising chiefly from the different cultural logic that these actors bring with them. Second, the government continues to insist on implementing conventional development plans for the region, intended to create infrastructure for the large-scale arrival of capital. Third, government policies for the protection of natural resources have consisted of conventional measures of expansion of natural parks or social forestry programs with little or no community participation. Only one small, but symbolically important, project for the conservation of biological diversity has attempted—even if in ambiguous ways—to incorporate the demands of the organized black communities.[19] Finally, the drug cartels are also entering the region in the form of large-scale mining, agro-industrial, and tourist projects, with enormous consequences that are still difficult to discern.[20]

In addition to highlighting these factors, it is necessary to point out that the organizational level of the black communities in the central and southern Pacific region is still low. Their vulnerability has been revealed in a variety of environmental, social, and cultural conflicts between local communities and timber, mining, and agro-industrial interests that have increased in number and intensity since the approval of Ley 70; nevertheless, movement organizations have extracted partial but important victories in some of these conflicts.[21] These cases have made manifest several important aspects of environmental policy and conflict. They have made evident not only the weakness of the state agencies in charge of the protection of natural resources but also the not infrequent collusion between their functionaries and the private interests exploiting the same resources they are mandated to protect. In a handful of cases, state functionaries have allied themselves with local businesses to repress movement organizations. Also, local government officials are hesitant to address the severe environmental problems that sometimes affect the communities under their jurisdiction. Finally, government measures aimed at controlling environmental abuses are frequently late and insufficient, or require the perpetrators to make only minor corrections to their environmentally destructive activities.[22]

It is important to highlight some of the conceptions of territory and biodiversity developed by the movement in their interaction with community, state, political, and academic sectors. As was already mentioned in the earlier discussion of the movement's principles, the territory is seen as a fundamental and multidimensional space for the creation and re-creation of the social, economic, and cultural values and practices of the communities. The defense of the territory is thus assumed within a historical perspective linking past and future. In the past, communities maintained a certain autonomy; they relied on forms of knowledge, worldviews, and ways of life conducive to certain uses of natural resources. Meanings and practices of nature go side by side in all cultures, producing particular "uses" and effects. This relationship between meanings and practices—and the social relations in which they are embedded—is being transformed today by the developmentalist onslaught that forces the loss of knowledge, territory, and cultural practices and that reduces nature into a commodity. Confronted with national and international pressures concerning the biodiversity, the natural and genetic resources, of the region, the organized black communities are preparing themselves for an unequal and strategic struggle to maintain control over the only remaining territorial space over which they still exert a significant cultural and social influence.

As part of their strategy for the demarcation of collective territories, activists have developed an important conception of the territory that highlights articulations between patterns of settlement, use of spaces, and practices of meaning-use of resources. Riverine settlements, for instance, evidence a longitudinal and discontinuous pattern along the rivers in which multiple economic activities (fishing, agriculture, small-scale mining and forestry, hunting and gathering, and subsistence and market activities) are combined and articulated according to the location of the settlement in the upper, middle, or lower segment of the river. This longitudinal dimension articulates with a horizontal axis regulated by the knowledge and utilization of multiple resources, from those close to the river margin that have been domesticated—including medicinal herbs and food crops—to the undomesticated species found in the various layers of forest away from the river. A vertical axis—from the infraworld to the supraworld, populated by benevolent as well as dangerous spirits—also contributes to articulating the patterns of meaning-use of resources. These various axes also depend on maintaining social relations between communities, which in some parts of the Pacific entail interethnic relations between black and indigenous communities.[23]

The defense of the territory entails the defense of this intricate pattern of social relations and cultural constructions, and is understood by movement activists in this light. It also implies the creation of a new sense of belonging linked to the political construction of a collective life project and the redefinition of relations with the dominant society. In the vision of the PCN, this possibility is more real in those communities encompassed under particular *palenques,* or networks of black organizations. At stake with Ley 70, in this way, is not "land" or even the territory of this or that community but the concept of territoriality itself as a central element in the political construction of reality on the basis of black experience. The struggle for territory is thus a cultural struggle for autonomy and self-determination. This explains why for many people of the Pacific the loss of territory would amount to a return to slavery or, worse perhaps, to becoming "common citizens."

The definition of "biodiversity" as "territory plus culture" made by movement activists incarnates an entire political ecology. This definition and the political practice that surrounds it are important contributions to today's intellectual ferment on the nature-society relation. It finds echo in current trends in political ecology concerning concepts such as territory, landscape, biodiversity, and "nature" itself. If territory is to be thought of as "the ensemble of projects and representations where a whole series of behaviors and investments can pragmatically emerge, in time and in social, cultural, aesthetic and cognitive space"—as an existential space of self-reference where "dissident subjectivities" can emerge (Guattari 1995, 23, 24)—it is clear that this project is being advanced by the social movements of the Pacific. Similarly, the definition of biodiversity proposed by the movement provides elements for reorienting biodiversity discourses according to local principles of autonomy, knowledge, identity, and economy (Shiva 1994). Finally, from the activists' efforts at theorizing local practices of use of resources, we learn that "landscapes" are not only surface phenomena but that they involve multiple worlds (Bender 1993), and that "nature" itself is not an entity "out there" existing outside human history but that it is produced in deep conjunction with the collective practice of humans who see themselves as integrally connected to it.

The Question of Development

From the PCN's perspective, development plans for the Colombian Pacific region have amounted to no more than material interventions on behalf of national and international economic interests. From the very first development plan for the region—the Plan for the Integral Development of the Pacific Coast, or PLADEICOP (DNP 1983), implemented between 1983 and 1993—to today's Plan Pacífico for Sustainable Development (DNP 1992), state intervention has been geared toward rationalizing the extraction of natural resources and structured by a homogenizing development discourse; it has in no way taken into account the diversity of cultures of the region, and actually acted against this diversity.[24]

As most other countries in Latin America and the world, Colombia has opened up its doors to the transnationalization of the economy. Despite the recognition of ethnic and territorial rights, the contradiction between the *apertura* policies and the interests of the black communities is clear, particularly in light of the geopolitical location of the region in the context of Pacific Basin integration and the wealth of its natural resources. Notwithstanding the protection afforded by the new Constitution, it is market forces that continue to determine the goals of development, including what has been rightly called "the merchandising of biodiversity" (Martínez-Alier 1996). The conflict between market-driven interests and the interests of ethnic groups is more visible in the Pacific rain-forest region than anywhere else in Colombia.

For the ethno-cultural organizations, development must be guided by principles derived from the rights and aspirations of the local communities and must propend for the affirmation of cultures and the protection of natural environments. These principles—compensation, equity, autonomy, self-determination, affirmation of identity, and sustainability[25]—also point toward restoring a sense of balance between the cultural, social, economic, and ecological contributions of black communities to the country and the scarce contributions made to the country by the central government. Similarly, development strategies must foster the communities' ethnic identity and decisionmaking capacity, including their creativity, solidarity, pride in their traditions, consciousness of their rights and forms of knowledge, and attachment to their territory. Any development alternative must articulate a vision of both a present and a future based on collective aspirations. It must go well beyond the creation of infrastructure and the improvement of material conditions to the strengthening of local cultures and languages.

PCN activists are by no means dismissive of goals such as health, education, communications, overall economic productivity, and distributing a fair share of public resources. These goals, however, are seen from the perspective of the need to defend the ancestral territories and maintain control over them, the rights of the communities to determine planning processes, and the overall goal of preserving cultural and organizational differences. "Sustainability" is not only an ecological, economic, and technological issue; it involves all of the principles stated above. It reflects the way in which the black communities of the Pacific continue to trust that life, peace, and democracy in Colombia will sacrifice neither nature nor cultural diversity (PCN 1994). The articulation of the ecological, the cultural, and the economic that underlies this vision constitutes a political ecology for the reconstruction of the relations between culture, nature, and society in this important part of the world. It also aims at a postdevelopment moment in which the unidimensional character of development—as an economistic project of social, cultural, and ecological transformation—is called into question.[26]

Conclusion

The Colombian Pacific coast region is witnessing the development of an important social movement, explicitly conceived from an ethno-cultural perspective. This movement has emerged at a particular moment in the regional, national, and international histories of the economic and the biological, and has been growing steadily in scope and complexity. The social movement of black communities is struggling against forces of Euro-Andean modernity—from colonizers to developers and narco-investors—that seek to impose in the region an extractivist regime. The movement constitutes, in this way, an important manifestation of the historical struggle for the autonomy of minority cultures and subjectivities, and for alternative regimes of nature construction—of weaving together the ecological, the cultural, and the techno-economic.

We have argued in this chapter that the social movement of black communities embodies a politicization of culture—a cultural politics—that has visible effects on established political cultures. The social and political crisis that Colombia—and most of Latin America—is undergoing finds in this movement a series of elements for reordering its imaginary and reorienting its project of nation building. The firm and radical yet pluralistic and nonviolent position of the movement can contribute toward processes of peace and solidarity with nature and each other so needed in the country. Despite the forces opposing the movement, in the current climate of certain favorable ecological and cultural conjunctures it is not far-fetched to think that the social movement of black communities actually represents a real defense of the social and biophysical landscapes of the Pacific region.

This defense advances through a slow and laborious construction of Afro-Colombian identities that articulate with alternative constructions of development, territory, and biodiversity conservation. The social movement of black communities can be described as one of cultural and ecological attachment to a territory, even as an attempt at creating new existential territories. Its reinterpretation of the history of local knowledge and practices; its critique of mainstream representations of blackness and of the Pacific region itself; and its articulation—still incipient and precarious, and yet illuminating—of alternative views of the link between culture, nature, and development, are all important elements for this project. In the long run, the movement can be seen as an attempt to demonstrate that social life, work, nature, and culture can be organized differently than as mandated by the dominant models of culture and the economy. The desires of an entire collectivity and even life itself are at stake.

Notes

1. We should make clear from the outset that our analysis refers only to the central and southern parts of the Pacific region, and to one movement strand only (the ethno-cultural organizations). This qualification will become clear as the chapter unfolds.

2. The number and quality of studies of black cultures of the Pacific region is increasing. For an introduction to the anthropological literature, see Friedemann and Arocha 1984; Arocha 1991; and Whitten 1986. For a critical assessment of the anthropological discourse on black culture, see Restrepo 1996.

3. Among the earlier expressions linked to the church was the Golconda movement promoted by the Bishop of Buenaventura, Gerardo Valencia Cano—known as "the red bishop"—whose social doctrine contributed to an incipient black consciousness; his legacy is strongly felt today among those sectors that work within the framework of the Afro-American pastoral. In urban and student circles, two organizations—the National Movement for the Rights of the Black Communities (Cimarrón) and Presencia Negra—succeeded in articulating a series of demands and in forming an urban militant base. Some of these aspects of the black movement in Colombia are discussed in Wade 1995.

4. The differences among black groups can be considered from various angles, such as the basis for mobilization (rural or urban), relations to traditional parties and the Left, the intellectual training of the activists, and geographical location. One of the main differences occurs between the organizations of the northern province of Chocó and its capital, Quibdó; and the southern provinces of Valle del Cauca, Cauca, and Nariño, with the port cities of Buenaventura, Guapi, and Tumaco, respectively, as their main black centers. As the only majority black province in Colombia, Chocó has an older and stronger link to the state and to traditional political parties than the rest of the region. Another important area of black mobilization is in the Norte del Cauca region, south of Cali.

5. The M-19 Alliance was formed as a result of the peace process of the late 1980s and the return to civilian politics of the M-19 guerrilla group. The development of this movement prior to 1991 is chronicled in Fals Borda 1992.

6. AT 55 stated that, within two years of the approval of the new Constitution, the Congress had to elaborate and approve "a law that recognizes the right to collective property to the black communities that have occupied *tierras baldías* ["empty," "unused," or public lands] in the rural riverine areas, in accordance with their traditional production practices. . . . The same law shall establish mechanisms for the protection of the rights and cultural identity of the same communities, and for the promotion of their social and economic development." The article also stipulated the establishment of a commission to draft the law, with the participation of the black communities, and the possibility of applying the law to other areas of the country with similar conditions.

7. The PCN is composed of regional *palenques;* a national coordinating committee; and technical teams at national and, in some cases, regional levels. Originally designating the autonomous territories of maroons or freed slaves in colonial times, today's *palenques* are spaces for discussion, decisionmaking, and policy orientation established in each of the regions with substantial black populations. They operate in conjunction with the Asamblea Nacional de Comunidades Negras, or ANCN (National Conference of Black Communities) and, together, constitute the Consejo Nacional de Palenques. Regional *palenques* are composed of two representatives from each of the region's organizations. The National Coordinating Committee is in charge of coordinating actions, implementing the decisions of the ANCN, and representing the PCN in national and international forums. The committee also coordinates the technical teams and the *palenque* representatives to the high-level commission in charge of regulating Ley 70. The technical teams contribute technical advice toward policy decisions in economic, development, environmental, and ethno-educational matters.

8. In an intelligent maneuver, a black senator from the Liberal Party got hold of the draft proposal for the enactment of AT 55 into law, prepared through the massive organizing process detailed here, and presented a version of it to Congress as her own.

9. Ley 70 is composed of sixty-eight articles distributed among eight chapters. Besides recognizing the rights to collective ownership of territory and to natural resources, Ley 70 explicitly recognizes Colombian blacks as an ethnic group with rights to its own identity and culturally appropriate education, and requires the state to adopt social and economic measures in accordance with black culture. Similarly, according to the law, any program on behalf of black communities must enlist their participation and respond to their particular needs, the preservation of the environment, and the development of local production practices. Development and the eradication of poverty should equally reflect black community aspirations. The law also outlined participatory mechanisms for its regulation and implementation (particularly the High Consultative Commission and its regional counterparts, with the participation of both government and black representatives) and created a special electoral system for electing two black candidates to the Chamber of Representatives. Some of these features are unprecedented in Latin America.

Ley 70 defines the black community as "the ensemble of families of Afro-Colombian descent possessing their own culture, sharing a history, and practicing their own traditions and customs within the rural-town relationship, who exhibit and maintain a consciousness of identity that sets them apart from other ethnic groups."

10. This and the succeeding quotations in this section are from the proceedings of the ANCN's Puerto Tejada conference held in September 1993.

11. Law 121 ratified the International Labor Organization's Agreement 169 concerning indigenous and tribal communities.

12. These include the Process of Black Communities (with which this part of the chapter is primarily concerned); the Working Group of Chocó Organizations; the Afro-Colombian Social Movement; the Social Movement of Black Communities; the Cimarrón National Movement; the National Afro-Colombian Home; the Afro-Colombian Social Alliance; Afro-South; Afro-Antioquia; Malcom; the Cali Black Community Council; Vanguard 21 of May; Raizales; and the Federation of Organizations of the Cauca Coast.

13. The problematic character of this view of the black experience has already been analyzed by Fanon in his discussion of a national culture (1968, 206–248).

14. The activists' interpretation of certain features of the river communities as showing a lack of interest in accumulation is in accordance with Marx's observation that only with the development of the class structure of capitalism does "accumulation for accumulation's sake" become a cultural imperative.

15. This articulation of movement strategy around culture and identity resonates with that of Mayan activists in Guatemala as discussed by Warren (in this volume). Black activists of the Pacific have also been criticized for their cultural approach in terms similar to criticisms of their Guatemalan counterparts, even if in Colombia the logic of "popular" leftist organizing is significantly different. There is much to be learned from comparative analyses of ethno-cultural mobilizations taking place in many parts of Latin America today (from the Zapatistas to the Mapuche and from the Pacific to the Amazon) in the context of the emergence of ethnic consciousness, constitutional reforms, Left-Right and class realignments, and particular processes of globalization.

16. See the day-long interview conducted by Arturo Escobar and co-researchers with leaders of the movement, including the two authors of this chapter, in which the question of gender occupied a prominent place, mostly as it was advanced by Libia Grueso, Leyla Arroyo, and other women activists. The interview took place in Buenaventura on January 3, 1994 (Escobar and Pedrosa 1996, chap. 10).

17. See, for example, Camacho's work (1996) and the dissertation in progress by Kiran Asher (1997).

18. One example is the effort spearheaded by the black writer Manuel Zapata Olivella in the 1960s.

19. This is the Proyecto Biopacífico for biodiversity conservation (see GEF/PNUD 1993). The project—conceived as a Global Environment Facility (GEF) program and funded by the Swiss government and the United Nations Development Program (UNDP)—has allowed a certain degree of participation by black organizations. Its initial three-year budget of US$9 million, however, is ridiculously low compared with the budget of the large-scale development plan, Plan Pacífico for Sustainable Development, during the same period ($256 million). One of the authors of this chapter, Libia Grueso, was the regional project coordinator for Proyecto Biopacífico in Buenaventura. For an analysis of the meaning of this project in the strategies of conservationist capital, see Escobar 1997.

20. In fact, movement activists feel the least equipped to deal with this tremendous force, which has already brought widespread changes to Colombia and elsewhere.

21. Some of these cases involved the construction of an oil pipeline ending in the port of Buenaventura; the suspension by the Ministry of the Environment of industrial gold mining in the Buenaventura area; the closing of a hearts of palm canning operation in the same area; and the design of a reforestation program in the south Pacific region (a particularly important ecological zone that suffers from intense timber activity). In all of these instances, despite tensions with other community organizations, the social movements

achieved partial but important victories. For a discussion of these cases and their impact on the movement, see Grueso 1995.

22. Juan Martínez-Alier (1995) suggests that the study of environmental conflict and its distributional effects should be a central task of political ecology. To this extent, the Pacific region of Colombia—and other rain-forest areas—have particularly important lessons for the field.

23. This brief presentation of what could be called "local models of nature" in the Pacific region is highly inadequate, and could be the topic of a separate study. Suffice it to say that the ensemble of meanings-practices (or "local models") of nature at play here are very different from modern systems. For a theoretical and political discussion of the importance of this difference, see Shiva 1994. For an detailed study of one such model in the Pacific, see Restrepo and del Valle 1996.

24. For an in-depth analysis of these plans, see Escobar and Pedrosa 1996.

25. These principles were laid out in February 1994 as part of the collective analysis by the PCN of the National Plan for the Development of Black Communities elaborated by the Colombian Department of National Planning (DNP). While there was some black representation in the commission that drafted the plan—including representatives from the PCN—the government rejected the PCN's request to have its own panel of experts and advisors included in the deliberations. As a result, the technocratic vision of the DNP and of conventional black politicians and experts prevailed in the overall conceptualization of the plan. This battle for the first "development plan for black communities" was thus lost by the movement, although not entirely, to the extent that some of their views were included.

26. The potential role of biodiversity conservation in the formulation of alternatives to development is analyzed by Escobar (1997).

References

Appadurai, Arjun. 1991. "Global Ethnoscapes." In *Recapturing Anthropology,* ed. R. Fox, 191–210. Santa Fe, N.Mex.: School of American Research.

Aprile-Gniset, Jacques. 1993. *Poblamiento, Hábitats y Pueblos del Pacífico*. Cali: Universidad del Valle.

Arocha, Jaime. 1991. "La Ensenada de Tumaco: Invisibilidad, Incertidumbre e Innovación." *América Negra* 1:87–112.

Asher, Kiran. 1997. "Constructing Afro-Colombia: Ethnicity and Territory in the Pacific Lowlands." Ph.D. diss., Department of Political Science, University of Florida.

Bender, Barbara, ed. 1993. *Landscape: Politics and Perspectives*. Oxford: Berg.

Camacho, Juana. 1996. "Black Women and Biodiversity in the Tribugá Golf, Chocó, Colombia." Final report presented to the MacArthur Foundation, Bogotá.

DNP (Departamento Nacional de Planeación de Colombia). 1983. *Plan de Desarrollo Integral para la Costa Pacífica, PLADEICOP*. Cali: DNP/CVC.

______. 1992. *Plan Pacífico. Una Estrategia de Desarrollo Sostenible para la Costa Pacífica Colombiana*. Bogotá: DNP.

Escobar, Arturo. 1995. *Encountering Development: The Making and Unmaking of the Third World*. Princeton: Princeton University Press.

______. 1997. "Cultural Politics and Biological Diversity: State, Capital, and Social Movements in the Pacific Coast of Colombia." In *Between Resistance and Revolution: Cultural*

Politics and Social Protest, ed. R. Fox and O. Starn, 40–64. New Brunswick, N.J.: Rutgers University Press.

Escobar, Arturo, and Alvaro Pedrosa, eds. 1996. *Pacífico: Desarrollo o Diversidad? Estado, Capital y Movimientos Sociales en el Pacífico Colombiano.* Bogotá: CEREC/Ecofondo.

Fals Borda, Orlando. 1992. "Social Movements and Political Power in Latin America." In *The Making of Social Movements in Latin America: Identity, Strategy, and Democracy,* ed. A. Escobar and S. Alvarez, 303–316. Boulder: Westview Press.

Fanon, Frantz. 1968. *The Wretched of the Earth.* New York: Grove Press.

Friedemann, Nina S. de, and Jaime Arocha, eds. 1984. *Un Siglo de Investigación Social en Colombia.* Bogotá: Etno.

García Canclini, Néstor. 1990. *Culturas Híbridas: Estrategias para Entrar y Salir de la Modernidad.* Mexico City: Grijalbo.

GEF/PNUD (Global Environment Facility/United Nations Development Program). 1993. *Conservación de la Biodiversidad del Chocó Biogeográfico. Proyecto Biopacífico.* Bogotá: DNP/Biopacífico.

Gonzáles Casanova, Pablo. 1994. *Globalidad, Neoliberalismo y Democracia.* Mexico City: UNAM.

Grueso, Libia. 1995. "Diagnósticos, Propuestas y Perspectivas de la Región del Chocó Biogeográfico en Relación con la Conservación y Uso Sostenido de la Biodiversidad." Unpublished report to Proyecto Biopacífico, Bogotá.

Guattari, Félix. 1995. *Chaosophy.* New York: Semiotext[e].

Hall, Stuart. 1990. "Cultural Identity and Diaspora." In *Identity, Community, Culture, Difference,* ed. J. Rutherford, 392–403. London: Lawrence and Wishart.

Harvey, David. 1989. *The Condition of Postmodernity.* Oxford: Blackwell.

Klandermans, Bert. 1992. "La Construcción Social de la Protesta y los Campos Pluriorganizativos." In *The Frontiers in Social Movement Theory,* ed. A. Morris and C. Mueller. New Haven: Yale University Press. Unpublished Spanish translation.

Leyva, Pablo, ed. 1993. *Colombia Pacífico.* Bogotá: Fondo FEN.

Lozano, Betty Ruth. 1996. "Mujer y Desarrollo." In *Pacífico: Desarrollo o Biodiversidad?* ed. A. Escobar and A. Pedrosa, 176–204. Bogotá: CEREC/Ecofondo.

Martínez-Alier, Juan. 1995. "Political Ecology, Distributional Conflicts, and Ecological Incommensurability." *New Left Review* 211:70–88.

______. 1996. "Merchandising Biodiversity." *Capitalism, Nature, Socialism* 7 (1):37–54.

Melucci, Alberto. 1989. *Nomads of the Present.* Philadelphia: Temple University Press.

PCN (Proceso de Comunidades Negras). 1994. *Documento para Discusión Frente al Plan Nacional de Desarrollo para Comunidades Negras.* Unpublished manuscript.

Pred, Alan, and Michael Watts. 1992. *Reworking Modernity.* New Brunswick, N.J.: Rutgers University Press.

Restrepo, Eduardo. 1996. "Economía y Simbolismo en el Pacífico Negro." Undergraduate anthropology thesis, Universidad de Antioquia, Medellín.

Restrepo, Eduardo, and Jorge I. del Valle, eds. 1996. *Renacientes del Guandal.* Bogotá: Biopacífico.

Robertson, Roland. 1992. *Globalization.* London: Sage.

Rojas, Jeannette. 1996. "Las Mujeres en Movimiento. Crónicas de Otras Miradas." In *Pacífico: Desarrollo o Diversidad?* ed. A. Escobar and A. Pedrosa, 205–219. Bogotá: CEREC/Ecofondo.

Serbin, Andrés. 1991. "Por Qué no Existe el Poder Negro en América Latina?" *Nueva Sociedad* 111:148–165.

Shiva, Vandada. 1994. *Monocultures of the Mind*. London: Zed Books.

Wade, Peter. 1993. *Blackness and Race Mixture: The Dynamics of Racial Identity in Colombia*. Baltimore: Johns Hopkins University Press.

______. 1995. "The Cultural Politics of Blackness in Colombia." *American Ethnologist* 22 (2):341–357.

Whitten, Norman. 1986. *Black Frontiersmen: Afro-Hispanic Culture of Ecuador and Colombia*. Prospect Heights, Ill.: Waveland Press.

Chapter Nine

Black Movements and the "Politics of Identity" in Brazil

OLIVIA MARIA GOMES DA CUNHA

To change is to change culturally
—Eduardo de Oliveira e Oliveira, 1974

Buy this or read this, because it is authentically black.[1]

In this chapter, I examine the experience of the Afro-Reggae Cultural Group (Grupo Cultural Afro Reggae), which, in a strict sense, cannot be easily classified under the rubric of the "black movement." The group does, however, consider itself a tributary of that movement, drawing upon its objectives and strategies to craft its own ideology and projects. The group's founders came to know one another within the recreational and activist circles of Rio de Janeiro's black movement and nongovernmental organizations (NGOs).[2] The principal objective of this chapter is to compare contemporary voices that deploy a "racial politics" within Brazil's new political-institutional environment to those voices that—under military rule, in the formative years of the black movement—advocated the advancement of "black culture" as a strategy for the *mobilization, politicization, and consciousness raising* of the black population. I will argue that, in their different contexts, intellectual and scholarly activities in race and race relations in Brazil served as crucial interlocutors for many of these movements, past and present.

I would like to thank the organizers of this collection, Sonia Alvarez, Arturo Escobar, and Evelina Dagnino for the invitation to participate in this volume as well as in the seminar "Culturas de Políticas / Políticas das Culturas: revistando os movimentos sociais na America Latina." During this seminar I was aided by the generous comments of this volume's editors. Additionally, I appreciate the feedback I received from "special readers" who aided me during the process of writing the final version. The concern, attention, and interest of John Burdick, Giralda Seyferth, Peter Fry, Flávio Gomes, Carlos Hasenbalg, and Verena Stolcke were of fundamental importance in aiding my efforts to complete this chapter.

Politics and Culture: Questions and Meanings

> In order to survive and develop, the group also had to learn from the popular classes. It had to continue to learn, to exchange. We are the reproducers of a culture they produce. . . . There is a prevailing idea that . . . "you take this music, this popular culture to the proletariat." This is a concept that has been used by all those who try to work with, take something to the popular classes. But this is not in fact the group's intention to the extent that, if they were to do that, they would be negating their work. They are not taking culture, they are identifying with the existing culture.[3]

The above quotation was taken from an interview given by a member of Grupo Vissungo to a leftist newspaper; the member's tone reflected the "popular" nature of his group's forms of communication with the public. Musicians from Grupo Vissungo conducted research on the Bantu roots of regional music in rural areas of the states of Minas Gerais and Rio de Janeiro. The musical forms they recovered were adapted and mixed with stories and musical instruments of African origin and then performed in concerts held both in formal artistic venues as well as in neighborhoods on the periphery of Rio de Janeiro. At the time, such musical performances represented one of the primary strategies utilized by black movement groups enabling movement leaders to establish a closer relationship with the poor residents of the periphery and shantytowns *(favelas)* of Rio de Janeiro.[4] The majority of these neighborhoods' residents are black. Grupo Vissungo emerged during a period in which the prevailing discourse of the black movement was dominated by ethnic and political issues; its proposals were intended to reconfigure the meanings, understandings, and interpretations of popular cultural and recreational forms within that prevailing discourse. Among the groups that comprised a varied and diverse "black movement," including Grupo Vissungo, this strategy revealed a rich and promising path. Weeklong art exhibitions and the presentation of traditional forms of samba by samba schools, as well as a type of conversion to a cultural universe inspired by Africa and Candomblé, were intermingled with conferences and debates about black organizations in the United States and revolutionary and postcolonial movements in Africa. These activities, taken together, characterized the black movement at this time (Hanchard 1991; Turner 1985; González 1985). The search for "Brazilian cultural roots" in Africa occurred, above all, in university environments and in the social circles of a small group of largely university-educated nonwhites, emerging in the same contemporary political-cultural scenario of what many now call the "rebirth" of the black movement.[5]

This movement emerged during the same period as many other social movements in Brazil, within a context of a slow opening of the military authoritarian regime (1964–1985). Countless groups organized around different and often newly established agendas during the latter half of the 1970s: women, unions, homosexuals, environmentalists, and neighborhood associations, among others. The emergence of these groups suggests a remapping of forms of organization and the transformation of diverse aspects of daily life into political issues (Winant 1993). Urban black groups of mainly university students, journalists, artists, and professionals began to insert themselves in a variety of ways into the discussion of the model of race relations then in place in Brazil. These debates, in many cases, began with critical analyses of the violence perpetrated by state police institutions. During this particular period, criticisms of the absence of individual liberties focused on the political dimension (Caldeira 1991). The struggle against the military regime responded initially to pressures for the defense of human rights and for freedom of expression. Black movement activists detected an opportunity within this struggle to advance criticisms of the authoritarian makeup of police institutions. These institutions, in the final analysis, penalized, with greater frequency, individuals who were doubly excluded: by poverty and by the color of their skin. The Unified Black Movement Against Racial Discrimination (Movimento Negro Unificado Contra a Discriminação Racial, or MNU) was established in response to the forms of violence that most greatly affected the black population.[6]

The MNU emerged at a time when many black associations (cultural, recreational, and entertainment) were promoting a variety of activities that lacked explicit (antiracist) political organizational objectives. Whereas the MNU's strategies and attempts to unify black movements were grounded in the understanding that racism was a political issue, these other black associations continued to emphasize culture and sociability, resisting the politicization of discourses about race. Grupo Vissungo, which emerged in the late 1970s as a "cultural group," in many ways sought to merge these two projects: They sought to transform "culture," in particular "black culture," into an instrument for raising the consciousness of poor and marginalized black populations. This shift was supported by various segments of the black movement due to its shift away from the strictly political issues that had occupied a central position in the discussion to that point.

Looking back at various texts produced by black activists during the late 1970s and the early 1980s (when Grupo Vissungo and the MNU first emerged), we can perceive that the discussion often focused on how the organizing strategies of the black movement revolved around the notion of "culture." In the following section, I will briefly describe three distinct positions advocated by intellectuals and activists associated with the black movement during the 1970s. Further, I will identify how the theme of culture was discussed and analyzed by these distinct perspectives within the black Movement.

In distinguishing between a "recreational-entertainment" position that was averse to politicization and an alternative position that viewed "culture" as a means of bringing intellectuals and activists into closer contact with black communities, Lélia González, then an MNU activist, called attention to the disputes about "culture" within the MNU and in the larger black movement at the time of MNU's founding. The first position emphasized the recreational and cultural aspects of black organizations; González argues, for example, that samba schools, "precisely because they were able to mobilize the masses, from our viewpoint, . . . were always the object of control by the 'authorities.' . . . However, the cultural organizations have been of great importance because they create the possibility of exercising political practices and preparing for the arrival of Black movements with an ideological focus" (1980, 22).

For González, the principal characteristic of these recreational associations was their oscillation between co-optation, principally among those groups that worked closely with the state, and the tendency to restrict themselves to "culturalist" or "assimilationist" practices (1980, 25). González established these differentiations in an effort to make a twofold claim. First, in order to legitimate those groups that prioritized political discourse over "culturalism," González maintained that "culturalist" activists would weaken the antiracist struggle and upheld its supposed illegitimacy. Second, González implied that each notion—"politics" as well as "culture"—when viewed separately, would be incapable of carrying out the transformation project that she was defending. In other words, she maintained that neither cultural events such as dance parties and celebrations nor the traditional political appeals of leftist parties and organizations had proven capable of mobilizing or raising the consciousness of the black population. According to González, in black "entertainment" associations, culture was a practice that reinforced traditional values or supported an ideology that obfuscated racial-social relations through the reification of the "myth of racial democracy." In contrast, the idea of "politics," as a practice of reflection and transformation, would function for González as a type of agent for potentializing meanings. The idea of *transformation,* in this view, thus reconfigures the relationship between culture and politics.

It is important to point out that the criticisms leveled at "culturalism" must be discussed in relation to what was thought to characterize the political culture of the relationship between the dominant and popular classes—co-optation. Discussions and criticisms of co-optation were not limited to the black movement. Rather, they formed a central part of the political *ethos* that characterized many social movements and leftist groups during the late 1970s and early 1980s. "Politicization," for example, which was a predominant trend during the political opening of the military regime, was the primary objective of social movements and the black movement as they sought to reorganize the popular classes. It was thought necessary to purify the personalistic and clientelistic links that were believed to constitute the relationship between political elites and socially marginalized sections of the population. Nowhere was this more evident than in the efforts to "reorganize" and "raise the consciousness" of the masses in order to establish democracy and win elections. Ideas such as *organization* and *mobilization* were vehicles that fostered discussions about how black movement activists could work more closely with the popular classes. As we will see, the reproduction of this dualistic authoritarian vision would provoke numerous internal criticisms and conflicts within the black movement over the course of the following decades (Duarte et al. 1993). For González and others who shared her vision, "culturalism" did not confront the profound social contradictions that plague Brazilian society; rather, it actually reinforced a benevolent image of a Brazil in which there is a homogenous racial and economic population.

The effort to raise consciousness, for a large number of black activists and intellectuals during this period, had one important implication. This was the reaction to the commercialization and banalization of culture by elites and the state. By labeling this vision of culture as "black," it gained a certain value in a particular market of symbolic goods, to the extent that it was assumed to be "pure" (not co-opted) and representing "resistance" (offering a political-social project for transformation). The process of *consciousness raising (concientização),* as seen from this point of view, consisted of both a kind of conversion to a militant ethos of sociability based on activism or religion (especially African-based religions such as Candomblé) as well as a reconfiguration of racial terms (with respect to nomenclature).

During this period, other questions regarding the necessary link between culture and politics that were important for the mobilization and organization of the black population were raised. For González, there were distinct positions in the debate about racism and the need to devise a political ideology that would create a vibrant and unified national movement. The central principle for her was that the "struggle" should be constructed around *diversity*. The first references to the notion of "difference," as an artifact demarcating distinct historical, cultural, and ethnic attributes, were sketched out. At the time, the idea of "difference" assumed an ontological status that could be explained by a mixture of cultural and historical elements determined by the origins and vicissitudes of the black presence in the Americas. If there was a privileged place within this debate, it was in the sphere of culture. *Cultural diversity,* as proposed by González, could be perceived and exemplified in the *quilombos,* in religious brotherhoods and samba schools.[7] *Difference* and *diversity* were attributes used to configure other possible "unified wholes" to be incorporated under a polymorphous notion of "black culture." This was an effort to create collective references capable of capturing, embracing, and reconfiguring the disparate ways in which the presence of blacks was felt in Brazilian society.

The concept of "black culture" as the "resistance against oppression" also appeared in discussions about the various forms of struggles undertaken by blacks against diverse forms of racial discrimination. "Black culture," then, would be something to be "redeemed," "valorized," and "promoted" while kept distant from efforts to "commercialize" it. The valorization of particular cultural aspects deemed "black" would constitute a strategy of politicization. The idea of "resistance" entailed a "distancing" from and negation of the racial ideology reflected by "the myth of racial democracy."[8] This redefinition shifts the perspective away from an ideology in which miscegenation was awarded the highest praise, thereby recharting the map of identity in which not only Africa but also *black culture* and *African* are relocated on the basis of a different type of cartography (Slater, in this volume). New tensions between various factions of the black movement resulted from this new cartography.

Returning to González's text, it is necessary to call attention to the political conjuncture in which she writes and to the meanings she attributes, in her analysis of the black movement, to key concepts that are privileged. González diverges from proposals that have minimal political content because she valorizes efforts to mobilize the "black masses." This point, in fact, made vital political and ideological connections, and as a result the debate was taken seriously by the majority of the Left (Gilroy 1993a). González explains the disjunction between the two tendencies, the "culturalist" and the "political":

> It is worthwhile to note that cultural organizations that, in some form, distance themselves from the MNU (because of disagreement with the MNU's proposals or because they lack political clarity) were obligated to make their positions more evident precisely because the MNU was able to enter into political spaces that demanded a clear positioning. Today it is not enough to merely support culturalist or intellectual positions that have become increasingly divorced from the reality experienced by the black masses. (1980, 64)

Another important point of discussion for activists and intellectuals was and continues to be the "end of the myth of racial democracy" as a prerequisite for the promotion of black mobilization and the education of all Brazilians concerning the existence of racism in Brazil. Among intellectuals, criticisms of Brazil's racial paradise were dominated by the insertion of social class either as preponderant or as determinant of social positions that are analogous to racial categories. I will not delve into this discussion, which has been sufficiently covered elsewhere, other than to point out that the literature produced after the UNESCO study made in the 1950s greatly enriched the terms and language of the debate.[9] The overwhelming majority of these studies strongly emphasized socio-economic inequalities to the detriment of explanations related to "color" and "race" (Winant 1993).

For black activists and intellectuals, these studies were preceded by the description of Brazilian society itself, in terms of its historical and cultural formation, as racially polarized. Thus, the "reality" uncovered through both quantitative and qualitative research sharply undermined claims supportive of racial democracy. This debate was grounded in the analytical studies and terms of a particular case study: race relations in the United States (Fry 1996).

The justification for this position, often implicit in the debate within the black movement, was to promote unity in the face of the fragmentation suggested by individual situations. The debate was initiated by the need to denounce the profound racial inequalities that mark Brazilian society. Sociologist Gilberto Freyre's theories of racial democracy mask these same racial relationships. Within the discourse on desirable forms of intervention and the utilization of the concept of "black culture" as a strategy of mobilization, efforts to characterize the "myth" as an official ideology have complex implications. Peter Fry, for example, questions the hierarchical ways in which the myth and reality are used in the literature on the subject. Moreover, he calls our attention to the dangerous reductionism that results from interpretations of "racial democracy" (1996). Curiously, this type of analysis was not absent from the activist debate of the 1970s. Black activist and historian Joel Rufino dos Santos calls attention to the need to separate the analysis of racial democracy as an ideal from efforts to prove its "inexistence" at the concrete level of race relations in Brazil.

It is in this context of the critique of the "myth of racial democracy," as the model for explaining the dynamics of inequalities in Brazil, that the United States referent became the prevailing paradigm of analysis on the subject of Brazilian race relations. The strategy utilized by many segments of the black movement was to portray Brazilian society in black and white terms. Important themes and issues such as color, phenotype, hair texture, and interracial relationships that shape race relations were ignored by accounts reducing the discussion of race in Brazil to black and white terms.

The activist and intellectual Eduardo de Oliveira e Oliveira, for example, defended a polarized vision of race relations and, consequently, of strategies to confront racial discrimination (1974). *Polarization* was explained and justified by the argument that the existing racism had similarly pernicious effects on blacks, mestizos, and mulattos. Thus, it was argued that racial relations were *relations of coercion.*[10] He proposed that multiple categories of racial classification be dropped in favor of a bipolar system of racial classification. Thus, the term *black*, as a social category, would encompass all of the variations of the nonwhite racial classifications prevalent in Brazilian discourses about race. The concept of culture, according to Oliveira e Oliveira, was in turn a crucial element in the construction of an "ethnicitized" reality (the "view of the Black"). Among "blacks," culture could thus be a powerful resource to withstand the pressures of co-optation, distinguishing the multiple classificatory nuances based on phenotype from those based on *difference*. It is important to note that if this conceptualization of *black culture* has a delimiting role, it is not only through it that black movement interventions into poor and black communities would occur but, principally, among those who consider themselves free of "hegemonic culture": black intellectuals.

Oliveira e Oliveira developed a theory of "intellectual commitment" in which he calls dedicated intellectuals, above all black intellectuals, to the task of "decolonization" (1977). In working with a "non-ethnocentric" conception of culture, the task of committed intellectuals would be to "decolonize" the minds and practices of their colleagues, since "Black intellectuals were corralled by their primary and primeval condition, as both subject and object of their inquiries and had no other option. They are not dealing with a particular subject (it is necessary that they understand this), but for a cause" (1977, 27). For Oliveira, the tension that permeated these efforts, at once political and intellectual, would create the possibility for the theoretical and analytical redirection of studies about blacks and their political mobilization in Brazil. Similar to Guerreiro Ramos in the 1950s, who defended a "critical sociology" in the intellectual production of race-related themes, Oliveira e Oliveira called the attention of intellectuals to their dual roles and to the need to formulate their own theoretical paradigms for research.[11] Although not in these precise terms, Oliveira e Oliveira suggested that the condition of the "eternal native" would create the possibility for a form of direct intervention in the debate. This new position established the basis for an authority that can generate new discussions about the conditions in which intellectual knowledge and theories are produced. In this text, Oliveira e Oliveira laid out the principal points for a "science for and not about blacks," in which one's "ethnic condition" would occupy a specific mode of insertion into the intellectual debate. Though the theoretical and methodological instruments of the Brazilian academy were premised on racist assumptions, according to Oliveira e Oliveira, black intellectuals must reappropriate their condition, transforming it into a *place* from which to produce a critique of "liberal bourgeois sociology" (1977, 26).

For the purposes of this chapter, two issues emerge prominently from this debate. First, the ambiguity of the categories of racial classification, it was argued, should be reduced to a single political category capable of articulating other social differences, such as gender and class, under the rubric of ethnicity. Second, issues that lie in the spheres of the historical, cultural, national, and transnational have connections whose mixture must be reappropriated through inclusionist methods. That is, parallel to the simplification of classification terms that had weakened the process of "raising the consciousness" of black Brazilians, political, cultural, and international references were being used as paradigms in the antiracist struggle in Brazil. Moreover, the definition used by González for "difference" and "diversity"—the historical forms and socially distinct ways of thinking about the ethnic question—can and should be subsumed under this dualist approach. The category "black" refers not only to a rereading of previous forms of social subordination but also to a *place* toward which all the varieties of racial classification terms could converge.

Referring to this strategy as "culturally inclusive," Gilroy (1993b) shows how the dualist vision and the consequent construction of a ethno-nationalist discourse, in the English context, avoids references to the categories of "hybrids" and "creoles." Similarly, though in a different context, R. Panikkar[12] examines the possibilities of an "inter-religious" dialogue between Hinduism and Catholicism and argues that in the face of the danger of losing identity, the discourse of analogy was substituted by one equivalency. These processes are important for our purposes since they force us to examine how cultural contact can be considered "impure" and "polluted" (Douglas 1977; Gilroy 1993b, 2). In other words, that which is created by a mixture can serve as the basis for the affirmation of a positive discourse supporting the "myth of racial democracy." The incorporation of that which is proximate, while different, can serve as a strategy of political affirmation.[13] As we shall see below, in the example of the Afro-Bahian *blocos,* this artifice of substituting equivalence for analogy was attempted in the 1980s. These two examples illustrate other discursive strategies evident in the texts of González and Oliveira e Oliveira. In the first place, with respect to the various adjectives used to define and utilize the concept of culture, this concept permits us to encompass all that is seen as "residual" and susceptible to appropriation by nationalist discourse. If "popular culture" featured prominently in the writings of the Left and in population education campaigns during the 1970s, "black culture" was "recovered" or "redeemed" by black organizations in their irreversible process of "raising consciousness" among the masses. As in the first case, this process preexisted, although obfuscated by commercialization and the impact of the media. The "popular" thus gains an ethnic status as it is transformed into "black." Thus, the task of "mobilization" is imbricated with another, whose character is vital.[14] As with Midas, everything that glitters is transformed into black rather than gold. Oliveira e Oliveira proposed this discursive resource as a method, an artifact for reading Brazil's complex racial system, in which it is necessary to define places, establish positions, and identify voices in order to demonstrate what is politically relevant in the struggle against racism. In doing this, he calls not on the "masses" but on black intellectuals, those who would be implicated in the very plot that they are trying to unravel. The "consciousness-raising task," entrusted to intellectuals, should be preceded by a moment of rupture and the forced choice between the primacy of the subjective and the imperative of the collective.

The historian and activist Maria Beatriz do Nascimento, in her article "Culturalismo e Contracultura" published in 1976,[15] differentiated between "culturalism," which has been a principal method for studying Brazilian society since the 1930s, and the "culturalizing" *(culturalizante)* focus, which appeared to gain a stronghold among various segments of the black movements in the 1970s.[16] The danger of the second notion lay in its potential to reinforce the ethnocentric assumptions of the first. These studies often support "traditional," "pure," and "unstained" aspects of the so-called Afro-Brazilian culture that had not been influenced by the processes of miscegenation and industrialization (Dantas 1988), Nascimento maintained, and ended up promoting a peculiar understanding of Brazil's ethnic diversity. It is this viewpoint that informed the earliest cultural policies, which recognized the "Afro-Brazilian" population as an integral part of the Brazilian nationality. Public policies inspired theories that valorized and sought to institutionalize a *pluralist* vision of Brazilian nationality.

The idea of *nation* as a kind of spatial (geographical-physical), ethnic, and historic *continuum,* as understood by Brazilian intellectuals such as Oliveira Viana or Gilberto Freyre, was a fundamental pillar in this discourse. It was assumed that Brazil, given the mixture of various "human currents/races," had created an actual tropical *melting pot,* erected upon the blood of whites, Indians, and blacks. The tropical character of the formation of the nation, while at once unique and multiple, gave meaning to everything that could not be defined by concepts. "Tropicality" *(tropicalidade)* as an analogy of indefiniteness, an elegy to celebrations, is a strong component in the work of Freyre: "In the light of the tropical sun concepts are obfuscated, by the most absurd manifestations of political instability, of fluctuations of opinion, of sudden reactions and unexpected victories. . . . tropical in the sense of restless instability, of suffering, of peculiarities, of its weaknesses, of its generosity, of its passion, of its baroque emphasis."[17]

There are many similarities between the geopolitical outlook of nationality, proposed by intellectuals linked to the Estado Novo, and the idealization of "national integration," as promoted by the military regime after 1964. Contrary to other situations, the Brazilian state recognized diversity as a national attribute. The "myth of the three races" was subject to many diverse forms of cultural expression, principally those that had an official character.

Nascimento rejected this interpretation insofar as it propitiated an astute pacification of the conflict by presenting the purported integration of the cultural sphere as evidence of the nonexistence of inequality in the realm of social relations. She warned of the "danger" of the exaltation of the "pure" and the "traditional," phenomena related directly to "archaic cultures" (1976, 5). Nascimento classified "traditional cultures" and "cultures of domination" as suffering from ethnocentric and culturalist biases and warned of the possible manipulation of the concept that could weaken its ability to be transformed into a "culture of resistance":

> It is pertinent to understand how Black groups currently organize themselves. We need to ask ourselves what limits our own culture, which is manipulated by the dominant system, presents for us? We must have a critical attitude before our culture. In truth, some of our practices, such as religion, incorporate representations of the dominant culture—as opposed to what happened with the "Kibanguismo" in the Congo or with "Peyotism" among Native Americans which created a third component with which the subordinate group articulated a process of transformation. Our *candomblé* and *umbanda,* by contrast, accommodated themselves to the process of integration. They did not create their own truths, they did not bring an ideology of salvation to the group. On the contrary, in the case of *candomblé,* religious leaders sought to maintain anachronistic elements and transformation was stymied. (1976, 5)

It is necessary to reiterate that not all visions of the role and significance of the category of "black culture," as a strategy for political mobilization, were conceptualized in the same way. Nascimento's vision was not restricted to the spaces of sociability and small political discussions privileged by black activists during this period. One must take into account that concepts such as "hegemony," "hegemonic culture," and "culture of resistance" gained importance in intellectual and activist circles at the end of the 1970s as explanatory categories for domination—at once political and cultural. The proximity of the black movement to leftist political parties was very close and intense. In intellectual debates, specifically those among black activists, the concept of hegemony was contrasted to another: the need to develop practices that would result in the creation of "counter-hegemonic" practices (Schelling and Rowe 1993). The concept of "black culture" was thus introduced into these circles as a racialized counterpoint to the idea of popular culture. The move reified "pure" black cultural practices as opposed to those seen to have been "commercialized" and manipulated. In some ways this debate can be understood as a protective artifact—the remapping of boundaries, the formulation of concepts and words of one's own—that would distance black movement discourse from the celebration of miscegenation.

Just who was actually responsible for the racial discrimination that nonwhites faced in everyday life was (and is), in fact, a difficult question to respond to in Brazil. One of the recurring ways of addressing this crucial question was to define practices and establish strategies of political intervention by drawing on particular theories and explanatory categories borrowed from the academic debate on race relations. It is important to point out that this dialogue between activist and intellectual environments, though tense, was appropriated and reconstituted in the discourses of the movement.

By the middle of the 1980s, this search for models of mobilization based on political-cultural practices appeared to have reached an impasse. As historian and activist Joel Rufino dos Santos put it, this search implied a quest for the "black signifier":

> The limits of the current Black movement are, then, on one the hand, the end of previous understanding of Brazil (from its period of intense economic and social acceleration) and on the other, the beginning of a new conception of Brazil (that Brazil has exhausted its possibilities of growth). Accepting this hypothesis, we must conclude that the Black movement, in its current stage, is the child of the current Brazilian crisis, in particular, the result of the myth of racial democracy. Thus, the ability of the Black movement to move to the next stage—when it will begin to grow again—depends on overcoming the Brazilian crisis which, quite logically, will demand a redefinition of the movement. (1985, 307)

This redefinition, curiously, was based on the same assumptions as in the previous period. That is, the difficulty in deciphering the enigma, for Santos, was the inability of the movement to understand *difference* within the appearance of racial *equality*. Perceiving the plurality of engagements and the subjectivity of projects in the face of constructed practices falls under the logic of the "politics of identity."

The crisis or impotency of which Santos spoke was also exemplified in the proliferation of groups and organizations that prioritized cultural activities—groups that bet on the didactic character of such experiences and on new models of identity. In an effort to comprehend the black movement at the end of the 1980s, Damasceno, Giacomini, and Santos (1988) have shown that the utilization of terms such as culture and *black culture* revealed a recurring bias in such organizations. If this change is attributable to a discourse of "crisis" or to the impasse then confronted by many social movements, it resulted in the reconfiguration of the very language used by black groups.

This reconfiguration permitted important shifts, since it allowed political projects and the construction of identity—individual as well as collective—to become more viable. This was extremely significant because it allowed for the political organization of different kinds of groups. Moreover, it also signaled the beginning of a discourse about the boundaries and limitations of the concept of identity, specifically the concept of "black identity," among black movements in Brazil. On the one hand, as Hall (1993a, 1993b) and Calhoun (1994) both show, a focus on the "politics of identity" produces politically viable categories that rearticulate small differences into rubrics capable of proposing antidiscriminatory polices. Yet, on the other hand, forms of struggle grounded in identity cannot account for the internal tensions that are constitutive of and refer to the individual and collective spheres. To conclude the first section of this chapter, I will briefly describe the experiences of the Afro-Bahian *blocos* in relation to questions of culture and identity.

Blocos Afro: "Culture" and "Community"

The process through which new *blocos*[18] developed has its roots in the city of Salvador, Bahia. Preceding the emergence of a local chapter of the MNU, a carnival *bloco* was founded whose most distinctive characteristic was its "afro" style. The style of this group—Ilê Aiyê—was subsequently adopted by other groups.[19] The novelty produced by the growth of these groups in the political and cultural atmosphere of Salvador was reproduced in other cities and contexts, and thus the trend became more than a localized phenomenon. The objective was to raise the consciousness of young blacks and mestizos through entertainment and cultural events—most notably carnival. An additional objective was to strengthen ties to youth through political and cultural activities by focusing on Afro-Brazilian themes.

Since the creation of Ilê Aiyê in 1974, every year during carnival thousands of participants, mainly blacks and mestizos, parade, dance, and sing while dressed in costumes alluding to African traditions.[20] Themes chosen revolved around the "history of resistance" by black Brazilians as well as the process of decolonization and liberation in the countries of black Africa. Within this trajectory, affiliations were established, myths retold, and alliances strengthened. Grupo Cultural Olodum, one of the most innovative *blocos,* drew upon influences ranging from cultural affinities between Brazil and Cuba to the black pharaohs of Egypt.

Different groups developed their own themes and styles so that each *bloco* had its own distinctive image. Whereas Ilê Aiyê redefined its links to Africa through its emphasis on the pervasiveness of black culture and religion in Brazil, the Afro Muzenza group looked to Jamaica. The members of this group crafted an image based on the colors, themes, and emblems of Rastafarianism, ultimately selecting Bob Marley as a kind of group patron. They thereby attracted a new generation of black youths who lived on the periphery of the city, who were not familiar with the discourse used by university-educated activists, and who were drawn to the *blocos* because of their innovative styles (Cunha 1991).

Within the persistent discussion regarding the utilization and limitations of culture as a strategy for political mobilization, there were two clearly defined positions. The tension between a "culturalist" position and a position that privileged a more strictly political focus was ongoing. It surfaced quickly during the early stages of the development of the *blocos*. The use of dance parties and celebrations as spaces to raise consciousness and to reaffirm identity gained an important place in activist discussions, first locally and then nationally.[21]

The style adopted by the *blocos afro* had an enormous impact on activists in other cities due to the centrality of the groups' message and their expanding scope of influence, which no longer depended solely on carnival. They also attracted an increasing number of nonwhites. The ties that bind the "participant," "sympathizer," and "parade reveler" were substantially more malleable than the ties that bind more traditional forms of political activism. From an institutional perspective, the *bloco* could simultaneously be in several different places at the same time, allowing for an extension of dialogues and partnerships into a variety of spheres. During the *blocos*' initial phase, their undefined racial character denoted—at least for those who defined themselves as political activists in a strict sense—the weakening of the political, the danger of misinterpretation ("culturalism" instead of cultural politics), and the possibility of co-optation (Risério 1981; Silva 1988; Cunha 1991).

By the beginning of the 1980s, new *blocos* and *afoxés* erupted throughout the periphery of Salvador, leading to what Antônio Risério called the "reafricanization" of the Bahian carnival. Some of these groups had other projects beyond the carnival celebrations. Nourishing dreams of community projects, they organized debates and cultural activities while simultaneously trying to enter regional media outlets commercially. The process of the "reafricanization" of carnival reinvigorated the music industry due to the proliferation of new rhythms and styles that were subsequently marketed under the rubric of "*axé* music."

Initially, the *blocos* were comprised of youths who were drawn into the groups through personal and neighborhood relationships, as more and more young people left the *afoxés* and the traditional *blocos de indios*. By contrast, a very different style of organizing occurred among embryonic groups of professionals, artists, and university-educated individuals who would form the basis of the MNU. This is why divisions, with respect to cultural or political proposals, marked the early period of the MNU in Salvador. Jônatas Silva, an MNU activist and a defender of the "political line" during this period, sums up the two conflicting visions:

> If the united efforts of the "culturalists" and the "politicos" did not yield fruit for the Unified Black Movement, the reason lies in the fact that each side was incomprehensible to the other. Black activist Luiz Alberto affirms that "the artistic faction did not understand the interaction between culture and politics and vice versa. Truthfully, no one at this time understood. In that particular moment it reflected the weakness of Black activism since no one understood the real dimensions of their struggle. This weakness was also reflected theoretically as Black activists worked with whatever was going on around them and interpreted reality superficially without addressing more profound questions such as the relationship of culture to politics. The role of culture within the political struggle was not understood and the role of pure political contestation was also not understood by the artistic sector." (1988, 286)

These questions were not confined to the MNU. They spilled over into the *blocos,* resulting in an increase of tension within the MNU leadership. Activists criticized the lack of politicization of certain *blocos* and the traditionalism of their agendas.[22] This criticism was based on the belief that traditional leadership supported the continuation of older religious practices such as *afoxés* and Candomblé, which had strong ties to conservative politics. A second criticism was that the "culturalists" within the *blocos (carnavalescos)* experienced difficulties bridging the gap between the political projects offered by the vanguard and the interests of the "communities" participating in the *bloco.*[23] Questioning the unity of the *blocos* and proposing to return to their "community" roots, the leadership of some *blocos* discouraged the presence of activists. Their highly politicized discourse was declared to have a divisive effect on the community. When both "culturalists" and "politicos" began to refer to a "crisis," a "loss of identity," and "diffusion," Ilê Aiyê, during the Fifth Congress of Blacks of the North and Northeast, declared that:

> We are the ones responsible for this dispersion. We have been involved and interested in the problematic of Blacks, but what have we done for the majority? We have limited our discussions to offices and meeting halls, to the small number of privileged and educated Blacks. . . . We are talking, people, about the majority of Blacks that live in distant neighborhoods suffering every type of humiliation and disrespect by the men who claim to run this country. It is for these Blacks that we must focus intellectual activities, looking for answers to our questions and then taking our answers to those who have a right to them. Our discussions can not remain on a distant plane since this does not contribute to the improvement and strengthening our race. We must find a more accessible *language* so that we will be understood. (italics mine)[24]

Questions related to the difficulties in crafting a language accessible to the general public remained a central point of conflict for many organizations. In Salvador during this period, the example of the *blocos* turned out to be a paradigmatic experience as the language that emerged from their practices was constructed for heterogeneous "publics." On the one hand, the notion of community is used to designate a conjunction of associations, organizations, and religious groups made up of blacks and mestizos dedicated to the discussion of racial issues. On the other hand, "community" is used to refer to the territorialized presence of *blocos* in certain neighborhoods. In the first sense, ethnicity is highlighted; in the second, the "popular" representativeness of the community is highlighted instead, which makes its links to the *bloco* so crucial. Thus, the ethnic quasi-exclusivity that had previously marked the definition of the black community is fragmented. The community attains new, spatial meanings as its subgroups assume the names of neighborhoods and locations where the *blocos* would develop their "community-based projects."

These projects, therefore, can only be understood by recalling the pre-1980 political environment in which the majority of the *bloco* leaders formed their vision of what comprised political activity and that deeply marked the practices of some of the most important groups. In general terms, we can say that the contemporary *blocos* were the result of the standoff in the 1970s between "culturalists" and their MNU colleagues who supported a more politicized approach.

Initially, this tension was ameliorated through a conciliatory strategy. Aware of the power of the market for goods categorized as "afro," Olodum and Araketu were the first groups to signal the gradual expansion of their areas of activity to exploit this commercial opportunity by selling records and tapes. They also promoted themselves in media outlets by emphasizing their cultural roots. These groups invested in local solidarity networks that stimulated voluntary participation and professionalization. These localities, largely neighborhoods on the periphery of the city and shantytowns lacking public services, gained visibility in song lyrics, in graphic materials, in becoming "emblems" of the groups. This practice of "reterritorializing" the music in specific localities implied a reevaluation of the purposes and objectives of the *blocos* and, as a consequence, of the black movement in Salvador. The idea of a local "political commitment" was superimposed on the strict definition previously used to define the struggle against racism. As David Slater argues in this volume, the limits of these geographic references are always relative and appear at distinct moments. Pelourinho, the neighborhood in which Grupo Cultural Olodum was founded and continues to maintain its educational and entertainment activities, was an important local reference point distinguishing Grupo Cultural Olodum from other groups. The internationalization of Bahia and, more specifically, Salvador placed Pelourinho on the map. The alterations and differential strategies of territorialization also implied redefinitions with respect to political alliances and affinities.

The dialogue between local participation and a broader political referent first developed in confronting the everyday problems faced by shantytown residents resulting from racial discrimination: police violence, poverty, unemployment, marginalization, the absence of public services, the lack of schools, and so on. At the same time, the "politicos" claimed that this strategy weakened *blocos'* ability to mobilize because the strategy was susceptible to paternalism, clientelism, and the tendency to rely on politicians for employment. Yet, given the low level of internal organization among the *blocos,* internal divisions grew. The more politicized sectors gradually lost ground in the leadership of the *blocos*. The redefinition of spaces of action, the prominence of solidarity networks, and the establishment of local support systems alongside the strengthening of a national antidiscrimination struggle were decisive issues in reconfiguring the limits and exposing the fragility of the new activism.[25] The entrance of new groups into this discussion provoked other types of conflicts that were not always political or visible. The divergence between those sets of groups that were at first realigned around the headings of "activists" and "culturalists" *(carnavlescos)* was typified by particularistic debates. Included in these debates were issues related to the influence of political parties and unions, the role of elections and black candidates, the unification of the black movement in Bahia, the emergence of small groups of black women and black homosexuals, and the relationship of these groups to the political and cultural institutions of the state.

In a subsequent phase, the *blocos* could no longer be seen as strictly cultural entities. They gained new profiles in the composition of their leadership, in their involvement in political activities beyond carnival, and, more recently, in their entrepreneurial activities as well. It is in this sense that these organizations ceased to be *blocos afro* and were transformed into "cultural groups." In the same sense, the changes spilled over into the groups that were more strictly political, thereby demonstrating that these groups are not immune to this process of change.

The first attempts at unifying the black movement occurred within the confines of the MNU, whose importance as one of the key spaces for the formation of leadership had initially been established under the military regime. However, the proliferation of groups dedicated to the antiracist struggle and the politicization of the *blocos* removed the MNU from its central and unifying position; it became instead one of many associations, groups, community organizations, *blocos,* and *afoxés* in the fight against racial discrimination. The experiences of *blocos afro* in Salvador became a point of reference for similar groups in other cities; though the circumstances in Salvador were seemingly unresolved, they were in fact managed more peacefully in other parts of the country.

"Ambiguity" began to incorporate a discourse of what was understood as *modernity*—the possibility of assimilating and transforming, of breaking from isolationism—as some activists of the 1970s had foretold.

The appropriation of international music genres—such as reggae—in the rhythmic and musical style of the *blocos* can be interpreted as a metaphor for this new discourse. Reggae is useful as a "diacritical sign" of particular aesthetic frontiers constructed by the *blocos*. The creation of "black culture" was no longer limited to the process of reclaiming African heritage, but now utilized invention. The most explicit and visible example of this new perspective is Grupo Cultural Olodum, which strengthened its ties to various social groups, arenas, and issues. Olodum was the first of the cultural groups to transform itself into an NGO in Salvador. Their objective was to engage in local and regional struggles to boost the visibility of and improve living conditions in specific neighborhoods as well as to develop their own educational, business, and entertainment programs.[26]

The introduction of reggae into the words, spaces, and events of the *blocos afro* initially incorporated a more complete vision of what must be called "modernity." The incorporation of reggae stands in opposition to the limits that are encased in "tradition." In this view, "tradition" is not only the result of the continuation of religious and cultural references but is also seen as the refusal to change. Reggae represented musical expressions, urban lifestyles, and political ideas that had been adopted internationally by young blacks.

Yet "modernity" did not indicate the absence of "political content." The members of Olodum, for example, were already by the end the 1980s (Cunha 1991) defining their music and their cultural projects as "postmodern." This "postmodernity" nonetheless was constituted on the basis of both the negation of the imperative of "tradition" among *blocos afro* and as an argument for space, support, alliances, and visibility. It could be understood as an attempt to incorporate diversity without aesthetic limits. The adoption of the term "postmodern" could be reduced to the idea that, in musical terms, Olodum could do anything and everything. But the form, though unlimited, must nonetheless correspond to particular meanings. Therefore, Olodum initially selected a repertoire that mixed utopia with history, tambourines with synthesizers. The pendular movement back and forth between form and content was constitutive of the actual process of the consolidation of reggae as a musical style in Salvador.

But the experience of the *blocos* was exemplary and transcended regional boundaries. The *blocos* soon offered different methods of participation. Their supporters were no longer exclusively comprised of blacks and mestizos. This signified the broadening of spaces and the need to recast the dialogue about what constitutes "culture" and "difference."

> Our unity, comprehension of the near future, political responsibility, self-esteem, Black pride and anti-racism are our weapons to confront the challenges of life. . . . The lessons of the new world order should leave no doubt: there are new ways to struggle on the planet. Those who do not realize this will remain in the past unable to find the doorways to the present and will not live to see tomorrow. The election of Nelson Mandela in South Africa closes a worldwide fight against racial and social apartheid in which we still live, in Brazil and Bahia, where the majority of the excluded survive on bread and water while a minority enjoys the wealth of the country. . . . It is necessary to fight and to dream. It is now our time. With strength and competence, alongside everyone who is against racism, after 299 years of the death of Zumbi and 196 [years] since the revolt of Alfaiates, we will lift our strong hands to join the battle for liberty. We will accomplish this golden dream, we will follow once again the eternal light of the sun, wake to a happy dawn and be born to an epoch in which all are equal in their differences.[27]

Although Olodum's vision does not represent consensus within the black movement, it is illustrative of the important shifts in a particular discourse about polarization. João Jorge Rodrigues speaks of *self-esteem, antiracism, citizenship,* the *new world order, excluded majority,* and *equality in difference.* In this text, which covers fifteen years of the group's history, there is only one reference to the "Afro-Brazilian community" and none to "black" as the popular basis of support for the group. As to investments in media, the fruits are "individual promotions" and "social starmanship," along with the internationalization of the black movement. It is important to note that there is a certain slippage in the usage of the ascriptive language to other terms, the referential bases of which appear to be less restricted. These changes, for the most part, were made possible by the prominence that the notion of "community" came to occupy in activists' efforts within these groups. Community became an important point of reference that helped to redirect the actual significance and roles of these groups.

In the following section I will describe the experience of Grupo Cultural Afro Reggae in Rio de Janeiro with regard to these issues. I will try to explain how these movements become delinked from specific places (Gray 1993; Clifford 1988; Hall 1993b) and are only possible in certain contexts.

The Stage Is the Shantytown: Grupo Cultural Afro Reggae

The *Afro Reggae Notícias (ARN),* first published in 1993, labeled itself as a "different newspaper." The difference rested, they explained, in the fact that they wanted to "raise the consciousness of people in special manner. With swing and rhythm."[28] Over the course of three years, *ARN* has published articles and interviews about reggae, rap, hip hop, *blocos afro,* dance, apartheid, and racism in Brazil and in other parts of the world. Curiously, the journal's style did not greatly differ from standards established by similar journals of the black movement published in the 1980s: political information intermixed with columns dedicated to music. Thus, the method of reaching out to the public was not significantly altered. However, music was the central element of the newspaper from the start.

The idea for the publication came from a group of youths who organized dance parties in the central districts of Rio de Janeiro. The dance parties revolved around African rhythms, most notably reggae and funk, and the group enjoyed a faithful following. At the first planning meeting of the "First Reggae Dance" of 1992, they resolved to publish a "cultural journal" that would not only provide information about their dance parties but also about other "Afro-Brazilian" cultural events. It is important to emphasize that the privileged concept of culture, as promoted by Grupo Cultural Afro Reggae (GCAR), was based on a nonexclusive definition. Rarely in *ARN*'s editorials or signed articles do we find references to the concept of a "black culture." In the journal's second issue we find a small indication of this important shift. The editorial does not refer to "Afro-Brazilian culture" but rather to "popular Brazilian culture":

> During this carnival it was more obvious than ever that popular Brazilian culture was badly treated. A true popular culture comes from the backyards, from the *organic meeting of the communities,* in their most creative organizational forms. . . . The most powerful forms of communication were so distant from carnival's designers and participants that they are unable to capture the essence of carnival. We are talking about the style called *axé* music: a curious rubric under which large record companies lump all Black rhythms coming from Bahia. . . . and as if this wasn't enough, they tried to create a fight between the samba schools and the *blocos afro,* forgetting that samba, as a matter of roots, is minimally the godfather of that Afro-Brazilian musical force. It was samba which opened the path for the new generation, extending the spaces in which they could play. For a long time samba was "something only for Blacks." Thus, our position was to put the black into the white *[botar o preto no branco].* We are indeed in the middle of a fight, but it is not this one. The fight is not between us, it is not between tribes and it is against a dominant minority which always selects one culture as better than others. (italics mine)[29]

But the "difference" with respect to the process of raising consciousness could only in fact be produced outside the pages of the journal. The founders of the journal had diverse educational backgrounds. During the period that this research was conducted (1994–1996), the group's governing board consisted of an unemployed chemical technician who made his living selling cassette tapes, compact discs, and silk-screened shirts; a mid-level public servant; a young man who had previously driven a taxi and delivered newspapers; a graduate student in the social sciences; a graduate student in education; a journalist; and a dentist. With one exception (who referred to himself as mestizo), all of the group's members used the term "black" to refer to themselves. This racial self-identification was understood as political and was not just constructed using "racial" criteria. It took into account a variety of influences such as education, life experiences, social origin, phenotypes, and world visions—elements that they imagined to comprise, in malleable form, an image. Although these influences delimited a certain profile that the majority identified as "black," they did not circumscribe the group's activities to a specific location—the "social location" to which Oliveira e Oliveira (1977) referred.

The group's definition of what is political was always enunciated as a subjective matter. The perception existed that their chosen and privileged references, both cultural and territorial, had various facets. In other words, the "social location," which according to Oliveira e Oliveira was constituted by the binomial race and class, became pulverized in the discourse of the members of Grupo Cultural Afro Reggae into a set of multiple possibilities for recasting the terms upon which racial and social contradictions were based. This relative autonomy and the negation of "social determinism" (Calhoun 1994)—be it in the ways they viewed themselves, Brazilian society, or the work they did—would determine the group's choice of collaborators and institutional linkages and its refusal to adopt what Ruben César Fernandes (1989) has called a "collective proper name."

Slater (in this volume) explores the distinction between "politics" and the "political," suggesting the emergence of new questions within an eminently subjective discourse. This does not imply the elimination of the social conditions in which their meanings were constructed. In fact, in the view of the GCAR, their choices with regard to *where* and *how* they should act were intimately related to both their personal histories and their exposure to and participation in what I call "the spaces of sociability of the black movement in Rio." Before they founded the GCAR, some of the members had contact with other black organizations and groups, but these contacts did not grow into any form of sustained activism. The narratives about the group's pre-formative period focus on how their choices were informed by what they identified as "wrong" or "misguided" in previous black activist strategies. Moreover, they identified possible political-institutional linkages according to their own life trajectories. In the various narratives about the emergence of the group, there are references to various, generally personal, encounters, in which without a doubt the contact with black movement activists and institutions appears as a paradigm of either what is rejected or what is desired. In the first case, critiques were directed at possible mistakes in the comprehension and implementation of the black movements' proposals. In the second case, what was highlighted was the success of particular black groups in widening their range of collaborators. In this sense, what could be interpreted as merely a criticism of an essentialist *ethos* regarding what was then conceived of as "black identity" should, in fact, be understood as a strategy to legitimate other types of partnerships and engagement with movement groups, NGOs, and institutions.

The following quotation was presented in a context in which the relationship of Grupo Cultural Afro Reggae to the black movement was questioned. It is understood here as a text that synthesizes my interpretation. Despite the subjective character of this narrative, its ideas are representative of those advanced in the group's journal. This more personal dimension of the narrative should be emphasized, as the role of the group and its future prospects seem to be related to individual life projects; the collective dimension of activism–social intervention is deemphasized. It is interpersonal relationships that propel political projects, no longer seen as "missions" but rather as possibilities for professionalization. In the narrative of an activist, who will be identified here as Paulo, we can find several ways in which individual and collective political projects interact:

> I was never interested in participating organically in these Black movement groups. I believed and continue to believe that these movements are important. It is very important that these movements and these debates exist. However, I have always believed that the theoretical foundations of most of these groups were wrong. In the first place, it is wrong to try to explain Brazil from a perspective grounded in the racial relations of the United States. This is something that has always made me very uncomfortable. Because, if, on the one hand, the question of defining *moreno, mulatto,* and *mestizos* is related to the question of "whitening," on the other hand, this is a concrete fact of our reality. Brazil is a country in which the majority of its population is heteroracial. This does not negate the fact of racism. I have always considered, and I have an example within my home, that racism does not impede sexual, cultural, or social mixing between the races. This is something that even today is called "cordial racism." It is precisely due to cordial racism that the definition of what it means to be a Black in Brazil today must be located within Brazilian reality. Now, how can we do this without weakening the political struggle and without downplaying the existence of racial prejudices? This is the dilemma which I see. But, on the other hand, the proposals of the Black movement did not satisfy me, did not respond to my needs. The projects of the Black movement, such as the movement for reparations or the introduction Nagô/Yorubá language in schools' curriculum, do not have a concrete basis in our reality. I believe that these types of activities are more coherent among the Xhosa in South Africa because you actually have people who speak the language in addition to English. I think that it is important that the Zulus maintain their identity but I do not believe that Nagô or Yorubá are fundamental to our ethnic identity. . . . I distanced myself from groups who organized culturally around African languages because I don't think their discourses say much to society. Today, in the po-

> litical struggle, you have to deconstruct a logic which no longer serves your needs. (interview with author, January 1996)

The GCAR did not necessarily break with its emphasis on racial issues as it reinvented its logic. It did, however, update discourses on race by conjugating them with other issues. Thus, we can perceive several crucial issues in Paulo's narrative. In the first place, the discourse of the black movement is of some concern to Paulo, a participant in the GCAR. This is exemplified in a clear manner, as are many of the themes that have been discussed in this chapter. In particular, whom do the black movements in Brazil imagine that they "represent," what are the privileged means through which this representation can become effective, and at what levels and in which public spaces and institutions should the struggle be carried out? One key question stands out in the narrative: Which language should be used to bring visibility to the racial discrimination and racism that exist in Brazilian society? On the one hand, the GCAR's "myth of origin" is grounded precisely in dance parties and celebrations, in leisure and entertainment; it is not exclusive to specific places or spaces. The need to create alternatives to the previous territorialization of the movement is central to the GCAR. It appears that they are proposing a "deconstructionist" position. In this sense, the black movement is one of the principal interlocutors of the group.

The second set of questions raised by Paulo is linked to a certain discursive logic in which some themes are more prominent from the vantage point of the observer-interviewer. In this sense, it is important to stress that we all speak from particular places. Those places inform the urgency with which we do or do not contemplate issues related to racism, which are, in turn, veiled by our personal projects and life histories. Nonetheless, while this "mixture" of references—either "collective" or "subjective"—appears to increasingly characterize possible interpretations of social movements, it can be seen as the reverse of the excessive use and abuse of categories, reference units, and "collective subjects" (Fernandes 1989) with the aim of establishing difference or distinctiveness.

We can thus understand another alteration operative in the lived experiences of GCAR members. What appears to be at stake is a displacement of a gaze that sees the "other" as an object of transformation from "traditional" into "modern," from "manipulable" into "articulated," from "poor" into "citizen," and from the innumerable racial denominations that inhabit a stream of fluid categories into "black." In other words, notions such as "fluidity," "residuality," and "fragmentation," most strongly identified with sociological discourse, are taken to be, in the words of one GCAR members, "facts of reality" in an effort to understand the obstacles that stood in the way of wider popular adherence to black movement proposals of the past. Curiously, this impasse between a social science discourse *about* blacks and a "reality" supposedly different from that advanced by the black movement's own analysis is revealed in the work of the GCAR in the shantytowns. It was precisely shantytown-based projects that provided examples of a "reality" distinct from the reality that had prevailed in the earlier analyses of the movement.

If the emphasis on the binomial mobilization-consciousness no longer appeared to be relevant or to be a clear objective of the group's project, its rationale was recontextualized by the use of the notion of "citizenship" *(cidadania)*. The guiding idea behind the project was to develop activities that stimulated self-esteem, primarily among children and youths, by providing cultural and educational opportunities as well as some type of occupational training. All of these programs were justified by the need to diminish the social and cultural distance between the residents of the shantytowns and those who live in *"o asfalto"* (literally, "the asphalt," or middle class neighborhoods). The objective was to steer youths away from criminal activities by creating other cultural and professional outlets and opportunities for them. These were seen as important steps to help transform youths from a marginalized inhabitants into citizens. Thus, if consciousness-raising projects and the construction of "black identity" found less emphasis in GCAR discourse, it was because it was replaced by a more contemporary and supposedly more universal concept. GCAR members speak of their intervention projects as promoting "work," "education," and the generation of income—conditions necessary for the activation of citizenship status.[30] GCAR, in claiming status as an NGO, inherited other traditions, associational practices, and strategies designed to encourage "popular participation." This approximation in the activities and discourse of the GCAR resulted in a model of intervention that attempts to patch together the diverse segments of the black movement and the organizational and activist mechanisms typical of NGOs.

This process, which Luís Fernando Dias Duarte (1993) has called "conversion," has important implications in the evaluation of the "citizenship" projects aimed at poor urban communities. Duarte calls attention to a possible analogy between such projects of citizenship and other disciplinary processes that are almost always practices of an authoritarian state. Verónica Schild, in her analysis of the role of the concept of citizenship among NGOs and some women's movements in Chile (in this volume), calls attention to centrality of "nation" in which all possible differences maintain some type of affiliation. In this sense, NGOs as "mediators" (Jelin, in this volume) have a fundamental privileged, intellectual responsibility to interpret and explain reality to those groups, mainly the popular classes, that do not share the same access to privileged forms of knowledge (E. Carvalho 1991). For Duarte, the "difference" between the agents of reason and the popular classes is always conditioned by a hierarchical vision of society; it does not have the permanence of the "resistant difference" of the popular classes. As Duarte says, "it was under the impact of growing disrepute of this model and the concomitant interest and valorization of 'difference' that the first positive concepts of a 'popular culture' were formulated" (1993, 11).

The expansion of public and partnership involvement in the GCAR's projects can be gleaned from their publications. In November 1993, the *ARN* informed its readers in an editorial that "the *ARN,* given the size to which it has grown in such a short time, is now a part of the Grupo Cultural Afro Reggae, which was founded by the same writers and editors of this journal. The GCAR already has various projects underway—always with the goal of producing cultural exchanges—and we will talk about these projects in future editions."[31] One of these projects was the Community Cultural Centers (Núcleos Comunitários de Cultura). The idea for this project developed in a partnership between the GCAR and several NGOs involved in the construction of the Peace House (Casa da Paz*)* in the shantytown of Vigário Geral.[32] The contact with these "communities" and the success of the journal led to the further development of such ideas:

> The need emerged to consolidate the relationship of the group with those populations which are predominately Black and are, therefore, producers of Afro-Brazilian culture, the prime material of the journal. But how to do this? The answer came out of the very heterogeneous composition of the group which was involved in the production of the journal. Cultural producers, social movement activists, journalists, students, etc., who come from different social classes, and who through their experiences—in the shantytowns and *"no asfalto"*—knew the creative potential of these communities. Combining experiences, they decided to bet on the growth of self-esteem through cultural means. They suggested the Community Cultural Centers and so that this project could enjoy a certain autonomy in relation to the journal, the GCAR was created.[33]

It was not only contact with the "communities" and with other NGOs that was fundamental to this change in status. Even before transforming themselves into a cultural group, the GCAR held their meetings at the office of an NGO—the Center for the Articulation of Marginalized Populations (CEAP)—whose links to other NGOs as well as to the black movement are quite strong. It was also as a consequence of this early contact with CEAP that the GCAR's transformation became more evident. The challenge imposed by this first attempt at institutionalization enabled new paths to be taken and new partnerships to be established. As one of the participants explained, there were "contacts" with the most varied social movement sectors, including other black movement groups.

In the narratives of several participants interviewed, issues regarding the role and place of the GCAR in the larger black movement do not appear to require rigid labels or political-institutional affiliations. These affiliations are always defined on the basis of the specific cultural activities developed in the "communities." The models and strategies of political involvement were altered. Grupo Cultural Afro Reggae, even as it rejected the exclusive label of a "black movement group" and began to describe itself as an NGO, has not stopped investing in the issues that define its emblematic support and explain its distinctiveness. It is in this situation that shantytowns appear as one of stages for the group's intervention.

The shantytown as a geographical reference and the "community" as a political reference became the new keys in the group's discourse. The "community" is no longer merely the territory in which the GCAR was formed; it has been transformed into an emblem of its presence—local as well as global. As is the case with numerous *blocos* from Bahia, the "community" is, instead, a conglomerate around which various boundaries, principally socioeconomic and geographic, have been established. To the "community" now belong all those who share an identity imposed by their exclusion and their marginalization. It preexists the intervention of the group and does not have an easily identifiable ethnic profile. It is its marginal character that confers a possible identity. The preferential action in shantytowns presupposes a type of "action in the communities" in which the group makes itself visible but from which it remains distinct.

These activities, therefore, are different from the creation of solidarity networks or the strengthening of political alliances in the face of oppression and marginalization, as described in this volume by Libia Grueso, Carlos Rosero, and Arturo Escobar (in a discussion of black communities on the Pacific coast of Colombia) and by Kay Warren (in a discussion of the Pan-Mayan movement in Guatemala). If there is something that these movements share in common, it is precisely their unique character and the different ways in which "communities" are perceived, constructed, or "imagined." With regard to the GCAR, we can perceive that the valorization of their members' work in shantytown communities becomes an artifact for legitimating their activities vis-à-vis those associational practices in which affinities are established exclusively through recreational activities grounded in an ethnic ethos and identity. In situating itself outside "the community," the GCAR conceives of itself as different from the groups with which it works. The analytical implications of this position are even richer when compared to the example of Oliveira e Oliveira (1974), who by contrast assumes that black identity is constructed as a racialized representation of a "social location." However, as Duarte has demonstrated, the usage of the term "community" to refer to a "conscious and responsible" unit that at the same time is in opposition to society constitutes a type of embarrassment: "When the activists help to construct these communities, they are perhaps effectively contributing to the consolidation of 'communities' which are, in the classical philosophical tradition, in opposition to citizenship" (1993, 15). In this sense, "community" reifies differences and creates boundaries between "us" and "them."

Conclusion

Writing this chapter stimulated me to think about the many "places" from which those who write about the Brazilian black movement speak. When I considered the diverse experiences that resulted in the descriptive and analytical texts written by black activists in the 1970s as well as my own ethnographic experiences with youths who did not intend to have their words crystallized in this fashion, I never imagined that it would be possible to do so from an invisible or untainted place, imposing my own interpretation as a type of "lazy divinity . . . contemplating its creation in order to observe it, register it, and interpret it" (Crapanzano 1991, 69). My intervention had more explicit objectives. I wished to place in question the continual interference of other discourses and positions constructed under explicitly subjective points of view. Borrowing from José Jorge Carvalho:

> Because of a unidimensional position in the politics of identity that has grown with the reality of late transnational capitalism, a politics of alterity that releases the essentialization that accompanies a belligerent posture toward the world has come be seen as archaic or unnecessary. The challenge consists of engineering an organizational form within which the Brazilian experience of *quilombos* might serve as another alternative to contemporary efforts to expand social movements without having to endure a process of conversion and a hardening of the heart. (1996, 6)

In a certain way, I was simultaneously socialized in the environments of social movements and of the social sciences. During the 1970s and 1980s, the discourses of each were only valued when imbricated with the other. Social movements tried to take advantage of the analytical tools provided by the social sciences under the guise of interpreting, describing, and classifying their own activities. In this context, disputes and fissures in the intellectual debate were accompanied by passion and anguish. This is what stands out from my readings of the texts of Eduardo de Oliveira e Oliveira, Beatriz Nascimento, and Lélia González, who were important symbols not only for black activists but also for students who, like me, greatly benefited from the fruits of this tension, which remained latent in subsequent intellectual debates on race that were imagined to be "free" of these impassioned positions.

Curiously, university students, a group to which I belonged during the 1980s, consumed both. What we imagined to be "passion" and "reason" were "converted" to a greater or lesser degree into different representations that both discourses had produced about Brazilian society. The polarization between the "official racial discourse" and the alternative, which would supposedly emerge through the "processes of consciousness raising" (implying cognitive and corporal transformations), hovered amid a spectrum of diffuse situations that ran through personal experiences. The subjective and relational character of these experiences were thus transformed by the assumption that they affected "white" or "black" intellectuals in different ways. If the former privileged the superiority of objectivity and rationality, the latter, if they did not agree, qualified the value of objectivity with the accusation that it was mediated by a kind of "guilt."

"Black intellectuals" were continually confronted with the question of "authenticity." The weight of always being "native," more or less "black," "whitened," "converted," or "representative of foreign discourses" was ever present in their work as scholars. But these visions are not necessarily unique to particular interlocutors. They were always present, although not always explicitly, in the passionate moments of debate about "race" and racism, and many times their presence resulted in arguments about the criteria for evaluating intellectual production. Oliveira e Oliveira (1977) believed that a double insertion conferred legitimacy and power before the object/subject. Beatriz Nascimento (1976) questioned whether it was necessary to take a critical stance on this position. González (1980) positioned herself from a more essentialist vision and argued for a "black point of view."

In this text, I have discussed the distinct positions of diverse interlocutors about culture and politics and the relationship between the two in order to clarify the action and outreach strategies of different segments of the black movement vis-à-vis the communities they purport to represent. In this way, I have tried to draw attention to the provisional character of these visions and their varied meanings as well as by whom they were articulated. The subjective character of the texts analyzed in some ways demonstrates that there was a certain caution in the necessarily partial treatment of texts in the analysis and assumptions of the movement produced by activists. It must be noted that this subjective dimension has always been countered with explicit models and analytical categories formulated by the academic debate. The tension between academic and activist discourses has been marked by efforts to demonstrate how "racial politics" and the "politics of identity" formulated by social movements are imbricated. This tension has also been made explicit in the dialogue among whites, nonwhites, Brazilians, "Brazilianists," leftists, intellectuals, federal agencies, and NGOs, among others.

One of the purposes of this chapter was to call attention to the fact that many of the important shifts in activist discourse accompanied shifts in the academic debate. If during the early years black activists relied upon concepts and terminology imported from Marxism such as "consciousness" and "mobilization," the 1980s saw their gradual substitution by the concept of "identity." Within the processes of "mobilization" and "consciousness raising," the concept of culture was just one aspect that reinforced the distinctive character of the antiracist struggle. During the 1980s, it would assume a central role. From then on, the notion of identity took on new importance. The focus on identity made it possible to articulate that which cannot be articulated: the diffuse, the shapeless. At the same time, it enabled the integration of subjective positions within a collective setting (Calhoun 1996).

Among Bahia's *blocos afro,* this shift resulted in simultaneous moves of divergence and convergence: the polarization between the configuration and primacy of a political *ethos* and the implosion of a multiplicity of more subjective spheres of action and participation. It is in this way that concepts such as *identity* cease to be "analytical categories" and are transformed into "native categories." Stuart Hall offers an analogous frame of reference: the utilization of identity in the discourse of intellectuals and activists in England. Here, instead of disappearing, it is possible to perceive a displacement of the "place" from which identity is enunciated, "no longer producing stability and totalities" (1993b). Parallel to this shift, Hall calls attention to the fact that the discourse of identity is produced by the observer, which has interesting implications for our discussion.

Finally, the case of Grupo Cultural Afro Reggae exemplifies another type of dislocation concerning the place, connections, and ambiguities of a discourse no longer grounded in *racial identity* but rather in *difference.* If the narratives about the black movement and its institutions had historically valorized what was imagined to constitute the *center* rather than the *margins* of antiracist discourse, the example of GCAR forces us to imagine other possible places where we may find the same issues and practices. This redirection only became possible when other connections were made. To speak of *citizenship* may have been a recourse to escape the "logic of identity" and may have called attention to the fact that other identities, not always hierarchically ordered, are at stake. Even though, as I have argued, this new discourse implies new arrangements that are problematic in their political and theoretical matrices, it is with clear impact that the new discourse has penetrated the spaces of the black movement.

Notes

1. "Editorial Comment: On Thinking the Black Public Sphere," *Public Culture* 7, no. 1 (1994):9.

2. My observation of the activities of this group began in December 1994 when I initiated a study about youth, entertainment, and violence in a shantytown in the northern part of Rio de Janeiro, Vigário Geral. During that time, I held a fellowship with the Rockefeller Foundation, the Instituto de Filosofia Ciências e Sócias, and the Universidade Federal do Rio de Janeiro's Race and Ethnicity program. I relied upon the help of a graduate research assistant who was also a member of the Afro-Reggae Cultural Group.

3. Grupo Vissungo, interview, *Versus* 22 (1978):41.

4. The Black Rio organization and the Quilombo samba school, while operating in distinct public spheres, are two important examples of these efforts. Black Rio united large numbers of black youths in dances whose principal theme was inspired by the soul music of the United States. Quilombo, founded by intellectuals and black artists, was committed to researching "black roots" while also resisting the appeal of the commercialization of music and political co-optation. For a further discussion of the origins of Black Rio and its connections to the founding of the "Rio Funk" dances, see Vianna 1988. For a general discussion of these movements and their relationship with black movement activists, see Hanchard 1991. See Lopes 1979 for a defense of Quilombo's proposals.

5. This "rebirth" has, as a point of reference, the varied organizational efforts of the black movement, such as attempts to found political parties and the publication of journals dedicated to debating and denouncing racism, which began early in the twentieth century and continued until the 1964 military coup.

6. See Cardoso 1978 for a discussion of police violence and the black movement.

7. *Quilombos* communities were formed by escaped slaves; they existed throughout Brazil during the seventeenth, eighteenth, and nineteenth centuries.

8. The analogy between resistance and isolation marks historical writings on Brazilian *quilombos*. For a more detailed discussion see Santos Gomes 1995.

9. A study funded UNESCO and carried out by Brazilian and foreign social scientists during the 1950s examined the reality of race relations in Brazil during the period known as "racial harmony."

10. Oliveira e Oliveira's argument makes reference to Carl Degler 1971. Degler addresses the relative malleability of the terms of racial classification and of miscegenation as positive characteristics in Brazil in comparison to the more rigid categories adapted in the United States. Oliveira e Oliveira chose the mulatto as the paradigm of the Brazilian racial impasse (or "epistemological obstacle") in which social ascension depended on a shift in phenotype criteria and the terms of racial self-identification.

11. See Ramos 1995.

12. See R. Pannikar, "Introduction: The Rhetoric of the Dialogue," in *The Intrareligious Dialogue* (New York: Paulist Press, 1978).

13. I agree with the need to rethink the terms of this discussion; it is important to emphasize the differences in how the Brazilian racial system has been constituted. I disagree with Hanchard when he insists that national characteristic should be considered "racial exceptionalism" (1995). Though I agree that we must rethink the terms upon which the discourse emphasizing differences in the Brazilian racial system is framed—which at times verges on vainglorious nationalism—I disagree with Hanchard's lumping of any and all efforts to analyze national vicissitudes under the rubric of "racial exceptionalism." Hanchard (1991) analyzes in greater detail the inability of black movements to either construct a project of popular mobilization or denounce the fallacy of the "myth of racial democracy." For important critiques of Hanchard's analysis, see Fry 1996 and Bairros 1996.

14. The notion of mobilization is not clearly defined in the texts analyzed. Fontaine has a different reading. He defines "mobilization," as defended by members of the MNU, as a transformative project that would unite blacks with other organizations in civil society. See Fontaine 1983, 1985.

15. Maria Beatriz do Nascimento presented her article at the "Week of Studies About the Contribution of Blacks in the Social Formation of Brazil," an annual event that took place for four consecutive years. The event was sponsored by students and intellectuals in the Fluminense Federal University (in the state of Rio de Janeiro). See M. B. Nascimento 1976 and Oliveira e Oliveira 1977.

16. Arthur Ramos, a physician from Bahia who was also known as an anthropologist, was the principal proponent of this position. He was responsible for the systemic "collection" of ethnographic material among Brazilians who were, at that particular time, known as "descendants of Africans" and as "carriers" of an African culture in Brazil. See Beatriz Góes Dantas 1988.

17. Gilberto Freyre, quoted in Chauí 1984, 33.

18. *Blocos* began as cultural and recreational associations of nonwhite youth, whose goal was to enact African and Afro-Brazilian themes in the carnival of the city of Salvador. In the 1980s, *blocos* became more complex as they became linked to other social actors (such as the state, political parties, social movements, and NGOs); some of them evolved into important "cultural groups." The first *afoxés* (to be discussed later) date to the first years of the century; they are almost exclusively black recreational groups staging Afro-Bahian cultural and religious themes in the streets of Salvador during carnival.

19. For a more detailed description of this process see Risério 1981; see also Silva 1988, 275.

20. The "Africanization" of carnival in Salvador was not invented by the *blocos afro*. Nina Rodriques demonstrates that in the beginning of the century (and Peter Fry, Sérgio Carrara, and Ana Luiza Costa demonstrate that in the 1980s) the "societies," "playing" *(tocças)*, and *"afoxés"* consisted of pioneering experiences since they drew upon African themes and Candomblé during carnival. Risério (1981) demonstrates that the *blocos afro* developed a new interpretation of Africa, distancing themselves from traditional rhythms and religions. Above all, the new interpretation was postcolonial and nonreligious. For an in-depth discussion of these issues see Rodriques 1939; Fry, Carrara, and Costa 1988; Morales 1988; Risério 1981.

21. The "Black Conferences" *(Encontros dos Negros)* held in the north and northeast and the south and southeast regions of Brazil are examples of meetings in which issues ranging from the agenda for making demands to the unification of the movement were discussed.

22. The conflict between the traditionalism of older black groups and a new generation of activists and leaders who created the *blocos afro* is discussed by Ana Maria Morales (1988). She makes an interesting comparison between the traditional *afoxé* Sons of Gandhi and the *bloco afro* Ilê Aylê whose membership was limited to blacks.

23. The distinction between activists and *carnavalescos* demonstrates an important difference between the objectives and practices of specific sectors of the black movement. These sectors were, initially, totally opposed to one another.

24. Bloco Carnavalesco Ilê Aiyê, "Pronunciamento do B. C. Ilê Ayiê"—V Encontro de Negros Norte e Nordeste (Salvador, Brazil, May 8, 1985, mimeographed), 2–3.

25. Many of the disputes in the *blocos* between the "culturalists" and the "politicos" occurred with the creation of the advisory committees that were intended to bridge the gap between proposals emphasizing carnival activities and those focusing on community and cultural work. These small working groups enabled leaders of the black movement to participate in the *blocos afro*. However, the role of these working groups was questioned by the *blocos*. In a paper presented by the group Ilê Aiyê at the Evento Secneb 82 entitled "O Conceito de Política Nos Blocos Negros e Afoxés," there was clear skepticism about the objectives and purposes of these new "advisors": "The make-up of the groups had little theoretical understanding of Black Africa and Blacks so they had to turn to white intellectuals who studied Blacks to obtain information about their own culture. These white intellectuals thus became advisors. They brought a particular vision of politics to the leadership, and thereby to the *bloco* and *afoxé* which was generally contrary to the aspirations of their members." In the same form, this conflict was almost always present in power relationships between the advisory committees and leaders of the *blocos*. "The traditional leader wanted the advisory committees to limit themselves to activities which would generate income and increase prestige of the *blocos*. *Négo; boletim informativo do MNU* 3 (March 1982):3; see also Cunha 1991.

26. For a brief overview of the internationalization of Olodum, see "Uma breve história do tempo," *Jornal do Olodum* 2, no. 5 (November 1994):1.

27. João Jorge Rodrigues, "Olodum 15 anos," *Jornal do Olodum* 2, no. 6 (December 1994):1.

28. *Afro Reggae Notícias* 1, no. 0 (January 1993):1.

29. "Preto no Branco," *Afro Reggae Notícias* 1, no. 1 (February-March 1993):2.

30. As Rubem César Fernandes and Leandro Piquet (1991) demonstrate, the principal efforts of NGOs in Brazil revolve around these issues. Sérgio Baierle (in this volume) described the experiences of NGOs in Porto Alegre, calling attention to the vision of citizenship as a passive value to be "redeemed."

31. *Afro Reggae Notícias* 1, no. 4 (November 1993): 2.

32. This project was founded in 1993 in the shantytown of Vigário Geral in Rio de Janeiro after twenty-one residents were assassinated during a police invasion. The House of Peace (Casa de Paz) was built on the site of a house badly damaged by heavy weaponry during the invasion. The house had been owned by a family of Pentecostalists who were killed during the massacre. As a result of the demands of area residents, the House of Peace was constructed through the combined efforts of community organizations, NGOs, churches, and intellectuals. Open every day to the residents of the shantytown, the House of Peace provides courses, lectures, videos, and medical services for children, as well as maintaining a library.

33. "A Cultura para sair do Gueto," *Afro Reggae Notícias* 2, no. 9 (1994):7.

References

Agier, Michel. 1992. "Ethnopolitique: Racisme, Statuts et Mouvement Noir à Bahia." *Cahiers d'Études Africaines* 125 (32):53–81.

Andrews, George Ried. 1992. "Black Political Protest in São Paulo." *Journal of Latin American Studies* 24:147–171.

Assumpção, Leilah Landim. 1993. *A Invenção das Ongs: Do Serviço Invisível à Profissão sem Nome*. Rio de Janeiro: Museu Nacional/Universidade Federal do Rio de Janeiro.

Bairros, Luiza. 1996. "Orfeu and Power: Uma Perspectiva Afro-Americana sobre a Política Racial no Brasil." *Afro-Ásia* 17:173–186.

Caldeira, Teresa Pires do R. 1991. "Direitos humanos ou privilégios de bandidos?" *Novos Estudos* 30:162–174.

Calhoun, Craig. 1994. "Social Theory and the Politics of Identity." In *Social Theory and Politics of Identity*, ed. C. Calhoun. Oxford: Blackwell.

______. 1996. "Multiculturalism and Nationalism, or Why Feeling at Home Is Not a Substitute for Public Space." Paper presented at a UNESCO conference, Cultural Pluralism, Identity, and Globalization, April 10–12, Rio de Janeiro.

Cardoso, Hamilton. 1978. "Cala Boca. Macaco! Polícia Paulista combate possível Pequena Burguesia Negra!" *Versus* 24 (42).

Carvalho, Eduardo Guimarães. 1991. *O Negócio da Terra*. Rio de Janeiro: Editora da UFRJ.

Carvalho, José Jorge. 1996. "Globalização e Simultaneidade de Presenças." Paper presented at the Conselho Internacional de Ciências Sociais/Conjunto Universitário Cândido Mendes, April 10–12, Rio de Janeiro.

Chauí, Marilena. 1984. *Seminários*. São Paulo: Brasiliense.

Clifford, James. 1988. *The Predicament of Culture*. Cambridge: Harvard University Press.

Crapanzano, Vincent. 1991. "Diálogo." *Anuário Antropológico* (Universidade de Brasília) 88:59–80.

Cunha, Olívia Maria Gomes da. 1991. *Corações Rastafari. Lazer, Política e Religião em Salvador*. Rio de Janeiro: Museu Nacional/Universidade Federal do Rio de Janeiro.

Damasceno, Caetana, Sônia Giacomini, and Micênio Santos. 1988. "Catálogo das Entidades do Movimento Negro no Brasil." *Comunicações do Iser* 7 (29).

Dantas, Beatriz Góes. 1988. *Vovó Nagô e Papai Branco*. Rio de Janeiro: Graal.

Degler, Carl. 1971. *Neither Black nor White: Slavery and Race Relations in Brazil and the United States*. New York: Macmillan.

Douglas, Mary. 1977. *Pureza e Perigo*. São Paulo: Perspectiva.

Duarte, Luís Fernando Dias, et al. 1993. "Vicissitudes e Limites à Cidadania nas Classes Populares Brasileiras." *Revista Brasileira de Ciências Sociais* 22 (8):5–19.

Fernandes, Rubem César. 1989. "Cultura Brasileira: Como Falar do seu Futuro?" *Comunicações do ISER* 8 (33):36–42.

Fernandes, Rubem César, and Leandro Piquet. 1991. *Ongs Anos 90: A Opinião dos Dirigentes Brasileiros*. Rio de Janeiro: Núcleo de Pesquisa do ISER.

Fischer, Michael M. 1986. "Ethnicity and the Post-Modern Arts of Memory." In *Writing Culture*, ed. J. Clifford and G. E. Marcus. Berkeley: University of California Press.

Fontaine, Pierre Michel. 1983. "Models of Economic Development and Systems of Race Relations: The Brazilian Development and the Afro-Brazilian Condition." In *Movimentos Sociais Urbanos, Minoriais Étnicas e Outros Estudos*, ed. L. A. Silva, et al. Brasília: ANPOCS.

Fontaine, Pierre Michel, ed. 1985. *Race, Class, and Power in Brazil.* Los Angeles: Center for Afro-American Studies, University of California at Los Angeles.

Fry, Peter. 1996. "O Que é Que a Cinderela Negra tem a Dizer Sobre a 'Política Racial' no Brasil." *Revista USP* 28:122–135.

Fry, Peter, Sérgio Carrara, and Ana Luiza Costa. 1988. "Negros e Brancos no Carnaval da Velha República." In *Escravidão e Invenção da liberdade; estudos sobre o negro no Brasil,* ed. J. J. Reis. São Paulo: Brasiliense.

Gilroy, Paul. 1992. "Cultural Studies and Ethnic Absolutism." In *Cultural Studies,* ed. L. Grossberg, C. Nelson, and P. Treichler. New York: Routledge.

______. 1993a. "The End of Antiracism." In "*Race,*" *Culture, and Difference*, ed. A. Rattansi and J. Donald. London: Sage.

______. 1993b. *The Black Atlantic: Modernity and Double Consciousness.* London: Verso.

Gomes, Flávio dos Santos. 1996. "Ainda os Quilombos: Repensando a Construção de Símbolos de Identidade Étnica no Brasil." In *Política e Cultura: visões do passado e perspectivas contemporâneas,* ed. E. Reis et al., 197–221. São Paulo: Hucitec/ANPOCS.

Gonzáles, Lélia. 1980. "O Movimento Negro na Útima Década." In *O Lugar do Negro*, ed. L. Gonzáles and C. Hasenbalg. Rio de Janeiro: Marco Zero.

______. 1985. "The Unified Black Movement: A New Stage in Black Political Mobilization." In *Race, Class, and Power in Brazil,* ed. P. Fontaine. Los Angeles: Center for Afro-American Studies, University of California at Los Angeles.

______. 1988. "A Categoria Político-Cultural da Amefricanidade." *Tempo Brasileiro* 92–93 (June-July): 69–82.

Gray, Herman. 1993. "African-American Political Desire and Seductions of Contemporary Cultural Politics." *Cultural Studies* 7 (3):364–373.

Guattari, Félix. 1981. *Revolução Molecular: Pulsações políticas do Desejo.* São Paulo: Brasiliense.

Hall, Stuart. 1992. "Cultural Studies and Its Theoretical Legacies." In *Cultural Studies,* ed. L. Grossberg, C. Nelson, and P. Treichler. New York: Routledge.

______. 1993a. "New Ethnicities." In "*Race,*" *Culture, and Difference,* ed. A. Rattansi and J. Donald, 252–259. London: Sage.

______. 1993b. "Old and New Identities, Old and New Ethnicities." In *Culture, Globalization, and the World-System,* ed. A. King. London: Macmillan; Albany: State University of New York Press.

Hanchard, Michael. 1991. "Orpheus and Power: The Movimento Negro in Rio de Janeiro and São Paulo, Brazil, 1945–1988." Ph.D. diss., Princeton University.

______. 1992. "Culturalism versus Cultural Politics: The Movimento Negro in Rio de Janeiro and São Paulo, Brazil, 1970–1988." In *The Violence Within: Cultural and Political Analyses of National Conflict,* ed. K. Warren. Boulder: Westview Press.

______. 1994. "Black Cinderella? Race and the Public Sphere in Brazil." *Public Culture* 7 (1):165–185.

______. 1995. "Fazendo a Exceção: Narrativas de Igualdade Racial no Brasil, no México e em Cuba." *Estudos Afro-Asáticos* 28:203–218.

Hasenbalg, Carlos, and Nelson do Valle Silva. 1993. "Notas Sobre Desigualdade Racial e Política no Brasil." *Estudos Afro-Asiáticos* 25:141–160.

Lopes, Nei. 1979. "Samba e ascensão social: uma utopia." *Revista de Cultura Vozes* 73 (3):43–50

Mitchell, Michael. 1977. *Racial Consciousness and the Political Attitudes and Behavior of Blacks in São Paulo, Brazil.* Ann Arbor: University of Michigan Press.

______. 1985. "Blacks and the Abertura Democrática." In *Race, Class, and Power in Brazil,* ed. P. Fontaine. Los Angeles: Center for Afro-American Studies, University of California at Los Angeles.

Morales, Ana Maria. 1988. "O Afoxé Filhos de Gandhi pede Paz." In *Escravidão e Invenção da liberdade; estudos sobre o negro no Brasil,* ed. J. J. Reis, 264–274. São Paulo: Brasiliense.

Nascimento, Maria Beatriz do. 1976. "Culturalismo e Contracultura." In *Semana de Estudos Sobre a Contribuição do Negro na Formação Social Brasileira,* ed. Grupo Cultural André Rebouças, 2–6. Niterói, Brazil: Universidade Federal Fluminense.

Nascimento, Maria Ercília do. 1989. *A Estratégia da Desigualdade: O Movimento Negro nos Anos 70.* São Paulo: Pontifica Universidade Catolica.

Oliveira e Oliveira, Eduardo de. 1974. "Mulato, um Obstáculo Epistemológico." *Argumento* 1 (3):65–73.

______. 1977. "Etnia e Compromisso Cultural." In *Semana de Estudos Sobre a Contribuição do Negro na Formação Social Brasileira,* ed. Grupo Cultural André Rebouças, 22–28. Niterói: Universidade Federal Fluminense.

Peirano, Mariza. 1986. "Sem lenço, Sem documento." *Sociedade e Estado* 1 (1):49–64.

Ramos, Guerreiro. 1995. "Para uma sociologia militante." In *Introdução Crítica à Sociologia Brasileira.* Rio de Janeiro: Editora UFRJ.

Risério, Antônio. 1981. *Carnaval Ijexá.* Salvador, Brazil: Corrupio.

Rodriques, Nina. 1939. *Os Africanos no Brasil.* São Paulo: Cia. Editora Nacional.

Sansone, Lívio. 1995. "Mudar o Imudável: Políticas Públicas e Desigualdades Raciais no Brasil." Paper presented at the nineteenth ANPOCS Annual Conference, October 21–27, Caxambu, Brazil.

Santos, Joel Rufino dos. 1985. "O Movimento Negro e a Crise Brasileira." *Política and Administração* 2 (July-September):285–308.

Santos Gomes, Flávio dos. 1995. "Quilmbos, Zumbi, e Palmares: Repensando a construção de símbolos de identidade étnica no Brasil" Paper presented at the nineteenth Reunião Anual de Associação Brasileira de Pós-Graduação em Ciência Sociais (ANPOCS), October, Caxambu, Brazil.

Schelling, Vivian, and William Rowe. 1993. *Memory and Modernity: Popular Culture in Latin America.* London: Verso.

Seyferth, Giralda. 1983. "Etnicidade e Cidadania: Algumas Considerações sobre as Bases Étnicas da Mobilização Política." *Boletim do Museu Nacional* 42:1–16.

Silva, Jônatas Conceição da. 1988. "Histórias de Lutas Negras: Memórias do Surgimento do Movimento Negro na Bahia." In *Escravidão e Invenção da Liberdade: Estudos Sobre o Negro no Brasil,* ed. J. Reis, 275–288. São Paulo: Brasiliense.

Turner, J. Michael. 1985. "Brown into Black: Changing Racial Attitudes of Afro-Brazilian University Students." *Race, Class, and Power in Brazil,* ed. P. Fontaine. Los Angeles: Center for Afro-American Studies, University of California at Los Angeles.

Vianna, Hermano, Jr. 1988. *O Mundo Funk Carioca.* Rio de Janeiro: Jorge Zahar.

West, Cornel. 1992. "The Postmodern Crisis of the Black Intellectuals." In *Cultural Studies,* ed. L. Grossberg, C. Nelson, and P. Treichler. New York: Routledge.

Wade, Peter. 1990. "'Race,' Nature, and Culture." *Man* 28:17–34.

Winant, Howard. 1993. "Rethinking Race in Brazil." *Journal of Latin American Studies* 24:173–192.

Chapter Ten

Beyond the Domestic and the Public: Colonas *Participation in Urban Movements in Mexico City*

MIGUEL DÍAZ-BARRIGA

No nos importó que los esposos se enojasen con nosotras, que nos bronqueran. Nosotros venimos arrastrando una cadena de miseria en este país, las gentes más jodidas. No tener casa implica una serie de problemas y los señores estaban acostumbrados a que las mujeres estábamos dispuestas a perder todo, menos el marido. Nomás que llegando aquí cambió totalmente la situación. . . . Entendimos que defender la familia significa ser ¡libres!, ¡no libertinas!, que mucha gente ha confundido la situación. . . . "Ah esas viejas revoltosas, izquerdistas, mitoteras, guerrilleras, marimachas." No es cierto, nosotras fuimos mujeres de no desprendernos de nuestras obligaciones de mujeres, pero nos dimos el tiempo para andar en la lucha. Hacíamos de comer en la noche y nuestros esposos no se quedaban sin comer.

It did not matter to us that our spouses got mad at us, that they fought with us. In this country we, the people who are the most screwed over, carry around a chain of misery. Not having a house implies a series of problems and men are accustomed to think that women are capable of losing everything, except their husbands. However, once we arrived here [to this neighborhood] this completely changed the situation. We understood that defending our family means being free, not being loose women. Indeed, many people have misunderstood our situation. They say, "Ah, these rebellious women, leftists, big-mouths, guerrillas, tomboys." This is not true! We were not women who put aside our responsibilities, we created time to participate in the struggle. We always prepared the evening meal and our husbands were never left without something to eat.

—Pilar, a participant in the urban movement of Campamento 2 de Octubre[1]

In Mexico City's low-income neighborhoods *(colonias populares),* women who involve themselves in urban movements are usually put down as *libertinas* (loose women), *viejas revoltosas* (rebellious old women), *mitoteras* (bigmouths), or *marimachas* (tomboys). Pilar, the author of this chapter's epigraph, who participated in the urban movement (UM) in Campamento 2 de Octubre during the 1970s, emphasizes the contradictory pressures that women faced as they attempted to maintain their traditional "domestic" responsibilities and at the same time engage in grassroots organizing. Pilar both justifies her participation in UMs *(significa ser libres, no libertinas)* and emphasizes her ability to fulfill her domestic tasks. Pilar's recounting of her participation in UMs thus challenges *and* reinforces traditional notions of women in the domestic sphere. My goal in this chapter is to characterize the contested terrain of the domestic and public spheres that resulted from women's participation in UMs. I start by describing how women have challenged traditional notions of the domestic-public and then show how transcending this dichotomy has involved generating new understandings of politics and development.

Initially, research on UMs in Latin America emphasized the structural factors behind the political marginalization of the poor and the lack of services and housing (Epstein 1973; Perlman 1976). This research described in detail the land tenure conflicts and urban service issues that conditioned the emergence of UMs. By the 1980s, urban researchers began shifting their focus from structural factors to the production of urban meaning and cultural identities (Canel 1992; Castells 1983; Díaz-Barriga 1996; Vélez-Ibáñez 1983). This shift was a result of both the widening of UM projects to include urban planning and gender issues, and the rise of new theoretical concerns in social movement research (Escobar and Alvarez 1992; Calderón and Reyna 1990; Calderón, Piscitelli, and Reyna 1992). At the same time, researchers began to rewrite the history of UMs by developing typologies and analyzing political strategies (Bennett 1992, 1993; Farrera Araujo and Prieto Hernández 1986; Hernández 1987; Perló and Schteingart 1984; Ramírez Saíz 1986, 1990; Tamayo 1989) and by focusing on women's participation in urban organizing (Massolo 1983, 1989, 1992; Stephen 1992). This focus, as Elizabeth Jelin notes, has included looking at how women have challenged dominant gender ideologies by generating new links between the domestic and public spheres.

> In the context of the ideology of the dominant patriarchal society, the two spheres [domestic and public] are seen as opposed: in order to participate outside the household the woman must neglect her domestic tasks, abandoning her family role. A deeper analysis of what happens in the domestic sphere reveals that, arising from the specific role of woman-housekeeper or wife-mother, women have a potential for organizing, participating and transforming that needs to be discovered and analysed. (Jelin 1990, 7–8)

To highlight these potentials, researchers have focused on the continuities that poor women have established between these spheres (Blondet 1990; Brugada 1986;

Caldeira 1990; Logan 1990) as well as on the processes through which women have identified first practical and later gender-based needs (Brugada 1986; Lind 1992; Molyneux 1985; Moser 1989). For the most part, theorizing on women's participation in UMs has explored how poor women have both deployed domestic discourses (such as motherhood) in the public domain and increasingly organized around gender needs and issues (Martin 1990). This focus on bridging domestic and public space and identifying broader sets of needs has, however, limited our understanding of the differing ways in which poor women *(colonas)* have conceptualized participation in UMs and contextualized understandings of needs.

In this chapter, I apply the "borderlands concept" to emphasize how, through a variety of strategies, *colonas* blur the distinction between the domestic and public spheres and simultaneously identify practical and gender needs. The borderlands concept, as developed for Chicana feminism by Gloria Anzaldúa (1987) and for the field of anthropology by Renato Rosaldo (1989), calls for attention to the creative ways in which social actors navigate the intersections of social experience. As Anzaldúa and Rosaldo note, borderland zones are a response to dominant ideologies and societies that attempt to order social experience into strict dichotomies—for example, the maintenance of a strict differentiation between European and Mexican cultures in the United States. Social actors who occupy the intersections of social experience, such as Chicanas/Chicanos, are engaged in processes of cultural hybridization that involve political struggle, improvisation, and a tolerance for ambiguity (Anzaldúa 1987, 79–80; Rosaldo 1989, 216–217). These borderland experiences represent not only the bridging of social experiences but also the transforming of cultural meanings and social relations. In the case of *colonas* participation in UMs, I apply the borderlands concept to highlight how women's involvement defies dichotomous representations of domestic and public life. I emphasize that in blurring distinctions between the domestic and public, *colonas* have both challenged and reinforced the cultural and political meanings of women's subordination as well as inhabited a social space wrought with ambiguity, irony, and conflict.

In what follows, I draw upon the personal accounts of three women who participated in UMs in Mexico City—Ursula, Doña Jovita, and Pilar—to describe how *colonas* have navigated the conflicts and violence associated with grassroots organizing. I specifically focus on how these *colonas* have redefined needs, welded everyday life *(lo cotidiano)* into development planning, and re/invented ways of doing politics. My findings are partially based upon field research that I conducted on the ethnohistory of UMs from 1970 to 1990 in a southern district of Mexico City. As part of my field research, I collected accounts of participation in UMs in the region, including that of Ursula, who was one of the best-known UM leaders in Mexico City during the 1970s—she led the UM in Lomas de Padierna. Unlike Doña Jovita and Pilar, Ursula became the leader of the UM in her *colonia,* one of the few women to direct a UM during this time. An activist group, the Revolutionary Movement of the People (Movimiento Revolucionario del Pueblo, or

TABLE 10.1 Sources for Case Studies

Colonia (Neighborhood)	*Account and Source*	*History*
Padierna	*Ursula* (Díaz Barriga 1995)	Díaz Barriga 1995
Ajusco	*Doña Jovita* (MRP n.d.)	Alonso 1980
Campamento 2 de Octubre	*Pilar* (Massolo 1992)	Castells 1983

MRP), published Doña Jovita's oral history as part of its attempt to organize women in the low-income neighborhoods (MRP n.d.). The account, which is well known among *colonas* active in grassroots organizing, describes Doña Jovita's participation in the UM in the *colonia* Ajusco during the 1970s. Alejandra Massolo, in her volume *Por Amor y Coraje: Mujeres en Movimientos Urbanos de la Ciudad de México* (1992), collected four accounts of women who participated in grassroots organizing during the 1970s. These accounts, which include Pilar's, focus on a variety of themes including initial attempts by women to organize themselves independently of the male-dominated structure of their respective UMs.[2]

Urban Movements in Mexico City

During the 1970s, UMs emerged in many low-income areas of Mexico City, including in the *colonias* Lomas de Padierna, Ajusco, and Campamento 2 de Octubre. To analyze the emergence of UMs in Mexico City during the 1970s, one must first understand the significance of the massacre of student activists at Tlatelolco on October 2, 1968. Indeed, the organization of UMs was the result of a change in the strategies of student activists that resulted from the massacre. Many activist groups changed their political programs from directly challenging the state to attempting to form a broader protest movement across society by working directly with *colonos, campesinos* (peasants), and *obreros* (workers). In their accounts of participating in grassroots organizing, Ursula, Doña Jovita, and Pilar all make reference to activists working in their *colonias.* Ursula, for example, talks about how activists helped her in formulating demands and in organizing community projects such as the maintenance of a popular school. Pilar talks about the legacy of the 1968 massacre, noting that Mexicans will never forget how the blood of those killed spawned many social movements (Massolo 1992, 247).

Activists from a variety of newly formed groups, including the Popular Independent Front (*Frente Popular Independiente,* or FPI), worked directly with *colonos* to organize marches and grassroots development projects as well as to help articulate demands for land rights (the FPI was active both in Lomas de Padierna and Campamento 2 de Octubre).[3] In many *colonias,* the police and landholders attempted to forcefully evict *colonos*—in Campamento 2 de Octubre they went so far as to burn down the *colonia.* Once *colonos* successfully resisted these attempts at eviction—by organizing defense committees and staging marches—the state began legalizing land tenure by charging *colonos* for land, a process known as land regularization.

During the 1970s, this process generated a whole new set of conflicts as *colonos* and the state disagreed over land prices, urban zoning issues, and plot sizes.

Paradoxically, for political activists who were attempting to form a social protest movement during the 1970s, demands for land rights ultimately involved state intervention and the eventual demobilization of many UMs. As Alan Gilbert and Peter Ward (1985) point out, state land regularization policies have had a mixed record of success in benefiting the urban poor. The regularization process "opens up the land market to higher-income groups unprepared to occupy illegal land" and sometimes involves charging land and service taxes at rates the poor cannot afford (251). In some cases land regularization may not have been necessary: "The wish to regularize land titles may emanate from the authorities. It may be linked to new taxes, it may encourage an attitude of support for the government in power. Rather than enjoying full legality the poor may be content with the knowledge that they will not be turned off their land." (251)

Although the goal of land regularization is to grant land tenure rights to *colonos,* the state has—through a combination of repression and co-optation—used the process to demobilize UMs (Pezzoli 1987, 385). It is within the history of these struggles for land and urban services that we must contextualize the participation of *colonas* in UMs. As we shall see in the accounts of women's participation in UMs, many *colonas* have conceptualized the corruption, co-optation, and repression that emerged during the land regularization process as aspects of a male-dominated public sphere. Women first organized in all three *colonias*—Lomas de Padierna, Campamento 2 de Octubre, and Ajusco—to demand land tenure and services. Indeed, Ursula, Doña Jovita, and Pilar all discuss their participation in UMs in terms of the struggles for land tenure and conflicts with land regularization agencies such as FIDEURBE (the Trust for Urban Development).

Ursula, Doña Jovita, and Pilar were each from migrant families who had moved to various areas of the city before participating in a land takeover to obtain housing. Ursula moved to the *colonia* Padierna in 1970 from another area in the center of Tlalpan (a political ward in the southern part of Mexico City). She arrived in Padierna as a single mother. Doña Jovita migrated to Mexico City with her husband from a village in Zacatecas while in her late teens or early twenties—she was married at seventeen and says that she and her husband moved to Mexico City a few years later (MRP n.d., 9). After being evicted from one area, they searched for another place to live, finally arriving at what is now the *colonia* Ajusco at a time when it was barely settled. Pilar, also after settling in another area of Mexico City, moved to Campamento 2 de Octubre in 1972, when the movement was beginning to reach its highest levels of intensity. Pilar, who worked as a manual laborer at a university, was also a single mother. By participating in grassroots organizing, these women partially challenged traditional constructions of gender identities based on women's roles in the domestic sphere. As Pilar's quotation at the beginning of this chapter suggests, the reality of the domestic-public dichotomy—as an ideology that aids in maintaining traditional gender relations—exists side by side with the possibilities for transforming its meaning. In the case of UMs, this reconfiguration has been mediated through a variety of strategies.

The Channeling of Needs

The reason why poor women, and the poor in general, participate in UMs is perhaps straightforward: they are seeking a way to satisfy basic needs such as housing, water, and economic subsistence. This answer, however, is more complex than it may seem because the politics of needs is linked to an array of power relations (Escobar and Alvarez 1992, 320). Scott Mainwaring (1987), in his research on UMs in Rio de Janeiro and São Paulo, rightly argues that the perception of needs does not directly lead to participation in social movements but rather is linked to a wide array of social forces, including activist groups organizing in the favelas. This is also true of UMs in Mexico City, where grassroots organizing, and indeed the spread of needs discourses, were the result of a collaboration between *colonos* and activists. As Vivienne Bennett points out in her history of UMs in Mexico City, activists and *colonos* criticized the state for being unable to satisfy the basic land and housing needs of the urban poor (1992, 245). This use of the term *necesidad* to describe grassroots organizing was evident in my fieldwork. For example, in a document distributed throughout Lomas de Padierna, activists defined the goals of the UM in terms of *necesidad:* "As in many other *colonias*, in Padierna we have waged a constant struggle in order to satisfy our *necesidades;* to obtain a piece of land where we can live, for the education of our children, for the legalization of our plots, and for the introduction of basic services like electricity, potable water, streets, and medical clinics along with other services."[4]

As I have shown in an earlier work, the discourse of *necesidad* is deployed by a variety of actors—including both grassroots activists and state agencies—to justify development programs and mediate land tenure conflicts (Díaz Barriga 1996).[5] Indeed, as Ursula, Doña Jovita, and Pilar discuss, there were many conflicts between activists, groups of *colonos,* and the state over strategies to provide land tenure and services.

Carolyn Moser (1989) and Amy Conger Lind (1992) have described how women's organizations within UMs have expanded their agendas from basic or practical needs to strategic needs. These strategic needs, according to Moser, are based on using gender identity to challenge the sexual division of labor (1989, 1803). Lind, in her overview of women's organizations in Ecuador, shows how "poor women in urban areas often base their politics on a certain set of 'needs' derived from their reproductive roles" (1992, 139). Lind demonstrates how these women's groups integrate practical and strategic needs in their struggles for housing, services, and gender equality. A similar process is described by Clara Brugada (1986) in her writing on UMs in Mexico City. Brugada points out that because of the lack of urban services, women begin to see the need for participating in UMs. This need, according to Brugada, becomes part of a series of strategic needs based on the opposition of family members, including husbands, to the reorganization of domestic tasks as women spend more time at protests and meetings (1986, 13–15). This linear relation between practical and strategic needs, however, represents only one possibility for their articulation. For Ursula, Doña Jovita, and Pilar there is a constant blurring and integration of needs so that it is difficult to represent their activism in terms of one set of needs leading to another. Indeed, as I will discuss, the very ways in which each woman contextualizes *necesidades* varies.

Ursula arrived to the *colonia* Padierna just as activists from the Popular Independent Front and *colonos* were beginning to mobilize. According to Ursula, she participated in grassroots organizing to resolve her need for housing. Because the land takeover occurred on the Padierna *ejido,* urban settlers were evicted on a number of occasions by *ejidatarios* (farmers on the *ejidos*). *Ejidos* were farms established by the Mexican government as part of a land reform program after the 1910–1920 revolution. A number of *ejidos* that formed near Mexico City were later incorporated into the expanding city—a process that was often violent as the urban poor sought to obtain land on *ejidos.*

I asked Ursula if she knew about the violence that was occurring as a result of *ejidatarios* evicting settlers. Ursula discussed how she became involved in urban politics in terms of the anger she felt when *ejidatarios* tore her house down.

> I did not know what the problems were when I came here. They [the leaders of the land invasion] told me, "We are going to give you a lot; you pick which one." I went looking around, not knowing what problems I was going to have. Then they brought me to the far side of the *colonia;* there were only rocks. I told them that I was single and did not have anyone to help me level the ground and remove stones. Then I saw a plot that had one wall and was level. I said to myself, "It is pretty here. I like it. Here is where I am going to stay." It was the biggest conflict that I have ever experienced. I was ignorant, new to the area. And here in front of me were the *ejidatarios* who were against us. I put up my shack and the next day the *ejidatarios* with their people tore it down. Well, there my *coraje* [anger, courage] began. When my home was destroyed something inside me awoke. Before this happened I was calm and passive, but afterwards I became angry. . . . This is when I began to get involved in the movement without even wanting to become involved![6]

Through her participation in the women's committee, whose worked focused mainly on the organization of a primary school, Ursula gradually rose to a leadership position in the *colonia.* She talked about her first experiences in UMs in terms of learning about the conflicts that the poor faced and the ways in which demands were made on the state. For example, in a meeting with other leaders of UMs, Ursula tells how she learned about making demands. I should note that the mention of Francisco de la Cruz in the following passage is significant since at that time he was the leader of Campamento 2 de Octubre.

> I remember the first time that I was sent as part of a commission. . . . the protest was organized by Francisco de la Cruz and I went as part of the commission from

> Padierna. . . . they gave me a pencil and they told me—I remember this very well—they told me, "here is your pencil and your card, write out your petitions" and I said, "petitions, what are petitions?" . . . Later Francisco de la Cruz told me that they were the *necesidades* that existed in our *colonia*. And I replied, "why didn't you say so?"[7]

Ursula then points out that in her original set of demands she did not include land regularization; she did not see this as part of the *necesidades* of the *colonia* such as potable water.

Although her participation clearly broke the stereotype of women's roles in UMs as followers rather than leaders, Ursula did not mention making gender issues a central focus of her political agenda. When I asked her about being a woman and leading the *colonia*, she insisted that she had been chosen by the community.

> I did not represent the *colonia*. I did not have an official post. I was a part of the committee of defense of the *colonia*. I was also working on the problem of water and the painting of the water barrels. A moment arrived when people began to come to see me about their problems. I would tell them, "Let's go and try to solve these problems," and we would organize ourselves and go see the government officials. We hung a bell at the school and whenever there was a problem we would ring it and the people would gather to see what was going on, to find out if the police or *ejidatarios* had torn down someone's house. The people started to come to see me if there was a problem.[8]

Led by Ursula, women became key actors in resisting attempts by the state to evict *colonos*. As Ursula pointed out, the police were less likely to detain or use physical violence against women. When I interviewed Ursula, she emphasized how *colonas* captured men who were attempting to evict their neighbors—in one case they even imprisoned, for three days, a group of men who attempted to evict a single mother. Ursula talked about the inability of male leaders in the *colonia* to argue with authorities; according to her, she rose to a leadership position because she was more willing to confront state officials.

Like Ursula, when Doña Jovita settled into her *colonia* she immediately became part of a conflict over land rights. These conflicts first revolved around various attempts to force *colonos* to pay for land as a prelude to the regularization of land tenure. As *colonos* settled in Ajusco they attempted to organize themselves, eventually allying with activist groups, in order to gain land tenure rights. The discourse of *necesidad* was employed by Doña Jovita to justify her participation in UMs despite criticism from community members and her family, especially her husband. In her account of participating in UMs, Doña Jovita tells how her husband opposed her attempts to organize women in her neighborhood (MRP n.d.). Doña Jovita points out, "Women have known how to form a dynamic organization in this neighborhood, we have known how to form a powerful movement as women, as mothers, because we have felt the *necesidad* of protecting, of caring for the patrimony of our children" (MRP n.d., 35). The use of the word "patrimony" *(patrimonio)* in this context is especially revealing because it shows the extent to which *necesidad* can be an aspect of reproducing traditional household relations. In this sense, Doña Jovita's testimony centers on, to use Carolyn Moser's phrase, the "practical needs" to maintain the household. Indeed, participation in land takeovers is especially difficult for women since, in many cases, they must maintain their household despite the lack of basic services such as water, electricity, and sanitation. Doña Jovita, however, simultaneously identifies "strategic needs." In her testimony, Doña Jovita constantly brings up how her husband initially criticized her for engaging in politics. She is critical of her husband and of men in general because they leave everything to women, including housework, the education of the children, and the procurement of a home and land (MRP n.d., 31).

In Campamento 2 de Octubre, as in Lomas de Padierna and Ajusco, there were sharp struggles over land tenure between *colonos,* the state, and landowners. These struggles often entailed pitched battles with the police. Pilar, in her oral history of participation in the UM in Campamento 2 de Octubre, explains how women worked together to demand land tenure rights while they simultaneously provided basic services for the community, such as a school. In one case, a group of women tore down a police guard station and used the materials to build a kindergarten. When the police questioned the women, they justified their actions in terms of *necesidad.*

> They [the police] had changes of the guard and during one change we said, "let's do it"—these guard houses of sheet metal weigh a lot but we were a huge number of women. When the police arrived they no longer had a guard station and we had a kindergarten for our children. There was a fight and we beat the police and left telling them, "We have this *necesidad*." They replied, "This is not possible, [the guard station] is here so that the police will not get sunburned or wet." And we replied, "That's too bad, we already took it." (Massolo 1992, 253)

Later, Pilar extends the *necesidad* argument to a range of women's issues including abortion rights.

> This is one need, among many, of Mexican society. This service ought to be free for all women. For example single women have *necesidades* that people do not understand. What do they want them to be, prostitutes? They see a single woman with a child and they say that this woman has become a prostitute. . . . Many people are beginning to understand this problem and the *necesidades* of their daughters, and of their daughters-in-law—we discuss these matters in our meetings—the women understand. But what happens! They go to church and there they are exposed to propaganda. (Massolo 1992, 276)

In both of these passages, Pilar expresses the hope that by recognizing people's *necesidades,* claims for urban services and reproductive rights can overcome the power of the police and the church.

For each of these *colonas, necesidad* forms part of a borderland region between the domestic and public spheres; between challenging perceptions of women as primarily maintainers of the household and criticizing the state for being unable to satisfy the urban poor's *necesidades*. The ways in which they contextualize these *necesidades* vary according to their experiences and individual perspectives. For Ursula, the need for housing moves her into wider conflicts and broader participation in grassroots organizing. Doña Jovita emphasizes the need to provide for a future for her children and criticizes men who do not allow women to participate in grassroots organizing. Finally, Pilar justifies political action in terms of *necesidad* and talks about wider gender issues, such as abortion rights, in terms of recognizing women's *necesidades*.

Welding Development Alternatives with *Lo Cotidiano*

A number of researchers of UMs have pointed to *lo cotidiano* (the everyday) as a means of generating alternative modes of development (Hiernaux 1988, 75; Sandoval 1991, 305).[9] Elizabeth Jelin argues that *lo cotidiano* represents an intersection between the institutionalized level of politics and identity, and local and family-based practices that both challenge and reproduce dominant culture (1987, 11). Research on *lo cotidiano,* as Arturo Escobar points out, is still at an incipient stage mainly because it implies a focus on culture as practice and involves understanding politics not only as what he terms the "macro aspects of protest" but as an attempt to reimagine everyday life (1992, 70–71). For the case of UMs, I would argue that the interaction of everyday life with the political-institutional must be understood in terms of the organization of urban space. As *colonos* settle into an area, there is an immediate attempt to plan the layout of their neighborhood, usually involving activist groups. As the state begins to negotiate with *colonos* about their remaining in the area by making land payments, a whole series of issues emerge over plot sizes, land prices, and spaces for public services. These planning issues, especially the state's attempts to charge market prices for land and control the allocation of plots, were a major point of conflict between the state and UMs during the 1970s. These conflicts often involved groups of *colonas* directly confronting the police.

There are a variety of levels in which the UMs in Lomas de Padierna, Ajusco, and Campamento 2 de Octubre can be understood as interrelating *lo cotidiano* with grassroots organizing and development issues. Here, I refer not only to the ways in which *colonos* organized to gain basic services such as a water supply but also to a wider set of issues about the design of their neighborhood. For example, when *colonos* took over land in Lomas de Padierna, they set aside areas for parks, playgrounds, and a primary school that they also administered; and they allocated plots at 500 square meters per family. *Colonos* also insisted that they maintain control over the design and construction of their own housing to allow for the building of extended family units as well as the cultivating of gardens.

By the mid-1970s, the state began to negotiate with *colonos* in Lomas de Padierna over land tenure rights through the newly created agency FIDEURBE (the Trust for Urban Development). A key issue for UMs became the spatial organization of the *colonia,* including such variables as plot sizes and parklands. These spaces, which defined the experiences of *lo cotidiano,* became a focal point of conflict. FIDEURBE proposed the building of subsidized housing units, small two-unit homes that would fit on plots of 250 square meters. This reduction of the plot size, as well as the design of standardized homes, were immediately rejected by *colonos.* With the larger plot sizes of 500 square meters, *colonos* would be able to build housing for their extended families as well as in many cases have space to raise animals and cultivate gardens. Ursula told me how *colonos* captured FIDEURBE engineers to protest the construction of subsidized housing.

> In 1974, the state made the policy that FIDEURBE would enter the *colonia* to build houses. They even did an exhibition of the homes they would build. They were going to put two homes on 250 square meters and they were going to sell us the homes. . . . We expressed our opposition but the engineers came anyway. In April of 1974 they entered the *colonia.* The bell was rung and *colonos* joined together; we removed them from the *colonia* for the first time. The second time . . . the bell started ringing to warn everyone that the police were coming. Well, down the street came a whole battalion of riot police to protect the engineers. We were united, and in one movement we captured the engineers and the riot police. We put them in their jeeps and conducted a march to the ward offices. We did not allow the police or engineers to get out of the jeeps until we arrived at the ward offices. With this action our movement began to gain respect.[10]

This story is one of the many that I collected about the conflicts that emerged as state planners attempted to reorganize urban space. Ursula's rejection of FIDEURBE's proposal and the capture of the police escort mainly by *colonas* point to a complicated articulation of *lo cotidiano* with the political-institutional. On the one hand, these actions show how the UM's demands had become centered on a traditional organization of urban space, individual family units, parks, and so on. On the other hand, they cast *colonas* in a major role in grassroots organizing that included engaging in pitched battles with the police and organizing protests against state agencies.

Doña Jovita also emphasizes the role of women in the conflicts with FIDEURBE. As in Lomas de Padierna, there were a series of disputes between FIDEURBE and the UM in Ajusco over land prices, the allocation of plots, and land taxes.[11] As the conflict became more heated, a group of women destroyed the post built to house FIDEURBE officials. Doña Jovita emphasizes that the role of women in this conflict is often forgotten: "Look at what people in the *colonia* say: 'they say that the post built for FIDEURBE was destroyed by a bus that was driven by a drunk driver, the bus exploded.' They never say, never, that a group of *viejas* [old women] destroyed the post!" (MRP n.d., 23). Throughout her account, Doña Jovita emphasizes that women were at the core of the struggles with FIDEURBE. These conflicts were not only about land prices but also about recognizing the role of *colonos* in planning and urbanizing the zones. Doña Jovita notes that *colonos* had constructed the *colonia*. "This was an inhospitable and inhabitable rocky area. We, us *colonos*, have come to give life to something so that it is now able to live. . . . And now comes a Trust that is going to sell us what is ours" (MRP n.d., 21).

In Campamento 2 de Octubre, conflicts between the state and *colonos* were especially severe because here the state sought to set an example for UMs that had become too powerful or too radical. As Manuel Castells points out:

> The squatters preserved their autonomy *vis-à-vis* the Administration and used their strong bargaining position to call for a general political opposition to the PRI's [the Institutional Revolutionary Party's] policies. They became the target of the most conservative sectors of the Mexican establishment. After a long series of provocations by paid gangs, the police attacked the *Campamento* in January 1976, setting fire to it and assaulting the squatters. Some days later, several hundred families returned to the settlement, reconstructed their houses, and started negotiating with the government to obtain a legal right to remain there. (1983, 272)

Castells is right to emphasize that the demands of the UM became relatively modest, including legalization of the settlement and the installation of services. Castells points out that to understand *colonos*' resistance to state policies and the state's harsh response to the UM, the larger issue of organizing and maintaining political autonomy must be considered. These conflicts were not simply about providing urban services but, more, the possibility of maintaining grassroots organizations that were autonomous from the state.

Beyond macro issues of political autonomy and power, as Pilar reminds us, these conflicts were also about women's participation in UMs and attempts to articulate new understandings of *lo cotidiano*. In talking about the burning of the *colonia*, for example, Pilar starts by noting that women played a large role in attempts to resist the police. After reporting how several women were beaten, including herself, she talks about how the burning destroyed the vision that *colonos* had developed of their *colonia*.

> It was the most brutal repression that the Campamento 2 de Octubre had suffered. I was in the kitchen. . . . we cooked every night so that in the mornings the school kids would pass by to have breakfast and our comrades that were going off to work would get lunch. There was always a popular kitchen: those who were invited ate, *colonos* that did not have money, the members of commissions that were leaving [for meetings or other business]. There was also a library; unfortunately the state destroyed many of the beautiful things that *colonos* had in mind to do, our *colonia* was going to be a model *colonia*. (Massolo 1992, 260–261)

Pilar's recounting of what *colonos* had "in mind"—a *colonia* with a popular kitchen and library, production cooperatives and facilities for raising chickens and rabbits, and other services such as a kindergarten maintained by *colonos* themselves—is given in the context of police repression. The kindergarten, which was constructed by *colonas,* was destroyed by riot police in 1975 (Massolo 1992, 226). In describing attempts to defend the kindergarten, Pilar emphasizes how its construction was the work of *colonas* (Massolo 1992, 228). In recounting the January 1976 burning, Pilar also emphasizes how she and a group of women attempted to defend the popular kitchen against the riot police (Massolo 1992, 260–262). In her account, Pilar uses the words for riot police *(granaderos)* and men *(hombres)* interchangeably. In both the cases of the popular kitchen and the kindergarten, attempts to reimagine *lo cotidiano* and devise new understandings of urban development are contrasted with the actions of male police.

New Ways of Doing Politics

In the literature on women's participation in UMs, the possibility of continuous social spaces that link the domestic and public are a major focus. Teresa Caldeira (1990), for example, argues that to understand the possibilities of continuous domestic and public spheres, it is necessary to look at how women seek to devise alternatives to the violent and corrupt public sphere of male politics. Caldeira begins her analysis by noting that the participation of women in UMs in Brazil, while undoubtedly based on needs, is also a result of meanings associated with the reorganization of the domestic sphere and the possibilities for transforming gender relations (1990, 62–63). She argues that poor women initially organized to reduce the conflicts at home that resulted from their participation in UMs. For Caldeira, the work of women's organizations in overcoming the opposition of husbands provides an initial impetus for challenging traditional notions of women's role in the domestic sphere. This organizing ultimately leads to poor women creating alternatives to traditional notions of "woman as housewife" and "man of politics."

> A new space is being created, not only to enable women to share the equally pervasive oppression and to identify common problems but also to construct an agreeable alternative. Within the social movements women are creating a new identity, as the discussion of their own distinctive topics acquires legitimacy. . . . We have already seen that this new identity contrasts with two other experiences: that of the traditional housewife and that of the man of politics. The situation of the housewife enclosed within the four wall of her home, frozen in time, totally dependent on the man—obviously a negative characterization—is offset against an "opening to the world" achieved by participating in local movements. (1990, 64)

The participation of women in grassroots organizing is therefore linked "not only to a number of meanings relating to the domestic and female universe (the home, the family, children, disinterested work for others, cooperation, among others) but also to the creation of a semantic space that separates their action in pursuit of certain demands from politics, as well as to living a new experience as women" (Caldeira 1990, 64).

Similarly, in discussing women's participation in UMs, Joann Martin argues that "continuity" should be a key metaphor for understanding the reconfiguration of the domestic and public spheres. In her research in Morelos, Mexico, Martin notes that poor women have rejected the public sphere of politics that is based on patron-client ties and corruption. Instead, they have opted for the expansion of the domestic sphere into politics.

> Years of involvement with the Mexican state had convinced Buena Vistans that in politics ties to community give way to the demands of patron-client relationships organized around corruption. Women's politics attempts to redeem the community by emphasizing ties between family and community over the connections between the community and the state. Emphasis on family and community does not mean that women support a policy of isolation from the state. Recognizing both the need and the danger of such external relationships, women suggest instead that only the power of a mother's devotion to her children can overcome the lure of self-interest and corruption. In short, Buena Vistan women assume a *continuity* between the domestic and public arenas that overrides the dichotomies anthropologists have frequently seen as explaining women's subordination. (1990, 471; my emphasis)

Martin's description of a continuity between the domestic and public spheres points to a creative reworking of the dichotomy's meaning. This strategy, however, is not without its critics. Kathleen Logan, for example, points out that poor women's reliance on traditional symbols in urban politics, such as parenthood, may ultimately limit possibilities for the transformation of gender identities (1990, 156).

To be sure, some *colonas* conceptualize grassroots organizing in terms of providing for one's children and contrast their participation with the corruption of the state. The metaphor of continuities, however, limits our understanding of the ways that *colonas* navigate the discourses and practices associated with the domestic and public realms. Rather than establishing continuities, *colonas* such as Ursula, Doña Jovita, and Pilar are constructing a borderlands zone that is laced with power and contradiction. This zone is not fixed by two social spheres but rather is a hybrid space that is marked by improvisation, heterogeneity, and even irony (see Rosaldo 1989, 207–217). For example, Ursula, Doña Jovita, and Pilar differ both in the emphasis they give to parenthood and in the ways in which they conceptualize co-optation and corruption. Ursula emphasizes her ability to confront authorities and to stress gaining services for *colonos* over questions of political ideology. Doña Jovita, in contrast, defines much of her political experience in terms of providing for the *necesidades* of her children and in terms of her Catholic faith. Pilar focuses on the possibilities for Mexican women to become more rebellious, to reject the gender ideologies of the state and church. All three women attempt to reimagine politics in ways that go beyond the male figure of political corruption, the *caudillo* (political boss).

Since the 1970s, *colonos* and urban activists have conceptualized the co-optation of leaders and the problem of political corruption in terms of the dynamic of *caudillismo.* The term *caudillo* is used to identify "natural leaders" *(dirigentes naturales)* who rule through charisma and repression and who are often affiliated with or co-opted by the state. In histories of UMs, activists often refer to the 1970s as the age of the *caudillo*. During this period, UMs were noted for their reformist tendencies and their lack of democratic structure. They were led by political strongmen, leaders whose decisions and powers were almost incontestable. In summing up the tendencies of UMs in the early 1970s, Javier Farrera Araujo and his colleagues write: "The spontaneous and local movements generally created leaders who ended up becoming *caudillos* because of their lack of political consciousness. They returned to the reformism that produced them and separated themselves from the rest of the movement; with frequency these *caudillos* were co-opted by components of the state" (Farrera Araujo et al. 1982, 30). Activists such as Farrera, who organized *colonos* in the southern part of Mexico City, viewed this type of political organizing as paternalistic and easily subject to manipulation.

Ursula was originally backed by members of the FPI working in Padierna because they saw her as counteracting the impact of the movement's first leader, Don Geraldo, who was labeled by activists as a *caudillo*. Ursula first participated in a committee of women that was involved in obtaining a regular water supply for the *colonia.* In talking about taking a leadership role in the *colonia,* Ursula refers to how men were unwilling to confront government officials, as I discussed earlier. She emphasizes how Don Geraldo became frightened and left the *colonia* after threats were made against him by *ejidatarios*. She notes that she learned to engage in urban politics without becoming corrupt. For example, in discussing her work with activists from the FPI, she states that she learned not to profit from politics.[12] Indeed, she speaks critically about how many former leaders of UMs had promised their support for the Institutional Revolutionary Party (Partido Revolucionario Institucional, or PRI) in exchange for local services. On the other hand, she argues that she was forced to stop working with students because of their political naïveté—their inability to see the necessity at some levels to cooperate with the state. In the end, Ursula evicted activists from the *colonia.*

The major point of contention between activists and *colonos* was participation in a state-organized Junta de Vecinos (Committee of Neighbors). During the late 1970s, most UMs resisted participating in the Junta de Vecinos, since these committees did not have any power and were controlled by the PRI. In response to a question I asked about the clearing of streets, Ursula began to discuss the issue of participation in the Junta de Vecinos.

> When I decided to enter the Junta de Vecinos there were kids *[muchachos]* that were activists, some were anarchists and others Maoists, and all of that . . . [pauses] . . . Well, I saw how the people were asking for water and other services and that the authorities were not helping us. I told my *compañeros* that it would not be a bad idea to enter the Junta de Vecinos so that we could gain services. The first time that I went to a meeting of the Junta, when I was named a representative of the *colonia,* there

> were many *compañeros* who said, "¡mucha política!" People said that I had sold out . . . that the authorities had given me money. Activists tried to organize the people against me. They even brought people in from other *colonias* in order to organize assemblies, which they held in the middle of the *colonia*, near the school. The block representatives told me about the assemblies and I told them, "We are not selling anything; it is not an issue of merchandise; we are not profiting. If they are organizing assemblies and the people want to go, let them go. We are going to continue working . . . working the administration of land regularization and demanding water and more schools."[13]

Ursula and her group of followers argued that they were completely independent of any political groups, that they only worked on practical issues and were unwilling to participate in PRI events unless guaranteed a concrete service for their *colonia.* Ursula is referred to by activists and many *colonos* as being a *caudilla*—a woman who once worked for the *necesidades* of her *colonia* but who betrayed the movement. Others *colonos,* however, defend her ability to bring services to the *colonia* and her political independence. It would be beyond the scope of this chapter to explore the intricacies of arguments on both sides (such as the lack of PRI symbolism in her office). What I want to emphasize is that the very debate over the nature of a *caudilla* as opposed to a *caudillo* points to a shifting of the terms of urban politics.

"I had the *necesidad* of having land, of having this security, of having this *patrimonio* for my children" (MRP n.d., 16). Doña Jovita constantly refers back to these dual perceptions, *necesidad* and providing for her children, in describing her participation in UMs. She describes many of the difficulties that she faced when she first moved to the *colonia*—when it was a barren area full of rocks—in terms of caring for children. She relates that because of *necesidad,* for example to get *masa* (dough) for preparing tortillas, women had to leave their children on the *cerro* (hill) (MRP n.d., 11). Sometimes mothers returning from work or shopping had to frantically search for their children, who had become lost in the *cerro.* In talking about her struggles with her husband, Doña Jovita emphasizes that her children did not hinder her participation in the UM. Rather, she emphasizes how her children aided her political participation, despite the opposition of her husband (MRP n.d., 32). She goes on to discuss the central role that women played in the UM.

> Here women organized the struggle! Men played a role but women were the majority of participants. Who organized us? We women did, women organized committees to try to gain a water supply; women prevented them [landowners and the state] from taking away our land . . . because we are the ones who suffered. Imagine being without water. . . . Would we not struggle to have this liquid that is so indispensable for food, for washing the children, to drink, for everything? (MRP n.d., 31–32)

According to Doña Jovita, the grassroots organizing of women remained autonomous from the dynamic of corruption and *caudillismo* that was prevalent among male leaders. Doña Jovita herself turned down several offers to become active in the government's community boards, saying that she had no motivation to become involved with the state. In praising other leaders, such as the well-known human rights activist Rosario Ibarra, she notes that such activists have never been involved in the government and that instead they are vocal in pressuring the state from below (MRP n.d., 41).

In discussing political leadership within the UM, Doña Jovita emphasizes the political naïveté of some leaders, the outright corruption of others, and the non-involvement of most political parties in UM politics. She ends by noting that *colonos* must develop a form of politics that goes beyond traditional political leadership: "We do not want *caudillos*, we want responsible people, people that feel our problems, that are capable of resolving the problems of the people" (MRP n.d., 41). She extends this argument by describing her move to Mexico City as a search for the promised land. Indeed, the UM had a strong religious component because of the activism of religious groups and priests from the local Catholic church (Alonso 1980, 381–382). This search for the promised land involved not only gaining services and land regularization—both of which occurred in the *colonia*—but building a better world for her children in which the poor do not face such a struggle for land and basic services. As in the case of Lomas de Padierna, the UM in Ajusco became divided; leaders were co-opted as a result of land regularization programs and the organization of the Junta de Vecinos. Doña Jovita continued to participate in UMs, as part of the Union of Popular Neighborhoods (Unión de Colonias Populares, or UCP) as well as of a political party. Like Pilar, she viewed the two forms of participation as being complementary.

According to Pilar, the UM at Campamento 2 de Octubre passed through two stages. Pilar describes the first stage in nostalgic terms; she talks about working with student activists and Francisco de la Cruz (Pancho), who led the movement in demanding land tenure and services. The second stage followed the January 1976 burning of the *colonia;* Pilar describes in critical terms the actions of both student activists and Pancho. On the one hand, she playfully criticizes student activists for being naïve while at the same time giving them credit for organizing *colonas.* On the other, she indignantly criticizes Pancho for becoming a *caudillo.* Much of the force of this indignation comes from the fact that she had been a great believer in Pancho's abilities as a leader: He was, Pilar ironically says, more than a mother to me.

In analyzing the UM in Campamento 2 de Octubre, Manuel Castells emphasizes that the students, with their "verbal radicalism," were at least partially responsible for the harsh repression that the movement faced (1983, 196). Pilar also points out that the students played a role in providing an excuse for the state to engage in repression. However, unlike Castells, Pilar also emphasizes that student activists played a large role in organizing women in the *colonia:* "They made us rebellious—we have to thank them for this because we were accustomed to being passive women, always in the house, obedient to our father, our mother, and later our husband, conformist old women. They made us rebels and loud mouths, many people who did not get a higher education obtained it here" (Massolo 1992, 255). Throughout her account, Pilar uses subtle irony and humor to express the contradictory situations that *colonos* faced. Thus her reference to students turning women into *boconas* (bigmouths) is an ironic play on a stereotype about women active in politics. Later, she ironically notes that student activists were "an accelerator" *(el acelere)*, a designation that denotes sarcasm. Students aided the movement but also gave it a reputation for being a guerrilla organization: "You know that the student is the accelerator, unfortunately because of the accelerator they took us here to be pseudo-guerrillas" (Massolo 1992, 255). This irony underlies a respect for the role the students played but also a recognition of the conflicts and differences that emerged between *colonos* and activists.

In talking about Pancho, Pilar ironically reports on her own initial devotion to his leadership. Not only was Pancho more than a mother to her (an expression that has many layers of meaning!) but he was also a "clay idol" (Massolo 1992, 265). Pilar uses these phrases to undermine her own naïveté in believing so thoroughly in one man (charisma is a major element of *caudillismo*). Throughout her interview she points out that *colonos* must stop thinking about grassroots organizing in terms of the personality of leaders and more in terms of the formation of democratic committees. This critique is similar to criticisms made by Alonso (1980), Castells (1983), and others, which emphasize the lack of democratic organizing within UMs during the 1970s. Pilar's own recounting of how Pancho became a *caudillo* integrates a discussion of gender dynamics with an analysis of political corruption. Pilar points out that after the 1976 burning, Pancho became involved with selling plots and running a taxi business that state agencies helped him establish. He distanced himself from women organizers and began evicting people who did not pay "contributions" to his organization. Pilar notes:

> It was during this time that Pancho de la Cruz, from my point of view, betrayed the movement, when he began to abuse *colonos*. When he formed the taxi group, the taxi drivers—the men—struggled against us, because Pancho told them, "look, if you evict these old women *[viejas]* you all can have their land." Therefore the women of the Campamento, accustomed to receiving blows from the riot police, well we became afraid and we began to buy gasoline, to have bottles of gasoline to make fires, in order to make them run. (Massolo 1992, 266–267)

In the above passage, Pilar clearly identifies the conflict within the *colonia* in terms of gender dynamics—male taxi drivers pitted against *colonas*. Pilar criticizes the ways in which Pancho abused the "contributions" he collected as a deviation from the politics of *necesidad*. She notes that there was no *necesidad* for finances and making a profit; Pancho squandered moneys that should have been used to make a better *colonia* for their children (Massolo 1992, 266).

As the UM became divided, Pancho evicted student activists. He was eventually imprisoned for selling land that he did not own. His legacy is still under debate; when he was released from prison in the mid-1980s, several letters to newspapers argued that he was not a *caudillo*. Indeed, Pilar points out that Pancho still has many followers. As the movement lost its intensity because of divisions between *colonos* and the provisioning of services, Pilar became more active in a leftist political party. During the 1980s, regional and national councils of UMs were established but Pilar says that she could not participate because councils wanted whole communities represented. She pointed out that she was an individual, a *colona,* and that she could not represent an entire *colonia*. She ironically remarks, "It became apparent to me that it was corrupt for me to go [to meetings of the various councils] because *I am not the Campamento 2 de Octubre,* I am nothing more than a material human being" (Massolo 1992, 254; my emphasis).

Webs of Political Participation

In the literature on UMs, studies of women's activism have relied upon a linear narrative about creating continuities between the domestic and public domains and identifying practical and gender-based needs. Discussions of gender dynamics have focused on groups of women as a whole—poor women, *faveladas,* Buena Vistans, and so on—and at a general level have considered whether gender identities are transformed in such movements, almost as a yes-or-no proposition. Likewise, research on social movements has debated whether these movements are new or old, autonomous or branches of political parties, without exploring how these boundaries are crossed and redefined. As Judith Adler Hellman notes, social-movement researchers must devise a more complex way of examining the histories and outcomes of grassroots organizing, one that goes beyond exploring newness and autonomy (1992, 55). For Ursula, Doña Jovita, and Pilar, their participation in grassroots organizing both sheds light on these debates and complicates the terms through which we think about UM history.

In the 1980s, Ursula remained the leader of her *colonia* and was granted a *colectivo* route by the state (*colectivos* are taxis for multiple riders with fixed routes). For many *colonos* and activists, the fact that she was granted such a route clearly indicates that she was co-opted. After Ursula evicted activists, the state attempted to remove her as the leader of the *colonia* but she remained in charge, with strong backing from many *colonos*. In discussing transformations of gender identity, I would point to her role as a leader of the *colonia* and to her emphasis on political pragmatism. When I first visited Ursula in 1987, she was convening a meeting of *colectivo* drivers; in the meeting, about fifty men listened to Ursula give them instructions about the maintenance of the route. Looking at reports published by the political wards, including transcripts of meetings of *colonia* representatives in the Junta de Vecinos, it is evident that Ursula is one of the few women leaders of a *colonia.* Like Pilar, Ursula is both thankful for and critical of her work with activists groups. Unlike Pilar, however, she views her attempts to create an autonomous political space not in terms of participation in leftist politics but as strict political pragmatism; according to Ursula, her position is free of political ideology and allegiance to any political party. Ursula noted various difficulties that she had with the PRI, including being pressured to provide people for rallies. She stated, in line with her emphasis on pragmatism, that she only played this role when the benefits for *colonos* were clear. This point is deeply contested.

In the 1980s, Doña Jovita remained active in her *colonia* even though the movement had become divided. She participated in the citywide UCP and became involved with a leftist political party, the Unified Socialist Party of Mexico (Partido Socialista Unificado de México, or PSUM). In her account of grassroots organizing, she emphasizes how the role of women is being forgotten despite the fact that women were, in reality, responsible for the movement. Her articulation of gender identities focuses on providing for her children as a major motivation for participating in grassroots organizations. She discussed her political identity in terms of struggling for land and creating new expressions of her religious beliefs, viewing politics as an attempt to construct the promised land here on earth.

Pilar begins her account by emphasizing that Mexican women must become more rebellious. She continually stresses this point throughout her account, exhorting *colonas* to see through the PRI's strategies of giving out breakfasts and other services in exchange for political support. Pilar, before moving to Campamento, had participated in the old Mexican Communist Party (Partido Comunista de México, or PCM), and throughout her participation in the UM she was active in political parties. She points out that participants in the UM were affiliated with various political parties but that the movement itself was autonomous. As the movement became increasingly divided, Pilar focused her activism on working with the PSUM while avoiding participation in the various councils of UMs organized in the late 1970s and early 1980s, such as the UCP, as discussed earlier.[14] Throughout her account, Pilar talks about the wider *necesidades* of women, including abortion rights. She notes that much of her participation in the PSUM is dedicated to pressuring for such *necesidades*. In 1982 she ran unsuccessfully as a PSUM candidate for the Chamber of Deputies.[15]

For all three women, a key element of their participation in grassroots organizing was their association with activist groups. Groups such as the FPI represented both continuities and breaks with "older" forms of political organizing based on parties, the proletariat, and peasants.[16] To be sure, activist groups of the 1970s introduced new forms of organizing as they began to work in the *colonias populares*. This organizing represented a response to the October 2, 1968, massacre and an attempt to construct a more broadly based opposition movement that went beyond parties and traditional labor organizations. The relation of these "new" movements, such as UMs, to more traditional political and labor organizations was varied and complex. In Mexico, as in other Latin American countries, the issue of autonomy from political parties was hotly debated and remained a bitter cause of conflict among UMs (Bennett 1992, 251).

Many *colonos*, as witnessed by Doña Jovita and Pilar, maintained ties to political parties (and other organizations) even though the UM they participated in had no official party affiliation. During the late 1970s and early 1980s, councils such as the UCP attempted to include within the UMs' agendas electoral politics and participation in party organizing.[17] Although these electoral issues are beyond the scope of this chapter, it is useful to point out that the activism of Ursula, Doña Jovita, and Pilar defies any simple dichotomization between the social (activism in a UM) and political (participation in a party). On the one hand, Ursula maintained a leadership role in Lomas de Padierna while viewing her relationship with the state on pragmatic grounds. On the other hand, Doña Jovita alternates between activism in UMs and opposition parties such as the PSUM. Finally Pilar, because of the divisions in Campamento 2 de Octubre, has moved into party politics. Her participation in the PSUM involved including UMs' and women's *necesidades* in the party agenda (Massolo 1992, 274–279).[18]

By the late 1980s, as Hellman notes, the links between social movements and political parties became stronger as seen in the various coalitions formed around the Cárdenas campaigns (1992, 258). Indeed, many UMs began to participate in elections for the first time (Bennett 1992, 254). In analyzing the outcomes of grassroots organizing, Hellman notes that the issue of autonomy is often reified to the point of denying the complexities of social movements' relationships with other organizations and the state. Hellman argues that narratives about social movements should not simply examine the maintaining or loosening of autonomy but rather should explore the historical changes that occur as movements confront the state (1992, 55). In this sense, the experiences of Ursula, Doña Jovita, and Pilar are instructive since they point to a variety of outcomes: from maintaining a leadership role and accommodating the state to merging social movements with opposition party politics.

Conclusions

I began this chapter by quoting Pilar, who describes the criticisms that women endure for their activism in grassroots organizing. Pilar transforms these stereotypes, such as the *bocona* (bigmouth), into a more positive aspect of rebelliousness. She takes a number of negative stereotypes and transforms their meaning, while ironically reporting on the various difficulties that *colonas* faced with the police and the leadership of the movement (Massolo 1992). Her use of irony, such as calling student activism "the accelerator," expresses her contradictory social experiences. Far from representing a continuity between the domestic and public spheres, Pilar's experiences express the ambiguities and contradictions of living in a borderlands space. Most studies of women's participation in UMs—including writings on testimonies—have not paid attention to such use of irony and ambiguity. Indeed, social-movement researchers must begin the task of describing and amplifying this source of cultural creativity.

In this chapter, I have provided an initial overview of the characteristics and dynamics of these borderland experiences. I started by noting the centrality of needs discourses in the political programs of UMs and the participation of *colonas* in grassroots organizing. Interpretations of needs, I noted, must be contextualized in a wide array of social relations including struggles over land tenure and critiques of sexism.

I then examined how Ursula, Doña Jovita, and Pilar engaged in strategies for carving out a borderlands experience that fused domestic and public discourses and practices, such as welding *lo cotidiano* and development issues and articulating new ways of doing politics. These strategies were clearly emergent in that they were ongoing processes that responded to institutional politics, distinct social experiences, and the exigencies of everyday life. Indeed, each *colona* interpreted her understanding of needs and politics with a different set of tools—from Ursula's pragmatism and Doña Jovita's religiosity to Pilar's emphasis on rebelliousness. And, as the UMs in their neighborhoods were weakened, each *colona* developed different ways of expressing their continuing political activism.

Finally, I should note that these accounts of grassroots participation call into question a number of dichotomies through which UMs and social movements in general are theorized. I refer here not only to the ways in which researchers have conceptualized the domestic and public but also the application of other dichotomies: practical needs/strategic needs, old movements/new movements, and parties (political)/urban (social) movements. To be sure, these dichotomies represent key elements of dominant ideologies and, perhaps, overly rigid notions of political activism. However, more attention needs to be given to the ways in which participants in grassroots organizing have navigated and, in some cases, reconfigured these dichotomies. Such a study would require a new way of understanding theory, beyond the development of conceptual dichotomies and linear narratives to an examination of the contradictory sets of practices and discourses that are generated at the intersections of social experience.

Notes

1. Massolo 1992, 256–257.

2. Working with narratives, of course, raises a series of methodological issues. In all three instances I have checked the accuracy of each account with case studies of UMs in each *colonia* (see Table 10.1). A real danger in social movement research is the tendency to exaggerate the unity and successes of grassroots organizing. Ursula, Doña Jovita, and Pilar are all open and frank about the divisions and difficulties that exist within their respective movements. Throughout the chapter, I compare and contrast interpretations of events with the accounts of other participants (in the case of Lomas de Padierna) and case studies (for Ajusco and Campamento 2 de Octubre). For example, I contrast Ursula's understanding of co-optation with that of activists and *colonos* in Lomas de Padierna. Both Doña Jovita and Pilar stress the role of women in UMs—a perspective barely mentioned in Alonso 1980 and Castells 1983. As I mention, Pilar views the UM in the Campamento 2 de Octubre not only as a struggle for political autonomy (Castells's perspective) but also as a conflict over gender relations and politics.

3. In my own work (Díaz Barriga 1995) I describe the history of the involvement of the FPI in Lomas de Padierna. Alejandra Massolo describes the work of the FPI in Campamento 2 de Octubre (1992, 225).

4. Letter from FPI activists to *colonos* in Lomas de Padierna, 1980.

5. Jeffrey Rubin (in this volume) points out that social movement activists, such as those in COCEI (Coalition of Workers, Peasants, and Students of the Isthmus), partially base their opposition to the ruling PRI (Institutional Revolutionary Party) on its inability to satisfy basic needs *(necesidades)*. Rubin rightfully points out that this justification of grassroots organizing can mask severe conflicts among social movement participants.

6. Ursula, taped interview, June 16, 1987.

7. Ibid.

8. Ibid.

9. In the literature on urban planning in Mexico City, there have been several attempts to link *lo cotidiano* to the possibilities of generating new forms of urban neighborhoods. Daniel Hiernaux (1988), for example, notes the limitations that various state agencies have imposed on the participation of citizens of Mexico City in decisions that affect their everyday lives. Hiernaux argues that certain services, such as running water, require centralized administration and great technical expertise. However, he notes that there are a series of decisions that should involve local communities. These decisions include the closing of streets to traffic, the establishing of parks, and the organizing of local markets (1988, 75). By creating forums for active community participation, Hiernaux argues that the initiatives of grassroots organizations could be better recognized and that communities could have more control over the urban spaces that define their everyday life. While Hiernaux argues for the integration of *lo cotidiano* and development planning at an institutional level, attempts to generate this relationship were already a major part of the political programs of urban movements in Mexico City.

10. Ursula, taped interview, June 16, 1987.

11. These disputes are described in detail in Alonso 1980, 379–439.

12. Ursula, taped interview, June 16, 1987.

13. Ibid.

14. The PCM was one of the political parties that created the PSUM.

15. The election was for the fifteenth electoral district of the Federal District. The PSUM received 10.5 percent of the vote. The PRI candidate won the election with 49.3 percent of the vote (Massolo 1992: 275).

16. See Calderón, Piscitelli, and Reyna 1992 for a discussion of old versus new social movements.

17. Vivienne Bennett describes the UCP in the following terms: "Between 1979 and 1981, three important coalitions of popular neighborhoods were constituted in the Valley of Mexico. The first was the *Unión de Colonias Populares* (UCP), formally constituted in July 1979 with 300 members from 7 *colonias* (although it has its roots in a previous UPM [urban popular movement], the Frente Popular Independiente). By the time of its first anniversary in 1980, the UCP had 1,100 members in 9 *colonias*. The organization worked to forge links with other groups, first with the Left through the Mexican Communist Party (PCM) and later with other popular organizations. The UCP was one of four groups that coordinated the first nationwide meeting of urban popular movements, held in Monterrey in 1980, and it has remained active in creating new political organizations" (1992, 250).

18. The PSUM joined the PMT (Mexican Workers Party) to form the PMS (Mexican Socialist Party). The PMS was part of the FDN (National Democratic Front) for the 1988 elections and later formed part of the PRD (Party of the Democratic Revolution).

References

Alonso, Jorge, ed. 1980. *Lucha Urbana y Acumulación de Capital*. Mexico City: Casa Chata.

Anzaldúa, Gloria. 1987. *Borderlands/La Frontera*. San Francisco: Spinsters/Aunt Lute.

Bennett, Vivienne. 1992. "The Evolution of Urban Popular Movements in Mexico Between 1968 and 1988." In *The Making of Social Movements in Latin America: Identity, Strategy, and Democracy,* ed. A. Escobar and S. Alvarez, 240–259. Boulder: Westview Press.

______. 1993. "Orígenes del Movimiento Urbano Popular Mexicano: Pensamiento Político y Organizaciones Políticas Clandestinas, 1960–1980." *Revista Mexicana de Sociología* 3:89–102.

Blondet, Cecilia. 1990. "Establishing an Identity: Women Settlers in a Poor Lima Neighborhood." In *Women and Social Change in Latin America,* ed. E. Jelin, trans. A. Zammit and M. Thomson, 12–46. London: Zed Books.

Brugada, Clara. 1986. *La Mujer en la Lucha Urbana y El Estado*. Mexico City: Equipo Mujeres en Acción Solidaria.

Caldeira, Teresa. 1990. "Women, Daily Life, and Politics." In *Women and Social Change in Latin America,* ed. E. Jelin, trans. A. Zammit and M. Thomson, 47–78. London: Zed Books.

Calderón, Fernando, and José Luis Reyna. 1990. "La Irrupción: Oye, Pedro, Te Hablo a Ti." *David y Goliath* 57:12–20.

Calderón, Fernando, Alejandro Piscitelli, and José Luis Reyna. 1992. "Social Movements: Actors, Theories, Expectations." In *The Making of Social Movements in Latin America: Identity, Strategy, and Democracy,* ed. A. Escobar and S. Alvarez, 19–36. Boulder: Westview Press.

Canel, Eduardo. 1992. "Democratization and the Decline of Urban Social Movements in Uruguay: A Political-Institutional Account." In *The Making of Social Movements in Latin America: Identity, Strategy, and Democracy,* ed. A. Escobar and S. Alvarez, 276–290. Boulder: Westview Press.

Castells, Manuel. 1983. *The City and the Grassroots: A Cross-Cultural Theory of Urban Social Movements*. Berkeley: University of California Press.

Díaz Barriga, Miguel. 1995. "Urban Movements in Mexico City: A Case Study of Urban Expansion, Ecology, and Development in the Ajusco Region, 1970–1990." Unpublished manuscript.

______. 1996. "*Necesidad:* Notes on the Discourses of Urban Politics in the Ajusco Foothills of Mexico City." *American Ethnologist* 23 (2):291–310.

Epstein, David. 1973. *Brasilia, Plan and Reality*. Berkeley: University of California Press.

Escobar, Arturo. 1992. "Culture, Economics, and Politics in Latin American Social Movements Theory and Research." In *The Making of Social Movements in Latin America: Identity, Strategy, and Democracy,* ed. A. Escobar and S. Alvarez, 62–85. Boulder: Westview Press.

Escobar, Arturo, and Sonia E. Alvarez, eds. 1992. *The Making of Social Movements in Latin America: Identity, Strategy, and Democracy*. Boulder: Westview Press.

Farrera Araujo, Javier, et al. 1982. "Movimientos Sociales Urbanos." In *Cuadernos de Dinámica Habitacional*. Mexico City: COPEVI.

Farrera Araujo, Javier, and Diego Prieto Hernández. 1986. "Hístorias Metropolitanas: cases sociales y lucha de clases frente al problema urbano en la Ciudad de México." Thesis, Escuela Nacional de Antropología e Historia, Mexico City.

Gilbert, Alan, and Peter Ward. 1985. *Housing, the Poor, and the State: Policy and Practice in Three Latin American Cities*. Cambridge: Cambridge University Press.

Hellman, Judith Adler. 1992. "The Study of New Social Movements in Latin America and the Question of Autonomy." In *The Making of Social Movements in Latin America: Identity, Strategy, and Democracy*, ed. A. Escobar and S. Alvarez, 52–61. Boulder: Westview Press.

Hernández, Ricardo. 1987. *La Coordinadora Nacional del Movimiento Urbano Popular: CONAMUP*. Mexico City: Equipo Pueblo.

Hiernaux, Daniel. 1988. "Planificación y Gestión: El Caso de la Ciudad de México." In *Política y Movimientos Sociales en la Ciudad de México*, ed. A. Cenecorta and A. Calvo, 59–76. Mexico City: Departamento del Distrito Federal.

Jelin, Elizabeth. 1987. *Movimientos Sociales y Democracia Emergente*. Buenos Aires: Centro Editor de América Latina.

Jelin, Elizabeth, ed. 1990. *Women and Social Change in Latin America*. Trans. A. Zammit and M. Thomson. London: Zed Books.

Lind, Amy Conger. 1992. "Power, Gender, and Development: Popular Women's Organizations and the Politics of Needs in Ecuador." In *The Making of Social Movements in Latin America: Identity, Strategy, and Democracy*, ed. A. Escobar and S. Alvarez, 134–149. Boulder: Westview Press.

Logan, Kathleen. 1990. "Women's Participation in Urban Protest." In *Popular Movements and Political Change in Mexico*, ed. J. Foweraker and A. Craig, 150–159. Boulder: Lynne Rienner.

Mainwaring, Scott. 1987. "Urban Popular Movements, Identity, and Democratization in Brazil." *Comparative Political Studies* 20 (2):131–159.

Martin, Joann. 1990. "Motherhood and Power: The Production of a Women's Culture of Politics in a Mexican Community." *American Ethnologist* 17 (1):470–490.

Massolo, Alejandra. 1983. "Las Mujeres en los Movimientos Sociales Urbanos de la Ciudad de México." *Iztapalapa* 9:152–167.

______. 1989. "La Mujer en la Ciudad de México: Mientras crecía, crecíamos." *Fem*. 13 (78):9–15.

______. 1992. *Por Amor y Coraje: Mujeres en Movimientos Urbanos de la Ciudad de México*. Mexico City: El Colegio de México.

Molyneux, Maxine. 1985. "Mobilization Without Emancipation? Women's Interests, State, and Revolution in Nicaragua." *Feminist Studies* 11 (2):227–254.

Moser, Carolyn. 1989. "Gender Planning in the Third World: Meeting Practical and Strategic Gender Needs." *World Development* 17 (11):1799–1825.

MRP (Movimiento Revolucionario del Pueblo). n.d. "Doña Jovita; un testimonio de la participación de las mujeres en las luchas urbanas." Mexico City. Mimeographed.

Perlman, Janice E. 1976. *The Myth of Marginality: Urban Poverty and Politics in Rio de Janeiro*. Berkeley: University of California Press.

Perló, Manuel, and Martha Schteingart. 1984. "Movimientos Sociales Urbanos en México." *Revista Méxicana de Sociología* 4:105–127.

Pezzoli, Keith. 1987. "The Urban Land Problem and Popular Sector Housing Development in Mexico City." *Environment and Behavior* 19 (3):371–397.

Ramírez-Saíz, Juan Manuel. 1986. *El Movimiento Urbano Popular en México*. Mexico City: Siglo XXI.

______. 1990. "Urban Struggles and their Political Consequences." In *Popular Movements and Political Change in Mexico,* ed. J. Foweraker and A. Craig, 234–246. Boulder: Lynne Rienner.

Rosaldo, Renato. 1989. *Culture and Truth: The Remaking of Social Analysis*. Boston: Beacon Press.

Sandoval, Juan Manuel. 1991. "Los Nuevos Movimientos Sociales y el Medio Ambiente en México." In *Servicios Urbanos, Gestión Local, y Medio Ambiente,* ed. M. Schteingart and L. d'Andrea, 305–335. Mexico City: El Colegio de México.

Stephen, Lynn. 1992. "Women in Mexico's Popular Movements: Survival Strategies Against Ecological and Economic Impoverishment." *Latin American Perspectives* 72 (19):73–96.

Tamayo, Sergio. 1989. *Vida Digna en Las Ciudades: El Movimiento Urbano Popular en México 1980–1985*. Mexico City: Ediciones Gernika.

Velez-Ibáñez, Carlos. 1983. *Rituals of Marginality: Politics, Process, and Culture in Central Urban Mexico, 1969–1974*. Berkeley: University of California Press.

Chapter Eleven

Defrocking the Vatican: Feminism's Secular Project

JEAN FRANCO

Discussions over the use of words often seem like nit-picking, irrelevant to "real" struggles. Yet the power to interpret, and the active appropriation and invention of language, are crucial tools for emergent movements seeking visibility and recognition for the views and actions that filter out from their dominant discourses. In recent decades, for example, the once derogatory word "queer" has been transformed into a statement of pride and a declaration of intent. Though many of us have been irritated by seemingly endless debates over the use of the words "Latin" American or "*mestizaje,*" such debates are themselves symptoms of the perturbing actuality of racial difference in which supremacy has been defined according to race and color.

But the struggle for interpretive power is now played not on a level playing field but on a terrain dominated by conservative media who push their own clamorous narrative. In the United States, a notorious example of this uneven struggle has been the debate over political correctness. "Political correctness" was a designation initially used by liberals and the Left to prevent hate speech and to make people think twice before using abusive terms such as "nigger," "wog," or "dyke." For the Right, however, "political correctness" is identified with notions of a new "thought police," with the paradoxical result that people are encouraged to be politically *in*correct and to demonstrate their freedom, particularly on radio talk shows, by using the very hate speech that political correctness was intended to curb. The resignification of political correctness as permission to "talk dirty," far from being merely an abstract issue, has had real effects in exacerbating already sharp racial divisions.

The struggle for interpretive power was never more in evidence than in the debates over gender that preceded the 1995 Beijing Conference on Women.[1] The financialization of global and neoliberal policies has placed feminism in a strategic position in opposition to fundamentalists seeking to preserve women's natural subordination and the global capitalism that has incorporated women at the lowest level of the workforce. During the preparations for the Beijing conference, serious attempts were made by the Vatican and conservative forces to undermine feminism by staging an apparently trivial sideshow—namely, an attack on the use of the word "gender." What the outcome revealed was reminiscent of the emperor's new clothes—the nakedness of the Vatican position. More importantly, it revealed the desperation of an ancient global institution (Orbis et Urbe) threatened by this jenny-come-lately—feminism—now claiming global citizenship. What was at stake in this struggle over a word? What does it tell us about the Vatican's position in relation to neoliberalism and about feminism's aspiration to "global citizenship"? How are both these positions related to the heterogeneous politics of nation-states as they attempt to implement neoliberal economic policies?

As part of its campaign against feminism, particularly feminists in its own congregations, the Vatican attacked what it believed to be the very foundation of feminist theory—gender interpreted as the socially constructed difference between feminine and masculine. The preparatory document for the Beijing conference had used the term "gender" "to refer to awareness of the difference between masculine and feminine as distinct from anatomical sex; but not as a euphemism for sexual orientation as some critics charge." It notes that "differences between women's and men's achievements and activities are still not recognized as the consequences of socially constructed gender roles rather than biological differences" and calls on governments to "integrate gender perspective in legislation, public policies, programs and projects."[2]

The Vatican's attack was motivated not only by the increasing power of feminism but also by their attempts to restage the Church as a bulwark against a "savage capitalism." By putting feminist struggles into the same bag as the population control policies of international organizations, it hoped to show that both were foreign to Hispanic tradition. The Church was helped by the fact that the Spanish and Portuguese word for gender, *"género,"* did not carry the same range of meanings as in English. As Donna Haraway has pointed out, the English word "gender" is not an easy word to translate: "The substantives 'Geschlecht,' 'gender,' 'genre,' and 'género' refer to the notion of sort, kind, and class. In English, 'gender' has been used in this 'generic' sense continuously since at least the fourteenth century. In French, German, Spanish, and English, words for 'gender' refer to grammatical and literary categories. The modern English and German words, 'gender' and 'Geschlecht,' adhere closely to concepts of sex, sexuality, sexual difference, generation, engendering, and so on, while the French and Spanish seem not to carry those meanings as readily."[3] But the use of "género" or "género sexual" to refer to the socially constructed difference between masculine and feminine was also important to Latin American feminists, as Marta Lamas argued in a lucid account of the genealogy of the term. Lamas emphasized the cultural symbolization of anatomical difference and its real effects on "practices, ideas, discourse and social representation which attribute objective and subjective behavior to people according to sex." It is through the process of the constitution of gender that society reproduces the idea of what men and women should be and what is proper to each sex. "Gender cannot be separated from signification and operates in all spheres, accounting not only for the symbolization of masculine and feminine but for the 'naturalization' of heterosexuality and the criminalization of 'unnatural behavior.'"[4] Lamas distinguishes between the deep psychological formation of the human subject and the transformable social effects that follow from the "logic of gender." The deconstruction of "the logic of gender" is crucial to what she regards as the "ethical and political goals of feminism," which are to refashion "symbolically and politically a new definition of what it is to be a person—a human being and a subject, whether in the body of a woman or a man." Thus Lamas makes the understanding of the logic of gender crucial not only to feminism but to humanity at large. As Lamas acknowledges, however, gender can be used strategically to avoid the consequences of female separatism. Gender may thus simply indicate the fact that the "feminine" cannot be discussed without also referring to the "masculine," a usage that became important in U.S. academic circles and later in Latin America in order to avoid the marginalization of women's studies. The problem here is that "gender" then comes to be used instead of "women." This substitution, which may divert attention from problems specific to women, has been criticized, although the criticism relates more to strategy and implementation than to theory.[5] It is also a fact that as feminism expands, diversifies, and reflects on itself, older theoretical constructs are bound to come into question.[6]

The Vatican was, of course, not particularly concerned with the finer points of the argument within feminism. Rather, its attack on gender was a reaction to the growing number and influence of feminists on women's movements, some of which had developed under Church auspices. There are now thousands of women's movements, NGOs, and feminist organizations worldwide. The delegates at the Beijing conference from Brazil alone represented over a thousand women's and feminist organizations.[7] The Mexican delegation to Beijing included 250 feminist groups who, much to the disgust of the conservative National Action Party (PAN), gave their support to the "concept of the Lesbian family as a legal option in juridical and economic terms."[8] This is certainly one reason why the Vatican and conservative forces found "gender" to be objectionable; as Judith Butler points out, "if gender is the cultural meanings that the sexed body assumes, then a gender cannot be said to follow from a sex in any one way."[9] In other words, the use of the word "gender" underscores the fact that heterosexuality is no longer the only option. The Vatican quite correctly deduced that the use of the word "gender" might have practical consequences ranging from legalized abortion to the acceptance of homosexuality, the recognition of irregular families, and the collapse of family values.

Interestingly enough, the Vatican began focusing on social construction precisely at a time when it was also attempting to modify its attitude toward women because of women's increasing visibility in United Nations global conferences and also for practical reasons, because the Church was losing its congregations to evangelical sects. The Vatican needed to attract women (but not feminists), and one way of doing this was to separate women from feminism, which in the past had been stigmatized as an aggressive "unfeminine" movement. Women, the Vatican believed, could be steered away from the dangerous excesses of feminism once it was shown that the language of feminism embraced unnatural practices. But what made the Vatican's hand a little too visible was that in the two months leading up to the Beijing conference, objections to the word "gender" had reached a crescendo, making it clear that the attack on the word was centrally orchestrated. For instance, in July 1994 several members of an Argentine government planning committee, which had been formed to draw up changes in the national curriculum, resigned when they found that changes had been made in their proposal, apparently by the Minister of Education. Mention of Darwin and Lamarck had been eliminated, references to sex education had been erased, and the word "gender" had been replaced by "sex." It was the auxiliary bishop of Buenos Aires who came to the defense of these excisions, arguing that the use of the word "gender" was "intended to provoke an ideological shift and to generate a new conception of the human person, of subjectivity, marriage, the family and society. In short, what is proposed is a *cultural revolution.*" Using the word "gender" "as a purely cultural construct detached from the biological," the bishop warned, "makes us into *fellow travelers* of radical feminism." And he went on to quote U.S. feminist Shulamith Firestone's *The Dialectics of Sex* in support of his argument that feminism was more extreme than Marxism.[10] Thus gender was, in his view, associated with sinister foreign influence.

Although it may be amusing to think of the Catholic hierarchy wading through feminist theory, its attempts to demonize feminism and prohibit the word "gender" must be seen in the context of the global arena. The Vatican has observer status at United Nations summit conferences and is an active lobbyist. It pressures governments to select pro-life delegates and was successful in persuading President Menem of Argentina to support pro-life resolutions at a summit of Latin American presidents in Cartagena, Colombia. At the Rio Conference on Environment in 1992, the Vatican joined with delegates from Islamic countries to secure the elimination of a section of the final document that referred to family planning. The Vatican also brought pressure to bear before the Conference on Population and Development in Cairo, where its preoccupation with abortion obscured other issues. The Vatican found allies among Islamic fundamentalists when it attempted to scuttle documents favoring reproductive rights. When it was unsuccessful in its bid to erase certain clauses from the final documents, the Vatican resorted to insisting on bracketing phrases it considered controversial, a tactic that it continued to employ during the preparations for the Beijing conference. Gayatri Chakravorty Spivak, a member of the Asian Human Rights Council at the Cairo conference, remarked that the attempts of her group to relate questions of population to development were thwarted; because of "the controversy generated by the Pope, the northern-domination women's caucus could only discuss population in terms of abortion rights."[11]

Because the Church's position is so rigid (neither abortion nor contraception are sanctioned), and is so removed from practical life, the Vatican has had to go to considerable lengths to overcome the disaffection in its own ranks, in which an effective pro-choice constituency had developed. Pope John Paul II's *Letter to Women,*[12] for example, represented one attempt to mend misogynistic policies by praising women's mission as mothers, wives, daughters, workers, and nuns. In his letter, the Pope recognizes that women have frequently been marginalized and even reduced to slavery because of male domination, and he expresses regret that certain "sons of the Church" might have contributed to women's oppression in the past. However, he refrains from exploring the reasons for the subordination of women on the grounds that "it would not be easy to attribute precise responsibility considering the strength of cultural sedimentations that, through the centuries, have formed people's mentalities." What the Pope does not seem to realize is that, when he refers to the obstacles that impede women's full incorporation into social, political, and economic life, he needs the word "gender" in order to explain the "cultural sedimentations" that account for inequalities. But to use "gender" would entail the acknowledgment that heterosexuality is also socially constructed.

One tactic that the Vatican employed unsuccessfully was the anticolonialism card; it charged that gender, in the feminist sense, was "foreign" to non-Western countries and to Latin America. The Vatican foreign minister claimed that the draft Platform for Action would impose a "Western type of household" in which the family is "often characterized by an absence of children and not infrequently by deviations which cause psychological imbalances and weaknesses in its most vulnerable members."[13] In a major press conference before the start of the Beijing conference, Vatican spokesman Joaquín Navarro-Valls described the draft Platform for Action as "ideologically unbalanced," saying that it would "impose a Western model of femininity that does not take due account of the value of women in the large majority of the world's countries." It also placed too much emphasis on "gender" and "sexuality" and not enough on "motherhood."[14] The Archbishop of Tegucigalpa and President of the Latin American Episcopal Conference, Oscar Rodríguez, asserted that the aim of the Beijing conference was "to force society to accept five types of gender: masculine, feminine, lesbian, homosexual and transsexual." As the pro-choice Catholics would point out, the preparatory document gives no evidence to support such a claim.

The Catholic Church's position on abortion and birth control is, of course, divorced from actual practices even among the faithful. For instance, a poll taken in Lima after President Alberto Fujimori's recent decision to make contraception available to poor families showed that 95 percent of the population believed in God, yet 80 percent also believed that Peruvians were in agreement with the use of contraceptives.[15] Likewise, the Church considers abortion "a grave sin"—yet it is a major form of birth control in the region. In Chile, there are an estimated 170,000 abortions each year. One out of every three pregnancies in Peru ends in abortion. Since abortions are performed clandestinely and often in less than optimal conditions, this is also a pressing health issue. Abortion is the fourth most common cause of maternity deaths and the third most common cause of hospitalization during pregnancy in Mexico. In Colombia, 74.5 percent of maternal deaths are the result of botched abortions.[16] The "family" as defined by the Church also has little relation to actual experience. Households headed by women are the rule rather than the exception in the poorer sectors of society. In Chile, 40 percent of all families are not headed by a married couple. Of every seven babies born in that country, one is the child of an adolescent, and in 61 percent of those cases, the baby is the offspring of an unmarried mother.[17] The Vatican's position on abortion ignores the fact that for many women it is a desperate remedy and not sexual liberation. But the Church cannot, without delegitimizing itself, renounce the divine handiwork in the creation of nature and the two sexes. In the end it spuriously mimics the theology of liberation with a superficial commitment to the poor while deflecting attention from its policy on reproductive rights.

Interestingly it was in Chile, the flagship country for neoliberalism in Latin America, that the debate over gender became most ardent. It began even before Josefina Bilbao, minister of the National Women's Service (SERNAM), had published the government position paper. In an interview with *Política y Sociedad,* she tried to wriggle out of the controversy by defining gender according to the *Dictionary of the Royal Academy* as "a group of beings who have one or various characteristics in common." Bilbao was in a difficult position. As a representative of a neoliberal country with a high stake in modernization, she would not want to present an anachronistic impression to the world. But neoliberalism in Chile is also backed by powerful conservative forces that were not prepared to entertain the legitimization of divorce, abortion, or same-sex marriage. Bilbao attempted to sidestep the issue of gender altogether, focusing instead on the conference themes of poverty, education, and political participation, the topics of the paper she later presented at the Beijing conference.[18] However, a group of conservative senators attacked her position paper because in it she had used the offending word, "gender." The senators complained that:

> Many people use the word without further clarification, claiming that masculine and feminine respond merely to cultural and sociological constructions and not to biological conditions that constitute the psychology of woman and man. According to this conception, the difference between the sexes does not have a natural origin, a view that has consequences for the individual, for the family, and for society.

These ambiguous ideas were declared unacceptable. The alternative that the senators came up with, although it was eventually defeated, illustrates what lies behind the struggle over the meaning of gender. Every Chilean, said the dissident senators, had the constitutional duty to preserve "the essential values of Chilean tradition." They claimed to be defending that tradition against "value-oriented totalitarianism" (in other words, feminism), which, they argued, would encourage the proliferation of unnatural practices. These senators defined the family as the stable union of men and women within marriage, and they deemed inadmissible any term or action that threatened the family or "admitted that persons of the same sex might constitute a family."[19] Even though the objecting senators were in a minority, they effectively blocked a more openly secular position on the family and reproductive rights.

As it happened, this was a rearguard action. The Vatican approved the Beijing decisions with reservations. Joaquín Navarro-Valls, on behalf of the Holy See, deplored the unexpected obsession with reproductive rights, saying that "on the one hand those responsible want dignity and freedom for women and on the other they take a paternalist attitude to women." (Imagine the Vatican accusing the United Nations of paternalism!) Clearly battle-scarred, the Vatican explained that in associating itself with the document, it hoped to elevate and develop the authentic and the useful while vigorously denouncing what is "false and damaging to human development."[20]

Even though the Vatican view did not prevail, their campaign raises questions about the role of fundamentalist and conservative religions *in alliance with* neoliberalism, despite the contradiction between the Church's attitude to reproductive rights and the demographic policies of international organizations (such as the World Bank and the Inter-American Development Bank) whose population control policies are of a piece with strategies of capitalist development. What explains this alliance is the ethical vacuum of late-twentieth-century capitalism; with the welfare state delegitimized, there is not much left to hold the dike against the rising tide of poverty. The organization of societies with high unemployment gives rise to repressive measures in nominally democratic societies. Yet advanced capitalism stimulates desires without discrimination or distinction so that the poor are constantly confronted with a cornucopia of consumer goods. The cost of capitalist globalization also exacts a particularly high price on women who are now an important part of the labor force at the lowest and least protected levels.

In Chile, the Church earned goodwill as a protector of human rights during the military regime, but in the postdictatorship period it is an ally of the government of "concertación," which cannot quite hide the iron fist. The Vatican presents itself as the protector of the poor, and the Pope seems to embrace the ancient anticapitalist tradition of the Church when he takes up the issue of poverty in order to rebuke the greedy. However, this is more than anything a rhetorical gesture, and it is significant that the most visible media icon of self-abnegation is not Saint Francis but Mother Theresa, who provided the poor with a place to die in and who consorted with the mighty.

The situation of the poor in advanced capitalist societies is evidently a cause for alarm since it suggests the possibility of rebellion and disturbance of the kind exemplified by neo-Zapatismo in Mexico, which declared itself "the first rebellion against neoliberalism." The responses of national governments are varied but nearly always involve forms of surveillance and control. In the United States, the employed middle class increasingly enclose themselves in fortified enclaves and tacitly accept increased policing and imprisonment of the marginalized; in many parts of the world the free market has not hindered outright authoritarianism; while in some parts of Europe attempts are made to maintain some vestiges of a welfare state. In Latin America, one option for neoliberalism is to embrace the free market while relying on the Church to act as a moral conscience, even though the Church is plainly opposed to the politics of the World Bank and the Inter-American Development Bank. In Argentina, where President Menem depends on popular support from a still largely Catholic interior (a support that is rapidly vanishing), the government has strongly endorsed the Vatican position on the "right to life," as of course have Presidents Violeta Barrios de Chamorro and Arnoldo Alemán of Nicaragua.

The implementation of population policies (as understood by the World Bank and the Inter-American Development Bank) in Latin America necessarily entails a confrontation with the Church, a confrontation that few governments are willing to initiate. Only in Peru, where President Fujimori has dispensed with the pretense of democracy, could radical measures be put into effect without fear of opposition. In his inaugural address to the nation on July 28, 1995, Fujimori unexpectedly broke ranks with other Latin American countries on the issue of birth control, announcing that the state would facilitate access to family planning for poor families. "We have been and shall continue to be a pragmatic government, without taboos or 'sacred cows,'" he said in a pointed reference to the Church. "Peruvian women must be in control of their own destinies." Fujimori played the modernization card, appealing to multilateral lending institutions by promising that by the year 2000 poverty would be reduced by 50 percent and that 50 percent of social spending would be targeted for women. A government document drawn up in 1993 and obtained by the Peruvian newspaper *Oiga* revealed exactly how large the population problem loomed in the government's scheme of things. The document forecast that, at its current growth rate, within four decades Peru would have to support "a population of eight million hungry uneducated and unemployed people in a climate of absolute poverty and deeply inured delinquency." For those belonging to this "social surplus," the document recommended vasectomies for men and tubal ligation for women. Not surprisingly, this language led to comparisons between Fujimori's population control drive and the Nazi's "final solution." Church leaders denounced it as a proposal for the "mutilation" of men and women by the power of darkness.[21]

Fujimori answered his critics in a speech in Beijing, in which he represented himself as a "blue-jeans president" in touch with contemporary problems. He announced that a "social miracle," which would boost women's status from that of mere survival to that of productive development, would follow his "economic miracle."[22] However, his claim to be protecting women rings hollow given that Fujimori has demolished workers' rights in Peru, including health and safety regulations for women in the workplace.[23] Both multinational lending institutions and feminist groups are in favor of promoting sex education, making contraception widely available women, and decriminalizing abortion; however, as far as Latin American feminists are concerned, the goals of these two different kinds of organizations are not comparable. For feminists, population control cannot be separated from social issues, including the protection of human rights and the improvement of living and working conditions. This point was emphasized by the head of the official Mexican delegation to Beijing, José Gómez de León, who, in defending Mexico's support for the Beijing resolutions, also stated that the real theme of Beijing was human rights and not abortion.[24]

The Beijing conference and its official delegations was an hour's distance from the Forum Huairou, where a vast spectrum of opinion was represented. However, press coverage in the West and especially in the United States was largely devoted to Chinese suspicion and defensiveness about human rights issues raised at the non–state-sponsored Forum Huairou. Because of this, the most significant decisions made by the forum were not always reflected in the media.[25] These included "a more complex view of poverty in relation to its feminization; a substantial broadening of human rights, incorporating the rights of women and including the reproductive and sexual rights of persons and also the recognition that these rights are essential to democracy; further, domestic and sexual violence were declared incompatible with any proposal for peace and therefore for any construction of democracy."[26] Virginia Vargas Valente described the Huairou Forum as a practical example of global citizenship and argued that women's struggle for citizenship was an aspect of the more general problems of Latin American modernization and democracy. This led her to the conclusion that, for any real democratization to take place, the relationship between the state and society and the role of the state in public policies and citizens' welfare must be rethought. "Vast" public spaces, in which different social groups identify their needs, elaborate their demands, negotiate their proposals, and force governments to act on measures that have been agreed to, must also be constituted.[27] But the difficulties of enacting even modest changes can be gauged by the fate of the Mexican delegation, which incorporated a diversity of groups representing many different interests. On his return from Beijing, José Gómez de León, General Secretary of CONAPO (Consejo Nacional de Población) and head of the Beijing delegation, chose to reply in circumspect fashion when asked if the abortion laws would be repealed; he said that that the "Beijing agreement does not represent a mandate for any country."[28] The prudent tone of this reply was certainly a response to the attack from the Right. The Mexican experience, like that of Chile, illustrates that a minority expressing views that are counter to modernization can still hinder change and make global citizenship virtual rather than actual.

The demand for global citizenship also confronts feminists, once again, with the difficult problem of whether they can really represent the underclass. As Gayatri Chakravorty Spivak writes,

> Because the limits and opening of a particular civil society are classically tied to a single state, the transnationalization of global capital requires a post-state class-system. The use of women in its establishment is the universalization of feminism of which the United Nations is increasingly becoming the instrument. In this re-territorialization, the collaborative non-governmental organizations are increasingly being called an "international civil society," precisely to efface the role of the state, and to mask the functioning of "economic citizenship." Thus elite, upwardly mobile (generally academic) women of the new diasporas join hands with similar women in the so-called developing world to celebrate a new global public or private "culture," often in the name of the underclass, and keep in place the immiseration of grassroots Southern women.[29]

It is significant that Spivak couches the problem in terms of "women" and not "gender," because gender is not a concept that is particularly useful in this debate. Indeed it is possible that feminists may have no particular interest in defending the use of a term that has now lost even its theoretical rigor.[30] However, there are three reasons for not disposing of "gender" too rapidly. The first is that, as Marta Lamas points out, the "logic of gender" still operates powerfully in the structuring of both the social imaginary and everyday life in ways that are prejudicial to constituting a better society; thus it is important to dismantle the binary opposites that support these structures.[31] The Vatican objections clearly highlighted the importance of this process. Second, even though gender may become little more than a code word for anti-essentialism, it still has its value in this regard. And third, in the context of the crisis of neoliberalism in the university, "gender" provides a space for criticism and knowledge production outside traditional disciplines.[32]

Feminism is not *a* theory and it is not *a* social movement. This is what makes feminism unique. Although global in scope, feminism is necessarily shaped by national and regional cultures, politics, and economics. Perhaps rather than describing feminism simply as a movement with a set of objectives, one should describe it as a position (not exclusive to women) that destabilizes both fundamentalism and the new oppressive structures that are emerging with late capitalism. As a secular nonessentialist and counterhegemonic movement, it must confront other global institutions, not only the Vatican but also the World Bank, a confrontation that involves more urgently than ever the struggle for interpretive power.

Notes

1. See the essay by Sonia E. Alvarez in this volume; see also Virginia Vargas Valente, "Disputando el espacio global. El Movimiento de Mujeres y la IV Conferencia Mundial de Beijing," *Nueva Sociedad* 141 (January-February 1996): 43–53.

2. "Draft Platform for Action" (Fourth Conference on Women, United Nations, New York, May 24, 1995).

3. Donna Haraway, "Gender for a Marxist Dictionary," in *Simians, Cyborgs, and Women: The Reinvention of Nature* (New York: Routledge, 1991), 130.

4. Marta Lamas, "Cuerpo: diferencia sexual y género," *Debate feminista* año 5, 10 (September l994).

5. Ana Alice Alcántara Costa and Cecilia Maria Bacellar Sardenberg, "Teoria e praxis feminista na academia. Os núcleos de estudos sobre a mulher nas universidades brasileiras" (unpublished article).

6. Judith Butler, *Gender Trouble: Feminism and the Subversion of Identity* (New York: Routledge, l990). Butler's critique focuses on the production of "woman" as the subject of feminism. She argues that "the presumption of a binary gender system implicitly retains the belief in a mimetic relation of gender to sex whereby gender mirrors sex or is otherwise restricted by it" (6).

7. Sonia Alvarez, personal communication.

8. "Las feministas exigen al gobiernto que cumpla los acuerdos de Beijing," *Proceso* (Mexico City), January 2, 1995, p. 34.

9. Butler, *Gender Trouble,* 6.

10. *La Nación* (Buenos Aires), June 12, l995, p. 11.

11. Gayatri Chakravorty Spivak, personal communication.

12. Pope John Paul II, *Letter to Women,* June 29, l995.

13. "The Campaign for a Conservative Platform," *Conscience: A Newsjournal of Prochoice Catholic Opinion* 16, no. 3 (Autumn l995):15.

14. Joaquín Navarro-Valls, "Distortion of the Draft Platform for Action," *Conscience* (Autumn 1995):3.

15. *Washington Post,* October 11, l975.

16. "Católicas por el derecho a Decidir de Bogotá, 'Demandas a la Jerarquía Eclesiástica,'" *Conciencia Latinoamericana* (September-December 1994):l6.

17. Myriam Donoso P. y Laura Sau A., "Asignatura pendiente de la transición chilena," *Conciencia Latinoamericana* (September-December 1994):l9.

18. Josefina Bilbao, interview, *Política y Sociedad* (July 1995).

19. *La Epoca* (Santiago), August 19, 1995. For an account of this debate in relation to the reorganization of the university under neoliberalism, see the excellent article by Kemy Oyarzún, "Estudios de Género: saberes, políticas, dominios," *Revista de Critica Cultural* 12 (July 1996).

20. *El Mercurio* (Santiago), September 16, 1996.

21. *Oiga* (Lima), August 4, 1995, p. 12. This policy almost must be considered within the unique context of Peru, in which women's movements have been extremely active, particularly in food distribution programs. For a history of feminism and women's movements, see Virginia Vargas, "Las actuales vertientes del movimiento de mujeres," in *Detras de la puerta; hombres y mujeres en el Perú de hoy,* ed. Patricia Ruiz-Bravo (Lima: Pontifica Universidad Católica del Perú, 1996), 105–143.

22. "Discurso del Señor Presidente de la República del Perú ante la Cuarta Conferencia de la Mujer," *El Peruano* (Lima), September 15, 1995.

23. Delia Zamora, *Piel de mujer* (Lima: Fomento de la Vida, 1995). Delia Zamora is a union leader.

24. *Proceso* (Mexico City), October 2, 1995, p. 32.

25. Clara Jusidman, "Mexico y la IV Conferencia de la Mujer," *Debate feminista* año 6, 12 (October 1995).

26. Valente, "Disputando."

27. Ibid., 141.

28. *Proceso* (Mexico City), October 2, 1995, p. 32.

29. Gayatri Chakravorty Spivak, from a speech given at the Socialist Scholars Conference, March 1996, New York.

30. Both Judith Butler in *Gender Trouble* and Roger Lancaster in *Life is Hard: Machismo, Danger, and the Intimacy of Power in Nicaragua* (Berkeley: University of California Press, 1992), esp. 117–118 n, are critical of the sex-gender distinction and propose ways of retheorizing sex.

31. Lamas, "Cuerpo." See also María Ragúz, "Masculinidad, femenididad y género. Un enfoque psícologico diferente," in *Encrucijadas del saber: Los estudios de género en las ciencias sociales,* ed. Narda Henríquez (Lima: Pontificia Universidad Católica del Perú, 1996), 31–73.

32. See Oyarzún, "Estudios de Género"; see also Narda Henríquez, ed., *Encrucijadas del saber: Los estudios de género en las ciencias sociales* (Lima: Pontificia Universidad Católica del Perú, 1996).

Part Three

Globalization, Transnationalism, and Civil Society

Chapter Twelve

Latin American Feminisms "Go Global": Trends of the 1990s and Challenges for the New Millennium

SONIA E. ALVAREZ

Most of the more than 1,800 Latin Americans who attended the NGO Forum of the Fourth World Conference on Women (FWCW)—held in August–September 1995 in the small backwater town of Huairou, China—appeared to revel in an effusive celebration of post–Robin Morgan "global sisterhood."[1] A festive climate of mutual recognition, exchange, and solidarity—reminiscent of the Latin American feminist *encuentros* of the 1980s[2]—prevailed among many forum participants, who not only had encountered a planetary venue in which to call attention to the needs of women in their own countries but also had discovered their commonalities and differences with women's struggles around the world. Women from every conceivable sector of the Latin American women's movements' "mosaic of diversity"[3] and from every country in the region organized numerous workshops, demonstrations, and cultural events on themes ranging from racism and black and indigenous women's struggles to women's growing impoverishment and to sexuality and reproductive rights. Though the professed goal of the forum was to influence the proceedings and conclusions of FWCW, most at the Latin American "regional tent"—one of the liveliest and most heavily programmed of the dozens of thematic and regional meeting spaces in Huairou—appeared little concerned with and mostly minimally informed about the workings of the UN conference itself.

In marked contrast, some seventy kilometers away in the city of Beijing, a relatively small subset of the Latin American participants—mostly from highly professionalized, thematically specialized, and transnationalized feminist non-governmental organizations (NGOs)—focused their energies primarily on influencing the international Platform for Action, to be drafted by official delegations to the FWCW, and helped articulate the "global women's lobby." A cadre of Latin American feminists appeared to have acquired considerable skill in navigating the often murky waters of global and regional policy arenas. The Regional Coordination of Latin American and Caribbean NGOs—whose six subregional "focal points" had labored tirelessly for nearly two years to try to impact the Beijing conference—held endless (and often closed) strategy meetings and planning sessions; plotted tactical moves; drafted and redrafted innumerable documents, press releases, and lobbying instruments; and worked closely with other international women's networks, whose energies had been similarly directed toward incorporating feminist demands into the UN process. And in maneuvering the circuitous corridors of influence at the FWCW, Latin American NGO lobbyists were able to enlist the support of a significant number of new allies among the official delegates—many of them feminists (sometimes former "sisters-in-struggle") who, over the course of the past decade, had been appointed to government ministries responsible for women's issues or elected to parliament, or who had become staff members of UN agencies or other sectors of the international aid and development establishment.

The different faces of feminism reflected in the contrast between the Latin American "tent" and the regional women's "lobby"—along with the endless organizing, coalition-building, and lobbying efforts; the intricate political negotiations; and the contentious strategic debates about preparations for Huairou and Beijing—distilled many of the important gains as well as new tensions that typified Latin American feminisms and gender politics in the 1990s.[4] Though this essay cannot possibly do justice to the richness, diversity, and complexity of what I shall hereafter refer to as the "Beijing process" in Latin America, I draw examples from distinct moments and events of that process—specifically from the Brazilian movements' preparations for Beijing from 1993 through 1995, the regional preparatory meetings held in Mar del Plata in September 1994, and Latin American women's participation in the NGO Forum in Huairou and in the FWCW in Beijing in August and September 1995—in an effort to analyze five relatively recent trends in the region's feminist politics.[5]

First, I will suggest that the Beijing process highlighted the dramatic proliferation or *multiplication* in the 1990s of the spaces and places in which women who call themselves feminists act and wherein, consequently, feminist discourses circulate—underscoring the reconfiguration of the distinct, and somewhat narrowly defined, Latin American feminist political identity that had congealed in the 1970s and early 1980s. Second, Beijing brought to light the relatively rapid *absorption* of (the more digestible) elements of feminist discourses and agendas by dominant cultural institutions, parallel organizations of civil society, political society and the state, and the international development establishment—all spheres in which feminists can today be found. Third, the increased professionalization and specialization of significant sectors of feminist movements—what I shall call "NGOization"—was also amply evident in Beijing-related coalitions, events, and activities in most countries in the region. Fourth, the increased *articulation* or networking among the varied spaces and places of feminist politics was also made apparent during the Beijing process. Individual activists, groups, specialized feminist NGOs, and their counterparts elsewhere in the region and the globe are today linked through a wide variety of heteronomous movement networks. Indeed, Latin American feminisms increasingly form (a still somewhat marginal) part of that much-celebrated late-twentieth-century phenomenon, "global civil society"; the *transnationalization* of movement discourses and practices is the fifth and final trend I will discuss in what follows.

I shall maintain that, on the one hand, these trends signal a healthy decentering of Latin American feminism, a once relatively isolated and restricted movement, which—like many of the region's so-called new social movements emerging in the 1970s and 1980s in the context of authoritarian or exclusionary (or even formally democratic) regimes—can now more aptly be characterized as an expansive, polycentric, heterogeneous *field of action* that spans into a vast array of cultural, social, and political arenas. These feminisms' proactive capacities and cultural-political influences have expanded significantly. On the other hand, I will argue that these recent developments in gender politics on a national and global scale have triggered profound contradictions within the contemporary Latin American feminist movement field—generating new conflicts (and exacerbating old ones) concerning the appropriate sites, targets, and goals of feminist politics and how and by whom movement priorities should be set. The wide-ranging Latin American feminist field of the 1990s, I will submit, is increasingly mined by uneven power relations among women.

In conclusion, I will suggest that the different logics informing the Latin American tent and the regional women's lobby revealed a growing rift between the two foundational dimensions of the transformational project that inspired second-wave Latin American feminism from the 1970s through the mid-1980s—between what I shall call its ethical-cultural and its structural-institutional dimensions. To contextualize my analysis of contemporary movement advances and contradictions, it is first necessary to trace briefly how Latin American feminists configured a distinct cultural-political identity during the 1970s and early 1980s.

Forging a Latin American Feminist Identity in the Singular

To improve the situation of women in a region marked by egregious social and economic inequalities, most founding members of Latin American feminism's second wave[6] asserted the need to engage fully in the "general struggle" for social justice and against "savage capitalist" models implanted by military and civilian political elites and their imperialist and ruling class allies during the 1960s and 1970s. Most turned their backs on the state and eschewed the conventional political arena—then (rightly) viewed as exclusionary, oppressive, and self-evidently inimical to any and all claims for social justice, let alone gender justice. Many enlisted in clandestine leftist organizations and legal opposition parties and focused their energies on promulgating poor and working-class women's participation in community women's groups, grassroots survival struggles, militant trade unions, and human rights movements—working closely with the women from the popular sectors who constituted what later came to be known as the *movimiento de mujeres* or larger women's movement.[7]

But because both the dominant political culture and that of much of the intellectual and militant Left were permeated by sexism, early feminists also came to understand women's oppression as profoundly cultural, crosscutting all public and private discourses and spaces—including those of the male-dominant opposition, where women and "their issues" too often were consigned to the sidelines of would-be structural-institutional transformations. As Nicaraguan feminist María Teresa Blandón summed up during a presentation at the Huairou NGO Forum, "the feminist movement appeared questioning out-of-date or decrepit ways of doing politics *[formas caducas de hacer política]* . . . and was born with a very radical perspective of criticizing the Left."[8] Given their male *compañeros'* neglect and often outright dismissal of matters of particular concern to women—such as domestic and sexual violence, publicly financed day care, and reproductive rights—early second-wave feminists proclaimed the need to also center their politics on such issues, waging a "specific struggle" for women's rights and human dignity.

Within the larger Latin American women's movement, the boundary between feminists and nonfeminists came to be identified with this dual emphasis on both the "general" and the "specific," the "political" and the "cultural," with the feminist refusal to privilege one struggle over the other. As the hierarchical, militaristic political culture then prevalent on the Left came to be identified as masculinist, and therefore as part of the problem, early feminists further declared the need to invent "new ways of doing politics." Feminist struggle, they asserted, must also be pursued at the level of daily life, of interpersonal and social relations, of "consciousness"—and not just at the level of structures and institutions of (class) domination. Hence, strategies aimed at "*conscientización*"—cultural-political interventions such as promoting workshops and courses on gender power relations, addressing sexual discrimination in the workplace, teaching reproductive health, and helping participants in popular women's organizations who faced domestic violence—were also deemed crucial to the struggle against women's oppression.

Reacting to both exclusionary and often repressive regime institutions and to the "democratic centralism" of the leftist opposition, feminists fashioned a distinct cultural politics that valued radical democratic practices and organizational autonomy. The resulting "feminist culture," according to Maria Luiza Heilborn and Angela Arruda (1995), was

> imbued by such values, manifest, for example, in the decentralization of the movement and its autonomy vis-à-vis other actors. Such decentralization expressed itself in the debates about representation, direct and equitable participation, non-monopoly of the spoken word or of information, in the rotation of occasional tasks and responsibilities, the non-specialization of functions, the non-delegation of power. In sum, organizational horizontalism was extolled as the perfect incarnation of the organizational principles of radical democracy. (20)

Whereas during the early years of Latin American feminism's second wave, movement practices often mirrored the organizational hierarchies inherited from the Left—for example, organizing women's "congresses" and centralized "coordinations" in which different sectors of the larger women's movement would be "represented," "manifestos" would be drafted, and "*palavras de ordem*" (marching orders) would be "consensually" agreed upon—by the 1980s, feminists had adopted more fluid, less hierarchical practices. Representational schemes of all sorts were increasingly shunned, and emphasis placed on each woman "speaking for herself" and not in the name of her feminist group, party, or class organization. Periodic meetings or "*encuentros*," where feminists came together to share experiences, "exchange ideas, express feelings, thoughts and emotions" (Sternbach et al. 1992, 208), rather than to vote on "the" movement's "strategic priorities," increasingly replaced more formal gatherings. In organizational terms, early feminists also emphasized absolute autonomy in relation to the Left, the larger opposition, and, of course, the state—rejecting "any and all injunctions, control or submission to any and all instances external to the women involved" (Heilborn and Arruda 1995, 20)—even as they retained important ideological affinities to the Left-opposition project of structural-institutional transformation.

In Brazil, for example, a distinct feminist identity thus began to be articulated *from within* that opposition by a few women scholars and professionals and some (mostly) white, middle-class women who were active in clandestine opposition parties and radical student movements in the mid-1970s; this identity had distinguished itself from other contemporary gender identities by the beginning of the next decade. Brazilian feminism defined itself in relation to and/or in contrast to: the Left (both the "militant" or revolutionary Left and the theoretical-academic Left, which insisted on relegating gender oppression to the status of a "secondary contraction"); to nonfeminist women also active in the opposition, then known as the "*políticas*," who insisted on prioritizing the "general struggle" and adamantly proclaimed themselves to be "*femeninas não feministas*" (feminine, not feminist); to the hundreds of grassroots women's groups—many times linked to the (antifeminist, even when otherwise progressive) Catholic Church—then proliferating throughout Brazil, who organized around family and community survival issues and constituted privileged publics for feminist cultural-political interventions; and to the media-distorted image of "man-hating, bourgeois, imperialist" feminist movements then emergent in North America and Europe.[9]

Being a feminist, then, came to denote centering one's politics on a particular set of issues of *specific* concern to women, adhering to particular organizing norms (such as direct participation, procedural informality, and the lack of functional specialization), and acting in particular public spaces (for instance, in autonomous feminist organizations) to deepen the analysis of gender oppression and, in the larger *movimiento de mujeres,* to promote widespread consciousness of that oppression. The then common practice of "double militancy"—whereby many feminists participated both in a party or class organization to advance the general struggle *and* in feminist and women's groups to promote changes of specific concern to women (Sternbach et al. 1992, 217)—underscored the sharp boundary constructed between the distinct Latin American feminist political identity and nonfeminist identities and practices.

Of course, that boundary continued to be hotly contested throughout the 1980s, particularly when—as will be discussed below—the return of civilian regimes and electoral democracy to much of the region led growing numbers of "independent" feminists to look toward political parties, legislatures, and the state as potentially viable arenas in which to promote changes in women's status. Brazilian feminist identity, for instance, was originally configured in a still-authoritarian political conjuncture, where the spaces for its political articulation—particularly outside the opposition—were highly restricted. By the late 1970s and early 1980s, however, as legal opposition parties gained electoral strength and came to power in several states and municipalities, the radically "autonomous" organizational and political feminist identity described above was deeply shaken; many feminist activists flocked to electoral politics, began pressuring for the adoption of progressive gender policies, and even went to work for some of the new local opposition governments.

Latin American Feminism "Goes Plural"

The Latin American Beijing process appeared to signal a *vertiginous multiplication of the spaces and places in which women who call themselves feminists act today and a reconfiguration of feminist identities*—suggesting that by the mid-1990s, the boundary demarcating what constituted feminist versus nonfeminist practices had been further unsettled. As the leftist opposition field in which early feminism was inserted itself became less homogeneous, less unified, and more diversified in its discourses and practices[10] over the course of the past decade, so, too, did the region's feminist movements. With the return of electoral democracy (however flawed and still restricted) and liberal rights discourses (however hollow and "neo") to much of the region, the potential spaces available for the articulation of a feminist politics appeared to have dramatically expanded.

The more than one thousand participants in the Mar del Plata NGO Forum appeared to embody the growing heterogeneity of feminist practices in the region and their dense imbrication with multiple spaces of action—within and without the larger women's movement. Among them were self-professed "Peronist feminists" and party activists of all ideological persuasions who seemed to have embraced core aspects of a liberal feminist "women's equality" agenda; black feminists from Peru, Bolivia, Colombia, Nicaragua, Brazil, the Dominican Republic, and Uruguay who declared allegiance to both black and women's rights movements; prominent feminist scholars—including Argentina's Maria del Carmen Feijoó and Chile's Teresa Valdés—now serving as "consultants" advising governments, foundations, and UN agencies how best to promote "gender equity"; erstwhile members of clandestine opposition parties in the 1960s and 1970s who had founded feminist collectives in the early 1980s and who were now "professionals" in national and international women's, environmental, human rights, and development NGOs; "founding mothers" of Latin American feminism's second wave—including Peru's Roxana Carrillo and Brazil's Branca Moreira Alves and Ana Maria Brasileiro—now working for UNIFEM (the United Nations Development Fund for Women) and other UN and development agencies; working-class leaders from popular movements in Peru, Brazil, Nicaragua, and Mexico who proclaimed themselves "popular feminists"; directors and staff from specialized government agencies addressing women's issues, some of whom—like Bolivia's Sonia Montaño or Chile's Maria Elena Valenzuela—had extensive prior trajectories as autonomous feminists; and Catholic theologians and lay activists from Católicas por el Derecho a Decidir—the Latin American affiliate of Catholics for Free Choice, with branches in Mexico, Brazil, and Uruguay—who were intent on defying the Church's dogmatic antifeminism.

In short, the Beijing process made abundantly clear a significant *decentering* of contemporary Latin American feminist practices.[11] The process revealed that—in contrast to the early years of feminism—many women who proclaim themselves "feminist" today no longer undertake their cultural-political interventions primarily or exclusively within autonomous feminist groups or organizations of the *movimiento de mujeres*. Rather, by the mid-1990s, many feminists claimed to be taking their transformational discourses and practices into a wide variety of sociocultural and political arenas. And the erstwhile prevalent practice of double militancy appeared to be giving way to more integrated feminist practices aimed at impacting or transforming dominant political cultural discourses and practices from within.

This decentering of feminist practices, moreover, also appeared to have contributed to a redefinition and expansion of the feminist agenda for social transformation. Many activists now affirmed that feminist struggles should no longer be confined to a set of specific issues of primary or exclusive concern to women—such as sexual violence and abortion—but, as proclaimed by one of the Brazilian movement's slogans during their preparations for Beijing, should also seek to "see the world through the eyes of women," to view the "general struggle" through a gendered lens. As one long-time Argentine feminist who in recent years has worked in government put it during a workshop at the Huairou NGO Forum, "we must develop more than just a feminist policy agenda; we must strive to develop a feminist agenda for public policy." Latin American and Caribbean Regional NGO

Forum coordinator and long-time feminist activist from Peru, Virginia Vargas, reaffirmed this position in her speech to the assembled government delegates at the FWCW:

> There are no topics that are exclusively women's, nor can there be themes about which we are prohibited from opining and deciding. The great global preoccupations concern us. Human rights, nuclear and military disarmament, the eradication of poverty, the deepening of democracy grounded in the respect for difference, and a sustainable development centered on people are key for the future of humanity. Concrete measures to achieve gender justice must be specified.[12]

Carmen Tornaría, national coordinator of the Grupo Iniciativa Peking-Uruguay, further argued that feminists must recast their historic claims in response to contemporary national and international discursive frameworks concerning citizenship rights, and that feminist discourses and strategies "should vary according to the historical moment." Rather than advocating women's right to abortion exclusively on the historic feminist grounds that "our bodies belong to us," she contended, feminists today must also couch "sexual rights, the decriminalization of abortion . . . as themes related to the construction of citizenship and affirm the idea that States should be secular and that there should be as much freedom as possible so that each person can exercise her sexuality or maternity as she pleases."[13]

This kind of gendered perspective on "the general" has enabled feminists to develop innovative advocacy strategies—for example, they have argued successfully for the inclusion of women's rights within the framework of international human rights law.[14] Building on the Vienna Platform for Action and the UN Declaration on the Elimination of Violence Against Women—which recognized that the rights of women and girls are an inalienable, integral, and indivisible part of universal human rights—the final document of the Mar del Plata forum proclaims, for example:

> Violence against women, beyond being a violation of human rights, restricts women's citizenship, obstructs their development and substantially affects the quality of life of societies. . . . The social cost of violence practiced against women translates into lost work days, expenditures in services to victims, but even more, in the enormous costs incurred in human suffering and has the long-term effect of perpetuating a violent and unequal social structure.[15]

The Beijing process further revealed that the once-rigid boundary between feminists and nonfeminists was also being challenged by new movement actors who insisted on resignifying feminism and who claimed to enact their feminist politics in a wide range of arenas. With the expansion of black feminism, lesbian feminism, popular feminism, ecofeminism, Christian feminism, and so on,[16] the mid-1980s and 1990s witnessed the proliferation of new actors whose political-personal trajectories often differed significantly from those of earlier feminists (now referred to as the *"históricas,"* or historic feminists), whose discourses emphasized the ways in which race/ethnicity, class, sexuality, age, and so on are *constitutive* of gender identities, and whose practices sometimes differed from the cultural politics of the early years of Latin American feminism.

Afro–Latin American women participants at the Mar del Plata NGO Forum, for example, proclaimed that racism deeply marks black women's lives and entreated all Latin American women's movement activists to embrace their particular struggle:

> Racism as an ideological form which sustains the domination of one sector of the population by another, is one of the fundamental causes which blocks the sustainable development of non-white sectors of Latin American and Caribbean populations, who make up the majorities of our continent. This has not been alien to the women's movement, since it refers to an ideology inscribed in our social structures. Considering the struggle and participation of Black women in the construction of our societies, we call on all women to incorporate themselves into our struggle to eradicate another form of discrimination.[17]

Afro–Latin American women—whose political trajectories often traversed both black movement and feminist organizations—participated in the Beijing process in expressive numbers, proclaiming that "Any strategy for development, peace, or equality must necessarily consider the particularities of Black women" and promoting the formation of national networks that would guarantee "the active participation of diverse ethnic and racial sectors of women" in the Beijing meetings (Red de Mujeres 1994). Some lesbian feminists similarly saw participation in the preparatory process as an opportunity to insist that "it is necessary to break the isolation and marginality imposed on lesbians. It is therefore necessary for the women's movement . . . to incorporate . . . [lesbian] specificity as an issue of relevance to all women."[18] Black women and lesbians organized several sessions at the NGO Forum in Mar del Plata and also caucused separately to ensure that their specific demands were included in the forum's recommendations to ECLAC (the Economic Commission on Latin America and the Caribbean).

While declaring their affinity with many aspects of the feminist political imaginary, many self-proclaimed popular feminists and rural and urban female trade unionists participating in the Beijing process nonetheless affirmed an identity distinct from that of the predominantly white, middle-class, university-educated *históricas*. In evaluating her experience at the Mar del Plata NGO Forum, one working-class activist from Brazil stated that although participating in a legal training course offered by feminist attorneys "[had helped to] redeem my self-esteem, to be conscious of citizenship, to struggle for my rights, to make my own history, to be my own woman *[ser dona de mim],"* she had also seen "rich women talking about the difficulties and violences lived by poor women, and I thought to myself that no matter how hard they tried to be authentic they were far from knowing what we in the [urban] periphery, from the less privileged classes, experience."[19] On the one hand, this statement suggests that feminist interventions in the larger women's movement arguably have had important cultural-political effects; yet, on the other hand, it also makes clear that feminism is being resignified as it is appropriated by women whose life experiences differ significantly from those of the founding mothers of Latin American feminism's second wave. As Teresa Aparcana—president of the Coordenadora Metropolitana del Programa de Vaso de Leche in Lima—aptly put it during a presentation at the Mar del Plata forum: "Before, talking about feminism was taboo among women of the popular sectors. . . . yes, we are feminists today, but we are feminists of a new world . . . and we will not subject ourselves to other women."

Most of the national and regional movement documents generated during the Beijing process emphasized the "plural," "multicultural," and "pluriethnic" character of Latin American and Caribbean societies and women's movements. The final Brazilian movements' preparatory document proclaimed the women's movement to be a "kaleidoscope"; declared that it had "multiplied, is heterogeneous and plural"; and featured extensive references to the "specific demands of Black women, young women, indigenous women, lesbians, [and] disabled women."[20] And "diversity" was *the* central theme around which activities were structured at the Latin American and Caribbean tent at the NGO Forum in Huairou.

The Absorption of (Select) Feminist Discourses and Agendas by Organized Civil Society, Political Society, and National and International Policy Arenas

The multiplication of spaces in which Latin American feminists were active in the 1990s was both a cause and consequence of the relatively *rapid appropriation or absorption of some new and historic feminist ideas and issues by the mainstream of contemporary Latin American states and societies.* The tireless efforts of feminists—now dispersed throughout the fabric of Latin American societies—to bring their claims to bear on male-dominant civil and political society and the state would appear to have borne fruit.

In the last decade, virtually all Latin American governments established specialized state agencies, ministries, and secretariats charged with improving the status of women and "incorporating" them into "development."[21] Many of the region's new "democratic" constitutions contain clauses promoting women's equality in the family, the workplace, and the polity.[22] Specialized police precincts have been set up in Brazil, Nicaragua, Peru, and several other countries to prosecute crimes against women.[23] The full spectrum of political parties—progressive, centrist, and conservative—today feel compelled to pay at least lip service to women's concerns. Parliaments in countries such as Argentina and Brazil have passed legislation establishing quotas for women's representation on party electoral lists.[24] Some unions—like the progressive Central Unica dos Trabalhadores (CUT), the largest trade union in Brazil, with over 17 million members—have also established representational quotas to enhance women's participation among union leadership. CUT has also adopted some feminist banners as its own, recently declaring its determination to combat sexual harassment in the workplace.[25]

The UN process itself lent newfound or renewed legitimacy to many domestic and regional feminist demands for gender justice. A wide gamut of long-standing feminist claims—ranging from demands for nonsexist educational policies to more equitable participation in public and family life to reproductive rights—were rife in the language of the numerous official UN, ECLAC, and national government documents produced to evaluate progress toward "gender equity" over the course of the previous decade. The ECLAC Program for Action, for instance, proclaimed that its central objective was to "[a]ccelerate the achievement of gender equity and the total integration of women into the development process, as well as the full exercise of citizenship within the framework of a sustainable development, with social justice and democracy."[26]

The issue of violence against women, which just a decade ago was not even mentioned at the Nairobi Platform for Action, featured prominently in Beijing-related national and regional documents and was now framed as a "human rights" issue.[27] The regional platform also acknowledges the "[p]ersistence of cultural models that exclude, silence or distort the identity and understandings of women in all areas of social life, and which are expressed in the family, in education, the mass media and art"[28] and, for the first time, enjoins governments to adopt measures to "[p]romote cultural equality and the respect for cultural diversity so as to stimulate the visible and equitable participation of women and men of all ethnic groups."[29]

In several countries, moreover, feminist scholars and NGO professionals were incorporated into their governments' preparatory processes and could be found among the official delegates to both the Mar del Plata and Beijing conferences in unprecedented numbers. For the first time in the history of Brazil's participation in UN conferences, for example, the Foreign Ministry recruited prominent feminist scholars to draft its official report and invited dozens of women's movement activists to participate in a number of government-sponsored public seminars on women's issues. Many of the women's movement's recommendations found their way into the official reports to the UN, and the Brazilian government ultimately approved the Beijing platform without reservations.

Moreover, African-Brazilian feminists participating in the Beijing process succeeded in persuading their government to include the race-specific data and policy recommendations in its official report to the UN. They played a key role in both Mar del Plata and Beijing in getting race and ethnicity included in the regional and global Platforms for Action, and they were represented among the official delegates to both the ECLAC and Beijing conferences. Black feminist Nilza Iraci underscored the significance of African-Brazilian women's participation, stressing that the fact that race and ethnicity had been introduced "to 181 countries through the initiative of the official Brazilian delegation [to the FWCW] establishes new parameters for the discussion of the racial question. It represents the Brazilian government's recognition, at the international level, of the fallacy of racial democracy."[30]

The incorporation of select feminist claims at the level of official UN and government discourse and policy, of course, hardly translates into effective implementation or enforcement. Brazilian feminists are quick to point out, for instance, that Brazil has signed but seldom complied with prior international agreements on women's equality (such as the Convention to End Discrimination Against Women, or CEDAW). They note, further, that since the return of civilian rule in 1985, Congress has enacted much progressive gender legislation that has yet to be fully implemented. As neoliberalism rolls back the state and enthrones the (gendered) logic of the market, it is unlikely that the necessary resources will be allocated to the promotion of gender equality by male-dominant states and international regimes—at least, not in the absence of political will and the pressure from organized mass constituencies that might help generate such will.

The absorption of feminist discourses has also been, at best, partial and selective—and, as Verónica Schild (in this volume) poignantly reminds us, the consequences of selective appropriation are often less than benign. Although by the 1990s many Latin American governments might more readily be persuaded that women should be "incorporated into national development" or that educating women is "good for economic modernization," most remain hesitant to embrace feminist claims—for reproductive choice, sexual self-determination, alternative family structures, lesbian rights, and so on—because to do so would significantly unsettle prevailing gender power arrangements. This resistance was also amply evident in the Beijing process, as the governments of Argentina, Ecuador, and Honduras, in particular, lined up behind the Vatican and took reactionary positions on every conceivable issue that might undermine "Christian family values."[31]

The Re/configuration of the Latin American Feminist Movement Field in the 1990s

Although feminist demands are, invariably, resignified—and often radically tergiversated—when they "enter" the state or the UN arena, the inclusion of many feminists and some of their core issues into the official Beijing preparatory process in Latin America cannot merely be viewed as evidence of "co-optation," and it is certainly not the consequence of the male-dominated governments' "largesse." Rather, this inclusion must at least partially be attributed to the effectiveness of relentless interventions by that growing number of feminists who have "occupied," if not "conquered," a multitude of male-dominant publics in recent years. In other words, feminist discourses now circulate in and potentially destabilize the dominant political cultures of a wide variety of social, cultural, and political actors and institutions in Latin America.

The notion of absorption—as opposed to co-optation—implies agency. That is, Latin American feminists who have chosen to work primarily or exclusively within government bureaucracies, parliaments, trade unions, and so on, are not (always) mere "dupes" who have been "bought off" or have "sold out" to masculinist political cultures. Instead, as Amy Lind persuasively argues, "in the past fifteen years . . . many [feminists] have come to realize that [the state] and other institutions as well, such as foreign banks and multinationals, play increasingly powerful roles in defining what can and cannot be placed on the development agenda" (1995, 217), and thus these institutions have become crucial arenas for feminist struggle. Drawing on Jean Franco, Lind contends that feminists acting within the state or traditionally male-dominant institutions of civil and political society are also engaged in struggles for "'interpretive power' in defining the discursive domain in which concrete decisions about development are made" (17).

Moreover, as Arturo Escobar maintains, "the production of new [official gender] discourses . . . is not a one-sided process; it might create conditions for resistance . . . even if these resistances take place within the modes of development discourse" (1995, 155). Though Schild (in this volume) persuasively argues that there is a "convergence between the concerted actions of the networks of women activists and professionals that make up a large segment of the women's movement" and neoliberal state's "cultural-political project," most feminists who dedicated their organizing efforts to the Beijing process over the course of early 1990s insisted that the minimally progressive official documents and platforms it generated provided potentially powerful (at least symbolic) tools with which to resist neoliberalism's cultural offensive and wage new domestic policy battles.

The decentering of feminist practices in the 1990s, coupled with the proliferation of feminist actors, issues, and claims, moreover had unsettled the distinct feminist cultural politics constructed in the 1970s and early 1980s, giving rise to a vast new range of practices and cultural-political interventions. The Beijing process amply testified to the expansive reach of feminist discourses into a panoply of cultural/political/quotidian spaces and places, suggesting a significant reconfiguration of the feminist movement field. Though "the heroic days of barricades and demonstrations seem to be over, at least for the time being," as Alícia Frohmann and Teresa Valdés argue, leading some analysts and historic activists to "go so far as to say that there is no longer a women's movement . . . and that democracy co-opted the feminist discourse and demobilized the movement" (1995, 291), one might argue instead that the changed national and international context—more receptive, at least rhetorically, to some feminist claims—has helped reshape feminist identities and discourses and redirected practices at new "targets" both within and beyond the larger women's movement field. The political demands, discourses, practices, and mobilizational and policy strategies of feminist movements are today spread widely, and sometimes invisibly, through the social fabric, constituting political-communicative movement webs[32] that stretch into and across feminist collectives and NGOs, popular women's organizations, trade unions, parliaments, the academy, the Church, the media, and other organizations and institutions.

In what follows, I will critically assess the extent to which this heterogeneous, multifaceted Latin American feminist field still demarcated "a common [ethical-political] field of references and differences for collective action and political contestation"[33]—a shared "discursive matrix," which, according to Eder Sader (1988), refers to "distinctive ways of approaching reality which imply different attributions of meaning." Do the *"femócratas"*[34]—as some activists refer to feminists from the movement who have entered the state or the development establishment—continue to share a "common field of references" with popular feminists, trade unionists, radical lesbians, and independent feminist collectives? I will suggest that, though Latin American feminisms remain informed by a shared normative imperative—namely, eradicating women's subordination—the diverse (and sometimes divergent) practices; growing power imbalances; and uneven access to cultural, material, and political resources of subjects differentially situated within the field represent serious contradictions and new challenges as Latin American feminisms approach the new millennium.

The "NGOization" of Latin American Feminisms

In the 1990s, a relatively new phenomenon—the feminist NGO—came to play a prominent and highly controversial role in sustaining and articulating the constitutive webs of the expansive Latin American feminist movement field. Indeed, the absorption of some of the more culturally acceptable items of the feminist agenda fostered the *increased specialization and professionalization* of growing numbers of feminist NGOs dedicated to intervening in national and international policy processes.[35] On the one hand, dominant institutions incorporated select items of that agenda, in part because growing numbers of feminist activists have devoted their organizational energies to that end over the course of the past decade. On the other hand, the very creation of governmental and intergovernmental institutions dealing with "women's issues," the proliferation of legislation targeting women, and other forms of institutionalization of the feminist transformational agenda during the 1980s generated increased demand for extragovernmental institutions that could produce specialized information about women's status to be more readily and effectively "fed into" the policy process—something that the autonomous feminist groups or collectives of yesteryear, guided by the more informal, antihierarchical, functionally undifferentiated "feminist culture" so aptly summarized by Heilborn and Arruda (1995) would have been hard pressed to accomplish.

The growing "developmentalization" of women as new "client groups" of states and international regimes (Escobar 1995, 155) moreover contributed to NGOization by infusing the more professionalized sectors of the feminist movement field with significant material resources. Maria Aparecida Schumaher and Elizabeth

Vargas (1993) maintain that the spread of NGOs in Brazil in recent years is intimately related to the erosion and inefficiency of the national state:

> The big multilateral agencies (United Nations, World Bank), in possession of voluminous funds for investment in the Third World, until the 1970s almost exclusively financed governments. The changing evaluation of the performance of official organs reoriented the flow of such resources. . . . The wastefulness, malversation of funds, the rotativity of government technical personnel, are at the origin of this shift. Thus, organizations of civil society came to represent an interesting alternative. Presenting a clearer action profile and presenting themselves as available for better defined partnership relations, the NGOs appear as an efficient mechanism for the implementation of public policies, be they progressive or not. (362–363)

As specialized governmental agencies such as SERNAM (the National Women's Bureau) in Chile, CNDM (the National Council on Women's Rights) in Brazil, CONAMU (the National Women's Council) in Venezuela, and DINAMU (the National Women's Directorate) in Ecuador were typically understaffed, underfunded, and often far removed from centers of power within the state, they increasingly delegated or subcontracted data gathering, policy assessment (and, increasingly, implementation), and other forms of "project management" to feminist NGOs.[36] Although many advances in gender policy can be attributed to the organizational efficiency and political pragmatism of these new movement actors, critics note that in taking on research or service activities commissioned by state and international agencies, feminist NGOs sometimes act like "neo-" rather than "nongovernmental" organizations. In other words, some NGOs are seen to be providing public services that formerly were (and still ought to be) the purview of the state.[37]

Although the concept of nongovernmental organization is indiscriminately deployed in development discourse to refer to any social actor *not* clearly situated within the realm of the state or the market—from peasant collectives and community soup kitchens to research-oriented policy think tanks—within contemporary Latin American women's movements, the term "feminist NGO" has come to denote particular kinds of groups with orientations and practices distinct from those of the historic feminist groups of the 1970s and early 1980s. Indeed, most Beijing-related documents produced by both movements and governments echoed the ever more common distinction made among feminists between NGOs and "the movement" in recent years. The former characteristically have functionally specialized, paid, professional staff and, sometimes, a limited group of volunteers; receive funding from bilateral and multilateral agencies and (usually foreign) private foundations; and engage in pragmatic strategic planning to develop "reports" or "projects" aimed at influencing public policies and providing advice or *asesoría* to the *movimiento de mujeres* and varied services to low-income women.[38] Though sometimes engaging in similar *asesoría* and policy-oriented activities, the feminist movement is commonly understood to be made up of militant feminist groups or collectives that fit more neatly into the foundational feminist mold described above. They have largely volunteer and often sporadic participants (rather than "staff"), more informal organizational structures, and significantly smaller operating budgets; their actions (rather than "projects") are guided by more loosely defined, conjunctural goals and objectives.

Feminist NGOs decidedly took center stage during the Latin American Beijing process. It was these relatively new movement actors—whose numbers have risen dramatically since the mid-1980s—who were called in as consultants by ECLAC and many national governments to provide "expert" input into official preparatory documents; it was they who received (often sizable) grants from bilateral and multilateral aid agencies and private national and international foundations to organize Beijing-related activities, produce reports and publications, and so on; and it was NGOs, according to most women's movement participants and observers, who dominated the political and organizational dynamics and who controlled the purse strings of the women's movements' parallel Beijing preparatory process in Latin America and elsewhere. Indeed, in a highly controversial move, the U.S. Agency for International Development (USAID)—the primary bilateral funder of the Latin American NGOs' participation in the coordination for the Beijing conference—insisted on disbursing funds through "focal points" consisting of a single NGO or a consortium of NGOs in each of six subregions.[39] In most countries, NGOs skilled in the art of lobbying—and who possessed policy-specialized staff, who had previous experience in the UN process, and who earned handsome foreign funding—were the ones who orchestrated national and regional Beijing-related events, defined the larger women's movement's Beijing agenda, and organized the pre-FWCW coordination described below.

The Increased Articulation and Transnationalization of Latin American Feminist Organizations, Agendas, and Strategies

The Beijing process itself induced activists—most often at the initiative of or under the leadership of feminist NGOs—to forge new local, national, regional, and global coalitions, reinforcing the growing tendency to transform the largely informal linkages fashioned during the 1980s through numerous local and regional *encuentros* into the more formal, structured *redes* (networks) or "articulations" of the 1990s. To be sure, NGO participation in and global coalition building for the UN process "was dramatically intensified as a consequence of the [rapid] sequence of world conferences of the 1990s."[40] And this process of participation and articulation of "global civil society" was actively encouraged by bilateral and multilateral agencies and private philanthropy alike. As one Uruguayan feminist put it, the veritable funding frenzy for UN-related activities reflected the shifting "cycles of fashion of the agencies of international cooperation . . . which went from [support for] research centers, to grassroots organizations, to NGOs, to local networks, to regional networks, and now global networks."[41]

In Brazil, a few feminist NGOs professionals who had participated in previous UN conferences began organizing for Beijing in the fall of 1993. With the support of UNIFEM, they held a national meeting in Rio de Janeiro in January 1994 to develop strategies for Beijing. Close to one hundred representatives of women's groups from eighteen states voted to create a coordinating body charged with overseeing movement efforts to "bring Beijing home to Brazil." They formed a national coalition—the Articulation of Brazilian Women for Beijing '95—and launched an unprecedented nationwide effort focused on drawing public attention to the importance of international conventions on women's rights and raising public awareness of gender inequality.

With the professed goal of enhancing the domestic impact of the Beijing conference, this coalition secured funding from international foundations such as the Ford Foundation, the McArthur Foundation, German and other European agencies, and over half a dozen others and promoted the creation or reactivation women's movement forums[42] in twenty-five of Brazil's twenty-six states and the Federal District. State women's forums promoted ninety-one local meetings and debates to evaluate progress toward women's equality over the course of the two UN-designated "decades for women" and to take stock of the obstacles still faced in the struggle for gender justice. Over eight hundred women's organizations were involved in this unprecedented national articulatory process, unquestionably infusing renewed mobilizational energies into local women's movements—especially in more remote areas of Brazil where the movement was still weak or incipient. More than seven hundred local delegates traveled from the far reaches of Brazil to attend the National Conference of Brazilian Women Toward Beijing held in Rio de Janeiro in June 1995. And approximately three hundred Brazilian women ultimately made their way to the NGO Forum in Huairou (as compared to the mere thirty or so who had participated in the forum during the Third World Conference on Women in Nairobi in 1985), with some forty of these staying on to participate in the "global women's lobby" at the FWCW.

National and regional issue-specific networks (or "identity" networks), also largely articulated by feminist NGOs—linking black women's organizations, indigenous women, lesbian rights advocates, socialist feminists, domestic workers, feminists in political parties, and individuals and groups working on issues ranging from feminist ecology to violence against women to reproductive rights—similarly have propagated dramatically in recent years[43] and also played a prominent role in the Beijing process. Between 1993 and 1995, preexisting specialized networks and pro-Beijing coalitions alike held innumerable seminars and conferences specifically oriented toward drafting and voting on "documents" that would contribute to official government reports to the UN as well as, ultimately, to the Beijing Platform for Action. And, in marked contrast to the more fluid, informal feminist *encuentros* of yesteryear, participation in these preparatory meetings was typically restricted to card-carrying members of feminist networks, feminist social scientists, policy analysts and other "specialists," and designated "representatives" of local women's groups and forums (in the case of Brazil) or of subregional focal points (in the case of the Latin American and Caribbean NGO coordination regions).

Though only a relatively small number of feminist NGO professionals were directly involved, the unprecedented number of specialized strategy meetings held by the Regional Coordination organizers themselves reflected the fact that *feminist advocacy efforts have become increasingly transnationalized* in recent years.[44] As one internationally prominent Brazilian NGO professional stated, "Beijing confirms the notion that the gender agenda is an agenda without frontiers . . . it generated a global agenda." Regional coordination members and the innumerable documents they produced made continual reference to the salience of intervening in "planetary policies" through the "construction of an international civil society."

For Mar del Plata NGO Forum coordinator Ana Falú, Beijing represented the first time that Latin American women had come to a world summit with such a highly organized, formally structured regional network. Although globalization and the various regional economic integration initiatives certainly worked to enhance feminist awareness of the importance of impacting transnational policy arenas, Falú further suggested that "international cooperation" had helped foster this process because "USAID's convocation was appropriated by the movement."[45] The Beijing process also strengthened the region's heretofore tenuous links to international feminist NGOs outside Latin America—which had experienced a significant boost when a Brazilian national feminist network, the Coalition of Women's NGOs for the Environment, Population, and Development, hosted the global women's lobby, dubbed *Planeta Fêmea* (female planet), at the Rio de Janeiro conference in 1992. Funding from North America for Beijing-related preparatory activities enabled Latin American NGO professionals to participate in North American feminist-controlled global meganetworks (both "virtual" and "real"; see Lins Ribeiro, in this volume)—such as Bella Abzug's Women's Environment and Development Organization (WEDO)—on a more even footing than ever before.

As evidenced by the selective inclusion of feminist demands in the Mar del Plata and Beijing platforms, the growing articulation and transnationalization of some actors within the Latin American feminist movement field, coupled with the movement's increased NGOization, have arguably bolstered the proactive capacity of feminism in national and international policy processes and augmented its influence in global, regional, and national policy arenas. To be sure, feminists have been central actors in the configuration of what Keck and Sikkink (1992) have dubbed "transnational issue networks":

> A transnational issue network includes a set of relevant actors working internationally on an issue who are bound together by shared values, a common discourse, and dense exchanges of information and services. Such networks are most prevalent in issue areas characterized by high value content and informational uncertainty. They involve actors from non-governmental, governmental, and intergovernmental orga-

> nizations. What is novel in these networks is the ability of non-traditional international actors to mobilize information strategically so as to gain leverage over much more powerful organizations and governments. (Sikkink 1995, 3–4)

The Beijing process suggests that the increasingly formalized linkages between Latin American feminists working in NGOs and those acting within male-dominant policy arenas, political parties, state institutions, and multilateral agencies have significantly improved the leverage of feminist rights advocates in recent years.

Global Feminism and Its Discontents: Tensions and Contradictions in an Expansive, Heterogeneous Social Movement Field

While the trends discussed above represented significant advances for feminist politics in the region, they also posed new challenges and triggered fresh tensions within an increasingly diverse, complex, and often factious social movement field. The proliferation of spaces of feminist action—which now include transnationalized, formalized networks; professionalized NGOs; the state; and international development apparatuses—is not easily reconciled to historic feminist cultural-political practices, triggering continual re/negotiations of, and often contentions debates over, the appropriate sites, targets, and goals of feminist politics, and indeed over the very "meaning" of feminism itself.

The contrasting discourses and practices engaged in by the Latin American tent at Huairou and the Beijing regional lobby were viewed by many as emblematic of a growing rift between differentially situated actors within the Latin American feminist movement field. Although many heralded the absorption of movement demands in the FWCW and ECLAC platforms and in official government reports to the UN as a triumph, "a qualitative leap," others insisted that "feminist demands are not exhausted in the transformation of the State." Many feminist critics and activists in the larger *movimiento de mujeres* condemned what they viewed as excessively narrow, state-centric strategies that appeared to respond more to the "logic of patriarchal domination" than to an alternative "feminist worldview" and that seemed to underplay the importance of continued feminist struggle in the realms of fomenting gender consciousness and challenging patriarchal cultural norms. As one Uruguay feminist proclaimed during the Mar del Plata forum, "we have to work to transform the patriarchal cultural logic . . . we cannot only intervene in the institutional."

In an essay that circulated widely during the Sixth Latin American and Caribbean Feminist *Encuentro* held in November 1993 in El Salvador, Chilean feminist Margarita Pisano foreshadowed many of the criticisms later leveled during the Beijing process by feminist activists wary of the prospect that, as one Brazilian expressed it, "the feminist movement is becoming a U.N. conference":

> Political pressure strategies based on lobbies have a subtle and dangerous limit, a not too well demarcated frontier with the traffic of influence. If we direct our energies at influencing the system and its powers, we profoundly weaken the power of social movements like feminism and its possible allies, which have been constructing a transformative project of civilizational change. . . . Groups in power are very clear on this game. It involves . . . an intentionality of dividing to impede the connections among transformative projects. . . . It is ingenious to think that with the logic of lobbies and negotiation, we will achieve a utopia that can permeate the human imaginary. For that we need a force capable of putting forth as a realizable desire a utopia that breaks with the dynamic of domination.[46]

Pisano's "*feministas cómplices*"—an informal network of radical women from throughout the region who declare "a great discomfort before current discourses, their proposals for 'change' and the lack of imagination and creativity they contain"—pointedly distance themselves from "the others," the "*institucionalizadas,*" who, according to the *cómplices,* "in part feel themselves to be producers of this [masculine] culture and adhere to the projects and systems it has produced."[47] Indeed, new boundaries *within* the Latin American feminist field were apparently being re/drawn, and sharp, dualistic distinctions were rife in activist discourses concerning the Beijing process: the "bureaucratic-institutional movement" versus "independent feminists"; "the specialists" versus "*las metafóricas*";[48] "the *movimiento de mujeres*" versus "the *movimiento de proyectos de mujeres*" (the movement of women's projects); "*las ongistas*" (the NGOers) versus "*el movimiento.*"

Some regard feminists who have entered the state as constituting a new "gender technocracy" that is abandoning core foundational feminist principles. As one Paraguayan feminist expressed with dismay during a Huairou workshop, "I see my feminist comrades going down a completely alienated path . . . rebelliousness is being done away with . . . we are conforming to their rules." Her concern was echoed by a Mexican feminist during a Huairou workshop entitled "Latin American Feminisms: Twenty Years Later": "Feminism has ceased to be marginal and is now institutional . . . the cost of this institutionalization has been great . . . it seems that we have forgotten about process . . . the most urgent of our problems will not be resolved here [in Beijing] . . . I don't think we should wager so much on a conference . . . we must go back and look in the mirror."

The latest form of institutionalization, in the form the feminist NGOs, has been particularly controversial within the larger feminist field, and the Beijing process exacerbated existing tensions between the "*ongistas*" and the "others." During a Huairou forum workshop entitled "Metaforo: Las Cumbres Mundiales y el Movimiento de Mujeres" (Metaforum: World Summits and the Women's Movement), organized by Grupo Iniciativa Peking-Uruguay to critically discuss the implications of feminist participation in the UN process, a Peruvian feminist suggested that "this 'Summits' thing caught us very disorganized; this has to do with the genesis of NGOs in Latin America . . . we moved very quickly from consciousness-raising groups to NGOs . . . and this has created new tensions." The differential power wielded by some NGOs and their predominance during the Beijing process was criticized by a Chilean participant: "We entered this process in a very disordered fashion. Some NGOs had a greater protagonism because they obtained funding. . . . There are some who have taken control *[han tomado el mando]*."

To be sure, the Beijing process suggested that because resources provided by the international development community enabled some feminist NGOs to gather policy-relevant information and maintain permanent staff charged with "interfacing" with UN, government, and media representatives, these more professionalized, policy-oriented strands of the feminist field have become privileged interlocutors with public officials, the media, and bilateral and multilateral aid and development agencies. Acknowledging that "women's NGOs have been occupying an important space," a Bolivian activist asked to whom NGOs were accountable, as they appeared to her to be principally "legitimated by the patriarchal powers."

Even when feminist NGOs explicitly deny that they represent the women's movement, they are too often conveniently viewed as doing so by elected officials and policymakers who can thereby claim to have "consulted civil society" by virtue of involving a handful of NGOs in a particular policy discussion. As one longtime Brazilian activist put it:

> It has been common to refer to the NGOs as if they constituted the feminist movement proper. And it is also frequently that the members of NGOs portray themselves as "representatives" of the feminist movement. Suddenly we forgot all of our reflections on the necessity of expressing plurality and difference have been forgotten. A new relationship of power has been established within the movement. We now form part of a scenario in which some possess the information, have access to sources of funding and its allocations, therefore, they are the ones who effectively decide. (Borda, quoted in Schumaher and Vargas 1993, 363–364)

The problem of representativeness is further complicated by the fact that Latin American NGOs typically are not membership organizations, and they generally adopt routine procedures or mechanisms that would make their actions more accountable to larger movement constituencies on behalf of whom they profess to act.

Given these new divisions and power imbalances within the feminist movement field, forging minimally unified or consensual movement strategies, even around conjunctural activities like preparing for the FWCW, has become an ever more vexing challenge. Considerable controversy surrounded the very creation of the Articulation of Brazilian Women for Beijing '95, its sources of funding, and its political objectives, for example. Some feminists objected to the very idea of creating a centralized coordination at the national level—maintaining that no such body could adequately "represent" the movement and fearing that a national coordination might be vulnerable to political "manipulation" and "co-optation."

The predominance of professional, internationally funded NGOs among those advocating such a coordination further fueled suspicion among grassroots groups and less-institutionalized sectors of the women's movements—who increasingly see themselves as further removed from national and international policy arenas and funding sources.

The issue of funding was also fraught with contention, as many in the movement objected to the designation of USAID—believed responsible for supporting the military dictatorship and promoting population control and sterilization abuse in Brazil—as the principal bilateral funder for Latin American participation in the Beijing process. Still others opposed the USAID exigency that funds for the Beijing process be administered by a single national "focal point"—fearing, again, excessive centralization and potential manipulation.

Finally, conflict raged about the ultimate objective of organizing around the Beijing conference. Some insisted on the importance of increasing feminist input into the government's document to the UN, which they saw as crucial in developing more effective future advocacy efforts in the policy realm. Others preferred instead to prioritize the remobilization and revitalization of the women's movement itself, focusing their organizational efforts toward "changing culture" and influencing public opinion.

Though the Articulation of Brazilian Women was successful in mobilizing thousands of women around Brazil,[49] this movement network—along with other pro-Beijing and thematically specialized national and regional networks—was widely criticized for failing to fully "democratize" information about the Beijing process, "centralizing" decisionmaking, and "monopolizing" resources and representation of the women's movement. From the outset, some São Paulo feminists stridently objected to "the First World countries' imposition" of an agenda for Beijing and organized their own "encounter-like" meetings to assess the UN-designated "women's decades," arguing that who "should speak about the twenty years of women's struggles should be the women who lived through this history. Until now, we have seen an elite of the movement getting together and making proposals to us."[50]

Contending that the Latin American and Caribbean regional coordination was controlled by "small groups of privilege" *(grupitos de privilegio)* and was plagued by "masculinist vices," dissident activists from Argentina, Bolivia, and Mexico organized a parallel meeting during the Mar del Plata forum, alleging that "there had been a process of exclusion of autonomous movement groups and those that are most contestatory." During a Huairou workshop called to evaluate the preparatory process, a Chilean NGO feminist echoed these sentiments: "There was a gap in terms of information, people who have felt excluded . . . information about the conference did not reach the base . . . and therefore the process has weakened the movement." Such criticisms were tempered by the growing recognition that, as one Uruguayan stressed, "we have to overcome the populist mentality that we must include everybody in all processes . . . there is a need to specialize this type of [lobbying] work . . . we have to overcome a confrontational mentality . . . leave aside *principismo*."

While acknowledging that specialized articulations have greatly enhanced the policy effectiveness of the movement, a number of participants in the Beijing process further complained that national, regional, and global feminist networks are often less inclusive, internally democratic, or fluid than the term "network" would appear to imply. The Colombian feminist theorist Magdalena León argued that "the movement today is a tangle of networks *[un enredo de redes]*"; and a Bolivian activist maintained that the "networks are ensnaring us" *(las redes nos estan enmarañado)* and that, though actively promoted by international funders, many regional networks lack "a real presence in our countries."

Still other critics argued that feminist NGOs' and networks' increased focus on national and international policy arenas has distanced them from the grass roots, from the needs and concerns of local women—leading, as one Peruvian put it, to "a divorce between the popular movement and the feminist NGOs. . . . Beijing means very little to most women in our countries." Some complained that "global agendas" were not being set by the movement and asked with concern: "Up to what point are we being accomplices? Are they channeling the movement toward the form of functioning of the UN?" As representatives of subregional focal points and NGO professionals spent the better part of the early 1990s traveling around the region and the globe to "strategize" for Rio de Janeiro, Vienna, Cairo, Copenhagen, and Beijing, it seemed as though some among the more transnationalized sectors of the Latin American feminist field had inverted the classic slogan—"think globally, act locally"—and seemed instead to be "acting globally" and "thinking locally."

Concluding Reflections

The NGOization and transnationalization of the Latin American feminist field appeared to have led increasing numbers of feminists to privilege some spaces of feminist politics, such as the state and the international policy arenas, over efforts to transform prevailing representations of gender, emphasize changes in consciousness, and promote cultural transformation through local grassroots-oriented organizing and mobilizational activities. The danger, as foretold by some of the critical voices cited above, is that the cultural-ethical dimension of the foundational feminist transformational project might be increasingly neglected by growing numbers of feminists and ignored (and ultimately silenced) by dominant political, cultural, and economic institutions. Though the battles waged by the so-called "*institucionalizadas*" within the conventionally defined political arena must be understood as cultural struggles over the meaning of received notions of "citizenship," "development," "the family," and "gender," as the enactment of one of many possible sorts of feminist cultural politics, the neglect or silencing of other forms of cultural-political intervention—such as local mobilization and *conscientización* work with women of the popular classes—might ultimately compromise the very quest for more "equitable" gender policy. In the absence of such work, feminists might lack the broad social base or political constituencies that would enable them to press more effectively for the implementation of the many new rights and entitlements recently earned through increased engagement in political-institutional arenas on a national, regional, and global scale.

Still, I have also tried to emphasize that recent feminist advances in the realms of policy and rights are themselves a consequence of the dramatic decentering of the Latin American feminist movement field into a vast range of institutional and extra-institutional spaces and places, of relatively successful feminist cultural-political incursions into the discursive terrain of male-dominant parallel organizations of civil society, political society, the state, and international institutions. Moreover, the Beijing process suggests that this profusion of feminist spaces has not necessarily led to a "fragmentation" of feminisms. Rather, though feminist ideas, energies, and activities are today diffused into a variety of new realms, the Beijing process confirmed that they remain articulated through increasingly formalized political-communicative networks or webs that configure the ever more heterogeneous, spatially and organizationally dispersed, and polycentric Latin American feminist field.

These multilayered articulations can be viewed as constituting what Nancy Fraser (1993) has called "subaltern counterpublics" that, in turn, are increasingly imbricated with dominant publics. These alternative publics have helped widen "discursive contestation"[51] around issues of concern to different groups of women that might otherwise have remained excluded from dominant publics. Moreover, because the multiple threads of feminist movement webs span vertically as well as horizontally, they construct crucial linkages between movements and institutional political arenas, linkages that have enabled movement demands and discourses to be translated into programmatic items on party and union platforms and into national policies and international conventions.

I would suggest that some of the other so-called new social movements that emerged in Latin America over the past two decades—such as the environmental and human rights movements—may have been similarly reconfigured since the late 1980s. Perhaps such movements have not merely "disappeared" or been "coopted" or "swallowed up" by dominant institutions, as some scholars have maintained.[52] Rather, if we were to remap the recent trajectories of their activists, their issues, their discourses, we might well find that they are still very much present in new arenas—such as national and international NGOs or specialized government agencies—while still operating within a "discursive matrix" that is at least partially shared with a wide range of other actors in a particular movement field.

However, the preceding analysis of the Latin American Beijing process should prompt us to explore the continual discursive contestations and power struggles that often characterize such expansive, heterogeneous fields of movement action. Clearly, some of the new spaces/places wherein feminist politics are today enacted (such as the state, professionalized NGOs, and the development establishment) confer greater access to power—as well as differential access to material, cultural, and political resources—than others (such as grassroots organizations). Though the many different women who transit within the Latin American feminist field still "recognize" one another as such—even when they frequently doubt the "ontological legitimacy" of the "other"—new hierarchies and power relations are being forged within that vast, complex field, and the parameters of legitimacy, interlocution, accountability, and representation are continually renegotiated and contested. In other words, the decentering of the Latin American feminist field has been accompanied by an intensification of power imbalances among women acting at different levels and occupying different spaces within that field. As we enter the new millennium—which, in Beijing-speak, "*será de las mujeres*" (will belong to women)—devising effective mechanisms and procedures for democratizing relations *within* that field constitutes one of the most formidable challenges faced by the region's feminisms.

Finally, the manifold democratic contradictions made evident by the Beijing process should further caution us against uncritically extolling the virtues of "global civil society," for it, too, is a terrain mined with highly unequal relations of power. Though feminist theorist and international NGO professional Charlotte Bunch declared Huairou to be a "global town meeting" of women, some (few) women clearly had greater access to the town's coffers and the town's male elders than (most) others. Though civil society is certainly crucial to the democratization of dominant national and international publics, it must remain a central "target" of the democratizing efforts of feminists and other progressive activists worldwide.[53]

Notes

1. In 1984, the radical American feminist Robin Morgan published *Sisterhood is Global: The International Women's Movement Anthology* (Garden City, N.Y.: Anchor Books). The collection was subsequently subjected to considerable criticism from Third World feminists inside and outside the United States for its Eurocentric, homogenizing vision of women's oppression.

2. On the Latin American and Caribbean feminist *encuentros,* see Sternbach et al. 1992 and Fischer 1993.

3. I borrow this metaphor from Calderón, Piscitelli, and Reyna 1992.

4. As noted in our analysis of the Latin American feminist *encuentros,* "It is, of course, difficult, if not dangerous, to generalize across countries in a region as diverse as Latin America when discussing any sociopolitical phenomenon" (Sternbach et al. 1992, 208). The trends discussed below certainly are pronounced to differing degrees in the various countries in the region. Still, one of the arguments advanced later in this chapter is precisely that there is an increasing "unity-in-difference" in the multifaceted, heterogeneous feminisms found in the diverse national settings of Latin America, and that something called "Latin American and Caribbean feminism" is today recognized to exist as such by both participants and external observers.

5. The ensuing analysis draws primarily on documents, interviews, and personal observations relating to various events, held in several Brazilian cities between October 1993 and August 1996, concerning the Beijing conferences and other feminist-related topics. These events include the NGO Forum in Mar del Plata in September 1994; the third UN PrepCom for Beijing in New York in March 1995; and the Huairou NGO Forum and the Beijing FWCW in August–September 1995. During this period, I was on leave from the University of California at Santa Cruz and was serving as Program Officer in Rights and Social Justice for the Brazil office of the Ford Foundation. As Ford prioritized Beijing-related "programming" in its offices around the world, my position as a "grant-maker" enabled me to accompany the Latin American Beijing process quite closely. My simultaneous "positionalities" as program officer, long-time student of Latin American feminisms, and Latina feminist-activist—though at times difficult to reconcile—offered a unique perspective on this process. Still, my role as a "funder" of some of the activities observed at times meant that I was not privy to other kinds of strategic information. This research forms part of a larger ongoing project on social movements and alternatives to "actually existing" democracy in contemporary Latin America. As always, I am greatly indebted to many Brazilian and Latin American feminist activists for their rich analytical insights and their support of my research, especially Vera Soares, Schuma Schumaher, Eunice Gutman, Inês Magalhães, Hildésia Medeiros, Claudia Ferreira, Sueli Carneiro, and Nilza Iraci. I am also grateful to colleagues who commented on earlier drafts of this essay: Natalie Lebon, Marysa Navarro, Vera Soares, and especially Claudia Lima Costa. Finally, I thank colleagues and staff at the Rio de Janeiro office of the Ford Foundation—particularly Bradford Smith, Sarah Hawker Costa, and Janice Rocha—for their support of my efforts to continue to pursue scholarly research during my tenure at the foundation.

6. See Sternbach et al. 1992 for a succinct account of the origins and development of Latin American feminisms in the 1970s and 1980s. See also Léon 1994; Jaquette 1994; Vargas 1994.

7. On the *movimiento de mujeres,* see Díaz-Barriga, in this volume; Jelin 1990.

8. Unless otherwise specified, textual quotations are based on field notes and informal interviews conducted by the author. This and all other translations from the Spanish and Portuguese are my own.

9. See Alvarez 1990, 1994 for a detailed analysis of the multiple factors shaping the early development of Brazilian feminist movements. See also Soares et al. 1995; Soares 1994, 1995; Schumaher and Vargas 1993.

10. See Dagnino, in this volume.

11. See Stein 1995 on a similar dynamic in U.S. lesbian-feminist movements.

12. "Discurso pronunciado por Virginia Vargas, Coordinadora de las ONGs de la Región de América Latina y el Caribe," photocopy.

13. Carmen Tornaría, interview, Beijing, September 13, 1995.

14. See Sikkink 1995; Friedman 1995; CLADEM 1992.

15. Coordinación Regional de ONGs de América Latina y el Caribe, "Foro de ONGs de América Latina y el Caribe—Informe," Mar del Plata, September 1994, 30–31.

16. See Castro 1995; Carneiro 1995; Lamas et al. 1995; Ribeiro 1995; Roland 1995; Vargas 1995; Nunes 1995; Oliveira and Carneiro 1995; ISIS International 1993.

17. "Propuestas de las Mujeres Negras, Latinoamericanas y Caribeñas para Beijing," distributed at the Mar del Plata NGO Forum, September 9, 1994, and signed by black women from nineteen countries in the Americas.

18. Coletivo de Feministas Lésbicas, "Lésbicas no Brasil," *Enfoque Feminista* no. 7 (January 1995): 19.

19. These comments are part of a personal evaluation of the Mar del Plata forum by Marli Medeiros, one of the "grassroots paralegals" working with Themis, a feminist legal, research, and educational NGO based in Porto Alegre, Brazil. They were submitted as part of a 1995 annual report to the Ford Foundation and are cited with permission of the author.

20. Articulação de Mulheres Brasileiras, "Síntese do Documento das Mulheres Brasileira—IV Conferência Mundial das Nações Unidas sobre a Mulher," September 1995.

21. Lind 1995; Alvarez 1990, 1996; Schumaher and Vargas 1993; Friedman 1997.

22. Méndez 1994; Alvarez 1994.

23. Americas Watch 1991; Blondet 1995; Chinchilla 1994; Nelson 1997; Linhares Barsted 1994

24. Pinto 1994; Feijoó 1994; Alvarez 1995.

25. Castro 1995.

26. Naciones Unidas, Comisión Económica para América Latina y el Caribe. Regional Program of Action for Women in Latin America and the Caribbean, 1995–2001. Twentieth Meeting of the Board of Directors of the Regional Conference on Women's Integration to Social and Economic Development in Latin American and the Caribbean. Santiago, November 16–18, 1994, Section 1C, p. 7.

27. Sikkink 1995; Friedman 1995; Jelin 1996.

28. Naciones Unidas, Section 7, para. 124a, p. 33.

29. Ibid., para. 126, p. 34.

30. Nilza Iraci, "A Conferência de Beijing e o Mito da Democracia Racial," *Fêmea* 3, no. 32 (September 1995):9.

31. See Franco, in this volume.

32. For further elaboration of the notion of social movement webs, see Alvarez, forthcoming.

33. See Baierle 1992; see also Doimo 1993 and 1995.

34. During her presentation at a workshop at the Huairou forum entitled "Vertientes del Movimiento de Mujeres: Oficial y Autónomo en América Latina," Gloria Bonder attributed the coining of this term to Australian feminists.

35. On the proliferation of NGOs in other movements, see Landim 1993; Fernandes 1994; Oliveira and Tandon 1995; MacDonald 1992.

36. Lind 1995, 145; see also Lebon 1996; Friedman forthcoming; Schild, in this volume; Frohmann and Valdés 1995; Alvarez 1995.

37. See Schild, in this volume; Barrig 1994, 1995.

38. See esp. Tarrés 1995; Lind 1995; Frohmann and Valdés 1995; Lebon 1993, 1996.

39. The USAID-defined subregions were Mexico, Central America, the Caribbean, the Andean region, the Southern Cone, and Brazil.

40. Sônia Correa, "Mesa: De Nairobi a Beijing: Estagnação ou Avanço?" (speech delivered at the Revista Estudos Feministas Seminar on Beijing, Rio de Janeiro, November 14, 1995). Correa is a "historic" Brazilian feminist and NGO professional. The UN conferences of the early 1990s included the Environment and Development Summit in Rio de Janeiro, 1992; the Human Rights Summit in Vienna, 1993; the UN Conference on Population and Development in Cairo, 1994; and the Social Development Summit in Copenhagen, 1995. On Latin American participation in UN women's conferences from 1975 through 1995, see Navarro 1996; ISIS International, 1995.

41. Carmen Tornaría (comment at the workshop "Metaforo: Las Cumbres Mundiales y el Movimiento de Mujeres," organized by Grupo Iniciativa Peking-Uruguay, NGO Forum, Huairou, China, September 6, 1995).

42. Several of these city- or statewide movement forums—typically monthly gatherings, open to all interested participants, in which women activists shared information, devised short-term strategies, and forged conjunctural coalitions—had been active long before the initiation of the Beijing preparatory process. But Beijing infused new purpose into some forums that had been relatively dormant and sparked the creation of new movement forums and local coalitions in states and regions of Brazil where they had not previously existed.

43. See Keck and Sikkink 1992 on "transnational issue networks." Sikkink (1995) refers to women's movements as the quintessential network.

44. On the "transnationalization" of other social movements, see Lins Ribeiro, in this volume; Ghils 1992; Lipschutz 1992.

45. Ana Falú (speech delivered at the Latin American and Caribbean Plenary—Regional Action Plans, NGO Forum on Women, Huairou, China, September 7, 1995).

46. Margarita Pisano (essay circulated at the Sixth Latin American and Caribbean Feminist *Encuentro,* San Salvador, November 1993), 7.

47. Ibid.

48. This distinction was drawn—in a humorous spirit—by a participant at the conclusion of the Huairou forum workshop entitled "Metaforo: Las Cumbres Mundiales y el Movimiento de Mujeres," organized by Grupo Iniciativa Peking-Uruguay to critically and collectively discuss the implications of feminist participation in the UN process.

49. The Articulation's relative success stemmed in large part from its ability to reconcile the above-cited divergent perspectives on the Beijing process. First, at the founding meeting, state representatives—elected by local women's forums on a rotational basis—voted to reject USAID support and seek alternative funding sources. Second, the alternation of Articulation delegates sought to enhance representativeness and promote the inclusion of all interested sectors of the movement. And, finally, the Articulation's goal of "bringing Beijing home to Brazil" was pursued in a two-pronged fashion. On the one hand, emphasis was placed on promoting local- and state-level events that would enable women to "evaluate the decade" from their "own specific perspective" and remobilize local movement organizations. On the other, the Articulation sought to enhance women's movement input into and participation in the Brazilian government's official preparatory process.

50. "Carta de São Paulo," *Boletim do Centro Informação Mulher* no. 13 (July 1994).

51. See this volume's Introduction.

52. Some of this literature is discussed in Baierle and in this volume's Introduction.

53. Cohen and Arato (1992) maintain that civil society must be understood as both a terrain and a target of social movements.

References

Alvarez, Sonia E. 1990. *Engendering Democracy in Brazil: Women's Movements in Transition Politics*. Princeton: Princeton University Press.

______. 1994. "The (Trans)formation of Feminism(s) and Gender Politics in Democratizing Brazil." In *The Women's Movement in Latin America: Participation and Democracy,* ed. J. Jaquette. Boulder: Westview Press.

______. 1995. "Género, Poder y Participación en América Latina: Algunos Retos Teóricos para la Agenda de Investigación Feminista Pós-Beijing." Paper presented at the NGO Forum of the FWCW in Huairou, China, August 30–September 8, 1995; and at the Nineteenth International Congress of the Latin American Studies Association, September 28–30, Washington, D.C.

______. 1996. "Concluding Reflections: 'Redrawing' the Parameters of Gender Struggle." In *Emergences: Women's Struggles for Livelihood in Latin America,* ed. J. Friedman, R. Abers, and L. Autler. Los Angeles: Center for Latin American Studies, University of California at Los Angeles.

______. 1997. "Reweaving the Fabric of Collective Action: Social Movements and Challenges to 'Actually Existing Democracy' in Brazil." In *Cultures of Protest,* ed. R. Fox and O. Starn.

Americas Watch. 1991. *Criminal Injustice: Violence Against Women in Brazil.* New York: Human Rights Watch.

Baierle, Sérgio. 1992. "Um Novo Princípio Ético-Político: Prática Social e Sujeito nos Movimentos Populares Urbanos em Porto Alegre nos Anos 80." Master's thesis, Universidade Estadual de Campinas, São Paulo.

Bairros, Luiza. 1995. "Nossos Feminismos Revisitados." *Revista Estudos Feministas* 3 (2):458–463.

Barrig, Maruja. 1994. "The Difficult Equilibrium Between Bread and Roses: Women's Organizations and the Transition from Dictatorship to Democracy in Peru." In *The Women's Movement in Latin America: Participation and Democracy,* ed. J. Jaquette. Boulder: Westview Press.

______. 1995. "Women, Collective Kitchens, and the Crisis of the State in Peru." In *Emergences: Women's Struggles for Livelihood in Latin America,* ed. J. Friedman, R. Abers, and L. Autler. Los Angeles: Center for Latin American Studies, University of California at Los Angeles.

Basu, Amrita, ed. 1995. *The Challenge of Local Feminisms: Women's Movements in Global Perspective.* Boulder: Westview Press.

Blondet, Cecilia. 1995. "Out of the Kitchens and Onto the Streets: Women's Activism in Peru." In *The Challenge of Local Feminisms: Women's Movements in Global Perspective,* ed. A. Basu. Boulder: Westview Press.

Calderón, Fernando, Alejandro Piscitelli, and José Luis Reyna. 1992. "Social Movements: Actors, Theories, Expectations." In *The Making of Social Movements in Latin America: Identity, Strategy, and Democracy,* ed. A. Escobar and S. Alvarez, 19–36. Boulder: Westview Press.

Carneiro, Suely. 1995. "Gênero, Raça e Ascensão Social." *Revista Estudos Feministas* 3 (2):544–552.

Castro, Mary Garcia. 1995. "Gênero e Raça no Movimento Sindical: Reflexões Caminho a Beijing." Paper presented at the First Seminario de Mulheres Negras—Emancipação, Trabalho e Cidadania, Mulheres Mobilizadas para a IV Conferência Internacional sobre Mulheres, Pequim 95, May 13, Salvador, Brazil.

Chinchilla, Norma Stoltz. 1994. "Feminism, Revolution, and Democratic Transitions in Nicaragua." In *The Women's Movement in Latin America: Participation and Democracy,* ed. J. Jaquette. Boulder: Westview Press.

CLADEM (Comité Latinoamericano de Defensa de los Derechos de La Mujer). 1992. *Mulher e Direitos Humanos na América Latina.* São Paulo: CLADEM.

Cohen, Jean L., and Andrew Arato. 1992. *Civil Society and Political Theory*. Cambridge: MIT Press.

Doimo, Ana Maria. 1993. "O 'Movimento Popular' no Brasil Pos–70: Formação de um Campo Ético-Político." Ph.D. diss., University of São Paulo.

______. 1995. *A Vez e a Voz do Popular: Movimentos Sociais e Participação Política no Brasil pós–70*. Rio de Janeiro: Relume-Dumará/ANPOCS.

Escobar, Arturo. 1995. *Encountering Development: The Making and Unmaking of the Third World*. Princeton: Princeton University Press.

Escobar, Arturo, and Sonia E. Alvarez, eds. 1992. *The Making of Social Movements in Latin America: Identity, Strategy, and Democracy*. Boulder: Westview Press.

Feijoó, María del Carmen. 1994. "La Trampa del Afecto: Mujer y Democracia en Argentina." In *Mujeres y Participación Política: Avances y Desafios en América Latina*, ed. M. León. Bogota: Tercer Mundo Editores.

Fernandes, Rubem Cesar. 1994. *Privado, porem Público: O Terceiro Setor na América Latina*. Rio de Janeiro: Relume-Dumará.

______. 1995. "Elos de uma Cidadania Planetária." *Revista Brasileira de Ciências Sociais* 10 (28):15–34.

Fischer, Amalia. 1993. "Los Encuentros Feministas: En Busca del Rumbo Perdido o de uno Nuevo." In *Feminismos: Gestos para una Cultura Tendenciosamente Diferente*, ed. X. Bedregal, A. Fischer, E. Gabiola, G. Gargallo, and M. Pisano. Photocopy.

Fraser, Nancy. 1993. "Rethinking the Public Sphere: A Contribution to the Critique of 'Actually Existing Democracy.'" In *The Phantom Public Sphere*, ed. B. Robbins. Minneapolis: University of Minnesota Press.

Friedman, Elisabeth. 1995. "Women's Human Rights: The Emergence of a Movement." In *Women's Rights/Human Rights: International Feminist Perspectives*, ed. J. Peters and A. Wolper, 18–35. New York: Routledge.

______. 1997. "Gendering Transitions: The Paradoxical Political Opportunities of Women's Organizing in Latin American Democratization." Ph.D. diss., Stanford University.

Frohmann, Alicia, and Teresa Valdés. 1995. "Democracy in the Country and in the Home: The Women's Movement in Chile." In *The Challenge of Local Feminisms: Women's Movements in Global Perspective*, ed. A. Basu. Boulder: Westview Press.

Ghils, Paul. 1992. "International Civil Society: International Non-Governmental Organizations in the International System." *International Social Science Journal* 133:417–429.

Heilborn, Maria Luiza, and Angela Arruda. 1995. "Legado Feminista e ONGs de Mulheres: Notas Preliminares." In *Gênero e Desenvolvimento Institucional em ONGs*, ed. Núcleo de Estudos Mulher e Políticas Públicas. Rio de Janeiro: IBAM/Instituto de la Mujer.

ISIS International, ed. 1993. *Despejando Horizontes: Mujeres en el Medioambiente*. Santiago: ISIS International.

______. 1995. *De Nairobi a Beijing: Diagnósticos y Propuestas*. Santiago: ISIS International.

Jaquette, Jane E., ed. 1994. *The Women's Movement in Latin America: Participation and Democracy*. 2nd ed. Boulder: Westview Press.

Jelin, Elizabeth. 1996. "Women, Gender and Human Rights." In *Constructing Democracy: Human Rights, Citizenship, and Society in Latin America*, ed. E. Jelin and E. Hershberg. Boulder: Westview Press.

Jelin, Elizabeth, ed. 1990. *Women and Social Change in Latin America*. London: Zed Books.

Keck, Margaret, and Kathryn Sikkink. 1992. "International Issue Networks in the Environment and Human Rights." Paper presented at the Eighteenth International Congress of the Latin American Studies Association, September, Los Angeles.

Lamas, Marta, Alicia Martínez, María Luisa Tarrés, and Esperanza Tuñon. 1995. "Building Bridges: The Growth of Popular Feminism in Mexico." In *The Challenge of Local Feminisms: Women's Movements in Global Perspective,* ed. A. Basu. Boulder: Westview Press.

Landim, Leilah. 1993. "A Invenção das ONGs: Do Serviço Invisível à Profissão sem Nome." Ph.D. diss., Programa de Pós-Graduação em Antropologia Social, Universidade Federal do Rio de Janeiro/Museu Nacional.

Lebon, Nathalie. 1993. "The Brazilian Feminist Movement in the Post-Constitutional Era: Assessing the Impact of the Rise of Feminist Non-Governmental Organizations." *Florida Journal of Anthropology* 18:17–26.

______. 1996. "The Professionalization of Women's Health Groups in São Paulo, Brazil: The Troublesome Road to Diversity." Photocopy.

León, Magdalena, ed. 1994. *Mujeres y Participación Política: Avances y Desafios en América Latina.* Bogota: Tercer Mundo Editores.

Lind, Amy C. 1995. *Gender, Development, and Women's Political Practices in Ecuador.* Ph.D. diss., Cornell University.

Linhares Barsted, Leila de Andrade. 1994. "Violência contra a Mulher e Cidadania: Uma Avaliação das Políticas Públicas." *Cadernos CEPIA,* no. 1.

Lins Ribeiro, Gustavo. 1994. "The Condition of Transnationality." Working Paper No. 173, Federal University of Brasília, Brasília.

Lipschutz, Ronnie D. 1992. "Reconstructing World Politics: The Emergence of Global Civil Society." *Millennium: Journal of International Studies* 21 (3):389–420.

MacDonald, Laura. 1992. "Turning to the NGOs: Competing Conceptions of Civil Society in Latin America." Paper presented at the Eighteenth International Congress of the Latin American Studies Association, September, Los Angeles.

Méndez, Norma Villareal. 1994. "El Camino de la Utopía Feminista en Colombia, 1975–1991." In *Mujeres y Participación Política: Avances y Desafios en América Latina,* ed. M. León. Bogota: Tercer Mundo Editores.

Navarro, Marysa. 1996. "Feminism and the United Nations Fourth World Conference." Collins Lecture, May 1, Dartmouth College, Hanover, New Hampshire. Photocopy.

Nelson, Sara. 1997. "Policing Women." Ph.D. diss., University of Washington.

Nunes, Maria José Fontelas Rosado. 1995. "Gênero: Saber, Poder e Religião." *Mandrágora* 2 (2):9–15.

Oliveira, Miguel Darcy, and Rajesh Tandon, eds. 1995. *Cidadãos: Construindo a Sociedade Civil Planetária.* Washington, D.C.: CIVICUS, World Alliance for Citizen Participation.

Oliveira, Rosângela de, and Fernanda Carneiro, eds. 1995. *Corpo: Meu Bem, Meu Mal. III Seminário de Direitos Reprodutivos: Ética e Poder.* Rio de Janeiro: ISER.

Pinto, Celi Regina Jardim. 1994. "Mulher e Política no Brasil: Os Impasses do Feminismo enquanto Movimento Social, face as Regras do Jogo da Democracia Representativa." *Revista Estudos Feministas,* special issue (October):256–270.

Pisano, Margarita. 1993. "Introducción a un Debate Urgente." In *Feminismos: Gestos para una Cultura Tendenciosamente Diferente,* ed. X. Bedregal, A. Fischer, E. Gabiola, G. Gargallo, and M. Pisano. Photocopy.

Red de Mujeres Afrocaribeñas y Afrolatinoamericanas. 1994. "Las Mujeres Negras Hacia la Conferencia Mundial." *Boletina Informativa* 1 (4):2–4

Ribeiro, Matilde. 1995. "Mulheres Negras Brasileiras: de Bertioga a Beijing." *Revista Estudos Feministas* 3 (2):446–458.

Roland, Edna. 1995. "Direitos Reprodutivos e Racismo no Brasil." *Revista Estudos Feministas* 3 (2):506–514.

Sader, Eder. 1988. *Quando Novos Personagens Entraram em Cena.* São Paulo: Paz e Terra.

Schumaher, Maria Aparecida, and Elisabeth Vargas. 1993. "Lugar no Governo: Alibi ou Conquista?" *Revista de Estudos Feministas* 1 (2):348–365.

Sikkink, Kathryn. 1995. "Transnational Networks on Violence Against Women." Paper presented at the Nineteenth International Congress of the Latin American Studies Association, September 28–30, Washington, D.C.

Soares, Vera. 1994. "Movimento Feminista: Paradigmas e Desafios." *Revista Estudos Feministas,* special issue (October):11–24.

______. 1995. "O Contraditório e Ambíguo Caminho a Beijing." *Revista Estudos Feministas* 3 (1):180–191.

Soares, Vera, Ana Alice Alcantara Costa, Cristina Maria Buarque, Denise Dourado Dora, and Wania Sant'Anna. 1995. "Brazilian Feminism and Women's Movements: A Two-Way Street." In *The Challenge of Local Feminisms: Women's Movements in Global Perspective,* ed. A. Basu. Boulder: Westview Press.

Stein, Arlene. 1995. "Sisters and Queers: The Decentering of Lesbian Feminism." In *Cultural Politics and Social Movements,* ed. M. Darnovsky, B. Epstein, and R. Flacks. Philadelphia: Temple University Press.

Sternbach, Nancy Saporta, Marysa Navarro-Aranguren, Patricia Chuchryk, and Sonia E. Alvarez. 1992. "Feminisms in Latin America: From Bogota to San Bernardo." In *The Making of Social Movements in Latin America: Identity, Strategy, and Democracy,* ed. A. Escobar and S. Alvarez. Boulder: Westview Press.

Tarrés, Maria Luisa. 1995. "Construyendo Ciudadania en un Sistema de Partido Unico: Las ONGs de Mujeres y su Contribuición a la Democracia Mexicana." Paper presented at the Nineteenth International Congress of the Latin American Studies Association, September 28–30, Washington, D.C.

Valdés, Teresa. 1994. "Movimiento de Mujeres y Producción de Conocimientos de Género: Chile, 1978–1989." In *Mujeres y Participación Política: Avances y Desafios en América Latina,* ed. M. León. Bogota: Tercer Mundo Editores.

Vargas, Virginia. 1994. "El Movimiento Feminista Latinoamericano: Entre la Esperanza y el Desencanto." In *Mujeres y Participación Política: Avances y Desafios en América Latina,* ed. M. León. Bogota: Tercer Mundo Editores.

______. 1995. "Una Mirada del Proceso Hacia Beijing." *Revista Estudos Feministas* 3 (1):172–179.

Chapter Thirteen

Cybercultural Politics: Political Activism at a Distance in a Transnational World

GUSTAVO LINS RIBEIRO

Globalization, the information era, and non-governmental organizations are highly complex, much-debated topics that are both the causes and the results of many changes in political, social, cultural, and economic life. In this chapter, I will explore the entanglement of these issues to shed light on the emergence of another dimension of political and cultural life, the virtual imagined transnational community that can be better understood through an analysis of cybercultural politics. My aim is to advance two powerful political dimensions: witnessing at distance and activism at distance. I locate my own discussion within the growing literature on global citizenship and planetary civil society, and on the impact of new communications technologies on the formation of new subjectivities; collectivities; social, economic, and institutional needs; ideologies; utopias and dystopias; and flows of people, goods, and information.[1] Although this approach cannot be circumscribed to a given region of the world, most of my examples are marked by a Latin American perspective.

Since my interest is to examine how cyberspace alters the cultural politics of collective and individual political actors in a shrinking world, I will limit myself to presenting a few arguments concerning globalization and transnationalism that are central to my reasoning. I will then briefly describe two computer networks that, among many, are important loci of political information and action for non-governmental organizations (NGOs). My choice is based upon the fact that these networks are not only intimately and functionally related but are also highly in-

Reginaldo Ramos de Lima and Gabriel O. Alvarez assisted me in gathering data on the Internet and in discussing this work on different occasions.

fluential within the environment in which they operate. The Association for Progressive Communications (APC), which is intended to be global in scope, is a consortium of eighteen nationally based networks. Alternex, a member of APC, is also of international scope (given the interconnections currently available for networks on the Internet), but it is primarily designed to serve Brazilian NGOs. Before concluding, I will consider these issues in light of the experiences of activists of one of Brazil's most well-known NGOs, the Brasília-based Institute of Socioeconomic Studies (INESC).

Globalization and Transnationalism

The adage that the world is shrinking is certainly an apt one. The development of the transportation, communications, and information industries; the globalization of financial markets; and the diffusion of segments of productive processes through different areas of the world have led to an increase in the circulation of capital, information, and people never experienced before in world history. At the same time that the control of scientific and technological development intensifies an often unequal competition among economic actors, there is a noticeable growth of the importance of services in the economy. This is an era of flexible accumulation, of post-fordist capitalism (Harvey 1989), that corresponds to a variety of economic and political actors with new ideologies and goals.

A significant number of social scientists, economists, and geographers are explicitly working with transnationalism and with its close relative, globalization.[2] For the purposes of making an analytical distinction, I consider globalization mostly as a historical economic process directly related to the expansion of capitalism, to the "shrinking of the world." In this connection, the process of globalization creates the economic and technological basis that makes possible the existence of transnationalism. Although it obviously has cultural and political implications, globalization differs from transnationalism in the sense that politics and ideology are the privileged realms of the latter. The organization of people within imagined communities; their relationships to power institutions; and the reformulation of identities, subjectivities, and the relationships between the private and public spheres are the main thrust of the discussion on transnationalism. Citizenship, for instance, is an issue more pertinent to transnationalism than to globalization.

Institutions and political subjects geared to the logics of fordist capitalism are undergoing profound transformations with diverse impacts on their power of agency. An often-mentioned illustration refers to the relative weakening of the nation-state vis-à-vis the unleashing of transnational forces and actors. The emergence of global fragmented space generates new relationships between different localities—in spite of the mediation of the nation-states where they are situated—and between these localities and the world system. New communication media, especially the Internet, create, under the aegis of computer-and-electronic capitalism, possibilities for the existence of a virtual imagined transnational community (Ribeiro 1996).

Levels of Integration, Transnationalism, and Imagined Communities

The social representation of membership to a level of integration is often expressed in terms of an inclusive logic that may be analytically simplified as the relationships between local, regional, national, and international levels of integration.[3] The appearance of novel forms that relate space to politics (the nation-state, for instance) generally puts into jeopardy the modes of representing membership to sociocultural and political-economic units. In his analysis of the changing relationships between processes of individual and collective formation prompted by contemporary global integrative forces, Norbert Ellias (1994, 148) considers that the transition to a new level of total integration of humankind, with a more complex and wider type of human organization, generates, like in similar situations, "conflicts of loyalty and consciousness," given, among other things, the resulting representational and institutional instability as well as the concomitant presence of disintegrating processes and the transference of power from one level to another.

The transnational level of integration does not obey the same classificatory logic of inclusiveness as other levels do. It crosscuts, as a transversal axis, the different levels of integration in such a manner that it is extremely difficult to positively relate transnationalism to a circumscribed territory. Its space can only be conceived as diffused, disseminated in a web or a network. I can thus say that a transnational level of integration does not correspond to spatial realities as the other levels do. In fact, transnationalism typically manifests itself through a different articulation of real space and through the creation of a new domain of political contestation and cultural ambience that is not equivalent to the space we normally experience: the so-called cyberspace and cyberculture. This is why the technosymbolic basis for the emergence of what I call the virtual imagined transnational community is the global computer network, commonly known as the Internet.

Many factors concur in the creation of the transnational condition. In a previous article, I considered the existence of six clusters of conditions that create the constraints through which transnationality can exist: historical, economic, technological, ideological-symbolical, social, and ritual (Ribeiro 1994b). In Appadurai's vision (1990), the "global cultural economy" develops from the disjunctive interplay of different "scapes": ethnoscapes, mediascapes, technoscapes, finanscapes, and ideascapes. Sklair (1991, 6), in order to avoid state centrism, bases her analysis on three different "levels" of transnational practices: "the transnational corporation (TNC) is the major locus of *transnational economic practices;* . . . the transnational capitalist class is the major locus of *transnational political practices;* and the major locus of *transnational cultural-ideological practices* is to be found in the culture-ideology of consumerism" (my emphasis). Other considerations are equally important: processes of deterritorialization and reterritorialization, inter- and transnational migratory flows, identity fragmentation, the introduction of new political and social actors, the advent of new individual skills, and the development of an international pop culture geared to the mass media and entertainment industry (Basch, Schiller, and Blanc 1994; Gupta 1992; Ortiz 1994; Rosenau 1992).

But, at this point, I wish to highlight what I deem to be the emergence of a new *imagined* community. For this reason I must focus on communications technologies that are also technologies of community creation (Stone 1992), especially on the newest and most powerful manifestation of interactive communication operating at a global scale, the Internet. Only thus we will be able to understand how cybercultural politics enhances interplay between political actors anchored in different levels of integration, transnational flows of political information and articulation, and "witnessing and political activism at distance." Benedict Anderson (1991) showed, in retrospect, how important print capitalism was to the creation of an imagined community that would develop into a nation. I suggest that electronic and computer capitalism is the necessary environment for the development of a transnation.

Anderson emphasized the central role that visual representations, printed languages, the proliferation of publishing houses, the mass production of books and newspapers ("print-as-commodity" traded in "the vernacular print-market"), and the coalition between Protestantism and print-capitalism played in eroding the previously existing "sacred imagined communities" and in creating national imagined communities. These forces displaced Latin (the elite language) as the only written language, thereby greatly enlarging the numbers of readers, and engendered new administrative vernaculars closer to common speech. They also generated communion and imagined linkages by fixing an "assemblage" of related vernaculars and dialects and by creating a sense of simultaneity, of "unified fields of exchange and communications" (Anderson 1991, 47) between fellow readers who "gradually became aware of the hundreds of thousands, even millions, of people in their particular language-field, and at the same time that only those . . . so belonged. These fellow-readers, to whom they were connected through print, formed, in their secular, particular, visible invisibility, the embryo of the nationally-imagined community." For me, cyber-fellows are the embryo of the transnationally imagined community.

The Internet and the Virtual Imagined Transnational Community

First developed as part of an American defense project, the Internet, the network of networks, is presently interconnecting millions of people all over the globe; it has become the most powerful symbolic transnational means of interactive communication. In practice, the Internet's global distribution is skewed, especially considering regions of the world such as the Middle East, Latin America, and Africa. In the United States, where more than 50 percent of the world's Internet-connected computers reside (the rest are dispersed throughout more than a hundred other countries), white middle-class males predominate among a pool of users who are seen as a market of affluent, educated consumers (Bournellis 1995)[4]. For a world elite, virtual reality now exists in an "on-line," "parallel" world, a sort of hyper-postmodern universe, where time, space and, geography are nonexistent or nonimportant (Escobar 1994; Laquey and Ryer 1994).

Computer networks have generated their own culture and space that are frequently, but not exclusively, designated as "cyberculture" and "cyberspace." For Arturo Escobar (1994, 214), *cyberculture* "refers specifically to new technologies in two areas: artificial intelligence [particularly computer and information technologies] and biotechnology." The diffusion of new technologies brings into light two regimes of sociality, technosociality and biosociality, that "embody the realization that we increasingly live and make ourselves in technobiocultural environments structured by novel forms of science and technology." *Cyberspace,* on the other hand,

> refers to the growing networks and systems of computer-mediated environments. As a spatialized, computer-mediated network of interactions, cyberspace is seen as "enabling full copresence and interaction of multiple users, allowing input and output from and to the full human sensorium, permitting situations of real and virtual realities, remote data collection and control through telepresence, of intelligent products and environments in real space." (Novak 1991, 225; Escobar 1994, 216).[5]

Cyberspace is thus the universe a *user* enters when plugging into a network. There, the user will not only feel within a high-tech virtual world but will also meet other *users,* norms, worldviews, procedures, and discourses that comprise a cyberculture subdivided into many different subcultures. The Internet is a global virtual archipelago within an electronic ocean that calls for navigators who embody its virtues and who are fascinated by these same virtues. It exposes the "Internaut" to the dazzling works of speed, simultaneity, and virtuality; to the immediate, conscious experiencing of the shrinking of the world; to the mesmerizing sensation of access to an infinite availability of information and interlocution (with the opposite feeling of information overload, its frustrating counterpart). Cyberculture takes to paroxysm some of the most powerful promises of modernity, including the assumption of a single global diversified community, existing in real time, in a parallel dimension, with its many fragments, unified only through abstractions, imploding over actors' heads haunted by former pretensions to resolved and organic identities. The reconfiguration of bodies and identities, made possible by the virtual global crowd and virtual, global, decentered, fragmented space, potentializes the anonymous cosmopolitan experience within the planetary virtual web. The manipulation of identity is now as easy as playing video games, a fact that partially accounts for the expressive numbers of teenagers on the Internet. Identity manipulation and the fascination with the infinite availability of information and interlocution (without the exposure to the dangers that may accompany facing difference in the real world), together with the feeling that you are here and in many other places at the same time, that you can choose to create universes of your own, provide a sensation of self-enlargement that is even more understandable when combined with the growing predominance of loneliness in mass societies. The enlarged self is now ready to colonize the real world from the virtual one.

Virtuality is a key concept in understanding the type of culture generated by the transnational community.[6] Sensitivity to virtuality seems to be a general characteristic of human beings, since we are capable of being symbolically transported to other places, imagining what is not here and, more, creating realities from structures that are pure abstractions before they become empirical facts. Virtual communities and apparatuses existed prior to computer networks. Moviegoers, radio listeners, TV watchers, and ham radio enthusiasts can be counted among these. One result of the development of technology is a quantitative and qualitative enhancement of the virtual universe.

But what is the difference between an imagined community and a virtual one? The difference lies in the fact that an imagined community is an abstraction symbolically and politically constructed, while the virtual community is more than that: It is a reality of a different kind, an intermediate, parallel state between reality and abstraction where simulation and simulacra have lives of their own.[7] The virtual reality is "there"; it can be experienced, manipulated, and lived as if it were real. Once you have finished your sojourn in the virtual universe, you can reenter the real, hard world. There is a "hybridization" between the "real and the virtual, between the synthetic and the natural" (Quéau 1993, 96).

The culture of the network, with its codes, protocols, and emerging writing styles, also presupposes the existence of a linguistic competence, something that, as Bourdieu noted (1983, 161ff.), cannot be separated from power analysis. Who speaks, to whom, through what media, and in what constructed circumstances are vital elements of any communication process. Some studies (for instance, Weber 1994; Edwards 1994; Stone 1992) indicate that people have to be "socialized" into newsgroups. "Lurkers" (people who read postings to newsgroups without interacting themselves) "first write in an apologetic and respectful fashion. Their writings may ask for welcome or claim membership. They explicitly acknowledge the rules and conventions . . . [of the newsgroup], and the need for 'safety' on the group" (Weber 1994, 2). Like in other situations, "the creation of criteria of inclusion and exclusion to control and delimit the group" (Williams 1989, 407) is also at stake in the structuring of virtual communities.

As a means of transnational communication, the Internet raises the interesting question of the emergence of an "international auxiliary language," to borrow a 1931 phrase from Edward Sapir (1956). The development of "computer English," a transnational creole (that is not threatening the presence of many national languages), points to a process of "debabelization" that is occurring within the virtual imagined transnational community. In such a context, however, we may imagine three likely scenarios. In one, English gains autonomy as the Internet language, reinforced by the consolidation of its global commercial, military, scientific, and diplomatic functions, and by other phenomena such as the expansion of cable TV and of mass pop culture hegemonized by the United States. A second scenario would see "computerese" gain autonomy, given impetus by user-friendly software based primarily on the utilization of icons. Finally, a third possibility would be the development of a "Tower of Babel" software program capable of translating all languages on the Internet.

The sociolinguistic issue is rapidly becoming a cultural and political one. In Latin America, for instance, there are groups such as Hispanored dedicated to promoting the *hispanización* of the Internet and to discussing "the future of our culture in the information age." There are initiatives along similar lines in different countries (Argentina, Cuba, Peru, Mexico) and among the Latino community in the United States (the Midwest Consortium for Latino Research, for example).[8] Still, hybrid situations often occur in which a sort of bilingual interaction develops: One reads a message in Spanish and answers in English (or vice-versa). In Hispanored there was the case of a Brazilian who, after apologizing for his poor Spanish, used a translation software program to recast his message originally written in Portuguese.

Members of transnational political imagined communities, like members of other imagined communities, especially ideologues, tend to have hyperbolic opinions about their role in the real world (see, for example, Laquey and Ryer 1994). They often think of themselves as capable of freely manipulating the system once they are entitled as "users" of this new order, just as people probably felt in the prehistory of bourgeois democracy, nation-states, and the free market. Children of both globalism and the computer age see themselves as creating a new world, a new situation, mediated by high technology, where access to the network is simultaneously a sort of postmodern liberation and an experience of a new democratic medium that empowers people to flood the world system with information, thereby checking the abuses of the powerful. NGOs everywhere praise this potentially liberating force.

But every technological innovation is ambiguous, containing in itself both the potential for utopia and dystopia (Feenberg 1990). The Internet does not fit the image of a liberal free market—uncontrolled and responsive only to individual manipulation. Although we should explore the idea of a decentralized control mechanism, it may be argued that the Internet is controlled by a "hierarchy of connections," the highest points of which are located in the U.S. government, in security agencies, and in private corporations that in case of necessity may always exercise their digital power. Giuseppe Cocco, in an article on the relationships between information, communication, and new forms of capitalist accumulation (1996, 23), states that the Internet "may be interpreted as an attempt to transform the partial advantage accumulated by the U.S. in the first phase of the emergence of the information economy, into a new hegemonic project at the industrial, political and cultural levels." Herbert Schiller (1996, 92–93), working along similar lines, notes the long-standing recognition by the U.S. leadership of the "centrality of information control for gaining world advantage" and that "the free flow of information, in its implementation, has meant the ascendance of U.S. cultural products worldwide." American dominance in the satellite and electronic information industry has its roots in pragmatic imperial geopolitics: "Control of information instrumentation, invariably, goes hand in hand with control of the message flow, its content, surveillance capability, and all forms of information capability" (93). Schiller concludes that:

> the strength, flexibility, and range of global business, already remarkable, will become more so. The capability of the state, including the still very powerful United States, to enforce its will on the economy, domestic or international, will be further diminished. This may be partly obscured for a time because the National Security State will have at its disposal an enhanced military and intelligence capability, derived from the new information technologies. For this reason, the American state will be the least vulnerable, *for a time,* to the forces undermining states everywhere. (103)

More prosaic factors limit the implementation of virtual democracy: the cost of computers, related equipment, and services; access and knowledge to the codes of the network; education; knowledge of the English language; and the control of the functioning of the system by many different computer centers.[9]

Perhaps it is a common characteristic of all imagined communities that they give the impression that everyone is equal once qualified with the necessary competence. However, the virtual imagined transnational community shares, so far, many more "primordial sentiments," ties, and characteristics with the emerging new states (Geertz 1963), than with civil ones. This is why it is more interesting to investigate this community's cultural politics than its political culture.

Cybercultural Politics

Cybercultural politics can be divided into two different, but interrelated, realms. One is defined by the political activity within the Internet itself; the other by the relationship between computer networks and political activism in the real world. These realms will increasingly become more imbricated given the new configuration of interdependency of electronic and magnetic means where economy, information, and politics circulate in a fashion that is vulnerable to the anarchical or organized manipulation of individuals and groups (Schwartau 1995).

The Net: Cyberpolitics and Cyberactivism

The Internet's prehistory involves four different stories of origin. Besides the *military,* the Internet is often associated with the community of computer and electronics *engineers* and with the *scientific and academic community,* who have a need to exchange information. Finally, there are the heirs of the *California counterculture,* with their dreams of an alternative media that would empower a highly democratic and secondarily anarchical community. These origins still inform the Internet's cultural politics, along with the different discourses of the groups struggling to impose a hegemonic interpretation over its purposes and destiny. Issues such as freedom of speech versus censorship, public space versus private space, and large corporations and capitalist interests versus community needs are some of the most hotly debated topics around which many cyberactivists organize. At the same time, the rapid commercialization of cyberspace is increasingly transforming the Internet into a virtual shopping mall, with e-money as the global currency with which one can buy anything from pornography to information on stock markets.[10] Since my primary goal in this article is to discuss the relationship between NGOs and electronic networks—the second realm of cybercultural politics—in this section I will explore a few of the different ways in which the Internet is opening a new field of political conflicts and contestation.

Arthur Kroker and Michael Weinstein are two of the most provocative analysts of the power struggles occurring over the Internet. They point to the advent of new fetishes and power systems, of the "wired body," of what they call the "virtual class" (1994). Notwithstanding their quasi-delirious rhetoric and hypercriticism that sometimes reify technopower, Kroker and Weinstein are acid demolishers of cyber-authoritarianism and of the hysteria created by "technotopia" in favor of the Internet, the privileged space for the exercise of power by the virtual class. Mainly composed of "pure capitalists" and "visionary capitalists specialized in computers," this class is grounded in the communications industry. Once the expansion of the electronic frontier is established, the virtual class seeks to subdivide cyberspace for the purposes of capitalist accumulation and political control. What is at stake is a competition for rights to intellectual property. The democratic possibilities of the Internet comprise the initial seduction for the construction of the digital superhighway (the "privileged monopoly of global data communication") and for the subordination of the network to the "predatory commercial interests" of the virtual class.

A fierce struggle is occurring within the Internet between the virtual class and its opponents. For Kroker and Weinstein, the "wireless body" or the "hyper-texted body" is the locus of "the major political and ethical conflict of late twentieth- and early twenty-first-century experience" (1994, 17). A sort of humanist residue within the universe of cybernetic fetish, the "wireless body" is "a moving field of aesthetic contestation for remapping the galactic empire of technotopia."[11]

Based upon the disseminated, fluid, and fragmented characteristics of the Internet, a group of cyberactivists, the Critical Art Ensemble, proposes a new interpretation of the dynamics of power in the present and a mode of counterbalancing it: the electronic disturbance. For them, power does not consolidate any longer in bunkers that can be taken over. Sedentary structures, typical of former modes of exercising and circulating power, are at service of a "nomadic power" exercised by a nomadic elite that "moves from centralized urban areas to decentralized and deterritorialized cyberspace," transforming itself into a "transcendent entity that can only be imagined" (Critical Art Ensemble 1994, 17). Therefore:

> Nomadic power must be resisted in cyberspace rather than in physical space. . . . a small but coordinated group of hackers could introduce electronic viruses, worms and bombs into data banks, programs and networks of authority, possibly bringing the destructive force of inertia into the nomadic realm. Prolonged inertia equals the collapse of nomadic authority on a global level. Such strategy does not require a unified class action, nor does it require simultaneous action in numerous geographic areas. The less nihilistic could resurrect the strategy of occupation by holding data as hostage, instead of property. By whatever means the electronic authority is disturbed, the key is to totally disrupt command and control. Under such conditions, all dead capital in the military/corporate entwinement becomes an economic drain, material, equipment and labor power, all would be left without a means of deployment. Late capital would collapse under its own excessive weight. (25)

Another point that is necessary to consider is the fascination with information availability within the network. For the Critical Art Ensemble (1994, 132), although the current situation can be partly described as information overload, it is also defined by insufficient access to information, creating

> a peculiar case of censorship. Rather than stopping the flow of information, far more is generated than can be digested. The strategy is to classify or privatize all information that could be used by the individual for self empowerment, and to bury the useful information under the reams of useless junk data offered to the public. Instead of the traditional information blackout, we face an information blizzard, a white-out. This forces the individual to depend on an authority to help prioritize the information to be selected. This is the foundation for the information catastrophe, an endless recycling of sovereignty back to the state under the pretense of informational freedom.

To avoid whiteout and locate relevant information within the opaque, overwhelming mazeways of the Internet, activists need to have a clear agenda and a precise definition of their interests.[12]

Most activists in "physical space" are unaware of the political discussions and struggles that are occurring within cyberspace. Many different actors including government agencies, political parties, unions, and NGOs, all with different ideologies, whether progressive, conservative, or repressive, make use of computer networks. Workers, for instance, may find on the Internet a perfect ambience to resurrect their presence in a globalized and transnational economy in a manner relatively free of corporate and national constraints, as demonstrated by an online newspaper, the San Francisco Free Press (http://www.ccnet.com/SF_Free_Press/welcome.html), produced by San Francisco strikers in 1994 and read by unionists around the world (Lee 1995, 64). Many trade unions, federations, and confederations have their own networks in countries such as Australia, Brazil, Canada,

Great Britain, Israel, South Africa, and the United States. Eric Lee (1995, 67) ends his article on the forging of worldwide solidarity in an optimistic vein: "Thanks to the Internet, a century-long decline in internationalism has already been reversed, and for thousands of trade unionists who log-in every day, internationalism already has been reborn."

But I will focus on the use that NGO activists, particularly environmentalists, make of electronic networks, because these actors are highly sensitive to new ways of enhancing political action and to ideologies that boost transnationalism.

The Internet and NGO Political Activism

The realization that ecological frontiers do not coincide with political ones, together with the identification of many supranational and global environmental problems (such as acid rain, nuclear hazards, the depletion of the ozone layer, and global warming) have provided environmentalism with a clear transnational discourse. "One planet, one globe" and "think globally, act locally" are slogans that epitomize this propensity and the need to articulate on a global level.

Environmentalist NGOs often act like brokers between different actors involved in the developmentalist drama. Local populations, social movements, government agencies, political parties, unions, and multilateral agencies make up the political field where NGOs intervene. Reliable and up-to-date information, obtained in the transactions between these actors, is one of the most valuable assets that enable NGOs to carry out their activities. In this connection, they are highly dependent on communications to operate properly. NGOs are also known for their capacity to establishing different, often ad hoc coalitions between various actors in the political field when they intervene to achieve specific goals. To the extent that this flexibility permits pragmatic and heterodox alliances that prove to be effective in many circumstances, it is also responsible for a certain ideological and political fuzziness that may result in endless debates about tactics, strategic initiatives, and appropriate discourses.

Networking pragmatism, thus, is an effective instrument, reflected by the NGOs' strong ability to move from local to national, international, and transnational scenarios; but it also engenders a relative loss of homogeneity in the resulting political subjects who often exist as target-oriented coalitions that are dismantled once the given task is accomplished. This is why NGOs and their networks may be characterized as pragmatic, fragmented, disseminated, circumstantial, and even volatile political actors. Their strength comes from these characteristics that enable them to match the fluidity of a changing political field with more effectiveness than traditional political actors, who are often bound by the dictates of internal ideological, organizational, and political coherence and cohesiveness (with consequent weight and institutional investment of energy), which provides an external identity qualifying these political actors as representative of a segment, of a corporation, or of precisely delimited interests. But the NGOs' primary weakness also derives from these characteristics, since networking pragmatism dissolves them as political actors who could have a larger presence if they were consolidated into a more homogeneous and coherent subject with a shared programmatic objective. Thus NGOs and their networks are a new political subject creating new forms of action and impasses to older mechanisms of political representation and action. Since they are not invested with the claims of universal or corporate representation typical of the Enlightenment's metanarrative responsible for the institutional and ideological profiles of most of the "traditional" political actors and apparatuses, NGOs can indeed be an effective fragmented, decentered, political subject in a postmodern world, but the cost of flexibility, pragmatism, and fragmentation may well be reformism—their capability to promote radical change may weaken.

The pragmatism inherent in the interconnection of different nodal points of agency within a temporary, circumscribed field is also one of the pivotal forces of the structuring of electronic networks. Thus, accustomed to networking in "physical space" and hungry for effective means of communication and for information, NGOs rapidly found electronic networks to be another useful and powerful milieu for their organizational and political needs. Networking in real politics seems to find an ideal mirror in the many possibilities of networking in cyberspace. Coalitions may be formed with various actors operating at different levels of agency; transnational communications and alliances can be effective with little or no control by nation-states.

Conscious of the potential of this new means of communication and integration, NGOs promoted and praised its use. Articles published in *Le Monde Diplomatique* by leaders of "Third World NGOs" highlight the electronic networks' potential for worldwide empowerment and democratization of information. The news of the assassination of the Brazilian environmental leader Chico Mendes in 1988; the denouncement of brutalities against arrested Russian unionists in 1993; and the worldwide mobilization against the Clinton administration's interpretation of the Rio-92 Convention on Biological Diversity, also in 1993, are examples of the effective use of the Internet given by Carlos Alberto Afonso (1994) and Roberto Bissio (1994).[13] Both authors value the emergence of virtual communities and the speed, simultaneity, low operational costs, and capability to retrieve texts from different addresses as powerful weapons available to global civil society. For Bissio:

> The participation in an electronic debate has a clear democratic characteristic. The point of view of a large "world" institution has exactly the same weight, considering its visual presentation, as that of a popular group working at the village level. Without the attraction exerted by fancy paper and editing, readers are sensitive only to arguments. Documents from both sides are simultaneously transmitted to the whole world, and receivers can immediately react with their own commentaries.

Bissio is also aware that the need to diffuse access to this new technology must be accompanied by the diffusion of new equipment and telecommunications infrastructure if the gap between North and South is not to widen.

Until now, the United Nations Conference on Environment and Development (UNCED), held in Rio de Janeiro in 1992, has been the largest stage to demonstrate the significance of NGOs and electronic networks in contemporary cultural politics.[14] The UN granted unprecedented visible participation to NGOs in the official conference and installed a computer network that kept the transnational virtual community informed of the events and decisions being made in Rio de Janeiro. Environmentalist activists who could not attend the Global Forum, the assembly of transnational citizens that paralleled UNCED (commonly known as the Earth Summit), could participate in this mega-global ritual of the transnational community via cyberspace (Ribeiro 1994b). The UNCED also revealed an important actor, the Association for Progressive Communications (APC), a network that from Rio-92 through Beijing-95 has been responsible for linking UN conferences with the virtual imagined transnational community.

Electronic Networks for NGOs

Cyberactivists count on different organizations to promote and defend their interests, such as the Electronic Frontier Foundation, the Internet Communications Affairs Association, the Internet Society, the Association of Online Professionals (in the United States), the Association for Community Telematics (in Australia), the Digital Citizens' Movement of the Netherlands, the Network Society of New Zealand, Community (in Great Britain), and many others.[15] These institutions are often more oriented toward what I previously defined as the political activity within the Internet (cyberpolitics and cyberactivism). But, as we know, cybercultural politics also involves actors who struggle to enhance the political efficacy of computer networks for civil society in "physical space." Here the APC is certainly prominent, not only because it has gathered an impressive number of members and affiliates but also because of the power it has been capable of garnering (based on its political and technical know-how) in the process of becoming an institution representative of NGO opinions on these subjects and a broker between powerful governmental organizations and supranational agencies of global governance such as the UN.[16]

In the 1980s, several nonprofit computer networks were set up in different countries. Many environmental NGOs took leadership roles in establishing networks to serve their information and communications needs. From 1987 to 1990, the following networks emerged: the Institute for Global Communications (or IGC, in the United States);[17] Greennet (Great Britain); Pegasus (Australia); Web (Canada); Nicarao (Nicaragua); Nordnet (Sweden) and Alternex (Brazil). According to Afonso (1994), these were led by NGOs that collaborated to establish international e-mail services in order to exchange information on the environment. In May 1990, APC was founded as a nonprofit organization to coordinate the operation and development of these seven independent networks and to stimulate the creation of others. By August 1995, the APC had become a consortium of eighteen international member networks serving 30,000 community activists, scientists, natural-resource managers, educators, policymakers, nonprofit organizations, and NGOs in over 130 countries. It is the largest global computer networking system dedicated to social and environmental issues and to enhancing the effectiveness, organizational ability, and capacity of NGOs.[18]

The IGC and APC are divisions of the Tides Foundation, a nonprofit, charitable institution based in the United States. The APC's organizational structure comprises the North American regional office in the United States, the International Secretariat in Brazil, and the APC Coordinating Council (or Board of Directors). It is a flexible organization that allows its members to operate in autonomous fashion; it fosters ideological pluralism and the development of new international networks. The APC Coordinating Council experiments with its own medium: It formulates policy primarily on-line, also holding quarterly "meetings" and voting on-line. The council only holds one face-to-face meeting a year. The APC is maintains a multinational political structure that promotes transnational forms of political integration within cyberspace.

APC leadership and members have connections with different segments and initiatives of electronic capitalism. Members of the IGC have worked with Hewlett-Packard and have received funding and computers from Apple. IGC technicians, assisted by technical staff from other APC networks, have developed an "APC Unix-based Software" that is provided free or at low cost to APC members. In 1994, the IGC advisory board was searching for "one member with significant business expertise, who is also well connected to the computer industry" (Sallin 1994). Greennet, the British network, at one time ran commercial networks for Apple UK. In addition, Sun Microsystems has donated equipment to some networks.

Compared to systems such as Compuserve and American Online, each with millions of users, APC appears to be a small undertaking. But it would be tedious to list all the users who benefit from the association; I will mention but a few. They include a variety of environmental interest groups, industries, commercial groups, federal and state government offices, universities, and scientific and research groups. EcoNet users, for instance, include the Environmental Defense Fund, Earth First, the Rainforest Action Network, Greenpeace, Amnesty International, Oxfam, the Third World Network, the World Resources Institute, the World Wildlife Fund, the Center for our Common Future, the National Audobon Society, the Army Corps of Engineers, Dow Chemical, The Cable News Network (CNN)'s Network Earth, the Atlantic Richfield Company, and the U.S. Department of Energy.[19]

The diversity of users of these networks facilitates not only a rich exchange of information but also the establishment of several partnerships between different actors. Web, a Canadian network that encompass hundreds of environmental organizations, all levels of government, and many businesses, is involved with many projects of the federal government and the Ontario provincial government. The latter created a fund of Can$100 million to develop networks and networking infrastructure.

APC users include a range of people and groups active in the environmental political field including governmental organizations, NGOs, scientists, private corporations, and concerned individuals. The APC is an demonstration that this kind of computer network can be a diversified, fragmented, albeit unified subject, hegemonized politically and administratively by NGOs. This structure is replicated in less-inclusive organizations such as Alternex, the Brazilian network of NGOs and an APC founding member.

Alternex was created in 1989 in Rio de Janeiro by one of the most prominent Brazilian NGOs, the Brazilian Institute of Social and Economic Analysis (Ibase), in partnership with the IGC and with the support of the United Nations Development Program (UNDP), the Brazilian Agency of Cooperation (of the Ministry of Foreign Affairs), the Italian Agency of Cooperation (Cesvi), and other international organizations.[20] In November 1990, together with the Federal University of Rio de Janeiro, Ibase participated in a project to install and operate an Internet node in Rio de Janeiro, becoming "the first computer network service operated by an NGO in Latin America to have a permanent connection with the Internet, a privilege for the Brazilian civil society" (Carlos Alberto Afonso, quoted in Aguiar 1995). Although in 1994 80 percent of Alternex users were based in Brazil, the network had accounts in more than thirty-five countries, mostly in Latin America, where its staff helped to create other networks (Sallin 1994). Today, the Alternex server allows access to other APC networks, the Internet, and the Brazilian national computer networks (RNP), exclusively run (until recently) by a federal agency, the Brazilian Council for Scientific and Technological Development (CNPq).

Within Alternex, individual users predominate over institutions. Among the latter, more than 70 percent are nonprofit organizations; other institutional users include government, corporate, and business groups mostly related to the computer industry. Individual users are primarily professionals, university professors, scientists, and political activists. Alternex regional distribution replicates Brazil's uneven development; the largest number of users is concentrated in the rich southeastern region (1,778 as of April 1995) and the smallest figure (54) being found in the Amazon region (see Aguiar 1995).

Alternex's twenty-two public conferences in Portuguese and Spanish represent only 30 percent of all the public conferences within the network, but since they were initiated they have been fueled by more than 120 institutions, of which the great majority are NGOs. Predominant among these is a group of 44 institutions acting in "the areas of transference of information/knowledge/technologies," followed by 40 environmental and ecological organizations (Aguiar 1995). The largest and most influential Brazilian NGOs use Alternex as a medium of communication. Among these I chose the Institute of Socioeconomic Studies (INESC), a Brasília-based NGO, to examine how electronic networks are actually used by political activists.

Activism and Electronic Networks

INESC is primarily dedicated to monitoring the activities of Brazil's National Congress on issues involving human rights, the environment, Indian rights, popular movements, agrarian reform, and the advancement of democracy. Its office in Brasília is completely computerized, and a systems manager oversees the operation of the computer system. INESC has a highly experienced staff composed of anthropologists, sociologists, journalists, economists, lawyers, and other professionals. In the late 1980s INESC, long a member of Alternex, participated in the first discussions about the need to socialize and democratize advanced systems of communication for Brazilian NGOs.[21]

INESC activists define their organization as basically an information and communications NGO that makes available to social movements, political parties, other NGOs, intellectuals, and concerned citizens critical information on the day-to-day activities of Brazil's National Congress. Thus, their need for information and communications capabilities is high. All activists recognize the great importance of computer networks for their activities. E-mail is a predominant form of interoffice communication, saving paperwork and time that was previously spent in meetings and in disseminating crucial information among all members of the organization. E-mail also allows coordinators to control the internal flow of information and to ensure that each staff member receives their messages and acts accordingly.

Alternex is used to distribute e-mail, to participate in virtual conferences, and to send and receive documents. Together with letters, bulletins, newspapers, and other printed matter; regular and cellular telephones; and the fax machine, the network is considered a necessary communications tool for INESC's political and administrative work. In this sense, the network did not act as a substitute for another medium but represented a welcome addition, since it opened up new and different possibilities.

First, the network is viewed as a very inexpensive medium. Although it is recognized that the installation of computer equipment and networks in general reproduces the stratification already existing in the NGO community in Brazil, the largest NGOs having joined electronic networks long ago and owning more and better equipment and software, it is also believed that Alternex empowers smaller NGOs since it provides regional, national, and international communications at very low cost. Second, the dissemination and capillarity of the global electronic networks, together with their speed and simultaneity, are characteristics cherished by a community highly dependent on information, contacts, and exchanges with qualified sources. Furthermore, the Internet allows for the storage and organization of information. Other possibilities not explicitly mentioned by INESC activists but discovered by Cristina Inoue in her research on NGOs and electronic networks include "finding information otherwise unavailable" and obtaining "global access to information on local facts, and local access to global issues," especially to UN and World Bank related activities (1995, 116).

For INESC activists, the Internet is most valuable for establishing and maintaining contacts at the national and international levels. Although the Internet is also used at the local level, the telephone and face-to-face interactions are still more highly valued since they are in the end more effective than "colder," more impersonal forms of communication. Trust, friendship, reputation, predictability, hierarchical position within a social network, and even charisma are elements of political activity that certainly cannot be reduced to technologies of communication.[22] There are features of face-to-face interaction (gestures, tone, pitch, indexicality) and even of telephone conversation that are highly informative; these features are concealed in computer-based interactions. In some crisis situations, the intensity of communication is highly amplified when activists recur to all means available: letters, faxes, telephone calls, e-mail, and personal visits.

Since computer networks are part of the apparatuses of time-space compression, it is not surprising that the annihilation of distance, speed, and simultaneity play a central role in users' evaluations. One environmentalist said that hours before a preparatory meeting of the UNCED in New York, he could retrieve vital official UN information at the last minute that gave him political leverage vis-à-vis other negotiators, such as officials of Brazil's Foreign Ministry. The use of the electronic network, thus, allowed him to influence the results of that important meeting.[23]

In this connection, it would be expected that in faraway places Alternex would become a more decisive factor. However, one activist who worked with another NGO for almost two years in the Amazon region reported that although the local office where she was placed had computers connected to Alternex, the staff did not know how to use them. Furthermore, the local telecommunications infrastructure was so inadequate that even fax transmissions were frequently interrupted. These are not uncommon drawbacks. On the contrary, perhaps the two strongest obstacles to the diffusion of computer technologies and networks are users' ignorance and antiquated telephone systems. The installation of up-to-date high-tech telecommunications infrastructures is clearly related to macro development policies and replicates the unequal distribution of wealth within and across nations. The diffusion of computer literacy, although related to wider determinations such as standards of living and education, is a phenomenon that also takes place via informal mechanisms of socialization encountering different structures of personality.

Inoue (1995, 113) considers that the present time is an "adaptation" period in which there is a "mismatch between the [Internet's] potential and what is effectively used." Indeed, a greater degree of computer literacy is, today, a valuable asset for NGO activists with different impacts on hierarchical structures. It is becoming a condition for self-achievement. Another differentiating factor is proficiency in English. Given the transnational and international fields in which most NGOs operate and the crucial importance of foreign funds and partnerships, this is hardly surprising. Within electronic networks such as Alternex and other APC affiliates, as well as the Internet, the overwhelming predominance of English is recognized as a limitation. Aguiar, for instance, states that the problem with this large offering of information

> is that the greatest amount of the "hundreds of conferences existing within the system" . . . is capable of being accessed only by a selected number of persons that dominate the English language, since only 30% of the conferences are in Portuguese. This is radically against the primordial objective of democratization of information to civil society . . . since it excludes, for instance, thousands of union and community leaders, high-school teachers, municipal administration employees, amongst many other "multiplying agents" that should be stimulated to use the Net. The scarcity of material in Portuguese is also related to the treatment of subjects of interest to the Brazilian user, to the need of critical analysis of the national reality and even of a Brazilian perspective on world issues. In the present . . . what is being primordially disseminated is the worldview of certain foreign NGOs and social movements (above all from the U.S.) and the thoughts of the United Nations on international relations and on important structural issues of poor countries.

One INESC activist said that computer literacy and English proficiency are decisive since they enable individuals to have access to more information, in a milieu where information and power are components of the same equation. These linguistic and techno-symbolic objective factors, rooted in globalization and transnationalization processes, may thus have unforeseen impacts on organizations' cultural politics, hierarchical structures, needs, and demands. They also provide another indication that the virtual transnational imagined community represents a world elite even when we consider its most progressive members and institutions. But we must recall that global political articulations, notably those promoted by the environmental movement, be they virtual or real, also empower local actors, often giving them a national and global visibility/capability that they would hardly otherwise achieve (Wapner 1995; Albert 1995).

Linguistic and cultural issues will remain a major political battlefield in cyberspace, and some activists are aware of this. Demands for the translation of major documents affecting a nation or its politics and economy, what an INESC activist called the "democratization of language," are already being negotiated with large multilateral agencies such as the World Bank. We are again facing the dual, paradoxical movement of globalization: the simultaneous fostering of integration and fragmentation (Rosenau 1992).

Conclusions

Computer networks undoubtedly enhance the capabilities of political activists. They allow virtual coalitions, a swift and inexpensive means of communication with global capillarity, and data availability that multiplies the opportunities for individuals and groups to denounce, articulate, and campaign. The virtual communities that networks create are powerful weapons for generating transnational solidarity on many pressing issues. The Internet, thus, is an important tool for empowering individuals and groups by linking them "into distant developments," making them "more aware of how micro actions might aggregate to collective outcomes" and affording them a "multitude of access to the course of events" (Rosenau 1992, 285–286).

Besides the fact that the Internet is based upon a very special, "intelligent," and interactive machine, the possibility of manipulating networks is also a result of the history of the diffusion of computers, which, in turn, generated the context for the discussion of "electronic democracy" and the empowerment of "digital citizens." Only after computers had already become relatively common domestic appliances did they begin to be used in networks as communications media. This made possible, as Rheingold (1994) maintains, the establishment of a medium of communication "of many to many," in which a centralization by powerful political and economic agencies has not occurred; or, perhaps, in view of the growing commercialization and censorship on the Internet, I should say has not occurred *yet.*

Indeed, given the intelligent characteristics of the electronic network and of some of the segments of its virtual community, the vulnerability of economic, political, and military information is such that it engenders various problems of security, with the consequent appeals to cryptography and the restriction of freedom of speech and circulation within cyberspace. In this connection, "war of information" scenarios (Schwartau 1995) are created, where keepers of the establishment may confront hackers, cyber–Robin Hoods for some and heroes for others. The interest that American security forces have in the Internet is already a well-known fact. David Corn (1996) comments on a paper written by an official of the Department of Defense calling attention to "cyber-smart lefties" and to the potential use of the Internet for counterintelligence and disinformation purposes. The IGC is particularly pinpointed due to its reputation as an "alternative news source" and its worldwide connections. According to Corn, the paper "refers to IGC conferences that might be considered noteworthy by the Pentagon, including ones on anti-nuclear arms campaigns, the extreme right, social change, and 'multicultural, multi-racial news.'" At the same time, there are recurrent news items on the Internet indicating the control and censorship the Chinese government exerts over computer networks. According to one Internet source, such control entails, among other things, the registration of Internet users at their local police station. In Latin America, Guatemala is mentioned as a country whose government has policies discouraging the widespread dissemination of the Internet.

Inoue (1995, 79) quotes a passage by Tehranian (1990, xiv, xv) that summarizes the dual and paradoxical role information technologies play, since they "can extend and augment our powers, for good and evil, for better or worse, for democracy or tyranny. . . . On one hand, they have provided the indispensable tools and channels for the centralization of authority, control, and communication typical of modern industrial state. But on the other hand, they have also supplied the alternative channels of cultural resistance and ideological mobilization for the oppositionist forces."

The discussion on the role of the new technologies of communication and information is bound to endure and to provoke many exchanges between "apocalypticists" and "integrationists" (Eco 1976). But I agree with Lévy when he states that "unfortunately, the image of technique as an evil potency, isolated and against which it is impossible to struggle, reveals itself to be not only false but catastrophic, it disarms the citizen in front of the new prince who knows very well that the redistributions of power are negotiated and disputed in *all* terrains and that nothing is definitive" (Lévy 1993, 12). This is why I offer the notions of witnessing and political activism from a distance. A Latin American example will provide a necessary innuendo.

The use that the Ejército Zapatista de Liberación Nacional (or EZLN, of Chiapas, Mexico) made of the Internet on several occasions is a powerful illustration of how cyberpolitics can intervene in real politics.[24] For instance, the FZLN was able to halt an impending attack of the Mexican army by alerting the transnational virtual community, which responded by flooding the Mexican government's electronic mailboxes with protests. Mexico's secretary of foreign affairs, recognizing the effectiveness of this initiative, stated that "the war in Chiapas was an Internet war" (*Proceso* 991 [October 30, 1995]:48). Such an outcome is only possible because of the existence of what I call "witnessing at distance," or the virtual power of global public opinion, of the transnational community.

Communications technologies (including texts, paintings, photos, and records), given their capacity to disperse and enlarge a subject (Lévy 1993; Stone 1995), have allowed for the transmission of audiovisual information that was not directly witnessed by the subject. In a sense, thus, witnessing at distance is nothing new. However, under the empire of the mass media, in the age of information and electronic reproduction dominated by the immediacy of the image and the circulation of simulacra, witnessing at distance operates to a much larger degree than ever before. It has become a powerful political weapon of mass societies, enhanced by the development of the means of communication.[25] The latecomer is the global computer network that, alongside exchanges of written, visual, and audio information, stimulates the creation of the transnational virtual community.

Witnessing, besides being an existential and empirical force, activates different forms of commitment embedded in moral and sometimes religious values. Wapner, while commenting upon the use that "transnational environmental activist groups," especially Greenpeace, make of mass media to bring "hidden spots of the globe into people's everyday lives," asserts that this enables "people to 'bear witness' to environmental abuse" (1995, 321). Furthermore, Wapner shows that "bearing witness is a type of political action that originated with the Quakers. It requires that one who has observed a morally objectionable act (in this case an ecologically destructive one) must either take action to prevent further injustice or stand by and attest to its occurrence; one may not turn away in ignorance" (the moral importance of "bearing witness" is certainly not exclusive to Quakers). But witnessing at distance cannot only be conceived of as a floating entity, a segment of a moral economy, that appeals to enlightened individuals' indignity. It needs to transform its moral outrage into changes in the real world, into action. And this is what the Internet allows: the existence of "activism at distance" with a strong capability of intervening in the course of real events. Only the Internet allows for instantaneous, collective, decentered "activism at distance." In another paradoxical operation of cyberspace, it enlarges the public sphere and political action through the virtual world and reduces them in the real one.

Images of violence perpetrated by political or institutional agents and the possibility that related information will be widely disseminated represent an effective means of controlling abuses. But neither witnessing nor activism at distance are entirely efficient weapons at the disposal of political activists. This recognition brings up the difficult topic of the relationship between power and information. First, a ruler may dispose of a large quantity of information indicating positions against the ruler's own real or presumed actions, although this does not mean that the ruler will necessarily take them into consideration. Second, pressure exerted by activism at distance capable of harming those in power is part of the reality of politics, but it can reasonably be assumed that decisions made by those power holders are mostly measured in terms of real-world power alliances and calculations. Finally, all political subjects struggle for visibility in mass societies' battlefields and resort to different media to achieve their goals. What determines whether an issue gains wide recognition is a complex amalgamation of social energies deriving from many different contexts, including fortuitous events.

It is true that the diffusion of information is positively correlated to the democratization of access to power. However, if we take into consideration that books, public education, and the mass media have destroyed neither the profound existing social inequalities nor the abuse of power, we can predict that computer networks will come no closer to representing a true libertarian panacea. In spite of virtual reality's growing importance in the contemporary world, power is, in the last instance, defined by social, economic, and political relationships that are played out in the real world.

Notes

1. See Alvarez 1995; Appadurai 1990, 1991; Aranha Filho 1996; Canclini 1995; Carey and Quirk 1996; Cocco 1996; Commission on Global Governance 1995; Edwards 1994; Ellias 1994; Escobar 1994; Feenberg 1990; Fernandes 1995; Hakken 1993; Hannerz 1992; Inoue 1995; Leis 1995; Lévy 1993; Rheingold 1994; Ribeiro 1994a, 1994b, 1996; Rosenau 1992; Roszak 1994; Schiller 1996; Stallabrass 1995; Stone 1992, 1994, 1995; Wapner 1995. For a related set of works see note 2 below.

2. A brief list would include Barnet and Cavanaugh 1994; Breton 1994; Featherstone 1990; Giddens 1990; Harvey 1989; Ianni 1995; Mattelart 1994; Monetta 1994; Ortiz 1994; Santos et al. 1994; Sassen 1991; Sklair 1991. Works such as Wolf 1982 and Nash 1981, 1983 may be con-

sidered as part of an anthropology of the world system. More recently, in anthropology, there are the following works: Alvarez 1995; Appadurai 1990, 1991; Basch, Schiller, and Blanc 1994; Canclini 1994, 1995; Edwards 1994; Foster 1991; Gupta 1992; Rothstein and Blim 1992; Rouse 1995; Ruben 1995. For a review essay on anthropology, globalization, and transnationalism see Kearney 1995. For related references see note 1 above.

3. A diagram of these levels of integration (that in reality are always condensed) would have the shape of concentric circles. If I were supposing a unilineal and evolutive relationship between the levels of integration, I would remain within the framework of cultural diffusionism. The power of structuration of the different levels of integration operates in a multilinear and heteroclite manner, unequally distributing itself in geographical and social terms.

4. Surveys on the profiles of virtual shoppers found varied but generally high average yearly incomes, mostly above US$50,000 (Bournellis 1995).

5. Stone (1992, 609) defines cyberspace as "a physically inhabitable, electronically generated alternate reality, entered by means of direct links to the brain, that is, it is inhabited by refigured human 'persons' separated from their physical bodies, which are parked in 'normal' space. . . . The 'original' body is the authenticating source for the refigured person in cyberspace: no 'persons' exist whose presence is not warranted by a physical body back in 'normal' space."

6. The imagined and virtual transnational community can only be understood if we consider the difficult question of virtuality, a complex state that intervenes in different ways in social and psychological life. From a symbolic perspective, the dynamics of virtuality are the hard core of the transnational community (Ribeiro 1996).

7. The imagined community cannot be reduced to the virtual one since once a person exits cyberspace, that person can still imagine that the virtual community is "there" and is ready to be (re)entered. Furthermore, virtuality is to some extent more "real" than imagination. See my discussion on the subtle relationships between reality, virtuality, and imagination (Ribeiro 1996). According to Howard Rheingold (1994: 5), "*virtual communities* are social aggregations that emerge from the Net when enough people carry on those public discussions long enough, with sufficient human feeling, to form webs of personal relationships in cyberspace."

8. The Cuban National Library of Science and Technology, together with the Autonomous National University of Mexico, produced a *Directory of Networks and Information Systems and Communication on Latin America and the Caribbean,* with information on eighty networks and information systems in the region. See also the *E-Mail Directory of Labor Organizations in Latin America and the Caribbean,* produced by the Instituto Laboral de Educación Sindical of Puerto Rico [RazaNet@sfstate.edu].

9. For yet another critical position see Stallabrass 1995. For him, "cyberspace is also likely to be, in flagrant contradiction to its postmodern apologists, the embodiment of the totalizing system of Capital" (29). And more, cyberspace "is merely a literal expression of the situation of the individual in contemporary society, and more specifically of business people and their camp followers (engineers and intellectuals) spinning universalizing fantasies out of their desire to ride the next commercial wave. This wondrous but specious technology threatens to act as another curtain between those who consume it and the condition of the world: as the poor are excluded from cyberspace, and will appear on it only as objects, never as subjects with their own voices, there is a danger that they recede even further from the consciousness of the comfortable. As the real world is left to decline, the air once again becomes full of phantoms, this time digital, promising at the last moment to

pluck utopia from apocalypse" (30). The interplay between visions of utopia and dystopia on the Internet will endure and deepen in a way analogous to what happened with other discussions on new technologies of communication (Carey and Quirk 1996). Electronic computer networks, since their very beginning, have been hampered by conflicts stemming from their corporate conception, use, and control and by those individuals and groups adapting the technology to their own interests (Feenberg 1990).

10. The Internet's commercial domain (*.com) has been the fastest growing segment since 1994 and is now the largest domain, education being the second largest (Bournellis 1995). Total sales between September 1994 and August 1995 were estimated at US$118 million.

11. John Perry Barlow, a "Cognitive-Dissident and Co-Founder of the Electronic Frontier Foundation," wrote a manifesto condemning the commercialization of cyberspace, which circulated on the Internet. Here some passages: "Governments of the Industrial World, you weary giants of flesh and steel, I come from Cyberspace, the new home of Mind. On behalf of the future, I ask you of the past to leave us alone. You are not welcome among us. You have no sovereignty where we gather. We have no elected government, nor are we likely to have one, so I address you with no greater authority than that with which liberty itself always speaks. . . . We are forming our own Social Contract. This governance will arise according to the conditions of our world, not yours. . . . Ours is a world that is both everywhere and nowhere, but it is not where bodies live. . . . Your legal concepts of property, expression, identity, movement and context do not apply to us. They are based on matter. There is no matter here. Our identities have no bodies, so, unlike you, we cannot obtain order by physical coercion. We believe that from ethics, enlightened self-interest, and the commonweal, our governance will emerge."

12. It is important to note that "information overload" has existed at least since the first libraries were built.

13. Other examples often cited to illustrate how, in crisis situations, the Internet evades official censorship and provides independent information are the Tiananmen Square conflict in Beijing in 1989, the coup attempt in Moscow in 1991, and the Gulf War of 1990–1991.

14. "In the preparation of UNCED, during and after it, electronic networks contributed to NGO's networking. NGOs had access to and exchanged information and documents, discussed positions, articulated actions within and through networks during the entire Rio–92 process" (Inoue 1995, 93). This author quotes Shelley Preston's opinion that, through electronic networks, "citizens from around the world were able to access and share information related to the planning and substance of UNCED" (1994).

15. The Online Activism Organizations List kept by ACTION (ACTIvism ONline, action@eff.org) enumerated, in November 1995, a total of ninety-seven "international, national, regional and local groups supporting the online community." The great majority were based in the United States, but they are also found in Australia, Austria, Canada, England, France, Ireland, Italy, the Netherlands, New Zealand, Norway, Scotland, and Spain. Some of their most representative goals are to enhance computer use and literacy as well as Internet extensions and applications; to develop low-cost access to computer networking; to ensure the independence of Internet affairs and bring the entire Internet community together as a whole; to enhance democracy on-line and off-line; to develop community-based computer networks; to defend freedom of expression and oppose governmental censorship and regulation of on-line media; to affirm and protect constitutional rights for "electronic citizens"; and to promote the protection of privacy and data security.

16. The following is mostly based upon the study of the APC made by Susanne Sallin (1994).

17. In 1995, five networks comprised the IGC: PeaceNet, EcoNet, ConflictNet, LaborNet, and WomensNet.

18. Besides the above-mentioned seven founding networks, the other APC members are as follows: Comlink (Germany), Glasnet (Russia), Equanex (Ecuador), Chasque (Uruguay), SangoNet (South Africa), Wamani (Argentina), GLUK (Ukraine), Histria (Slovenia), LaNeta (Mexico), Colnodo (Colombia), and PlaNet (New Zealand).

19. Among the many services that can be found in APC networks are the Pacific News Service, the Peacenet World News Service, Greenpeace News, the Environmental News Service, InterPress Service (IPS, the largest news agency in the developing world), conferences of the International Institute for Sustainable Development, and information related to UN conferences. EcoNet's electronic conferences and databases provide information on energy policy, global warming, rain-forest preservation, water quality, toxic waste, and environmental education.

20. Ibase is one of Brazil's largest and most influential NGOs, working on different political and social issues such as hunger, human rights, popular movements, and environmental problems. The information on Alternex is mostly based upon Aguiar 1995.

21. The following discussion is based upon interviews I conducted of INESC officers, namely its systems manager and its environmental and Indian rights staff.

22. A Dutch activist told Inoue that "you wouldn't dream of planning a strategy campaign if the others involved are not known to you" (1995, 112).

23. Given the plural composition of networks and the interconnections available within the Internet, the opposite situation can also happen. An activist justified to Inoue his opinion on the importance of face-to-face relations by mentioning "the case of people from the World Bank that secretly get to know the contents of electronic conferences in order to anticipate NGOs' reactions to Bank projects" (1995, 112).

24. The FZLN can be understood as a globalized local movement that was able to become a localized global movement due to its ability to use mass media and especially the Internet to deterritorialize its claims, disseminating them to a much wider audience. In this vein, it is interesting to see the rhetorical strategies of a summons, distributed on the Internet since May 1996, calling for an Intercontinental Encounter for Humankind and Against Neoliberalism (held from July 27 to August 3, 1996), a humorous document written in five different versions to match the characteristics of what the FZLN deemed to be a diversified universe of sympathizers. For a work on the Zapatista movement, see Barabas 1996.

25. It is useful to recall the role that images played in mobilizing American and international opinion against the Vietnam War. This is one reason why the media coverage of the Gulf War was so intensively controlled.

References

Afonso, Carlos Alberto. 1994. "Au Service de la Société Civile." *Le Monde Diplomatique,* July 16.

Aguiar, Sonia. 1995. "Avaliação Preliminar do Alternex." Rio de Janeiro. Mimeographed.

Albert, Bruce. 1995. "O Ouro Canibal e a Queda do Céu: uma crítica xamânica da economica política da natureza." Série Antropologia (University of Brasília), no. 174.

Alvarez, Gabriel Omar. 1995. "Los Límites de los Transnacional: Brasil y el Mercorsur. Una Aproximación antropológica a los procesos de integración." Série Antropologia (University of Brasília), no. 195.

Anderson, Benedict. 1991. *Imagined Communities: Reflections on the Origins and Spread of Nationalism*. Rev. ed. London: Verso.

Appadurai, Arjun. 1990. "Disjuncture and Difference in the Global Cultural Economy." In *Global Culture,* ed. M. Featherstone, 295–310. London: Sage.

______. 1991. "Global Ethnoscapes: Notes and Queries for a Transnational Anthropology." In *Recapturing Anthropology: Working in the Present,* ed. R. Fox, 191–210. Santa Fe, N.Mex.: School of American Research Press.

Aranha Filho, Jayme. 1996. "Tribos Eletrônicas: metáforas do social." *Comunicação & Política* 3 (1):64–74.

Barabas, Alicia M. 1996. "La Rebelión Zapatista y el Movimiento Indio en Mexico." Série Antropologia (University of Brasília), no. 208.

Barnet, Richard J., and John Cavanagh. 1994. *Global Dreams: Imperial Corporations and the New World Order*. New York: Simon and Schuster.

Basch, Linda, Nina Glick Schiller, and Cristina Szanton Blanc. 1994. *Nations Unbound: Transnational Projects, Postcolonial Predicaments, and Deterritorialized Nation-States.* Langhorne, Pa.: Gordon & Breach.

Bissio, Roberto. 1994. "Cyberespace et Démocratie." *Le Monde Diplomatique* (July 16).

Bourdieu, Pierre. [1977] 1983. "A Economia das Trocas Linguísticas." In *Pierre Bourdieu,* ed. R. Ortiz. São Paulo: Editora Ática.

Bournellis, Cynthia. 1995. "The Internet's Phenomenal Growth Is Mirrored in Startling Statistics." *Internet World* (November):47–52.

Breton, Gilles. 1994. "La Globalización y el Estado: algunos conceptos teóricos." In *Globalización, Integración e Identidad Nacional,* ed. M. Rapoport, 19–32. Buenos Aires: Grupo Editor Latinoamericano.

Canclini, Néstor García. 1994. "Identidad Cultural Frente a los Procesos de Globalización y Regionalización: México y el Tratado de Libre Comercio de América del Norte." In *Las Reglas del Juego: América Latina, Globalización y Regionalismo,* ed. C. Monetta. Buenos Aires: Corregidor.

______. 1995. *Consumidores y Ciudadanos: Conflictos Multiculturales de la Globalización.* Mexico City: Editorial Grijalbo.

Carey, James W., and John J. Quirk. 1996. "A História do Futuro." *Comunicação & Política* 3 (1):102–123.

Cocco, Giuseppe. 1996. "As Dimensões Produtivas da Comunicação no Pós-Fordismo." *Comunicação & Política* 3 (1):20–33.

Commission on Global Governance. 1995. *Our Global Neighbourhood.* Oxford and New York: Oxford University Press.

Corn, David. 1996. "Pentagon Trolls the Net." *The Nation* (March 4). Electronic reproduction.

Critical Art Ensemble. 1994. *The Electronic Disturbance*. Brooklyn, N.Y.: Autonomedia.

Eco, Umberto. 1976. *Apocalípticos e Integrados*. 2nd ed. São Paulo: Perspectiva.

Edwards, David B. 1994. "Afghanistan, Ethnography, and the New World Order." *Cultural Anthropology* 9 (3):345–360.

Ellias, Norbert. 1994. "Mudanças na Balança Nós-Eu (1987)." In *A Sociedade dos Indivíduos*. Rio de Janeiro: Jorge Zahar Editores.

Escobar, Arturo. 1994. "Welcome to Cyberia: Notes on the Anthropology of Cyberculture." *Current Anthropology* 35:211–231.

Featherstone, Mike, ed. 1990. *Global Culture: Nationalism, Globalization, and Modernity*. London: Sage.

Feenberg, Andrew. 1990. "Post-Industrial Discourses." *Theory and Society* 19 (6):709–737.

Fernandes, Rubem César. 1995. "Elos de uma Cidadania Planetária." *Revista Brasileira de Ciências Sociais* 28:15–34.

Foster, Robert J. 1991. "Making National Cultures in the Global Ecumene." *Annual Review of Anthropology* 20:235–260.

Geertz, Clifford. 1963. "The Integrative Revolution: Primordial Sentiments and Civil Politics in the New States." In *Old Societies and New States: The Quest for Modernity in Asia and Africa*, ed. C. Geertz, 105–157. New York: Free Press.

Giddens, Anthony. 1990. *The Consequences of Modernity*. Stanford: Stanford University Press.

Gupta, Akhil. 1992. "The Song of the Nonaligned World: Transnational Identities and the Reinscription of Space in Late Capitalism." *Cultural Anthropology* 7 (1):63–79.

Hakken, D. 1993. "Computing and Social Change: New Technology and Workplace Transformation, 1980–1990." *Annual Review of Anthropology* 22:107–132.

Hannerz, Ulf. 1992. "The Global Ecumene." In *Cultural Complexity: Studies in the Social Organization of Meaning*, 217—267. New York: Columbia University Press.

Harvey, David. 1989. *The Condition of Post-Modernity*. Oxford: Blackwell.

Ianni, Octávio. 1995. *A Sociedade Global*. 3rd ed. Rio de Janeiro: Civilização Brasileira.

Inoue, Cristina Yumie Aoki. 1995. "Globalização, Organizações Não-governamentais e Redes de Comunicação por Computador: um estudo exploratório." Master's thesis, University of Brasília.

Kearney, Michael. 1995. "The Local and the Global: The Anthropology of Globalization and Transnationalism." *Annual Review of Anthropology* 24:547–565.

Kroker, Arthur, and Michael A. Weinstein. 1994. *Data Trash: The Theory of the Virtual Class*. New York: St. Martin's Press.

Laquey, Tracy, and Jeanne C. Ryer. 1994. *O Manual da Internet: Um Guia Introdutório para acesso às redes globais*. Rio de Janeiro: Campus.

Lee, Eric. 1995. "Workers Unite." *Internet World* (August):64–67.

Leis, Héctor Ricardo. 1995. "Globalização e Democracia. Necessidade e Oportunidade de um espaço público transnacional." *Revista Brasileira de Ciências Sociais* 28:55–69.

Lévy, Pierre. 1993. *As Tecnologias da Inteligência: O Futuro do Pensamento na Era da Informática*. Rio de Janeiro: Editora 34.

Mattelart, Armand. 1994. *Comunicação Mundo: História das Idéias e das Estratégias*. Petrópolis, Brazil: Vozes.

Monetta, Carlos J., ed. 1994. *Las Reglas del Juego: América Latina, Globalización y Regionalismo*. Buenos Aires: Corregidor.

Nash, June. 1981. "Ethnographic Aspects of the World Capitalist System." *Annual Review of Anthropology* 10:393–423.

______. 1983. "The Impact of the Changing International Division of Labor on Different Sectors of the Labor Force." In *Women, Men, and the International Division of Labor*, ed. J. Nash and M. Fernández-Kelly, 3–38. Albany: State University of New York Press.

Novak, Marcos. 1991. "Liquid Architecture in Cyberspace." In *Cyberspace: The First Steps*, ed. M. Benedikt, 225–254. Cambridge: MIT Press.

Ortiz, Renato. 1994. *Mundialização e Cultura*. São Paulo: Brasiliense.

Preston, Shelley. 1994. "Electronic Global Networking and the NGO Movement: The 1992 Rio Summit and Beyond." *Swords & Ploughshares: A Chronicle of International Affairs* 3 (2).

Quéau, Philippe. 1993. "O Tempo do Virtual." In *Imagem-Máquina,* ed. A. Parente, 91–99. Rio de Janeiro: Editora 34.

Rheingold, Howard. 1994. *The Virtual Community: Homesteading on the Electronic Frontier*. New York: Harper Perennial.

Ribeiro, Gustavo Lins. 1994a. *Transnational Capitalism: Hydropolitics in Argentina*. Gainesville: University Press of Florida.

______. 1994b. *The Condition of Transnationality*. Série Antropologia (University of Brasília), no. 173.

______. 1996. "Internet e a Comunidade Transnacional Imaginada-Virtual." *Interciencia* 21 (6):277–287.

Rosenau, James N. 1992. "Citizenship in a Changing Global Order." In *Governance Without Government: Order and Change in World Politics,* ed. J. Rosenau and E. Czempiel, 272–294. New York: Cambridge University Press.

Roszak, Theodore. 1994. *The Cult of Information: A Neo-Luddite Treatise on High Tech, Artificial Intelligence, and the True Art of Thinking*. Berkeley: University of California Press.

Rothstein, Frances Abrahamer, and Michael Blim. 1992. *Anthropology and the Global Factory: Studies of the New Industrialization in the Late Twentieth Century*. New York: Bergin & Garvey.

Rouse, Roger. 1995. "Thinking through Transnationalism: Notes on the Cultural Politics of Class Relations in the Contemporary United States." *Public Culture* 7:353–402.

Ruben, Guillermo. 1995. "Empresários e Globalização." *Revista Brasileira de Ciências Sociais* 28:71–87.

Sallin, Susanne. 1994. "The Association for Progressive Communications: A Cooperative Effort to Meet the Information Needs of Non-Governmental Organizations." Case study, Harvard-CIESIN Project on Global Environmental Change Information Policy, Cambridge. Electronic reproduction.

Santos, Milton, Maria A. De Souza, Francisco C. Scarlato, and Monica Arroyo, eds. 1994. *O Novo Mapa do Mundo: Fim de Século e Globalização*. São Paulo: Hucitec/ANPUR.

Sapir, Edward. [1931] 1956. "The Function of an International Auxiliary Language." In *Culture, Language, and Personality,* 45–64. Berkeley: University of California Press.

Sassen, Saskia. 1991. *The Global City: New York, London, Tokyo*. Princeton: Princeton University Press.

Schiller, Herbert I. 1996. *Information Inequality: The Deepening Social Crisis in America*. New York: Routledge.

Schwartau, Winn. 1995. *Information Warfare: Chaos on the Electronic Superhighway*. New York: Thunder's Mouth Press.

Sklair, Leslie. 1991. *Sociology of the Global System*. Baltimore: Johns Hopkins University Press.

Stallabrass, Julian. 1995. "Empowering Technology: The Exploration of Cyberspace." *New Left Review* 211:3–32.

Stone, Allucquère Rosanne. 1992. "Virtual Systems." In *Incorporations,* ed. J. Crary and S. Kwinter, 609–621. New York: Zone.

______. 1994. "Will the Real Body Please Stand Up? Boundary Stories About Virtual Cultures." In *Cyberspace: First Steps,* ed. M. Benedikt, 81–118. Cambridge: MIT Press.

______. 1995. *The War of Desire and Technology at the Close of the Mechanical Age.* Cambridge: MIT Press.

Tehranian, Majid. 1990. *Technologies of Power: Information Machines and Democratic Prospects.* Norwood, N.J.: Ablex.

Wapner, Paul. 1995. "Politics Beyond the State: Environmental Activism and World Civic Politics." *World Politics* 47:311–340.

Weber, H. L. 1994. "The Social Organization of an Electronic Community: A Case Study." Paper presented at the Ninety-Third Meeting of the American Anthropological Association, December, Atlanta.

Williams, Brackette F. 1989. "A Class Act: Anthropology and the Race to Nation Across Ethnic Terrain." *Annual Review of Anthropology* 18:401–444.

Wolf, Eric R. 1982. *Europe and the People Without History.* Berkeley: University of California Press.

Chapter Fourteen

The Globalization of Culture and the New Civil Society

GEORGE YÚDICE

In this chapter I will explore ways in which the transdisciplinary field of cultural studies can address changing patterns of cultural identity. I will particularly focus on how the current processes of globalization have generated discussions about the role of civil society as the medium through which the conventional compromise between the state and the diverse sectors of the nation—the *e pluribus unum*—is renegotiated. This revision is often brought to the fore by localities that have the most to gain or the most to lose from the vicissitudes wrought by globalization. Civil society has become the concept of choice as many movements for reform and revolution have been chastened by the eviction of socialism as a political alternative, at least into the near future. The current dominance of neoliberalism—the set of policies that include trade liberalization, privatization, the reduction (and in some cases near elimination) of state-subsidized social services like health care and education, the lowering of wages, and the evisceration of labor rights—has contributed to the Left's shift in political attention from the takeover of state power (which in many cases has not resolved the question of sovereignty) to issues of civil and human rights and quality of life. Conventional and even progressive political parties have succeeded in doing very little to counter these policies, both because the institutionalized political process is largely dysfunctional in responding to social needs and because enormous pressures from international financial interests not only have discouraged reform but have actually worsened conditions, such as the ever increasing gap in income distribution. Consequently, the most innovative actors in setting agendas for political and social policies are grassroots movements and the national and international nongovernmental organizations (NGOs) that support them. These actors have put a premium on culture (defined in a myriad of ways), a resource already targeted for exploitation by capital, and have established a foundation for resistance against the ravages of that very same economic system. In what follows, I first outline a brief history of how cultural studies has dealt with the issue of cultural identity. Next I go on to review how globalization has altered the objects and methods of the study of culture, particularly in relation to Latin America. Then I look into the specific effects of neoliberalism on Latin American political and social movements Finally, I examine the Zapatistas in Chiapas, Mexico, as a new kind of indigenous movement that departs from conventional notions of both leftist political movements and grassroots organizations.

Globalization and Cultural Studies

Until the 1980s, most cultural studies traditions in Europe and the Americas had a national frame. Greater emphasis on the global context of cultural practices in the 1980s and 1990s is the result of the effects of trade liberalization, the increased global reach of communications and consumerism, new kinds of labor and migration flows, and other transnational phenomena. Also significant in this regard was the implosion of the communist bloc, brought about in part by propaganda and by economic and even military warfare on the part of the United States and its allies. This world historical event not only focused the world's gaze on global economic restructuring and its ideological underpinnings but it also brought to light a series of conflicts that appeared to be new: the rise of presumably dormant nationalisms, the emergence of religious and ethnic fundamentalisms, and the determination to redraw geopolitical boundaries as a response to globalization. Some of these observations have been factored into assessments of political and cultural conflicts in the United States and Europe, particularly in reference to the rightward turn in politics and the recrudescence of racial and ethnic strife. They have been less important in analyses of the ongoing transformation in the rest of the Americas. However, other aspects of globalization have been particularly significant. Most importantly, long-standing institutional arrangements, from government proprietorship of industry to public subvention of culture and education, have been undergoing considerable change. This alteration is most often attributed to economic restructuring, particularly policies such as the reduction of the public sector, the privatization of national enterprises and social services, and the evisceration of labor laws that create new opportunities for profit and reduce the operating expenses of capital. These have been seen as the means to integration in a streamlined U.S. economic bloc that can compete with the renewed economic muscle of Europe and East Asia. Other global trends considered significant in the transformation of Latin America are: the new global division of labor ensuing from global economic restructuring, deregulation, the development of capital markets, the denationalizing impact of new technologies on telecommunications and the mass media, the rise of global marketing, the exponential growth of international travel and the tourism industry, and the political and social effects of an expanded narco-traffic industry that has permeated the centers of power not just in Colombia, Peru, and Bolivia, but also in Brazil, Mexico, and, some have argued, even Cuba.

Such a focus on the global was certainly not part of the framework of cultural studies as the field emerged in the late 1950s and was institutionalized in the early 1960s at the Birmingham Centre for Contemporary Cultural Studies. Its frame was English, to the exclusion of other subnations or colonies of the United Kingdom. Richard Hoggart (1992), Raymond Williams (1958, 1965, 1977), E. P. Thompson (1963), and others were interested primarily in helping to shift the focus of national culture away from the tradition of "the best that has been thought and said," characteristic of the legacy of Matthew Arnold, toward a valorization and study of the practices of working-class Britons. In later, Gramscian-inflected characterizations of the enterprise, this shift was described as a complex struggle for hegemony, that is, the shaping of meaning into an articulated whole that makes sense to diverse sectors of the nation, although within that whole the interests of the dominant classes, though contested, are ultimately served (Gramsci 1971). Unlike the more conventional notion of ideology (the worldview of the dominant classes, in its simplest formulation), culture, in this view, was defined as the struggle over meaning. That is, culture is no one's or no one group's property (as would be the case in ideology) but is rather a stratified process of encounter. The founders of cultural studies no longer saw culture as a civilizational achievement but as the strategies and means by which the language and values of different social classes reflected a particular sense of community while nevertheless adapting to the place made available to that community within the contest of cultures that makes up the nation.

Transdisciplinary fields of study, like communications and American studies in the United States or the anthropological and sociological study of culture in Latin America, were also conceived within a national framework up to the 1970s. The major exceptions were the dependency theory of the 1950s and 1960s and the critique of cultural imperialism, prevalent among leftist academics particularly in the 1960s and 1970s in Latin America as well as in other "peripheral" or Third World regions, and among the minority academics and intellectuals who struggled to establish ethnic studies departments in the United States. Dependency theorists focused on the unequal exchange imposed by central economies on those of the periphery (Baran 1958; Dos Santos 1970) as well as on the influence that this asymmetry has in structuring internal class relations within dependent countries (Cardoso and Faletto 1973). Cultural dependency is derived from this model insofar as not only class interests but also class tastes and values are thought to be determined by the cultural models of the center (Franco 1975). This perspective was echoed and taken further in books like *Para leer al Pato Donald* [How to Read Donald Duck]. The authors, Ariel Dorfman and Armand Mattelart, like many others at the time, saw the U.S. media as a weapon in the service of U.S. imperialism. Similarly, the Black Power, Chicano, and (Nuyorican) Young Lords movements of the late 1960s attacked the collusion of the media with the military-industrial complex as well as the racist imperialism at the heart of American society and foreign policy. With their focus on the power of institutions of production and distribution to spread capitalist and colonialist values, most of these critics gave little attention to the processes of reception—how readers and viewers might resist, appropriate, or otherwise modify mass-mediated messages. In the British context, even Hoggart, who sought to demonstrate (and advocate) the resilience of British working-class culture, worried that the "newer," American-style "mass art" would lead to a "subjection [that] promises to be stronger than the old because the chains of cultural subordination are both easier to wear and harder to strike away than those of economic subordination." He saw this as a cultural colonization that promised "progress . . . as a seeking of material possessions, equality as a moral levelling, and freedom as the ground for endless irresponsible pleasure" (Hoggart 1992, 187, 263).

In tune with the radical tenor of the period but drawing quite different conclusions from it, Marshall McLuhan, as if dismissing the kind of backward-looking resiliency advocated by Hoggart, urged educators to accept the cultural implications of the new electronic technologies of mass culture. To do so, he argued, would better prepare youth for participation in a media-saturated public culture. Also anticipating the anti-imperialist charges made by Dorfman, Mattelart, and others, he counterargued that "Hollywood is often a fomenter of anticolonialist revolutions" and quoted Sukarno to back up his point: by showing that a "people have been deprived of even the necessities of life . . . [Hollywood] helped to build up the sense of deprivation of man's birthright, and that sense of deprivation has played a large part in the national revolutions of postwar Asia." McLuhan's new world order did not portend greater inequality; instead it was envisioned to be conducive to a "recreat[ion of] the world in the image of a global village" (McLuhan and Fiore 1967, 100, 131, 67).[1]

McLuhan's global dreams, which were unabashedly utopian, resurface now and then, particularly in the participatory visions that the Internet produces in its most enthusiastic surfers. But even as these dreams are blown to galactic proportions, there are critics like Richard J. Barnet and John Cavanagh, Leslie Sklair, Saskia Sassen, and others who examine the mayhem that hovers at the frontiers of utopia. The protagonists of globalization, according to these critics, are not the new technologies per se but the global corporations that have brought about a simultaneous integration of economies, the disintegration of politics, and a decrease and downgrading of employment, thus leading to the proletarianization of the middle classes and the greater immiseration of the poor as corporations thrive. As Barnet and Cavanagh note, the technologies (informatics, telecommunications, biotechnology) on which social transformation is premised are "anything but labor-intensive," thus adding to the scarcity of jobs already effected by economic restructuring (Barnet and Cavanagh 1994, 426). For Sklair, it may not be accurate to consider consumers "cultural dupes" or to characterize capitalist consumerism as U.S. cultural imperialism; however, national corporations like Mexico's Televisa and Brazil's Globo do just as well or better in promoting the "culture-ideology of consumerism" in these countries (Sklair 1993, 32). Sassen (1991) shows how finance and media conglomerates have altered the material and social spaces of global cities, including those in the periphery like São Paulo and Mexico City, forming or deepening new spatial arrangements whereby pockets of wealth are surrounded by stretches of inner cities and shantytowns whose residents provide the cheap labor that underwrites the lifestyle of the professional-managerial classes.

Although most leftist views of globalization are pessimistic, the turn to civil society in the context of neoliberal policies, and the uses of the new technologies on which globalization relies, have opened up new forms of progressive struggle in which the cultural is a crucial arena of struggle. The multiclass Viva Rio movement in Rio de Janeiro, for example, has converted most of the areas of social life abandoned by the neoliberal state—health care, labor, neighborhood development, facilities for street children and the homeless—into an agenda for organizing civil society. Their most innovative and risky premise is the bridging of concerns of the middle class and the poor. For example, middle-class apprehensions about security (greater and more effective policing) are linked to the poor's demands for civil and human rights (protests against police brutality). Viva Rio also brought poor youth groups, particularly enthusiasts of funk music and dance, who were feared by the middle classes together with other sectors of society in a project to disseminate funk music as one of the most important cultural features of the city. Although there are risks that such a linking of concerns might yield preference to the demands of elites (as occurred when the military occupied the city's favelas in late 1994), Viva Rio's emphasis on neighborhood development for the poor serves as an effective counterweight (Yúdice forthcoming[b]). The Zapatistas, whom I will treat in detail below, have made use of the Internet and other media in new ways to create wide-ranging networks of solidarity, not only to foster the rights of indigenous groups and democratization in Mexico but also to organize a worldwide movement against neoliberalism.

Globalization and Culture in Latin America

In the past two decades, new approaches to the study of culture in Latin America have begun to consider globalization, although the two unconventional examples mentioned above (Viva Rio and the Zapatistas) have yet to be incorporated into this new scholarship. As I mentioned at the beginning of this chapter, most interpretations of Latin American cultures have been carried out from a national perspective. The major exceptions, dependency theory and anti-imperialism, ultimately hark back to appeals to the purity and health of the authentic nation in the face of foreign cultural contamination. By the late 1970s and early 1980s, as several Latin American countries were making the transition from authoritarian dictatorships to democracy (or, more exactly, to electoral politics without the oversight of the police state), anti-imperialism was left behind as an ineffective analytical framework that did not adequately engage a series of new realities, such as the actions of international NGOs with agendas that addressed human rights, gender and racial equality, the landless, street children, and the environment. This international linkage to certain social movements, as well as the transnational flows of communications, information, gendered identity images and lifestyles, and their relation to the breakdown of formal politics, created a new imaginary that could not be faithfully captured by the anti-imperialist framework. This is not to say, of course, that enormous inequalities ceased to exist between North and South.

This shift was registered in the very conception and practice in the cultural sphere. As the hold of the national imaginary ebbed due not only to the pull of the transnational but also to the tug of grassroots initiatives, the cultural sphere became increasingly important. The imbrication of the transnational and the grassroots (most evident in the action of NGOs) produced situations in which culture could no longer be seen predominantly as the reproduction of the "way of life" of the nation as a discrete entity separate from global trends. Taking these circumstances into account, Chilean sociologist José Joaquín Brunner, for example, rejected the idea that modernization is inherently foreign to a supposedly "novohispanic," baroque, Christian, and mestizo cultural ethos. For traditional elite intellectuals (including major exponents of the literary world), this ethos becomes inauthentic as it is "colonized" by other ethical values. In Brunner's assessment, certain folkloric stereotypes had been folded into a *representation* of the popular as an inherent magical realism, which ultimately smacked of essentialism. The literati put forward this imaginary of the transcultural and hybrid as a means to valorize, and thus legitimize, the contradictory mixtures typical of Latin American cultural formations. This is not to say that the literati were wrong about Latin American national cultural formations; they are in fact hybridized. The critique focuses, rather, on the representations and ideological uses made of that mixture, uses that moreover are historically contingent.[2] Brunner argued that these mixtures were generated by the differentiation in modes of production, the segmentation of markets of cultural consumption, and the expansion and internationalization of the culture industry. Latin America's peculiar forms of hybridity were therefore not cause for an essentialist celebration of their marvelous qualities or for a denunciation of their inauthenticity. Brunner preferred to focus on those features that, from a more historical and sociological perspective, register the emergence of a modern, transnationalized cultural sphere in heterogeneous societies (1987, 4).

Echoing Ernesto Laclau and Chantal Mouffe, Brunner argues that the intellectual of today must necessarily abandon the traditional role of articulating a national common sense, especially if that sense is based on some representation of a generalized popular that *assimilates* a myriad of differences:

> The national-popular preserves the old desire to give culture a unifying ground, be it a class, racial, historical or ideological one. When culture begins to deterritorialize, when it becomes more complex and varied, assumes all the heterogeneities of society, is industrialized and massified, loses its center and is filled with "lite" and transitory expressions, is structured on the basis of a plurality of the modern; when all this takes

> place, the unifying desire becomes reductionist and dangerously totalitarian or simply rhetorical. (1990, 21)

Brunner redefines the terrain of cultural activity such that it necessarily encompasses areas that have been outside of the domain of traditional intellectuals (including the literati) and also areas that, in the current conjuncture, run the risk of being left to the experts of techno-bureaucratic engineering of not only economic but also social and cultural "development." In other words, appeals to the "national-popular" may actually make it more difficult to address and take some measure of control over the transnational phenomena that increasingly define the culture. It is incumbent on intellectuals and critics, then, to understand how these phenomena are produced and not disdain them because they do not conform to an idealized critical discourse thought to be necessary for the conduct of society.

This is the task that Jesús Martín-Barbero takes on in the realm of the media, particularly in relation to urban youth cultures, whose symbols depart quite markedly from those of the national-popular. Many activists and scholars of grassroots social movements seem to have a measure of disdain for youth cultures because they seem to fly in the face of the kind of sovereign culture that affords the nation a foundation for resistance to cultural imperialism.[3] Martín-Barbero's *De los medios a las mediaciones* put forth an important critique of the idea that transnationalization was just a new and more sophisticated form of imperialism. Transnationalization, despite its homogenizing tendencies, has also been an important factor in helping to see through the "blackmail of the state" and in breaking through the older "totalizing political strategies" of the Left, thus enabling a critique of the fetishizations of the "popular" and its reconstitution as the democratic action of "political subjects" (1987, 225–226). In order to register the possibilities of democratic action in these media-saturated civil societies, it is necessary to criticize and move beyond the limiting ideological and theoretical positions that presented "the relations and conflicts between culture industries and popular cultures as external to each other or simply as a question of resistance." If we can get beyond this Manichaean dichotomy, it becomes possible to "rethink the relations between culture and politics . . . to connect cultural politics to the transformations in political culture, particularly in relation to the latter's communicational implications, that is, to the weave of interrelations that social actors constitute" and thus to think of mass communications not as "mere problem of markets and consumption" but rather as the "decisive space in which it is possible to redefine the *public* and to construct democracy." It is precisely in this endeavor that "Cultural Studies and media studies speak to each other" (Martín-Barbero 1993). The possibility of a progressive politics of mass communications is not only evident in the recontextualized reception characteristic of youth cultures; it is perhaps the most salient aspect of Zapatista activity, as is proposed below.

Situating his media analysis in the context of postmodernity and transnationalization, Martín-Barbero emphasizes two results—one "positive" and the other "negative"—of the fragmentations, decenterings, heterogenizations, and hybridizations brought about by these phenomena. On the one hand, insofar as the "traditional spaces of collective gathering are disarticulated, [a process that] de-urbanizes everyday life and makes the city less likely to be used," the audiovisual media, especially television, become the "means to return the city to us, to relocate us in it," in its "imaginary territories" (Martín-Barbero 1993). The funk youth cultures about which Vianna (1988) and I (Yúdice 1994) have written make use of pop music and dance as a means to "take back" the city, which, according to the elites, does not belong to them. Furthermore, the mass media can recover "the traces which can enable the recognition of '*pueblos*' [both people and country] and the dialogue between generations and traditions." Martín-Barbero also advocates the study of the "changes in images and metaphors of the national, the devaluation, secularization and reinvention of myths and rituals through which this contradictory but still powerful identity is unmade and remade both from a local and transnational perspective" (Martín-Barbero 1992, 50).

Néstor García Canclini's *Culturas híbridas* (translated as *Hybrid Cultures*) (1990) is probably the best-known study of Latin American hybridization in a transnational era. His *Consumidores y ciudadanos* (1995b) and many other books and articles tackle problems presented by processes of globalization and regional integration. Already by the late 1970s, García Canclini had framed his study of Mexican popular cultures, especially the artisanal production of indigenous peoples, within the framework of globalization. It should be noted that in Latin America, the term "popular culture" refers to the cultural practices of sundry "subordinate cultures," rather than to "mass culture," as in the United States. This does not mean that popular culture is necessarily considered authentic and untouched by the mass culture industries, a claim that García Canclini, like Brunner and Martín-Barbero, rejects out of hand. On the contrary, García Canclini argues that these "subordinate" cultures "are not allowed any autonomous or alternative development, and their production and consumption as well as social structure and language are reorganized in order to make them receptive to capitalist modernization" (García Canclini 1982, 29; 1993, 8). In Mexico, this process has been brokered by the state, coextensive with the Institutional Revolutionary Party (PRI), which has ruled uninterruptedly for almost seventy years. The institutionalization of the ideology of *Indigenismo* was carried out as a compromise solution to popular struggles in the aftermath of the Mexican Revolution. Under Lázaro Cárdenas's centralization of a populist state in the 1930s, real gains were made in the redistribution of land to indigenous groups and in labor laws for the emergent industrial proletariat. However, as the state apparatus grew to mammoth proportions, it increasingly put the interests of modernization and development over those of the popular sectors. This ultimately resulted in a sorry situation whereby the peasantry, in particular indigenous peoples, retained their status as the symbolic base of the nation but were excluded from effective participation and were left out in the distribution of resources by the very same state that "represented" them.

The ability of the Mexican state to negotiate its contradictory existence began to founder in the 1960s, as a series of labor and student strikes challenged state repression and corruption. In October 1968, at least four hundred but possibly over one thousand students were massacred at the Plaza of Three Cultures in Tlatelolco. By the late 1970s a coterie of anthropologists and sociologists including Guillermo Bonfil Batalla and García Canclini challenged institutionalized indigenism as well as the role of intellectuals and academics. Bonfil Batalla, for example, called for a redefinition of the "researcher" as a collaborator in the projects of subaltern communities. He proposed this collaboration as a needed retooling for social scientists who were seeing their traditional functions disappear, not only due to the paradigm crisis in the social sciences but also to recent political and economic transformations (such as the advent of neoliberalism and privatization). These changes displaced anthropologists from their function as facilitators of national integration in the pact that had been struck between the state and civil society in the postrevolutionary period under Cárdenas (Bonfil Batalla 1991, 18–19). García Canclini, in turn, called not only for refashioning the institutions of the organization, production, marketization, and consumption of popular culture but also for the creation of a new public sphere and even a new tourism industry from which to rethink and reexperience culture (1982, 161; 1993, 114).

Culture Under Neoliberalism

Such calls for rethinking the relation of the state and civil society have become even more relevant since the early 1980s, when the Mexican government adopted neoliberalism. They have also had an enormous impact on cultural identity, particularly since the terms by which the state addressed its national constituency have changed significantly. Under Miguel de la Madrid (1982–1988), Carlos Salinas de Gortari (1988–1994), and now Ernesto Zedillo (1994–), nationalist, anti-imperialist discourse was dropped along with trade barriers, long thought to be the bulwark of sovereignty. Now free trade with the United States was courted and decentralization implemented. In this context, for example, emerging private and public institutions in search of new legitimacy altered their approach to the national identity of culture, which was now put to work in the global arena, as in the "Splendors of Thirty Centuries" blockbuster exhibition. The cultural difference expressed by means of art was no longer used to take a nationalist, defensive position vis-à-vis the dominant models of Western modernity, particularly the United States (as in the case of the muralists), but rather for staging showcases that demonstrated that Mexico was on a civilizational par with its trading partner to the north. This seems to have been the purpose of the "Myth and Magic" exhibition at Monterrey's Museo de Arte Contemporáneo, exemplar of would-be first-world art institution (Yúdice forthcoming[a]).

Anthropological institutions and the discipline of anthropology itself, like the art world, also found it necessary to "reconvert" in the context of globalization and shifts in the self-perceptions of the Mexican nation. The role of the anthropologist vis-à-vis state institutions like the Instituto Nacional Indigenista changed, which added to the crisis of social scientists and intellectuals discussed above. The transnationalization of the media, evident in Televisa's offerings, and the prevailing consumerist ethos contributed to changes in cultural identity, evident in the growing preference for Hollywood and other U.S. audiovisual imports (García Canclini 1995b). Privatization initiatives, downsizing, and the decentralization of the public sector, particularly in relation to culture, have begun to shift the center of attention away from a centralized, national context toward regional cultures, a process that is given impetus by the geographically differential impact of the North American Free Trade Agreement (NAFTA). Although it may not be advisable to speak of the culture of neoliberalism, these changes have taken place under neoliberal policies. Before going on to examine new cultural manifestations in this context, a brief account of neoliberalism is in order.

Neoliberal economic policies found fertile terrain in Latin America under the draconian conditions of the early 1980s. An enormous foreign debt had accrued as a result of state-led development and the failure of import substitution in the face of a fierce competitiveness unleashed by the global imposition of market values and free trade. The reduction of a state that guaranteed employment and regulated capital, the privatization of state-owned enterprises and services, the targeting of scarce resources, and decentralization were instituted as part of the structural adjustment programs prescribed by such international finance institutions as the World Bank and the International Monetary Fund, institutions that had the power to sanction investment. Economic integration into the world economy meant reduced state power to shield citizens from the ups and downs of the world market, the disciplining of labor by the criterion of competitiveness, and the unprecedented dissemination of the ideology of the free market. The irony is that trade liberalization, which, it was argued, would increase employment, has not only not done so in the three NAFTA countries but has led to a decrease in real wages and jobs since the early 1980s (Shorrock 1996).

According to Alejandro Foxley, neoliberal policies like stabilization, trade liberalization, and privatization, if implemented successfully, should lead to a final stage of increased investment and productivity. Crucial to the ability to move from one phase of development to another is political legitimacy, which is countered by increasing poverty and unemployment. Stabilization of the economy in the face of the debt crisis, for example, was carried out by a set of policies that decelerated growth, which in turn led to unemployment, lowered wages, and reduced government expenditures in the social sector. The other phases have also had a negative impact on the quality of life of the general populace, particularly the lower classes. Privatization, for example, is deployed as a means to increase productivity, since state-owned enterprises that are favorable to labor are taken over by private concerns that initiate downsizing and technological modernization, both of which lead to unemployment and a competitive labor market (i.e., lower wages) that enhances participation in the world economy. These social hardships, Foxley argues, must be offset by "a strong social component that will neutralize the negative equity effects" of the first two phases (1996, 3).

The question that remains is whether the transition to the third phase of increased investment and productivity can be achieved with a more egalitarian income distribution. For Foxley this depends on the handling of exchange rate and fiscal policies. Reducing inflation by adjusting the exchange rate can produce a trade deficit and, as in the case of Mexico, diminish foreign currency reserves until they become insufficient to back up foreign investment. Devaluation, which is the usual remedy for this problem, is instituted by increasing interest rates and reducing government expenditures, both of which lead to further unemployment and the fraying of the safety net. But even without devaluation, privatization itself leads to a shrinkage of the safety net and greater hardship for low-income sectors, since the state has virtually relinquished its capacity to regulate enterprises it once owned.[4]

The question then might be why social capital has not been increased. Foxley suggests that a vigorous civil society may be able to develop the needed social capital to democratize economic and political life. This might beg the question of what will foster that civil society. In many Latin American countries, it is less the state than grassroots initiatives and considerable aid from NGOs, many of which are foreign, that has nourished civil society. We might say that just as the state must manage the contradictions of neoliberalism, so also must civil society, for it has been assigned the role of ensuring "stability along with transformation" (Ronfeldt 1995). Civil society has a double origin: in neoliberalism's need for stability and political legitimation, and in grassroots organization for the sake of survival in the face of structural adjustment. There are thus two kinds of civil society activity, or at least two directions in which civil society might move: toward stability or toward ungovernability, both terms used by those analysts, usually on the economic and political Right, who favor the transition to neoliberalism.

Ronfeldt has formulated a model of national evolution through four "mentalities": *tribal,* which constitutes the basis of identity; *institutional,* which provides efficient decisionmaking and control; *market,* which generates greater productivity and social diversification; and *network,* which fosters "mutual collaboration among members of a distributed, multi-organizational network" resulting in a strengthened civil society through the actions of social movements as well as "environmental, peace, human-rights, and other networks of nongovernmental organizations" (Ronfeldt 1995). This form of civil society offers the stability that the state can no longer provide in periods of great (and painful) restructuring. But this last mentality may also result in the strengthening of "uncivil society," which Ronfeldt exemplifies by reference to subversive groups such as criminal networks (e.g., narco-traffickers), terrorists, and rightist militias, as well as leftist organizations and insurgents like the Zapatistas.

What is instructive in Ronfeldt's analysis is the notion that civil society must be *managed* in the interest of maximizing political stability and economic transformation. For Ronfeldt and other advocates of neoliberalism, civil society should be linked to the market in order to nudge it in the direction of maintaining the capitalist system, which is thought to be the only soil fertile enough for democracy to take root. Consequently, even a civil society that works against neoliberalism—for example, the Canadian, U.S., and transnational NGOs that provide support for the Zapatistas—is ultimately a benefit to market society because it "corrects" the excesses of the market and thus stabilizes and legitimizes the system. Civil society will in the long term—if not in the medium term—help Mexico evolve into a "true" market society. Such activity will in turn further destabilize the corrupt, inefficient, and institutionalized interests of the PRI, which has ruled for nearly seven decades. It also promotes the diversity that, according to Ronfeldt, is necessary for the market system to operate. The function of the state, then, is to *manage,* not eliminate, these forces of civil society so as to keep "ungovernability" (or, rather, the demands of democratization) at bay. We see here a rightist version of Laclau and Mouffe's vision of radical democracy (1985), but with the significant difference that the "multiplication of antagonisms" that would presumably further the process of democratization ends up working in the interests of capital.

The contradictory conditions under which civil society is fostered—the state manages and controls third-sector organizations by means of official certification,[5] and these flourish in opposition to or in spite of the state—hold simultaneously as NGOs that have state sanction nevertheless attempt to undermine the very means by which the state attempts to co-opt them. This is the case in organizations such as the *museos comunitarios* (about which I say more below) that are funded by the state yet in some cases maintain covert relations with contestatory groups, including the Zapatista National Liberation Army (EZLN). This is also typical of journals and university and cultural organizations that work to disseminate the information that flies in the face of the government's and the international finance institutions' interpretations of social conditions. Many such organizations receive funding from federal arts and cultural funding agencies.

The Zapatistas and the Struggle for Civil Society

Although it is true that a renewed civil society—composed of new social movements—emerged in the 1970s as a force mobilized against authoritarian states in Latin America and eastern Europe, it is under neoliberalism that this new society has flourished and integrated with the state and the market. Hence the significance of a movement that would challenge the new status quo precisely on its very own terms. However, the possibility of rethinking politics and culture in Mexico received an unanticipated shot in the arm with the insurgency of the EZLN on January 1, 1994. Their action consolidated the frustrations with one-party authoritarian rule, and to this date the calls for reform and relinquishment of that rule have not disappeared from public discussion. The state, together with the media conglomerates, particularly Televisa, had blanketed public space with neoliberal hype (a reversal of former nationalist stances) in support of NAFTA.[6] The Zapatistas took the opportunity presented by NAFTA and capitalized on the public's attention by timing the onset of their insurgency for the day on which the agreement went into effect. Although the Zapatistas engaged in battle in the first month and in sporadic skirmishes over the next two years, they are not a guerrilla army in the conventional Latin American style, like Castro's rebels, the Sandinistas, the Salvadoran Farabundo Martí National Liberation Front (FMLN), or even the Shining Path. More than armed combat, they have engaged in a struggle over the definition of the public good, both national and transnational, and have demonstrated an expert use of global resources, particularly the news media and the Internet. As such, they have initiated the kind of intervention into civil society that Bonfil Batalla, García Canclini, and many others had called for but that was impossible to achieve from a purely intellectual or political standpoint.

The Zapatistas made the call to institute a new civil society on January 1, 1996, in the "Fourth Declaration of the Lacandon Jungle," as a response to a "national plebiscite for peace and democracy" that they had conducted in the fall of 1995. The EZLN created the Zapatista Front of National Liberation (FZLN), "a civil and nonviolent organization, independent and democratic, Mexican and national, which struggles for democracy, liberty, and justice in Mexico." The aim of the front is to organize the demands and proposals of all sectors of the opposition (although not the conservative National Action Party, or PAN) against the "state-party system [which] is the main obstacle to a transition to democracy in Mexico." Furthermore, the front will draft a new constitution that addresses the demands of the Mexican people and that retains Article 39 of the current constitution. This article states that "national sovereignty resides essentially and originally in the people. All public power derives from the people and is instituted for their benefit. The people have, at all times, the inalienable right to alter or modify their form of government" (EZLN 1994, 34). The Zapatistas' call for a "nation of many worlds" contrasts with the bankrupt national project of the PRI: "In the world of the powerful there is no space for anyone but themselves and their servants. In the world we want everyone fits. In the world we want many worlds to fit. The Nation which we construct is one where all communities and languages fit, where all steps may walk, where all may have laughter, where all may live the dawn" (Henríquez and Rojas 1996). More recently, however, the government has adopted much of this multicultural discourse. This is evident in the Programa de Cultura 1995–2000 announced in January 1996 by Rafael Tovar y de Teresa, president of the Consejo Nacional de la Cultura y las Artes, which states that "culture contributes to the manifestation of the ethnic and social diversity of the country" (Poder Ejecutivo Federal 1996a, 2; see also Poder Ejecutivo Federal 1996b).

The Zapatista program is unabashedly utopian, particularly its decision to stay out of electoral politics and yet to wield influence over Mexican society—to help create a national forum in which diversity is recognized. This is a new way of conceiving of power, a social power rather than a coercive power. FZLN representative Priscilla Pacheco Castillo characterizes the question of power thus: "When we say we don't want to take power, we don't mean we will remain neutral about power. When we talk of organizing society, we are talking of power, but a different kind of power. We have a different conception of power; it is more a social kind of power. It does not have to be represented in a government" (Spencer 1996). The major result of Zapatista actions has been to establish dialogue among the many sectors of civil society as well as to compel the government to join these discussions (Henríquez and Pérez 1995). Their only safeguard has been the watchful eye of the world, whose attention they have been able to secure by threatening to expose the state's lack of commitment to democracy. By launching their offensive when they did, the Zapatistas "blackmailed" the state, which would otherwise have probably wiped them out, unfettered by the rhetoric of democratization that accompanied NAFTA. Just as importantly, the Zapatistas planned an artful guerrilla media war. In a country in which the media are oriented to the state and its policies, the Zapatistas have been able to carve a spaçe for themselves and their civil society project by remaining newsworthy—virtually rewriting the manual for marketing—and pushing the normally unidirectional means of communication into a back and forth dialogue (López 1996, 30–31).

The emphasis on direct speech, as if a "real" public sphere in a mass-mediated society were possible, has been criticized for its romanticization of indigenous cultural practices (e.g., the priority of face-to-face, collective decisionmaking over electoral representation). When the Zapatistas publish a communiqué in which they state that "the flower of the word will not die . . . because it comes from the depths of history and the land and can no longer be usurped by the arrogance of power" (Henríquez and Rojas 1996), they are couching a sophisticated bid for public reception in a language that resonates with the cultural legitimation of premodern discursive forms. The "Zapatista Manifesto in Nahuatl" not only lays claim to a prominent place in the Mexican nation but also affirms that democracy will come when the culture of the nation is refashioned from the perspective of indigenous peoples. This entails dredging up the claims to recognition and dignity made throughout history in the many tongues silenced by the reigning culture, the official *Indigenismo* of the mestizo state. "But the rebellion that rises with a brown face and a true tongue was not born today. In the past it spoke with other tongues and in other lands . . . in nahuatl, paipai, kiliwa, cúcapa, cochimi, kumiai, yuma. . . . By speaking in its Indian heart, the nation maintains its dignity and its memory" (Henríquez and Rojas 1996).

The Mexican state's adoption of neoliberalism is expressed not only by a new set of rhetorics but also by policies that depart from the consensus of the past. The 1992 constitutional reform of Article 27, for example, reorganized land tenure and permitted title holders of *ejidos* (land vested in the community) to enter into commercial contracts, thus introducing corporate capital into collective farming. Although this measure pushed some landholding farmers into export production, particularly the larger ones, most small farmers were "isolated from the institutional and financial supports that [would have] allowed them to continue to farm in the face of unfavorable market conditions" (Barkin 1995). The result was a further erosion of the material base of rural society, which ultimately contributed to the Zapatista rebellion. Neoliberalism, in fact, has been seen by the Zapatistas and other opposition groups as a threat to their continued existence. The "national dialogue" convened by the EZLN on the rights and culture of indigenous peoples emphasized that the "culture of neoliberalism" must be dismantled if indigenous peoples were to gain autonomy under a "new federalism" (Pérez and Morquecho 1995).

The Zapatistas have been able to make common cause with many sectors of the Mexican population in this united front against neoliberalism, especially since the government's policies have had a disastrous effect on the vast majority of the population. The Zapatistas have also extended their opposition to neoliberalism to the international arena, calling for an "Intercontinental Forum Against Neoliberalism" in their January 1996 "First Declaration of La Realidad" (*La Jornada* 1996). Besides the meeting held from July 27 to August 3, 1996, other anti-neoliberalism meetings are being planned for Berlin, Tokyo, an African city yet to be determined, Sydney, and Mexico City. An important feature of the agenda is to organize a broadly based internationalist culture ("a new international of hope") to counter the culture of neoliberalism. The culture should include: "All individuals, groups, collectives, movements, social, citizen, and political organizations, neighborhood associations, cooperatives, all leftist groups, non governmental organizations, groups in solidarity with the struggles of the peoples of the world, bands, tribes, intellectuals, musicians, workers, artists, teachers, peasants, cultural groups, youth movements, alternative media, ecologists, squatters, lesbians, homosexuals, feminists, pacifists."

The discontent with neoliberalism has even driven many members of the ruling PRI to fall over themselves in the rush to criticize, opportunistically, their own party's economic policies and to call for a "recomposition of the political system," concurring with the opposition that Mexico's sovereignty is at stake ("La política debe ser instrumento"). The PRI brought the crisis on itself, but the new consensus that there must be reform has to be credited to the Zapatistas more than to any other sector of the opposition. What exactly, however, does a "recomposition of the political system" mean in Mexico? From a U.S. perspective, one might imagine a system of representation whereby all manner of interest groups, including the so-called identity groups of multiculturalism, gain proportional representation in the myriad institutions of the state, the corporate sector, and civil society. However, this U.S.-style representational mode of "distributional equity" has not been adapted by the newly born Movement of National Liberation (MLN) and the Broad Oppositional Front (FAO). The latter is formed independently, albeit with EZLN guidance, from over five hundred organizations (Correa and López 1996).

Even the recently signed agreement with the government on Indian rights, particularly regarding political and cultural autonomy, "the right to adopt their own forms of government in their communities or towns according to their customs" (Preston 1996), is not conceived within such a system of representation. The agreement includes the right to multicultural education (whatever that might mean in the Chiapanecan or Mexican context), including teaching in indigenous languages. However, the Zapatistas have stressed again and again that they are not an identity group and that their efforts are aimed at transforming the entire nation, at reinvigorating civil society for all. The autonomy they seek is *neither integrationist nor separatist,* as even the government negotiators have come to accept (Rojas 1996). This marks a significant departure from the terms of *Indigenismo,* which had presumably integrated indigenous communities since the establishment of the Instituto Nacional Indigenista. As Rodolfo Stavenhagen explains, "the real identity and unity of the indigenous peoples of Mexico is provided at the community level." The administration of municipalities that include indigenous communities will require the negotiation of satisfactory juridical-constitutional formulas. Autonomy, like integration in the United States, however, "does not produce miracles: it is but a juridical framework within which the national State and indigenous peoples can freely and constructively confront the large-scale problems of poverty and well-being, identity and equality" (Stavenhagen 1995).

Unlike African Americans before the civil rights era, indigenous peoples in Mexico had been represented by indigenist ideology as an *integral* part of the nation. Integration via the Instituto Nacional Indigenista has operated more like an asylum than a home, however. While community was the Indians' own criterion for identity, the state rearticulated that identity in keeping with its own nationalist project, reifying customs as objects and beliefs as myths and institutionalizing them in such neutered spaces as the National Museum of Anthropology. The very notion of "patrimony"—Whose? For what purposes? For whose observation?—has, indeed, become a contested category, as diverse groups seek to wrest control of the means of symbolization from the state institutions that claim proprietary rights over customs, habits, ritual objects, and so on. Mexican critics have spoken of the Mexican state's pyramidal cultural apparatuses, and none could be more emblematic than the National Museum of Anthropology. It will be instructive, therefore, to briefly examine the terms according to which a new museological movement has been generated among indigenous communities.

The *museo comunitario* (community museum) movement, which began in 1986, although facilitated by national and international professional museological institutions, has sought its raison d'être in local practices and, thus, has been relatively independent of the proprietary-conservationist ethos of the ideology of national patrimony. As a recent report issued by organizers from these museums explains, the indigenous people who established them valorize the objects and practices to be displayed and enacted in relation to the needs of their community, to the reproduction of the community. To the degree that this is the case, "that valorization may contain features that go beyond scientific and aesthetic principles, and [may be legitimized] by the sacred" (Barrera Bassols et al. 1995, 28, 33).

The first *museo comunitario* was established in Tlalocula, Oaxaca, by the decision of the community. After an archeological find was made in their community, the Shan Dany residents decided to set aside a space where they could record and concentrate their activities, including an exhibition of the work of artisans and the systematization of their healing practices. Until they established their museum, this community had not revealed in public the activities that are now displayed and enacted. The museum itself is not identified by a building, a collection, or a particular audience. Its "display" is the interaction of the community with itself and with other communities. The exhibits are not laid out in writing but are the result of much organization and cultural activity that adheres to the community's sociopolitical, mythic, and religious rhythms. In many cases, the museological practice is so intertwined with the reproduction of the community itself that the "exhibition" may consist of practices that further the local economy, such as the systematization of the knowledge involved in coffee growing and the opening up of the community to tourism. The exhibition "La vida en un sorbo: El café en México" [A Sip of Life: Coffee in Mexico], for example, was initiated by the National Coordinating Committee of Coffee Growing Organizations (CNOC), which is composed mainly of indigenous producers. The museum not only reproduced the ritual coffee growing techniques but also provided a place for growers to sell their coffee and thus dispense with the intervention of intermediaries such as distributors.

The community museums are interesting in and of themselves. But I raise this example because the community I am referring to participated in an international discussion that demonstrates the degree to which even the smallest of indigenous groups can be inserted into transnational networks that have an impact on questions of identity and representation. This community was invited by the Smithsonian Institution's National Museum of the American Indian (NMAI) to participate in a discussion entitled "Ethnic Identity, Community Museums, and Development Programs" in September 1995. Twenty-five other Latin American Indian groups were invited. The discussion was meant to be the first event in an attempt to expand the concept of the "American Indian" beyond the borders of the United States. What makes this meeting interesting is that it raised many problems about the conceptualization of identity, ethnicity, and nomenclature that may not become evident until two or more systems of thinking about these issues come into contact.

The director, Richard West, explained that these groups were invited to educate the Smithsonian about the real meaning of the objects that were housed there. The Smithsonian took the guiding premise that a museum should consult the people who provide the objects on exhibit and not just collect the objects (Barrera Bassols and Vera Herrera 1996, 23–24). The participants were told that the Smithsonian would use this knowledge in order to represent native peoples exactly as they themselves wanted to be represented. This motive raised many concerns and elicited doubts from some that their cultures could be adequately represented. A

Mam from Guatemala raised objections about the representativity of the collection and said: "We did not come to exhibit ourselves, we are not objects." Another participant opined that preserving the bones of his forebears was counterproductive. Yet another, a Shuar from Ecuador, objected to the idea that the museum should document indigenous cultures because they are disappearing. What is needed, he said, is to document culture for the cultural self-development of the community. The notion of a disappearing culture is erroneous, "surely put forward by an anthropologist" (Barrera Bassols and Vera Herrera 1996, 24–25). The most heated discussions, however, involved nomenclature and the criteria for assuming the identity of an Indian. The museum officials variously used the terms Indian, indigenous, Native American, tribal, people, community. These terms made some of the participants feel uncomfortable, as if it did not matter what they called themselves. One participant from Peru said that his neighbors only referred to each other using the term "peasant." Instead of *el día de la raza* [day of the race], they should celebrate *el día del campesinado* [day of the peasant] (Barrera Bassols and Vera Herrera 1996, 26). An observer of a similar event, the Festival of American Folklife, organized by the Smithsonian's Center for Folklife Programs and Cultural Studies and held in June and July 1994, reported that "the system of racial representations, conflicts, and transactions of U.S. society . . . tends to racialize the lives of other peoples . . . ," a "very complex matter that must be examined in relation to workings of international and transnational agencies" (Mato 1995a, 23).

The differences in systems of identity categorization were commented on with great concern when the participants were told that in the United States one can be an Indian on the basis of blood even if one doesn't "belong" to an indigenous community. For the NMAI, the problem of representativity is solved because 50 percent of its board members have at least one-sixteenth Indian blood. The participants expressed their view that such an institution should be administered by Indian communities. It's not enough, they argued, for the director to be a Cheyenne, which raised the question of what is important in the constitution of identity. Some groups considered participation, instead, as the way to determine belonging. The Latin American Indian participants were not impressed by the racial component of the so-called ethnic minorities at the Smithsonian. They argued that this was not a blood or race issue. Instead, it is a "wide-ranging set of assumptions, presuppositions, beliefs, myths, values, experiences and ties that researchers themselves have defined as the 'horizon of intelligibility' or 'territory of meaning'" (Barrera Bassols and Vera Herrera 1996, 37). Structures of feeling are what produce group belonging. Not even the use of the "same" language is sufficient to nurture this sense of belonging.

This discussion brings to the surface the complex negotiations of cultural reproduction and identity, particularly for marginalized or subordinate groups, that are now negotiated in a transnational sphere. I have referred to this process as "transnational cultural brokering" in a study on the exhibition of the work of

Latin American artists in U.S. museums and galleries (Yúdice forthcoming[a]). The process, however, is endemic wherever "metropolitan" institutions (whether national or international) seek to help out local communities, most often with best of intentions.[7] This is evident in the "mixed" agenda put together by the cosponsors of the Festival of American Folklife, on which I have been commenting. The Inter-American Foundation, for example, seems to have a different agenda from that of the Smithsonian. According to reports, the former organization took a somewhat technocratic approach to questions of community development. One participant, "a development specialist at a multilateral banking institution . . . said [he] was very pleased with the program, and added: 'This is not a program on culture and development, but on how the Inter-American Foundation understands culture and development'" (Mato 1995a, 28). Although not necessarily accepting the framing terms of the discussions, the participants did not conflict in any significant ways with the hosts. Mato hypothesizes that the lack of conflict reflects a degree of satisfaction with the kinds of projects included in the program, a desire not to offend one's hosts, and most importantly the "develop[ment of] attitudes of trying to satisfy expectations that [funding recipients] attribute to the donor agencies" (1995a, 40).

An interesting contrast is provided by some of the EZLN communiqués. Subcomandante Marcos, who has sought out the aid of "international civil society" (i.e., NGOs and solidarity groups from North America), is keenly attuned to the predicaments that arise in the kinds of situations reviewed above. He refers in one communiqué, for example, to two photographers who showed up in the Lacandon jungle to "take some shots of Zapatista life in order to present it in a global event on the Internet." They justified their visit by presenting themselves as journalists with "testimonial and artistic intentions." Marcos, in somewhat tongue-in-cheek fashion—yet quite seriously, as becomes evident as the narrative progresses—finds the photographers guilty of perpetrating the "crime" of "image theft." To undo their crime, Marcos takes the camera into his own hands and turns it on the photographers, whom he considers apocryphal agents of public history. By focusing the instrument of representation on them, he aims to "reach the world that looks at their photographs." This reversal, the communiqué continues, is an attempt to bridge the distance between spectator or photographer and the Zapatistas, the objects of their prurience. Marcos proposes establishing a different kind of relationship by turning the gaze back onto the spectators and photographers. On this bridge, they are themselves transformed into actors who, by definition, must assume a role. Like one of Julio Cortázar's narrators, Marcos propels the viewers and readers into the story as actors who must choose a side: to engage in the always institutionalized quagmire of representation or to act out the relation to civil society in a different way.

Marcos's little allegory does not assume that images tell the truth. Rather, it is in the taking hold of the instruments of image making and framing that one can challenge the truth of representations. This is, of course, a tale familiar to anthropologists and media critics who have challenged the conditions under which subjects are turned into represented objects and are thus bereft of the power to tell their own story. In fact, the report on community museums makes explicit reference to the new forms of negotiation of Indian rights that the Zapatistas, careful not to be taken in by the intermediary role, initiated (Barrera Bassols et al. 1995, 29). In this particular case, Marcos is referring to the indigenous peoples who make up the mass of the EZLN and who heretofore have "only appeared as images in museums, tourist guidebooks, crafts advertising." "The eye of the camera seeks them out," the text goes on, "as an anthropological curiosity or a colorful detail of a remote past." What is it that has altered the terms of representation? "The eyes [sights] of the rifles that they have taken up have forced the eyes of the cameras to look in a different manner." The Zapatistas may not own the means of representation, but they have found creative ways of exercising a measure of control over representations of their activities. In good part, this measure of control depends on the solidarity of other agents, particularly sympathetic newspapers like *La Jornada* but also local radio stations and transnational media, especially the Internet. We have come full circle from the anti-imperialist denunciations and fears of Dorfman and Mattelart. The Zapatistas' expert handling of the electronic media shows that there is no inherent contradiction between technological modernization and grassroots mobilization (Halleck 1994; Cleaver forthcoming). In fact, the Internet has allowed the Zapatistas to question spectators and readers, to "travel through cyberspace and invade, like a modern virus, the memories of machines, and of men and women" (Halleck 1994).

A word of caution is in order. Subcomandante Marcos and other members of the Zapatista directorate are also intermediaries, and as such are themselves susceptible to the critiques discussed here. They are, of course, aware of this; for this reason they have said: "We the Zapatistas want everything for everyone, and nothing for ourselves." It is also for this reason, perhaps, that although they identify themselves as indigenous people and demand political and cultural autonomy, they have not set the terms of the representation of Indian identity. Their agenda is the organization of civil society.

Conclusion

The organization of civil society, as I argued above, is not an uncontradictory feature of progressive action. It is to a large degree imposed by neoliberalism, and as such its success can only be limited, especially if we gauge it against the dreams of power of traditional leftist movements. Many of the arguments reviewed here concerning new kinds of social movements, particularly those that concentrate on organizing civil society, must stand the test of history. Currently there is much enthusiasm and hope that civil society will serve as the basis for renewing the state-nation compact. The problem is that the results can be contradictory. Will the state reform called for by the Zapatistas—which the PRI signed in July 1996—

give greater political leverage to the conservative PAN? Will the decentralization of the state's monopoly of cultural representation create openings for the media and private enterprise to extend their reach? And does not the effervescence of NGOs cut two ways: helping to buttress a public sector evacuated by the state and at the same time making it possible for the state to steer clear of what was once seen as its responsibility? There is also the uncertainty that ensues from a movement that has to date waged its most effective battles in the realm of publicity. To what degree does such activity depart from the already overdetermined character of publicity in a capitalist society? Of course, there is no reason why consumer capitalism cannot be wielded against itself. The production of a CD-ROM, announced in July 1996, will allow interested parties to walk through the Lacandon jungle and get to know the Indians and their plight. But will such a medium take on the character of interactive electronic entertainment?

Such questions form part of a larger context in which any action must be evaluated. Michel Foucault (1983) coined the term "governmentality" to refer to the ways in which action is already channeled by the institutional arrangements of a society.[8] This concept points out the limits to action. Even if the PRI were to be separated from the state, would the arrangements that have held for almost seventy years be altered enough for true democratization to take place in Mexico? Can action in the terrain of civil society bring about such an alteration of institutional arrangements?

The notion of governmentality is more or less neutral with respect to social change. That is, it does not evaluate such change negatively, as does the concept of governability. What it does emphasize, however, is that all action moves along the tracks of structures of possibility provided by institutional arrangements. This structuring accounts for why the movements may not have the same significance in countries where institutional arrangements are different. One might ask why a movement like the Zapatistas has not emerged in a country like Brazil where there are significant numbers of landless groups. There is a movement of landless rural workers (the Movimento Sem Terra) that has gotten the attention of the government, which has promised action on its behalf. However, the differences and potentials of the Zapatistas and the Movimento Sem Terra are quite marked. The Zapatistas achieved the attention of the entirety of the Mexican nation and indeed of the world precisely because Mexico had entered a free trade agreement with the United States. That agreement gave the Zapatistas a certain leverage—a chance to "blackmail" the state (rather than forcing it militarily) into meeting some of its demands. Another feature of the Mexican nation-state is, as I have explained above, a seven-decade-old practice of situating national culture in centralized, pyramidal institutions. Transnational processes, in conjunction with the demands of grassroots organizations, have resulted in numerous protests against that centrality. Brazilian cultural institutions are not similarly centralized, and the Brazilian state does not invest as much as the Mexican state in subsidizing the intellectual artist class, which ultimately keeps this class buffered in a sphere of perhaps ineffective critique. The Zapatista movement, therefore, marks a significant departure from the protagonism of intellectuals.

There are some similarities, of course. The electronic media are monopolized by one meganetwork in each country, Televisa in Mexico and Globo in Brazil. But the control of publicity by these networks has been cannily sidestepped by the Zapatistas. Their use of the Internet, facilitated to a large degree by solidarity groups in the United States and Europe as well as by sympathetic intellectuals in Mexico, can serve as an example to movements in other countries. It remains to be seen whether other movements will earn the same degree of legitimacy currently enjoyed by the Zapatistas.

Notes

1. It is significant that McLuhan conceived this global village within the tradition set forth by one of the major formulators of the cultural legacy against which the Birmingham Centre for Contemporary Cultural Studies worked: T. S. Eliot, in particular his "Tradition and the Individual Talent." The reworking of tradition, which is how Eliot conceives the act of poetry, is invoked by McLuhan to characterize the means by which the new electronic media will organize the global village as a work of art (McLuhan and Powers 180 n. 3).

2. In contrast to more affirmative assessments of "marvelous realism," such as that of Michael Taussig (1987, 165–167), I, along with other critics of literary and intellectual production in Latin America, find that much of the discourse on the Latin American "marvelous" was produced in a contentious relation to a supposedly stultifying and inauthentic European surrealism. Such a contention is at the very heart of, for example, Alejo Carpentier's novel *Los pasos perdidos (The Lost Steps)* and his programmatic preface to *El reino de este mundo (The Kingdom of This World)*. Carpentier resorts to essentialism of the most crass type when he embodies Latin American origins in his protagonist's newfound lover in the heart of the jungle (a stand-in for the "real" Latin America), the indigenous mother-earth Rosario. She stands for everything that negates the culture of the protagonist's upper-class European father. Consequently, the binary representations that Carpentier wields in this novel are ultimately beholden to the European model that they would undo. Such a narrative strategy is typical, in my view, of Latin American elites in search of a national cultural identity that supports the independence from Europe that these elites sought. But such an autonomy, which reflects by means of narrative allegory the will to economic sovereignty evident in the work of dependency theorists and advocates of import substitution, is a far cry from any effective advocacy of or collaboration with the popular or subaltern classes in Latin American nations. It is this kind of imaginary, projected by the intelligentsia, that the indigenous movements have repudiated. Such a surrogate manifestation of culture is ultimately a drawback for the uses of culture by grassroots groups. This is an argument, as I explain below, that the *museos comunitarios* movement in Mexico has made.

3. This point needs greater analysis, which I cannot provide here. Suffice it to say that youth cultures, whose very existence runs counter to the rejection of capitalism typical of many grassroots movements, flourish *within* consumerist capitalism, despite the fact that the majority of these youth do not have much buying power to speak of. Their culture, like that of grassroots movements, is one of survival, but much more identified with using to their own advantage the structures that capital opens up for others, the elites. Studies of

youth cultures tend to work within the "practices of everyday life" framework laid out by Michel de Certeau (1984). See, for example, Vianna 1988, Franco 1993, and Yúdice 1994. Other more Marxist approaches that deal sympathetically with youth cultures are Valenzuela Arce 1988, 1993.

4. Victor Bulmer-Thomas summarizes these contradictions of the new economic model thus: "Privatisation leads to rising unemployment, but labour market reform may not be sufficient to absorb surplus labour. Export promotion requires a depreciation of the real effective exchange rate, but inflation stabilisation may require the opposite. Technological modernisation requires access to capital, but the reform of domestic capital markets may make the needed investments more expensive. Fiscal reform requires increases in revenue, but tariff reductions and the elimination of employment taxes lead to a fall" (Bulmer-Thomas 1996, 12).

5. The recently instituted process of certification of NGOs under the Ley de Fomento a las Activities de Bienestar y Desarrollo Social in Oaxaca is an example of government control. The junta established by this law has the authority to create, modify, and eliminate NGOs, which must even pay fees for the maintenance of the junta (Montesinos 1996). It is obvious, then, that civil society does not function in practice as a "Third Sector" independent of government and productive enterprises, as the recently formed Mexican Center for Philanthropy (CEMEFI) would have it (*Directorio de Instituciones Filantrópicas* 1995, ix), but rather as the handmaiden of both.

6. During visits to Mexico in 1992 and 1993, I saw many television and print commercials that advised citizens to meet the challenge of economic adulthood (NAFTA) with social maturity. The commercials urged viewers to keep the streets clean, get to work on time, and so on.

7. Transnational brokering is even more complicated, as Daniel Mato points out in his study on the phenomenon. Not only are there the foreign and national metropolitan agents (such as banks, the UN, and government institutions) on the one hand and local and social movement agents as well as the target community on the other, but there is also an entire spectrum of intermediary organizations, particularly NGOs. All of these agents constitute "complexes of brokering" that must negotiate a plethora of competing agendas (1995b, 8). Even among NGOs there is great diversity, starting with the difference between INGOs (international nongovernmental organizations) and NGOs. For example, "[u]nlike the INGOs, many of the Latin American human rights organizations have close ties to political parties," including commissions created by governments, which adds another dimension: the degree to which these organizations are independent of the governments that created them (Torres and Toro 1992, 20–21).

8. "Governmentality" should not be confused with "governability." The latter term is of utmost concern to conservatives and all those who see social change in the direction of democratization as a form of chaos. This is exactly the way in which Ronfeldt (1995) assessed the activities of civil society organizations, or what he called the network society.

References

Baran, Paul. 1958. "On the Political Economy of Backwardness." In *The Economics of Underdevelopment,* ed. A. N. Agarwala and S. P. Singh, 75–91. Bombay: Oxford University Press.

Barkin, David. 1995. "The Spectre of Rural Development." On-line posting. Available from <http://www.igc.apc.org/nacla/devel/dbarkin.html>.

Barnet, Richard J., and John Cavanagh. 1994. *Global Dreams: Imperial Corporations and the New World Order*. New York: Simon and Schuster.

Barrera Bassols, Marco, Iker Larrauri Prado, Teresa Márquez Martínez, and Graciela Schmilchuk. 1995. "Museos AL REVÉS: Modalidades comunitarias y participativas en la planificación y el funcionamiento de museos." Report submitted to Fideicomiso para la Cultura México/USA, Mexico City.

Barrera Bassols, Marco, and Ramón Vera Herrera. 1996. "Todo rincón es un centro: Hacia una expansión de la idea del museo." Unpublished manuscript.

Bonfil Batalla, Guillermo. 1991. "Desafíos a la antropología en la sociedad contemporánea." *Iztapalapa* 11 (24).

Bradsher, Keith. 1995. "Low Ranking for Poor American Children." *New York Times,* August 14, A9.

Brunner, José Joaquín. 1987. "Notas sobre la modernidad y lo postmoderno en la cultura latinoamericana." *David y Goliath* 52.

______. 1990. "Seis Preguntas a José Joaquín Brunner." *Revista de Crítica Cultural* 1 (May).

Bulmer-Thomas, Victor. 1996. "Introduction." In *The New Economic Model in Latin America and Its Impact on Income Distribution and Poverty*, ed. V. Bulmer-Thomas, 7–26. New York: St. Martin's Press.

Bulmer-Thomas, Victor, ed. 1996. *The New Economic Model in Latin America and Its Impact on Income Distribution and Poverty*. New York: St. Martin's Press.

Cardoso, Fernando Henrique, and Enzo Faletto. 1973. *Dependência e Desenvolvimento na América Latina: Ensaio de Interpretação Sociológica*. Rio de Janeiro: Zahar.

Carpentier, Alejo. 1949. *El reino de este mundo*. Mexico City: Edición y Distribución Iberoamericana de Publicaciones.

______. 1953. *Los pasos perdidos*. Mexico City: Edición y Distribución Iberoamericana de Publicaciones.

CEMEFI (Centro Mexicano para la Filantropía). 1995. *Directorio de Instituciones Filantrópicas*. Mexico City: Centro Mexicano para la Filantropía.

Cleaver, Harry. Forthcoming. "The Zapatistas and the Electronic Fabric of Struggle." In *The Chiapas Uprising and the Future of Revolution in the Twenty-First Century*, ed. J. Holloway.

Correa, Guillermo, and Julio César López. 1996. "500 organizaciones, en la gestación de una 'gran fuerza social y política.'" *Proceso* 1002 (January 15):28.

de Certeau, Michel. 1984. *The Practice of Everyday Life*. Berkeley: University of California Press.

Dorfman, Ariel, and Armand Mattelart. 1972. *Para leer al Pato Donald: Comunicación y colonialismo*. Mexico City: Siglo XXI.

Dos Santos, Teotônio. 1970. "The Structure of Dependence." *American Economic Review* 60 (5):235–246.

EZLN (Zapatista National Liberation Army). 1994. "Declaration of the Lacandon Jungle." In *Documentos y comunicados: 1º de enero / 8 de agosto de 1994*. Mexico City: Era.

______. 1995. "Communiqué of the Clandestine Committee." November 17. Reproduced in Elio Henríquez and Rosa Rojas, "Queremos ser parte de la nación mexicana, como iguales," *La Jornada*, November 18, 1995.

Featherstone, Michael, ed. 1990. *Global Culture: Nationalism, Globalization, and Modernity*. London: Sage.

Foucault, Michel. 1983. "The Subject and Power." In *Michel Foucault: Beyond Structuralism and Hermeneutics,* ed. H. L. Dreyfus and P. Rabinow, 208–226. Chicago: University of Chicago Press.

Foxley, Alejandro. 1996. "Preface." In *The New Economic Model in Latin America and Its Impact on Income Distribution and Poverty,* ed. V. Bulmer-Thomas, 1–6. New York: St. Martin's Press.

Franco, Jean. 1975. "Dependency Theory and Literary History: The Case of Latin America." *Minnesota Review* 5 (Fall):65–79.

______. 1993. Paper presented at the First Meeting of the Inter-American Cultural Studies Network, May 3–5, Iztapalapa, Mexico City. Quoted in George Yúdice, "Cultural Studies and Civil Society," in *Reading the Shape of the World: Toward an International Cultural Studies,* ed. H. Schwarz and R. Dienst (Boulder: Westview Press, 1996).

García Canclini, Néstor. 1982. *Las culturas populares en el capitalismo.* Havana: Casa de las Américas.

______. 1990. *Culturas híbridas: Estrategias para entrar y salir de la modernidad.* Mexico City: Grijalbo.

______. 1993. *Transforming Modernity: Popular Culture in Mexico.* Austin: University of Texas Press.

______. 1995a. *Hybrid Cultures.* Minneapolis: University of Minnesota Press.

______. 1995b. *Consumidores y ciudadanos: Conflictos multiculturales de la globalización.* Mexico City: Grijalbo.

Gramsci, Antonio. 1971. *Selections from the Prison Notebooks.* Ed. and trans. Q. Hoare and G. Smith. New York: International Publishers.

Halleck, Deedee. 1994. "Zapatistas On-Line." *NACLA Report on the Americas* 28 (September-October):30–32.

Henríquez, Elio, and Matilde Pérez. 1995. "La transición democrática no la determinará el gobierno, dijo el 'sucomandante' en un video." *La Jornada,* August 9.

Henríquez, Elio, and Rosa Rojas. 1995. "Queremos ser parte de la nación mexicana, como iguales." *La Jornada,* November 18.

______. 1996. "Fourth Declaration of the Lacandon Jungle." On-line posting. Available from <http://www.eco.utexas.edu:80/Homepages/Faculty/Cleaver/chiapas952.html>.

Hoggart, Richard. [1957] 1992. *The Uses of Literacy.* New Brunswick, N.J.: Transaction.

Laclau, Ernesto, and Chantal Mouffe. 1985. *Hegemony and Socialist Strategy: Towards a Radical Democratic Politics.* London: Verso.

La Jornada. 1996. "Contra el Neoliberalismo y por la Humanidad." On-line posting. Available from <http://serpiente.dgsca.unam.mx/jornada/1995/oct95/951021/cara.html>.

López, Julio César. 1996. "Interview with Subcomandante Marcos." *Proceso* 1002 (January 15).

Martín-Barbero, Jesús. 1987. *De los medios a las mediaciones: Comunicación, cultura, hegemonía.* Barcelona: Gustavo Gili.

______. 1992. "Communication: A Strategic Site for the Debate on Modernity." *Border/Lines* 27:47–52.

______. 1993. "La comunicación en las transformaciones del campo cultural." Paper presented at the First Meeting of the Inter-American Cultural Studies Network, May 3–5, Iztapalapa, Mexico City.

Mato, Daniel. 1995a. "Beyond the Mall: A View of the Culture and Development Program of the 1994 Smithsonian's Festival of American Folklife in the Context of the Globalization Process." Paper presented at the Center for Folklife Programs and Cultural Studies, Smithsonian Institution.

______. 1995b. "Complexes of Brokering and the Global-Local Connections: Considerations Based on Cases in 'Latin' America." Paper presented at the Nineteenth International Congress of the Latin American Studies Association, September 28–30, Washington, D.C.

______. Forthcoming. "Procesos culturales y transformaciones socio-políticas en América 'Latina' en tiempos de globalización." In *América Latina en Tiempos de Globalización*, ed. D. Mato, E. Amodio, and M. Montero. Caracas: UNESCO-CRESALC.

McLuhan, Marshall, and Quentin Fiore. 1967. *The Medium Is the Massage: An Inventory of Effects*. New York: Bantam Books.

McLuhan, Marshall, and Bruce R. Powers. 1989. *The Global Village: Transformations in World Life and Media in the 21st Century*. New York: Oxford University Press.

Montesinos, El Centro Antonio de. 1996. "Mexican Government Controls Non-government Organizations." On-line posting. Available from [chiapas-l@profmexis.sar.net].

Pérez, Matilde, and Gaspar Morquecho. 1995. "El diálogo nacional convocado por el EZLN ya empezó: invitados zapatistas." *La Jornada* On-line posting. Available from <http://serpiente.dgsca.unam.mx/jornada/1995/oct95/951021/cara.html>.

Poder Ejecutivo Federal. 1996a. *Programa de Cultura 1995–2000*. Mexico City: Consejo Nacional para la Cultura y las Artes.

______. 1996b. *Programa de Desarrollo Educativo 1995–2000*. Mexico City: Consejo Nacional para la Cultura y las Artes.

Preston, Julia. 1996. "Mexico and Insurgent Group Reach Pact on Indian Rights." *New York Times*, February 15, A12.

Rojas, Rosa. 1996. "Tello: para los indios, política del Estado." *La Jornada*. On-line posting. Available from <http://serpiente.dgsca.unam.mx/jornada/1995/oct95/951021/cara.html>.

Ronfeldt, David. 1995. "The Battle for the Mind of Mexico." Unpublished paper, Rand Corporation. On-line posting. Available from [chiapas@mundo.eco.utexas.edu].

Sassen, Saskia. 1991. *The Global City: New York, London, Tokyo*. Princeton: Princeton University Press.

Shorrock, Tim. 1996. "Drop Seen in Real Wages in All Three NAFTA Countries." *Journal of Commerce* (May 29). Available from the Institute for Agriculture and Trade Policy, [iatp@igc.apc.org].

Sklair, Leslie. 1993. "Consumerism Drives the Global Mass Media System." *Media Development* 2:30–35.

Spencer, Neville. 1996. "Zapatistas Work to Establish Political Front." Interview with Priscilla Pacheco Castillo of the FZLN. *Green Left Weekly* 241 (August 7). On-line posting, New York Transfer News Collective. Available from [nyt@blythe.org].

Stavenhagen, Rodolfo. 1995. "Buenas noticias de Chiapas." On-line posting. Available from <http://www.eco.utexas.edu:80/Homepages/Faculty/Cleaver/chiapas952.html>.

Taussig, Michael. 1987. *Shamanism, Colonialism, and the Wild Man: A Study in Terror and Healing*. Chicago: University of Chicago Press.

Thompson, E. P. 1963. *The Making of the English Working Class*. London: Victor Gollancz.

Torres, Blanca, and Celia Toro. 1992. "The Renewed Centrality of the United States in Inter-American Relations: The Issues and the Actors." Paper presented at the Conference on Rethinking Development Theories, March 11–13, Institute of Latin American Studies, University of North Carolina at Chapel Hill.

Unomásuno. 1996. "La política debe ser instrumento de solución de conflictos: Oñate." *Unomásuno*, January 15, p. 5.

Valenzuela Arce, José Manuel. 1988. *¡A la brava ése! Cholos, punks, chavos banda*. Tijuana: El Colegio de la Frontera Norte.

______. 1993. "Mi barrio es mi cantón. Identidad, acción social y juventud." In *Nuevas identidades culturales en México,* ed. G. Bonfil Batalla. México City: Consejo Nacional para la Cultura y las Artes.

Vianna, Hermano. 1988. *O Mundo Funk Carioca.* Rio de Janeiro: Zahar.

Williams, Raymond. 1958. *Culture and Society: 1780–1950.* New York: Columbia University Press.

______. [1961] 1965. *The Long Revolution.* Harmondsworth, England: Penguin Books.

______. 1977. *Marxism and Literature.* Oxford: Oxford University Press.

Yúdice, George. 1994. "The Funkification of Rio." In *Microphone Fiends: Youth Music and Youth Culture,* ed. T. Rose and A. Ross. New York: Routledge.

______. 1996. "Cultural Studies and Civil Society." In *Reading the Shape of the World: Toward an International Cultural Studies,* ed. H. Schwarz and R. Dienst. Boulder: Westview Press.

______. Forthcoming(a). "El impacto cultural del Tratado de libre comercio norteamericano." In *Culturas en globalización: América Latina–Europa–Estados Unidos: libre comercio e integración,* ed. N. García Canclini. Caracas: Editorial Nueva Sociedad.

______. Forthcoming(b). *We Are Not the World: Identity and Representation in an Age of Global Restructuring.* Durham, N.C.: Duke University Press.

Chapter Fifteen

Rethinking the Spatialities of Social Movements: Questions of (B)orders, Culture, and Politics in Global Times

DAVID SLATER

Contemporary currents in social theory and cultural studies increasingly reflect a pervasive sense of time-space compression. Concepts of velocity and mobility and the remapping of territorial identities and cultural dispositions mark the terrain of much recent analysis in this regard. Moreover, terms such as "globalization," the "global-local nexus," "critical globalism," and the "global condition"[1] all reflect a widening sensibility of the need to reach beyond national boundaries. Stretching across these boundaries and making global connections has been a characteristic of some of the new forms of mobilization, of resistance and movement—movements that have been contextualized as "nomads of the present" (Melucci 1989), capturing an important sense of fluidity and flexibility. Resistances and oppositions have increasingly been seen as independent from any encapsulating universalist discourse. Archipelagos of resistance and reverse discourses that have the potential to be connected across space, but that are also distinct, specific, and embedded in local and regional contexts, have emerged in many different societies, encouraging in some cases the use of the term "new social movements."[2]

Leaving aside for the moment the question of how these social movements might be interpreted and in what manner their origination and continuing presence could be treated theoretically, it is abundantly clear that their existence has been connected to a range of significant themes from development to democracy, from citizenship to culture, and from environment to emancipation. These sites of knowledge have their own intersections, but it is a reflection of the growing interest in movements that their investigation and critical analysis connect to an ever growing gamut of themes and issues. As the centrality of class has waned, the revival of interest in civil society, and in state-society relations in general, has been accompanied by a search for alternative forms of "doing politics" in a variety of cultural contexts and against a backdrop of normalizing projects of global order and power. As I shall argue below, and as is discussed in this volume as a whole, the connections between social movements and cultural politics, and in particular the cultural framing of "doing politics," have become a key theme of inquiry, which can be expanded and rethought by incorporating a spatial imagination.

Movements and the Remapping of the Political

One potential area of inquiry that has remained underexposed concerns what I shall refer to as the imbrication of geopolitics and social movements. Thus, in some discussions of the interconnections between movements and democracy, or development, or cultural change, the territoriality or more generally the spatiality of movements, power, and politics has been marginalized.[3] It is certainly the case that the way we can think about politics and the political has been connected to movements and to resistances, but in the literature on social movements, the difference that the *geo*political can make has not always been taken as a significant issue. I will argue here that the geopolitical has a certain duality and can be examined in relation to the territoriality of politics within national boundaries as well as to the transnational flows and penetrations of different kinds of power. In the context of social movements, struggles for the decentralization of political power within a given national territory and for a radical restructuring of the territorial power of the state can be identified as exemplifying the more inner-oriented form of the geopolitical. This is not meant to suggest that there are no links to the transnational or global contexts of political contestation; rather, the primary focus is on the "inside," whereas there are other instances, other kinds of movements that, although also having an "inside," are deeply involved in a transnational arena as well, as can be seen in the example of some environmental movements. Falk (1993, 39) has referred to this phenomenon as "globalization from below." In a parallel way, it is possible to argue that in the analysis of democracy and processes of democratization there is also an inside, the territorialization of democracy within a given nation-state, and an outside, the struggle for a democratization of institutions that operate at the global level but that have multiple effects within the territorial polities of the countries of the South. Clearly, in the cases of social movements and democracy, the inside and outside of the geopolitical are not to be realistically seen as separate but as overlapping and intertwined in a complex of relations.

Connolly (1991a) has maintained that democratic political theorists and international relations theorists would seem to have little to say to one another. On the one hand, intrastate political theory tends to concentrate on "internal" issues such as rights, justice, community, obligation, identity, and legitimacy; whereas on the other, interstate theory examines "external" questions of security, alliances, violence, war, and subversion. For Connolly, this particular discursive division of labor allows the effects of changes in the contemporary era to fall through the gaps of democratic theory. What is then needed is a realization that democratic politics must extend into global issues because, increasingly, the most fundamental issues of life are not resolvable within the confines of the territorial state.[4] More generally, it is contended that one of the key requirements of the current period is to supplement and challenge structures of territorial democracy with a politics of nonterritorial democratization of global issues. Here, one can think of a number of movements that re-inscribe the meanings and practices of democratization.

Feminist movements that continue to struggle for the liberation of women from all types of oppression have constructed new forms of organization and solidarity that connect transnationally. In Latin America, for example, the biannual feminist *encuentros* held since 1981 have consistently expanded, taking on a variety of themes from autonomy to issues of community leadership (Alvarez, in this volume and Jaquette 1994). Along another path, as García (1992) and Wapner (1995) have both indicated, transnational environmental groups extend their activities beyond the territorial confines of a given country. In these two examples, gender relations and environmental issues have become focal points in the rethinking of the spatialities of democratization. For Connolly, these kinds of movements would exemplify the point that nonterritorial democratization can ventilate global issues through the creative interventions of nonstate actors. In their turn, these interventions could potentially reinvigorate the internal democracy of territorial states. However, nonterritorial democratization lacks a secure regional base and, it can be argued, is less firmly anchored in the terms of its accountability. Democratization beyond a territorial anchorage, as Held (1995) has indicated, also tends to emerge as a series of demands and claims that are still relatively nascent in their formation, although this would certainly be less true of the women's movement. In contradistinction, the territorial state, in global times, tends to rest on increasingly fragile and precarious ground, with pressures from below often opening up fissures in its territorial control while the globalization of financial, economic, and cultural power increasingly impinges on it from above.[5]

It is particularly important to emphasize the continuing ways in which much social and political theory—in the context of interpreting social movements, or democracy, or the state—has tended to evade the difficult question of the inside and the outside and their dialectic. In a related intervention, Connolly (1991b) draws our attention to the way in which a certain rather pervasive undercurrent of political theory constructs a boundary between an inside (self) and an outside (other). Behind the boundary we have our own world of community, membership, internal understandings, morality, distributive mechanisms, democratic accountability, obligations, and allegiances. On the other side, outside our own constructed world, there are alternative worlds of strangers, hazards, external principles, and uncertain moralities. There would not be very much that connects these other worlds to us politically, morally, or culturally. The threat of anarchy and alterity outside would intensify the inclination to regard shared understandings and common principles of membership as adequate norms of political judgment within the state and would fortify the view of the territorial state as the highest unit of political loyalty, identification, and democratic participation. In this kind of context, there would be little room for the possibility of what Campbell (1996) has referred to as "radical interdependence" across borders.

While Connolly's critique of the split between an inside and an outside, which is constitutive of much political theory, is highly relevant for a whole series of issues, not least for those interpretative modes that classify and contextualize social movements within a self-containing inside, it is equally worthwhile to note that the theory Connolly is evaluating is Western, and that the forms in which political theory has evolved in the societies of Europe and North America cannot be realistically divorced from the colonial and imperial imaginations and projects that are rooted in those societies. Thus, although the heterogeneities and complex differences within the categories of West and non-West or North and South have to be constantly kept in mind, geopolitical memory—the recalling and re-presentation of those crucial divides in the nature, scope, and magnitude of power relations—needs to be taken as a central part of our own contemporary project of critical analysis.[6] It is here too that the cultural practices and forms of representation that are inscribed within power relations give a further specificity to the development of spatial politics. As Ortner (1995) has suggested in a timely intervention, one of the salient themes in rethinking our analyses of resistance concerns the question of cultural dynamics and the ways in which the forms, moments, and absences of resistance need to be linked to what is referred to as the thickness of the cultural process, within which there may well be a complex of shifting loyalties, shifting alliances, and also shifting categories.

If modern politics is a spatial politics, with its crucial condition of possibility being the distinction between an inside and an outside, between the citizens, communities, and movements within and the enemies, others, and absences without, it is also the case that the characteristic universalisms of so much Western social and political theory have expressed a continuing amnesia toward the geopolitical penetrations, fragmentations, and power relations within which modern accounts of universality have been articulated. Furthermore, when modern politics has been viewed as world politics, many accounts have tended to assume that "world politics" refers not only to some determining structure but more relevantly to processes that occur in realms somewhere "beyond" society. In contrast, social movements have frequently been seen as phenomena that occur within society, existing in juxtaposition to those key political structures that give them their essential meaning—namely, states and the state system. Moreover, within this inner realm of society, social movements have tended to be interpreted as part of civil society, which in turn has been distinguished as separate from the political affairs of the modern state. In this sense, the ways in which social movements have been analyzed have tended to reproduce an approach to politics that is confined to a pre-given realm implicitly constructed as nonproblematic.

Social movements may well be linked to the political domain through their impact on state policies or on the priorities of political parties, but any connection to global politics would characteristically be made through the mediation of the inner political system. This particular perspective tends to treat politics as a domain that is separate from the economic and the social and to draw demarcating lines between an inner national political realm and an outer domain of world politics. In an earlier series of comments on this theme, I suggested that a binary division has often been drawn between the realm of the political, bounded within the state, and political parties; and the space of the social, framed around the family, the school, religion, the individual, movements. Alternatively, I argued that the political dimension could be endowed with a certain duality, whereby it could be seen as inscribed within the different spheres of the social whole and also as constitutive of the terrain on which the fabric and fate of the social whole is decided (Slater 1994). Hence, what is and is not political at any moment changes with the emergence of new questions posed by new modes of subjectivity—for instance, "the personal is political" and different kinds of social relations. This is not meant to imply that the political eliminates the social conditions from which its meaning can emerge; gender, religious belief, the environment, nationality, regionalism, and so on, may become political at certain moments, but they are not only political. Furthermore, cultural heterogeneity across societies will alter the ways in which the political is constituted; for example, the specificity of religious practices, as in the case of Brazil, has affected the mode of oppositional expression (Krischke 1991), and in the context of indigenous movements, the historicity of cultural meanings and practices has a crucial political impact (see, for example, Warren, in this volume).

A primary feature of the political relates to the questioning of the socially given, of what appears to be socially natural and uncontested. When "the given" is not accepted as such but referred back to its earlier constitution, its potential instability is revealed and reactivated (Laclau 1990, 212). That instability is inseparably bound up with the pluralization of the origin or with the disruption of the implicit notion of a singularity of foundational meaning; as Foucault (1984, 79) expressed it in his discussion of genealogy and Nietzsche, "what is found at the historical beginning of things is not the inviolable identity of their origin . . . it is disparity." The desedimentation of the social entails laying bare its political content, and since the social is expressed through a plurality of forms, the desedimentation of the socially given, in its plurality, reveals the potentially protean nature of the political. In this context, it has been remarked that contemporary social movements have challenged and redrawn the frontiers of the political. This can mean, for example, that movements can subvert the traditional givens of the political system—state power, political parties, formal institutions—by contesting the legitimacy and the apparently normal and natural functioning of their effects within society. But, also, the role of some social movements has been to reveal the concealed meanings of the political encased in the social. Social struggles can be seen as "wars of interpretation" within which the orientation and significance of their demands and revindications are constructed through their practice. It is within a related approach to social movements that Walker (1994, 674–675), in his imaginative intervention, argues that perhaps the most interesting element of social movements concerns the ways in which they may contribute to the "reconfiguration of the political under contemporary conditions."

Issues of Interpretation

Perhaps one of the most fascinating and complex questions surrounding any treatment of the conjunction of social movements and the political concerns the issue of interpretation itself. For Walker (1995, 311), much analysis of the novelty of social movements is characterized by a crucial limitation, which is that "the horizon of enquiry is already given by historically specific understandings of what it means to speak of community, a class, an interest, an identity, or a movement of action." As a consequence, one tends to encounter questions of whether social movements constitute a break from or a continuation of class politics; whether they reflect a reinvigoration of civil society or an abandonment of the state; whether they constitute mobilizations that are free from previous forms of populism, or whether they capture a continuation of liberal pluralism. In these kinds of positionings, social and political phenomena are not infrequently insinuated with implicitly pre-given and consensual meanings. Walker goes on to assert that for all its sophistication, the literature on social movements still seems bound by framings of political possibility that preclude casting doubt on established conceptions of political community and identity. Thus the possibility of the newness of social movements is circumscribed by a "specific rendition of what it means to be political, and of where the political is to be found" (Walker 1995, 312).

Looking at some of the recent discussions of social movements (Munck 1995; Jordan 1995; Scott 1995; Shefner 1995; Weyland 1995), one can find examples of the basic thrust of Walker's critical contention, and one is struck above all by a common assumption that politics and political strategy, as well as class and materiality, are somehow already pre-given in their significance and location in the broader analytical arena. It is also as if certain categories exist on a prediscursive terrain whereby conceptual markers such as class and materiality are constructed as the radically unconstructed. Butler (1990), in her influential analysis of feminism and the subversion of identity, argues that in the cultural interpretation of sex and gender, the production of sex as the prediscursive must be understood in terms of the power relations that produce the effect of a prediscursive sex, thereby concealing the very operation of discursive production. Similarly, with certain kinds of arguments about social movements and political change, one still encounters interpretations that implicitly grant a prediscursive, independent meaning to categories of class, materiality, and agency, thus drawing a screen over the way in which those concepts have been discursively constructed. As Butler (1992, 13) notes in a subsequent article, agency can be viewed as belonging to a mode of thinking about persons as instrumental actors who confront an external political field, and "if we agree that politics and power exist already at the level at which the subject and its agency are articulated and made possible, then agency can be *presumed* only at the cost of refusing to inquire into its construction."

One of the primary questions emanating from these kinds of arguments concerns the definition of politics and the political and their relation to our theoretical understanding of social movements. In many contributions to the debate on social movements, no distinction is made between politics and the political, and as noted above it is quite often the case that politics is referred to in a way that already presumes a meaning that is consensual and foundational. However, I would not suggest that there is an already fully formed theoretical framework that we can grasp and immediately apply. Our conceptual and thinking spaces are striated by a series of destabilizations and uncertainties that make any such quick alternative framing quite inappropriate. There is a sense in which many of the concepts employed to explain social and political phenomena appear increasingly precarious and partial. In times of rethinking, re-visioning, reimagining, the notion of taking "soundings," or the emphasis on fluidity if not vertigo within the fields of analytical inquiry, reflect the presence of a shifting, mobile terrain. Previously staked-out domains of knowledge, lined by the contours of linked categories and constructs, are being increasingly destabilized and disrupted by ideas coming out of the border zones that traverse and transgress these older and erstwhile ensured domains. One such idea concerns the way in which we may rethink politics and the political.

Mouffe (1995, 262–263), for instance, in a viewpoint that connects to Lefort's earlier work (1988), writes that for her "the political" relates to the antagonistic dimension that is inherent in all human society—an antagonism that can take many different forms and that can be located in diverse social relations. In contrast, "politics" can be taken to refer to the ensemble of practices, discourses, and institutions that seek to establish a certain order and to organize social life in conditions that are always potentially subject to conflict precisely because they are affected by the dimension of "the political." In this light, politics can be seen as the attempted pacification of the political, or the installation and embodiment of order and sedimented practices in a given society. Depoliticization is the most established task of politics, and, as writers such as Honig (1993) and Rancière (1995) have suggested, it can be argued that key branches of political philosophy and theory have displaced the political as a means to realize the closest approximation of political "Good" in the midst of the disorder of empirical politics. Rancière's suggestive notion of the pacification of the political can be exemplified in a number of additional ways that are specifically relevant to our own discussion.

First, in the context of many societies of the South wherein social conflicts, material polarization, violence, and a growing disillusionment with formal institutions manifest themselves in ways that appear to be steadily more problematic, new policies of "good governance" and the attempt to introduce Western-style arrangements for democratization can be taken as one form of the external ordering and containment of the political. At the same moment, within some African societies, for example, new networks of solidarity are being established and new mentalities are taking shape such that, as Monga indicates in his discussion of democratization in francophone Africa, "we are now witnessing a complete transformation of the conditions in which politics emerge" (1995, 360). What we see in these instances are simultaneous but deeply contrasting attempts to realign the relations between politics and the political.

Second, in a sharply differing example, the Cuban experience of postrevolutionary order has been characterized by the continuing attempts of a one-party state to neutralize points of potential antagonism by positioning government as the synthesis of society. The imperative of order and security has been translated into policies of integration and assimilation whereby difference has been equated with destabilization. In the contrasting case of Nicaragua, an initial attempt to integrate the ethnic minorities of the Atlantic coast into the Sandinista project was subsequently radically altered and replaced by a conversation in which the government came to recognize the rights of difference and autonomy. In the general history of Marxist projects in the Third World, the drive to centralize has been predominantly rooted in an ideological suspicion of the local and the regional, and the pacification of the political has been an immanently territorial project.

Third, in a number of Andean countries—Bolivia, Colombia, and Peru being clear examples—in the last fifteen to twenty years there have been a series of mobilizations, protests, and movements emerging at the local and regional levels that have challenged the existing territoriality of the state (Fals Borda 1992; Laserna 1986; Slater 1989). In particular, new associations have been made between democratization and decentralization, and in the struggle against centralism new forms of spatial subjectivity and identity have emerged. These new forms, which contest the given territoriality of the political system, can be viewed as reflections of the political expressed spatially. In response, central state administrations have introduced a variety of reforms that have sought to contain and incorporate these local and regional resistances. By seeking to realign and restructure the territorial power of the central state, a variety of governments in these countries have sought to contain and pacify the geopolitical within their already constituted boundaries.

Overall, in these examples and more generally, the most salient point of my argument is to stress the interactive nature of politics and the political—to posit their distinction but also their essential interconnectedness. Hence, the reference to the political does not entail a marginalization of the formal sphere of politics; rather, it calls for a distinction between two registers that implicate and involve each other. Politics has its own public space—it is the field of exchanges between political parties, of parliamentary and governmental affairs, of elections and representation, and in general of the type of activity, practices, and procedures that take place in the institutional arena of the political system. The political, however, as Arditi (1994, 21) has proposed, can be more effectively regarded as a type of relationship that can develop in any area of the social, irrespective of whether or not it remains within the institutional enclosure of "politics." The political then is a living movement, a kind of "magma of conflicting wills" or antagonisms; it is mobile and ubiquitous, going beyond but also subverting the institutional settings and moorings of politics.

In an important sense, the idea of the imbrication of politics and the political reflects the continuing debate about the relations between the state and civil society. Let us for a moment refer to a recent passage from Ernesto Laclau. In an interview concerning the paradoxes of contemporary politics, Laclau emphasizes that the contemporary situation can be characterized by the blurring of the division between the state and civil society. For Laclau, currents circulate between the spheres of state and civil society, "making illusory the idea of a confrontation or even a delimitation between the two as fully fledged autonomous entities" (1994, 45). As an example, Laclau refers to the radicalization of the democratic process, arguing that it would be unacceptable to go along with the view that equates the radicalization of democracy with the deepening of the division between civil society and the state, since in many instances the advance of democracy requires progressive legislation that goes against deep-seated interests anchored in civil society itself. On the other hand, it would also be inapposite to accept the idea that the public sphere is the "locus of an absolute and omnipotent popular will"; instead, "democratic politics requires many and complex strategic moves which cut across the two spheres and dissolve the clear-cut differentiation between the two" (46).

Laclau's attempt to underscore the importance of an interweaving of moves that merge and dissolve the civil society–state distinction is particularly relevant in the analysis of social movements, since civil society has not infrequently been essentialized in a positive frame as the terrain of the good and the enlightened. The emphasis on imbrication is also pertinent to our discussion of politics and the political since their interaction transgresses the civil society–state divide. The merging and interweaving noted here can be illustrated in the context of the relation between sedimentation and reactivation. Politics, for example, can be thought of as the institutionalization of an order that is designed to overcome or at the least to confine the threatening conflicts of the political—a case of sedimentation. But "order" or "governance" is always a series of regulative and sedimented procedures, practices, codes, and categories that can never be absolutely fulfilled. This is the case since the political—the possibilities of subversion, questioning, opposition, refusal, and resistance—can never be fully overcome; the interruption of desedimentation, or interventions that constitute a reactivation of the instability that "order" sought to pacify, reflect the inseparability of politics and the political. In this conceptual context, the political is always that irremovable inner periphery at the heart of politics.[7]

In a similar theoretical vein, one could invoke here Foucault's concept of "governmentality," which is seen as at one internal and external to the state, "since it is the tactics of government which make possible the continual definition and redefinition of what is within the competence of the state and what is not, the public versus the private and so on" (1991, 103). Here, "governmentality" could be viewed as a kind of attempted pacification of the political, and the resistances and oppositions to such a pacification—different kinds of movements, which Foucault referred to as "reverse discourses"—could then be taken as the equivalent of "the political." In Foucault's account of governmentality, there are a number of references to "the West," but the difference that the non-West might make, or more generally the impact of cultural differences on the modalities of governmentality, was not a theme of his analysis. Similarly, in the work referred to above, where a theoretical move is made to defend a distinction between politics and the political, the difference that the cultural might make remains unexplored. I shall return to this theme below.

Locating the Geopolitical

One question that can be immediately posed at this juncture concerns the potential relevance of the spatial for any demarcation of politics and the political. What difference would the prefix "geo-" make to my argument above? Inscribing a spatial dimension into this notion of politics could lead us into a discussion of the internal territoriality of constructed institutional orders through, for example, a consideration of the local-regional constitution of national political systems. In addition, a critical examination of the relations between nation-states, located within a posited world system of such units, which have been traditionally regarded as the building blocks of geopolitics, could form a related path of inquiry. Also, we might want to go beyond these "containers" and think of geopolitics in terms of the global processes that transgress the boundaries of states (Held 1995; Taylor 1995).

Furthermore, we can go on to denote two connected expressions of the geopolitical that relate to Arditi's metaphor of the "magma," to those underlying, unstable, fluid "substances" that may break the ordered surface and provoke reorderings, restructurings, or, in certain moments, transformative ruptures, as created by past revolutionary insurgencies. The first expression of the geopolitical can be defined within the ostensibly inner bounded realm of the territorial state. Here, as briefly alluded to above, there have been examples in a range of peripheral societies of certain kinds of movements that have challenged and continue to challenge established territorial orderings of the state (see, for example, Grueso, Rosero, and Escobar's analysis, in this volume). In some instances, such movements have been intimately rooted in ethnic identities, as has been the case in the Atlantic coast region of Nicaragua. In the previously mentioned examples of Bolivia, Colombia, and Peru, however, whereas indigenous communities have been differentially involved in the struggles against a centralized state, the local and regional movements of these societies have been unpredictably heterogeneous and have embraced a highly diverse range of demands. This tentative distinction is not meant to imply that the "indigenous" or the "communal" are somehow uniform. Often, as Agrawal (1995) reminds us, the idea of the "indigenous" is deployed in a way that masks an important heterogeneity that lies within. And heterogeneity (or internal differences), conflicts, and ambiguities need to be given more analytical attention in all our discussions of resistances and movements (see, for example, Rubin's contribution, in this volume).

In those specific cases where a concerted challenge has been made to the centralized nature of state power, as has occurred in Bolivia, an eventual legislative response (in this case, the 1995 Law on Administrative Decentralization) does not bring to a close territorial protest and contestation; instead, the continuing interwoven nature of geopolitics and the geopolitical is taken into a new phase. And we should not assume that the challenges, in the Bolivian case, to the centralization of power are of a singular orientation, since the various departmental *comités cívicos* have articulated their demands in ways that have not always achieved interdepartmental unity.[8] Similarly, at the local level, the Popular Participation Law of 1995, which ostensibly decentralizes power and resources to new rural municipalities, has evoked a variety of responses from grassroots indigenous organizations (Albó 1996).

In a different societal context, regional movements in Peru in the 1970s called for a new level of territorial power—the establishment of regional governments in a unitary state. Their impact, and their challenge to the given spatio-political order, created the conditions for a protracted national debate and eventual legislation to install a new version of government. However, the influence of these various movements, often embodied in the form of "regional fronts," was slowly undermined by growing violence, social dislocation, and acute instability. Specifically, Sendero Luminoso, with its practice of "armed stoppages" at local and departmental levels, created an atmosphere characterized by violent confrontations, making it increasingly difficult for regional movements to organize peaceful and effective protests.[9]

A guerrilla organization and a series of loosely grouped regional fronts, operating at the same moment, represented two very different expressions of a geopolitical challenge to the existing institutional order in Peru. The former challenge came to overshadow all other forms of political contestation, and with a change in government in 1990 followed by President Alberto Fujimori's "auto-golpe," the intensity of the threat to the political order was used to justify a recentralization of power and a sharp reduction in the importance of the newly established regional governments. In the Peruvian case, in sharp contrast to Bolivia, the emergence of a deep association of violence and terror with a movement that initiated its actions in a quintessentially peripheral region of the Andes has greatly facilitated the renewal of a centralist project. Moreover, any counterproject aimed at deepening and broadening democratic structures, of "territorializing democracy," may well be haunted by signs of "terror" hidden in the naming of "territory."[10]

A second instance of the geopolitical relates to the original constitution of national sovereignties. Significantly, the geopolitical in this context can be used to destabilize some of the meanings previously attached to the political, since in many of these conceptualizations the analysis of the relation between politics and the political is worked out within the confines of an implicitly Western territorial state. Here, there is an assumption of pre-given territorial integrity and impermeability. But in the situation of peripheral polities, the historical realities of external power and its effects within those systems are much more difficult to ignore. What this contrast points to is the lack of equality in the full recognition of the territorial integrity of nation-states. Predominantly, those underlying, mobile, unstable, disrupting currents that can fundamentally shift the terrain of politics are located within the implicitly bounded space of one nation-state, which is invariably Western in its origin. Missing is the possibility that externally based forces could also constitute the magma of the political. Such an absence reflects a governing supposition, rooted in modern political theory, that the context is formed by full territorial sovereignty; "quasi-sovereignty," in contrast, would be applicable to non-Western states (Jackson 1993).

For the societies of Latin America, Africa, and Asia, the principles governing the constitution of their mode of political being were deeply molded by external penetration. Colonialism, for example, represented the imposition and installation of principles of the political that violated the bond between national sovereignty and the constitution of societal being. The framing of time, and the ordering of space, followed an externally imposed logic, the effects of which still resonate in the postcolonial period. The struggles to recover an autochthonous narrative of time and an indigenous ensemble of meanings for the territory of the nation have formed an essential part of postindependence politics.[11]

In what were referred to as "wars of national liberation," the struggle to breathe new life into the time-space nexus of independence lay at the core of the anti-imperialist movement. At the same time, however, it must be stressed that the struggles against imperialism in peripheral societies have always assumed a variety of forms, as witnessed in Latin America, where the meanings given to cultural imperialism by Sendero Luminoso in Peru contrast markedly to the Sandinista discourse of the 1980s or to today's Zapatistas in Chiapas, Mexico. Furthermore, of course, contemporary struggles to redefine the geopolitical take place in an era marked, as noted above, by the hegemony of neoliberal ideas.

Examined broadly, neoliberal discourse not only enframes development in its notions of structural adjustment and good governance but reaches out and gives contemporary meaning to projects for democracy. This attempt to construct a global agenda has been specifically criticized by Bikhu Parekh, who observes that to insist on the universality of liberal democracy is to impose on other countries systems of government unrelated to their skills and talents, reducing them to "mimics, unable and unwilling to be true either to their tradition or . . . imported alien norms"; he germanely adds that the "cultural havoc caused by colonialism should alert us to the dangers of an over-zealous imposition of liberal democracy" (1993, 168).[12]

Inside/Outside and Zones of Resistance

In the above outline of the geopolitical, themes of power, culture, inside/outside, and movements intersect in a way that can be further developed, and the uprising in Chiapas can be taken as one particularly illustrative example of these kinds of intersections. In this context, it is possible to identify the interweaving of "levels of analysis" so that the global, the regional, and the local can be interpreted as deeply imbricated, with the notion of the "borderization" of the world underlining the fragility of settled spatial orders.

The armed uprising of between three to four thousand Indians in Chiapas on January 1, 1994, and the seizure of seven towns was timed to coincide with Mexico's entry into the North American Free Trade Agreement (NAFTA) with the United States and Canada. One of the first communiqués of the Ejército Zapatista de Liberación Nacional (EZLN) stated that NAFTA "is a death certificate for the Indian peoples of Mexico, who are dispensable for the government of Carlos Salinas de Gortari" (quoted in Harvey 1995, 39). The validity of this vision was subsequently captured in a leaked Chase Manhattan Bank memorandum for early 1995, which argued that the Mexican government "will need to eliminate the Zapatistas to demonstrate their effective control of the national territory and of security policy."[13]

Clearly, we have here a pivotal example of the importance of connecting inside with outside, of seeing the global and the local and regional as intimately intertwined rather than as separate and unconnected worlds. In an earlier analysis, EZLN Subcomandante Marcos described Chiapas in a regional/national/global context, outlining an approach that rekindled many previous *dependentista* arguments. In a language that evoked Eduardo Galeano's classic text, Marcos wrote:

> Chiapas is bled through thousands of veins: through oil ducts and gas ducts, over electric wires, by railroad cars, through bank accounts, by trucks and vans, by ships and planes, over clandestine paths, third-rate roads, and mountain passes. . . . [O]il, electric energy, cattle, money, coffee, bananas, honey, corn, cocoa, tobacco, sugar, soy, melons, sorghum, mamey, mangos, tamarind, avocados and Chiapan blood flows out through a 1,001 fangs sunk into the neck of southeastern Mexico. . . . [B]illions of tons of natural resources go through Mexican ports, railway stations, airports and road systems to various destinations: the United States, Canada, Holland, Germany, Italy, Japan—but all with the same destiny: to feed the empire.[14]

The presence of a geopolitical imagination that fuses a variety of spatial arenas—the global, the national, the regional, and the local—is again strongly evident in an interview with the Zapatista subcomandante published in August

1995, from which three crucial observations can be highlighted. First, it is argued that current processes of globalization have the potential to break nation-states and to accentuate internal regional differentiations, as reflected in the divergence between the northern, central and southeastern zones of Mexico. Second, with reference to questions of war, it is commented that political confrontation and the battle for ideas has acquired more significance than direct military power, echoing the Gramscian contrast between a war of position and a war of maneuver and crucially foregrounding issues of cultural difference and conflict. And third, pivotal importance is given to the role of the means of communication. If a movement or a resistance can be made to appear dead or moribund, irrespective of the reality on the ground, this constitutes a greater threat than superior military strength.[15] It is in this situation that the use of e-mail and the Internet have assumed an alternative potential (see Yúdice, in this volume, for a related account).

I have quoted at some length from one of the key Zapatista leaders in order to underscore the way the thinking within a resistance movement can reflect the interlocking nature of issues that resonate transnationally. Also, as researchers such as Dietz (1995), Harvey (1995), and Zermeño (1995) have reminded us, the Zapatista rebellion is anchored in a long regional history of social struggle and opposition, which provide it with a deep political sustenance. Furthermore, its leadership expresses a respect for difference and plurality that displays a sharp contrast to previous revolutionary movements, and its recent sixteen popular demands concerning land, housing, work, food, health, education, culture, information, independence, democracy, freedom, justice, peace, security, anticorruption, and environmentalism have been articulated through an emphasis on dialogue and the recent organization of a *consulta nacional*.[16]

The wave of massive support that initially greeted the Zapatista insurgency had both an urban and rural component. Moreover, as Gunther Dietz points out (1995, 46), the new alliances of indigenous communities in Michoacán, Guerrero, Oaxaca, Veracruz, and Morelos convened regional assemblies in which the recourse to armed struggle was viewed with "understanding," while it was added that the worsened situation of their own regions hardly differed from that leading to the insurrection in Chiapas.[17] The struggles for territorial autonomy, embodied in organizations such as the Independent Front of Indian Peoples (FIPI) and the Indigenous National Convention (CNI), contain both an ethnic and regional dimension that connect with the Chiapas rebellion and reinforce the overall growing significance of the cultural within the geopolitical. A symptomatic feature of the validation of culture in this context relates to the reassertion of indigenous languages, as reflected, for example, in the fact that the recent "Manifesto of Aguas Blancas" of the state of Guerrero's Popular Revolutionary Army was read in Spanish and the Nahuatl language (*Latinamerica Press* 28, no. 26 [July 11, 1996]).

In the example of the Zapatista resistance and its challenge to the existing institutional order, it is evident that our conceptualization of the geopolitical assumes two linked meanings if we remain within an internal realm. First, the Chiapas uprising and its condensation of deeply rooted social opposition can be seen as representing a radical questioning of the territorial functioning of the contemporary Mexican state. Its list of demands, and its prioritization of a radical democracy and a just society, have been articulated in a context of territory and power and have established bonds between the regional, the national, and the global. Second, the Zapatistas represent a movement that, through its naming, reconnects to one of the founding moments of the Mexican Revolution. In a continuing act of radical remembrance, it subversively reframes the themes of land, justice, and democracy. Through a process of reactivation of contested meanings, it presents itself as a moment of resistance that is both cultural and geopolitical. At the same time, the effects of globalization, and through NAFTA the bringing into question of national sovereignty, provide an example of an externally generated geopolitics that crucially impinges on the internal, so that the timing of the uprising and the trajectory of Zapatista discourse cannot be understood outside the interwoven webs of inside and outside. This point can be further elaborated in relation to issues of democracy, justice, and the impact of neoliberalism.

At the beginning of 1996, the EZLN formed the Zapatista Front of National Liberation (FZLN), "a civil and nonviolent organization, independent and democratic, Mexican and national, which struggles for democracy, liberty and justice in Mexico." In the Fourth Declaration of the Lacandon Jungle, the Zapatistas called for a nation of many worlds and affirmed that democracy will come when the culture of the nation is refashioned from the perspective of indigenous peoples. At the same time, not only have the Zapatistas made common cause with many sectors of the Mexican population in their opposition to neoliberalism but, more notably, they have also extended their strategy to the international arena, calling for the convening of an "Intercontinental Forum Against Neoliberalism." Meetings were planned for Berlin, Tokyo, an African city, Sydney, and Mexico City. A significant feature of the agenda was to organize a broadly based internationalist culture to counter the culture of neoliberalism. Invitees included "all individuals, groups, collectives, movements, social, citizen and political organizations, neighborhood associations, cooperatives, all leftist groups, non governmental organizations, groups in solidarity with the struggles of the peoples of the world, bands, tribes, intellectuals, musicians, workers, artists, teachers, peasants, cultural groups, youth movements, alternative media, ecologists, squatters, lesbians, homosexuals, feminists, pacifists" (quoted in Yúdice, in this volume). Hence, the Zapatista struggle for democracy, justice, and national sovereignty is intimately linked with their opposition to neoliberalism and to NAFTA. They have made connections among the global, national, regional, and local and do not restrict their geopolitical vision to any one level of analysis or action.

In a comparative sense, if we limit ourselves to the idea of an internal territorial domain, for example the inner ambits of the territorial state, I want to suggest that the questioning, disrupting, destabilizing effects of the movements I have briefly referred to in this chapter can be thought of in terms of three modalities of the geopolitical. First, as strongly evidenced in the cases of Bolivia and Peru, there are regional movements that challenge the existing territorial power of the central state and call for a spatial extension and deepening of the democratic process. The fluidity and heterogeneity of these resistances, and in some instances their elusive transience, have led some investigators to belittle their effects in the "real world of politics." Nevertheless, they continue to move, to challenge existing cultural patterns of centralized power, and to call into question many of our established modes of analysis.[18]

Second, as described in the Mexican case, an armed uprising—a guerrilla movement that is regionally rooted but that is not confined to its region—can constitute another modality of the geopolitical that crosses borders between inside and outside having effects in a connected series of spheres. This is only one example; other guerrilla rebellions, such as the Sendero Luminoso movement in Peru, which was also regionally based but not limited to its original region, constructed a very different set of meanings and practices to confront centralized state power. Moreover, the 1980s also witnessed a series of guerrilla movements in Central America, where the territorial power of internal states was effectively fractured.

Third, the growth in indigenous demands for territorial autonomy in a number of Latin American societies combines an interrogation of existing spatial ordering with a profound questioning of the founding of the state itself. Autonomy was the major demand of Mexico's indigenous peoples when they called for the creation of a National Plural Indigenous Assembly for Autonomy, claiming that for centuries the Mexican government has been trying to integrate them into a homogeneous nation that has never existed. Although the call for autonomy is not new to Latin America's indigenous peoples, who have always demanded the right to self-government, today it is a highly charged issue because it is viewed by central governments as a call for secession and the breakup of territorial states. Autonomy is contingent on indigenous peoples having the right to their traditional land; this issue has been a key stumbling block for centuries. Land, in the indigenous cosmovision, is the source and mother of life, and many argue strongly that a guarantee to territory and to environmental conservation is crucial for the economic and cultural continuity of indigenous peoples (Collinson 1996). Land, territorial autonomy, and the reassertion of indigenous identities coalesce in ways that reemphasize the close intersections between the cultural and the geopolitical.

These three kinds of challenges to the territorial politics of the state are not to be seen as always separate, since the actual paths of struggle have sometimes overlapped. All three challenges represent the potential to undermine and weaken the solidity of contemporary political systems, and they have sometimes intersected with other social movements concerned with, for example, environmental and human rights issues. The intertwining of inside and outside has obviously varied among these movements, as have the degrees of connection between different kinds of struggle within the same society. "Archipelagos of resistance," where linkages may be tenuous, intermittent, or broken, would be a more accurate depiction of the situation than the notion of territorial coalitions.

Knowledge and Movements: Some Concluding Remarks

In times of acute political turbulence and precarious affinities, the placing of social movements has become increasingly problematic. Calderón (1995, 122) writes of the heterogeneous, plural, multiple nature of social movements, which he thinks may well be provoking a break in the totalizing, excluding, singular conceptualizations of Latin American destiny that have prevailed for so long. In those small, everyday, cultural spaces of resistance, it may be possible to discern the emergence of collectivist values and the social forms of self-government and solidarity—the seeds perhaps of continuing oppositions and the reconstruction of "historical subjects." Our optimism of the will encourages us to agree with Calderón, whereas our "realism of the intellect" leads us, as it does his own analysis, to emphasize that there is great diversity and unpredictability. Moreover, within the diversity, as a number of authors have shown, there can be conflict, dissonance, and the absence of democracy (see, for example, Rubin, in this volume; see also Hellman 1994). The development of a series of detailed case studies on particular social movements has demonstrated the complexity of the issues involved in any characterization of the political trajectory of oppositional imaginations. In this context, Ortner's recent observations on the need to avoid any romanticization of politics and to stress the importance of "culturally thick" portrayals of subjectivity are particularly apposite (1995). It is here too that the role of the "observer," researcher, academic is rather central. There are those who have been chided for "romantically listening to the movements," while conversely others have been criticized for remaining "trapped in the well-worn grooves of class analysis." Increasingly, more questions have been posed concerning the applicability of Western-based social theories to non-Western contexts. It is certainly the case that much of the Western discussion of social movements has proceeded as if such phenomena have rarely surfaced in the societies of the South. But not only is the object of knowledge confined to a Western or Northern terrain, the agents of knowledge are also predominantly of occidental origin. The prevailing regime of representation is Euro-Americanist, whereby the underlying assumption is that knowledge, and in particular theoretical knowledge, is a Western property.

The category "Euro-Americanist" is itself symptomatic of the problem of subsuming the Americas under the heading "America," and the modified "Euro-North-Americanist," leaving aside its cumbersome quality, still raises the question of the difference between Canada and the United States. In relation to my argument in this chapter, what is specifically significant here is the way in which the inside/outside thematic connects with questions of knowledge, culture, and representation. If, as Sonia Alvarez, Evelina Dagnino, and Arturo Escobar propose in their Introduction to this volume, we are to think a new cultural studies of the Americas, a project that would recognize the infinite complexities of such a "fractal structure with manifold political cultures," this invites us to consider the way we imagine different worlds and construct new analytical meanings. Often absent in investigations of movements and mobilizations has been the continuing impact of the power over other societies, the effects of invasive discourses of control and reordering. The project of neoliberal globalization represents the most recent of such discourses and contains the attempted subordination of different modes of thought and interpretation. The alternative development of critical knowledge incites the crossing of borders and the connecting of inside and outside, but it does so in a frame that requires recognition and reciprocity and in a context that transcends containment. Such a development should not be seen as offering an uncontaminated, authentic alternative but perhaps a further reflection of the need for hybridity in thought and analysis. One of our future challenges is to combine the insights to be gained from the hybridization of knowledges with a continuing interrogation of the multiple forms of power and resistance.

Notes

1. Robertson (1992), for example, argues that much of world history can be considered as sequences of "miniglobalization" in the sense that historic empire formation involved the unification of previously sequestered territories and social entities. He goes on to suggest a series of phases in the development of globalization and stresses the point that "there is a general autonomy and 'logic' to the globalization process, which operates in *relative* independence of strictly societal and other more conventionally studied sociocultural processes" (60). For other surveys dealing with the relations between globalization and culture and between democracy and global order, see King 1991 and Held 1995 respectively.

2. Such a description first emerged in a European context, but rapidly acquired a wider geographical application. The issue of "newness" has sparked off a variety of debates on historical continuities and discontinuities and has provoked a number of interesting exchanges on the theoretical bases for understanding social movements in general. Themes of North-South divergences and the problems of comparative analysis have also been introduced into the overall discussion; see Calderón 1995 for a recent text on social movements in Latin America set in an international context and Slater 1991, 1994 for a consideration of the question of novelty and theoretical divergences.

3. I reserve the term "territoriality" for contexts implying the space within nation-states, whereas "spatiality" is used in this paper to refer to multiple contexts both within and across nation-states. Furthermore, I will argue that the term "geopolitical" can be interpreted in a double sense, referring to both external and internal instances; it does not need to be contained exclusively within an inter- or transnational frame.

4. John H. Herz has provided one of the first, and subsequently most widely quoted, papers on the territorial state in the postwar period (1957). He was particularly concerned with the peculiar unity, compactness, and coherence of the modern nation-state, and he related these features to what he called the substratum of statehood, where the state "confronts us . . . in its physical, corporeal capacity: as an expanse of territory encircled for its identification and its defense by a 'hard shell' of fortifications. . . . [I]n this lies what will here be referred to as the 'impermeability', or simply the 'territoriality' of the modern state" (474). Herz considered this territoriality and protection given by the modern state to its

citizens to be a basic feature of the historical development of the political system in general. Interestingly, and symptomatically, generalizations are made on the basis of a certain reading of the European experience, and issues of the violation of the territorial integrity of non-European nation states are not taken into account.

5. It is always necessary to bear in mind when referring to globalization that the processes involved are uneven, and, as Mosquera (1994) has noted, we live in a world of "axial globalization" and "zones of silence," so that, for example, in many African situations, cultural and communicative linkages tend to flow directly back to European metropolises, leaving many African countries separated from each other, or only tenuously connected.

6. Jameson (1992) usefully distinguishes Third World cultures from those of the "developed" world in the sense that the former have far more difficulty in remaining independent from the gaze and penetration of the metropolitan cultures of the North. The latter cultures can throw up their barriers and erect their fortresses; similarly, the social scientists of North America and Europe can more easily neglect the intellectual life of the South. Implicit and explicit notions of the self-contained but universally relevant nature of occidental knowledge and especially theoretical knowledge are deeply rooted in Western culture.

7. It also must be added here that discussions of the political and politics have been characterized by a wide variety of conceptual perspectives. Frequently, for instance, the political has been defined in relation to the state (Ricoeur 1995), and there is a long history of seeing the private sphere as outside the political realm. More recently, notions of the diffusion of the political in society have gained more support and reflect an expanding discussion of the "frontiers of the political" (Morin 1995); for an earlier and classic treatment, see Schmitt 1976.

8. This was particularly evident in November 1993 when, at a meeting attended by a majority of the country's *comités* in Santa Cruz, differences emerged over the strength of anticentrist feeling and over the differing political party alignments of the committees. For background discussion of regionalization issues in Bolivia, see Slater 1995; and for a recent examination of many of Bolivia's key social themes, see Calderón and Laserna 1994.

9. For an analysis of the Sendero Luminoso (Shining Path) guerrillas, see Starn 1995.

10. "Territory" can be taken to refer to land, earth, or sustenance, but the form of the word, as Connolly points out (1994, 24), can also be related to a derivation of *terrere*, to terrorize.

11. On the question of time and the colonial encounter, see Fabian's pathbreaking text (1983) and Norton's recent article on "ruling memory" (1993). For a stimulating discussion of spatial aspects of culture and imperialism, see Said 1993.

12. In a related argument, Jacques Derrida writes that the exacerbation of foreign debt and related mechanisms are "starving or driving to despair a large portion of humanity. . . . [T]hey tend thus to exclude it simultaneously from the very market that this logic nevertheless seeks to extend. . . . [T]his type of contradiction works through many geopolitical fluctuations even when they appear to be dictated by the discourse of democratization or human rights" (1994, 82).

13. A copy of the Chase memorandum was obtained by the *Independent;* in a connected passage, the memo stated that while the insurrection in Chiapas "does not pose a fundamental threat to Mexican political stability, it is perceived to be so by many in the investment community. . . . [W]hat Mexico needs . . . is a more authoritarian government rather than more democracy." L. Doyle, "Did U.S. Bank Send In Battalions Against Mexican Rebel Army?" *Independent* (London), March 5, 1995, p. 14.

14. This quotation is taken from a work distributed in 1992 entitled "The First Wind," translated by Bardacke and López (1995, 32–33).

15. Subcomandante Marcos, interview, *La Jornada* (Mexico City), August 27, 1995, pp. 10–11.

16. The "national consultation," which took place on August 27, 1995, elicited a response from nearly 825,000 people; 97.7 percent approved of the sixteen demands and over 90 percent were in favor of political reforms. In addition, 56.2 percent expressed the view that the EZLN should convert itself into an independent political force. *La Jornada* (Mexico City), August 29, 1995, p. 5.

17. Harvey provides some indices of poverty for Chiapas, noting, for example, that 41.6 percent of homes were without drinking water in 1992, while 33.1 percent were without electricity and 58.8 percent were without drainage; the national averages were 20.6 percent, 12.5 percent, and 36.4 percent respectively (1995, 48).

18. As Routledge and Simons nicely remind us, "social science has been a key tool for taming spirits of resistance" (1995, 475).

References

Agrawal, A. 1995. "Dismantling the Divide Between Indigenous and Scientific Knowledge." *Development and Change* 26 (July):413–439.

Albó, X. 1996. "Bolivia: Making the Leap from Local Mobilization to National Politics." *NACLA Report on the Americas* 29 (March-April):15–20.

Arditi, B. 1994. "Tracing the Political." *Angelaki* 1 (3):15–28.

Bardacke, F., and L. López, eds. and trans. 1995. *Shadows of Tender Fury: The Letters and Communiqués of Subcomandante Marcos and the Zapatista Army of National Liberation.* New York: Monthly Review Press.

Butler, J. 1990. *Gender Trouble.* London: Routledge.

_______. 1992. "Contingent Foundations: Feminism and the Question of 'Postmodernism.'" In *Feminists Theorize the Political,* ed. J. Butler and J. Scott, 3–21. London: Routledge.

Calderón, F. 1995. *Movimientos Sociales y Política.* Mexico City: Siglo XXI.

Calderón, F., and R. Laserna. 1994. *Paradojas de la Modernidad: Sociedad y cambios en Bolivia.* La Paz: Fundación Milenio.

Campbell, D. 1996. "The Politics of Radical Interdependence: A Rejoinder to Daniel Warner." *Millennium: Journal of International Studies* 25 (1):129–141.

Collinson, H., ed. 1996. *Green Guerrillas: Environmental Conflicts and Initiatives in Latin America and the Caribbean.* London: Latin America Bureau.

Connolly, W. 1991a. *Identity/Difference: Democratic Negotiations of Political Paradox.* Ithaca: Cornell University Press.

_______. 1991b. "Democracy and Territoriality." *Millennium: Journal of International Studies* 20 (3):463–484.

_______. 1994. "Tocqueville, Territory, and Violence." *Theory, Culture and Society* 11 (1):19–40.

Derrida, J. 1994. *Specters of Marx.* New York and London: Routledge.

Dietz, G. 1995. "Zapatismo y Movimientos Étnicos-Regionales en México." *Nueva Sociedad* 140 (November-December):33–50.

Fabian, J. 1983. *Time and the Other*. New York: Columbia University Press.

Falk, R. 1993. "The Making of Global Citizenship." In *Global Visions: Beyond the New World Order,* ed. J. Brecher, J. Brown, and J. Cutler, 39–50. Montreal: Black Rose Books Ltd.

Fals Borda, O. 1992. "Social Movements and Political Power in Latin America." In *The Making of Social Movements in Latin America: Identity, Strategy, and Democracy,* ed. A. Escobar and S. Alvarez, 303–316. Boulder: Westview Press.

Foucault, M. 1984. "Nietzsche, Genealogy, History." In *Foucault Reader,* ed. P. Rabinow, 76–100. New York: Pantheon Books.

______. 1991. "Governmentality." In *The Foucault Effect: Studies in Governmentality,* ed. G. Burchell, C. Gordon, and P. Miller, 87–104. London: Harvester/Wheatsheaf.

García, M. P. 1992. "The Venezuelan Ecology Movement: Symbolic Effectiveness, Social Practices, and Political Strategies." In *The Making of Social Movements in Latin America: Identity, Strategy, and Democracy,* ed. A. Escobar and S. Alvarez, 150–170. Boulder: Westview Press.

Harvey, N. 1995. "Rebellion in Chiapas: Rural Reforms and Popular Struggle." *Third World Quarterly* 16 (1):39–73.

Held, D. 1995. *Democracy and the Global Order.* Cambridge, England: Polity Press.

Hellman, J. A. 1994. "Mexican Popular Movements, Clientelism, and the Process of Democratization." *Latin American Perspectives* 21 (2):124–142.

Herz, J. H. 1957. "Rise and Demise of the Territorial State." *World Politics* 9 (4):473–493.

Honig, B. 1993. *Political Theory and the Displacement of Politics.* Ithaca: Cornell University Press.

Jackson, R. H. 1993. *Quasi-States: Sovereignty, International Relations, and the Third World.* Cambridge: Cambridge University Press.

Jameson, F. 1992. *The Geopolitical Aesthetic: Cinema and Space in the World System.* Bloomington: Indiana University Press.

Jaquette, J. S. 1994. "From Transition to Participation: Women's Movements and Democratic Politics." In *The Women's Movement in Latin America: Participation and Democracy,* ed. J. Jaquette, 1–11. Boulder: Westview Press.

Jordan, T. 1995. "The Unity of Social Movements." *The Sociological Review* 43 (4):675–692.

King, A. D., ed. 1991. *Culture, Globalization, and the World System.* London: Macmillan.

Krischke, P. 1991. "Church Base Communities and Democratic Change in Brazilian Society." *Comparative Political Studies* 24 (July):186–210.

Laclau, E. 1990. *New Reflections on the Revolution of Our Time.* London: Verso.

______. 1994. "Negotiating the Paradoxes of Contemporary Politics: An Interview." *Angelaki* 1:3, 43–50.

Laserna, R. 1986. "Movimientos Sociales Regionales (Apuntes para la Construcción de un Campo Empírico)." *Pensamiento Iberoamericano* 10:83–105.

Lefort, C. 1988. *Democracy and Political Theory*. Cambridge, England: Polity Press.

Melucci, A. 1989. *Nomads of the Present: Social Movements and Individual Needs in Contemporary Society*. London: Hutchinson/Radius.

Monga, C. 1995. "Civil Society and Democratisation in Francophone Africa." *The Journal of Modern African Studies* 33 (3):359–379.

Morin, E. 1995. "Fronteras de lo Político." *Revista de Occidente* 167 (April):5–18.

Mosquera, G. 1994. "Some Problems in Transcultural Curating." In *Global Visions: Towards a New Internationalism in the Visual Arts,* ed. J. Fisher, 133–139. London: Kala Press.

Mouffe, C. 1995. "Post-Marxism: Democracy and Identity." *Environment and Planning D: Society and Space* 13:259–265.

Munck, G. L. 1995. "Actor Formation, Social Co-Ordination, and Political Strategy: Some Conceptual Problems in the Study of Social Movements." *Sociology* 29 (4):667–685.

Norton, A. 1993. "Ruling Memory." *Political Theory* 21 (3):453–463.

Ortner, S. B. 1995. "Resistance and the Problem of Ethnographic Refusal." *Comparative Studies in Society and History* 37 (1):173–193.

Parekh, B. 1993. "The Cultural Particularity of Liberal Democracy." In *Prospects for Democracy,* ed. D. Held, 156–175. Cambridge, England: Polity Press.

Rancière, J. 1995. *On the Shores of Politics.* London: Verso.

Ricoeur, P. 1995. "La Persona: Desarrollo Moral y Político." *Revista de Occidente* 167 (April):129–142.

Robertson, R. 1992. *Globalization: Social Theory and Global Culture.* London: Sage.

Routledge, P., and J. Simons. 1995. "Embodying Spirits of Resistance." *Environment and Planning D: Society and Space* 13:471–498.

Said, E. W. 1993. *Culture and Imperialism.* London: Chatto and Windus.

Schmitt, C. 1976. *The Concept of the Political.* Trans. G. Schwab. New Brunswick, N.J.: Rutgers University Press.

Scott, A. 1995. "Culture or Politics? Recent Literature on Social Movements, Class, and Politics." *Theory, Culture and Society* 12 (3):169–178.

Shefner, J. 1995. "Moving in the Wrong Direction in Social Movement Theory." *Theory and Society* 24 (4):595–612.

Slater, D. 1989. *Territory and State Power in Latin America: The Peruvian Case.* London and New York: Macmillan.

______. 1991. "New Social Movements and Old Political Questions: Re-thinking State-Society Relations in Latin American Development." *International Journal of Political Economy* 21 (1):32–65.

______. 1994. "Power and Social Movements in the Other Occident: Latin America in an International Context." *Latin American Perspectives* 21 (2):11–37.

______. 1995. "Democracy, Decentralization, and State Power: On the Politics of the Regional in Chile and Bolivia." In *C.L.A.G. Yearbook 1995* (Conference of Latin Americanist Geographers), ed. D. J. Robinson, 49–65. Austin: University of Texas Press.

Starn, O. 1995. "Maoism in the Andes: The Communist Party of Peru. Shining Path and the Refusal of History." *Journal of Latin American Studies* 27:399–421.

Taylor, P. J. 1995. "Beyond Containers: Inter-nationality, Inter-stateness, Inter-territoriality. *Progress in Human Geography* 19:1–15.

Walker, R. B. J. 1994. "Social Movements/World Politics." *Millennium: Journal of International Studies* 23 (3):669–700.

______. 1995. "International Relations and the Concept of the Political." In *International Relations Theory Today,* ed. K. Booth and S. Smith, 306–327. Cambridge, England: Polity Press.

Wapner, P. 1995. "Politics Beyond the State: Environmental Activism and World Civic Politics." *World Politics* 47 (April):311–340.

Weyland, K. 1995. "Social Movements and the State: The Politics of Health Reform in Brazil." *World Development* 23 (10):1699–1712.

Zermeño, S. 1995. "Zapatismo, región y nación." *Nueva Sociedad* 140 (November-December):51–57.

Part Four

Theoretical and Methodological Reflections on the Cultural and the Political in Latin American Social Movements

Yet the scenario is much more complex. Let me begin with a basic factual reality: Of all regions of the world, Latin America has the most inequitable income distribution. And more, polarization and economic inequality are increasing, in spite of the substantial political democratization that took place during the 1980s and in spite of some indications of economic growth, however uneven and discontinuous, in several countries. Reality is paradoxical: Economic growth, formal democracy, and increasing inequality (and therefore growing poverty) seem an unlikely combination of outcomes. Something must be wrong, in either one or another of these dimensions. What follows are some reflections about the relationship between social movements, democracy, and inequality, based on the realities of Latin America in the 1990s.

Democracy and Inequality: Polarization, Fragmentation, Marginality

The issue is a classic one: Can political democracy be instituted without guaranteeing a basic minimum level of economic well-being? Are basic economic rights part of the contents of basic *human* rights? Can people enjoy their civil and political rights if they do not have access to the basic conditions (the absence of hunger and pain and access to relevant information) that ensure the possibility of exercising such rights? This theme concerns more than the relationship between political democracy and economic dimensions such as equity and growth. It is a key aspect of the conditions that are required for the emergence of individual and collective self-reflective subjects (of rights).

The theoretical and ideological debate about the nature of rights and the definition of human rights—particularly whether human rights includes socioeconomic rights—tends to obscure one central question: What is the limit? Is there a "threshold of humanity"? What are the minimum qualifications that human beings, defined as a biological species, must meet to qualify as "human" social subjects? Obviously, mere physical survival is such a condition. Hunger, physical pain, torture and bodily injury, and extreme victimization transform the human subject into a body, annihilating its cultural dimension.

At another level, the *human condition* involves a sense of belonging to a political community.

> The fundamental deprivation of human rights is manifested first and above all in the deprivation of a place in the world [a political space] which makes opinions significant, and actions effective. . . . We became aware of the right to have rights . . . and a right to belong to some kind of organized community, only when millions of people emerged who had lost and could not regain those rights because of the new global situation. . . . Man, as it turns out, can lose all so-called Rights of Man without losing his essential quality as man, his human dignity. Only the loss of a polity expels him from humanity. (Arendt 1949; quoted in Young-Bruehl 1982, 257)

The sense of belonging and the possibility of interaction lie at the core of humanity. In other words, human society exists when there exists "the other" and a public sphere of interaction.

In this light, faced with extreme poverty, how can we be sure that we are still within the realm of humanity? Isn't extreme poverty a sign of dehumanization? Exclusion and indigence lie at the opposite edge of democracy, implying the denial of fundamental rights. It is the contrary of social actors and scenarios. The excluded are outside society, or are simply considered nonexistent.

The data on poverty and exclusion in Latin America are well known. The fact is that "democratization with adjustment" is leaving out masses of people; this does not seem to be a passing, frictional phenomenon but rather part and parcel of a process of structural marginalization.

This poses a puzzle: Defined as outsiders by the powerful, subordinate peoples (even slaves) have always been part of the political and social community. Historically, they have gained access to public sociopolitical space through their struggles. Yet social struggles involve collective actors and resources, which are absent in cases of extreme poverty and exclusion. No social movement of the oppressed can grow without having first gained a minimum of access and a minimum of humanity (in the sense of belonging to a community and of a self-reflexive capacity involved in identity building). A first response among the excluded, then, is apathy and passivity, the isolation and loneliness of misery, the lack of social ties among hungry people.

History and anthropology have documented the everyday forms of protest and boycott of subordinate groups. When power relations are extremely hierarchical and asymmetrical, subordinate people develop hidden forms of action, alternative social spaces where they can express their dissidence. In such spaces, in the backyards and alleys, in the invisible shapes and shadows, in what Scott (1992) calls *hidden transcripts,* a sense of dignity and autonomy vis-à-vis domination and power is constructed and sheltered. These are the protoforms of politics, the *infrapolitics of the powerless,* through which dignity and a sense of community are constructed. In fact, such practices show some degree of autonomy and reflexive capacity. Insofar as these are hidden practices, it becomes difficult to recognize them and distinguish them from apathy and subservience, until they become more explicit, when the process of transformation into collective movements is under way: that is, when the process of formation of social actors and movements is already taking place.

Both the human rights movement during the dictatorships and the feminist movement during the last two decades evolved in part in this way as outcomes of what initially were resistance practices. Something similar happened in the initial stages of the labor movement, of the antislave movements, of the movements of indigenous groups and peasants, all of which have a rich tradition in Latin America. In all these cases, boycotts and hidden resistances converged with ideologically driven "liberating" proposals, creating collective movements with a clear presence in the public space. Many other "protomovements" remained in the backyards and graveyards of history.

During the dictatorships of the 1960s and 1970s, many activities of political opposition had the character of resistance practices. Insofar as political opposition was multiclass, economic survival was not an issue, at least for part of the opposition movement. Practices of resistance to dictatorship easily turned into political acts. Or rather, resistance was, from the very beginning, a political act. Under authoritarianism, the logic of domination was clear: The lines of the *us* and the *they* could be drawn easily. There was no pretense of inclusion of "the other." Yet the transparent nature of political opposition obscured and veiled the other face of domination: poverty and economic violations of rights.

Transition to democracy brings confusion and bewilderment. A new space opens up for democratic discourse, for elections and participation. While democratic discourse becomes hegemonic, the reality of economic relations is in contradiction to it. Indeed, there is a double discourse: a discourse of participation and a nondiscourse of economic exclusion.

Under such conditions, the historically constructed "threshold of humanity" is threatened. Marginalized and excluded people may then refuse to accept the rules of the democratic game, or accept them only partially. Their response may then become social *violence*. The economically excluded do not become individual or collective subjects in the newly emerging public and political sphere: They may resist and protest, living under different rules, the rules of violence. Their (limited) energies and resources are not geared to integration, "acting out" instead of participating; at times, this is manifest in forms of communitarian resistance.

There are other forms of violence that do not involve the economically excluded. On the one hand, violence is generated by those who do not accept democratic rules for personal or group interests (such as drug trafficking and corruption); on the other hand, it is generated by the totalitarian rejection of the right of "others" to participate in the public sphere, with attempts to annihilate the other—state terrorism and racist violence do not disappear magically with the political transition to democratically elected governments.

The processes of impoverishment and exclusion, and their consequences in hampering the formation of social movements ready to initiate conflicts in terms of *societal* tensions and social relations, create the conditions for the emergence of racism. "Downwardly mobile" social sectors live with the threat of those who are below them (immigrants, blacks); elites define social problems in racial terms (it is "foreigners" who create problems), as a way to disguise their own domination and class exclusion (Wieviorka 1992).

Often, violence is understood as a last resource, when words and dialogue become impossible. It can also be conceived as a form of discourse, as an extreme way of talking, as a language of expression of conflict and social relations, in an attempt to participate in the definition of the political scenario. In such cases (the Ejército Zapatista de Liberación Nacional, or EZLN, is perhaps the latest and clearest case), violence is the voice of a collective actor with a strong sense of identity, resorting to a political discourse, that forces itself upon the powerful. In this way, the actor gains its place in the theater of the sociopolitical game. A real breakthrough in the handling of social and political conflict will take place if and when, heard and recognized by others, the discourse of violence is transformed into a discourse of dialogue and negotiation—and when the powerful learn to listen to other languages before messages are translated into the discourse of violent action.

Accepting the line of reasoning just presented has significant implications for the emerging democracies: Political democratization does not automatically produce a strengthened civil society, a culture of citizenship, and a sense of social responsibility. In fact, the vitality of civil society requires that people not fall below the thresholds that mark the possibility of their participation in the political community. One can be a nonparticipant in the community either through exclusion or through choice (by engaging in alternative, unlawful channels). At the same time and in a circular way, the vitality of civil society becomes the guarantee for the functioning of political democracy.

Actors and Spokespersons: Social Movements and NGOs in the 1990s

The circumstances of social actors around the world has profoundly changed during the last two decades. Until the 1970s, the primacy of the political system was undisputed: Political parties, elections, and revolutionary wars were the strategies for change. The state was at the center, and the question was how to gain state power. Even traditional corporatist actors (entrepreneurs and the labor movement, the military, and the clergy) were looked at in terms of their capacity to intervene in the political space of the state. Other actors were weak—social demands were put directly to the state, and what was left outside, spaces for sociability and local cultural reinforcement, was less "important."

Internationally, states were also the central actors and agents. Numerous international conventions and pacts were promoted and ratified by democratic governments. Society had little room in these accords; there was limited societal space. Underneath this reality, however, something different, something hidden and muddled, was boiling. In 1975, the world witnessed with astonishment the ferment of women in Mexico, at the time of the International Conference on Women in Mexico City. The action was not in the intergovernmental conference but outside, in the multiplicity of events and proposals with which the international women's movement was challenging the *official* conference. Since then, this pattern of parallel activities has become a widespread practice, and the power of nongovernmental social organizations started to grow. At the United Nations Conference on Environment and Development (UNCED) in Rio de Janeiro in 1992, at the human rights conference in Vienna in 1993, and at conferences in Copenhagen, Cairo, and Beijing in 1995, the struggle of nongovernmental organizations (NGOs) is not for the right to have a forum but for the incorporation of the demands and voices of the parallel forums in the official proceedings and resolutions.

The international visibility and recognition of NGOs is an indication of broader organizational and institutional changes. Since the 1970s, new forms of interest expression emerge in the public sphere; they direct their claims to the state, yet do not act through political parties. This was understandable under dictatorial regimes, when political parties had very limited room for action. Social movements could then emerge as forces in opposition to dictatorship, and they became significant actors in the transitions to democracy in many countries. Often they actually were collective actions with quite specific and limited objectives and demands.[1] During the transition to democracy, some urban movements became institutionalized social actors, especially at the level of local governments. There are now many places that provide spaces for the expression of citizens' demands, for citizens' control and monitoring of municipal administration, and for joint participation of social organizations and local government in city management (Raczynski and Serrano 1992).

Other social movements followed different paths during the 1980s. Several demands of the women's and human rights movements were incorporated into the social and political agendas of the transition. Thus, the critical stands of the feminist movement penetrated state bureaucracies, labor unions, business organizations, and even the Church. The debate on issues of gender discrimination, the logic of equality and equity, and discussions about judicial reform—including political and social recognition of violations of women's rights such as domestic violence (although not yet marital rape)—has taken root in Latin American societies. Even the issue of reproductive rights is openly debated in the region.

Also, insofar as the human rights discourse has been adopted by large sectors of society and is no longer limited to a small group of militants and activists, the very definition of success or failure of a social movement comes into question. Indeed, both the women's and the human rights movements weakened during the transition. There were internal conflicts over strategies between those who wanted to participate in the power structure of the state and those who were inclined to maintain the autonomy of the movement, even at the cost of remaining outside the loci of power.[2] At the same time, the issues raised by these movements expanded significantly and became generalized in the population, which is a clear indication of success. As a result, new themes were absorbed and appropriated by society at large, but the organizations became weak and conflict-ridden.

In more general terms, when the "new" social movements started to gain visibility nationally and locally, the question that generated interest and attention referred to the future of the links between the new demands and the political system. Would the movements be able to maintain their autonomy? Would they ultimately be coopted by political parties and the political system? Would their demands be appropriated by existing political and social institutions? Clearly, the links between social movements and political institutions are extremely unstable. What is clear is that they are more permanent and have stronger roots than what their role as instrumental alternatives to political parties during the time of the authoritarian regimes would have anticipated. In spite of the heterogeneity of the current scenarios, some significant trends, anchored in transnational processes, can be detected.

At the world level, the growth of international solidarity networks, geared to intervene in situations of economic exclusion and political oppression in the South (and increasingly in eastern Europe), was astonishing. Although some of these networks are highly asymmetrical (North American and European donors define the targets and select the recipients and channels of aid to the South), others are starting to evidence greater reciprocity and symmetry, not in terms of the flow of resources but in ideas and priorities. This is clearly so in the area of human rights and women; the environmental movement is younger but is hopefully moving in the same direction.

In Latin America, the collective protests and localized movements that prevailed two decades ago began to change, turning into formal organizations—the so-called *third sector,* different from the state and from the market, composed of private nonprofit organizations, self-managed, geared to intervene in favor of discriminated and dispossessed social sectors (Scherer-Warren 1993; Fernandes 1994). Structurally, these organizations are *intermediaries* and are related to each other through *networks.* At the local and national levels, they are becoming the mediators between the excluded and the state; between international movements and organizations, and local demands; between international cooperation and the final recipients of aid. These networks, both nationally and internationally, have a substantial organizational structure, following their own rules. They are increasingly recognized as legitimate organizations by governmental agencies. (In some countries, NGOs are even selected by international programs as channels for the transfer of resources, preferring them over governmental agencies in recipient countries.) In that vein, local and national NGOs, and their international links, through the formation of a class of professional staff members and voluntary workers, are becoming a major actor in the arena of social issues and processes.[3]

The density of organizations and the presence of international aid organizations vary among countries; they are more visible and have more impact in smaller countries. In bigger and more developed countries, international cooperation has less economic and political weight, and local NGOs constitute only *one* of the organizational forms of civil society. Their dynamism and strength depends then on how the state, political parties, and other organizations relate to each other and how they define the space for NGOs. In the 1990s, given the prevalence of neoliberal economic policies that curtail the scope of welfare and social policies, the actual role of NGOs is increasing; they are becoming intermediaries between the dispossessed and the state, and they act to "compensate" or fill the vacuum left by the curtailment of state services. While assuming the role of representing the voiceless, they become spokespersons—at times authorized voices; at times, self-appointed— of victims (of human rights violations under dictatorial regimes, of economic exclusion in dictatorships and democracies, of discrimination against minorities, of alienation and expropriation of natural resources, of pollution, and so on), re-presenting these victims vis-à-vis the power structure. At times, these processes are part of the democratizing movements; at other times, they reproduce patriarchal, populist, or authoritarian forms of relationship between subordinate and powerful sectors of society.

Thus, as is the case with most social organizations, the nature of social movements and of NGOs is quite heterogeneous: they not only vary in their aims and ideological commitments but they also vary in the degree of grassroots participation, in their degree of centralization, in their democratic or authoritarian practices. Cases of "authoritarian technocracy" *on behalf of* the poor *(we know what is good for you and will make sure that you comply)* are innumerable.

I must introduce a word of caution and concern. Within the hegemonic neoliberal discourse (including that of the international financial community), in which the state is "subsidiary" and should be as small as possible, this "third sector" is put forth as a model, as the basic road to *strengthening civil society.* I see a big danger in identifying this third sector with civil society (a conceptual danger, but with significant political and ethical implications). The fact is that NGOs and "private-yet-public" organizations do not have a built-in mechanism of accountability. They do not have a constituency or membership composed of their "sovereign citizens." They are financially accountable to those who provide funds and to their own ideology and consciousness, hopefully (but *only* hopefully) based on "good" values, solidarity, compassion, and commitment. Given this relative absence of institutional and societal accountability, there is always the danger of arbitrary action, of manipulation, of lack of transparency in objectives and practices. There is also a concern with rationality and efficiency: Given the scarcity of resources, are these organizations the most efficient way to handle social development issues?

Although in general this is not the case—NGOs are in fact playing a major role in the processes of democratization—I want to call attention to this built-in structural difficulty: Nobody obliges NGOs to guide their activities according to democratic and participatory principles, and no sovereign body, including the final beneficiaries, has the right to define the agenda of NGOs. This implies that *the state cannot and should not renounce its function and obligation to promote citizenship rights and participation. And social movements and collective participatory action on the part of societal movements cannot be totally institutionalized, be it through state-oriented channels or through "concerned" NGOs.*

Social Movements at the Turn of the Century

In a medium-term perspective on Latin America, the social demands expressed in collective movements have changed their profile. The labor movement and peasant movements, at their peak, forwarded projects for "total" societal transformation (Calderón and Jelin 1986). Since the 1970s, with the end of the developmental model of import substitution and the expansion of authoritarian political regimes, the space and scope of social movements has been changing. The heterogeneity and multiplicity of actors and meanings has become more visible; grievances have become more specific; the "identity" of social movements (Evers 1984) has begun to surface; the patterns of everyday life have become the focus of attention. What attracted the attention of analysts was that these specific and very concrete everyday concerns and demands often became major challenges to the basic principles of social and political organization (Calderón 1986; Escobar and Alvarez 1992). These were highly heterogeneous and diversified movements, which combined the logic of collective identity at the symbolic level with specific instrumental interests and demands.

Recent transformations and current processes—marked by the transition to democracy and to an open-market economy—point to new changes, to still more diversified patterns, to multiple meanings, to fragmentation. One can hear very often the argument that links apathy and the weakening of the social bond to individualistic market economies. *But,* this is not a lineal and total process. There is room for other expressions and other meanings, for collective actors who are searching for their identities and struggling for their legitimate space in the sociopolitical scenario: indigenous groups, youths, women, and ethnic and racial minorities. Themes and issues also continue to attract and convene: human rights, the environment, poverty, and exclusion.

In this new context, social actors and movements have a double role: On the one hand, they are collective systems of reciprocal recognition, expressing old and new collective identities, with important cultural and symbolic components. On the other hand, they are nonpartisan political intermediaries who bring the needs and demands of unarticulated voices to the public sphere, linking them to state institutions. The expressive role in the construction and collective identities and social recognition, and the instrumental role that challenges the existing institutional arrangements, are both essential for the vitality of democracy. Rather than interpreting the inability shown by political parties and formal institutions to coopt them as a weakness of democracy, social movements and nonpartisan organizations should be seen as a way to ensure a *dynamic* democracy—one that includes a self-contained device for expanding its own frontiers.

Notes

1. Analyzing Brazilian urban movements, Cardoso (1983) shows that these movements invariably approached the state in terms of specific demands. Insofar as their demands were met by the authoritarian state, they rapidly lost their belligerent and potentially oppositional character. Cardoso's analysis was important in demythifying the alleged contestatory nature of urban movements.

2. For a discussion of the human rights movements in Argentina, see Jelin 1994.

3. This statement must be qualified. The fragility of NGOs is linked to their lack of financial autonomy. It is the international aid organizations (governmental and nongovernmental organizations of the North that channel governmental funds, and international private financial links) who ultimately decide what their priorities will be. The current emphasis on "organizational sustainability" should be seen with concern, as a prelude to a restriction of funds leading to a changing orientation toward projects in which economic returns will become the measuring rod of investments (Scherer-Warren 1993).

References

Arendt, Hannah. 1949. "The Rights of Man: What Are They?" *Modern Review* 3 (1):24–37.

Calderón, Fernando. 1986. *Los Movimientos Sociales ante La Crisis.* Buenos Aires: CLACSO.

Calderón, Fernando, and Elizabeth Jelin. 1986. *Clases y Movimientos Sociales en América Latina: Perspectivas y Realidades.* Buenos Aires: Estudios CEDES.

Cardoso, Ruth. 1983. "Movimentos Sociais Urbanos: Balanco Critico." In *Sociedade e Política No Brasil Pos–64,* ed. B. Sorj and M. de Almeida. São Paulo: Brasiliense.

Escobar, Arturo, and Sonia E. Alvarez, eds. 1992. *The Making of Social Movements in Latin America: Identity, Strategy, and Democracy*. Boulder: Westview Press.

Evers, Tilman. 1984. "Identity: The Hidden Side of New Social Movements in Latin America." In *New Social Movements and the State in Latin America,* ed. David Slater. Dordrecht, the Netherlands: Foris Publications/CEDLA.

Fernandes, Rubem César. 1994. *Privado Porém Público: O Terceiro Setor Na América Latina.* Rio de Janeiro: Relume-Dumará.

Jelin, Elizabeth. 1994. The Politics of Memory: The Human Rights Movement and the Construction of Democracy in Argentina. *Latin American Perspectives* 21 (2):38–58.

Raczynski, Dagmar, and Claudia Serrano, eds. 1992. *Políticas Sociales, Mujeres y Gobierno Local.* Santiago: CIEPLAN.

Scott, James C. 1992. *Domination and the Arts of Resistance: Hidden Transcripts*. New Haven: Yale University Press.

Scherer-Warren, Ilse. 1993. "ONGs na América Latina: Trajetória e Perfil." Universidade Federal de Santa Catarina, Florianopolis, Brazil. Mimeographed.

Wieviorka, Michel. 1992. *El Espacio del Racismo*. Barcelona: Paidós.

Young-Bruehl, Elizabeth. 1982. *Hannah Arendt: For Love of the World*. New Haven: Yale University Press.

Chapter Seventeen

Final Comments: Challenges to Cultural Studies in Latin America

PAULO J. KRISCHKE

Many scholars and activists in Latin America have tended to consider some leading contemporary trends (such as "globalization" and "neoliberalism") as general blueprints that do not require detailed research of local political conditions before being applied. Social actors and movements were then "structurally" considered as the necessary opponents of national and international oppression. The authors of this book take a different stand on these issues. They certainly recognize that those general trends are common and indeed dominant in the Latin American countries, with a host of negative effects on the polity and the society. However, they do not posit social movements as the bearers of structural resistance and national emancipation from international domination. They prefer to look at the unfolding of a nonlinear cultural process of social and political change in which "ambiguity" is a key word (Yúdice; Schild; Alvarez; Rubin). The book portrays social actors as the subjects and interpreters responsible for the meanings and the political relevance of their actions, in their specific national contexts.

In fact, trends toward globalization can only be properly understood in their effects on social movements at the local and national levels (as the chapters by Yúdice, and by Grueso, Rosero, and Escobar, clearly demonstrate). One obvious reason for this is that there are not, as yet, international power structures capable of replacing, in Latin America, the national states as the *loci* of political life—in spite of the growing importance of regional cooperation and worldwide communications (Ribeiro). Therefore, the authors of this book rightly emphasize the importance of national specifications in order to evaluate the impact of general international trends on social movements (Jelin). Of course, there is always an expectation that national differences and social diversity may be gauged through a comparative outlook, and this book selects a "cultural studies" approach as its focus of analysis (Introduction).

The contributions of this book are conceived as "cultural studies" mainly to emphasize "that the cultural politics of social movements enacts cultural contestations or presupposes cultural difference" (Introduction). The editors of the book maintain that "cultural politics is enactive and relational . . . when movements deploy alternative conceptions of woman, nature, race, economy, democracy, or citizenship that unsettle dominant cultural meanings." This is an innovative approach, which firmly questions the "objectifying" trends of previous studies on "political modernization" and "political development" that imposed rigid "Westernizing" categories on comparative research, such as the "civic culture" of advanced Western democracies. Moreover, this cultural focus is firmly grounded methodologically, through an openness to the meanings and ends social actors attribute to their actions. It thus takes a definite stance for the political emancipation of Latin American "subaltern counterpublics" (Introduction). One may hope that this new focus on "cultural studies" will be evaluated in the years to come in the same vein as studies by British counterparts (particularly Stuart Hall and his associates), who were assessed by an inner participant in a (not unsympathetic but often very rigorous) comprehensive overview:

> Gramscian work has opened a number of areas to critical inspection in a novel and interesting way. It has been responsible for the emergence of a critical sociology of culture and for the politicisation of culture, and these developments have generated very successful academic programmes of research and course construction. However . . . there are also a number of tendencies towards closure in Gramscianism too. (Harris 1992, 195)[1]

The new cultural approach to Latin American social movements certainly learned from previous cultural studies in Great Britain and elsewhere to avoid the trends toward "closure." Perhaps this is the reason why "hegemony" (that "fashionable floating signifier"; Harris 1992, 44) is ruled out by the book's editors in the Introduction because "dominant political cultures in Latin America—with perhaps a few short-lived exceptions—cannot be seen as examples of hegemonic orderings of society."

To be certain, this book's approach to "cultural politics" introduces an understanding of the polity that is more open ended and sophisticated than the interpretation of politics made by most previous studies of social movements in Latin America. Previous studies have usually relied on a rigid dichotomy between civil society and the state (which was certainly relevant during the times of authoritarian military rule). This book's authors introduce a more flexible and nuanced understanding of politics. The essays by Cunha, Schild, Rubin, and Jelin emphasize, in turn, the ambiguities and nonlinear development of the relations between social movements and the state, in different historical contexts. All the book's essays also take into account national institutional change, constitutional democratization, and/or related transformations of the political structures. Slater even introduces a useful distinction between politics and "the political" in order to emphasize the specific political dimension of social movements. These contributions go far beyond the usual binary polarization between civil society and government that was sustained by many previous studies of social movements in Latin America. Alvarez, Dagnino, Jelin, Baierle, and the book's general editors develop the concept of the "public sphere" as an extension or expansion of institutional politics outside the boundaries of government. These are important conceptual innovations, which improve our understanding of the political relevance of social actors and movements.

The next step in this revalorization of politics, for the study of social movements, will be the recognition that an interpretation of both social and political democratization entails the adoption of a comparative scale to gauge "political development" (again, this contentious word!). I realize that "cultural studies" has a certain (and perhaps justified) resistance to words that imply quantifying, objectifying, or linear-geometrical comparing and that take the conventions of the advanced Western countries as their "benchmark." But I do not imply that one should return to the "modernization" illusions of the 1950s and 1960s or even to the outmoded Gramscian "theorems" of sociopolitical organization (typical of early-twentieth-century strategic approaches) held by both the Left and the Right. What I have in mind is Kholberg's and Jürgen Habermas's "moral/cognitive development" and its correspondence in sociopolitical democratization (Habermas 1987), which I have proposed elsewhere as a viable approach to the study of social movements during Latin American democratization (Krischke 1993). My point here is that the establishment of formal democratic rights in postauthoritarian regimes has allowed an expansion of the public sphere beyond the frontiers of government whereby social actors and movements are acquiring (and developing) new strategies, identities, and . . . a "civic culture"! In short, there is a process of social learning of democratic rights that may be assessed cross-culturally in specific political contexts (Krischke 1990), through the famous stages of "moral-cognitive development" (see Chilton 1990 for a methodological approach adopted in this research; see also Krischke forthcoming).[2]

Of course, poststructuralists also put up much resistance to approaches that emphasize institutional analysis or any kind of "development" that is not granted by "articulatory practices." This may be due to poststructuralism's "linguistic turn," conceived by some as a radical epistemic break between "discourses" and normatively grounded institutional analyses. David Harris provided a sharp (though somewhat one-sided) account of related influences of "post-marxism" on British cultural studies:

> First, post-marxism diffuses and dilutes "politics" to mean almost any antagonism. . . . Second, a (linked) theoretical void lies at the heart of discourse theory, seen best

> in its attempt to reject all kinds of essentialism. . . . Third, the notion of "articulation" is also incoherent; the issue is whether the connection between the elements in an articulatory practice are merely contingent or somehow necessary. (1992, 34)

This book's Introduction carefully avoids any lapse into "discourse radicalism." Nevertheless, much work is yet to be done to clarify how the articulations between social practices and discourses of "subaltern counterpublics" can influence democratic institutionalization in Latin America.

James Bohmann has suggested that Habermas's definition of "democracy as an institutionalization of discourses" implies that "discourses are institutionalized to the extent that a social setting is created that permits collective, post-conventional agreements which, in turn, create whatever shared structures actors may have" (Habermas 1979, 74). Democracy is thus seen as a "practical hypothesis" describing how a collective will may be formed in public processes of deliberation and not as a restrictive and exclusionary institutionalization of the public sphere (as the authors of this book's Introduction have suggested)—for democratic institutions are the loci where a collective will "ties the development of social systems to control through a politically effective institutionalization of discourse" (Habermas 1973, 398).

To be sure, Latin American democratic institutions are more distant from this "practical hypothesis" than those institutions of advanced Western democracies studied by Habermas. However, they are also the "institutionalization of discourses" that are striving to establish and expand democracy as part of a process of social evolution. In this sense, it is worth remembering that Habermas's theory of social evolution is guided by two basic tenets. The first is that "learning is the basic evolutionary mechanism in culture"; the second is that "homologous patterns exist on ontogenetic and phylogenetic levels for the cognitive development" of individuals and of societies (Habermas 1979, 99, 205). Moreover, Habermas's theory is multidimensional so as to include a cognitive dimension (the development of worldviews), a moral dimension (the development of moral and legal constructs), and a subjective dimension (the development of more complex personality structures and identities).

It is not possible to dwell here on the specifics of a research program on "moral/cognitive development" in Latin America. In any case, this is only one example of the kinds of proposals that may enhance the effectiveness of "cultural politics" in tackling personal, social, and political democratization from an overall perspective. However, it has the merit of facing another methodological problem seldom considered by previous studies on social movements in Latin America: the issue of the unit of analysis. This issue has been especially debated outside Latin America under the rubric of "reductionism" or "methodological individualism" (cf. Levine, Saber, and Wright 1987; Birnbaum and Leca 1990), and studies in North America on "resource mobilization" have raised it since the influential work of Olson (1965) on the "logic of collective action." Some of this book's authors have indirectly addressed the issue, in terms of "a new concept of citizenship" (e.g., Paoli and Telles; Dagnino). Paoli and Telles perceive it as a notion of citizenship that differentiates itself from the liberal conception and is conceived as an active collective participation in dialogue and negotiation related to the whole of society and its inequities. Dagnino defines this collective citizenship as the constitution of "active social subjects (political agents)." All the book's authors seem to endorse social conceptions of citizenship, in some cases side by side with the more conventional interpretation of citizenship as the individual exercise of basic civil, political, and social rights.

This definition of social participation as a form of collective citizenship is certainly relevant and accompanies the reappraisal and expansion of the political sphere already noted above. Moreover, the "enactive and relational" approach that this book takes to cultural politics goes far beyond the "monological" analyses of individual and social actors held by most previous studies on social movements. Nevertheless, a comprehensive debate on overall democratization is still wanted in comparative studies. And the new emphasis on "collective citizenship" runs the risk of simply renaming an old bias of previous studies of Latin American social movements, namely their refusal to integrate the personal and the individual into their focus of analysis. This refusal has often been justified as an opposition to egocentric interests, the focus of "rational choice" and "methodological individualism" (though Elster; Birnbaum and Leca; Levine, Saber, and Wright; and others have, from different points of view, rejected this criticism). Whatever the merits of this debate, it would be ironic if a line of "cultural studies" that intends to underlay the subjective dimension of social and political democratization (among other cultural aspects of politics) forgets the individual interests and personal motivations that drive people into social and political participation.

In fact, we must come to terms with the fact that social actors and movements are composed of individuals. And most previous studies of social movements in Latin America have tended, in an opposite direction, to attribute to social actors the characteristics of personalities and individuals—thus "reifying" or "essentializing" their actions and orientations. This lapse may be similar to previous Marxist conceptualizations of social classes (Kowarick 1995). The poststructuralist focus of this book is capable of identifying many peculiarities and diversities within social groups and movements, according to gender, age, and race. For example, Warren argues against the unified Marxist anticapitalist paradigm in its approach to indigenous groups, Cunha argues similarly about black movements in Brazil, and the Introduction mentions some related positive advancements in studies of "resource mobilization" in the United States. But more should be done to account for individual and personal differences within Latin American social groups and movements. A research approach to cognitive-moral development and its correspondence in the sociopolitical and normative spheres could provide such a comparative standpoint on overall democratization.

Finally, I would like to mention another relevant contribution of these new "cultural studies" on social movements in Latin America. In this volume, Ribeiro,

Yúdice and Cunha stress the importance of the imaginary, of myth and utopia, for the cultural life of social movements. Would it not also be important to introduce "ambiguity" into the sphere of the imaginary? In this sense, Paoli and Telles's suggestion, to look at present social conflicts and negotiations in Brazil as part of a "social contract" that is being worked out through the expansion of the public sphere, is valuable. This kind of concrete utopia has the advantage of being amenable to empirical analysis through an evaluation of its outcomes. Contract relations may be considered an operative myth or utopia that offers and produces specific results, which may partly actualize the hope of equity implied by the ideal of contract (cf. Rawls 1993 for the debates on Rawlsian neocontractarian analysis). Both Bohmann (1990) and Benhabib and Cornell (1987) have shown, in different ways, that the "Generalized Other" of the contractarian utopia's equity has to take into account the inequalities and diversities of every "concrete other"—thus correcting Rawls and Kohlberg from a Habermasian perspective on "communicative action."

The focus on contract relations may thus enhance our understanding of Latin American democratization in the context of "non-liberal or hierarchical societies" (Rawls 1993). For this focus provides one of the "ideoscapes" (Yúdice, in this volume), or "material processes through which imagined communities interact." Therefore, one may hope that these pioneer "cultural studies" on Latin American social movements will encourage new groundwork toward the understanding that democracy is possible, for it is already being built, right in the midst of outrageous social inequity and other forms of political oppression.

Notes

1. Harris adds: "Very briefly, gramscianism for me is far too ready to close off its investigations of social reality, to make its concepts prematurely identical with elements of that reality in various ways. . . . [They] are liable to premature closure by being too 'strategic' for me, as well—by letting a politics privilege analysis, both an explicit national politics, and a less explicit local academic polities. Such closures have benefits, but there are also considerable losses" (Harris 1992, 195).

2. James Bohmann (Baynes, Bohmann, and McCarthy 1986) and Seyla Benhabib (Benhabib and Cornell 1987) offer valuable theoretical insights on this project, which was inspired originally by Claus Offe's national evaluation of social movements in Germany (1985).

References

Barry, Brian. 1973. *The Liberal Theory of Justice: A Critical Examination of Principal Doctrines of a Theory of Justice in John Rawls*. Oxford: Oxford University Press.

Baynes, Kenneth, James Bohmann, and Thomas McCarthy, eds. 1986. *After Philosophy*. Cambridge: MIT Press.

Benhabib, Seyla, and Durcilla Cornell, eds. 1987. *Feminism as Critique*. New York: Blackwell.

Birnbaum, Pierre, and Jean Leca, eds. 1990. *Individualism, Theories, and Methods*. Oxford: Clarendon Press.

Bohmann, James. 1990. "Communication, Ideology, and Democratic Theory." *American Political Science Review* 84:93–109.

Chilton, Stephen. 1990. *Grounding Political Development*. Boulder: Lynne Rienner.

Elster, Jon. 1987. *Making Sense of Marx*. Cambridge: Cambridge University Press.

Gramsci, Antonio. 1971. *Selections from the Prison Notebooks*. Ed. Q. Hoare and G. Smith. New York: International Publishers.

Habermas, Jürgen. 1973. *Kulture und Kritik*. Frankfurt: Suhrkamp.

______. 1979. *Communication and the Evolution of Society*. Boston: Beacon Press.

______. [1984] 1987. *The Theory of Communicative Action*. Boston: Beacon Press.

Harris, David. 1992. *From Class Struggle to the Politics of Pleasure: The Effects of Gramscianism in Cultural Studies*. London: Routledge.

Kowarick, Lucio. 1995. "Investigação Urbana e Sociedade." In *Pluralismo, Espaço Social e Pesquisa,* ed. E. Reis, M. Tavares, and P. Fry. São Paulo: Hucitec/ANPOCS.

Krischke, Paulo J. 1990. "Movimentos Sociais e Democratizaçào no Brasil: Necessidades Radicais e Ação Comunicativa." In *Ciências Sociais Hoje*. São Paulo: ANPOCS-Cortez.

______. 1993. "Actores Sociales y Consolidación Democrática en América Latina: Estratégias, Identidades y Cultura Cívica." *Fermentum* (Universidad de Mérida) 3 (6-7):1–25.

______. Forthcoming. "Democratização, Cidadania e Opinião Pública, o Caso de Santa Catarina." In *Novas Democracias, Opinião Pública e Cultura Política,* ed. M. Alvaro. São Paulo: University of São Paulo.

Levine, Andrew, Elliot Saber, and Erik Ollin Wright. 1987. "Marxism and Methodological Individualism." *New Left Review* 162 (March-April).

Offe, Claus. 1985. "New Social Movements: Challenging the Boundaries of Institutional Politics." *Social Research* 52 (4):817–868.

Olson, Mancur. 1965. *The Logic of Collective Action: Public Goods and the Theory of Groups*. Cambridge, MA: Harvard University Press.

Rawls, John. 1993. "The Law of Peoples." In *On Human Rights,* ed. S. Shute and S. Hurley. New York: Basic Books.

Chapter Eighteen

Third World or Planetary Conflicts?

ALBERTO MELUCCI

A Prologue on Culture, Politics, and Domination

A book on social movements and culture in Latin America is in itself an event worth noting, a visible sign of the change in the social and political climate that has taken place over the last ten years in Latin America. Only a few years ago a book in the English language that included various North American authors and that issued from a project partially funded by the Rockefeller Foundation would have been considered one of the many efforts made by international capitalism to impose its economic power and cultural manipulation in a disguised form. Moreover, a book addressing the theme of social movements as a scientific subject and not just as a flag for revolutionary militancy is also a sign of a new relationship between collective action, culture, and politics in Latin America. Over the last decade, the theme of democracy has acquired a centrality in scientific and political debate that cannot be ignored—in the substantive sense because it highlights the democratization of politics and the guaranteeing of rights as the crucial condition for the nonsubordinate inclusion of Latin America in ongoing global processes, and in the symbolic sense because it signals that analysis of the forms assumed by democracy must necessarily address the cultural dimension of social conflicts and movements. This book is therefore already indicative that a public arena has opened up in Latin America for debate on democracy that goes beyond its institutional forms and strikes at the roots of the relationship between society, culture, and politics.

However, while recognizing the importance of the changed sociopolitical context in which this book is located, it is also important to point out the limitations of a debate that concentrates exclusively on the political dimension of democratization processes. Together with the rest of the world, Latin America is caught up in changes that invest the profound structures of social and cultural life: The severity of economic problems, the magnitude of inequalities, and the still-marked restriction of fundamental civil and political rights should not induce us to forget the impact of the global processes now affecting the continent. This creates unprecedented problems that overlap and interweave with other problems that are better known and more widely debated in Latin America today. If attention is focused solely on the theme of democracy (which seems to have taken the place of other themes predominant in previous decades, like class differences, inequality, and revolution), we may lose sight of the fact that new forms of domination and exploitation add themselves to older forms still unresolved and still so dramatically evident in various Latin American societies.

Today, the problem of how to deal with cultural power and cultural differences is an issue constantly subsumed by any reflection on contemporary social movements, especially because collective action today has a great deal to do with the ways in which we name the world. Who are the actors deciding the language used to name reality and choosing the codes that organize it? This is the central issue of power and conflict in a society in which information is becoming the core resource of social life. It applies to the First, the Second, the Third, and the nth Worlds (the distinction between these divisions grows increasingly blurred, and we no longer know where to plot the boundaries!). In a globalized world system, society has become a whole, a planetary society. The various forms assumed by power and social conflict affect this planetary space in its entirety, albeit in different ways in different parts of the world and, as regards different social groups, with disequilibria and inequalities that I shall discuss below. Today, it is this planetary space that frames every discussion of collective action and social movements.

The Meaning of Collective Action

When discussing social movements, we refer to highly heterogeneous phenomena that are investigated from various points of view. A first important theoretical step is to acknowledge that every definition is a map and as such is closely conditioned by the eye and hand of its draftsman. In the case of social movements in particular, it is necessary to move from a historical-empirical view to an analytic interpretation—in the awareness, that is to say, of the fact that every definition constructs its own object, and that certain dimensions or certain features of the phenomena observed are selected according to the analytical point of view adopted by the observer and according to the questions that the observer asks. Collective action is a terrain of passions, commitments, and alignments; we almost always find ourselves ranged on one side or the other, and this makes it all the more necessary to adopt an analytical point of view that breaks the empirical unity of phenomena down into its components.

In everyday usage, the term "movement" has come to coincide with anything that moves in collective form in a social environment. The empirical phenomena that we observe are never homogeneous entities, and the work of analytic decomposition forces us to abandon the romantic idea of movements and accept that collective phenomena are made up of multiple motivations, relations, and orientations. Their origins and outcomes are equally heterogeneous, and it is not easy to arrange them into a scenario ensuring a happy ending for all. Indeed, the history of collective phenomena teaches that these phenomena often give rise to new forms of power, violence, and injustice. We must therefore jettison the romantic and hyperrealistic view of collective phenomena and perceive them instead as composite forms of action to be explained in terms of different systems of social relations.

Two questions can be asked concerning collective action, both legitimate but each radically different from the other. One concerns the meaning of action; the other concerns the results that will ensue from the action. These questions are often confused because the tendency still persists to study movements in terms of how they can change society. From the theoretical-epistemological perspective that I propose, it is the question about the meaning of collective action that must be answered first, while the empirical unity of phenomena must be broken down in order to address the second question relative to their effects.

The confusion of these two questions has often prevented analytical issues from being framed in an appropriate form. Collective action has been collapsed into its more radical political forms, thereby generating a mythology of movements that does not correspond to the manner in which they are actually constituted. Moreover, it has fostered a sort of abstract voluntarism among intellectuals: In their desire to identify with movement actors and to share their life-conditions, while nevertheless enjoying a position of relative privilege in society, intellectuals have often imagined that they can take the place of the actors themselves, ending up by transforming themselves into ideologues or pedagogues of collective action.

Addressing collective action from an analytic perspective has immediate consequences for our understanding of contemporary phenomena. Since I was to some extent responsible for introducing the notion of "new social movements" into the sociological literature some twenty years ago, I have with alarm watched a fundamentally misconceived debate grow up around the concept. For the reasons set out above, so-called "new social movements" are never entirely "new"; they are always the outcome of a society's history, and in their empirical reality they are a highly heterogeneous mixture of diverse patterns and levels of action. By concentrating on the "novelty," or otherwise, of recent collective phenomena, the debate has ignored the truly important question—namely, whether in contemporary societies there are relations and social structures that can no longer be explained within the framework of industrial capitalist society as defined by the classical models of sociology. Therefore, what theoretical tools, what concepts are available to us to explain this possible discontinuity, this possible nonreducibility of certain features of contemporary phenomena to the historical and analytical model of industrial capitalism? This is a question that I regard as theoretically and politically crucial, and that the debate on the "new social movements" has simply removed from the scene; the debate, in fact, has developed into a confrontation between the defenders and opponents of "novelty" as the substantive, quasi-metaphysical attribute of contemporary movements.

My work of the last twenty years has explicitly addressed this theoretical challenge, seeking to identify *the elements* of contemporary collective action that require a conceptual framework *other* than that provided by industrial capitalism. On the one hand, contemporary societies founded on information produce increasing resources of autonomy for individual and collective actors. Complex systems can only work if the information produced circulates internally to them and if actors are able to receive this information, interpret it, and transmit it. On the other hand, complex systems require forms of power and control that ensure their integration, and this power must extend itself to the most intimate level at which the meaning of individual and collective action is formed. It is not enough to control manifest action; it is necessary to intervene in its motivational, cognitive, and affective roots; to manipulate the profound structure of the personality and perhaps even the biological structure itself.

Complex systems based on information must therefore disseminate independence and create dynamic conditions that enable autonomous actors to function as the reliable terminals of information networks. But at the same time they must transfer control to the formation of the meaning of action itself.

From this perspective, social conflicts mobilize actors who struggle to appropriate the possibility of giving meaning to their action—actors who seek to become the subjects of their own action and to produce autonomous meanings in relation to space and time, to life and death, to sexuality and reproduction. Confronting them are forms of power that grow increasingly neutralized within apparatuses, that impose their rationality and that force meaning to coincide with the technical-scientific procedures that characterize them. The action of contemporary movements has begun to make these dimensions of domination visible and to bring the autonomy needs of individuals and groups to the fore.

Conflicts, Inequality, Democracy

The conflicts just described are eminently relational, dynamic, and cultural because they invest the sphere of meaning formation; but they are nevertheless structural in character because they affect the forms of domination of a society based on information. The problem thus immediately arises of the relationship between these types of conflict and their empirical manifestations, which always come about in the context of concrete historical societies—that is, within a national state, a political system, a class structure, a specific cultural tradition. The problem becomes even more acute when we refer to developing societies, in which all these features are marked by economic dependence and by the weight of traditional power and inequality structures. Consequently the question to address is the form that these conflicts assume when they become empirically visible within a concrete society, especially in societies like those of Latin America.

There are two important aspects to consider when answering this question: first, the nature of the political system and of the state; second, the structure of inequalities and the mechanisms that produce and maintain poverty in the Latin American countries.

As regards the first aspect, the question concerns the relationship that arises between the emerging forms of collective action and their political expression. In developing societies, the democratization process and the theme of citizenship occupy center stage. During the last ten years, in fact, a process of "autonomization" of the political sphere has laboriously gotten under way: on the one hand, this process is no longer simply identified with the state; on the other, it has escaped the grasp of the oligarchic elites who used the state as the instrument through which they maintained their supremacy. It is therefore impossible, in Latin America today, to separate collective action from struggles for citizenship, for civil and democratic guarantees, for the attainment of forms of participation that translate into new rules and new rights.

But it would be an error to collapse collective action into politics, because it is precisely toward the desacralization and limitation of politics that complex systems are moving. From the analytic perspective that I use, the political system is not coterminous with society, and the dimension of social relations is analytically broader than political relations. The latter concern the processes whereby rules and decisions are shaped by the competition and negotiation of interests. Neoliberalism, too, seemingly proposes an approach that tends to reduce the scope of political relationships and to desacralize politics, but in fact it continues to nurture the myth that social demands can be straightforwardly translated into decisionmaking through an allegedly open competition. This thus fosters an ever more procedural version of democracy, which serves to conceal new forms of domination and power. It is instead the nontransparency of political processes that the analysis of collective action reveals to us. Collective action makes conflicts visible, and it reminds us that politics is not solely representation—it is also power. It also reminds us that the transformation of social demands into new rules and new rights is an open-ended task of democracy, a never-accomplished process. The transparent translation of social demands never occurs; a quota of conflict still persists in society to remind us of this shortfall. The distinction between systems of representation and decisionmaking on the one hand, and the forms of collective action irreducible to them on the other, is therefore one of the necessary conditions for contemporary complex systems to keep themselves open.

The second point concerns the enormity of the inequality and poverty in Latin American societies. Class analysis is still able to interpret the mechanisms and structure of many of these inequalities, and collective action in these societies necessarily involves the mobilization of marginalized and excluded social groups. But in this case, too, we must accomplish a quantum leap in our capacity for analysis. In fact, the traditional structure of material inequalities, in Latin American societies as well, is part of a new inequality structure based on the unequal distribution of the resources possessed by an information society. This new inequality involves disparities in access to the means with which the meaning of action is defined, individual and collective identity constructed, and native culture safeguarded. Those who are excluded, therefore, are not only deprived of material resources but even more of their capacity to be subjects; material deprivation combines with entirely subordinate inclusion in mass consumption, with the televisual-religious manipulation of consciousness, with the imposition of lifestyles that destroy, once and for all, the roots of popular cultures.

An important task for theory and research, therefore, is the analysis of this interweaving between old and new—analysis, however, that requires that categorical leap without which one remains trapped in old schemes of thought.

Poverty provides a good example of this interweaving. The intolerable poverty suffered by large swathes of the population in developing societies has generated waves of mobilization involving various categories of "the poor" (the landless, the inhabitants of the favelas, and so on). But the issue of poverty has mainly mobilized the urban middle classes, who have launched numerous organizations, campaigns, exemplary actions, and other efforts. Poverty has thus become an issue that concerns the definition of rights itself and the notions of "humanity" and of "being human." It is an issue, therefore, that certainly concerns the material conditions of the excluded, but that also and simultaneously involves a typically "postmaterial" cultural and ethical question: What is meant by being "human" and who has the right to apply this definition? The matter becomes tragically important when one realizes that poverty is inevitably bound up with the "defensive" violence unleashed by developing societies against the threat raised by the excluded (against the street children of Brazil, against the natives in Chiapas, and countless others).

Another example is provided by the emergence of the ethnic issue in Latin American societies via the mobilization of the native populations or of certain minorities (as in Chiapas and Colombia). In mobilizations that assert claims simultaneously involving ethnicity and land, there mix and merge the struggle against economic discrimination, political claims for territorial autonomy, and the symbolic appeal championing traditional language and culture. The ecological issue creates a bridge between these various dimensions because the appeal to native culture introduces the traditional values of knowledge of, and respect for, nature and contraposes them to "modernizing" technological innovation; traditional culture thus also becomes the means to save bioecological systems from destruction.

The Dilemmas of a Planetary Society

These examples demonstrate the interweaving of meanings in contemporary conflicts. They show how difficult it is to imagine definitive solutions to these conflicts. We can hope to reduce the severity of problems by making them more manageable; we can act to enlarge the sphere of democratic participation and of rights. But the questions that confront the planetary system will inevitably resurface in different forms.

The more society diversifies, the more conflicts become internal to the system and the more they involve the entire range of the social system. This means that conflicts tend increasingly to transform themselves into dilemmas, making manifest polarities in the system that cannot be eliminated because they define its very structure. The expectation that the society of the future would resolve the contradictions of present society was the great myth and the great hope of industrial society: a still not entirely socialized time and space fueled the project of capitalist-industrial conquest or revolution. The planetary system has now reached its spatiotemporal limits. It internalizes its conflicts because it can no longer project them into a future time and an external space.

Conflicts become dilemmas, therefore, and we can longer choose between nature and technology, for example, or between identity and difference. We must enable these polarities to coexist in permanent tension; but their coexistence is not linear and is constantly made manifest by social conflicts. The idea of a final stage in which society becomes transparent to itself has never been matched by the opaque and imbalanced reality of social relations, and it certainly cannot describe change in complex systems. Today, society can only measure itself against its conflicts, and politics becomes not the dream of making society transparent but the choice of which models of coexistence are able to reduce the amount of violence and inequality that social relationships necessarily produce.

Democracy today consists of the question of how best to reduce inequality and violence within a form of communal living that does not cancel out conflicts but that must instead wait to see them reborn regardless of the political adjustments that the system is able to accomplish. The degree of democracy in a society is measured by its capacity to redefine institutions and rights, thereby gradually reducing the inequality and violence that society itself produces. Considering democratic arrangements as always revisable obviously does not prevent priorities and value-criteria from being established as regards the goals pursued. For example, reducing injustice in strongly segmented societies may be a priority objective in terms of democracy, but it should not foster the illusion that the new system does not re-create forms of power and inequality.

Conflicts and the movements that express them are the main channels of information about the new patterns of inequality and the new forms of power that society re-creates. Instead of cultivating the illusory hope that democratic advances signify the elimination of power from society, we should ask ourselves what forms of power are more visible and therefore more negotiable than others. This is the problem of democracy in complex societies, and it is in these terms that the democratization process should be examined, if we do not wish merely to reproduce the shortcomings of liberal democracy. Movements perform an essential role vis-à-vis the political system in this process. If everything comes about internally to the political system, power is entirely self-legitimated and comes to coincide with its procedures. If there is some element that remains outside the political system so that conflicts become visible, power may be called into question and negotiated in new forms. It becomes possible to produce new rules, new criteria for inclusion, new rights, new forms of representation, and new decisionmaking processes that incorporate those dilemmas that society is able to handle.

We must rid ourselves of the idea that dilemmas can be resolved once and for all, so that we can start working in earnest for a more livable society—one in which freedom and justice, peace and environmental sustainability, the coexistence of differences, are not totalizing ideals for a transparent future but the normative criteria that shape our action in the present. This ethical commitment, and a sharp awareness of the tensions and limitations of social action, are today vital conditions for a viable democratic society.

Chapter Nineteen

Where To? What Next?

MARY LOUISE PRATT

In Western orthodox scholarly practice, theories are evaluated in terms of their capacity to generalize. This is often referred to as "explanatory power," understood as the ability to explain a maximum range of cases with a minimum number of axioms. The momentum of theory, or rather of theorizing as an institutional and intellectual activity, then, tends toward reducing heterogeneity. There to an important degree lie its powers of disorientation and illumination. It follows that theories, once articulated, resist heterogeneity; only under pressure do they augment the categories and propositions they deploy. *Someone* must insist on the existence and importance of cases that the theory does not explain or that contradict it. The stability and mutability of theories depends in part on who has and hasn't access to being that "someone."

In keeping with these norms, occidental social theory, in its orthodox varieties, has sought to build itself around a maximally uniform concept of the human subject and a concept of human collectivities that privileges homogeneity. Often, homogenization is achieved in social theory by locating relations of difference outside the domain of the social. In the *Politics,* for instance, Aristotle homogenizes the terrain for his social theorizing by locating women, children, and slaves in a domestic sphere ruled by natural laws that dictate a priori the subordination of each of these groups to the husband, father, and master, respectively. These three categories in turn intersect in a single subject: *the citizen*. The citizen (the free adult male subject) becomes the normative subject of society, of social theory, and of a maximally homogeneous collectivity whose bonds are based on sameness. (Sociobiology is used to reassert this configuration today.)

The gesture is only partially effective. The eminently social character of the excluded categories continuously asserts itself, in voices and actions of the naturalized noncitizens; in the efforts required to suppress and silence them; in contradictions and inconsistencies in the theory itself; and in the efforts required to suppress these. Aristotle, for instance, explicitly recognizes evidence contradicting his concept of natural slavery (the fact, for starters, that war prisoners who were citizens in one city-state could find themselves slaves in another). He simply chooses not to confront the issue.[1]

The study of "new social movements" has involved important confrontations with the homogenizing habits of mind social theory has traditionally fostered. It has engaged the heterogeneity of Latin American social formations and of social-political agency. Against the homogenizing momentum of theory, scholars studying these movements have been challenged to conceive social formations as constituted by (rather than in spite of) heterogeneity and to reconceive social bonding as constituted by (rather than in spite of) difference. The shift has provoked both panic and exhilaration. The 1992 volume to which the present collection is in some ways a sequel included a brilliant essay by Fernando Calderón, Alejandro Piscitelli, and José Luis Reyna that registered these responses.[2] "When we review the enormous number of social movements throughout Latin America and the Caribbean today," they begin, "the multiplicity of actors, themes, conflicts and orientations is overwhelming; beyond that, we are overwhelmed because the questions they raise have little to do with those we observed a quarter century ago" (19). The authors provide a catalogue of new cases to be accounted for, a list designed to provoke panic and exhilaration in the reader as well: Rastafarian movements, the Mothers of the Plaza de Mayo, oppositional women's movements, Sendero Luminoso, the Katarista indigenous movement in Bolivia, the industrial workers' movement in São Paulo, ecology movements, neighborhood democratizing organizations, and more. For good measure "youth, rock, salsa, student and ethno-cultural movements," as well as "those of ruling classes and those by region" are added. "How," the authors ask, "can such movements be interpreted?"—a broad question that in the very same sentence is rephrased as: "That is, are they regression or progress?" (22).

This abrupt reduction to a conventional political binary is revealing, mostly for its automatic, unconscious character. Binarism is the one form of heterogeneity that traditional theorizing tolerates. How often do attempts to analyze the crisscrossing of identities and lines of conflict and connection reduce to binarized discussions of men versus women; indigenes versus whites; rural versus urban; progressive versus reactionary; "new" versus "old" social movements—all of which in turn reduce to the binary Self versus Other, where the position of the Self is occupied by the citizen-subject, and his alter ego, the metropolitan theorist.

These positionings are destabilized by this new set of essays on (the no longer "new") Latin American social movements. These studies both enable and impose a significant decentering of intellectual perspective and political understanding. In contrast with the panic and exhilaration of the 1992 collection, the present volume, only partly a sequel, offers an often sobering reality check. Many of the articles adopt noticeably pragmatic, anti-idealist, antiprescriptive perspectives. Neither utopianism nor dystopianism prevail (or even occur, it seems). This deflated rhetoric might appear to reflect political resignation or the depressed state of mind to which the metropolitan leftist intellectuals are certainly entitled these days. But it is likely that something else is also at stake, namely the attempt to *reposition* the metropolitan intellectual with respect to the field of the social and particularly with respect to its traditional hinterlands and peripheries. The concept of the cultural, I will suggest below, plays a strategic role in bringing about this repositioning.

Let me elaborate. In what can sound like a rhetoric of disillusionment, many writers in this volume willfully refuse to judge the movements they discuss by presumed standards of progressiveness or other political criteria that might be taken for granted by metropolitan intellectuals or their readers. The writers do assert judgments expressed by other actors in the situation under study, however. Díaz-Barriga, for instance, quotes what the *colonas* say about student activists and what the activists say about the *colonas*. Alvarez quotes delegates at Huairou criticizing loss of militancy and co-optation by networking. Warren summarizes the Pan-Mayan's view of the *popular* movement and the latter movement's criticisms of the Pan-Mayanists. Da Cunha quotes the debate between political and cultural agendas within the black movement but does not take sides herself.

This withholding of judgment involves, it appears, a refusal of higher authority on the part of the academics, though not a refusal of authority per se. What is important and revealing, it is suggested, is not what metropolitan intellectuals think about a situation or how they might resolve a debate, but what the actors in the situation think and how they resolve debates. An effort is made to shift the center of gravity of knowledge, understanding, and judgment to the participants. Baierle makes the shift explicit when he rejects both programs and analyses that prescribe the integration of subaltern groups into processes specified or set in motion by others. The participants themselves, he argues, must generate the process and define its meaning.

Many of the essays are concertedly pragmatic and anti-idealist in tone. Alvarez and Schild incisively discuss the limits of NGOs, once seen as the basis for a new civil society. Díaz-Barriga underscores that the movements he studies are driven by what they define pragmatically as *necesidades*. Nearly all the writers seek to be "realistic"—that is, anti-idealistic—about the potential of grassroots movements to produce radical or large-scale change, or to win in open confrontations with market imperatives or with the state. Expectations, and even hopes, of large-scale or systemic change are willfully withheld; utopianism and revolutionary rhetoric are completely offstage. Here again one senses an effort to vacate a site of metropolitan intellectual authority, the site from which the intellectual finds in the actions of others the realization of his own dreams. These essays refuse to interpret movements on the periphery as signifiers whose signified rests in the metropolis. The pragmatism and anti-idealism the academics express here reproduces, as it reports on, that of the social movements themselves.

The characteristics of realism, anti-utopianism, anti-idealism, and antiprescriptivism derive in part from the authors' commitments to analyses that are resolutely *local,* or better, *localized.* In contrast with widely felt imperatives to describe globalization in global terms, the essays in this collection insist on the need to *localize* critiques of capitalism and calls for redress. The current phase of capitalist expansion, and its political consequences, are being lived out in vastly different ways by people in different places and situations. The advent of *maquila* labor, for instance, will be lived out differently by young women integrated into the wage labor force (and possibly freed from restricted possibilities back home), by the parents and siblings they leave behind, by the older women whom they displace from their jobs, by the businesses who benefit from their increased consumer power, by the men who sexually exploit them, by the companies who profit from their cheap labor, and so on. Movements to redress injustices and inequities must, so the argument goes, be generated from particular conditions, experiences, and situations that develop particular forms and possibilities of agency. If there is a "big picture," and there most certainly is in these essays, the metropolitan academy is only one among many positions from which it may be viewed and reflected upon.

The commitment to localism explains, perhaps, why so many of the essays seem to presuppose the goals of working for small changes and the impossibility of confronting the system in any wholesale way. This is overwhelmingly the way the system is lived. Only local circumstances provide referents for terms like equality, exploitation, empowerment, and democracy. This is not to say that radical thought or utopian imaginings are impossible. But the intellectuals here refuse to read them into the situation. Some readers will be critical of this abdication; others will see it as reflecting a stage in the process of intellectual repositioning that these chapters have undertaken.

While all the writers here work from positions of solidarity with the movements they study, the chapters register clear differences between "outsider" intellectuals who are studying social formations other than their own and "insider" intellectuals who are studying societies and movements of which they see themselves as members. The Brazilian intellectual-activists writing on developments in Porto Alegre (such as Sérgio Baierle) and the Colombians writing on the Pacific coastal movements there (Libia Grueso and Carlos Rosero) claim a stronger form of intellectual authority than the outsiders. These essays do express optimism and the hope of developing a template that could be deployed elsewhere. The Colombian activists are aware of being part of the larger ethnic movements that developed especially around the Columbus Quincentennial and, in Colombia, in relation to the new constitution. The Porto Alegre case is the lone instance in the book in which the movement under study belongs to a political party (the PT, or Workers' Party). The writers of these essays clearly believe that the Porto Alegre experience constitutes an important experiment in participatory democratic citizenship. Here elections are not that which produce democracy, but that which, if the right party wins, create conditions under which democracy may be pursued. Otherwise in this volume, party politics remain part of the problem, not the solution.

I spoke above about the effort to reposition the intellectual that is evidenced in this book. To grasp the importance of this process, it is necessary to comprehend one of the more curious, if overdetermined, characteristics of academic theorizing: It tends unconsciously to reproduce the structure of power that holds in the situation being theorized, *even when the goal is a critique of that structure.* Theorizing and social analysis are commonly (and unconsciously) done from the point of view of the party in authority in the situation being studied, even when the project is a critique of that authority. As Catharine MacKinnon so deftly argues in *Toward a Feminist Theory of the State,* "society has been theorized from the point of view of those it privileges";[3] the theorist unconsciously adopts the point of view of the empowered citizen. Intellectual authority produces itself by cloning that empowerment. Many of the writers in this volume seek to undo this unconscious identification and the metropolitan-centered "higher authority" it underwrites.

Key to this repositioning is the strategic use of the category of *the cultural.* This is the new element this book consciously attempts to introduce into the study of social movements. The question "What can cultural analysis tell us about social movements?" can be rephrased as "What does the category of the cultural enable us to reflect on?" The most immediate answer is "democracy." Nothing could be more important than the call (in this volume's Introduction) for "expanding and deepening" the idea of democracy, at a moment when neoliberal discourse has forcibly emptied it of meaning, until the mere presence of elections remains its lone defining characteristic. Building democracies and ending inequality are ultimately what is at stake for the writers in this book.

For Warren; Grueso, Rosero, and Escobar; and others, the category of the cultural enables the analyst to reconceptualize material needs and conditions. These have commonly been treated as transparent universals, governed—like Aristotle's women—by natural laws rather than constituted by culturally and historically shaped interactions between human communities and the material world. For Cunha, Rubin, and others, the cultural enables the analyst to localize and relativize political agendas by seeing them as embedded in political cultures. Oppositional movements, so the argument goes, work against dominant power structures, but they work within political cultures shared with the dominant power structures. This perspective raises the possibility of intervening not only in the dominant power structures but in the shared political culture that underwrites both dominant and oppositional movements. The insights of feminism have been, and remain, crucial to revealing the cultural dimensions of the political.

The category of the cultural also enables analysts to take the *everyday* as a point of departure for analyzing and evaluating social movements—the everyday becomes not the contingent and incidental, but *that which is at stake* for those living out the circumstances that have given rise to the movement. In related fashion, the category of the cultural enables the analyst to reflect on the domain of the *experiential,* often seen as the essential "other" to theory. Categories like "belonging" and "structure of possibilities" (Schild) identify experiential parameters that operate with tremendous force in shaping human desire and agency. Finally, the cultural enables analysts to talk about *consciousness,* that imponderable black box that tends to show up in political theory as the variable that will somehow change on its own after the election, the revolution, or the coup d'état has taken place. In this book, patterns of consciousness can be reflected on as part of political culture, as key, for instance, in making violent and unequal orders meaningful to people, in securing their resignation or compliance, and in defending alternative and resistant ways of being. Warren, and Grueso, Rosero, and Escobar, for instance, discuss movements working with non-Western cosmologies and epistemologies.

The category of the cultural also enables the authors to reflect on neoliberalism as a cultural and not just as an economic and political intervention. The essays only hint at the challenge of understanding how, for instance, neoliberalism creates categories of belonging, structures of possibility, forms of agency; how it seeks to reorganize the everyday; how it generates needs and conditions for fulfilling them (or not); how it creates meaningful political agendas that redefine citizenship and legitimate inequality. These dimensions are crucial to understanding the potency of the neoliberal paradigm—and also to identifying its weaknesses and fissures. As the editors observe in the Introduction, "neoliberalism is not a coherent, homogeneous, or totalizing project." Do crises of agency result when the imposition of consumerism creates new desires and meanings, while economies are structurally adjusted so that only small minorities can actually act on those desires and meanings? If not, why not?

I began these remarks with a reflection on the homogenizing momentum of orthodox theorizing. Theory, I suggested, resists heterogeneity and multiplies its terms and categories only if someone with access to the process insists on the need to do so. What one might call the "heterogenization" of the social as an object of study is a direct result of the diversification of access to the academy itself, a process to which this volume bears witness. Here again, point of view is important. From the normative, homogenizing point of view of the citizen-theorist, the imperative to recognize heterogeneity has the effect of fragmenting the social field—the way the new social movements were seen as fragmenting the binarized field of conventional political thought. From this position, the process is often seen as one of disintegration and loss of cohesion. But from the point of view of the excluded or invisible groups, the noncitizens now claiming belonging, the process is likely to be seen as the exact opposite: as one of inclusion and integration. The picture diversifies because others—the Others—are now in it. Indeed, for the noncitizens, fragmentation and disintegration better describe what existed before, when the categories of the social or the political were homogeneously defined through structures of exclusion and willful ignorance. When women lack legal rights, or when indigenous people lack access to schools, or when rural and urban worlds occupy distinct galaxies, or when the media only speak Spanish and you only speak Quechua, or when the price of belonging is ethnic, linguistic, or sexual suicide—*this* is fragmentation and incoherence.

These simultaneous integrations and disintegrations pose important intellectual challenges, which this book reflects both in its engagements (with the local, the cultural, the issue of citizenship) and its reticences (from theorizing, from self-reflection, from utopianism and revolutionism, from the critique of capitalism). I do not believe this collection of essays sees itself as a stopping-off place. The authors prepare the terrain for necessary reflections on the agency of scholars and intellectuals, their possible roles in struggles against inequality in whose outcomes they too have a stake, the effects of the production and distribution of academic knowledge, the place of speculative inquiry, the necessity of theorizing locally and perspectivally, and the need for epistemological mediators and methods of mediation. This collection is a signpost on a route toward a critical cultural practice, and a constructive reworking of the role of intellectuals in struggles against inequality.

Notes

1. Mary Louise Pratt, "La heterogeneidad y el pánico de la teoría," *Revista de Crítica Literaria Latinoamericana,* 1996. For further reflection in these issues, see also Mary Louise Pratt, "Daring to Dream: New Visions of Culture and Citizenship," in *Critical Theory and the Teaching of Literature,* ed. James Slevin and Art Young (Urbana, Ill.: National Council of Teachers of English, 1996.)

2. Fernando Calderón, Alejandro Piscitelli, and José Luis Reyna, "Social Movements: Actors, Theories, Expectations," in *The Making of Social Movements in Latin America: Identity, Strategy, and Democracy,* ed. Arturo Escobar and Sonia E. Alvarez (Boulder: Westview Press, 1992).

3. Catharine MacKinnon, *Toward a Feminist Theory of the State* (Cambridge: Harvard University Press, 1989), 162.

About the Editors and Contributors

Sonia E. Alvarez is associate professor of politics at the University of California at Santa Cruz. She is the author of *Engendering Democracy in Brazil: Women's Movements in Transition Politics* (Princeton University Press, 1990) and coeditor with Arturo Escobar of *The Making of Social Movements in Latin America: Identity, Strategy, and Democracy* (Westview Press, 1992). Her writings on feminist movements and democratization have appeared in *Signs, Feminist Studies, Revista Estudos Feministas, Debate Feminista,* and several edited collections. Alvarez's current research centers on challenges to democratic theory and practice posed by the (re)configuration of social movements and national and transnational civil society in Latin America.

Sérgio Gregório Baierle is a member of the board of directors of CIDADE (Centro de Assessoria e Estudos Urbanos), a Porto Alegre–based NGO that advises popular movement organizations. He received an M.A. in political science from the State University of Campinas (Unicamp) in São Paulo in 1992, and is currently employed by the Banco Central do Brasil.

Evelina Dagnino holds a Ph.D. in political science from Stanford University. She teaches at the State University of Campinas in São Paulo, where she helped create the Culture and Politics Doctoral Program. She has been visiting professor at Yale University, edited *Os Anos 90: Política e Sociedade no Brasil* (1994), and has published several articles on the relationships between culture and politics, social movements, democracy, and citizenship.

Miguel Díaz-Barriga is associate professor of anthropology at Swarthmore College. He holds a Ph.D. in anthropology from Stanford University. His writings on land tenure conflicts, popular culture, the press, and grassroots organizing in Mexico City have appeared in *American Ethnologist, Estudios Mexicanos/Mexican Studies, Alteridades,* and other journals. He is currently working on a monograph on the history of urban movements in the Ajusco region of Mexico City and on an edited volume on Central American critiques of neoliberalism.

Arturo Escobar is associate professor of anthropology at the University of Massachusetts at Amherst. He is the author of *Encountering Development: The Making and Unmaking of the Third World* (Princeton University Press, 1995) and coeditor (with Sonia Alvarez) of *The Making of Social Movements in Latin America: Identity, Strategy, and Democracy* (Westview Press, 1992) and (with Álvaro Pedrosa) of *Pacífico: Desarrollo o Divesidad? Estado, Capital, y Movimientos Sociales en el Pacífico Colombiano* (1996). His interests include political ecology and the anthropology of development, social movements, and technoscience. He has been working in the Pacific coast region of Colombia since the early 1990s, including more than a year of fieldwork.

Jean Franco is professor emerita of Columbia University, where she held a chair from 1982 to 1994. She holds a doctorate from the University of London (1964) and has held professorships at the University of Essex (1968–1972), Stanford University (1972–1982), and Columbia. She was president of the Latin American Studies Association from

1989–1991 and has served on committees for the Guggenheim, Rockefeller, and Social Science Foundations. Her books include *Plotting Women: Gender and Representation in Mexico* (1989); *Cruzando Fronteras, Marcando Diferencias* (1996); *Cesar Vallejo: The Dialectics of Poetry and Silence; Introduction to Spanish American Literature;* and *The Modern Culture of Latin America.* She coedited with Juan Flores and George Yúdice *On Edge: The Crisis of Contemporary Latin American Culture* (1992) and is now one of the editors of the Minnesota Press series on cultural studies in Latin America. She is working on a book on the effects of globalization, tentatively entitled "Border Patrol."

Olivia Maria Gomes da Cunha is a Ph.D. candidate in social anthropology at the Museo Nacional/Federal University of Rio de Janeiro.

Libia Grueso is a member of the Process of Black Communities, or PCN (a network of black community organizations from the Pacific coast region of Colombia), a member of the PCN's environmental technical team, and a long-time cultural and political activist in the Valle del Cauca Pacific region. She is a social worker with a master's degree in political science and has worked as regional coordinator of the Project for Biodiversity Conservation in Colombia's Pacific coast region.

Elizabeth Jelin is a sociologist and senior researcher at the Instituto de Investigaciones Sociales Gino Germani, the University of Buenos Aires, and at CONICET (Consejo Nacional de Investigaciones Científicas y Técnicas). She has published extensively on social movements, citizenship, gender politics, and democratization, among many other topics. Her recent publications include *Vida Cotidiana y Control Institucional en la Argentina de los '90* (Nuevo Hacer, 1996) and *Constructing Democracy: Human Rights, Citizenship, and Society in Latin America*, with Eric Hershberg (Westview Press, 1996).

Paulo J. Krischke received his Ph.D. in political science from York University in 1983. He is currently visiting professor of political science at the Federal University of Rio Grande do Sul, senior researcher for the National Council of Research and Development (CNPq, Brasília), and director of the Center for the Study of Democracy in Florianópolis, Santa Catarina. He is the author and editor of several books, including *O Contrato Social, Ontem e Hoje* (Cortez, 1993).

Gustavo Lins Ribeiro is associate professor of anthropology at the Federal University of Brasília. He is also a visiting professor at the graduate program in anthropology at the National University of Misiones (Argentina) and visiting scholar (1996–1998) at the Institute for Global Studies in Culture, Power, and History at the Johns Hopkins University. He holds a Ph.D. in anthropology from the City University of New York (1988). His doctoral dissertation on transnational migratory flows, the articulation of transnational capital, and the economic and political agents within and around the construction of the Yacyreta Hydroelectric High-Dam (Argentina/Paraguay) won the 1989 prize of the Brazilian Association of Graduate Programs in the Social Sciences and was published in Brazil, the United States, and Argentina. He has published several articles on development, environmentalism, and modernity in different periodicals in Latin America, the United States, and India.

Alberto Melucci holds doctoral degrees in sociology and clinical psychology. He is professor of cultural sociology at the University of Milan and professor of clinical psychology at the postgraduate school of clinical psychology. He has extensively taught in Europe, the United States, and Latin America. He is the author of more than fifteen books, the most recent in English including *The Playing Self: Person and Meaning in the Planetary Society* (1996); *Challenging Codes: Collective Action in the Information Age* (1996); and *Nomads of the Present: Social Movements and Individual Needs in Contemporary Society* (1989).

Maria Celia Paoli is professor of sociology at the University of São Paulo and senior researcher at the Núcleo de Estudos dos Direitos de Cidadania. She has published extensively on Brazilian working-class history and social movements.

Mary Louise Pratt teaches in the Departments of Spanish and Portuguese and Comparative Literature at Stanford University. She works in areas of Latin American literature and culture; theory; and culture and imperialism. She is author of *Imperial Eyes: Travel Writing and Transculturation* (1992); coauthor of *Women, Culture, and Politics in Latin America* (1990), and coeditor of *The Committed Critic: Essays on Politics and Culture*, with Jean Franco (forthcoming, 1997). She is currently completing a book on the history of Latin American women writers and intellectuals titled "Genero y ciudadania: las mujeres en dialogo con la nacion."

Carlos Rosero is member of the Colombian national coordinating committee of the Process of Black Communities, or PCN; he has worked as an ethno-cultural activist for many years, particularly in the Valle del Cauca Pacific region of Colombia. An anthropologist from the National University of Colombia in Bogota, he was the black communities' candidate to the National Constituent Assembly in 1991.

Jeffrey Rubin has taught at Amherst College and Yale University. In 1997 he was a Rockefeller Fellow in the Program in Culture and Politics at the State University of Campinas, São Paulo. His research interests include social movements, popular culture, and democratization in Mexico and Brazil. He has written articles on grassroots radicalism in Juchitán, Mexico; retheorizing the Mexican regime; and everyday forms of resistance. His book *Decentering the Regime: History, Culture, and Radical Politics in Juchitán, Mexico* is forthcoming from Duke University Press.

Verónica Schild is assistant professor of political science at the University of Western Ontario. Born in Chile, she studied in the United States and Canada, obtaining a Ph.D. in political science from the University of Toronto. She has published on the Chilean women's movement in a time of political transition as well as on the problematic treatment of civil society in democratization debates, and is presently working on a book on women and neoliberal state formation in Chile.

David Slater is professor of social and political geography at Loughborough University, England. Previously he was attached to the Interuniversity Center for Latin American Research and Documentation in Amsterdam. He is author of *Territory and State Power in Latin America* (St. Martin's Press and Macmillan, 1989) and editor of two special issues of *Latin American Perspectives* on social movements and political change in Latin America, published by Sage (1994). Currently he is working on the geopolitics of power and North-South relations.

Vera da Silva Telles is professor of sociology at the University of São Paulo and senior researcher at the Núcleo de Estudos dos Direitos de Cidadania. She has published extensively on urban poverty and local government in Brazil.

Kay B. Warren is chair and professor of anthropology at Princeton University. Her current research focuses on public intellectuals, social movements, ethnic nationalism, and documentary films made for TV. She has authored *The Symbolism of Subordination*, coauthored *Women of the Andes*, and edited *The Violence Within*. Her new book deals with Mayan resurgence and public intellectuals in Guatemala. Professor Warren has received recent awards from the Guggenheim Foundation, the Institute for Advanced Study, the Wenner-Gren Foundation, and the MacArthur Foundation.

George Yúdice is professor of American studies and Spanish and Portuguese at New York University. He is the author of the forthcoming *We Are Not the World: Identity and Representation in an Age of Global Restructuring* (Duke University Press); coeditor with Jean Franco and Juan Flores of *On Edge: The Crisis of Contemporary Latin American Culture;* and author of numerous essays on U.S. and Latin American culture and intellectual discourse. He is director of the Inter-American Cultural Studies Network.

Index